BRUNO DE HOGUES / GETTY IMAGES ©

A / GETTY IMAGES ©

(left) Place de la Concorde (p97)

(above) Jardin du Luxembourg (p234)

(right) Hall of Mirrors in Château de Versailles (p274)

PETE SEAWARD / GETTY IMAGES ©

Welcome to Paris

Paris has a timeless familiarity for visitors, with architectural icons, exquisite cuisine, chic boutiques and priceless artistic treasures.

Iconic Architecture

The wrought-iron spire of the Eiffel Tower, the broad Arc de Triomphe guarding Paris' most glamorous avenue, the Champs-Élysées, the gargoyled Notre Dame cathedral, lamplit bridges spanning the Seine and art nouveau cafes spilling onto wicker-chair-lined terraces are indelibly etched in the minds of anyone who's visited the city – and the imaginations of anyone who hasn't (yet). But despite initial appearances, Paris' cityscape isn't static: there are some stunning modern and contemporary icons too, from the inside-out, industrial-style Centre Pompidou to the *mur végétal* (vertical garden) gracing the striking Musée du Quai Branly.

Glorious Food

Paris' dining is also iconic: France's reputation for its cuisine precedes it, and whether you seek a cosy neighbourhood bistro or a triple-Michelin-starred temple to gastronomy, you'll find every establishment prides itself on exquisite preparation and presentation of quality produce, invariably served with wine. Enticing patisseries, *boulangeries* (bakeries), *fromageries* (cheese shops) and crowded, colourful street markets are perfect for packing a picnic to take to the city's parks and gardens. A host of culinary courses offer instruction for all schedules, abilities and budgets.

Stylish Shopping

Parisians are synonymous with style and fashion shopping is the city's forte. Paris remains at the forefront of international trends, and browsing emerging and established designer boutiques and flagship *haute couture* houses is a quintessential part of any visit. You'll also find uberhip concept stores, quirky homewares shops, and resplendent art nouveau department stores, along with a trove of vintage shops and flea markets, atmospheric bookshops, adorable children's wear and toy shops, art and antique dealers, venerable shops selling state-of-the-art professional cookware, and, of course, gourmet food and wine shops galore.

Artistic Treasures

With an illustrious artistic pedigree – Renoir, Rodin, Picasso, Monet, Manet, Dalí and Van Gogh are but a few of the masters who lived and worked here over the years – Paris is one of the great art repositories of the world, harbouring treasures from antiquity onwards. In addition to big-hitters like the incomparable Louvre, the Musée d'Orsay's exceptional impressionist collection, and the Centre Pompidou's cache of modern and contemporary art, there are scores of smaller museums housing collections in every imaginable genre, and a diverse range of venues mounting major exhibitions through to off-beat installations.

DOMINGO LEIVA / GETTY IMAGES ©

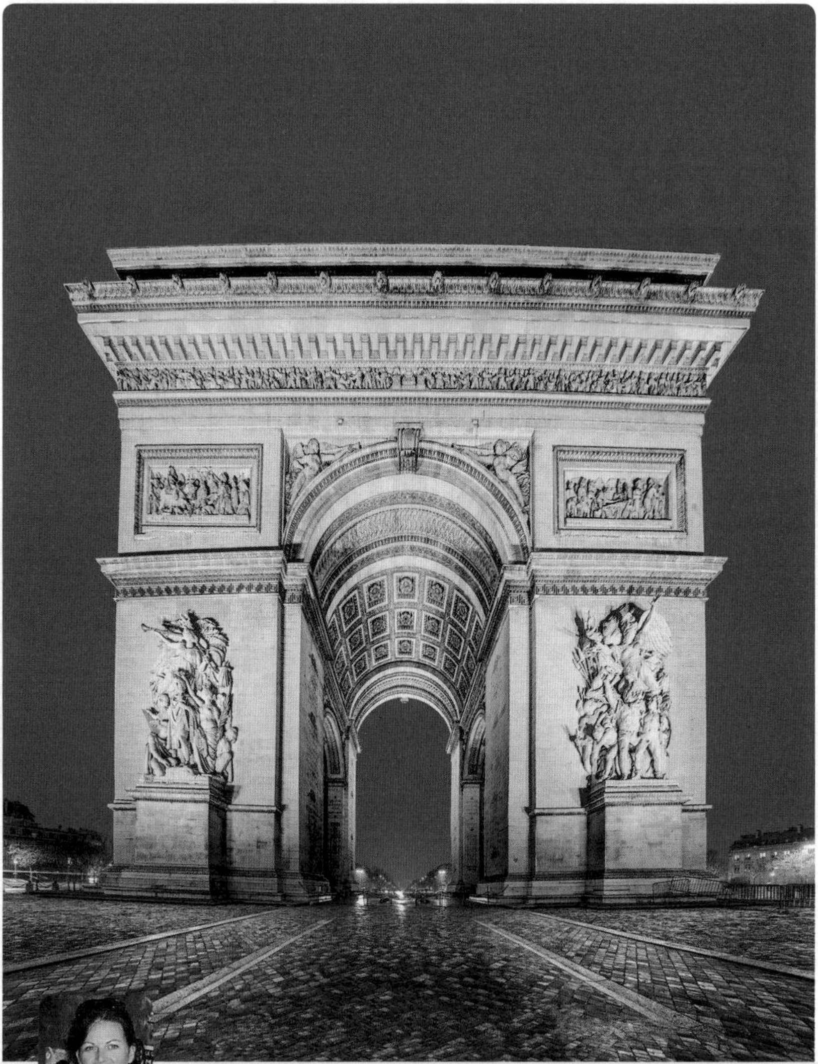

Why I Love Paris

By Catherine Le Nevez, author

Paris' grandeur is inspiring but what I love most about the city is its intimacy. Its *quartiers* (quarters) are like a patchwork of villages, and while it's one of the world's major metropolises – with all of the culture and facilities that go with it – there's a real sense of community at the local shops, markets and cafes that hasn't changed since my childhood. Yet because every little 'village' has its own evolving character I'm constantly discovering and rediscovering hidden corners of the city.

For more about our authors, see p432.

Top: Arc de Triomphe (p95)

Paris' Top 16

1

Eiffel Tower *(p82)*

1 No one could imagine Paris today without its signature spire. But Gustave Eiffel only constructed this graceful tower – then the world's tallest, at 320m – as a temporary exhibit for the 1889 Exposition Universelle. Luckily, its popularity assured its survival beyond the World Fair and its elegant art nouveau webbed-metal design has become the defining fixture of the city's skyline. Head here at dusk for the best day and night views of the glittering city, and toast making it to the top at the sparkling champagne bar.

Eiffel Tower & Western Paris

Arc de Triomphe *(p95)*

2 If anything rivals the Eiffel Tower as the symbol of Paris, it's this magnificent 1836-built monument to Napoléon's 1805 victory at Austerlitz. The intricately sculpted triumphal arch stands sentinel in the centre of the Étoile (star), the world's largest roundabout – just be sure to use the pedestrian tunnels below ground to reach it! Some of the best vistas in Paris radiate from the top, including sweeping views along the luxury shop-lined Champs-Élysées, Paris' most glamorous avenue.

Champs-Élysées & Grands Boulevards

PAWEL LIBERA / GETTY IMAGES ©

2

NAZRIE ABU SEMAN / GETTY IMAGES ©

3

4

Notre Dame *(p202)*

3 A vision of stained-glass rose windows, flying buttresses and frightening gargoyles, Paris' glorious cathedral on the larger of the two inner-city islands is the city's geographic and spiritual heart. This Gothic wonder took nearly 200 years to build, but would have been demolished following damage during the French Revolution had it not been for the popularity of Victor Hugo's timely novel, *The Hunchback of Notre Dame*, which sparked a petition to save it. Climb its 400-odd spiralling steps for magic rooftop views.

The Islands

The Louvre *(p109)*

4 The *Mona Lisa* and the *Venus de Milo* are just two of the priceless treasures resplendently housed inside this fortress turned royal palace turned France's first national museum. Stretching along the Seine, this immense museum can seem overwhelming, but there are plenty of ways to experience it even if you don't have nine months to glance at every artwork and artefact here. One of the best is its thematic trails – from the 'Art of Eating' to 'Love in the Louvre'.

Louvre & Les Halles

Parisian Dining *(p44)*

5 There's a reason that boxes of leftovers aren't done in Paris, and it has nothing to do with portion sizes. Whether you're at an unchanged-in-decades neighbourhood haunt, a beautiful art nouveau brasserie, a switched-on, experimental neobistro or a fêted *haute cuisine* establishment helmed by a legendary chef, the food and the dining experience are considered inseparable. France pioneered what is still the most influential style of cooking in the Western world and Paris is its showcase *par excellence*. Do as Parisians do and savour every moment.

ABOVE: SHOPS AND BISTROS IN RUE MOUFFETARD (P222), IN THE LATIN QUARTER

Eating

Basilique du Sacré-Cœur *(p137)*

6 Sacré-Cœur is a place of pilgrimage in more ways than one. Staircased, ivy-clad streets climb the hill of the fabled artists' neighbourhood of Montmartre to a funicular gliding up to the dove-white domes of Basilique du Sacré-Cœur (Sacred Heart Basilica). The chapel-lined basilica – featuring the shimmering apse mosaic *Christ in Majesty* – crowns the 130m-high Butte de Montmartre (Montmartre Hill). Its lofty position provides dizzying vistas across Paris from the basilica's front steps and above all, from up inside its main dome.

Montmartre & Northern Paris

Musée d'Orsay *(p230)*

7 The Musée d'Orsay's celebrated canvases by impressionist and post-impressionist masters including Renoir, Gaugin, Cézanne, Sisley, Manet, Monet, Degas and Toulouse-Lautrec might not have changed, but magnificent renovations at the Musée d'Orsay now make them appear as if they're hung in an intimate home. The grand former railway station (the Gare d'Orsay) housing the museum is an exemplar of art nouveau architecture, of course, but France's treasured national collection of masterpieces from 1848 to 1914 is the star of the show.

St-Germain & Les Invalides

6

Musée Rodin *(p236)*

8 The lovely Musée Rodin is the most romantic of Paris' museums. Auguste Rodin's former workshop and showroom, the 1730-built Hôtel Biron, is filled with Rodin's own sculptural masterpieces such as the marble monument to love, *The Kiss*, as well as creations by his protégé, sculptor Camille Claudel, and other artists whose works Rodin collected, Van Gogh and Renoir among them. But the real treat is the mansion's rambling, rose-scented sculpture garden, which provides an entrancing setting for contemplating works such as *The Thinker*. LEFT: *THE KISS* BY RODIN

St-Germain & Les Invalides

Canal St-Martin *(p143)*

9 Bordered by shaded towpaths and traversed by iron footbridges, the charming, 4.5km-long Canal St-Martin was slated to be concreted over (when barge transportation declined) until local residents rallied to save it. The quaint setting lured artists, designers and students, who set up artists' collectives, vintage and offbeat boutiques and a bevy of neo-retro cafes and bars. Enduring maritime legacies include old swing-bridges that still pivot 90 degrees when boats pass through the canal's double-locks, and a canal cruise is the best way to experience Paris' lesser-known waterway.

Montmartre & Northern Paris

The Seine *(p74)*

10 The city's most beautiful 'boulevard' of all, the Seine, flows through the city's heart, flanked by landmarks including the Eiffel Tower, Louvre and Notre Dame. Taking to the water on a cruise or Batobus ferry is an idyllic way to acquaint or reacquaint yourself with the city. Its 37 bridges and Unesco World Heritage–listed riverbanks are perfect for promenading, particularly along the new car-free stretch Les Berges de Seine, incorporating floating gardens on 1800 sq metres of artificial islands. Entertainment options abound, including summertime beaches.

The Seine

Specialised Shopping *(p60)*

11 Paris, like any major city, offers international chains (including icons that originated here). But what really sets Parisian shopping apart is its incredible array of specialist shops. Candles from the world's oldest candle maker, pigments from the art supply shop that developed 'Klein blue' with the artist, soft leather handbags made in the hip Haut Marais, green-metal *bouquiniste* (secondhand bookshop) stalls lining the banks of the Seine and fashions displayed beneath the stained-glass dome of *grande dame* department store Galeries Lafayette are just some of the goodies in store. BOTTOM RIGHT: GLASS DOME OF DEPARTMENT STORE GALERIES LAFAYETTE (P105)

Shopping

10

11

Centre Pompidou

(p117)

12 The primary-coloured, inside-out building, designed by architects Renzo Piano and Richard Rogers, houses France's national modern and contemporary art museum, the Musée National d'Art Moderne (MNAM), containing works from 1905 through to the present day, including works by Picasso, Matisse, Chagall and Kandinsky as well as cross-Atlantic artists such as Kahlo, Warhol and Pollock plus edgy installation pieces, sculpture and videos. The centre's cutting-edge cultural offerings include temporary exhibition spaces, a public library, cinemas and entertainment venues. Topping it off is the spectacular panorama radiating from the roof.

Louvre & Les Halles

12

13

14

Jardin du Luxembourg *(p234)*

13 The Jardin du Luxembourg offers a snapshot of Parisian life. Couples stroll through the chestnut groves. Children chase wooden sailboats around the octagonal pond and laugh at the antics of engaging marionettes. Old men play rapid-fire chess with cherished pieces at weathered tables. Students pore over books between lectures. Office workers snatch some sunshine, lounging in sage-green metal chairs. Musicians strike up in the bandstand. Joggers loop past stately statues. And friends meet and make plans to meet again.

St-Germain & Les Invalides

Cimetière du Père Lachaise *(p161)*

14 Paris is a collection of villages and this sprawl of cobbled lanes and elaborate tombs, with a population (as it were) of more than one million, qualifies as one in its own right. The world's most visited cemetery was founded in 1804, and initially attracted few funerals because of its distance from the city centre. The authorities responded by exhuming famous remains and resettling them here. Their marketing ploy worked and Cimetière du Père Lachaise has been Paris' most fashionable final address ever since.

Le Marais, Ménilmontant & Belleville

Street Markets (p191)

15 Stall after stall of cheeses, punnets of raspberries, stacked baguettes, sun-ripened tomatoes, freshly lopped pigs' trotters, horsemeat sausages, spit-roasted chickens, glass bottles of olives and olive oils, quail eggs, duck eggs, boxes of chanterelle mushrooms and knobbly truffles, long-clawed langoustines and prickly sea urchins on beds of crushed ice – along with belts, boots, wallets, cheap socks, chic hats, colourful scarves, striped T-shirts, wicker baskets, wind-up toys, buckets of flowers... Paris' street markets, such as the wonderful Marché Bastille, are a feast for the senses.

Bastille & Eastern Paris

15

16

Versailles (p274)

16 No wonder revolutionaries massacred the Château de Versailles palace guard and ultimately dragged King Louis XVI and his queen Marie Antoinette back to Paris to be guillotined: this monumental, 700-room palace and sprawling estate – with its fountained gardens, ponds and canals – could not have been in starker contrast to taxpayers' average living conditions at the time. A Unesco World Heritage–listed wonder, Versailles is easily reached from central Paris; try to time your visit to catch musical fountain displays and equestrian shows.

Day Trips from Paris

What's New

Legendary Hotels

Landmark hotel openings include illustrious addresses such as Les Bains, formerly thermal baths and later a steamy nightclub, and the art deco swimming pool now housing the Hôtel Molitor. And reopenings see the 2015 return of the Hôtel de Crillon (www.crillon.com), with two suites designed by Karl Lagerfeld, as well as belle époque beauty the Ritz (www.ritzparis.com), following head-to-toe renovations of its rooms, bars, restaurants, gardens and Ritz Escoffier cooking school. (p289)

Eiffel Tower Refit

On the 1st floor of Paris' emblematic tower, two glitzy new glass pavilions house interactive history exhibits; outside them, peer d-o-w-n through glass flooring to the ground below. (p82)

Riverside Renaissance

A breath of fresh air, the former expressway Les Berges de Seine has fitness areas, floating gardens and a string of bars, restaurants and clubs, and also hosts year-round activities and events. (p240)

Institute des Cultures d'Islam

Art exhibitions and a hammam top the billing at the new Institut des Cultures d'Islam cultural institute in northern Paris' Goutte d'Or neighbourhood. (p143)

Coffee Revolution

Bitter Parisian coffee is becoming a thing of the past thanks to local roasteries such as Belleville Brûlerie and Coutume, with a wave of cafes citywide now producing world-class brews. (p178)

Hip Hostels

For years, Paris' crash pads were as good as its coffee was(n't), but that's changing too with the opening of state-of-the-art flash pads such as St Christopher's. (p295)

Moveable Feasts

Street food is taking the city by storm as food trucks specialising in everything from French favourites such as *tartiflette* to gourmet burgers and wildly flavoured ice creams roll out across Paris. (p52)

Visionary Architecture

Frank Gehry's Fondation Louis Vuitton building topped by 3600 glass panels forming 12 giant 'sails' competes for attention with the artistic creations inside. (p89)

Stirring Symphonies

For a classical concert to remember, visit the 2400-seat, Jean Nouvel–designed Philharmonie de Paris when it opens in the Parc de la Villette in 2015. (p139)

Treasure Hunts

Tours with a twist organised by THAT-Lou challenge participants to undertake themed treasure hunts in high-profile museums and neighbourhoods. (p350)

Forum Overhaul

On the site of Paris' old wholesale markets, a rainforest-inspired giant glass canopy and meadow-like gardens atop the rejuvenated subterranean mall Forum des Halles will reach final completion in 2016. (p122)

For more recommendations and reviews, see **lonelyplanet.com/paris**

Need to Know

For more information, see Survival Guide (p345)

Currency
Euro (€)

Language
French

Visas
Generally no restrictions for EU citizens. Usually not required for most other nationalities for stays of up to 90 days.

Money
ATMs widely available. Visa and MasterCard accepted in most hotels, shops and restaurants; fewer accept American Express.

Mobile Phones
Check with your provider before you leave about roaming costs and/or ensuring your phone's unlocked to use a French SIM card (available cheaply in Paris).

Time
Central European Time (GMT/UTC plus one hour).

Tourist Information
The main branch of the Paris Convention & Visitors Bureau (Office du Tourisme et des Congrès de Paris; www.parisinfo.com; 27 rue des Pyramides, 1er; ⌚9am-7pm May-Oct, 10am-7pm Nov-Apr; Ⓜ Pyramides) sells tickets for tours, several attractions, museum and transport passes, and can book accommodation.

Daily Costs

Budget: under €100
- Dorm bed €25–50
- Coffee/glass of wine/cocktail/*demi* (half-pint of beer) from €2/3.50/8/3.50
- Excellent self-catering options, especially markets
- Frequent free concerts and events
- Public transport, stand-by theatre tickets

Midrange: €100–250
- Double room €130–250
- Two-course meals €20–40
- Museums free to around €12
- Admission to clubs free to around €20

Top End: more than €250
- Historic luxury hotels
- Gastronomic restaurants
- Designer boutiques
- The sky is the limit!

Advance Planning

Two months before Book accommodation, organise opera, ballet or cabaret tickets and make reservations for high-end/popular restaurants.

Two weeks before Sign up for a free, local-led tour, book a sight-seeing balloon 'flight' and start narrowing down your choice of museums, pre-purchasing tickets online where possible.

Two days before Pack your comfiest shoes!

Useful Websites

- **Lonely Planet** (www.lonelyplanet.com/paris) Destination information, bookings, traveller forum and more.
- **Paris Info** (www.parisinfo.com) Comprehensive tourist-authority website.
- **Secrets of Paris** (www.secretsofparis.com) Loads of resources and reviews.
- **Paris by Mouth** (http://parisbymouth.com) Foodie heaven.
- **My Little Paris** (www.mylittleparis.com) Little-known local treasures.

WHEN TO GO

Spring and autumn are ideal. Summer is the main tourist season but many places close during August. Sights are quieter and prices lower during winter.

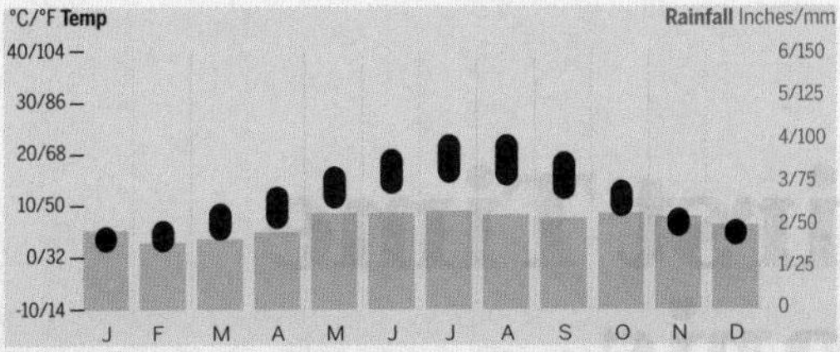

Arriving in Paris

Charles de Gaulle Airport Trains (RER), buses and night buses to the city centre €5.70–17.50; taxi around €50–65.

Orly Airport Trains (Orlyval then RER), buses and night buses to the city centre €7.50–12.50; T7 tram to Villejuif-Louis Aragon then metro to centre (€3.40); taxi around €40–65.

Beauvais Airport Buses (€17) to Porte Maillot then metro (€1.70); taxi at least €100 (probably more than the cost of your flight!).

Gare du Nord Train Station Within central Paris; served by metro (€1.70).

For much more on **arrival** see p346.

Getting Around

Walking is a pleasure in Paris, but the city also has one of the most efficient and inexpensive public transport systems in the world.

- **Metro & RER** The fastest way to get around. Runs from about 5.30am and finishes around 12.35am or 1.15am (and to around 2.15am on Friday and Saturday nights), depending on the line.
- **Bicycle** Virtually free pick-up, drop-off Vélib' bikes operate across 1800 stations citywide.
- **Bus** Good for parents with prams/strollers and people with limited mobility.
- **Boat** The Batobus is a handy hop-on, hop-off service stopping at eight key destinations along the Seine.

For much more on **getting around** see p348.

Sleeping

Paris has plenty of accommodation, but it's often *complet* (full) well in advance. Reservations are recommended year-round, and essential during the warmer months (April to October) and during all holidays. Accommodation outside central Paris is marginally cheaper than within the city, but travelling to and fro can consume time and money. Choose somewhere within Paris' 20 *arrondissements*, to experience Parisian life the moment you step out the door.

Useful Websites

- **Lonely Planet** (www.lonelyplanet.com/france/paris/hotels) Our top choices.
- **Paris Hotel** (www.hotels-paris.fr) Well-organised site with lots of user reviews.
- **Paris Hotel Service** (www.parishotelservice.com) Specialises in boutique gems.
- **Paris Hotels** (www.parishotels.com) Loads of options and locations.
- **Paris Attitude** (www.parisattitude.com) Thousands of apartment rentals; professional service, reasonable fees.

For much more on **sleeping** see p289.

ARRONDISSEMENTS

Within the Périphérique (ring road), Paris is divided into 20 *arrondissements* (city districts), which spiral clockwise like a snail shell from the centre. *Arrondissement* numbers (1er, 2e etc) form an integral part of all Parisian addresses, including in our reviews. Each *arrondissement* has its own personality, but it's the *quartiers* (neighbourhoods), which often overlap *arrondissement* boundaries, that give Paris its village atmosphere.

First Time Paris

For more information, see Survival Guide (p345)

Checklist

- Check passport validity and visa requirements
- Arrange travel insurance
- Confirm airline baggage restrictions
- Book ahead for accommodation and popular restaurants
- Buy tickets online for the Louvre, Eiffel Tower etc
- Organise international roaming on your phone if needed

What to Pack

- Comfortable shoes – Paris is best explored on foot
- Phrasebook – the more French you attempt, the more rewarding your visit will be
- Travel plug (adaptor)
- Bike helmet (not supplied with Vélib' bikes, so you may want to bring your own)
- Pocketknife with corkscrew (corked wine bottles are the norm; screw caps are rare. Don't forget to pack it in your checked baggage for flights)
- Washcloths (hotels/apartments don't provide them)

Top Tips for Your Trip

- An unforgettable introduction to the city is a river cruise (or the hop-on, hop-off Batobus) along the Seine, floating past Parisian landmarks including the Eiffel Tower, Louvre and Notre Dame.
- The metro is safe, clean and super-easy to use. Local buses are a scenic alternative.
- Prebook attractions online wherever possible to avoid standing in long ticket queues.
- Above all, don't try to cram too much into your schedule. Allow time to soak up the atmosphere of Paris' neighbourhoods – lingering over a coffee on a cafe terrace and exploring the backstreets are as much a part of the Parisian experience as visiting major sights.

What to Wear

As the cradle of *haute couture,* Paris is chic: don your smarter threads (and accessories). You'll also stand out less as a tourist and therefore be less of a target for pickpockets. Dress up rather than down for the 'nicer' restaurants, clubs and bars – no jeans, shorts or trainers/sneakers.

Bring sturdy shoes whatever the season – cobbled streets aren't kind on high heels or thin soles.

When visiting religious sites such as Notre Dame, be sure to dress respectfully.

Be Forewarned

- A substantial number of Paris' restaurants, smaller shops and various other venues close around August when Parisians traditionally head to the countryside or coast on summer holidays. Precheck establishments' seasonal closures to avoid disappointment.
- For a big city, Paris is generally exceptionally safe but pickpockets are an ever-present menace, particularly in tourist hotspots. Keep an extra-close eye on your belongings.
- Parisian hotel rooms are infamously small and expensive. Price-comparison online booking sites can save you a bundle, or consider a short-stay apartment. In both apartments and hotels, amenities such as air conditioning and lifts/elevators come at a premium.

Money

Visa and MasterCard are the most widely used credit cards; American Express is only accepted by upmarket establishments such as international chain hotels, luxury boutiques and department stores.

Chip-and-pin is the norm for card transactions – few places accept swipe-and-signature. Some foreign chip-and-pin-enabled cards require a signature – ask your bank before you leave. ATMs (*points d'argent* or *distributeurs automatiques de billets*) are everywhere; withdrawals incur international transaction fees.

You can change cash (and travellers cheques) at some banks, post offices and *bureaux de change* (money-exchange offices). Many shops don't accept €200 and €500 bills.

For more information, see p354.

Taxes & Refunds

Prices displayed in shops etc invariably include France's TVA (*taxe sur la valeur ajoutée;* value-added tax).

Non-EU residents can often claim a refund (p356) of TVA paid on goods.

Tipping

➡ **Taxis** Optional, but many round up to the nearest euro.

➡ **Restaurants** A 15% service charge is usually in the bill, though many people leave a few euros.

➡ **Bars & Cafes** Not necessary at the bar. If drinks are brought to your table, tip as you would in a restaurant.

➡ **Hotels** Bellhops usually expect €1 to €2 per bag.

Language

Although English is increasingly widespread in Paris, you'll have an infinitely more rewarding experience if you address locals in French, even simply '*bonjour, parlez-vous anglais*?' ('hello, do you speak English?'). See our Language chapter (p360).

1 What are the opening hours?
Quelles sont les heures d'ouverture?
kel son lay zer doo·vair·tewr

French business hours are governed by a maze of regulations, so it's a good idea to check before you make plans.

2 I'd like the set menu, please.
Je voudrais le menu, s'il vous plait.
zher voo·dray ler mer·new seel voo play

The best-value dining in France is the two- or three-course meal at a fixed price. Most restaurants have one on the chalkboard.

3 Which wine would you recommend?
Quel vin vous conseillez?
kel vun voo kon·say·yay

Who better to ask for advice on wine than the French?

4 Can I address you with 'tu'?
Est-ce que je peux vous tutoyer?
es ker zher per voo tew·twa·yay

Before you start addressing someone with the informal 'you' form, it's polite to ask permission first.

5 Do you have plans for tonight/tomorrow?
Vous avez prévu quelque chose ce soir/demain?
voo za·vay pray·vew kel·ker shoz ser swar/der·mun

To arrange to meet up without sounding pushy, ask friends if they're available rather than inviting them directly.

Etiquette

➡ Communication tends to be formal and reserved but shouldn't be mistaken for unfriendliness.

➡ Always greet/farewell anyone you interact with, such as shopkeepers, with '*Bonjour* (*bonsoir* at night)/*Au revoir*'.

➡ Particularly in smaller shops, staff may not appreciate you touching the merchandise until invited to do so, nor taking photographs.

➡ Parisians don't speak loudly – modulate your voice to a similarly low pitch.

➡ *Tu* and *vous* both mean 'you' but *tu* is only used with people you know very well, children or animals. Use *vous* until you're invited to use *tu*.

➡ Talking about money (eg salaries or spending outlays) is generally taboo in public.

➡ Never use '*garçon*' ('boy') to summon a waiter, rather 'Monsieur' or 'Madame'.

Top Itineraries

Day One

Louvre & Les Halles (p107)

Start with a stroll through the elegant **Jardin des Tuileries**, stopping to view Monet's enormous *Waterlilies* at the **Musée de l'Orangerie** and/or photography exhibits at the **Jeu de Paume**. IM Pei's glass pyramid is your compass point to enter the labyrinthine **Louvre**.

Lunch Nip out for contemporary cooking at Racines 2 (p129).

Louvre & Les Halles (p107)

Visiting this monumental museum could easily consume a full day but once you've had your fill, browse the colonnaded arcades of the exquisite **Jardin du Palais Royal**, and visit the beautiful church **Église St-Eustache**. Tap into the soul of the former Les Halles wholesale markets along backstreet legacies such as the former oyster market, **rue Montorgueil**. Linger for a drink on **rue Montmartre**, then head to the late-opening **Centre Pompidou** for modern and contemporary art and amazing rooftop views.

Dinner Frenchie (p127) and Verjus (p127) offer walk-in wine-bar dining.

Le Marais, Ménilmontant & Belleville (p159)

There's a wealth to see in Le Marais by day (**Musée Picasso**, **Musée Carnavalet**, **Musée des Arts et Métiers**...) but the neighbourhood really comes into its own at night, with a cornucopia of hip bars and clubs.

Day Two

Champs-Élysées & Grands Boulevards (p93)

Climb the mighty **Arc de Triomphe** for a pinch-yourself Parisian panorama. Promenade down Paris' most glamorous avenue, the **Champs-Élysées**, and give your credit card a workout in the **Triangle d'Or**, **Galeries Lafayette** or **place de la Madeleine** before catching edgy art exhibitions at **La Pinacothèque**.

Lunch Café Branly (p91): casual yet classy, with ringside Tower views.

Eiffel Tower & Western Paris (p80)

Check out indigenous art as well as the awesome architecture of the **Musée du Quai Branly**. This cultural neighbourhood is also home to the world's largest Monet collection at the **Musée Marmottan-Monet**, contemporary installations at the **Palais de Tokyo**, and Asian treasures at the **Musée Guimet**. Sunset is the best time to ascend the **Eiffel Tower**, to experience both the dizzying views during daylight and then the glittering *la ville lumière* (the City of Light) by night.

Dinner Cracking Modern French fare at Le Casse Noix (p263).

Montparnasse & Southern Paris (p256)

Detour for a drink at an historic Montparnasse brasserie such as **Le Select** or continue straight down the Seine to party aboard floating nightclubs including **Le Batofar**.

Day Three

The Islands (p200)

Starting your day at the city's most visited sight, **Notre Dame**, gives you the best chance of beating the crowds. In addition to its stained-glass interior, allow around an hour to visit the top and another to explore the archaeological **crypt**. For even more beautiful stained glasswork, don't miss nearby **Sainte-Chapelle**. Cross the **Pont St-Louis** to buy a **Berthillon** ice cream before browsing the Île St-Louis' enchanting boutiques.

Lunch Deliciously Parisian hangout Café Saint Régis (p209).

St-Germain & Les Invalides (p228)

Swoon over impressionist masterpieces in the magnificent **Musée d'Orsay**, scout out the backstreet boutiques and storied shops of St-Germain, sip coffee on the terrace of literary cafes such as **Les Deux Magots** and laze in the lovely **Jardin du Luxembourg**, the city's most popular park.

Dinner French classics in the art nouveau jewel Bouillon Racine (p243).

Latin Quarter (p211)

Scour the shelves of late-night bookshops including the fabled **Shakespeare & Company**, then join Parisian students and academics in the Latin Quarter's bars, cafes and pubs on **rue Mouffetard** or hit jazz club **Café Universel**.

Day Four

Montmartre & Northern Paris (p135)

Montmartre's slinking streets and steep staircases lined with crooked ivy-clad buildings are enchanting to meander, especially early morning when tourists are few. Head to the hilltop **Sacré-Cœur** basilica, then brush up on the area's fabled history at the **Musée de Montmartre**.

Lunch Locals' fave Le Miroir (p146) offers fantastic lunchtime *menu* specials.

Montmartre & Northern Paris (p135)

Stroll the shaded tow-paths of cafe-lined **Canal St-Martin**, and visit the futuristic **Parc de la Villette**, the kid-friendly **Cité des Sciences** museum and the instrument-filled **Musée de la Musique**, within the **Cité de la Musique**. Sailing schedules permitting, hop on a **canal cruise** to Bastille.

Dinner Sublime 'small plates' at Le 6 Paul Bert (p192).

Bastille & Eastern Paris (p187)

The Bastille neighbourhood calls for a cafe crawl: classics include the cherry-red **Le Pure Café** and absinthe specialist **La Fée Verte**. Salsa your socks off at the 1936 dance hall **Le Balajo** on nightlife strip **rue de Lappe** or catch electro, funk and hip hop at **Badaboum**.

If You Like...

Markets

Marché Bastille Arguably the best open-air market in the city. (p191)

Marché d'Aligre Wonderfully chaotic market with all the staples of French cuisine. (p191)

Marché St-Quentin Covered market dating back to 1866. (p151)

Rue Montorgueil Street stalls front the food shops of this pedestrianised strip. (p126)

Marché aux Enfants Rouges Glorious maze of food stalls with ready-to-eat dishes from around the globe. (p168)

Marché aux Fleurs Reine Elizabeth II Fragrant flower market. (p210)

Marché Raspail Especially popular for its fabulous Sunday organic market. (p247)

Marché aux Puces de St-Ouen Europe's largest flea market, with more than 2500 stalls. (p157)

Rue Mouffetard Atmospheric commercial street with food shops and stalls galore. (p222)

Marché de Belleville Open-air market in business since 1860, in one of Paris' most multicultural, up-and-coming 'hoods. (p173)

Churches

Église St-Eustache Architecturally magnificent and musically outstanding, this church has sent souls soaring for centuries. (p120)

JOE DANIEL PRICE / GETTY IMAGES ©

Lower chapel of Sainte-Chapelle (p207), in the Palais de Justice (Law Courts) on Île de la Cité

Cathédrale Notre Dame de Paris Paris' mighty cathedral is without equal. (p202)

Basilique du Sacré-Cœur The city's landmark basilica lords over Montmartre. (p137)

Église de la Madeleine Neoclassical landmark with wondrous concerts. (p99)

Église St-Pierre de Montmartre Where the Jesuit order was founded. (p140)

Sainte-Chapelle Classical concerts provide the perfect opportunity to truly appreciate Sainte-Chapelle's beauty. (p207)

Basilique de St-Denis France's first major Gothic structure and still one of its finest. (p141)

Église St-Germain des Prés Built in the 11th century, this is Paris' oldest church. (p238)

Église St-Sulpice Frescoes by Delacroix and a starring role in *The Da Vinci Code*. (p238)

Cathédrale Notre Dame – Chartres Renowned for its brilliant-blue stained glass. (p286)

Romance

Jardin du Palais Royal With its arcaded galleries and gravel walkways embraced by the neoclassical Palais Royal, there is no urban garden more elegant or romantic. (p122)

Le Grand Véfour Savour the romance of 18th-century Paris in one of the world's most beautiful restaurants. (p127)

The Islands Paris' islands harbour a trove of hidden romantic spots. (p200)

Île aux Cygnes The city's little-known third island has wonderful Eiffel Tower views. (p260)

Eiffel Tower There's a reason the top platform sees up to three marriage proposals an hour. (p82)

Canal St-Martin Stroll the shaded towpaths or sit on the banks and watch the boats float by. (p143)

Place St-Sulpice The *place* (square) in front of Église St-Sulpice is an enchanting spot to linger. (p238)

Musée Rodin Swoon over Rodin's marble monument to love, *The Kiss*, and stroll the museum's rose-clambered, sculpture-filled garden. (p236)

Le Pradey With its deep red walls, frilly bedspread and heart-shaped door frame, the themed Moulin Rouge room at this design hotel is pure romance. (p294)

Literature

Maison de Victor Hugo Visit the elegant home of celebrated novelist and poet Victor Hugo overlooking one of Paris' most sublime city squares. (p165)

Maison de Balzac Balzac's residence and writing studio from 1840–47 is a charmer. (p87)

St-Germain literary addresses Take a literary-loop walking tour through this fabled part of the Left Bank. (p242)

Latin Quarter literary addresses The Latin Quarter is scattered with seminal literary addresses. (p218)

Montparnasse literary addresses Writers, artists and political exiles flocked to Montparnasse's brasseries in its early-20th-century heyday. (p269)

Shakespeare & Company Attend a reading by established and emerging authors, curl up in the reading library or browse the shelves of this magical bookshop–writers' hub. (p225)

Bibliothèque Nationale de France France's national library frequently mounts literary exhibitions. (p261)

Panoramas

Eiffel Tower Each of Paris' landmark tower's three viewing platforms offers a different perspective of the city. (p82)

Tour Montparnasse The views over Paris are the redeeming feature of this soulless skyscraper. (p259)

Galeries Lafayette Some of the best free views of the city are from the top of this grand department store. (p105)

Le Printemps This magnificent department store also has mesmerising rooftop views for free. (p105)

Parc de Belleville Climb to the top of the hill in this little-known Belleville park to savour some of the best views of the city. (p167)

Arc de Triomphe Sweeping views along the Champs-Élysées. (p95)

Centre Pompidou Although only six storeys high, the Centre Pompidou rooftop's views across low-rise Paris are phenomenal. (p117)

Le Ballon Air de Paris Airborne views from a balloon. (p260)

For more top Paris spots, see the following:

- ➡ Museums & Galleries (p40)
- ➡ Eating (p44)
- ➡ Drinking & Nightlife (p54)
- ➡ Shopping (p60)
- ➡ Entertainment (p65)

Basilique du Sacré-Cœur The superb views from Sacré-Cœur's steps get even better from inside its central dome. (p137)

Art Nouveau

Eiffel Tower The graceful latticed metalwork of Paris' 'iron lady' is art-nouveau architecture at its best. (p82)

Abbesses metro entrance Hector Guimard's finest remaining glass-canopied metro entrance, illuminated by twin lamps. (p338)

Musée d'Orsay The 1900-built former railway station housing this monumental museum justifies a visit alone. (p230)

Le Train Bleu Resplendent restaurant inside the Gare de Lyon. (p196)

Musée Carnavalet Fouquet's stunning art-nouveau jewellery shop from rue Royale inside the city's leading history museum is a real treat. (p164)

Galeries Lafayette Glorious department store topped by a stunning stained-glass dome. (p105)

Le Carreau du Temple This old covered market in the Marais reopened in 2014 as a cutting-edge cultural and community centre. (p180)

Bofinger Nothing quite so tasty as dining between art-nouveau brass, glass and mirrors in Paris' oldest brasserie. (p175)

Modern & Contemporary Architecture

Centre Pompidou Designed inside-out by Renzo Piano and Richard Rogers in the 1970s, Paris' premier cultural centre is still cutting-edge today. (p117)

La Défense The only place in the city to see a forest of skyscrapers. (p87)

Musée du Quai Branly Striking Seine-side museum designed by Jean Nouvel. (p84)

Institut du Monde Arabe The building that established Nouvel's reputation blends modern and traditional Arab elements with Western influences. (p216)

Fondation Cartier pour l'Art Contemporain Stunning contemporary art space courtesy of Nouvel. (p259)

Fondation Louis Vuitton Frank Gehry–designed fine-arts centre, topped by a giant glass 'cloud'. (p89)

Louvre glass pyramid Egypt's original pyramid builders couldn't have imagined this. (p109)

Bibliothèque Nationale de France The national library's four towers are shaped like half-open books. (p261)

Cité de l'Architecture et du Patrimoine Inside the 1937-built Palais du Chaillot, the exhibits not only cover Paris' architectural past and present but also its future. (p85)

Parks & Gardens

Jardin du Luxembourg Paris' most popular inner-city oasis. (p234)

Jardin des Tuileries Meet Monet and revel in Paris at its symmetrical best. (p119)

Promenade Plantée The world's first elevated park, atop a disused 19th-century railway viaduct. (p189)

Maison et Jardins de Claude Monet The flower-filled gardens surrounding Monet's former home take on a palette of hues come spring. (p288)

Parc de la Villette Canal-side 35-hectare pavilion-filled 'park of the future' with state-of-the-art facilities for kids and adults. (p139)

Parc des Buttes-Chaumont Hilly, forested haven in Northern Paris. (p142)

Versailles Designed by André Le Nôtre, the château's gardens are fit for a king. (p274)

Jardin des Plantes The city's beautiful botanic gardens shelter rare plants and greenhouses. (p214)

Bois de Vincennes Paris' eastern woods were once royal hunting grounds. (p190)

Bois de Boulogne Explore Paris' western woods by rowboat or bicycle. (p89)

French Revolution–Era History

Place de la Bastille Site of the former prison stormed on 14 July 1789, mobilising the Revolution. (p189)

Versailles The October 1789 March on Versailles forced the royal family to leave the château. (p274)

Conciergerie Louis XVI's queen Marie-Antoinette was one of the aristocratic prisoners tried and imprisoned here. (p208)

Place de la Concorde Louis XVI and Marie-Antoinette were among thousands guillotined where the obelisk now stands. (p97)

Parc du Champ de Mars This former military training ground was the site of Revolutionary festivals. (p85)

ESCUDERO PATRICK / HEMIS. / GETTY IMAGES ©

(Above) Obelisk, place de la Concorde (p97)
(Below) Jardin des Tuileries (p119)

JEAN-PIERRE LESCOURRET / GETTY IMAGES ©

Musée Carnavalet Paris' history museum offers a comprehensive overview of this pivotal time in the city's history. (p164)

Concorde metro station Ceramic tiles spell out the text of the Declaration of the Rights of Man and of the Citizen, setting forth the principles of the French Revolution. (p338)

Caveau de la Huchette Long a swinging jazz club, this cellar was used as a courtroom and torture chamber during the Revolution. (p224)

Medieval History

Le Marais The Marais' medieval streets largely escaped Baron Haussmann's reformation. (p159)

Notre Dame Constructed between 1163 and the early 14th century. (p202)

Louvre Immense fort-turned-palace-turned-museum, constructed 1190–1202. (p109)

Sainte-Chapelle Consecrated in 1248. (p207)

Sorbonne University founded in 1253. (p214)

Musée National du Moyen Âge Partly housed in the 15th-century Hôtel de Cluny, Paris' finest civil medieval building. (p213)

Basilique de St-Denis Work on this Gothic wonder started around 1136. (p141)

Cathédrale Notre Dame – Chartres France's best-preserved medieval cathedral, built in the 13th century. (p286)

Château de Vincennes The only medieval castle in Paris. (p190)

Month by Month

TOP EVENTS

Paris Plages, July

Bastille Day, July

Banlieues Bleues, March

Rock en Seine, August

Nuit Blanche, October

January

The frosty first month of the year isn't the most festive in Paris, but fashion shows – as well as the winter *soldes* (sales) – certainly brighten the mood.

Louis XVI Commemorative Mass

On the Sunday closest to 21 January, royalists and right-wingers attend a mass at the Chapelle Expiatoire (www.monuments-nationaux.fr) marking the execution by guillotine of King Louis XVI in 1793.

Chinese New Year

Paris' largest lantern-lit festivities and dragon parades take place in the city's main Chinatown in the 13e in late January or early February. Parades are also held in Belleville and Le Marais.

February

Festivities still aren't in full swing in February, but couples descend on France's romantic capital for Valentine's Day, when restaurants offer special menus and more 'love locks' decorate (or, rather, desecrate) the city's bridges.

Salon International de l'Agriculture

Appetising nine-day international agricultural fair (www.salon-agriculture.com) with produce (and animals) from all over France turned into delectable fare at the Parc des Expositions at Porte de Versailles, 15e, from late February to early March.

March

Blooms appear in Paris' parks and gardens, leaves start greening the city's avenues and festivities begin to flourish. And days get longer – the last Sunday morning of the month ushers in daylight-saving time.

Banlieues Bleues

Big-name acts perform during the 'Suburban Blues' (www.banlieuesbleues.org) jazz, blues and R&B festival from mid-March to mid-April at venues in Paris' northern suburbs.

Printemps du Cinéma

Selected cinemas across Paris offer film-goers a unique entry fee of €3.50 per session over three days sometime around the middle of March (www.printempsducinema.com).

April

Sinatra sang about April in Paris, and the month sees the city's 'charm of spring' in full swing, with chestnuts blossoming and cafe terraces coming into their own.

Foire du Trône

Dating back some 1000 years (!), this huge funfair (www.foiredutrone.com) is held on the Pelouse de Reuilly of the Bois de Vincennes from around early April to early June.

Marathon International de Paris

On your marks…the Paris International Marathon (www.parismarathon.com), usually held on the second Sunday of April, starts on the av des Champs-Élysées, 8e, and finishes on av Foch, 16e, attracting more than 40,000 runners from more than 100 countries.

Foire de Paris

Gadgets, widgets, food and wine feature at this huge contemporary-living fair (www.foiredeparis.fr), held from late April to early May at the Parc des Expositions at Porte de Versailles, 15e.

May

The temperate month of May has the most public holidays of any in France. Watch out for widespread closures, particularly on May Day (1 May).

La Nuit Européenne des Musées

Key museums across Paris stay open late for the European Museums Night (www.nuitdesmusees.culture.fr), on one Saturday in mid-May. Most offer free entry.

L'Olympiade des Garçons de Café

Waiters first began racing through central Paris balancing a glass and bottle on a tray in the early 20th century (www.olympiade-garcons-de-cafe.fr).

Portes Ouvertes des Ateliers d'Artistes de Belleville

More than 250 painters, sculptors and other artists in Belleville in the 10e open their studio doors to visitors over four days (Friday to Monday) in late May (www.ateliers-artistes-belleville.org).

French Open

The glitzy Internationaux de France de Tennis Grand Slam hits up from late May to early June at Stade Roland Garros (www.rolandgarros.com) at the Bois de Boulogne.

June

Paris is positively jumping in June, thanks to warm temperatures and long daylight hours. Come evening, twilight lingering until nearly 11pm is the stuff of midsummer-night dreams.

Festival de St-Denis

Book ahead for this prestigious cycle of classical-music concerts at the Basilique de St-Denis (www.festival-saint-denis.com) and nearby venues held throughout the month.

Fête de la Musique

This national music festival (http://fetedelamusique.culture.fr) welcomes in summer on the solstice (21 June) with staged and impromptu live performances of jazz, reggae, classical and more all over the city.

Gay Pride March

Late June's colourful Saturday-afternoon Marche des Fiertés (www.gaypride.fr) through the Marais to Bastille celebrates Gay Pride Day with over-the-top floats and outrageous costumes.

Paris Jazz Festival

Free jazz concerts swing every Saturday and Sunday afternoon in June and July in the Parc Floral de Paris (www.parisjazzfestival.paris.fr); park entry for adults/under 25s of €5.50/2.75 applies.

La Goutte d'Or en Fête

Rai, reggae and rap feature at this three-day world-music festival (www.gouttedorenfete.org) on square Léon in the 18e's Goutte d'Or neighbourhood in late June.

July

During the Parisian summer, 'beaches' – complete with sun beds, umbrellas, atomisers, lounge chairs and palm trees – line the banks of the Seine, while shoppers hit the summer sales.

Paris Cinéma

Rare and restored films screen in selected cinemas city-wide during this 12-day festival (www.pariscinema.org) in the first half of July. It also hosts premiers, an international competition and outdoor events.

Bastille Day

Paris celebrates France's national day on 14 July with a morning military parade along av des Champs-Élysées accompanied by a fly-past of fighter aircraft and helicopters, and *feux d'artifice* (fireworks) lighting up the sky above the Champ de Mars by night.

Paris Plages

From mid-July to mid-August, 'Paris Beaches' take over the Right Bank between the Louvre, 1er, and Pont de Sully, 4e; and the Rotonde de la Villette and rue de Crimée, 19e. All beaches are open from 8am to midnight.

☆ Tour de France

The last of 21 stages of this legendary, 3500km-long cycling event (www.letour.com) finishes with a dash up av des Champs-Élysées on the third or fourth Sunday of July.

August

Parisians desert the city in droves during the summer swelter when, despite an influx of tourists, many restaurants and shops shut. It's a prime time to cycle, with far less traffic on the roads.

☆ Rock en Seine

Headlining acts rock the Domaine National de St-Cloud on the city's southwestern edge at this popular three-day, late-August music festival (www.rockenseine.com).

September

Tourists leave and Parisians come home: *la rentrée* marks residents' return to work and study after the summer break. Cultural life shifts into top gear and the weather is at its blue-skied best.

☆ Jazz à La Villette

This super two-week jazz festival (www.jazzalavillette.com) in the first half of September has sessions in Parc de la Villette, at the Cité de la Musique and at surrounding venues.

(Top) Celebrations for Bastille Day (p29)
(Bottom) Paris Plages (p29)

CHRISTIAN LIEWIG / CORBIS ©

PAWEL LIBERA / GETTY IMAGES ©

Festival d'Automne

Painting, music, dance and theatre take place at venues throughout the city from mid-September to late December as part of the long-running Autumn Festival of arts (www.festival-automne.com).

Journées Européennes du Patrimoine

The third weekend in September sees Paris open the doors of otherwise-off-limits buildings – embassies, government ministries and so forth – during European Heritage Days (www.journeesdupatrimoine.culture.fr).

Techno Parade

On one Saturday in mid-September floats carrying musicians and DJs pump up the volume between place de la République to place d'Italie during the Techno Parade (www.technoparade.fr).

October

October heralds an autumnal kaleidoscope in the city's parks and gardens, along with bright, crisp days, cool, clear nights and excellent cultural offerings. Daylight saving ends on the last Sunday morning of the month.

Nuit Blanche

From sundown until sunrise on the first Saturday and Sunday of October, museums and recreational facilities such as swimming pools stay open, along with bars and clubs, for one 'White Night' (ie 'All Nighter').

Fête des Vendanges de Montmartre

The grape harvest from the Clos Montmartre in early October is followed by five days of festivities including a parade (www.fetedesvendangesdemontmartre.com).

Foire Internationale d'Art Contemporain

Scores of galleries are represented at the contemporary-art fair known as FIAC (www.fiac.com), held over four days in late October at venues including the Grand Palais.

November

Dark, chilly days and long, cold nights see Parisians take refuge indoors: the opera and ballet seasons are going strong and there are plenty of cosy bistros and bars.

Africolor

From mid-November to late December, this six-week-long African-music festival (www.africolor.com) is primarily held in surrounding suburbs, such as St-Denis, St-Ouen and Montreuil.

Beaujolais Nouveau

At midnight on the third Thursday (ie Wednesday night) in November – as soon as French law permits – the opening of the first bottles of cherry-bright, six-week-old Beaujolais Nouveau is celebrated in Paris wine bars, with more celebrations on the Thursday itself.

December

Twinkling fairy lights, brightly decorated Christmas trees and shop windows, and outdoor ice-skating rinks make December a magical month to be in the City of Light.

Salon du Cheval de Paris

Sporting events and competitions including show jumping and dressage, plus a horseback parade through Paris, are part of the Paris Horse Fair (www.salon-cheval.com) from late November to early December.

Christmas Eve Mass

Mass is celebrated at midnight on Christmas Eve at many Paris churches, including Notre Dame – arrive early to find a place.

Le Festival du Merveilleux

Normally closed to the public, the private Musée des Arts Forains (www.arts-forains.com), filled with yesteryear fairground attractions, opens for 11 days from late December to early January, with enchanting rides, attractions and shows.

New Year's Eve

Bd St-Michel (5e), place de la Bastille (11e), the Eiffel Tower (7e) and, above all, av des Champs-Élysées (8e) are the places to be to ring in the New Year.

With Kids

Paris is extraordinarily child-friendly, with an overwhelming choice of creative, educational, culinary and 'pure old-fashioned fun' things to see, do, experience. For information on courses (cooking, pétanque*) and guided tours (French Revolution, Dark Side of Paris), see p351.*

ESCUDERO PATRICK / GETTY IMAGES ©

Jardin des Plantes (p214)

Science Museums

Cité des Sciences (p142)

If you have time for just one museum, make it this. Book interactive sessions in advance to avoid disappointment.

Palais de la Découverte (p99)

Collections at this science museum are a perfect mix of interactive and academic; outstanding science-experiment workshops for over-10s.

Musée des Arts et Métiers (p166)

Crammed with instruments and machines, Europe's oldest science and technology museum is mesmerising. Activity- and experiment-driven workshops are top-notch.

Art Attack

Centre Pompidou (p117)

Urban ode to modern art with great exhibitions, art workshops (for kids three to 12) and teen events in Studio 13/16.

Musée en Herbe (p122)

Thoughtful art museum for children with excellent bookshop and art workshops for kids two to 12.

Palais de Tokyo (p85)

Interactive installations, art workshops (for kids six to 12) and storytelling sessions (for three- to five-year-olds).

Treasure Hunts with THATLou (p350)

Give the kids a burst of art adrenelin with a THATLou treasure hunt at the Louvre or equivalent THATd'Or hunt at the Musée d'Orsay. Play alone or in teams. Fabulous fun for all ages.

Hands-On Activities

Crafty Happenings at Musée du Quai Branly (p84)

Mask-making, boomerang-hurling and experimenting with traditional instruments: the *ateliers* (for kids three to 12) at

NOT FOR PARENTS

For an insight into Paris with kids, pick up Lonely Planet's *Not for Parents: Paris*, perfect for children aged eight and up, it opens up a world of intriguing stories and fascinating facts about Paris' people, places, history and culture.

this Seine-side museum devoted to African, Asian and Oceanic art and culture are diverse and creative.

Music at Cité de la Musique (p142)

Concerts, shows and instrument workshops are part of the world-music repertoire at the City of Music.

Bag Painting with Kasia Dietz

Design and paint a reversible, hand-printed canvas tote with Paris-based New Yorker **Kasia Dietz** (www.kasiadietzworkshops.com) during a half-day bag-painting workshop (€80) – ideal for fashion-conscious teens (and parents).

Model building at Cité de l'Architecture et du Patrimoine (p85)

Workshops at Paris' architecture museum see kids (from five to 16 years) build art-deco houses, chateaux and towers in miniature form.

Animal Mad

Equestrian shows (p274) at Versailles

World-class equestrian shows at Château de Versailles are mesmerising and magical – combine with a stable visit.

Sharks at Aquarium de Paris Cinéaqua (p87)

It's not the best aquarium, but Cinéaqua has a shark tank and 500-odd fish species.

Ménagerie du Jardin des Plantes (p215)

The collection of animals in the Jardin des Plantes includes snow panthers and pandas; combine with the neighbouring Natural History Museum (p214).

Parc Zoologique de Paris (p190)

Observe lions, cougars, white rhinos and a whole gaggle of other beasties unseen at this state-of-the-art zoo in Bois de Vincennes.

Parks & Outdoor Capers

Sailboats in Jardin du Luxembourg (p234)

Playgrounds, puppet shows, pony rides, chess and an old-fashioned carousel: this mythical park has pandered to children forever. But it is the vintage toy boats to sail that are the real heart-stealer.

Jardin des Tuileries (p119)

Light relief after the neighbouring **Louvre**, this Seine-side park stages kids' activities and a summertime amusement park.

Parc Floral de Paris (p190)

Easily the best playground for kids over eight: outdoor concerts, puppet shows and giant climbing webs, 30m-high slides and a zip line, among other high energy–burning attractions.

Jardin d'Acclimatation (p89)

This enormous green area with cycling paths, forest, lakes and ponds in the Bois de Boulogne is a family must. Renting a pedalo or rowing boat – bring a picnic – is a warm-weather treat and every child loves the faster-paced amusement park.

Locks on Canal St-Martin (p143)

Watching canal boats navigate the many locks is fun, fascinating and free. Lunch

BRUNO DE HOGUES / GETTY IMAGES ©

Jardin du Luxembourg (p234)

waterside on fish and chips from the Sunken Chip (p151).

Riverside Play on Les Berges de Seine (p240)

Giant board games, a climbing wall, a 20m-long blackboard to chalk on, Native American-inspired tipis and events 'n' shows galore.

Mystery Afloat the Seine

Every kid, big and small, loves a voyage down the Seine with **Bateaux-Mouches** (p352) or **Bateaux Parisiens** (p352). But there is something extra special about the one-hour 'Paris Mystery' tours designed especially for children by **Vedettes de Paris** (p352).

Screen Entertainment

Digital Exhibitions at Gaîté Lyrique (p180)

Digital-driven exhibitions, video games for older children and teens, laptops to use in the digitally connected cafe and a library with desks shaped like ducks for kids under five to sit at and draw while older siblings geek.

Comic Art at Art Ludique–Le Musée (p262)

Teens will appreciate this refreshingly different art museum dedicated to comics, video games, animation and live-action cinema.

Special-Effect Movies at Cité des Sciences (p142)

Two special-effect cinemas: Géode with 3D movies, and Cinéma Louis-Lumière screening animation and short films. Top it off with a cinematic trip through the solar system in the science museum's Planetarium.

Behind-the-Scenes Tour at Le Grand Rex (p133)

Whizz-bang special effects stun during behind-the-scenes tours at this iconic 1930s cinema. Stand behind the big screen and muck around in a recording studio.

Theme Parks

The obvious, best suited for children aged four to 10, is **Disneyland Resort Paris** (p280). The other hot shot is **Parc Astérix** (www.parcasterix.fr; 30km north of Paris, A1 motorway between exit 7 & 8; adult/3-11yr €46/37, parking €10; ⌚10am-6pm Jun, 10am-7pm Jul & Aug, 10am-6pm Wed, Sat & Sun May & Sep-early Oct), a theme park 30km north of Paris which – despite its Gaullish comic-book-inspired name – covers the whole gamut from prehistory to the 19th century with its six 'worlds', adrenalin-pumping attractions and shows for all ages.

An Afternoon at the Theatre

The city's diverse theatre scene stages bags of *spectacles* (shows), *théâtre classique* (classical theatre) and other performances for kids, some in English; weekly entertainment mag *Pariscope* (€0.50) lists what's on, including **puppet shows** for kids in Jardin du Luxembourg, Jardin d'Acclimatation, Jardin des Tuileries, Parc Floral and Parc du Champ du Mars.

Easy Eating

Pizza Picnic at Pink Flamingo (p150)

Where else are you sent away with a pink balloon when you order? Kids adore take-away pizzeria Pink Flamingo with outlets on Canal St-Martin and in Bastille and Le Marais.

Hand-Pulled Noodles at Les Pâtes Vivantes (p103)

Watching nimble-fingered chefs pull traditional Chinese noodles by hand at **Les Pâtes Vivantes** is spellbinding.

Le Jardin des Pâtes (p216)

This Left Bank address, steps from Jardin des Plantes, cooks up some of Paris' most creative and tastiest pasta.

Dip in at Chalet Savoyard (p194)

Everyone loves a bubbling pot of cheese, a basket of bread and a fondue fork.

Best Crêpes in Town

The best bit about **Breizh Café** (p171) in Le Marais is the Breton cider parents can sip while kids tuck into some of Paris' best crêpes.

Three-Course Dining

Historic at La Coupole (p265)

The historic 1927 setting might not over-impress kids, but the lavish children's *menu* and game-filled notebooks to entertain will.

Gourmet at Glou (p172)

How refreshing to find a hip wine bar in Le Marais that serves excellent food and fine wine (parents) *and* caters to children with their own gourmet *menu*, colouring pencils and paper.

Au Moulin Vert (p267)

Charming, neighbourhood dining room behind a small replica windmill in Montparnasse; excellent children's *menu*.

All Aboard Le Train Bleu (p196)

Few restaurants are as atmospheric as the belle époque Blue Train at Gare de Lyon, perfect for budding gourmet train-spotters.

Sweet Dessance (p171)

Three-course dining built solely from sweet bites and desserts. How could any child refuse?

Rainy-Day Ideas

A Winter Circus

Clowns, trapeze artists and acrobats have entertained children of all ages at the city's circus, **Cirque d'Hiver Bouglione** (☎01 47 00 28 81; www.cirquedhiver.com; 110 rue Amelot, 11e; ⏲Oct-Mar; Ⓜ Filles du Calvaire), in Le Marais since 1852. The season runs October to March; performances last around 2½ hours.

Musée des Égouts de Paris (p241)

Romping through sewerage tunnels, learning what happens when you flush a loo in Paris and spotting rats is all part of the kid-cool experience at this quirky museum.

Les Catacombes (p258)

Teens generally get a kick out of Paris' most macabre sight, but be warned: guided tours of this underground cemetery packed with more skulls than you can imagine is not for the fainthearted.

Muséum National d'Histoire Naturelle (p214)

No space is better designed for children (aged six to 12) than the inventive Galerie des Enfants inside Paris' first-class Natural History Museum.

Musée de la Magie (p167)

Pure magic!

Like a Local

Paris is the world's most visited city, but it's not just an urban resort. The city has the highest population density of any European capital, and its parks, cafes and restaurants are its communal backyards, living and dining rooms, while neighbourhood shops and markets are cornerstones of local life.

MATT MUNRO / LONELY PLANET ©

Pétanque players in place Dauphine

Dining Like a Local

Parisians are obsessed with talking about, shopping for, preparing and above all eating food. Quality trumps quantity, which is reflected by small, specialist gourmet food shops that not only survive but thrive.

Sunday lunch is traditionally France's main meal of the week, but Sunday (and often Saturday) brunch has become a fixture on the weekend's social calendar from around noon to about 4pm. Prebooking is recommended for popular venues.

For local dining tips, see How to Eat & Drink Like a Parisian (p47).

Drinking Like a Local

Paris' high concentration of city dwellers is why most bars and cafes close around 2am, due to noise restrictions, and why nightclubs in the inner city are few.

In Paris, meals are almost always washed down with wine but again it's quality not quantity that counts. For Parisians, alcohol is invariably something to be savoured rather than a means of intoxication. Parisians tend to go to bars with groups of friends, so you may find there's less mingling than in British-style pubs.

Conversing Like a Local

Food aside, conversations between locals often revolve around philosophy, art and sports such as rugby, football (soccer), cycling and tennis. Talking about money (salaries or spending outlays, for example) is generally taboo in public. For a witty – and very accurate – insight into Parisian interaction, get hold of a copy of Olivier Magny's book *Stuff Parisians Like*.

Debating Like a Local

Grappling with concepts such as existentialism is required for Parisians to pass the baccalaureat (school certificate) – hence the popularity of *philocafés* (philosophy cafes), where wide-ranging, brain-teasing discussions like 'what is a fact?' take place. The original is the **Café des Phares** (www.cafe-philo-des-phares.info) on place de la Bastille. Most *philocafé* sessions are in French, but there's a popular English-language version at Café de Flore in St-Germain des Prés on the first Wednesday of every month from 7pm to 9pm. Entry's free but you need to buy a drink. Sign up at www.philosophy.meetup.com/274.

Dressing Like a Local

It's nearly impossible to overdress in this fashion-conscious city. Parisians have a finely tuned sense of aesthetics, and take meticulous care in their presentation (you'll never see a Parisian leave their apartment with just-out-of-the-shower wet hair). Parisians favour style over fashion, mixing basics from chain stores such as H&M with designer pieces, vintage finds and statement-making accessories. Even Parisian dogs are fashionably outfitted from specialist doggie designers.

Hanging Out Like a Local

Parisians generally work to live rather than the other way round. The standard 35-hour working week, along with long annual leave (anything up to nine weeks), and a *lot* of public holidays means that without the impetus to make and spend money 24/7/365, friends, family and leisure activities all factor highly in Parisians' *joie de vivre* (spirited enjoyment of life).

Parisians' foodie obsession often involves unwinding in a cafe, bistro or restaurant, over a picnic or (less often, given the premium on space) at someone's home. Cinemas, theatres and concert venues as well as festivals and events draw huge local crowds.

Sunday is the main day of rest, when most workplaces (including the majority of shops) close and locals head to museums, to parks, and to *jardins partagés* (community gardens) – visit www.paris.fr for a list (and map) of gardens that are open to the public.

Year-round, you'll find locals kicking back all along the banks of the Seine but never more so than on warm summer evenings.

Getting Around Like a Local

Navigation

A few pointers to help navigate the city: street numbers notated *bis* (twice), *ter* (thrice) or *quater* (four times) are similar to the English a, b etc. If you're entering an apartment building, you'll generally need the alphanumeric *digicode* (entry code) to open the door. Once inside, apartments are usually unmarked, without any apartment numbers or even occupants' names. To know which door to knock on, you're likely to be given cryptic directions like *cinquième étage, premier à gauche* (5th floor, first on the left) or *troisième étage, droite droite* (3rd floor, turn right twice). In all buildings, the 1st floor is the floor above the *rez-de-chaussée* (ground floor).

Transport

Parisians of all walks of life – from students to celebrity chefs – use the metro. If you're in Paris for a week or more, get a Navigo pass to save money and zip through the turnstiles without queuing for tickets.

Virtually free Vélib' bikes have been hugely popular since they were introduced several years ago and Parisians flit all over the city on these pearly-taupe machines.

In the wake of the success of Vélib', Paris launched the world's first electric-car-share program, Autolib'. But this is one instance where you might not want to follow the locals' lead – negotiating the city's unlaned roundabouts, one-way streets and scooters and cyclists that appear from nowhere can be a nerve-wracking experience for the uninitiated. (Note too that Parisian drivers frequently ignore green pedestrian lights – take care crossing roads!)

If you'd rather let someone else drive, regular buses are a much more local alternative to tourist buses.

Thanks to (generally) clement weather and (generally) flat terrain, locals – even police officers – often whizz around the city on inline skates. Paris is also home to the world's largest mass-skate, Pari Roller.

For Free

Paris might be home to haute couture, haute cuisine *and historic luxury hotels, but if you're still waiting for your lottery numbers to come up, don't despair. There's a wealth of ways to soak up the French capital without spending a centime (or scarcely any, at least).*

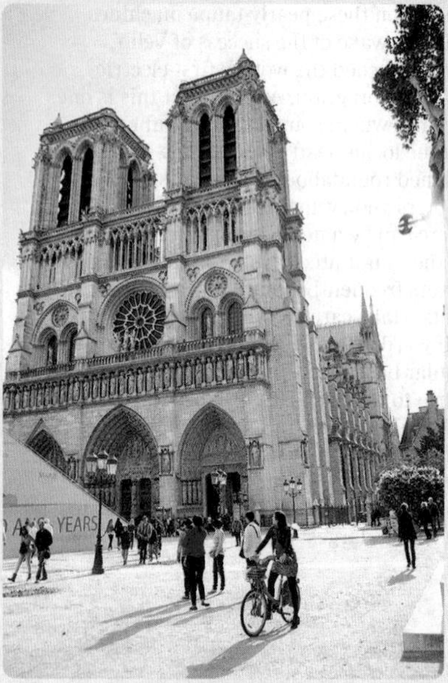

MATT MUNRO / LONELY PLANET ©

Cathédrale Notre Dame de Paris (p202)

Free Museums

If you can, time your trip to be here on the first Sunday of the month when you can visit the *musées nationaux* (www.rmn.fr) for free as well as a handful of monuments (some during certain months only).

European citizens under 26 get free entry to national museums and monuments.

At any time, you can visit the permanent collections of selected *musées municipaux* (www.paris.fr) for free.

Temporary exhibitions at both national and city museums always incur a separate admission fee. Some museums have reduced entry at various times of the day or week.

National Museum & Monument Free Days

The museums and monuments offering free admission on the first Sunday of the month:

- Arc de Triomphe (November to March)
- Basilique de St-Denis (November to March)
- Château de Versailles (November to March)
- Cité de l'Architecture et du Patrimoine
- Cité Nationale de l'Histoire de l'Immigration
- Conciergerie (November to March)
- Musée de la Chasse et de la Nature
- Musée de l'Orangerie
- Musée des Arts et Métiers (also free every Thursday from 6pm)
- Musée des Impressionnismes Giverny
- Musée d'Orsay
- Musée du Louvre (October to March)
- Musée du Quai Branly
- Musée Guimet des Arts Asiatiques
- Musée National d'Art Moderne (within the Centre Pompidou)
- Musée National du Moyen Âge (aka Musée de Cluny)
- Musée National Eugène Delacroix
- Musée National Gustave Moreau
- Musée Picasso
- Musée Rodin
- Panthéon (November to March)
- Sainte-Chapelle (November to March)
- Tours de Notre Dame (November to March)

Other Free Museums

Other freebies include Paris' fascinating town-planning and architectural centre, the Pavillon de l'Arsenal (www.pavillon-arsenal.com) in Le Marais, and the Musée du Parfum, which are free all year.

Admission to the Maison Européenne de la Photographie is free from 5pm every Wednesday evening.

Free Churches

Some of the city's most magnificent buildings are its churches and other places of worship. Not only exceptional architecturally and historically, they contain exquisite art, artefacts and other priceless treasures. Best of all, entry to general areas within them is, in most cases, free.

Do respect the fact that although many of Paris' places of worship are also major tourist attractions, Parisians come here to pray and celebrate significant events on religious calendars as part of their daily lives. Keep noise to a minimum, obey photography rules (check signs), dress appropriately and try to avoid key times (eg Mass) if you're sightseeing only.

Free Cemeteries

Paris' celebrity-filled cemeteries, including the three largest – Père Lachaise, Cimetière de Montmartre and Cimetière du Montparnasse – are free to wander.

Free Entertainment

Free Music

Concerts, DJ sets and recitals regularly take place for free (or for the cost of a drink) at venues throughout the city. Busking musicians and performers entertain crowds on Paris' streets, squares and even on the metro.

Free Literary Events

This literary-minded city is an inspired place to catch a reading, author signing or writing workshop. English-language bookshops such as Shakespeare & Company and Abbey Bookshop host literary events throughout the year and can point you towards others.

Free Fashion Shows

Reserve ahead to attend free weekly fashion shows at Galeries Lafayette's flagship department store. While you're here, don't miss one of the best free views over the Parisian skyline from Galeries Lafayette's rooftop. (Nearby department store Le Printemps also has amazing – and free – views from the roof.)

Free Festivals

Loads of Paris' festivals and events are free, such as the Paris Plages riverside beaches.

Getting Around

Walking

Paris is an eminently walkable city, with beautiful parks and gardens, awe-inspiring architecture, markets and shops to check out along the way.

For a free walking tour, contact Paris Greeters (p352) in advance for a personalised excursion led by a resident volunteer.

Cycling (Almost Free)

If you'd rather free-wheel around Paris, the Vélib' system costs next-to-nothing for a day's subscription, and the first 30 minutes of each bike rental is free.

Buses (Cheap as Chips)

Instead of a bus tour, simply hop on a local bus. Scenic routes include lines 21 and 27 (Opéra–Panthéon), line 29 (Opéra–Gare de Lyon), line 47 (Centre Pompidou–Gobelins), line 63 (Musée d'Orsay–Trocadéro), line 73 (Concorde–Arc de Triomphe) and line 82 (Montparnasse–Eiffel Tower). Time it to avoid peak commuting hours.

NEED TO KNOW

- Paris has hundreds of free wi-fi points (p353) at popular locations including parks, libraries, local town halls and tourist hotspots. Locations are mapped at www.paris.fr.
- Consider investing in a transport (p349) or museum (p353) pass.
- Theatre tickets are sold for half price on the day of performance.
- Paris' parks are perfect for picnics made from market fare.

Le 104 (p142)

Museums & Galleries

If there's one thing that rivals a Parisian's obsession with food, it's art. More than 200 museums pepper the city, and whether you prefer the classicism of the Louvre, the impressionists of the Orsay or detailed exhibits of French military history, you can always be sure to find something new just around the corner.

Paris Museum Pass

If you think you'll be visiting more than two or three museums and monuments while in Paris, the single most important investment you can make is the Paris Museum Pass (p353). The pass is valid for entry to some 38 venues in the city – including the Louvre, Centre Pompidou, Musée d'Orsay and the Musée Rodin (but not the Eiffel Tower). It will get you into another 22 places outside the city, including the châteaux at Versailles and Fontainebleau and the Basilique de St-Denis.

One of the best features of the pass is that you can bypass the long ticket queues at major attractions (but not always the security queues). But be warned, the pass is valid for a certain number of days, not hours, so if you activate a two-day pass late Friday afternoon, for instance, you will only be able to use it for a full day on Saturday. Also keep in mind that most museums are closed on either Monday or Tuesday, so think twice before you activate a pass on a Sunday.

The Paris Museum Pass is available online as well as at participating museums, tourist desks at the airports, branches of the Paris Convention & Visitors Bureau, Fnac outlets (www.fnactickets.com) and major metro stations. European citizens under 26 and children under 18 years get free entry to national museums and monuments, so *don't* buy this pass if you belong to one of those categories.

For Free

Municipal museums in Paris (eg Musée Carnavalet) are all free; many other museums have one free day per month (generally the first Sunday of the month). Note that temporary exhibits almost always cost a separate admission fee, even at free museums.

Performances

Many museums host excellent musical concerts and performances, with schedules that generally run from September to early June. Some of the top venues:

- **Musée du Louvre** (p109) A series of lunchtime and evening classical concerts throughout the week.
- **Musée d'Orsay** (p230) Chamber music every Tuesday at 12.30pm, plus various evening classical performances.
- **Musée du Quai Branly** (p84) Folk performances of theatre, dance and music from around the world.
- **Musée National du Moyen Âge** (p213) Medieval music performances twice a week.
- **Centre Pompidou** (p117) Film screenings and avant-garde dance and music performances.
- **Le 104** (p157) A veritable potpourri of everything from circus and magic to afternoon breakdancing.

Workshops

If you have kids in tow, make sure you check out the day's workshops *(ateliers)*. Although these are often in French, most activities involve hands-on creation, so children should enjoy themselves despite the language barrier. At major museums (eg Centre Pompidou), it's best to sign up in advance.

Dining

Although there are plenty of tourist cafeterias to be found in Paris, the dining options in museums are generally pretty good – some are destinations in themselves. Even if you're not out sightseeing, consider a meal at one of the following:

- **Les Ombres** (p90) and **Café Branly** (p91) These two dining options at the Musée du Quai Branly have ringside seats for the Eiffel Tower.
- **Tokyo Eat** (p90) Hip fusion food in the Palais du Tokyo.
- **Monsieur Bleu** (p90) The latest in the Palais du Tokyo features ubercool design and clientele.

NEED TO KNOW

Tickets

Consider booking online to avoid queues where possible (eg Musée d'Orsay, Centre Pompidou), but make sure you have a way to print the tickets. In some cases you can download the tickets onto a smart phone (eg BlackBerry, iPhone) but check before you make a purchase. Also ensure you can download more than one ticket onto your phone if need be.

If you can't book online, keep an eye out for automated machines at museum entrances, which generally have shorter queues. Note that North American credit cards (ie cards without an embedded smart chip) *won't work* in these machines.

City museums (eg Musée Carnavalet, Petit Palais, Musée Cognacq-Jay) are free.

Temporary exhibits almost always have a separate admission fee, even at free museums.

Ask if you qualify for a reduced-price ticket (*tarif réduit*): students, seniors and children generally get discounts or free admission.

Opening Hours

Most museums are closed on either Monday or Tuesday – it is vital that you verify opening days before drawing up your day's schedule.

General opening hours are from 10am to 6pm, though all museums shut their gates between 30 minutes and an hour before their actual closing times. Thus, if a museum is listed in this guide as closing at 6pm, make sure you get there before 5pm.

Major museums are often open one or two nights a week, which is an excellent time to visit as there are fewer visitors.

TIPS FOR AVOIDING MUSEUM FATIGUE

- Wear comfortable shoes and make use of the cloakrooms.
- Sit down as often as you can; standing still and walking slowly promote tiredness.
- Reflecting on the material and forming associations with it causes information to move from your short- to long-term memory; your experiences will thus amount to more than a series of visual 'bites'. Using an audioguide is a good way to provide context.
- Studies suggest that museum-goers spend no more than 10 seconds viewing an exhibit and another 10 seconds reading the label as they try to take in as much as they can. To avoid this, choose a particular period or section to focus on, or join a guided tour of the highlights.

- **Mini Palais** (p101) Gorgeous terrace and modern French cuisine in the Grand Palais.
- **Musée Jacquemart-André** (p143) Lunch or tea in the sumptuous dining room of a 19th-century mansion.
- **Le Bal Café** (p149) Modern British cuisine and superb coffee in an artsy, hidden hangout.
- **Le Saut du Loup** (p130) Views of the Louvre and Eiffel Tower are what it's all about here.
- **Cristal Room** (p86) Baccarat crystal meets Philippe Starck design in this Galerie-Musée Baccarat stunner.

Museums & Galleries by Neighbourhood

- **Eiffel Tower & Western Paris** (p80) The largest concentration of museums in Paris, from the Quai Branly to Musée Marmottan Monet.
- **Champs-Élysées & Grands Boulevards** (p93) Grand Palais, La Pinacothèque, Petit Palais and others.
- **Louvre & Les Halles** (p107) The Louvre, Centre Pompidou, Musée de l'Orangerie and others.
- **Montmartre & Northern Paris** (p135) Musée Jacquemart-André, Cité des Sciences, Le 104 and others.
- **Le Marais, Ménilmontant & Belleville** (p159) Musée Picasso and Musée Carnavalet.
- **Bastille & Eastern Paris** (p187) Cinémathèque Française and others.
- **Latin Quarter** (p211) Musée National du Moyen Âge, Musée National d'Histoire Naturelle, Institut du Monde Arabe.
- **St-Germain & Les Invalides** (p228) Musée d'Orsay, Musée Rodin and others.
- **Montparnasse & Southern Paris** (p256) Fondation Cartier and others.

Public Art

Museums and galleries are not the sole repositories of art in Paris. Indeed, art is all around you – from living walls (vertical gardens adorning apartment buildings) and yarn-bombed traffic poles to whimsical cows parading down the Champs-Élysées and 'invader' tags (tiled Space Invader–inspired creations) marking street corners. Enjoying art in Paris is simply a matter of keeping your eyes open.

While the smaller, anonymous works are among the most interesting and unique, there are plenty of big-name installations as well that have become destinations in their own right. Niki de Saint Phalle and Jean Tinguely's playful *Stravinsky Fountain* – a collection of 16 colourful, animated sculptures based on the composer's oeuvre – is located next to the Centre Pompidou. Daniel Buren's zebra-striped columns of varying heights at the Palais Royal is another beloved Paris fixture; the installation was originally greeted with derision but has since become an integral part of the historic site. Both the Jardin des Tuileries and the Jardin du Luxembourg are dotted with dozens of sculptures that date from the 19th and early 20th centuries; the Jardin des Tuileries also contains an area with more contemporary works from the likes of Lichtenstein and Magdalena Abakanowicz.

Interestingly, one of the best areas to go hunting for contemporary public art – and architecture – is out in the business district of La Défense, where you'll find some 60 works by well-known artists such as Miró, Calder and Belmondo. Metro stations, too, often contain some iconic or unusual additions, from Hector Guimard's signature art nouveau entrances to the crown-shaped cupolas at the Palais Royal.

Lonely Planet's Top Choices

Musée du Louvre (p109) The one museum you just can't miss.

Musée d'Orsay (p230) Monet, Van Gogh and company.

Centre Pompidou (p117) One of the top modern art museums in Europe.

Musée Rodin (p236) Superb collection of Rodin's masterpieces in an intimate setting.

Musée Picasso (p165) An incomparable overview of Picasso's work and life.

Best Modern Art Museums & Installations

Centre Pompidou (p117) Huge selection of modern art and big-name temporary exhibits.

Grand Palais (p97) Varied exhibitions inside a 1900 art nouveau beauty of a building.

Palais de Tokyo (p85) Interactive contemporary art exhibitions and installations against a stark concrete-and-steel backdrop.

Jeu de Paume (p119) Con-Photography exhibitions in the Jardin des Tuileries.

Best Unsung Museums

La Pinacothèque (p100) Shaking up the Paris art world with juxtaposed works and a diverse program of exhibitions.

Cité de l'Architecture et du Patrimoine (p85) Standout museum devoted to French architecture and heritage.

Musée Jacquemart-André (p143) Gorgeous 19th-century mansion hung with canvases by Rembrandt, Botticelli and Titian.

Musée des Lettres et Manuscrits (p238) Handwritten letters and works providing a powerful connection to their famous authors.

Best History Museums

Musée National du Moyen Âge (p213) Where medieval history and crafts come to life.

Musée Carnavalet (p164) A poetic ode to Parisian *histoire* secreted in a pair of remarkable *hôtels particuliers*.

Musée de l'Armée (p237) Within the monumental Hôtel des Invalides complex, commemorating French military history.

Musée de Montmartre (p140) Relive the days of Toulouse-Lautrec and Maurice Utrillo.

Best Museums for Non-European Art

Musée du Quai Branly (p84) Overview of indigenous art from around the world, presented in the most striking of manners.

Musée Guimet (p86) France's foremost Asian art museum.

Musée du Louvre (p109) Mesopotamian, Egyptian and Islamic artefacts.

Institut du Monde Arabe (p216) Art and artisanship from the Middle East and North Africa.

Best Small Museums

Musée de l'Orangerie (p119) For Monet's sublime *Water Lilies* series.

Musée Maillol-Fondation Dina Vierny (p239) Splendid museum focusing on the work of sculptor Aristide Maillol.

Cinémathèque Française (p189) Props, early equipment and short clips bring cinematic history to life.

Musée Marmottan Monet (p88) The world's largest Monet collection.

Musée de la Vie Romantique (p140) Dedicated to the work of two romantic-era artists.

Best Science Museums

Cité des Sciences (p142) Excellent science-related exhibits and attractions for all ages.

Muséum National d'Histoire Naturelle (p214) Dinosaur skeletons, taxidermied elephants and excellent temporary exhibits.

Palais de la Découverte (p99) Engaging, interactive children's science museum attached to the Grand Palais.

Musée des Arts et Métiers (p166) Europe's oldest science and technology museum.

Best Residence Museums

Musée National Eugène Delacroix (p238) The artist's home and studio contains many of his more intimate works.

Musée Cognacq-Jay (p166) Treasure trove of artwork and *objets d'art*.

Musée Nissim de Camondo (p141) Sumptuous mansion housing a private 19th-century collection of art and furnishings.

Musée Bourdelle (p259) Monumental bronzes displayed in the house and workshop of sculptor Antoine Bourdelle.

Maison de Victor Hugo (p165) Victor Hugo's former quarters, overlooking Paris' most elegant square.

Macarons prepared at La Cuisine Paris cooking school (p52)

Eating

The inhabitants of some cities rally around local sports teams, but in Paris, they rally around la table – and everything on it. Pistachio macarons, shots of tomato consommé, decadent boeuf bourguignon, a gooey wedge of Camembert running onto the cheese plate...food is not fuel here, it's the reason you get up in the morning.

Vegetable dish served at Le Dauphin (p174)

Paris: A Culinary Renaissance

Home to one of the world's great culinary traditions, France has shaped Western cooking techniques and conceptions of what good food is for centuries – whether it's a multicourse gourmet meal or a crusty baguette. Blessed with a rich and varied landscape, farmers with a strong sense of regional identity and a culture that celebrates life's daily pleasures, it's no surprise that French chefs have long been synonymous with gastronomic genius.

Over the past several decades, though, restaurant culture has started to slip. Frozen and industrially prepared ingredients, stultifying business regulations and an over-reliance on formulaic dishes led to a general decline in both quality and innovation. Alarmed by these foreboding trends, a new generation of chefs has emerged in the past several years, re-emphasising market-driven cuisine and displaying a willingness to push the boundaries of traditional tastes, while at the same time downplaying the importance of Michelin stars and the formal, chandelier-studded dining rooms of yesteryear.

Even more significantly, the real change that is taking place in Paris today is that more and more of these chefs – and, just as importantly, more and more diners – are open to culinary traditions originating outside of France. Some have trained abroad (in what is surely one of the greatest examples of Gallic pride-swallowing, French chef Gregory Marchand went to the UK to work for Jamie Oliver), while others aren't even French, originally hailing from Japan, the US or elsewhere. The latter group has come to Paris specifically because they love

NEED TO KNOW

Price Ranges

The symbols below indicate the cost for a two-course meal in our reviews.

€	less than €20
€€	€20-40
€€€	more than €40

Opening Hours

Restaurants generally open from noon to 2pm for lunch and from 7.30pm to 10.30pm for dinner. If you want to avoid the rush, remember that the peak Parisian dining times are 1pm and 9pm.

Most restaurants shut for one full day (usually Sunday) and sometimes an additional afternoon. August is the peak holiday month and many places are consequently closed during this time.

Reservations

You can generally find a free table for lunch at midrange restaurants, but it's best to show up before 12.30pm. It's always advisable to book in advance for dinner at a midrange restaurant, though often a day or two will suffice. At high-end restaurants, reservations for lunch or dinner are absolutely mandatory – sometimes up to one or two months in advance. On the phone, you should say: '*Je voudrais réserver une table pour une/deux/trois...personnes, s'il vous plaît*.' Big-name restaurants may require that you reconfirm on the day of your meal.

Tipping

A *pourboire* (tip) on top of the bill is not necessary as service is always included. But it is not uncommon to round up the bill if you were pleased with your waiter.

Paying the Bill

Trying to get *l'addition* (the bill) can be maddeningly slow in many cases. Do not take this personally. The French consider it rude to bring the bill immediately – you have to be persistent when it comes to getting your waiter's attention.

DAVID FREUND / GETTY IMAGES ©

Above: Classic Parisian bakery

Left: Fresh baguettes for sale at Marché Bastille (p191)

Eating by Neighbourhood

French cooking, but none are so beholden to its traditions that they are afraid to introduce new concepts or techniques from back home. French cuisine has finally come to the realisation that a global future doesn't necessarily mean a loss of identity – decadent work-of-art pastries and the divine selection of pungent cheeses aren't going anywhere. Instead, there is an opportunity to once again create something new.

How to Eat & Drink Like a Parisian

Eating well is of prime importance to most French people, who spend an inordinate amount of time thinking about, discussing and enjoying food and wine. Yet dining out doesn't have to be a ceremonious occasion or one riddled with pitfalls for the uninitiated. Approach food with even half the enthusiasm *les français* do, and you will be welcomed, encouraged and exceedingly well fed.

WHEN TO EAT

➡ **Petit déjeuner (breakfast)** The French kickstart the day with a *tartine* (slice of baguette smeared with unsalted butter and jam) and *un café* (espresso) or – for kids – hot chocolate. Parisians might grab a coffee and croissant on the way to work, but otherwise croissants (eaten straight, never with butter or jam) are more of a weekend or 4pm treat along with *pains au chocolat* (chocolate-filled croissants) and other *viennoiseries* (sweet pastries).

➡ **Déjeuner (lunch)** The traditional main meal of the day, lunch translates to a starter and main course with wine, followed by a short sharp *café*. During the work week this is less likely to be the case – many busy Parisians now grab a sandwich to go and pop off to run errands – but the standard hour-long lunch break, special *prix-fixe menus* and *tickets restaurant* (company-funded meal vouchers) ensure that many restaurants fill up at lunch.

THE FIVE BASIC CHEESE TYPES

'How can you govern a country that has 246 types of cheese?' Charles de Gaulle once quipped. A more relevant question for non-Frenchies: How do you come to grips with a shop that sells 246 types of cheese? The choices on offer at a *fromagerie* (cheese shop) can be overwhelming, but vendors will always allow you to sample before you buy, and they are usually very generous with their guidance and pairing advice. The following list divides French cheeses into five main groups – as they are usually divided in a shop – and recommends several types in each family to try.

➜ **Fromage à pâte demi-dure** 'Semi-hard cheese' means uncooked, pressed cheese. Among the finest are Tomme de Savoie, made from either raw or pasteurised cow's milk; Cantal, a cow's milk cheese from Auvergne that tastes something like Cheddar; St-Nectaire, a pressed cheese that has a strong, complex taste; and Ossau-Iraty, a ewe's milk cheese made in the Basque Country.

➜ **Fromage à pâte dure** 'Hard cheese' is always cooked and then pressed. Among the most popular are Beaufort, a grainy cow's milk cheese with a slightly fruity taste from Rhône-Alpes; Comté, a cheese made with raw cow's milk in Franche-Comté; Emmental, a cow's milk cheese made all over France; and Mimolette, an Edam-like dark-orange cheese from Lille that can be aged for up to 36 months.

➜ **Fromage à pâte molle** 'Soft cheese' is moulded or rind-washed. Camembert, a classic moulded cheese from Normandy that for many is synonymous with 'French cheese', and Brie de Meaux are both made from raw cow's milk. Munster from Alsace, mild Chaource and strong-smelling Langres from Champagne, and the odorous Époisses de Bourgogne are rind-washed, fine-textured cheeses.

➜ **Fromage à pâte persillée** 'Marbled' or 'blue cheese' is so called because the veins often resemble *persille* (parsley). Roquefort is a ewe's milk veined cheese that is to many the king of French cheeses. Fourme d'Ambert is a mild cow's milk cheese from Rhône-Alpes. Bleu du Haut Jura (also called Bleu de Gex) is a mild, blue-veined mountain cheese.

➜ **Fromage de chèvre** 'Goat's milk cheese' is usually creamy and both sweet and slightly salty when fresh, but hardens and gets much saltier as it matures. Among the best varieties are Ste-Maure de Touraine, a creamy, mild cheese from the Loire region; Crottin de Chavignol, a classic though saltier variety from Burgundy; Cabécou de Rocamadour from Midi-Pyrenées, often served warm with salad or marinated in oil and rosemary; and Chabichou, a soft, slightly aged cheese from Poitou.

➜ **Apéritif** Otherwise known as an *apéro*, the pre-meal drink is sacred. Cafes and bars get packed out from around 5pm onwards as Parisians wrap up work for the day and relax over a chit-chat-fuelled glass of wine or beer.

➜ **Diner (dinner)** Traditionally lighter than lunch, but a meal that is being treated more and more as the main meal of the day. In restaurants, the head chef will almost certainly be in the kitchen, which is not always the case during lunch.

MENU ADVICE

➜ **Carte** Menu, as in the written list of what's cooking, listed in the order you'd eat it: starter, main course, cheese then dessert. Note that an entrée is a starter, not the main course (as in the US).

➜ **Menu** Not at all what it means in English, *le menu* in French is a *prix-fixe menu*: a multi-course meal at a fixed price. It's by far the best-value dining there is and most restaurants chalk one on the board. In some cases, particularly at neobistros, there is no *carte* – only a stripped-down *menu* with one or two choices.

➜ **À la carte** Order whatever you fancy from the menu (as opposed to opting for a *prix-fixe menu*).

➜ **Formule** Similar to a *menu, une formule* is a cheaper lunchtime option comprising a main plus starter or dessert. Wine or coffee is sometimes included.

➜ **Plat du jour** Dish of the day, invariably good value.

Above: A selection of artisan cheeses on display

Right: Wine for sale on Rue Mouffetard (p222)

DENNIS K. JOHNSON / GETTY IMAGES ©

➡ **Menu enfant** Two- or three-course kids' meal (generally up to the age of 12) at a fixed price; usually includes a drink.

➡ **Menu dégustation** Fixed-price tasting menu served in many top-end restaurants, consisting of five to seven modestly sized courses.

DINING TIPS

➡ **Bread** Order a meal and within seconds a basket of fresh bread will be brought to the table. Butter is rarely an accompaniment. Except in the most upmarket of places, don't expect a side plate – simply put it on the table.

➡ **Water** Asking for *une carafe d'eau* (jug of tap water) is perfectly acceptable, although some waiters will presume you don't know this and only offer mineral water, which you have to pay for. Should bubbles be more your cup of tea, ask for *de l'eau gazeuze* (fizzy mineral water). Ice (*glaçons*) can be hard to come by.

➡ **Service** To state the obvious, France is not a service-oriented country. No one is working for tips here, so to get around this, think like a Parisian – acknowledge your *serveur*'s expertise by asking for advice (even if you don't really want it) and don't be afraid to flirt. In France flirtation is not the same as picking someone up, it is both a game that makes the mundane more enjoyable and a vital life skill to help you get what you want (such as the bill). Being witty and speaking French with an accent will often help your cause.

➡ **Dress** Smart casual is best. How you look is very important, and Parisians favour personal style above all else. But if you're going some place dressy, don't assume this means suit and tie – that's more business-meal attire. At the other end of the spectrum, running shoes may be too casual, unless, of course, they are more hip than functional, in which case you may fit right in.

Where to Eat

➡ **Bistro** (or *bistrot*) A small neighbourhood restaurant that serves French standards (duck confit, *steak-frites*). The setting is usually casual; if you're looking for a traditional French meal, a bistro is the place to start. Don't expect *haute-cuisine* service; most simply do not have the staff to cater to a diner's every whim.

➡ **Brasserie** Much like a cafe except it serves full meals, drinks and coffee from morning until 11pm or later. Typical fare includes *choucroute* (sauerkraut) and sausages.

➡ **Cafe** Many visitors will naturally gravitate towards cafes (which become bars around 5pm) because of the alluring ambiance and buzzy

Top: Patrons at a Paris cafe
Middle: Dessert crêpes
Bottom: Camion Qui Fume (p52), a Parisian food truck

DAILY BREAD

Few things in France are as tantalising as the smell of just-baked buttery croissants wafting out of an open bakery door. With roughly 1200 *boulangeries* (bakeries) in Paris – or 11.5 per sq km – you'll likely find yourself inside one at some point during your stay. And, as you'll notice in the extravagant display windows, bakeries bake much more than baguettes: they also sell croissants, chocolate éclairs, quiches, pizzas and an astounding array of pastries and cakes that you've likely never even heard of before. If you're eating lunch on the cheap or you're after a baguette sandwich to go, a trip to the closest bakery will do you right.

If it's the bread you're after, try to familiarise yourself with the varieties on sale while you're standing in the queue – not all baguettes are created equal. Most Parisians today will ask for a *baguette tradition* (traditional-style baguette), which is considerably better than the standard baguette. Other breads you'll see include *boules* (round loaves), *pavés* (flattened rectangular loaves), and *ficelles* (skinny loaves that are half the weight of a baguette).

sun-kissed terraces. Meals are inexpensive, but remember they often consist of industrially prepared food that's simply reheated, so stick to the drinks.

➡ **Crêperie** A quintessentially Parisian snack is the street crêpe made to order, slathered with Nutella and folded up in a triangular wedge. Crêpes can be so much more than this, however, as a trip to any authentic crêperie will reveal. Savoury crêpes, known as *galettes*, are made with buckwheat flour; dessert crêpes are made with white flour – usually you order one of each accompanied by a bowl of cider.

➡ **Gastronomic** Pierre Gagnaire, Alain Passard, Pascal Barbot...Paris has one of the highest concentrations of culinary magicians in the world. Designed to amaze your every sense, many of these restaurants are once-in-a-lifetime destinations – even for Parisians – so do your homework and make sure you reserve well in advance.

➡ **Market** Fantastic places to wander: here you'll find all the French culinary specialities in the same place, in addition to meals and snacks cooked on site. At last count there were 82 food markets in the city. Most are open twice weekly from 8.30am to 1pm, though covered markets keep general shop hours, reopening around 4pm.

➡ **Neobistro** Generally small and relatively informal, these are run by young, talented chefs who aren't afraid to experiment and push the envelope. The focus is on market-driven cuisine, hence choices are often limited to one or two dishes per course.

➡ **Wine bar/cave à manger** The focus is on sampling wine; the style of cuisine, while often excellent, can be wildly different. Some places serve nothing more than plates of cheese and charcuterie *(saucisson, pâté)*; others are full-on gastronomic destinations with a talented chef running the kitchen.

Vegetarians, Vegans & Gluten-Free

Vegetarians and vegans make up a small minority in a country where *viande* (meat) once also meant 'food', and they are not particularly well catered for. Specialist vegetarian restaurants are still few in number in Paris, and it's safe to say that vegetarians will still be met with looks of genuine bewilderment at some traditional French bistros. On the up side, more and more modern places are offering vegetarian choices on their set *menus;* another good bet is non-French cuisine. See www.happycow.net for a decent guide to veggie options in Paris.

Likewise, gluten-free dining isn't easy: try Noglu (p125) or Helmut Newcake (p151) for starters, but do your research ahead of time.

Cooking Classes

What better place to discover the secrets of *la cuisine française* than in Paris, the capital of gastronomy? Courses are available at different levels and durations; see the websites below for details.

Cook'n With Class (www.cooknwithclass.com) Nine international chefs, small classes and a Montmartre location.

École Le Cordon Bleu (www.cordonbleu.edu) One of the world's foremost culinary arts schools.

Artisan bread created at Poilâne Bakery (p243)

La Cuisine Paris (http://lacuisineparis.com) A variety of courses from bread, croissants and macarons to market classes and 'foodie walks'.

Le Foodist (www.lefoodist.com) Cooking classes, wine pairings and hosted dinners in the Latin Quarter.

Patricia Wells (www.patriciawells.com) Five-day moveable feast from the former *International Herald Tribune* food critic.

Food Trucks

Hour-long queues? Organic ingredients? TV spots? Welcome to the hip new world of Parisian food trucks. Find the day's location online or follow them on Twitter or Facebook.

Camion Qui Fume (www.lecamionquifume.com; burger & fries €10.50) The smoking food truck that started it all, with gourmet burgers grilled by SoCal chef (and now local food celeb) Kristin Frederick. Follow @lecamionquifume

Cantine California (www.cantinecalifornia.com; burger & fries €11) Organic burgers, tacos and homemade desserts from San Fran transplant Jordan Feilders. Follow @CantineCali

Mes Bocaux (www.mesbocaux.fr; 37 rue Marceau, 8e; 2-/3-course menu €11/13.50; Ⓜ Alma-Marceau) Savoyard chef Marc Veyrat upped the takeaway stakes when he put his small fleet of smart black food trucks on the road. Order gastronomic-to-go sandwiches and main dishes online before noon, then collect from the truck; the nearest stop to the Eiffel Tower is in front of the Anglo-American pharmacy at 37 rue Marceau, on the corner of rue de Chaillot. Dishes ooze the creative flair you'd expect of a former Michelin-starred chef – think ham, grated carrot, cumin, parmesan cheese and a wafer-thin slice of chocolate inside the '21st-century' sandwich.

Paris Food Bloggers & Useful Websites

Paris by Mouth (www.parisbymouth.com) Capital dining and drinking; one-stop surf for deciding where to eat.

Lonely Planet's Top Choices

Le 6 Paul Bert (p192) Dazzling dishes that change daily.

Restaurant David Toutain (p248) Mystery degustation courses showcasing creative high-end cooking.

Le Pantruche (p146) Superb modern French cuisine at fantastic value.

Bones (p193) Signature small plates or multicourse menus in stripped-back surrounds.

Hugo Desnoyer (p88) Feast for meat lovers courtesy of Paris' most famous butcher.

Best By Budget

€

La Pointe du Groin (p150) Off-the-wall humour and mouth-watering Breton tapas.

CheZaline (p191) Gourmet sandwiches and other gorgeous creations.

Au Pied de Fouet (p241) Bistro classics are astonishingly good value at this 150-year-old charmer.

Candelaria (p168) Hipster-favourite taqueria.

Les Deux Abeilles (p88) Old-fashioned lunch address.

€€

Frenchie Bar à Vins (p127) Can't get a booking at Frenchie? Try the wine bar instead.

Bistrot La Bruyère (p103) Unassuming but brilliant little bistro by rising-star chef Loïc Buisson.

Verjus Bar à Vins (p127) An oft-overlooked jewel by the Palais Royal.

Le Casse Noix (p263) Cosy retro interior, affordable prices and exceptional cuisine.

Dessance (p171) Paris' first dessert restaurant is stunningly sweet.

Blue Valentine (p173) Thoroughly modern bistro luring a hip crowd in the increasingly gourmet 11e.

€€€

Septime (p195) A beacon of modern cuisine.

Yam'Tcha (p129) Michelin-starred Franco-Cantonese creations from Adeline Grattard.

Le Grand Véfour (p127) The ultimate *haute cuisine* experience lives on at this 18th-century landmark.

Chez Françoise (p248) Old-school oyster specialist in the Air France building.

Le Jules Verne (p90) A magical, Michelin-starred address perched in the Eiffel Tower.

Best Traditional French

Philou (p152) Serious Gallic comfort food that changes with the seasons.

À la Biche au Bois (p193) Game, especially *la biche*, is the speciality of the countrified 'doe in the woods'.

Le Miroir (p146) Excellent French standards at this Montmartre favourite.

Bouillon Racine (p243) Art-nouveau jewel with traditional fare inspired by age-old recipes.

Robert et Louise (p168) 'Country inn' with red gingham curtains and meat cuts cooked on an open fire.

Best Neobistros

Pirouette (p128) A new spin for French cooking from Tomy Gousset.

Le Chateaubriand (p174) Elegant art-deco dining room with strikingly imaginative cuisine in the 11e.

Richer (p103) Smart setting and genius flavour combinations but no reservations, so arrive early.

Abri (p152) Unassuming temple to gastronomic wizardry.

Semilla (p244) Edgy, modern dishes from the open kitchen in factory-style premises.

Felicity Lemon (p173) A local Belleville pick, cooking creative, tapas-style dishes to share.

Best Wine Bars

Le Verre Volé (p152) Excellent wines, expert advice and hearty *plats du jour*.

Vivant (p153) Where else will you get to wine and dine in a century-old exotic bird shop?

Les Pipos (p219) A feast for all the senses.

Floquifil (p103) The back-street Parisian wine-bar dining experience of your imagination.

La Grande Crèmerie (p244) Rustic space serving the earthy flavours of the French countryside.

Best Boulangeries

Poilâne (p243) Turning out distinctive wood-fired, rounded sourdough loaves since 1932.

Besnier (p247) Watch baguettes being made through the viewing window.

Du Pain et des Idées (p150) Naturally leavened bread and short but sweet range of pastries.

Au 140 (p173) Crunchy-to-perfection baguettes and gourmet, wood-fired-oven breads.

MING TANG-EVANS / LONELY PLANET ©

Pink champagne

Drinking & Nightlife

For Parisians, drinking and eating go together like wine and cheese, and the line between a cafe, salon de thé (tearoom), bistro, brasserie, bar and even bar à vins (wine bar) is blurred. The line between drinking and clubbing is often nonexistent – a cafe that's quiet midafternoon might have DJ sets in the evening and dancing later on.

Le Saut du Loup (p130) cafe, in the Decorative Arts Museum

Drinking

Drinking in Paris as Parisians do means anything from downing a coffee at a zinc counter with locals, sipping tea in a chic *salon de thé*, meeting friends for *un verre* ('a glass') and a cheese and/or charcuterie platter on a pavement terrace, debating existentialism over an early evening *apéro* (*apéritif;* pre-dinner drink) in literary cafes, swilling martinis while listening to jazz or partying aboard floating clubs on the Seine…and much, much more.

COFFEE, TEA & HOT CHOCOLATE

Coffee has always been Parisians' drink of choice to kick-start the day. So it's surprising, particularly given France's fixation on quality, that Parisian coffee has lagged behind world standards, with burnt, poor-quality beans and unrefined preparation methods. But the city is in the throes of a coffee revolution, with local roasteries such as Belleville Brûlerie and Coutume priming cafes citywide for outstanding brews made by professional baristas, often using cutting-edge extraction techniques. Caffeine fiends are now spoilt for choice and while there's still plenty of substandard coffee in Paris, you don't have to go far to avoid it.

Surprisingly too, tea – usually associated with France's western neighbours, the UK and Ireland – is extremely popular in Paris. Tearooms offer copious varieties; learn about its history at the tea museum in the original Marais branch of Mariage Frères (p178).

For decadently rich hot chocolate, the *crème de la crème* is venerable tearoom Angelina (p235), with two branches two at Versailles.

NEED TO KNOW

Tiered Pricing

Drinking in Paris essentially means paying the rent for the space you take up. So it costs more to sit at a table than to stand at the counter, more for coveted terrace seats, more on a fancy square than a backstreet, more in the 8e than the 18e.

Average Costs

A coffee starts at around €2, a glass of wine from around €3.50, a cocktail generally costs €8 to €15 and a *demi* (half-pint) of beer between €3.50 and €7. In clubs and chic bars, prices can easily be double this. Admission to clubs is free to around €20 and is often cheaper before 1am.

Happy 'Hour'

Most mainstream bars and international-styled pubs have a 'happy hour' – called just that (no French translation) – which ushers in reduced-price drinks for a good two or three hours, usually between 5pm and 9pm.

Closing Times

Closing time for cafes and bars tends to be 2am, though some have licences until dawn. Club hours vary depending on the venue, day and event.

Top Tips

- Arrive early: come 10pm many cafes apply a pricier night rate.
- Although most places serve at least small plates (often full menus), it's normally fine to order a coffee or alcohol if you're not dining.
- The French rarely go drunk-wild and tend to frown upon it.

Coffee Decoded

- **Un café** A single shot of espresso.
- **Un café allongé** An espresso lengthened with hot water (usually, but not always, served separately).
- **Un café au lait** A coffee with milk.
- **Un café crème** A shot of espresso lengthened with steamed milk (closest thing to a caffè latte).
- **Un double** A double shot of espresso.
- **Une noisette** A shot of espresso with a spot of milk.

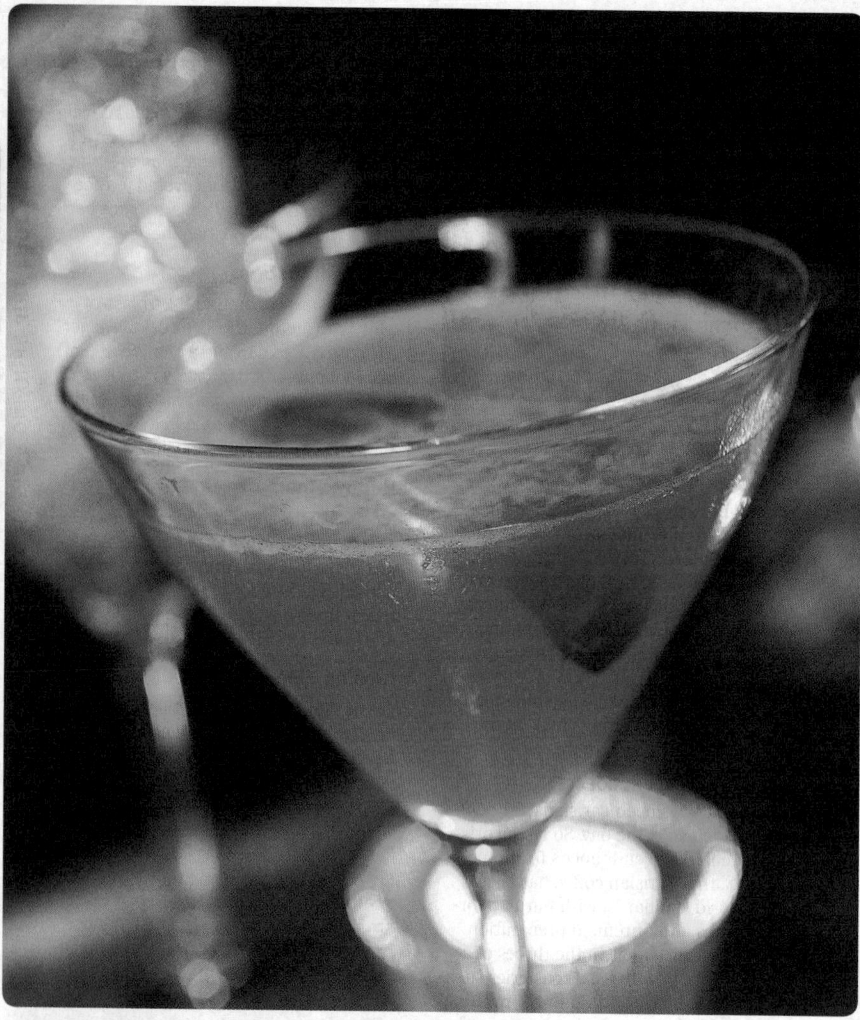

IMAGEBROKER / ALAMY ©

Above: Cocktail at the Experimental Cocktail Club (p131) in Les Halles

Left: L'Ebouillanté (p175)

Drinking by Neighbourhood

WINE

Wine is easily the most popular beverage in Paris and house wine invariably costs less than bottled water. Of France's dozens of wine-producing regions, the principal ones are Burgundy, Bordeaux, the Rhône and the Loire valleys, Champagne, Languedoc, Provence and Alsace. Wines are generally named after the location of the vineyard rather than the grape varietal. The best wines are Appellation d'Origine Contrôlée (AOC), meaning they meet stringent regulations governing where, how and under what conditions they're grown, fermented and bottled.

BEER

Beer hasn't traditionally had a high profile in France and the main French beer you're still likely to encounter is the mass-produced Kronenbourg 1664 (5.5%) premium lager, brewed in Strasbourg.

A handful of Parisian pubs produce their own microbrews. What's more, there's an emerging *bière artisanale* (craft beer) scene, with cafes beginning to offer limited-production brews on tap and by the bottle – La Fût Gueuze (p269) is a good place to start sampling. The city's inaugural artisan beer festival, La Paris Beer Week (http://laparisbeerweek.com), took place in brasseries, bars and specialist beer shops from late May to early June 2014 and is slated to become an annual event.

COCKTAILS

Recent years have seen a resurgence of cocktail bars across the city, from venerable establishments such as Harry's New York Bar, the original creator of the Bloody Mary, to glitzy bars and supercool backstreet speakeasies mixing up wildly inventive creations.

Nightlife

Paris' residential make-up means nightclubs aren't ubiquitous. Lacking a mainstream scene, clubbing here tends to be underground and extremely mobile. The best DJs and their followings have short stints in a certain venue before moving on, and the scene's hippest *soirées clubbing* (clubbing events) float between venues – including the city's many dance-driven bars.

But the beat is strong. Electronic music is of particularly high quality in Paris' clubs, with some excellent local house and techno. Funk and groove have given the predominance of dark minimal sounds a good pounding, and the Latin scene is huge; salsa dancing and Latino music nights pack out plenty of clubs. *Sono mondiale* (world music) has a huge following in Paris, where everything – from Algerian *raï* and other North African music to Senegalese *mbalax* and West Indian *zouk* – goes at clubs. Many venues offer salsa classes. R&B and hip-hop pickings are decent, if less represented than in many other European capitals.

Tea cannisters at Mariage Frères (p178)

BEFORE, L'AFTER & AFTER D'AFTERS

Seasoned Parisian clubbers, who tend to have a finely tuned sense of the absurd, split their night into three parts. First, *la before* – drinks in a bar that has a DJ playing. Second, they head to a club for *la soirée,* which rarely kicks off before 1am or 2am. When the party continues (or begins) at around 5am and goes until midday, it's *l'after*. Invariably, though, given the lack of any clear-cut distinction between Parisian bars and clubs, the before and after can easily blend into one without any real 'during'. *After d'afters,* meanwhile, kicks off in bars and clubs on Sunday afternoons and evenings, with a mix of strung-out hardcore clubbers pressing on amid those looking for a party that doesn't take place in the middle of the night.

CLUBBING WEBSITES

Track tomorrow's hot 'n' happening *soirée* with these finger-on-the-pulse Parisian nightlife links.

➡ **Paris DJs** (www.parisdjs.com) Free downloads to get you in the groove.

➡ **Paris Bouge** (www.parisbouge.com) Comprehensive listings site.

➡ **Parissi** (www.parissi.com) Search by date, then *la before, la soirée* and *l'after.*

➡ **Tribu de Nuit** (www.tribudenuit.com) Parties, club events and concerts galore.

NATURAL WINE

The latest trend in wine, *les vins naturels* (natural wines), have a fuzzy definition – no one really agrees on the details but the general idea is that they are made with as little human interference as possible. Quick translation? Natural wines contain little or no sulphites, which are added as a preservative in most wines. The good news is that this gives natural wines much more distinct personality (or *terroir,* as the French say), the bad news is that the wines can also be more unpredictable. For more specifics, see the website www.morethanorganic.com.

Lonely Planet's Top Choices

Le Mary Céleste (p174) There are few hipper places to drink than this fashionable Marais cocktail bar.

Le Baron Rouge (p196) Wonderfully convivial barrel-filled wine bar.

Experimental Cocktail Club (p131) Parisian style blended with New York street cred.

Holybelly (p155) The flag-bearer for Canal St-Martin's new crop of coffee houses.

Le Batofar (p268) Red-metal tugboat with a rooftop bar and portholed club beneath.

Best Coffee

Belleville Brûlerie (p186) Groundbreaking roastery with Saturday-morning tastings 'n' cuppings.

Coutume (p251) Artisan roasters of premium beans, with a fab flagship cafe.

La Caféothèque (p178) Maze of a coffee house with serious tasting notes and seating made to lounge on all day.

Tuck Shop (p155) Superb brews at this Aussie-run vegetarian hangout.

Telescope (p129) It may be small, but it packs a punch.

Fondation Café (p178) Teeny space with excellent coffee brewed from Belleville-roasted beans.

Best Tearooms

Le Loir dans La Théière (p178) Tasty tea in an enchanting, picture-book setting.

Mosquée de Paris (p220) Sip sweet mint tea and nibble sweet pastries in this peaceful haven.

Zen Zoo (p130) Taiwanese bubble tea in the City of Light.

Mariage Frères (p178) Paris' oldest and finest tearoom, founded in 1854.

Best Cocktails

Le Mary Céleste (p174) Ubercool cocktail bar with equally stunning cocktails and gourmet tapas.

Experimental Cocktail Club (p131) Fabulous cocktails in a setting that exudes spirit and soul.

Blue Valentine (p173) Beautifully crafted cocktails in the company of beautiful cuisine.

Candelaria (p168) Regulars swear by this achingly cool taqueria's Bloody Marys and cocktail-fuelled weekend brunches.

Artisan (p154) Sophisticated haunt at the foot of Montmartre.

Le Coq (p155) Signature cocktails mixing old-timey French liqueurs.

Best Nightclubs

ShowCase (p104) Cavernous venue beneath the Pont Alexandre III.

Le Rex Club (p130) Mythical house and techno club with a phenomenal sound system.

Rosa Bonheur (p157) Old-fashioned dance hall in the Parc des Buttes-Chaumont.

Best Wine Bars

Le Garde Robe (p131) Affordable natural wines and unpretentious vibe.

Chapeau Melon (p179) Stylishly cool wine cellar known for its natural French wines.

Le Barav (p175) Hipster *bar à vin* on one of the trendiest streets in the Haut Marais.

Best Pavement Terraces

Les Deux Magots (p249) Quintessential Left Bank literary cafe.

Chez Prune (p155) The boho cafe that put Canal St-Martin on the map.

Le Saut du Loup (p130) Sweeping summer terrace overlooking the Jardin du Carrousel and the Louvre.

Le Cap Horn (p174) Laidback Chilean bar with electric pavement terrace and fiery cocktails.

L'Ebouillanté (p175) Steps from the Seine.

Café Saint Régis (p209) Across from Notre Dame.

Best Neighbourhood Cafes

Le Petit Fer à Cheval (p174) Pocket-size cafe-bar with 1903 zinc bar and fervent crowd of regulars.

Aux Deux Amis (p179) Famed for its hand-cut horsemeat, served Fridays.

La Fée Verte (p196) Absinthe specialist.

Le Progrès (p154) Old-school Montmartre cafe loaded with ambiance.

Le Verre à Pied (p221) Pearl of a place where little has changed since 1870.

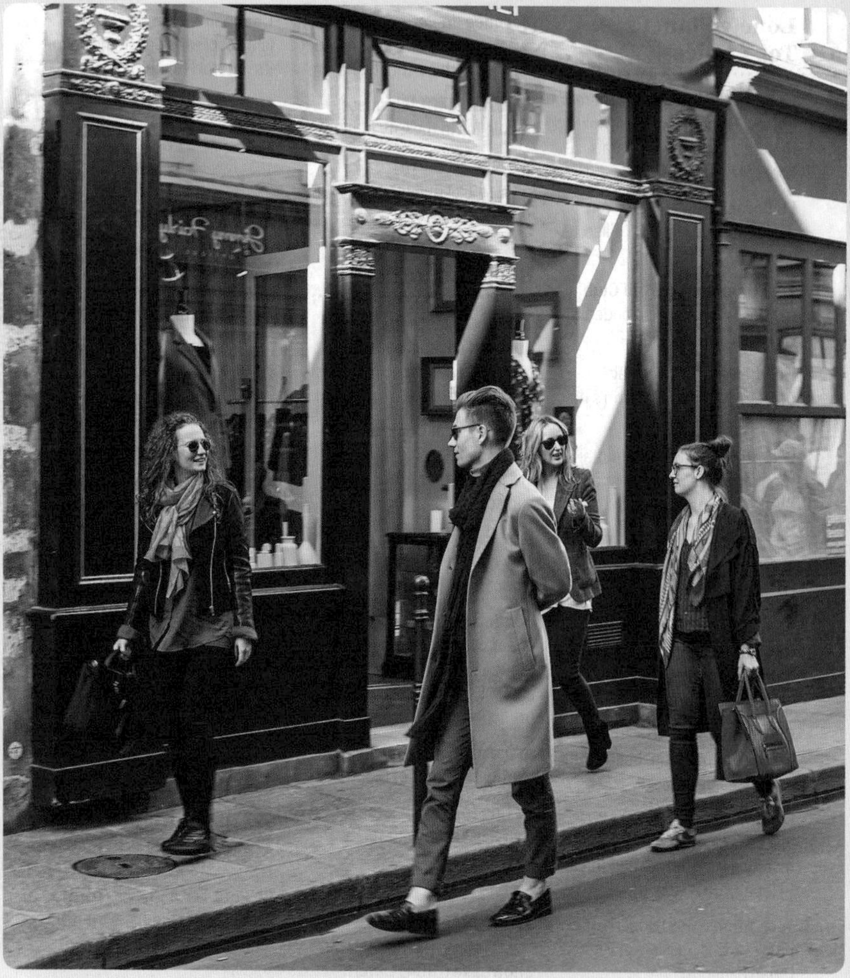

Parisians are renowned for their everyday sense of style

Shopping

Paris has it all: broad boulevards lined with international chains, luxury avenues studded with designer fashion houses, famous grands magasins (department stores) and fabulous markets. But the real charm lies in strolling the city's backstreets, where tiny speciality shops and quirky boutiques selling everything from strawberry-scented Wellington boots to heaven-scented candles are wedged between cafes, galleries and churches.

Grand department store Galeries Lafayette (p105)

Fashion

Fashion shopping is Paris' forte. Yet although its well-groomed residents make the city at times look and feel like a giant catwalk, fashion here is about style and quality first and foremost, rather than status or brand names.

A good place to get an overview of Paris fashion is at the city's famous *grands magasins* such as Le Bon Marché (p252), Galeries Lafayette (p105) and Le Printemps (p105).

FASHION SHOWS

Although tickets for Paris' high-profile *haute couture* and *prêt-à-porter* (ready-to-wear) fashion shows are like hens' teeth, you can still see some runway action: reserve ahead to attend free weekly fashion shows at Galeries Lafayette.

DRESSING FOR LESS

Parisian fashion doesn't have to break the bank: there are fantastic bargains at second-hand and vintage boutiques (generally, the more upmarket the area, the better quality the cast-offs), along with outlet shops selling previous seasons' collections, surpluses and seconds by name-brand designers.

Arcades

Dating from the 19th century, Paris' glass-roofed *passages couverts* (covered passages) were the precursors to shopping malls and are treasure chests of exquisite boutiques. Take a walk (p124) through some of the Right Bank's best-preserved arcades.

Markets

Nowhere encapsulates Paris' village atmosphere more than its markets. Not simply places to shop, the city's street markets are social gatherings for the entire neighbourhood,

NEED TO KNOW

Opening Hours

Shops generally open between 10am and 7pm Monday to Saturday. Smaller shops often shut all day on Monday and/or may close from around noon to 2pm for lunch. Many larger stores hold *nocturnes* (late-night shopping), usually (but not always) on Thursday, until around 10pm. Sunday shopping is limited; the Champs-Élysées, Montmartre and Le Marais are liveliest.

Sales

Paris' twice-yearly *soldes* (sales) generally last around five weeks; they start in mid-January and again in mid-June.

Tax Refunds

Non-EU residents may be eligible for a TVA (VAT; sales tax) refund (p356).

Top Shopping Tips

- The most exclusive designer boutiques require customers to get buzzed in – don't be shy about ringing the bell.
- Particularly in smaller shops, shopkeepers may not appreciate you touching the merchandise until invited to do so.
- Head to a *cabine d'essayage* (fitting room), or check sizes at www.onlineconversion.com/clothing.
- If you're happy browsing, tell sales staff '*Je regarde*' – 'I'm just looking'.
- Practically all shops offer free (and very beautiful) gift wrapping – ask for *un paquet cadeau*.
- A *ticket de caisse* (receipt) is essential for returning/exchanging an item (within one month of purchase).
- Bargaining is only acceptable at flea markets.

Parisian Souvenirs

For authentic quirky and/or nostalgic souvenirs, browse the City of Paris' Paris Rendez-Vous boutique (p181) or online store (http://boutique.paris.fr), which ships worldwide.

Above: Paris has many outdoor markets, such as this artist market near Montparnasse

Left: Concept store L'Éclaireur (p185) sells tableware and interior design items as well as clothing

Shopping by Neighbourhood

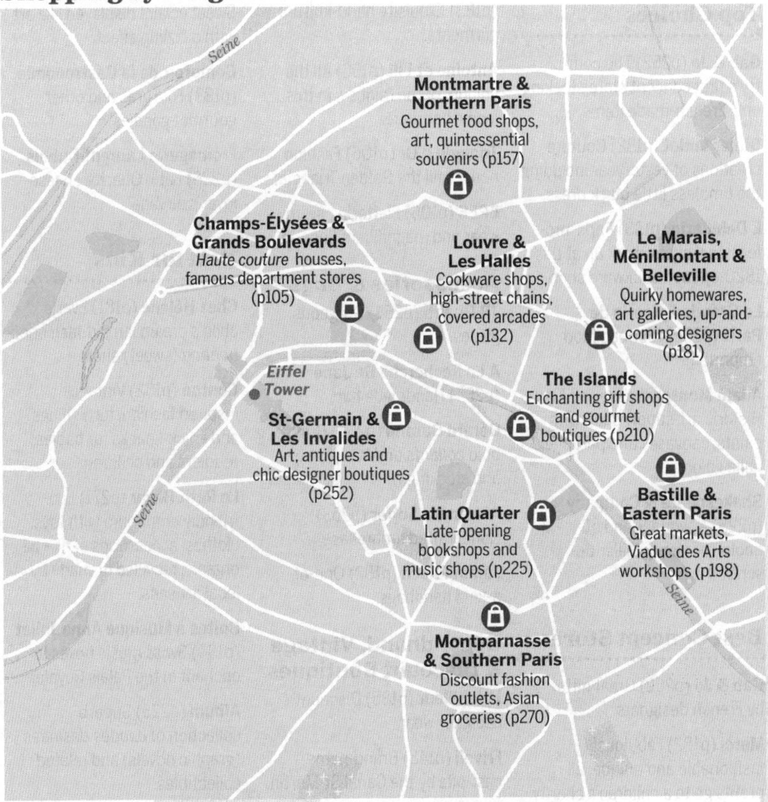

and visiting one will give you a true appreciation for Parisian life.

Nearly every little quarter has its own street market at least once a week (never Monday) where tarpaulin-topped trestle tables bow beneath fresh, cooked and preserved delicacies. *Marchés biologiques* (organic markets) are increasingly sprouting up across the city. Many street markets also sell clothes, accessories, homewares and more. Markets in Paris' more multicultural neighbourhoods are filled with the flavours and aromas of continents beyond Europe.

Bric-a-brac, antiques, retro clothing, jewellery, cheap brand-name clothing, footwear, African carvings, DVDs and electronic items and much more are laid out at the city's flea markets. Watch out for pickpockets!

The website www.paris.fr (in French) lists every market by *arrondissement,* including speciality markets such as flower markets. For a list of some of Paris' best markets, see p24.

Gourmet Goods

Food, wine and tea shops make for mouthwatering shopping. Pastries might not keep, but items you can take home (customs regulations permitting) include light-as-air macarons, chocolates, jams, preserves, foie gras and, of course, fabulous French cheeses. Many of the best *fromageries* (cheese shops) can provide vacuum packing.

Art, Antiques & Homewares

From venerable antique dealers to edgy art galleries, there are a wealth of places in this artistic city to browse and buy one-off conversation pieces and collectibles.

Paris also has a trove of unique homewares shops selling colourful, quirky innovations to brighten your living and/or working environment.

Lonely Planet's Top Choices

Gab & Jo (p252) The country's first concept store stocking only French-made items.

Didier Ludot (p132) Couture creations of yesteryear including the timeless little black dress.

E Dehillerin (p133) Paris' professional chefs stock up at this 1820-opened cookware shop.

La Grande Épicerie de Paris (p252) Glorious food emporium.

Adam Montparnasse (p270) Historic art-supply shop with paints, canvases and paraphernalia galore.

Shakespeare & Company (p225) A 'wonderland of books', as Henry Miller described it.

Best Concept Stores

Gab & Jo (p252) Great gifts by French designers.

Merci (p182) Fabulously fashionable and unique: all profits go to a children's charity in Madagascar.

Colette (p133) Uberhip designer fashion and basement water bar.

L'Éclaireur (p185) Part art space, part lounge and part deconstructionist fashion statement; for men and women in separate spaces.

Hermès (p253) Housed in an art-deco swimming pool.

Best Fashion

Boutiques

La Citadelle (p157) Multi-designer Montmartre shop with some real finds.

Andrea Crews (p183) Bold art and fashion collective.

La Boutique Extraordinaire (p183) Exquisite hand-knitted garments.

Antoine et Lili (p158) All the colours of the rainbow in this iconic boutique.

Triangle d'Or (p106) Fashion houses fill the Golden Triangle.

ERES (p106) Flattering swimwear and magnificent lingerie.

Accessories & Bags

JB Guanti (p254) Gorgeous gloves.

A La Recherche De Jane (p254) Handmade hats.

Gérard Durand (p255) Bright, bold *collants* and *bas* (tights and stockings).

Alexandra Sojfer (p253) Handcrafted umbrellas.

Jamin Puech (p182) One-of-a-kind handbags.

Secondhand, Vintage & Discount Boutiques

L'Habilleur (p185) Discount designer wear.

Frivoli (p148) Brand-name cast-offs by the Canal St-Martin.

Kiliwatch (p134) New and used streetwear; vintage hats and boots.

Chercheminippes (p254) Six specialist boutiques on one street.

Rue d'Alésia (p271) Seconds, samples and last season's stock.

Best Gourmet Shops

Place de la Madeleine (p102) Single-item specialist shops and famous emporiums.

La Manufacture de Chocolat (p198) Alain Ducasse's bean-to-bar chocolate factory.

Fromagerie Goncourt (p186) Contemporary *fromagerie* unusually styled like a boutique.

L'Éclair de Génie (p181) Sweet éclairs displayed like art with dazzling effect.

Comptoir de la Gastronomie (p133) Foie gras and other gourmet goodies.

Fromagerie Laurent Dubois (p226) Latin Quarter cheese-lover's nirvana.

Best for Kids

Chez Hélène (p181) Every child's dream: an old-fashioned *bonbon* (sweet) shop.

Bonton (p182) Vintage-inspired fashion, furnishings and knick-knacks for babies, toddlers and children.

Le Petit Bazar (p271) Eco-friendly emporium with toys, clothes, accessories et al – all organic, recycled or made by local artisans.

Boîtes à Musique Anna Joliet (p134) Swiss music boxes to enchant in the Palais Royale.

Album (p225) Superb collection of *bandes desinées* (graphic novels) and related collectibles.

Petit Pan Bébé (p184) Baby and children's wear stitched in a dazzling array of colours and fabrics.

Best Art & Antiques

Marché aux Puces de St-Ouen (p157) One of Europe's largest flea markets, with more than 2500 stalls.

Carré Rive Gauche (p253) Home to more than 120 specialised merchants.

Hôtel Drouot (p106) Famous auction house.

La Maison de Poupée (p252) Adorable antique dolls.

Deyrolle (p253) Taxidermist that starred in *Midnight in Paris*.

Point Éphémère (p156)

Entertainment

Catching a performance in Paris is a treat. French and international opera, ballet and theatre companies and cabaret dancers take to the stage in venues of mythical proportion, and a flurry of young, passionate, highly creative musicians, thespians and artists make the city's fascinating fringe art scene what it is.

NEED TO KNOW

Listings

Paris' two top listings guides *Pariscope* (€0.50) and **L'Officiel des Spectacles** (www.offi.fr; €0.50), both in French but easy to navigate, are available from newsstands on Wednesday, and are crammed with everything that's on in the capital.

Useful websites:

➡ **LYLO** (www.lylo.fr) Short for Les Yeux, Les Oreilles (meaning 'eyes and ears'), offering the lowdown on the live-music, concert and clubbing scenes.

➡ **Le Figaro Scope** (www.figaroscope.fr) Has a great search tool for concerts by *arrondissement* – click on the map.

➡ **Paris Nightlife** (www.parisnightlife.fr) All-encompassing listings site.

Tickets

The most convenient place to purchase concert, theatre and other cultural and sporting-event tickets is from electronics and entertainment megashop **Fnac** (☎08 92 68 36 22; www.fnactickets.com) – whether in person at the *billeteries* (ticket offices) or by phone or online. There are branches throughout Paris including in the Forum des Halles.

Tickets generally can't be returned or exchanged unless a performance is cancelled.

Discount Tickets

On the day of performance, theatre, opera and ballet tickets are sold for half price (plus €3 commission) at the central Kiosque Théâtre Madeleine (p105).

Cabarets

Whirling lines of feather-boa-clad, high-kicking dancers at grand-scale cabarets such as the can-can creator, the Moulin Rouge, are a quintessential fixture on Paris' entertainment scene – for everyone but Parisians. Still, the dazzling sets, costumes and dancing guarantee an entertaining evening (or matinee).

Tickets to these spectacles start from around €90 (from €130 with lunch, from €150 with dinner) and usually include a half-bottle of Champagne. Reserve ahead.

Moulin Rouge (p155)

Live Music

Festivals for just about every musical genre ensure that everyone gets to listen in. Street music is a constant in this busker-filled city, summer adding stirring open-air concerts along the Seine and in city parks to the year-round serenade of accordions.

JAZZ & BLUES

Paris became Europe's most important jazz centre after WWII and the city's best clubs and cellars still lure international stars.

Admission generally ranges from free to around €30 depending on the artist, time and venue.

Download podcasts, tunes, concert information and all that jazz from Paris' jazz radio station, **TFS** (89.9 MHz FM; www.tsfjazz.com).

FRENCH CHANSONS

While *chanson* literally means 'song' in French, it also specifically refers to a style of heartfelt, lyric-driven music typified by Édith Piaf, Maurice Chevalier, Charles Aznavour et al. You'll come across some rousing live covers of their most famous songs at traditional venues. Contemporary twists on the genre include the fusion of dance beats with traditional *chanson* melodies. The term also covers intimate cabarets such as Montmartre's Au Lapin Agile.

Admission generally ranges from free to around €30 depending on the artist, time and venue.

ROCK, POP & INDIE

Palais Omnisports de Paris-Bercy, Stade de France (p158) and Le Zénith in Parc de la

LOUISE HEUSINKVELD / GETTY IMAGES ©

Opéra Bastille (p198), designed by architect Carlos Ott

Villette are the largest venues but also the most impersonal; it's the smaller concert halls with real history and charm that most fans favour. Check http://gigsinparis.com for listings.

CLASSICAL MUSIC

The city hosts dozens of orchestral, organ and chamber-music concerts each week. In addition to theatres and concert halls, Paris' beautiful, centuries-old stone churches have magnificent acoustics and provide a meditative backdrop for classical-music concerts. Posters outside churches advertise upcoming events with ticket information, or visit www.ampconcerts.com, where you can make online reservations. Tickets cost around €23 to €30.

The Jean Nouvel–designed 2400-seat Philharmonie de Paris concert hall is expected to open in the Parc de la Villette (p139) in 2015.

Cinema

Paris has some wonderful movie houses to catch new flicks, avant-garde cinema and priceless classics.

Foreign films (including English-language films) screened in their original language with French subtitles are labelled 'VO' *(version originale)*. Films labelled 'VF' *(version française)* are dubbed in French.

Pariscope and *L'Officiel des Spectacles* list the full crop of Paris' cinematic pickings and screening times; online check out http://cinema.leparisien.fr.

First-run tickets cost around €11 for adults (€13 for 3D). Students, under 18s and over 60s get discounted tickets (usually about €7.70 or €9.70 for 3D) every night except Friday, and all day Saturday and for Sunday matinées. Most cinemas have across-the-board discounts on morning sessions.

Opera & Ballet

France's Opéra National de Paris and Ballet de l'Opéra National de Paris perform at Paris' two opera houses, the Palais Garnier and Opéra Bastille. The season runs between September and July.

Theatre

The majority of theatre productions in Paris, including those originally written in other languages, are – naturally enough –

performed in French. Only occasionally do English-speaking troupes play at smaller venues in and around town. Consult *Pariscope* or *L'Officiel des Spectacles* for details.

Buskers in Paris

Paris' gaggle of clowns, mime artists, living statues, acrobats, inline skaters, buskers and other street entertainers can be loads of fun and cost substantially less than a theatre ticket (a few coins in the hat is appreciated). Some excellent musicians perform in the long echo-filled corridors of the metro, a highly prized privilege that artists audition for. Outside, you can be sure of a good show at the following:

➡ **Place Georges Pompidou, 4e** The huge square in front of the Centre Pompidou.

➡ **Pont St-Louis, 4e** The bridge linking Paris' two islands (best enjoyed with a Berthillon ice cream in hand).

➡ **Pont au Double, 4e** The pedestrian bridge linking Notre Dame with the Left Bank.

➡ **Place Joachim du Bellay, 1er** Musicians and fire-eaters near the Fontaine des Innocents.

➡ **Parc de la Villette, 19e** African drummers at the weekend.

➡ **Place du Tertre, Montmartre, 18e** Montmartre's original main square is Paris' busiest busker stage.

Entertainment by Neighbourhood

➡ **Eiffel Tower & Western Paris** Entertainment options are limited in this refined residential area.

➡ **Champs-Élysées & Grands Boulevards** Famous revues and Paris' palatial 1875-built opera house take top billing here.

➡ **Louvre & Les Halles** Swinging jazz clubs, centuries-old theatres and cinemas mix it up with pumping nightclubs.

➡ **Montmartre & Northern Paris** Showstopping cabarets, mythologised concert halls and cutting-edge cultural centres scatter throughout Paris' northern quarters.

➡ **Le Marais, Ménilmontant & Belleville** Rockin' live-music venues, gay and lesbian clubs, DJs hitting the decks and old-style *chansons*.

➡ **Bastille & Eastern Paris** Salsa dancing, old-time tea dancing, and France's national cinema institute are big drawcards.

➡ **The Islands** Church concerts and street entertainers are the only entertainment options on Paris' islands.

➡ **Latin Quarter** Swing bands, cinema retrospectives and jam sessions are among the Latin Quarter's offerings.

➡ **St-Germain & Les Invalides** Atmospheric cinemas, cultural centres and theatres inhabit this chic, sophisticated neighbourhood.

➡ **Montparnasse & Southern Paris** Some of this area's most happening venues are aboard boats moored on the Seine.

Lonely Planet's Top Choices

Palais Garnier (p104) Paris' premier opera house is an artistic inspiration.

Point Éphémère (p156) Ubercool cultural centre on the banks of Canal St-Martin.

Moulin Rouge (p155) The can-can creator razzle-dazzles with spectacular sets, costumes and choreography.

Le 104 (p157) Cultural tour de force in a former funeral parlour.

La Flèche d'Or (p198) Former railway station club renowned for unearthing new talent.

Café Universel (p224) Brilliant jazz club showcasing a diverse range of styles.

Best Cinema

Cinéma La Pagode (p251) Paris' most unique cinema, in a converted 19th-century Japanese pagoda.

Cinémathèque Française (p198) The national cinema institute has a host of cinematic offerings.

Le Champo (p224) Beloved art-deco icon screening independent films.

Forum des Images (p132) The Paris film archive.

Le Grand Rex (p133) Art-deco landmark from the '30s.

Best Live Music

Jazz Clubs

Café Universel (p224) Intimate club with unpretentious vibe and no cover.

New Morning (p157) Solid and varied line-up of everything from post-bop and Latin to reggae.

Le Baiser Salé (p131) Reputable venue that focuses on Caribbean and Latin sounds.

Sunset & Sunside (p131) Blues, fusion and world sounds, as well as straight-up jazz.

Caveau de la Huchette (p224) Fun Latin Quarter cellar with swing dancing and an eclectic scene.

La Java (p180) Live salsa, rock and world music where Édith Piaf got her first break.

Rock, Pop & Indie

Le Trianon (p156) Old Montmartre theatre with great acts and an intimate setting.

Le Divan du Monde (p156) Great indie shows in Pigalle.

Cabaret Sauvage (p157) Giant yurt that hosts hip-hop, funk and world concerts.

Bus Palladium (p156) Eclectic rock venue.

La Maroquinerie (p180) Tiny but trendy venue in Ménilmontant with real cutting-edge gigs.

Le Nouveau Casino (p180) Underground and up-to-the-minute gigs.

French Chansons

Au Limonaire (p105) Perfect Parisian wine bar with *chansons* and French singer-songwriters.

Au Lapin Agile (p156) Mythic Montmartre cabaret.

Chez Louisette (p153) Classic *chansons* by the flea market.

Le Vieux Belleville (p181) Old-fashioned bistro and *musette* atop Parc de Belleville.

Classical

Salle Pleyel (p105) Highly regarded concert hall dating from the 1920s.

Église St-Eustache (p120) Sunday-afternoon organ concerts.

Église de la Madeleine (p99) Memorable organ recitals.

Best Cultural Centres

Centre Pompidou (p117) Irresistible cocktail of cutting-edge performances.

Gaîté Lyrique (p180) Unique and fascinating exhibitions create buzz at this vibrant cultural centre in Le Marais.

Le Carreau du Temple (p180) Covered market–turned–cultural centre, well worth a gander for its drop-dead-gorgeous art-nouveau ironwork alone.

L'Entrepôt (p270) Hosts everything from film screenings to concerts, poetry slams and art exhibitions.

Le Lucernaire (p251) Packed cultural agenda including popular Sunday concerts.

Best Theatre, Opera & Dance

Palais Garnier (p104) Fabled home of the phantom of the opera offering an unforgettable experience.

Opéra Bastille (p198) Paris' main, modern opera house, seating an audience of 3400.

Cité de la Musique (p157) Every imaginable type of music and dance.

Théâtre du Châtelet (p132) Operas, ballets, classical recitals and musicals.

Gay & Lesbian

The city known as 'gay Paree' lives up to its name. Paris is so open that there's less of a defined 'scene' here than in other cities where it's more underground. While Le Marais is the mainstay of gay and lesbian nightlife, you'll find venues right throughout the city attracting a mixed crowd.

Background

Paris was the first European capital to vote in an openly gay mayor (Bertrand Delanoë was elected in 2001), and the city itself is very open – same-sex couples commonly display affection in public and checking into a hotel room is unlikely to raise eyebrows. In fact, the only challenge you may have is working out where straight Paris ends and gay Paris starts, as the city is so stylish and sexy.

In 2013, France became the 13th country in the world to allow same-sex marriage (and adoption by same-sex couples). Despite protests by political and public opponents, polls show the majority of French citizens support marriage equality. Typically at least one partner needs to be a resident to get married here. And, of course, there's no end of romantic places to propose.

Drinking & Nightlife

Le Marais, especially the areas around the intersection of rue Ste-Croix de la Bretonnerie and rue des Archives, and eastwards to rue Vieille du Temple, has been Paris' main centre of gay nightlife for some three decades and is still the epicentre of gay and lesbian life in Paris. There's also a handful of bars and clubs within walking distance of bd de Sébastopol. The lesbian scene is less prominent than its gay counterpart, and centres on a few cafes and bars in Le Marais, particularly along rue des Écouffes. Bars and clubs are generally all gay- and lesbian-friendly.

Events

By far the biggest event on the gay and lesbian calendar is Gay Pride Day, in late June, when the annual Marche des Fiertés (www.gaypride.fr) through Le Marais to Bastille provides a colourful spectacle, and plenty of parties take place.

Year-round, check gay and lesbian websites or ask at gay bars and other venues to find out about events.

Organisations & Resources

Centre Gai et Lesbien de Paris Île de France (CGL; ☎01 43 57 21 47; www.centrelgbt-paris.org; 63 rue Beaubourg, 3e; ⏲centre & bar 3.30-8pm Mon-Fri, 1-7pm Sat, library 6-8pm Mon-Wed, 3.30-6pm Fri, 5-7pm Sat; Ⓜ Rambuteau or Arts et Métiers) Single best source of information for gay and lesbian travellers in Paris, with a large library of books and periodicals and a sociable bar. Also has details of hotlines, helplines, gay and gay-friendly medical services and politically oriented activist associations.

Lonely Planet's Top Choices

Open Café (p177) The wide terrace is prime for talent-watching.

Scream Club (p179) Saturday's the night at 'Paris' biggest gay party'.

La Champmeslé (p130) Cabaret nights, fortune-telling and art exhibitions attract an older lesbian crowd.

Queen (p104) Don't miss disco night!

Best Weekend in Le Marais

Loustic (p178) Among the best coffee (and espresso-bar interior design) in town.

Place des Vosges (p165) Charming city square.

Broken Arm (p171) Hipster address with fresh juice- and salad-driven cafe adjoining an achingly cool concept store.

Cimetière du Père Lachaise (p161) Oscar Wilde's winged-angel-topped tomb is a highlight.

La Belle Hortense (p176) Creative wine bar with modish mixed crowd and shelves of books.

Derrière (p171) Play ping-pong between courses at this stellar restaurant.

Best Shopping Sprees

Samuel Coraux (p182) Fabulous and occasionally outrageously kitsch jewellery for guys 'n' gals by one of Paris' funkiest jewel designers.

État Libre d'Orange (p182) Perfumery that screams Marais hipster, with scents bearing names such as Fat Electrician, Jasmin et Cigarette, and Delicious Closet Queen.

L'Éclaireur (p185) Part art space, part lounge and part deconstructionist fashion statement; fashion for men and women.

Best Apéros

L'Étoile Manquante (p177) Trendy, gay-friendly bar with retro interior and fabulous pavement terrace for obligatory after-work drinks.

Open Café (p177) With a four-hour happy hour kicking in daily at 6pm, how can you possibly go wrong?

Best Gay Hangouts

Le Cox (p177) The meeting place for an interesting (and interested) cruisy crowd throughout the evening from dusk onwards.

Best Lesbian Hangouts

3w Kafé (p178) Flagship cocktail bar-pub on a street with several lesbian bars; weekend dancing downstairs and themed evenings.

Les Jacasses (p179) Mellow music, hard-core evenings and a happy 'hour' that happily lasts for four.

Best Clubs

Open Café (p177) The only place to be late on a Saturday night.

Le Tango (p179) Mingle with a mixed and cosmopolitan gay and lesbian set in a historic 1930s dancehall.

NEED TO KNOW

Useful Websites

➡ **Paris-Gay.com** (www.paris-gay.com) Bang up-to-date site with bars, restaurants, shops, club nights, parties and other events.

➡ **Spartacus International Gay Guide** (www.spartacusworld.com) Travel site with solid recommendations for gay-friendly accommodation in particular.

➡ **CitéGay** (www.citegay.com) One of the best all-inclusive gay sites, with a heavily political agenda.

➡ **La France Gaie & Lesbienne** (www.france.qrd.org) 'Queer resources directory' covering cinema, music, art and more.

Publications

Many gay and lesbian magazines have folded but guys should look out for *Têtu*, a popular glossy monthly available at newsstands.

Best Party Spots Beyond Le Marais

Ménilmontant (p179) Edgy urban cool.

Pigalle (p154) Montmartre's sexy southern neighbour.

Champs-Élysées (p104) Glam bars and clubs.

Bastille (p196) Lively local vibe.

Canal St-Martin (p155) Arty, indie venues.

Belleville (p179) Increasingly hip, multicultural 'hood.

Parks & Activities

Ready to play with the Parisians? Take a break from the city concrete and check out the islands of green instead, where you'll be able to thwack a tennis ball, stroll in style, admire art or bust out some wine and cheese. And in true French form, you won't even need to break a sweat.

Parks

➡ **Jardin du Luxembourg** (p234) Paris' most iconic swath of green, where you can stroll among the statues, play tennis, jog in style and entertain the kids.

➡ **Jardin des Tuileries** (p119) Leafy Seine-side oasis, perfect for picnics, summer carnival rides, jogging and impossibly magnificent vistas.

➡ **Bois de Vincennes** (p190) The erstwhile royal hunting grounds east of Paris. Today it's home to a zoo, the kid-packed Parc Floral and pick-up football matches.

➡ **Bois de Boulogne** (p89) Haussmann's western oasis. Cycle, row, stroll the gardens, hit the amusement park or catch a steeplechase.

➡ **Jardin des Plantes** (p214) Natural history museum, botanic gardens and sprinkler-dodging picnics.

➡ **Parc des Buttes-Chaumont** (p142) Another Haussmann creation, this quirky local spot has a faux Greek temple, abandoned railway line, dance hall and tai chi vibes.

Spectator Sports

Paris hosts a great variety of sporting events throughout the year, from the French Open (www.rolandgarros.com) and BNP Parisbas Masters (www.atpworldtour.com) to local football matches. There are a handful of stadiums in and around the city; for upcoming events, follow the What's On link at http://en.parisinfo.com. Better yet, if you can read French, sports daily **L'Équipe** (www.lequipe.fr) will provide more depth. Local teams include Paris Saint-Germain (football; www.psg.fr) and the pink-clad Stade Français Paris (rugby; www.stade.fr). Catch France's national team, Les Bleus, at the Stade de France.

The city's three horsetracks can make for a thrilling afternoon. The Hippodrome d'Auteuil and the Hippodrome de Longchamp (www.france-galop.com) are in the Bois de Boulogne; the Hippodrome de Paris-Vincennes (www.letrot.com) is in the Bois de Vincennes.

Every October the Hippodrome de Longchamp hosts the Prix de l'Arc de Triomphe (www.prixarcdetriomphe.com), Europe's most prestigious horserace.

Cycling

Everyone knows that the Tour de France races up the Champs-Élysées at the end of July every year, but you don't need Chris Froome's leg muscles to enjoy Paris on two wheels. Between Vélib' (the Paris bike-share scheme; p349) and the hundreds of kilometres of urban bike paths, cycling around the city has never been easier. Sign up for one of the great city bike tours (p351) or hire a bike (p350) yourself. Some streets are closed to vehicle traffic on Sundays – great news for cyclists! Bring your own helmet.

Skating

The next most popular activity after cycling has to be skating, whether on the street or on ice. Rent a pair of in-line skates at Nomades and join the Friday evening skate (Pari Roller) that streaks through the Paris streets, or join the more laid-back Sunday afternoon skate (Rollers & Coquillages Ramble).

During the winter holidays several temporary outdoor rinks are installed around Paris – the most famous are located in front of the Hôtel de Ville and on the 1st floor of the Eiffel Tower. See www.paris.fr for other locations.

Hammams & Spas

Whether you want to hobnob with the stars at a *spa de luxe* or get a *savon noir* (black soap) exfoliation at the neighbourhood hammam, Paris has spaces to suit every whim.

A hammam generally charges an entrance fee, which grants you admission to a steam bath and sauna. Extras – exfoliation scrubs, orange-blossom massages, and mint tea and North African pastries – are tacked on to the initial price (but worth it!). Most hammams are primarily for women; if men are admitted it's usually only once or twice a week, and only rarely at the same time as women.

Swimming

If you want to go swimming at either your hotel or in a public pool, you'll need to don a *bonnet de bain* (bathing cap) – even if you don't have any hair. You shouldn't need to buy one ahead of time as they are generally sold at most pools. Men are required to wear skin-tight trunks (Speedos); loose-fitting Bermuda shorts are not allowed.

Boules

Don't be surprised to see groups of earnest Parisians playing *boules* (France's most popular traditional game, similar to lawn bowls) in the Jardin du Luxembourg and other parks and squares with suitably flat, shady patches of gravel. The Arènes de Lutèce *boulodrome* in a 2nd-century Roman amphitheatre in the Latin Quarter is a fabulous spot to absorb the scene. There are usually places to play at Paris Plages.

NEED TO KNOW

Where Can I Find...

The best single source of information on participatory sports in Paris can be found online at the city hall's website (www.paris.fr). Follow the *Practiquer un sport* link in the *Paris Loisirs* menu for info on everything from skating and badminton to stadiums and equipment rental. *Mairies* (town halls) in every *arrondissement* also have information on sports in their own patch. For an abbreviated version in English, head to http://en.parisinfo.com and follow the *Well Being* link in the *Practical Paris* menu.

Tickets

Tickets for big events can generally be purchased through the venue's website. In most cases you'll need to reserve well in advance, so this is best done before you leave for Paris. If you want to try your luck, head to the box office at the nearest Fnac store (www.fnac.com, follow the *Magasins* link to locate a branch near you), which should have a schedule of upcoming events.

River cruise boats on the Seine

The Seine

La ligne de vie de Paris (the lifeline of Paris), the Seine, sluices through the city, spanned by 37 bridges. Its Unesco World Heritage–listed riverbanks offer picturesque promenades, parks, activities and events, including sandy summertime beaches. After dark, watch the river dance with the watery reflections of city lights and tourist-boat flood lamps. You are in Paris.

Riverbank Rejuvenation

Paris' riverbanks have been reborn with the creation of Les Berges de Seine. On the Right Bank, east of the Hôtel de Ville, 1.5km of former expressway now incorporates walkways and cycleways. Even more revolutionary is the completely car-free 2.3km stretch of the Left Bank from the Pont de l'Alma to the Musée d'Orsay (newly linked to the water's edge by a grand staircase that doubles as amphitheatre seating).

A resounding success since it opened in 2013, this innovative promenade is dotted with restaurants and bars (some aboard boats), chessboard tables, hopscotch and ball-game courts, a skate ramp, kids' climbing wall, a 100m running track and floating gardens on 1800 sq metres of artificial islands (complete with knotted-rope hammocks where you can lie back and soak up the river's reclaimed serenity).

At any time of year, Les Berges de Seine also offers temporary events and activities as diverse as film screenings and knitting workshops, and even wintertime curling on ice.

Promenading & Pausing

The Seine's riverbanks are where Parisians come to cycle, jog, inline skate and stroll – staircases along the banks lead down to the water's edge.

Particularly picturesque spots for a riverside promenade include the areas around Paris' two elegant inner-city islands, the Île de la Cité and Île Saint-Louis. Up at street level, the banks are lined with the distinctive green-metal *bouquiniste* stalls selling antiquarian books, sheet music and old advertising posters. A lesser-known island stroll is the artificial Île aux Cygnes via its tree-shaded walkway, the Allée des Cygnes (walking from west to east gives you a stunning view of the Eiffel Tower).

The river also acts as a giant backyard for apartment-dwelling Parisians. All along its banks you'll find locals reading, picnicking, canoodling or just basking in the sunshine. Among the best-loved spots is the tiny, triangular park Square du Vert Galant beneath the Pont Neuf.

Summertime Beaches

Presaging the latest anti-auto revolution that ushered in Les Berges de Seine were the Paris Plages (Paris Beaches), with traffic supplanted by palm trees, bars, cafes, sun lounges, parasols, water fountains and sprays, and sand brought in by barges lining the river from mid-July to mid-August.

The Paris Plages were established in 2002 for Parisians who couldn't escape to the coast to cool off in the summer months. They now extend for more than 5km on sections of both banks during the season, and also incorporate activities such as *pétanque* (similar to bowls) and concerts.

Seine-Side Entertainment

In addition to Les Berges de Seine, entertainment options include floating nightclubs aboard boats moored in southern Paris, such as the red-metal tugboat Le Batofar, and even a floating swimming pool, Piscine Joséphine Baker.

On the banks, riverside venues include the Docks en Seine, home to the French fashion institute, the Institut Français de la Mode, which incorporates vast outdoor terraces, uberhip bars, clubs and restaurants, an entertainment-themed contemporary-art museum and more.

River Cruises & Tours

The best way, of course, to become acquainted with the Seine is to get out on it. A plethora of companies run day- and night-time boat tours (p352), usually lasting around an hour, with commentary in multiple languages. Many cruise companies also offer brunch, lunch and dinner cruises and the standard of cuisine is generally high (this is Paris, after all).

An alternative to traditional boat tours is the Batobus, a handy hop-on, hop-off service which stops at eight quintessentially Parisian attractions: the Eiffel Tower, Champs-Élysées, Musée d'Orsay, Musée du Louvre, St-Germain des Prés, Hôtel de Ville, Notre Dame and Jardin des Plantes. Single- and multiday tickets allow you to spend as long as you like sightseeing between stops.

NEED TO KNOW

The Seine's riverbanks are freely accessible around the clock, but bear in mind the following safety tips:

- ➡ There are no fences or barriers at the water's edge. If you're travelling with young children, keep a close eye on them to ensure they don't take an unexpected plunge.
- ➡ Swimming in the river is strictly forbidden, even during Paris Plages, due to boat traffic and the health hazards posed by the water quality (although it's better than it has been in a long time, with Atlantic salmon returning to the river).
- ➡ Stairs leading down to the water can be especially slippery after rain.

Explore Paris

PARIS'
TOP SIGHTS

Neighbourhoods at a Glance

❶ Eiffel Tower & Western Paris p80

Home to *very* well-heeled Parisians, this *grande dame* of a neighbourhood is where you can get up close and personal with the city's symbolic tower as well as striking new architecture in the high-rise business district of La Défense just outside the *Périphérique* (ring road) encircling central Paris.

❷ Champs-Élysées & Grands Boulevards p93

Baron Haussmann reshaped the Parisian cityscape around the Arc de Triomphe, from which 12 avenues radiate, including the glamorous Champs-Élysées. To its east are gourmet shops garlanding the Église de la Madeleine, the palatial Palais Garnier opera house and the Grands Boulevards' department stores.

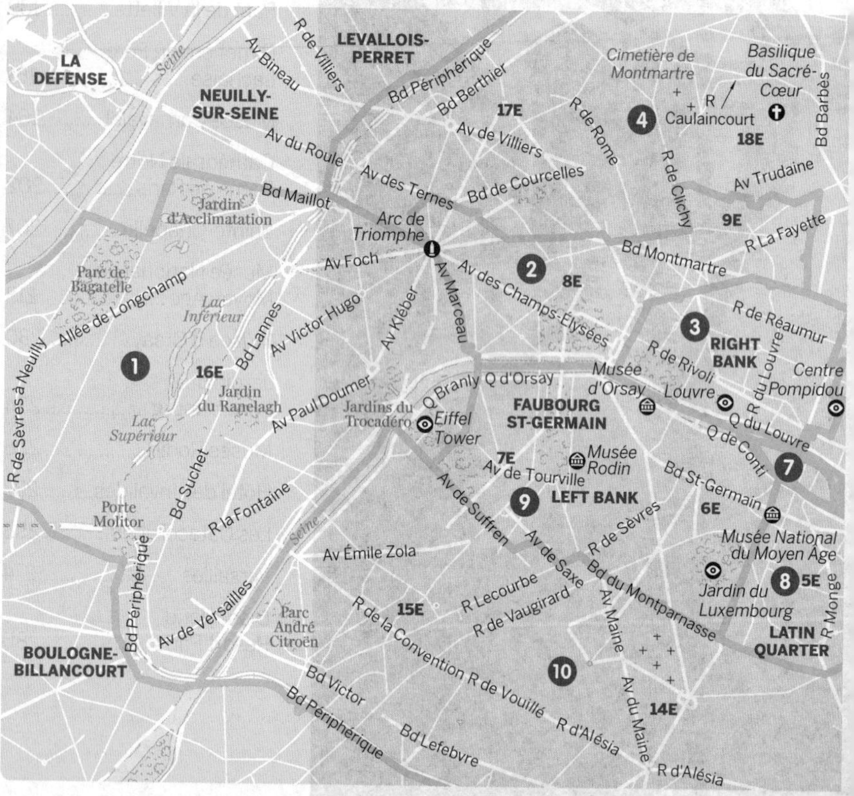

3 Louvre & Les Halles p107

Paris' splendid line of monuments, the *axe historique* (historic axis; also called the grand axis), passes through the Tuileries gardens before reaching IM Pei's glass pyramid at the entrance to the world's largest museum, the Louvre. Nearby, the Forum des Halles shopping precinct is undergoing a much-welcomed makeover.

4 Montmartre & Northern Paris p135

Montmartre's lofty views, wine-producing vines and hidden village squares have lured painters from the 19th century and onwards. Crowned by the Sacré-Cœur basilica, Montmartre is the city's steepest *quartier* (quarter), and its slinking streets lined with crooked ivy-clad buildings retain a fairytale charm. The Pigalle and Canal St-Martin areas are hotbeds of creativity.

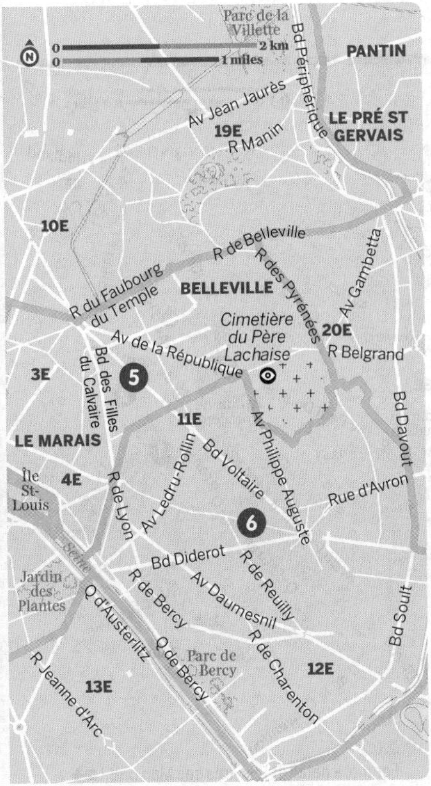

5 Le Marais, Ménilmontant & Belleville p159

Hip bars and restaurants, emerging designers' boutiques and the city's thriving gay and Jewish communities all squeeze into Le Marais' warren of narrow medieval laneways. Neighbouring Ménilmontant has some of the city's most happening nightlife, while Belleville is an up-and-coming hotspot.

6 Bastille & Eastern Paris p187

Fabulous markets, intimate bistros, and a disused 19th-century railway viaduct with artist studios below and an elevated park (Promenade Plantée) on top make this neighbourhood one of the best places to discover the Parisians' Paris.

7 The Islands p200

Paris' geographic and historic heart is here in the Seine. The larger of the two inner-city islands, the Île de la Cité, is dominated by Notre Dame. Serene little Île St-Louis is graced with elegant apartments and hotels and charming eateries and boutiques.

8 Latin Quarter p211

The hub of academic life in Paris, the Latin Quarter centres on the Sorbonne's main university campus. It harbours some fine museums and churches, and Paris' beautiful art deco mosque and botanic gardens.

9 St-Germain & Les Invalides p228

Literary buffs, antique collectors and fashionistas flock to this mythological part of Paris, where presences of writers such as Sartre, de Beauvoir and Hemingway still linger, and chic boutiques abound.

10 Montparnasse & Southern Paris p256

Montparnasse has brasseries from its mid-20th-century heyday and re-energised backstreets buzzing with local life, while Paris' largest Chinatown is filled with Asian grocers and eateries.

Eiffel Tower & Western Paris

EIFFEL TOWER & 16E | LA DÉFENSE

Neighbourhood Top Five

❶ Scaling the **Eiffel Tower** (p82) at dusk to watch its sparkling lights blink across Paris.

❷ Finding inspiration in the traditional art on display at the **Musée du Quai Branly** (p84).

❸ Wandering past cathedral portals, gargoyles and intricate scale models at the **Cité de l'Architecture et du Patrimoine** (p85).

❹ Exploring the **Bois de Boulogne** (p89): from bike rides, rowing boats and horse races to an amusement park kids will adore.

❺ Taking a trip out to the **Musée Marmottan Monet** (p88) to see the world's largest collection of Monet canvases.

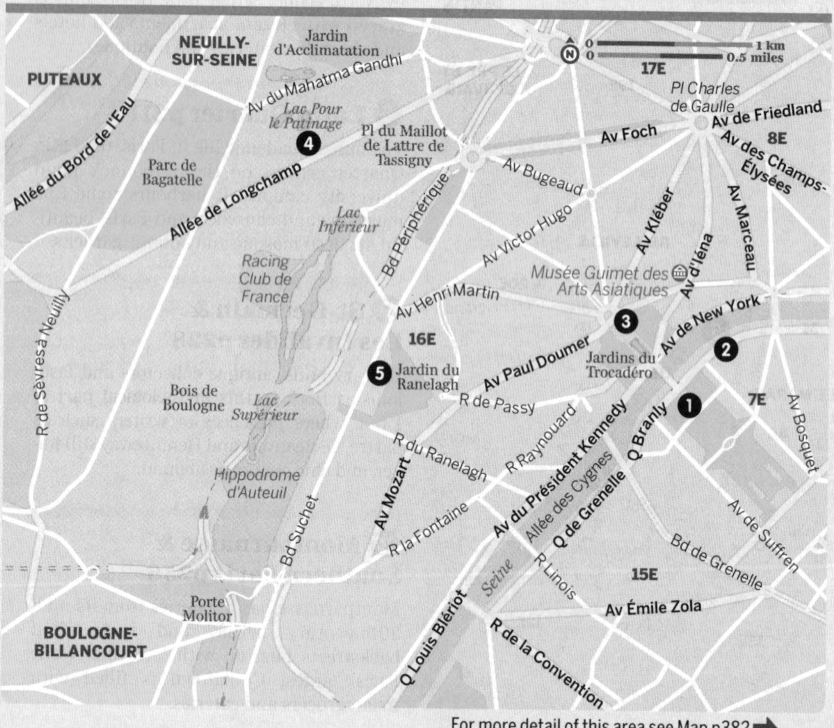

For more detail of this area see Map p382 ➡

Explore: Eiffel Tower & Western Paris

With its hourly sparkles that illuminate the evening skyline, the Eiffel Tower needs no introduction. Ascending to its viewing platforms will offer you a panorama over the whole of Paris, with the prestigious neighbourhood of Passy (the 16e *arrondissement*) stretching along the far banks of the Seine to the west. In the 18th and 19th centuries, Passy was home to luminaries such as Benjamin Franklin and Balzac. Defined by its sober, elegant buildings from the Haussmann era, it was annexed to the city only in 1860.

While most of the area today won't send the same frisson of excitement down your spine as taking the lift to the top of the tower, Passy is nonetheless home to some fabulous museums, and culture fans will certainly be busy. There's the Musée Marmottan Monet, with the world's largest collection of Monet paintings; the hip Palais de Tokyo, with modern-art installations; the Musée Guimet, France's standout Asian art museum; the underrated Cité de l'Architecture et du Patrimoine, with captivating sculptures and murals; and a host of smaller collections devoted to fashion, crystal, wine and even sub-Saharan art. On the Left Bank is the prominent Musée du Quai Branly, introducing indigenous art and culture from outside Europe, while at the city's western edge is the leafy refuge of the Bois de Boulogne. Beyond this lies the business district of La Défense.

Local Life

- **Museum hopping** Parisians flock to this part of town for its fine museums.
- **Green space** Leafy Bois de Boulogne is where city-dwellers escape the concrete on bikes, skates or by *footing* (jogging).
- **Daily commute** More than 150,000 people squeeze onto morning trains to La Défense, the city's business district, where skyscrapers rub shoulders with art.

Getting There & Away

- **Metro** Line 6 runs south from Charles de Gaulle–Étoile past the Eiffel Tower (views are superb from the elevated section); line 9 runs southwest from the Champs-Élysées.
- **RER** RER A runs west to La Défense; RER C runs along the Left Bank, with a stop at the Eiffel Tower.
- **Bus** Scenic bus 69 runs from the Champ du Mars (Eiffel Tower) along the Left Bank, crosses the Seine at the Louvre, and continues east to Père Lachaise.
- **Bicycle** Handy Vélib' stations include 2 av Octave Creard and 3 av Bosquet.
- **Boat** Eiffel Tower

Lonely Planet's Top Tip

There are excellent top-end restaurants in the 16e, but it is substantially more affordable – and fun in summertime – to follow the local flock and picnic. Build your own feast with sweet and savoury goodies from *boulangeries* and speciality food shops; grab a takeaway; or order a gourmet meal from Marc Veyrat's food truck.

Best Places to Eat

- Traiteur Jegado (p91)
- Hugo Desnoyer (p88)
- Monsieur Bleu (p90)
- Les Ombres (p90)
- 58 Tour Eiffel (p90)

For reviews, see p87

Best Picnic Spots

- Musée du Quai Branly garden (p84)
- Parc du Champ de Mars (p85)
- place des États-Unis, opposite Galerie-Musée Baccarat (p86)
- Bois de Boulogne (p89)

For reviews, see p85

Best Museums

- Musée du Quai Branly (p84)
- Cité de l'Architecture et du Patrimoine (p85)
- Musée Marmottan Monet (p88)
- Musée Guimet des Arts Asiatiques (p86)
- Musée Dapper (p85)

For reviews, see p85

SYLVAIN SONNET / GETTY IMAGES ©

TOP SIGHT
EIFFEL TOWER

There are different ways to experience the Eiffel Tower, from an evening ascent amid twinkling lights to a meal in one of its two restaurants. And even though some 6.7 million people come annually, few would dispute that each visit is unique – and something that simply has to be done when in Paris. A second-to-none, bird's-eye panorama of the city and discovering one of the world's most cherished icons at close quarters is what lures most visitors.

Metal Asparagus

Named after its designer, Gustave Eiffel, the Tour Eiffel was built for the 1889 Exposition Universelle (World Fair). It took 300 workers, 2.5 million rivets and two years of nonstop labour to assemble. Upon completion the tower became the tallest human-made structure in the world (324m or 1063ft) – a record held until the completion of the Chrysler Building in New York (1930). A symbol of the modern age, it faced massive opposition from Paris' artistic and literary elite, and the 'metal asparagus', as some Parisians snidely called it, was originally slated to be torn down in 1909. It was spared only because it proved an ideal platform for the transmitting antennas needed for the newfangled science of radiotelegraphy.

1st Floor

Of the tower's three floors, the 1st (57m) has the most space (hence its appealing museum-like layout) but the least impressive views. Two glass pavilions, **Pavillon Ferrié** and **Salle Gustave Eiffel** – open since summer 2014 – showcase

DON'T MISS

- Pavillon Ferrié, 1st floor
- 2nd-floor panorama
- Top-floor Champagne bar

PRACTICALITIES

- Map p382
- ☎08 92 70 12 39
- www.tour-eiffel.fr
- Champ de Mars, 5 av Anatole France, 7e
- lift to top adult/child €15/10.50, lift to 2nd fl €9/4.50, stairs to 2nd fl €5/3, lift 2nd fl to top €6
- ⏲lifts & stairs 9am-midnight mid-Jun–Aug, lifts 9.30am-11pm, stairs 9.30am-6.30pm Sep–mid-Jun
- Ⓜ Bir Hakeim or RER Champ de Mars-Tour Eiffel

interactive history exhibits, an immersion film and other features designed to help visitors learn more about the tower's ingenious design. Outside the pavilons, glass floors proffer a dizzying view of the ant-like people walking on the ground far, far below.

This level also hosts the affordable 58 Tour Eiffel restaurant.

Not all lifts stop at the 1st floor (check before ascending), but it's an easy walk down from the 2nd should you accidentally end up one floor too high.

2nd Floor

Views from the 2nd floor (115m) are the best – impressively high but still close enough to see the details of the city below. Telescopes and panoramic maps placed around the tower pinpoint locations in Paris and beyond. Story windows give an overview of the lifts' mechanics, and the vision well allows you to gaze through glass panels to the ground. Also up here are toilets, a souvenir shop and the Michelin-starred restaurant Jules Verne.

Top Floor

Views from the wind-buffeted top floor (276m) stretch up to 60km on a clear day, though at this height the panoramas are more sweeping than detailed. Celebrate your ascent with a glass of bubbly (€12 to €21) from the Champagne bar (open noon to 10pm). Afterwards peep into Gustave Eiffel's restored top-level office where lifelike wax models of Eiffel and his daughter Claire greet Thomas Edison.

To access the top floor, take a separate lift on the 2nd level (closed during heavy winds).

Tickets & Queuing Strategies

Ascend as far as the 2nd floor (either on foot or by lift), from where it is lift-only to the top floor. Pushchairs must be folded in lifts and you are not allowed to take bags or backpacks larger than aeroplane-cabin size.

Buying tickets in advance online usually means you avoid the monumental queues at the ticket offices. Print your ticket or show it on a smart-phone screen. If you can't reserve your tickets ahead of time; expect waits of well over an hour in high season.

Stair tickets can't be reserved online. They are sold at the south pillar, where the staircase can also be accessed: the climb consists of 360 steps to the 1st level and another 360 steps to the 2nd pillar.

If you have reservations for either restaurant, you are granted direct access to the lifts.

NIGHTLY SPARKLES

Every hour on the hour, the entire tower sparkles for five minutes with 20,000 gold-toned lights. They were first installed for Paris' millennium celebration in 2000 – it took 25 mountain climbers five months to install the current bulbs and 40km of electrical cords. For the best view of the light show, head across the Seine to the Jardins du Trocadéro.

Slapping a fresh coat of paint on the tower is no easy feat. It takes a 25-person team 18 months to complete the 60-tonnes-of-paint task, redone every seven years. Painted red and bronze since 1968, it's had six different colours throughout its lifetime, including yellow.

MAN ON WIRE

In 1989 tightrope artist Philippe Petit walked up an inclined 700m cable across the Seine, from Palais Chaillot to the Eiffel Tower's 2nd level. The act, performed before an audience of 250,000 people, was held to commemorate the French Republic's bicentennial.

TOP SIGHT
MUSÉE DU QUAI BRANLY

ARCHITECT: ATELIERS JEAN NOUVEL / PHILIPPE RUAULT ©

No other museum in Paris provides such inspiration for travellers, armchair anthropologists, and those who simply appreciate the beauty of traditional craftwork. A tribute to the incredible diversity of human culture, the Musée du Quai Branly presents an overview of indigenous and folk art from around the world. Divided into four main sections, the museum showcases an impressive array of masks, carvings, weapons, jewellery and more.

Oceania & Asia

The Oceania section, features remarkable carvings from Papua New Guinea and the surrounding islands, including a series of facade masks, daggers, jewellery, hair pieces and several ancestor skulls. Other cultures well represented here include the Maori and the Australian Aborigines.

Clothing, jewellery and textiles from ethnic minorities from India to Vietnam makes up the body of the Asian collection. One of the most striking articles is an Evenk shaman cloak from eastern Siberia.

Africa & the Americas

The Africa collection is particularly strong on musical instruments and masks, but there are some other unusual pieces, such as the life-size 11th-century sculpture of a hermaphrodite (Mali), which greets visitors with a raised arm. One of the more notable masks on display is a Krou mask from the Ivory Coast, which is said to have influenced Picasso.

Look for highlights from the great civilisations in the Americas collection – the Mayas, Aztecs and Incas – as well as objects from lesser-known peoples, such as the grizzly totem pole (Tsimshian) or the crazily expressive Kiiappaat masks (Greenland).

DON'T MISS

- The Papua New Guinea collection, Oceania
- The Evenk shaman cloak, Asia
- The Soninke hermaphrodite, Africa
- The grizzly totem pole, Americas

PRACTICALITIES

- Map p382
- www.quaibranly.fr
- 37 quai Branly, 7e
- adult/child €8.50/free
- ⌚11am-7pm Tue, Wed & Sun, 11am-9pm Thu-Sat
- Ⓜ Alma Marceau or RER Pont de l'Alma

SIGHTS

Eiffel Tower & 16e

EIFFEL TOWER LANDMARK
See p82.

MUSÉE DU QUAI BRANLY MUSEUM
See p84.

PARC DU CHAMP DE MARS PARK
Map p382 (Champ de Mars, 7e; M Champ de Mars–Tour Eiffel or École Militaire) Running southeast from the Eiffel Tower, the grassy Champ de Mars – an ideal summer picnic spot – was originally used as a parade ground for the cadets of the 18th-century **École Militaire**, the vast French-classical building at the southeastern end of the park which counts Napoleon Bonaparte among its graduates. The steel-and-etched glass **Wall for Peace memorial** (2000) is by Clara Halter.

MUSÉE DAPPER ART MUSEUM
Map p382 (www.dapper.com.fr; 35 rue Paul Valéry, 16e; adult/child €6/free; 11am-7pm Wed & Fri-Mon; M Victor Hugo) Focused on African and Caribbean art, this jewel of a museum is an invitation to leave Paris behind for an hour or two. Exhibits rotate throughout the year, but the permanent collection is superb: ritual and festival masks and costumes accompanied by several video presentations. The auditorium hosts film screenings, concerts, storytelling and other cultural events.

PALAIS DE TOKYO ART MUSEUM
Map p382 (www.palaisdetokyo.com; 13 av du Président Wilson, 16e; adult/child €10/free; noon-midnight Wed-Mon; M Iéna) The Tokyo Palace, created for the 1937 Exposition Universelle, has no permanent collection. Rather its shell-like interior of concrete and steel is a stark backdrop to interactive contemporary-art exhibitions and installations. Its bookshop is fabulous for art and design magazines, and its eating/drinking options are magic.

MUSÉE D'ART MODERNE DE LA VILLE DE PARIS ART MUSEUM
Map p382 (www.mam.paris.fr; 11 av du Président Wilson, 16e; 10am-6pm Tue, Wed, Fri-Sun, 10am-10pm Thu; M Iéna) FREE The permanent collection at Paris' modern-art museum

TOP SIGHT CITÉ DE L'ARCHITECTURE ET DU PATRIMOINE

In the eastern wing of Palais de Chaillot, directly across from the Eiffel Tower, is this standout museum devoted to French architecture and heritage. The burgundy walls and sky-lit rooms showcase 350 plaster casts taken from the country's greatest monuments, a collection whose seeds were sown following the desecration of many buildings during the French Revolution.

Some of the original details from which the casts were made, such as sculptures from the Reims Cathedral, were later destroyed in the wars that followed. Although not in situ, wandering through such a magnificent collection of church portals, gargoyles, and saints and sinners from around France is an incomparable experience for anyone interested in the elemental stories that craftspeople chose to preserve in stone.

On display on the upper floors are reproduced murals and stained-glass windows from some of France's most important monuments, which are arranged in an intriguing labyrinthine layout. One of the most beautiful reproductions in this section is the Cathédrale of St-Etienne cupola.

DON'T MISS...

- Casts Gallery
- Murals and Stained Glass Galleries
- Cathédrale of St-Étienne cupola

PRACTICALITIES

- Map p382
- www.citechaillot.fr
- 1 place du Trocadéro et du 11 Novembre, 16e
- adult/child €8/free
- 11am-7pm Wed & Fri-Mon, to 9pm Thu
- M Trocadéro

TOP SIGHT
MUSÉE GUIMET DES ARTS ASIATIQUES

France's foremost Asian arts museum, the Musée Guimet has a superb collection of sculptures, paintings and religious articles that originated in the vast stretch of land between Afghanistan and Japan. In fact, it's possible to observe the gradual transmission of both Buddhism and artistic styles along the Silk Road in some of the museum's pieces, from the 1st-century Gandhara Buddhas from Afghanistan and Pakistan to the later Central Asian, Chinese and Japanese Buddhist sculptures and art.

Other strong points of the museum include the Southeast Asian statuary on the ground floor (which has the world's largest collection of Khmer artefacts outside Cambodia), the Nepalese and Tibetan bronzes and mandalas, and the vast China collection, which encompasses everything from ink paintings and calligraphy to funerary statuary and early bronzes.

Part of the collection, comprised of Buddhist paintings and sculptures, is housed in the nearby **Panthéon Bouddhique** (Map p382; 19 av d'Iéna, 16e; ⌚10am-5.45pm Wed-Mon, garden to 5pm) FREE. Don't miss the wonderful Japanese garden here.

DON'T MISS...

- Afghan collection
- Southeast Asian statuary
- China collection
- Galeries du Panthéon Bouddhique

PRACTICALITIES

- Map p382
- www.museeguimet.fr
- 6 place d'Iéna, 16e
- adult/child €7.50/free
- ⌚10am-6pm Wed-Mon
- Ⓜ Iéna

displays works representative of just about every major artistic movement of the 20th and (nascent) 21st centuries, with works by Modigliani, Matisse, Braque and Soutine. The real jewel though is the room hung with canvases by Dufy and Bonnard. Look out for cutting-edge temporary exhibitions (not free).

FONDATION PIERRE BERGÉ-YVES SAINT LAURENT MUSEUM

Map p382 (www.fondation-pb-ysl.net; 3 rue Léonce Reynaud, 16e; adult/child €7/5; ⌚11am-6pm Tue-Sun; Ⓜ Alma Marceau) This foundation dedicated to preserving the work of the *haute couture* legend organises temporary fashion and art exhibitions.

MUSÉE DE LA MODE DE LA VILLE DE PARIS MUSEUM

Map p382 (www.galliera.paris.fr; 10 av Pierre 1er de Serbie, 16e; adult/child €8/free; ⌚10am-6pm Tue, Wed, Fri-Sun, 10am-9pm Thu; Ⓜ Iéna) Paris' Fashion Museum, housed in 19th-century Palais Galliera, warehouses some 100,000 outfits and accessories – from canes and umbrellas to fans and gloves – from the 18th century to the present day. The sumptuous Italianate palace and gardens dating from the mid-19th century are worth a visit in themselves, as are the excellent temporary exhibitions the museum hosts.

GALERIE-MUSÉE BACCARAT MUSEUM

Map p382 (www.baccarat.com; 11 place des États-Unis, 16e; adult/child €7/free; ⌚10am-6pm Mon & Wed-Sat; Ⓜ Boissière or Kléber) Showcasing 1000 stunning pieces of crystal, many of them custom-made for princes and dictators of former colonies, this flashy museum is at home in its striking new rococo-style premises designed by Philippe Starck in the ritzy 16e. It is also home to an upmarket restaurant called – what else? – Le Cristal Room.

FLAME OF LIBERTY MEMORIAL MONUMENT

Map p382 (place de l'Alma, 8e; Ⓜ Alma Marceau) This bronze sculpture, a replica of the one topping the Statue of Liberty, was placed here in 1987 as a symbol of friendship between France and the USA. More famous is its location, above the place d'Alma tunnel where, on 31 August 1997, Diana, Princess of Wales, was killed in a car accident. Graffiti remembering the princess covers the entire wall next to the sculpture.

MUSÉE DE LA MARINE NAVAL MUSEUM

Map p382 (Maritime Museum; www.musee-marine.fr; 17 place du Trocadéro et du 11 Novembre, 16e; adult/child €8.50/free; ⏲11am-6pm Wed-Mon, to 7pm Sat & Sun; Ⓜ Trocadéro) Located in the western wing of Palais de Chaillot, the Maritime Museum examines France's naval adventures from the 17th century until today and boasts one of the world's finest collections of model ships, as well as ancient figureheads, compasses, sextants, telescopes and paintings. Temporary exhibitions command an additional admission fee.

MUSÉE DE L'HOMME MUSEUM

Map p382 (Museum of Humankind; www.museedelhomme.fr; 17 place Trocadéro, 16e; Ⓜ Passy or Iéna) This museum inside Palais de Chaillot's western wing first opened in 1937. It focuses on human development, science and anthropology, with a varied collection spanning everything from Cro-Magnon fossils to *Vénus de Lespugue,* one of the earliest Palaeolithic works of art – beautifully presented under the palace's dazzling glass-and-steel roof dating to 1878. The museum reopens after renovations in late 2015.

AQUARIUM DE PARIS CINÉAQUA AQUARIUM

Map p382 (www.cineaqua.com; av des Nations Unies, 16e; adult/child €20.50/16; ⏲10am-7pm; Ⓜ Trocadéro) Paris' aquarium, on the eastern side of the Jardins du Trocadéro, has a shark tank and 500-odd fish species to entertain families on rainy days. Three cinemas screen ocean-related and other films (dubbed in French, with subtitles). Budget tip: show your ticket from the nearby Musée de la Marine to get reduced aquarium admission (adult/child €16.40/10.40).

MAISON DE BALZAC MUSEUM

Map p382 (www.balzac.paris.fr; 47 rue Raynouard, 16e; ⏲10am-6pm Tue-Sun; Ⓜ Passy or Avenue Président Kennedy) FREE This pretty, three-storey spa house is where realist novelist Honoré de Balzac (1799–1850) lived and worked from 1840 to 1847, editing the entire *Comédie Humaine* here. There's lots of memorabilia, letters, prints and portraits – perfect for die-hard Balzac fans.

MUSÉE DU VIN MUSEUM

Map p382 (☎01 45 25 63 26; www.museeduvinparis.com; 5 sq Charles Dickens, 16e; adult/child €10/free; ⏲10am-6pm Tue-Sun; Ⓜ Passy) The Wine Museum, headquarters of the prestigious International Federation of Wine Brotherhoods, introduces visitors to the fine art of viticulture with mock-ups and tool displays. End museum visits with a glass of AOP wine (€5) or a two-hour wine-tasting workshop (€63). If you lunch in the attached restaurant (noon to 3pm Tuesday to Saturday) museum admission is free.

⊙ La Défense

Architecture buffs will have a field day in Paris' business district, located in the western suburbs. Begun in the 1950s, today La Défense showcases extraordinary monumental art and is the only place in central Paris where you'll see skyscrapers.

GRANDE ARCHE DE LA DÉFENSE LANDMARK

(1 Parvis de la Défense; Ⓜ La Défense) La Défense's landmark edifice is the white marble Grande Arche, a cubelike arch built in the 1980s to house government and business offices. The arch marks the western end of the Axe Historique (Historic Axis), though Danish architect Johan-Otto von Sprekelsen deliberately placed the Grande Arche fractionally out of alignment. It's not possible to visit inside or access the roof.

MUSÉE DE LA DÉFENSE MUSEUM

(www.ladefense.fr; 15 place de la Défense; Ⓜ La Défense) FREE Set to reopen after renovation in early 2015, this museum evokes the area's development and architecture through drawings, architectural plans and scale models.

EATING

In addition to the pickings of the 16e *arrondissement*, the many restaurants of Les Invalides and buzzing market street of rue Cler, 7e, are a short walk from the Eiffel Tower – or, to shop for the perfect picnic, follow the local office crowd to rue de Chaillot. For a truly memorable experience, dine in the icon itself.

MARCHÉ PRÉSIDENT WILSON MARKET €

Map p382 (av du Président Wilson, 16e; ⏲7am-2.30pm Wed & Sat; Ⓜ Iéna or Alma Marceau) This open-air market across from Palais de Tokyo is the most convenient in the neighbourhood.

LES DEUX ABEILLES TEA ROOM €

Map p382 (☎01 45 55 64 04; 189 rue de l'Université, 7e; lunch menu €22, salads €14-18; ⏰9am-7pm; Ⓜ Alma or Champ de Mars-Tour Eiffel) There is no lovelier sanctuary from the Eiffel Tower crowds than this old-fashioned tea room, the elegant love child of a mother-and-daughter team who greet regulars with a *bisou* (kiss). Delicious homemade cakes and *citronnade* (ginger lemonade) aside, the Two Bees cooks up quiches, tarts and salads ensuring every table is full by 1pm. Breakfast and brunch available too.

CHOUX D'ENFER PATISSERIE €

Map p430 (☎01 47 83 26 67; cnr rue Jean Rey & quai Branly, 15e; bag sweet/savoury choux €5/7, with cream filling €6-17; ⏰10am-8pm; Ⓜ Bir-Hakeim or RER Champ de Mars-Tour Eiffel) This kiosk gives street food a whole new spin. The creation of top French chefs Alain Ducasse and Christophe Michalak, it cooks up *choux* (pastry puffs). Grab a brown paper bag of nine *choux salées* (savoury cheese puffs) spiced with pepper, curry or cumin; or go sweet with almond, cocoa, coffee, lemon and vanilla *chouquettes,* with or without cream filling.

LA MASCOTTE BRASSERIE €

Map p382 (☎01 40 36 03 86; 4 av du Président Wilson, 16e; mains €14-19; ⏰7.30am-midnight; Ⓜ Alma Marceau) In an area with few budget eating options, this buzzing neighbourhood brasserie with terrace in the lunchtime sun is a hot spot. Its kitchen prepares meal-size salads, steak tartare and other typical brasserie fare. Come dusk, after-work drinks kick in. Inside, a mezzanine with cushioned seating and shelves of books provides a peaceful sanctuary.

★**HUGO DESNOYER** BUTCHER €€

Map p382 (☎01 46 47 83 00; www.hugodesnoyer.fr; 28 rue du Docteur Blanche, 16e; menu €50, mains €16-32; ⏰7am-8pm Tue-Fri, 7am-7.30pm Sat; Ⓜ Jasmin) Hugo Desnoyer is Paris' most famous butcher and the trip to his shop in the 16e is well worth it. Arrive by noon or reserve to snag a table and settle down to a *table d'hôte* feast of homemade terrines, quiches, foie gras and cold cuts followed by the finest meat in Paris – cooked to perfection *naturellement.* Watch out for another Desnoyer opening in 2015.

TOP SIGHT
MUSÉE MARMOTTAN MONET

Housed in the duc de Valmy's former hunting lodge (well, let's call it a mansion), this intimate museum houses the world's largest collection of Monet paintings and sketches. It provides an interesting if patchy cross-section of his work, beginning with paintings such as the seminal *Impression Soleil Levant* (1873) and *Promenade près d'Argenteuil* (1875), passing through numerous water-lily studies, before moving on to the rest of the collection, which is considerably more abstract and dates to the early 1900s. Some of the masterpieces to look out for include *La Barque* (1887), *Cathédrale de Rouen* (1892), *Londres, le Parlement* (1901) and the various *Nymphéas* (many of these were smaller studies for the works now on display in the Musée de l'Orangerie, p119).

Temporary exhibitions, included in the admission price and always excellent, are generally shown either in the basement or on the 1st floor. Also on display are a handful of canvases by Renoir, Pissarro, Gauguin and Morisot, and a collection of 15th- and 16th-century illuminations, which are quite lovely if somewhat out of place.

DON'T MISS...

- *Impression Soleil Levant*
- *Promenade près d'Argenteuil*
- *Londres, le Parlement*
- The illuminations collection

PRACTICALITIES

- Map p382
- ☎01 44 96 50 33
- www.marmottan.com
- 2 rue Louis Boilly, 16e
- adult/child €10/5
- ⏰10am-6pm Tue-Sun, to 8pm Thu
- Ⓜ La Muette

BOIS DE BOULOGNE

The 845-hectare **Bois de Boulogne** (bd Maillot; Ⓜ Porte Maillot) owes its informal layout to Baron Haussmann, who, inspired by London's Hyde Park, planted 400,000 trees here in the 19th century. Along with various gardens and other sights, the park has 15km of cycle paths and 28km of bridle paths through 125 hectares of forested land.

Be warned that the area becomes a distinctly adult playground after dark, especially along the Allée de Longchamp running northeast from the Étang des Réservoirs (Reservoirs Pond), where all kinds of prostitutes cruise for clients.

The Bois de Boulogne is served by metro lines 1 (Porte Maillot, Les Sablons), 2 (Porte Dauphine), 9 (Michel-Ange-Auteuil) and 10 (Michel-Ange-Auteuil, Porte d'Auteuil), and the RER C (Avenue Foch, Avenue Henri Martin). Vélib' stations are found near most of the park entrances, but not within the park itself.

➡ **Jardin d'Acclimatation** (www.jardinacclimatation.fr; av du Mahatma Gandhi) Families adore this green and flowery amusement park on the northern fringe of wooded Bois de Boulogne. There are swings, roundabouts and playgrounds for all ages (included in the admission), as well as dozens of attractions such as puppet shows, boat rides, fun-fair rides, a small water park, pony rides, a little train and so on which cost extra.

➡ **Le Chalet des Îles** (Map p382; ☎01 42 88 04 69; Carrefour du Bout des Lacs; 30/60/90/120 minutes €6/10/15.50/19, plus €50 deposit; ⏲noon-5pm Mon-Fri, 10am-6pm Sat & Sun mid-Feb–Oct; Ⓜ Av Henri Martin) Rent an old-fashioned rowing boat to paddle around Lac Inférieur, the largest of Bois de Boulogne's lakes – romance and serenity guaranteed.

➡ **Parc et Château de Bagatelle** (rte de Sèvres à Neuilly, 16e; free Nov-Apr, adult/child €5/2 Jun-Oct; ⏲9.30am-8pm, shorter hours winter; Ⓜ Porte Maillot) These enclosed gardens, originally designed as the result of a wager between Marie-Antoinette and the Count of Artois, frame 18th-century **Château de Bagatelle** (rue de Sèvres à Neuilly; adult/child €6/free; ⏲tour 3pm Sat & Sun Apr-Oct), built for the younger brother of Louis XVI. Magnificent irises bloom in May, roses from June to October, and – perhaps most majestically of all – water lilies in August.

➡ **Pré Catelan** (Catelan Meadow; rte de Suresnes, 16e; ⏲9.30am-8pm, Jardin Shakespeare 2-4pm, shorter hours winter; Ⓜ Ranelagh) FREE This garden area within Parc de Bagatelle squirrels away the wonderful Jardin Shakespeare, where plants, flowers and trees mentioned in Shakespeare's plays are cultivated. Watch for summertime performances in the garden's small open-air theatre.

➡ **Jardin des Serres d'Auteuil** (av de la Porte d'Auteuil, 16é; ⏲8am-8.30pm summer, shorter hours otherwise; Ⓜ Porte d'Auteuil) Located at the southeastern end of the Bois de Boulogne are these impressive conservatories, which opened in 1898 and are home to a large collection of tropical plants.

➡ **Stade Roland Garros-Musée de la Fédération Française de Tennis** (www.fft.fr; 2 av Gordon Bennett, 16e; adult/child €10.50/8.50, with stadium visit €15.50/10.50; ⏲10am-6pm Wed, Fri-Sun; Ⓜ Porte d'Auteuil) The world's most extravagant tennis museum traces the sport's 500-year history through paintings, sculptures and posters. Tours of the stadium take place at 11am and 3pm in English; reservations are required.

➡ **Fondation Louis Vuitton** (www.fondationlouisvuitton.fr; av du Mahatma Gandhi, 16e) As exciting as the world-class works of art displayed in this stunning contemporary-art centre are, what really inspires is the 'iceberg' architecture design by Frank Gehry – 12 curvaceous giant 'sails' crafted from 3600 glass panels.

LE PETIT RÉTRO BISTRO **€€**

Map p382 (☎01 44 05 06 05; www.petitretro.fr; 5 rue Mesnil, 16e; mains €17-26, 2-/3-course menus €25/29; ⏲noon-2.30pm & 7-10.30pm Mon-Wed, to 11pm Thu-Sat; Ⓜ Victor Hugo) From the gorgeous 'Petit Rétro' emblazoned on the zinc bar to the ceramic, art nouveau folk tiles on the wall, this is a handsome old-style bistro. Its fare is French classic: for example, blood sausage, *blanquette de veau* (veal in a butter and cream sauce) and *oreilles de cochon* (pig's ears). Delicious.

TOKYO EAT FUSION €€

Map p382 (☎01 47 20 00 29; www.palaisdetokyo.com; Palais de Tokyo, 13 av du Président Wilson, 16e; mains €15-28; ⏲noon-2am Wed-Tue; MIéna) This artsy canteen attached to contemporary-art museum Palais de Tokyo is industrially chic, with colourful flying saucers hovering above the tables and changing art exhibits on the walls. Cuisine is unpredictable and fun – anything from chicken curry served on a banana leaf to caramelised chicory. DJs hit the decks some evenings.

MONSIEUR BLEU MODERN FRENCH €€

Map p382 (☎01 47 20 90 47; www.monsieurbleu.com; Palais de Tokyo, 20 av de New York, 16e; mains €15-20; ⏲noon-2am; MAlma Marceau) An 'in' address with the ubercool fashion set since opening in 2013, this darling of a restaurant has bags going for it – superb interior design by Joseph Dirand, excellent seasonal cuisine and a summer terrace with a monumental Eiffel Tower view. Find it inside Palais de Tokyo; reserve in advance.

58 TOUR EIFFEL BRASSERIE €€

Map p382 (☎01 45 55 20 04; www.restaurants-toureiffel.com; 1st level, Eiffel Tower, Champ de Mars, 7e; 2-/3-course lunch menu €21/26, dinner menu €66/75; ⏲11.30am-4.30pm & 6.30-11pm; MBir Hakeim or RER Champ de Mars–Tour Eiffel) If you're intrigued by the idea of a meal in the Tower, reserve a table at 58 Tour Eiffel. It may not be the caviar and black truffles of the tower's Michelin-starred address one floor up, but Alain Ducasse did sign off on the menu, ensuring it's far more than a tourist cafeteria.

LES OMBRES MODERN FRENCH €€€

Map p382 (☎01 47 53 68 00; www.lesombres-restaurant.com; 27 quai Branly, 7e; 2-/3-course lunch menu €32/42, dinner menu €68, mains €32-44; ⏲noon-2.15pm & 7-10.20pm; MIéna or RER Pont de l'Alma) This glass-enclosed rooftop restaurant on the 5th floor of the Musée du Quai Branly is named 'the Shadows' after the patterns cast by the Eiffel Tower's webbed ironwork. Dramatic Eiffel views are complemented by kitchen creations such as *gambas* (prawns) with black rice and fennel, or pan-seared Burgundy snails in watercress sauce. Reserve.

LE JULES VERNE GASTRONOMIC €€€

Map p382 (☎01 45 55 61 44; www.lejulesverne-paris.com; 2nd fl, Eiffel Tower, Champ de Mars, 7e; lunch/dinner menus €98/185-230; ⏲noon-1.30pm & 7.30-9.30pm; MChamp de Mars–Tour Eiffel or Bir Hakeim) Book way ahead (online only) to feast on Michelin-starred cuisine and the most beautiful view of Paris at this magical address, on the Eiffel Tower's 2nd level. Cuisine is contemporary, with a five- or six-course 'experience' menu allowing you to taste the best of chef Pascal Féraud's stunning gastronomic repertoire.

LOCAL KNOWLEDGE

THE ART OF LA DÉFENSE

More than just office space, La Défense is an engaging, open-air art gallery. Calder, Miró, Agam, César and Torricini are among the international artists behind the colourful and often surprising sculptures and murals that pepper the central 1km-long promenade. Pick up a map and excellent booklets in English outlining walks to discover its art and surprising green spaces at the **Info Défense** (☎01 47 74 84 24; www.ladefense.fr; place de la Défense; ⏲9am-6pm Mon-Fri, 10am-5pm Sat & Sun; MLa Défense) *kiosque*, to the side of the moon-shaped CNIT building on the main drag.

DRINKING & NIGHTLIFE

Ogling the illuminated Eiffel Tower aside, being in the wealthy and predominantly residential 16e after dark doesn't translate to much when it comes to buzzing bars and clubs. The pace picks up around Palais de Tokyo, and the lively bars and cafes of St-Germain are a short walk away.

★ST JAMES PARIS BAR

Map p382 (☎01 44 05 81 81; www.saint-james-paris.com; 43 rue Bugeaud, 16e; drinks €15-25, Sun brunch €65; ⏲7-11pm; 📶; MPorte Dauphine) It might be a hotel bar, but a drink at St James might well be one of your most memorable in Paris. Tucked behind a stone wall, this historic mansion opens its bar each evening to non-guests – and the setting redefines extraordinary. Winter drinks are in the library, in summer they're in the impossibly romantic garden.

LOCAL KNOWLEDGE

RUE DE CHAILLOT: BUDGET BEAUTIFUL, PICNIC PERFECT

In an area laden with offices and pricey dining options, savvy locals flock to rue de Chaillot at lunchtime to feast on a bevy of top-quality takeaway – perfect to picnic with in a grassy park. The delightful, chestnut tree–shaded park on place des États-Unis, the Seine, and the modernist gardens at the Musée du Quai Branly are not far away.

Here are three local favourites:

➡ **Mes Bocaux** Map p382 (www.mesbocaux.fr; 37 rue Marceau, 8e; Ⓜ Alma Marceau) Savoyard chef Marc Veyrat upped the takeaway stakes when he put his small fleet of smart black food trucks on the road. Order gastronomic-to-go sandwiches and main dishes online before noon, then collect from the truck; the nearest stop to the Eiffel Tower is in front of the Anglo-American pharmacy at 37 rue Marceau, on the corner of rue de Chaillot, where it pulls in at 11.50am. Dishes ooze the creative flair you'd expect of a former Michelin-starred chef: Veyrat's '21st-century' sandwich is a culinary cocktail of ham, grated carrot, cumin, parmesan cheese and a wafer-thin slice of chocolate.

➡ **Traiteur Jegado** Map p382 (☎01 47 20 23 83; www.traiteur-jegado.fr; 45 rue de Chaillot, 16e; salads & starters €13-16 per kg, mains €16-28 per kg; ⏲noon-2pm Mon-Fri; Ⓜ Alma Marceau or George V) The sign outside this busy canteen-style *traiteur* (caterer) simply reads *'plats cuisinés'* (cooked dishes), but there's no missing this top-choice takeaway address: just look for the lunchtime line snaking halfway down the street. Delicious salads, starters and hot dishes are cooked in its no-frills kitchen then bagged in plastic to go. To avoid queuing, order ahead online.

➡ **Malitourne** Map p382 (☎01 47 20 52 26; www.patisserie-malitourne.com; 30 rue de Chaillot, 16e; ⏲7.30am-7.30pm Mon-Fri, 8am-1pm Sat; Ⓜ Alma Marceau) Finish with something sweet from this great little *pâtissier*, chocolate-maker and *traiteur*. Going strong since 1976, it has the added bonus of street entertainment: watch chocolate-makers at work in their street-side kitchen with huge window designed to show them off.

BÔ ZINC CAFÉ CAFE, BAR

Map p382 (☎01 42 24 69 05; 59 rue Mozart, 16e; ⏲8am-midnight or 2am; Ⓜ Ranelagh) With its soft sage-green facade and buzzing pavement terrace, Bô Zinc is one of those great hybrid addresses – perfect for hanging with locals over coffee, tea or after-work cocktails. Seating is a mix of wooden bistro chairs and 'flop-in' armchairs, while potted palm trees – inside and out – add a touch of chic. Top-notch nosh too, served until 11pm.

CAFÉ BRANLY CAFE

Map p382 (27 quai Branly, 7e; ⏲9.30am-6pm Tue, Wed & Sun, to 8pm Thu, Fri & Sat; Ⓜ Pont de l'Alma or Iéna) This casual spot at the Musée du Quai Branly has ringside views of the Eiffel Tower and quality cafe fare (foie gras salad, XL *croque monsieur*) to tuck into over a drink or three. The setting, within the museum's modernist garden, is peaceful and fantastic.

UPPER CRÈMERIE CAFE, BAR

Map p382 (☎01 40 70 93 23; 71 av Marceau, 16e; ⏲noon-1am; Ⓜ Kléber or George V) The sun-flooded tables at this hybrid cafe-cocktail-bar in a quintessential Parisian pavement terrace heave at lunchtime and after work with a well-dressed crowd from surrounding offices. The place is hip, and the cocktails (and food) hit the spot just right. Inside, blue sofas and neon lighting reassure trendsetters that the place is anything but 'Paris-traditional'.

☆ ENTERTAINMENT

YOYO LIVE MUSIC, CINEMA

Map p382 (www.yoyo-paris.com; Palais de Tokyo, 13 av du Président Wilson, 16e; ⏲variable; Ⓜ Iéna or Alma Marceau) Be it street-art exhibitions, live music gigs, concerts, club nights or film screenings, this contemporary raw-concrete space inside Palais de Tokyo promises a great night out.

LES MARIONNETTES DU CHAMP DE MARS
PUPPET THEATRE

Map p382 (☎01 48 56 01 44; http://guignoldu-champdemars.centerblog.net; allée du Général Marguerite, 7e; admission €3.50; Ⓜ École Militaire) For time-honoured French entertainment, take the kids to a show in this Napoleon III–style puppet theatre. Shows are in French, but performances still amuse. Check the website for performance times – usually Wednesday, weekends and school holidays.

SHOPPING

PATRICK ROGER
CHOCOLATE

Map p382 (☎01 45 01 66 71; www.patrickroger.com; 45 av Victor Hugo, 16e; ⏲10.30am-7.30pm Mon-Sat; Ⓜ Kléber) The creations of chocolate artist and sculptor Patrick Roger are extraordinary – and often very large (80kg or so) – rendering a visit to his swish boutique an eye-opening experience. More modest, take-home boxes of one-bite chocolates, truffles, fruit jellies or coated almonds – flavoured with vanilla, caramel, Scottish whisky, oranges from Corsica and so forth – are as beautiful.

SPORTS & ACTIVITIES

STADE ROLAND GARROS
TENNIS

(www.billetterie.fft.fr; 2 av Gordon Bennett, 16e, Bois de Boulogne; Ⓜ Porte d'Auteuil) The French Open is held on clay at the 16,500-seat Stade de Roland Garros late May to mid-June.

HIPPODROME D'AUTEUIL
HORSE RACING

Map p382 (www.france-galop.com; Champ de Courses d'Auteuil, 16e, Bois de Boulogne; adult/child €3/free; Ⓜ Porte d'Auteuil) This horse-racing track in the Bois de Boulogne hosts steeplechases March to June and September to early December.

PARC DES PRINCES
FOOTBALL

(www.leparcdesprinces.fr; 24 rue du Commandant Guilbaud, 16e; Ⓜ Porte de St-Cloud) Home ground to Paris' top-division football team Paris St-Germain.

Champs-Élysées & Grands Boulevards

CHAMPS-ÉLYSÉES | GRANDS BOULEVARDS

Neighbourhood Top Five

❶ Climbing the **Arc de Triomphe** (p95) to survey the *axe historique,* extending from the Louvre to La Défense.

❷ Taking in a performance or touring the opulent 19th-century **Palais Garnier** (p97) opera house.

❸ Catching a free fashion show showcasing seasonal trends at the magnificent art nouveau department store **Galeries Lafayette** (p105), and admiring the rooftop panorama.

❹ Viewing exceptional art exhibitions at galleries like the **Grand Palais** (p97).

❺ Strolling the over-the-top **Champs-Élysées** (p97) – you can't leave Paris without doing it once.

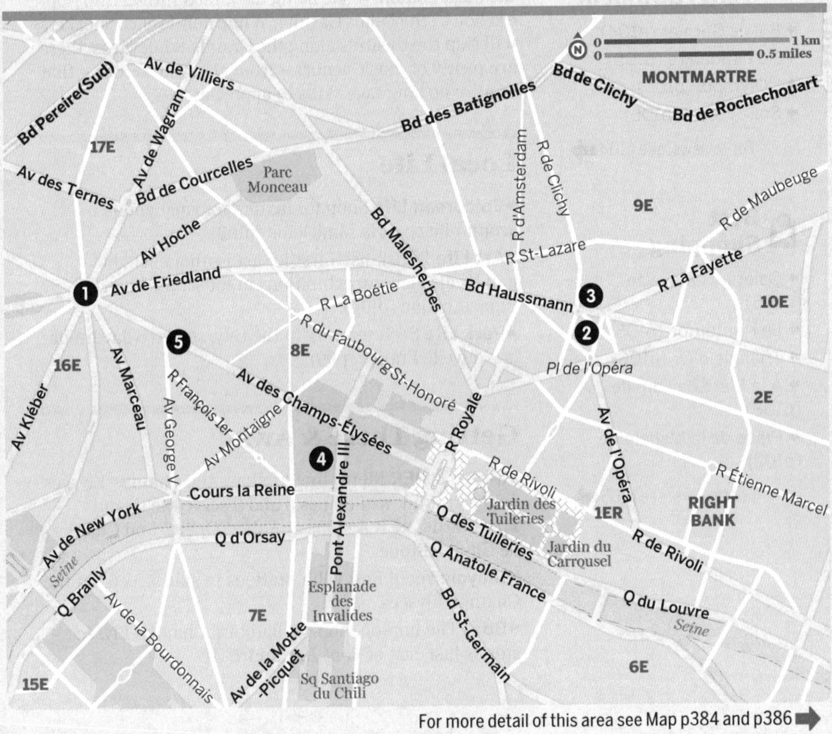

For more detail of this area see Map p384 and p386

Lonely Planet's Top Tip

Haute cuisine – and *haute* prices – are the rule in the 8e, but if you eat at one of the finer restaurants for lunch on a weekday, you'll save a bundle and still get to treat your taste buds to an extraordinary meal. Make sure to reserve.

Best Places to Eat

- Richer (p103)
- Le Hide (p101)
- Floquifil (p103)
- Bistrot La Bruyère (p103)
- Lasserre (p101)

For reviews, see p100

Best Entertainment

- Palais Garnier (p104)
- Au Limonaire (p105)
- L'Olympia (p105)
- Salle Pleyel (p105)

For reviews, see p104

Best Shopping

- Galeries Lafayette (p105)
- Le Printemps (p105)
- Triangle d'Or (p106)
- À la Mère de Famille (p106)
- Place de la Madeleine (p102)

For reviews, see p105

Explore: Champs-Élysées & Grands Boulevards

The Champs-Élysées and Grands Boulevards area is grandiose in layout – it's possible to play an epically proportioned game of connect the dots here. The main landmarks – the Arc de Triomphe, place de la Concorde, place de la Madeleine and the Opéra – are joined by majestic boulevards, each lined with harmonious rows of Haussmann-era buildings.

Monumental vistas will easily keep your eyes occupied but high-end shops and elegant department stores are this district's raison d'être and many will soon find their gaze slipping to the display windows of the luxury shops. Dior, Chanel, Louis Vuitton…fans of *haute couture* will find themselves pulled into the famed Triangle d'Or (Golden Triangle), south from the Champs-Élysées. Further east along the Grands Boulevards are the historic *grands magasins* (department stores) like Le Printemps and Galeries Lafayette, which will appeal to shoppers interested in a broader overview of French fashion.

But there's much more to this area than fashion overload. The vestiges of the 1900 World's Fair – the Grand Palais and Petit Palais (along with the bridge Pont Alexandre III) – play host to a variety of excellent exhibits.

Entertainment, too, has a strong tradition in this area, the most notable venue being the famed 19th-century opera house, the Palais Garnier. While non-French speakers will skip the theatres along the Grands Boulevards, there are plenty of music venues – from classical to rock – that require no language skills to appreciate.

Local Life

- **Epicurean Life** Shop for luxury gourmet goods around Place de la Madeleine (p102).
- **Art Life** Parisians' thirst for art is unquenchable – join locals viewing exhibitions in museums like La Pinacothèque (p100).
- **Park Life** Seek serenity in the tiny, secreted Jardin de la Nouvelle France (p99).

Getting There & Away

- **Metro & RER** Metro line 1 follows the Champs-Élysées below ground, while lines 8 and 9 serve the Grands Boulevards. RER A stops at Auber (Opéra) and Charles de Gaulle–Étoile.
- **Bicycle** You'll find Vélib' stations in side streets off the Champs-Élysées.
- **Boat** The hop-on, hop-off Batobus' Champs-Élysées stop is just east of Pont Alexandre III.

DUCEPT PASCAL / HEMIS.FR / GETTY IMAGES ©

TOP SIGHT
ARC DE TRIOMPHE

Napoléon's armies never did march through the Arc de Triomphe showered in honour, but the monument has nonetheless come to stand as the very symbol of French patriotism. The Tomb of the Unknown Soldier and the names of the numerous generals engraved onto the arch's inner walls pay homage to those who have fought and died for France. It's not for nationalistic sentiments, however, that so many visitors huff up the narrow, spiralling staircase every day. Rather it's the sublime panoramas from the top that make the arch such a notable attraction.

The arch was first commissioned in 1806 in the style of a Roman triumphal arch, following Napoléon's victory at Austerlitz the year before. At the time, the victory seemed like a watershed moment that confirmed the tactical supremacy of the French army, but a mere decade later, Napoléon had already fallen from power and his empire had crumbled. The Arc de Triomphe was never fully abandoned – simply laying the foundations, after all, had taken an entire two years – and in 1836, after a series of starts and stops under the restored monarchy, the project was finally completed. In 1840 Napoléon's remains were returned to France and passed under the arch before being interred at Invalides.

DON'T MISS

- Tomb of the Unknown Soldier
- Multimedia exhibit
- Viewing platform

PRACTICALITIES

- Map p384
- www.monuments-nationaux.fr
- place Charles de Gaulle, 8e
- adult/child €9.50/free
- 10am-11pm Apr-Sep, to 10.30pm Oct-Mar
- M Charles de Gaulle–Étoile

Beneath the Arch

Beneath the arch at ground level lies the **Tomb of the Unknown Soldier**. Honouring the 1.3 million French soldiers who lost their lives in WWI, the Unknown Soldier was laid to rest in 1921, beneath an eternal flame, which is rekindled daily at 6.30pm.

Also here are a number of bronze plaques laid into the ground. Take the time to try and decipher some: these mark significant moments in modern French history, such as the

ARCH ACROBATICS

On 7 August 1919, three weeks after the WWI victory parade, Charles Godefroy flew a biplane through the arch (14.5m wide) to honour the French pilots who had fought in the war. It was no easy feat: Jean Navarre, the pilot originally chosen to perform the flight, crashed his plane while practising and died.

Don't cross the traffic-choked roundabout above ground if you value your life! Stairs lead from the northern side of the Champs-Élysées to pedestrian tunnels (not linked to metro tunnels) that bring you out safely beneath the arch. Tickets to the viewing platform are sold in the tunnel.

BASTILLE DAY CELEBRATION

The military parade commemorating Bastille Day (14 July) kicks off from the arch (which is adorned by a billowing tricolour).

proclamation of the Third French Republic (4 September 1870) or the return of Alsace and Lorraine to French rule (11 November 1918). The most notable plaque is the text from Charles de Gaulle's famous London broadcast on 18 June 1940, which sparked the French Resistance to life: 'Believe me, I who am speaking to you with full knowledge of the facts, and who tell you that nothing is lost for France. The same means that overcame us can bring us victory one day. For France is not alone! She is not alone!'

The Sculptures

The arch is adorned with four main sculptures, six panels in relief, and a frieze running beneath the top. Each was designed by a different artist. The most famous sculpture is the one to the right as you approach from the Champs-Élysées: *La Marseillaise* (Departure of the Volunteers of 1792). Sculpted by François Rude, it depicts soldiers of all ages gathering beneath the wings of victory, en route to drive back the invading armies of Prussia and Austria. The higher panels depict a series of important victories for the Revolutionary and imperial French armies, from Egypt to Austerlitz, while the detailed frieze is divided into two sections: the *Departure of the Armies* and the *Return of the Armies*. Don't miss the multimedia section beneath the viewing platform, which provides more detail and historical background for each of the sculptures.

Viewing Platform

Climb the 284 steps to the viewing platform at the top of the 50m-high arch and you'll be suitably rewarded with magnificent panoramas over western Paris. From here, a dozen broad avenues – many of them named after Napoléonic victories and illustrious generals – radiate towards every compass point. The Arc de Triomphe is the highest point in the line of monuments known as the *axe historique* (historic axis, also called the grand axis); it offers views that swoop east down the Champs-Élysées to the gold-tipped obelisk at place de la Concorde (and beyond to the Louvre's glass pyramid), and west to the skyscraper district of La Défense, where the colossal Grande Arche marks the *axe*'s western terminus.

SIGHTS

Champs-Élysées

ARC DE TRIOMPHE LANDMARK

See p95.

AVENUE DES CHAMPS-ÉLYSÉES STREET

Map p384 (8e; MCharles de Gaulle–Étoile, George V, Franklin D Roosevelt or Champs-Élysées Clemenceau) No trip to Paris is complete without strolling this broad, tree-shaded avenue lined with luxury shops. Named for the Elysian Fields ('heaven' in Greek mythology), the Champs-Élysées was laid out in the 17th century and is part of the *axe historique*, linking place de la Concorde with the Arc de Triomphe. It's where presidents and soldiers strut their stuff on Bastille Day, where the Tour de France holds its final sprint, and where Paris turns out for organised and impromptu celebrations.

PLACE DE LA CONCORDE SQUARE

Map p384 (8e; MConcorde) Paris spreads around you, with views of the Eiffel Tower, the Seine and along the Champs-Élysées, when you stand in the city's largest square. Its 3300-year-old pink granite obelisk was a gift from Egypt in 1831. The square was first laid out in 1755 and originally named after King Louis XV, but its royal associations meant that it took centre stage during the Revolution – Louis XVI was the first to be guillotined here in 1793.

During the next two years, 1343 more people, including Marie Antoinette, Danton and Robespierre, also lost their heads here. The square was given its present name after the Reign of Terror in the hope that it would become a place of peace and harmony. The corners of the square are marked by eight statues representing what were once the largest cities in France.

GRAND PALAIS ART MUSEUM

Map p384 (www.grandpalais.fr; 3 av du Général Eisenhower, 8e; adult/child €13/9; 10am-10pm Tue-Sat, to 8pm Sun & Mon; MChamps-Élysées Clemenceau) Erected for the 1900 Exposition Universelle (World Fair), the Grand Palais today houses several exhibition spaces beneath its huge 8.5-ton art nouveau glass roof. Some of Paris' biggest shows (Renoir, Chagall, Turner) are held in the Galeries Nationales, lasting three to four months.

TOP SIGHT
PALAIS GARNIER

Few other Paris monuments have provided artistic inspiration in the way that the Palais Garnier has. From Degas' ballerinas to Gaston Leroux' Phantom and Chagall's ceiling, the layers of myth painted on gradually over the decades have bestowed a particular air of mystery and drama to its ornate interior. Designed in 1860 by Charles Garnier (then an unknown 35-year-old architect), the opera house was part of Baron Haussmann's massive urban renovation project.

The opera house is open to visitors during the day, and the building is a fascinating place to explore even if you're not taking in a show. Highlights include the opulent Grand Staircase, the library-museum (1st floor) and the horseshoe-shaped auditorium (2nd floor), with its extravagant gilded interior and red velvet seats. Above the massive chandelier is Chagall's gorgeous ceiling mural (1964), which depicts scenes from 14 operas.

Visits are generally unguided, though three days a week you can reserve a spot on an English-language guided tour. Staff advise showing up at least 30 minutes ahead of time. Check the website for updated schedules.

DON'T MISS...

- Grand Staircase
- Library-Museum
- Chagall's ceiling

PRACTICALITIES

- Map p386
- 08 25 05 44 05
- www.operadeparis.fr
- cnr rues Scribe & Auber, 9e
- unguided tour adult/child €10/6, guided tour €14/12.50
- unguided tour 10am-5pm, to 1pm on matinée performance days, guided tour by reservation
- MOpéra

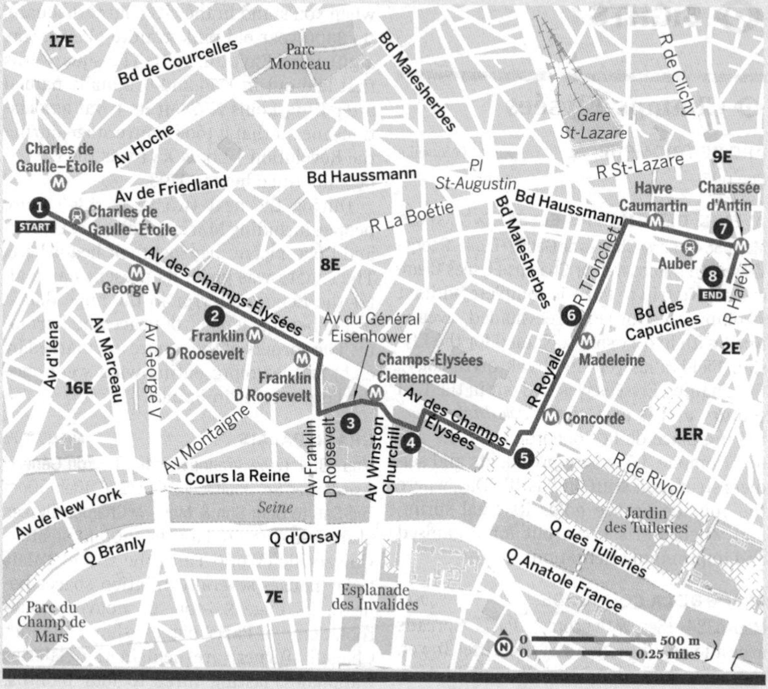

Neighbourhood Walk
Arc de Triomphe to Palais Garnier

START ARC DE TRIOMPHE
END PALAIS GARNIER
LENGTH 3.5KM; TWO HOURS

The city's sense of grandeur peaks beneath the mighty **1 Arc de Triomphe** (p95). Just don't try to cross the traffic-choked Étoile (star) roundabout above ground – use the pedestrian tunnels.

A dozen avenues radiate from the Étoile including the incomparable **2 av des Champs-Élysées** (p97). Take your time strolling this broad, tree-shaded avenue.

Parkland unfolds at the Champs-Élysées Marcel Dassault roundabout; turn right on av Franklin D Roosevelt then left on av du Général Eisenhower. On your right is the gorgeous, glass-roofed **3 Grand Palais** (p97), built for the 1900 Exposition Universelle.

Heading south across av Winston Churchill, you'll arrive at the smaller but equally striking art nouveau **4 Petit Palais** (p99), also built for the 1900 World Fair. Today it houses the city's fine arts museum.

Beyond the Petit Palais, turn left on av Dutuit and rejoin the Champs-Élysées, continuing east to **5 place de la Concorde** (p97), the vast square between the Champs-Élysées and the Jardin des Tuileries. In the centre, the pink granite obelisk stands on the site of a French Revolution guillotine.

Turn left on rue Royale to place de la Madeleine. The Greek-temple-style **6 Église de la Madeleine** (p99) dominates the centre, while the place itself is home to some of the city's finest gourmet shops, as well as the colourful Marché aux Fleurs Madeleine flower market, trading since 1832.

Continue north along rue Tronchet and right onto bd Haussmann. On your left you'll see the *grands magasins* (department stores) Le Printemps then **7 Galeries Lafayette** (p105), topped by a stained-glass dome – be sure to head inside and up to Galeries Lafayette's rooftop for a fabulous, free panorama over Paris.

Turn right on rue Halévy to reach the entrance to Paris' resplendent **8 Palais Garnier** (p97) opera house.

Hours, prices and exhibition dates vary significantly for all galleries. Those listed here generally apply to the Galeries Nationales, but always check the website for exact details. Reserving a ticket online for any show is strongly advised.

Other exhibit spaces include the imaginative Nef – which plays host to concerts, art installations, a seasonal amusement park and horse shows – and several other minor galleries. Renovations are ongoing and the monument will continue to develop its layout in the coming years, though it will remain open. There's also a fabulous restaurant, Mini Palais (p101).

PETIT PALAIS ART MUSEUM

Map p384 (www.petitpalais.paris.fr; av Winston Churchill, 8e; permanent collections free; ⌚10am-6pm Tue-Sun; Ⓜ Champs-Élysées–Clemenceau) FREE Like the Grand Palais opposite, this architectural stunner was also built for the 1900 Exposition Universelle, and is home to the Paris municipality's Museum of Fine Arts, the Musée des Beaux-Arts de la Ville de Paris. It specialises in medieval and Renaissance objets d'art such as porcelain and clocks, tapestries, drawings and 19th-century French painting and sculpture; and also has paintings by such artists as Rembrandt, Colbert, Cézanne, Monet, Gaugin and Delacroix.

PALAIS DE LA DÉCOUVERTE SCIENCE MUSEUM

Map p384 (www.palais-decouverte.fr; av Franklin D Roosevelt, 8e; adult/child €9/6; ⌚9.30am-6pm Tue-Sat, 10am-7pm Sun; Ⓜ Champs-Élysées–Clemenceau) Attached to the Grand Palais, this children's science museum has excellent temporary exhibits (eg moving lifelike dinosaurs) as well as a hands-on, interactive permanent collection focusing on astronomy, biology, physics and the like. Some of the older exhibits have French-only explanations, but overall this is a dependable family outing.

MUSÉE MAXIM'S MUSEUM

Map p384 (☎01 42 65 30 47; www.maximsmusee-artnouveau.com; 3 rue Royale, 8e; admission €15; ⌚tours 2pm, 3.15pm & 4pm Wed-Sun; Ⓜ Concorde) During *la belle époque*, Maxim's bistro was the most glamorous place to be in the capital. The restaurant has lost much of its cachet (though the food is actually excellent), but for art nouveau buffs, the real treasure is the upstairs museum. Opened by Maxim's owner, fashion designer Pierre Cardin, it's filled with some 550

LOCAL KNOWLEDGE

HIDDEN OASIS

Descending rustic, uneven staircases (by the white-marble Alfred de Musset sculpture on av Franklin D Roosevelt, or the upper garden off Cours la Reine) brings you to the tiny, 0.7 hectare **Jardin de la Nouvelle France** (Map p386; cnr av Franklin D Roosevelt & cours la Reine, 8e; ⌚24hr; Ⓜ Franklin D Roosevelt), an unexpected wonderland of lilacs, and lemon, orange, maple and weeping beech trees, with a wildlife-filled pond, waterfall, wooden footbridge and benches to soak up the serenity.

pieces of art nouveau artworks, objets d'art and furniture detailed during 40-minute guided tours (available in English).

LOUIS VUITTON ESPACE CULTUREL GALLERY

Map p384 (☎01 53 57 52 03; www.louisvuitton-espaceculturel.com; 60 rue de Bassano, 8e; ⌚noon-7pm Mon-Sat, 11am-7pm Sun; Ⓜ George V) FREE At the top of Louis Vuitton's flagship store is this contemporary art gallery with changing exhibits throughout the year. The entrance is via the mammoth store, which, of course, is something of a sight in itself.

◉ Grands Boulevards

ÉGLISE DE LA MADELEINE CHURCH

Map p386 (Church of St Mary Magdalene; www.eglise-lamadeleine.com; place de la Madeleine, 8e; ⌚9.30am-7pm; Ⓜ Madeleine) Place de la Madeleine is named after the 19th-century neoclassical church at its centre, the Église de la Madeleine. Constructed in the style of a massive Greek temple, 'La Madeleine' was consecrated in 1842 after almost a century of design changes and construction delays.

The church is a popular venue for classical-music concerts (some free); check the posters outside or the website for dates.

On the south side, the monumental staircase affords one of the city's most quintessential Parisian panoramas. From here, you can see down rue Royale to place de la Concorde and its obelisk and across the Seine to the Assemblée Nationale. The Invalides' gold dome appears in the background.

LOCAL KNOWLEDGE

THE UNSUNG MUSEUMS OF PARIS

Marc Restellini, director of the excellent La Pinacothèque, filled us in on his favourite art museums in Paris.

➡ **Musée d'Art Moderne de la Ville de Paris** (p85) An intelligent museum with high-quality, original exhibits, it carries out its mission as a modern-art museum with courage.

➡ **Musée Dapper** (p85) The greatest collection of African art in the world, imbued with a magical setting. It's a small museum, but when you leave it's as if you're returning from an incredible journey.

➡ **Musée Jacquemart-André** (p143) The second major private museum in Paris along with La Pinacothèque, it stages real art-history exhibits that are both original and daring.

LA PINACOTHÈQUE

ART MUSEUM

Map p386 (www.pinacotheque.com; 28 place de la Madeleine, 8e; adult/child from €12.30/10.80; 10.30am-6pm Sat-Tue & Thu, to 9pm Wed & Fri; M Madeleine) The top private museum in Paris, La Pinacothèque organises three to four major exhibits per year. Its nonlinear approach to art history, with exhibits that range from Mayan masks to retrospectives covering the work of artists such as Edvard Munch, has shaken up the otherwise rigid Paris art world and won over residents used to more formal presentations.

Although the focus is primarily on temporary exhibits, make sure to visit the permanent collection as well. Displayed thematically, it presents artwork rarely seen side by side in most other museums.

MUSÉE NATIONAL GUSTAVE MOREAU

ART MUSEUM

Map p386 (www.musee-moreau.fr; 14 rue de la Rochefoucauld, 9e; adult/child €5/free; 10am-12.45pm & 2-5.15pm Mon, Wed & Thu, 10am-5.15pm Fri-Sun; M Trinité) Symbolist painter Gustave Moreau's former studio is crammed with 4800 of his paintings, drawings and sketches – although symbolism received more attention as a literary movement in France (Baudelaire, Verlaine, Rimbaud). A particular highlight is *La Licorne* (The Unicorn), inspired by *La Dame à la Licorne* (The Lady with the Unicorn) cycle of tapestries in the Musée National du Moyen Âge. Present a Palais Garnier or Musée d'Orsay ticket for reduced admission.

MUSÉE DU PARFUM

MUSEUM

Map p386 (www.fragonard.com; 9 rue Scribe, 9e; 9am-6pm Mon-Sat, to 5pm Sun; M Opéra) FREE If the art of perfume-making entices, stop by this collection of copper distillery vats and antique flacons and test your nose on a few basic scents. Run by the parfumerie Fragonard, it's located in a beautiful old *hôtel particulier* (private mansion); free guided visits are available in multiple languages. A short distance south, a separate wing in a 20th-century theatre, the **Théâtre-Musée des Capucines** (Map p386; 39 bd des Capucines, 2e; 9am-6pm Mon-Sat; M Opéra), concentrates largely on the bottling and packaging side of perfume production.

MUSÉE GRÉVIN

MUSEUM

Map p386 (www.grevin.com; 10 bd Montmartre, 9e; adult/child €23.50/16.50; 10am-6.30pm; M Grands Boulevards) This large (and expensive) waxworks inside the passage Jouffroy has some 300 wax figures. They largely look more like caricatures than characters but, still, where else do you get to see Marilyn Monroe, Charles de Gaulle and Spiderman face to face, or the original death masks of some of the French Revolution leaders?

EATING

The Champs-Élysées area is known for its big-name chefs (Alain Ducasse, Pierre Gagnaire) and culinary icons (Taillevent), but there are a few under-the-radar restaurants too, where Parisians who live and work in the area dine on a regular basis. You'll also find good restaurants inside Publicis Drugstore (p105). Healthy budget options include branches of the Parisian sandwich-shop chain Cojean. Head to the Grands Boulevards for a more diverse selection – everything from hole-in-the-wall wine bars to organic cafes.

Champs-Élysées

★LADURÉE PATISSERIE €

Map p384 (www.laduree.com; 75 av des Champs-Élysées, 8e; pastries from €1.50; ⌚7.30am-11.30pm Mon-Fri, 8.30am-12.30am Sat, 8.30am-11.30pm Sun; Ⓜ George V) One of the oldest patisseries in Paris, Ladurée has been around since 1862 and was the original creator of the lighter-than-air macaron. Its tearoom is the classiest spot to indulge on the Champs. Alternatively, pick up some pastries to go – from croissants to its trademark macarons, it's all quite heavenly.

AUBRAC CORNER DELICATESSEN €

Map p384 (www.maison-aubrac.com/aubrac-corner; 37 rue Marbeuf, 8e; sandwiches from €5, burgers €9-11; ⌚7.45am-6.30pm Mon-Fri, 11am-6pm Sat; Ⓜ Franklin D Roosevelt) At this gourmet deli of famous steakhouse Maison Aubrac, burgers come with bowls of fries or *aligot* (mashed potatoes with melted cheese); take them downstairs into the hidden wine cellar, a refuge from the nonstop commotion outside. Afterwards, browse the deli for Laguiole (the special *aligot* cheese).

RAOUL MAEDER BOULANGERIE, PATISSERIE €

Map p384 (www.raoulmaeder.fr; 111 bd Haussemann, 8e; ⌚7am-7.30pm Mon-Fri, 7.30am-7pm Sat; Ⓜ St-Augustin) Alsatian specialities by this acclaimed *boulanger-pâtissier* include puffy pretzels, sweet or salted *kougelhopf* (marble cake), latticed cinnamon and raspberry *linzer torte* and shortbread, as well as award-winning breads.

LE HIDE FRENCH €€

Map p384 (☎01 45 74 15 81; www.lehide.fr; 10 rue du Général Lanrezac, 17e; 2-/3-course menus €25/34; ⌚noon-2pm Mon-Fri & 7-10pm Mon-Sat; Ⓜ Charles de Gaulle–Étoile) A perpetual favourite, Le Hide is a tiny neighbourhood bistro serving scrumptious traditional French fare: snails, baked shoulder of lamb with pumpkin purée or monkfish in lemon butter. Unsurprisingly, this place fills up faster than you can scamper down the steps of the nearby Arc de Triomphe. Reserve well in advance.

PHILIPPE & JEAN-PIERRE TRADITIONAL FRENCH €€

Map p384 (☎01 47 23 57 80; www.philippeetjean-pierre.fr; 7 rue de Boccador, 8e; 4-/5-course menus €40/50, mains €24-26; ⌚noon-2.15pm & 7.15-10.45pm Mon-Sat; Ⓜ Alma Marceau) Philippe graciously oversees the elegant, parquet-floored, white tableclothed dining room, while co-owner Jean-Pierre helms the kitchen. Seasonal menus incorporate dishes like cauliflower cream soup with mushrooms and truffles, sautéed scallops with leek and Granny Smith sauce, and melt-in-the-middle *moelleux au chocolat* cake. Given the service, quality and gilt-edged Triangle d'Or location, prices are a veritable bargain.

MINI PALAIS MODERN FRENCH €€

Map p384 (☎01 42 56 42 42; www.minipalais.com; av Winston Churchill, 8e; lunch menus €28, mains €22-45; ⌚10am-2am, kitchen to midnight; Ⓜ Champs-Élysées Clemenceau or Invalides) Set inside the fabulous Grand Palais, the Mini Palais resembles an artist's studio on a colossal scale, with unvarnished hardwood floors, industrial lights suspended from ceiling beams and plaster casts on display. Its sizzling success means that the crowd is anything but bohemian; dress to impress for a taste of the lauded modern cuisine.

PAD THAI THAI €€

Map p384 (☎01 43 80 20 52; www.padthai.fr; 32 rue Brey, 17e; ⌚2-/3-course lunch menus €14.50/17.50, 3-course dinner menus €20.50, mains €12-20; Ⓜ Ternes) The eponymous Thai classic *pad thai* (rice noodles stir-fried with prawns, eggs, tamarind, fish sauce, chillis and palm sugar, garnished with lime and peanuts) is the signature dish of this local spot. Other artfully presented takes on Thai street food include chicken *massaman* curry and fish with *pla yang* chilli paste.

LE BOUDOIR FRENCH €€

Map p384 (☎01 43 59 25 29; www.boudoirparis.fr; 25 rue du Colisée, 8e; 2-/3-course lunch menus €30/33, mains €26-30; ⌚12.30-3.30pm Mon-Fri, 7.30-11.30pm Mon-Sat; Ⓜ St-Philippe du Roule or Franklin D Roosevelt) Spread across two floors, the quirky salons – Marie Antoinette, Palme d'Or, le Fumoir – are individual works of art with a style befitting the name. Expect classy bistro fare (quail stuffed with dried fruit and foie gras, chateaubriand steak with chestnut purée) prepared by chef Arnaud Nicolas, a recipient of France's top culinary honour, Meilleur Ouvrier de France.

LASSERRE GASTRONOMIC €€€

Map p384 (☎01 43 59 02 13; www.restaurant-lasserre.com; 17 av Franklin Roosevelt, 8e; lunch

GOURMET FOOD SHOPS

Ultragourmet food shops garland **Place de la Madeleine** (Map p386; Ⓜ Madeleine); many have in-house dining options too. Notable names include truffle dealers **La Maison de la Truffe** (Map p386; ☎01 42 65 53 22; www.maison-de-la-truffe.com; 19 place de la Madeleine, 8e; ⊙10am-10pm Mon-Sat; Ⓜ Madeleine); luxury food shop **Hédiard** (Map p386; www.hediard.fr; 21 place de la Madeleine, 8e; ⊙9am-8pm Mon-Sat; Ⓜ Madeleine); mustard specialist **Boutique Maille** (Map p386; ☎01 40 15 06 00; www.maille.com; 6 place de la Madeleine, 8e; ⊙10am-7pm Mon-Sat; Ⓜ Madeleine); and Paris' most famous caterer, **Fauchon** (Map p386; ☎01 70 39 38 00; www.fauchon.fr; 26 & 30 place de la Madeleine, 8e; ⊙8.30am-8.30pm Mon-Sat; Ⓜ Madeleine), selling incredibly mouth-watering delicacies, from foie gras to jams, chocolates and pastries. Nearby is 'honey house' **La Maison du Miel** (Map p386; ☎01 47 42 26 70; www.maisondumiel.com; 24 rue Vignon, 9e; ⊙9.30am-7pm Mon-Sat; Ⓜ Madeleine).

menus €90-120, degustation menus €220, mains €82-125; ⊙noon-2pm Thu & Fri, 7-10pm Tue-Sat; Ⓜ Franklin D Roosevelt) Since 1942, this exceedingly elegant restaurant in the Triangle d'Or has hosted style icons like Audrey Hepburn and is still a superlative choice for a twin-Michelin-starred meal to remember. A bellhop-attended lift/elevator, white-and-gold chandeliered decor, extraordinary retractable roof and flawless service set the stage for head chef Christophe Moret's and pastry chef Claire Heitzer's inspired creations. Dress code required.

MAKOTO AOKI TRADITIONAL FRENCH €€€

Map p384 (☎01 43 59 29 24; 19 rue Jean Mermoz, 8e; lunch menus €22, mains €34-38; ⊙noon-2pm Mon-Fri, 7.30-9.30pm Tue-Sat; Ⓜ Franklin D Roosevelt) In an *arrondissement* known for grandiose interiors and superstar chefs who are often elsewhere, this intimate neighbourhood restaurant is a real find. The Japanese chef is a French-trained *haute cuisine* perfectionist; lunch might include an extravagant bacon-morel brioche; dinner a divine risotto with John Dory or truffles.

Grands Boulevards

LE VALENTIN TEAROOM €

Map p386 (www.le-valentin.fr; 30-32 passage Jouffroy, 9e; dishes €4-14; ⊙8.30am-7.30pm Mon-Sat, 10am-7pm Sun; Ⓜ Grands Boulevards) Inside beautiful covered-arcade passage Jouffroy, this enchanting, two-storeyed *salon de thé* slash patisserie slash *chocolaterie* is an equally lovely spot for breakfast, light lunches like quiches, salads, *feuilletés* (savoury-filled puff pastries) and *brochettes* (skewers), and dozens of varieties of tea, accompanied by exquisite *tartelettes* and delectable cakes.

STANZ BAGELS €

Map p386 (http://stanzbagel.com; 56 rue La Fayette, 9e; bagels €3.80-8.50; ⊙10am-8.30pm Mon-Sat, 11am-5pm Sun; Ⓜ Cadet) All-natural, handmade bagels, in classic and mini sizes, are given the Parisian gourmet treatment, with toppings such as smoked ham with honey mustard, rocket and pickles or chicken and preserved lemon. Sweet varieties range from pink praline to chocolate chestnut.

CHEZ PLUME ROTISSERIE €

Map p386 (www.chezplume.fr; 6 rue des Martyrs, 9e; dishes €3.50-8.50; ⊙10.15am-2.45pm Mon-Fri, 5-8pm Tue-Fri, 9.30am-8.30pm Sat, 9.30am-3pm Sun; Ⓜ Notre Dame de Lorette) This rotisserie specialises in free-range chicken from south-west France, prepared in a variety of fashions: simply roasted, as a crumble, or even in a quiche or sandwich. It's wonderfully casual: add a side or two (potatoes, polenta, seasonal veggies) and pull up a counter seat.

LE ZINC DES CAVISTES WINE BAR €

Map p386 (☎01 47 70 88 64; 5 rue du Faubourg Montmartre, 9e; lunch menus €15.50, mains €13.50-18; ⊙kitchen noon-11pm; Ⓜ Grands Boulevards) Don't tell the masses standing dutifully in the queue at the iconic, old-fashioned restaurant Chartier that there's a much better restaurant right next door. Local secret Le Zinc des Cavistes is as good for a full-blown meal (duck confit with mash, chicken fricassee with crushed potatoes) as it is for sampling new vintages.

SUPERNATURE ORGANIC €

Map p386 (☎01 47 70 21 03; www.super-nature.fr; 12 rue de Trévise, 9e; 2-/3-course lunch menus €17/20; ⊙noon-2.30pm Mon-Fri, 11.30am-3.30pm Sun; Ⓜ Cadet or Grands Boulevards) Clever veggie creations at this funky organic cafe include curried split-pea soup, and cantaloupe, pumpkin seed and feta salad but, being France, it's not all legumes – you can still order a healthy cheeseburger with sprouts. A takeaway branch two doors down (at 8 rue de Trévise, 9e) serves sandwiches, salads and thick slices of sweet-potato and gorgonzola quiche.

LES PÂTES VIVANTES
CHINESE €

Map p386 (www.lespatesvivantes.net; 46 du Faubourg Montmartre, 9e; noodles €9.50-12; ⊗noon-3pm Mon-Fri, noon-3.30pm Sat & Sun, 7-11pm daily; MLe Peletier) This is one of the only spots in Paris for *là miàn* (hand-pulled noodles) made to order in the age-old northern Chinese tradition. It packs in a crowd, so arrive early to stake out a table on the ground floor and watch the noodle maker work his magic.

★RICHER
NEOBISTRO €€

Map p386 (2 rue Richer, 9e; mains €16-25; ⊗kitchen noon-2.30pm & 7.30-10.30pm; MPoissonière or Bonne Nouvelle) Run by the same team as across-the-street neighbour L'Office, Richer's pared-back, exposed-brick decor is a smart setting for genius creations like trout tartare with cauliflower and tomato and citrus mousse, and quince and lime cheesecake for dessert. It doesn't take reservations, but if it's full, Richer posts a list of recommended local addresses outside. Fantastic value.

FLOQUIFIL
TRADITIONAL FRENCH €€

Map p386 (☑01 84 19 42 12; www.floquifil.fr; 17 rue de Montyon, 9e; mains €14-25; ⊗11am-midnight Mon-Fri, from 6.30pm Sat; MGrands Boulevards) If you were to envision the ultimate backstreet Parisian wine bar, it would probably look a lot like Floquifil: table-strewn terrace, dark timber furniture, aquamarine-painted walls and bottles galore. But while the by-the-glass wines are superb, you're missing out if you don't dine here (on rosemary-roasted lamb with ratatouille or at the very least a chacuterie platter).

BISTROT LA BRUYÈRE
BISTRO €€

Map p386 (☑09 81 22 20 56; 31 rue la Bruyère, 9e; 2-/3-course lunch menus €18/21, dinner menus €28/35; ⊗noon-2.30pm & 7.30-10.30pm Mon-Sat; MSt-Georges) Young-gun chef Loïc Buisson is the wunderkind behind winning dishes like tomato gazpacho, pig's trotter pancakes with apple chips, tuna with fried leeks, and beef from celebrated butcher Hugo Desnoyer at this unassuming but brilliant little bistro. One to watch.

CAILLEBOTTE
MODERN FRENCH €€

Map p386 (☑01 53 20 88 70; 8 rue Hippolyte Lebas, 9e; 2-course lunch menus €19, 3-/5-course dinner menus €35/49; ⊗noon-2.30pm & 7.30-10.30pm Mon-Fri; MNotre Dame de Lorette) Although named for impressionist painter Gustave Caillebotte, the clattering interior – slate tiles, blond wood and tightly packed marble-topped tables – means this isn't the place for a romantic meal. But it is the place for amazing flavour combinations like scallops with creamy fennel and coffee purée and sea urchin foam, by the same team as Le Pantruche (p146).

L'OFFICE
MODERN FRENCH €€

Map p386 (☑01 47 70 67 31; 3 rue Richer, 9e; 2-/3-course lunch menus €22/27, dinner menus €28/34; ⊗noon-2.30pm & 7.30-10.30pm Mon-Fri; MPoissonière or Bonne Nouvelle) Don't judge this one by the simple chalkboard descriptions ('beef/polenta'), which belie the rich and complex flavours emerging from the kitchen. The market-inspired menu is mercifully short – as in there are only two choices for lunch – but outstanding. Alternatively, cross the street to its newer, sleeker sibling, Richer.

LES COULISSES VINTAGE
BISTRO €€

Map p386 (☑01 45 26 46 46; www.restolescoulisses.fr; 19 rue Notre Dame de Lorette, 9e; 2-course lunch menus €16, 2-/3-course dinner menus €32.50/39.50; ⊗noon-2.30pm Mon-Fri, 7-11pm Mon-Sat; MSt-Georges) Framed by red curtains tied back with gold tassels, Les Coulisses Vintage has a loyal local following for its excellent value-for-money dishes that straddle the divide between traditional and modern – foie gras in gingerbread crumbs, roast cod with porcini mushrooms, and chocolate soufflé or sublime cheeses for dessert.

LE J'GO
REGIONAL CUISINE €€

Map p386 (☑01 40 22 09 09; www.lejgo.com; 4 rue Drouot, 9e; 2-/3-course menus €16/22, mains €13.50; ⊗noon-3pm & 6-11.30pm Tue-Sat; MRichelieu Drouot) With sunflower-coloured walls decorated with bull-fighting posters, this contemporary bistro magics you away to southwestern France (perfect on a grey Parisian day). Flavourful regional cooking is based around the rotisserie and other Gascogne standards like *cassoulet* and foie gras. The roasting takes a minimum 20 minutes, giving you the opportunity to sample a choice selection of sunny southern wines.

NOUVEAU PARIS-DAKAR SENEGALESE €€

Map p386 (☎01 42 46 12 30; www.lenouveauparisdakar.com; 11 rue de Montyon, 9e; mains €14-18, lunch menus €10.90, menus €25-36; ⊙noon-3pm & 7pm-1am; Ⓜ Grands Boulevards) Specialities at this slice of Senegal include *yassa* (chicken or fish marinated in lime juice and onion sauce) and *maffé Cap Vert* (lamb in peanut sauce). Live African music some nights.

BISTROT DU SOMMELIER BISTRO €€€

Map p384 (☎01 42 65 24 85; www.bistrotdusommelier.com; 97 bd Haussmann; lunch menus €34-55, dinner menus €70-118; ⊙noon-2.30pm & 7-10.30pm Mon-Fri; Ⓜ St-Augustin) If you like *haute cuisine* with your wine (rather than the other way around), this freshly refurbished brainchild of star sommelier Philippe Faure-Brac offers superb degustation menus with pre-paired wines. Fridays are an institution, offering a three-course tasting lunch with wine for €55 and five-course dinner with wine for €75 (reservations essential).

DRINKING & NIGHTLIFE

Champs-Élysées

AUTOUR D'UN VERRE WINE BAR

Map p386 (☎01 48 24 43 74; 21 rue de Trévise, 9e; ⊙10.30am-10.30pm Tue-Sat; Ⓜ Cadet or Grands Boulevards) You'd be forgiven for thinking that Autour d'un Verre is one of those pop-up places: the interior doesn't appear to have been renovated since the 1950s. But that's all part of its undercover appeal – and after a few glasses of Clos du Tue-Boeuf, who cares about decoration anyway?

CHARLIE BIRDY PUB

Map p384 (www.charliebirdy.com; 124 rue de la Boétie, 8e; ⊙noon-5am; ; Ⓜ Franklin D Roosevelt) This kick-back brick-walled place just off the Champs Élysées is easily the most inviting pub in the neighbourhood. The usual array of bar food (burgers, hot dogs, more burgers…) is available; DJs hit the decks on weekend nights.

LE MADAM CLUB

Map p384 (http://lemadam.com; 128 rue de la Boétie, 8e; ⊙11.45pm-7am Fri & Sat; Ⓜ St-Philippe du Roule) Carve up the dance floor at this 300-capacity party venue (with plenty of tables when you need a breather). Usually no cover charge, but dress to impress to get in.

QUEEN CLUB

Map p384 (☎01 53 89 08 90; www.queen.fr; 102 av des Champs-Élysées, 8e; ⊙11.30pm-6.30am; Ⓜ George V) These days this doyen of a club is as popular with a straight crowd as it is with its namesake clientele but Monday's disco nights are still prime dancing queen territory. While right on the Champs-Élysées, it's not nearly as inaccessible as the other nearby clubs.

SHOWCASE CLUB

Map p384 (www.showcase.fr; Port des Champs-Élysées, 8e; ⊙11.30pm-6am Thu-Sat; Ⓜ Invalides or Champs-Élysées Clemenceau) This gigantic electro club has solved the neighbour-versus-noise problem that haunts so many Parisian nightlife spots: it's secreted beneath the Pont Alexandre III bridge alongside the Seine. Unlike other exclusive Champs backstreet clubs, the Showcase can pack 'em in (up to 1500 clubbers) and is less stringent about its door policy, though you'll still want to dress like a star.

Grands Boulevards

LE FORUM COCKTAIL BAR

Map p386 (www.bar-le-forum.com; 4 bd Malesherbes, 8e; ⊙6pm-1am Mon, noon-1am Tue-Thu, noon-2am Fri, 7pm-2am Sat; Ⓜ Madeleine) More than 80 cocktails are detailed on the menu of this classy, dark timber-panelled cocktail bar footsteps from place de la Madeleine. All are painstakingly made to order and, in this neighbourhood, they don't come cheap, but are worth the wait and the price.

AU GÉNÉRAL LA FAYETTE BRASSERIE

Map p386 (52 rue la Fayette, 9e; ⊙10am-3am Mon-Sat, to 2am Sun; Ⓜ Le Peletier) With its archetypal belle époque decor (brass fittings, polished wood, large murals) and excellent wines by the glass, this old-style brasserie is an atmospheric spot for an afternoon coffee or evening drink.

ENTERTAINMENT

PALAIS GARNIER OPERA

Map p386 (☎08 92 89 90 90; www.operadeparis.fr; place de l'Opéra, 9e; Ⓜ Opéra) The city's original opera house is smaller than its Bastille counterpart, but has perfect acoustics. Due to its odd shape, some seats have limited or no visibility – book carefully. Ticket prices and conditions (including last-minute discounts) are available from the **box office** (Map p386; cnr rues Scribe & Auber; 11am-6.30pm Mon-Sat).

AU LIMONAIRE LIVE MUSIC

Map p386 (01 45 23 33 33; http://limonaire.free.fr; 18 cité Bergère, 9e; 6pm-2am Tue-Sat, from 7pm Sun & Mon; M Grands Boulevards) This perfect little wine bar is one of the best places to listen to traditional French *chansons* and local singer-songwriters. Performances begin at 10pm Tuesday to Saturday and 7pm on Sunday. Entry is free; reservations are recommended if you plan on dining.

L'OLYMPIA LIVE MUSIC

Map p386 (08 92 68 33 68; www.olympiahall.com; 28 bd des Capucines, 9e; M Opéra) Opened by the founder of the Moulin Rouge in 1888, the Olympia has hosted all the big names over the years, from Édith Piaf to Jimi Hendrix and Jeff Buckley, though it's small enough to put on a fairly intimate show.

SALLE PLEYEL CLASSICAL MUSIC

Map p384 (01 42 56 13 13; www.sallepleyel.fr; 252 rue du Faubourg St-Honoré, 8e; box office noon-7pm Mon-Sat, to 8pm on day of performance, 11am to 2hrs prior to performance Sun; M Ternes) Dating from the 1920s, this highly regarded hall hosts many of Paris' finest classical-music recitals and concerts.

FOLIES-BERGÈRE LIVE MUSIC

Map p386 (www.foliesbergere.com; 32 rue Richer, 9e; M Cadet) This is the legendary club where Charlie Chaplin, WC Fields and Stan Laurel appeared on stage together one night in 1911, and where Josephine Baker – accompanied by her diamond-collared pet cheetah and wearing only stilettos and a skirt made from bananas – bewitched audience members including Hemingway. Today, shows span solo acts such as Ben Harper to musicals.

KIOSQUE THÉÂTRE MADELEINE DISCOUNT TICKETS

Map p386 (opp 15 place de la Madeleine, 8e; 12.30-8pm Tue-Sat, to 4pm Sun; M Madeleine) Pick up half-price tickets for same-day performances of ballet, opera and music at this freestanding kiosk.

SHOPPING

Global chains line the Champs-Élysées, but it's the luxury fashion houses in the Triangle d'Or that have made Paris famous. The area around Opéra and the Grands Boulevards is where you'll find flagship *grands magasins* (department stores).

PUBLICIS DRUGSTORE CONCEPT STORE

Map p384 (www.publicisdrugstore.com; 133 av des Champs-Élysées, 8e; 8am-2am Mon-Fri, 10am-2am Sat & Sun; M Charles de Gaulle–Étoile) An institution since 1958, Publicis incorporates cinemas and late-opening shops including an *épicerie* (specialist grocer), pharmacy, beauty counter, international newsagent, *cave* (wine cellar) and cigar bar. At street level there's a glassed-in brasserie and steakhouse, but its newest and chicest dining space is downstairs at the glossy black and red Étoile branch of L'Atelier de Joël Robuchon.

GALERIES LAFAYETTE DEPARTMENT STORE

Map p386 (http://haussmann.galerieslafayette.com; 40 bd Haussmann, 9e; 9.30am-8pm Mon-Sat, to 9pm Thu; M Auber or Chaussée d'Antin) *Grande dame* department store Galeries Lafayette is spread across the main store (whose magnificent stained-glass dome is over a century old), **men's store** (Map p386) and **homewares** (Map p386) store, and includes a gourmet emporium. Catch modern art in the **gallery** (Map p386; www.galeriedesgaleries.com; 1st fl; 11am-7pm Tue-Sat) FREE, or take in a **fashion show** (bookings 01 42 82 30 25; 3pm Fri Mar-Jul & Sep-Dec by reservation); a free, windswept rooftop panorama; or a break at one of its 19 restaurants and cafes.

LE PRINTEMPS DEPARTMENT STORE

Map p386 (www.printemps.com; 64 bd Haussmann, 9e; 9.35am-8pm Mon-Wed, Fri & Sat, to 10pm Thu; M Havre Caumartin) Famous department store Le Printemps encompasses Le Printemps de la Mode (women's fashion), **Le Printemps de l'Homme** (Map p386; men's fashion), both with established and up-and-coming designer wear, and Le Printemps de la Beauté et Maison (beauty and homewares), offering a staggering display of perfume, cosmetics and accessories. There's a free panoramic rooftop terrace and luxury eateries including Ladurée.

HISTORIC HAUTE COUTURE

A stroll around the legendary **Triangle d'Or** (bordered by avs Georges V, Champs-Élysées and Montaigne, 8e) constitutes the walk of fame of top French fashion. Rubbing shoulders with the world's top designers are Paris' most influential French fashion houses:

➜ **Chanel** (Map p384; www.chanel.com; 42 av Montaigne, 8e; ⏱10am-7pm Mon-Sat; Ⓜ George V) Box jackets and little black dresses, chic ever since their first appearance in the 1920s.

➜ **Christian Dior** (Map p384; www.dior.com; 30 av Montaigne, 8e; ⏱10am-7pm Mon-Sat; Ⓜ George V) Post-WWII, Dior's creations dictated style, re-establishing Paris as the world fashion capital.

➜ **Givenchy** (Map p384; www.givenchy.com; 3 av George V, 8e; ⏱10am-7pm Mon-Sat; Ⓜ George V) The first to present a luxurious collection of women's prêt-à-porter.

➜ **Hermès** (Map p384; www.hermes.com; 24 rue du Faubourg St-Honoré, 8e; ⏱10.30am-6.30pm Mon-Sat; Ⓜ Concorde) Founded in 1837 by a saddle-maker, Hermès' famous scarves are *the* fashion accessory.

➜ **Jean-Paul Gaultier** (Map p384; www.jeanpaulgaultier.com; 44 av George V, 8e; ⏱10.30am-7pm Mon-Sat; Ⓜ George V) A shy kid from the Paris suburbs, JPG morphed into the enfant terrible of the fashion world with his granny's corsets, men dressed in skirts and Madonna's conical bra.

➜ **Lanvin** (Map p384; www.lanvin.com; 22 rue du Faubourg St Honoré, 8e; ⏱10.30am-7pm Mon-Sat; Ⓜ Concorde) One of Paris' oldest fashion houses, established in 1909.

➜ **Louis Vuitton** (Map p384; www.louisvuitton.com; 101 av des Champs-Élysées, 8e; ⏱10am-8pm Mon-Sat, 11am-7pm Sun; Ⓜ George V) Take home a real McCoy canvas bag with the 'LV' monogram.

➜ **Yves Saint Laurent** (Map p384; www.ysl.com; 38 rue du Faubourg St-Honoré, 8e; ⏱11am-7pm Mon, 10.30am-7pm Tue-Sat; Ⓜ Concorde) One of the top Parisian designers from the 1960s on, YSL was the first to incorporate non-European styles into his work.

À LA MÈRE DE FAMILLE — FOOD, DRINK

Map p386 (www.lameredefamille.com; 35 rue du Faubourg Montmartre, 9e; ⏱9.30am-8pm Mon-Sat, 10am-1pm Sun; Ⓜ Le Peletier) Founded in 1761, this is the original location of Paris' oldest chocolatier. Its beautiful belle époque façade is as enchanting as the rainbow of sweets, caramels and chocolates inside.

GUERLAIN — PERFUME

Map p384 (☎spa 01 45 62 11 21; www.guerlain.com; 68 av des Champs-Élysées, 8e; ⏱10.30am-8pm Mon-Sat, noon-7pm Sun; Ⓜ Franklin D Roosevelt) Guerlain is Paris' most famous parfumerie, and its shop (dating from 1912) is one of the most beautiful in the city. With its shimmering mirror and marble art-deco interior, it's a reminder of the former glory of the Champs-Élysées.

CHLOÉ — FASHION

Map p384 (www.chloe.com; 44 av Montaigne, 8e; ⏱10.30am-7pm Mon-Sat; Ⓜ Franklin D Roosevelt) Bold prints, bohemian layers and uneven hemlines have given street cred to this 1950s-established Parisian label.

LANCEL — ACCESSORIES

Map p384 (www.lancel.com; 127 av des Champs-Élysées, 8e; ⏱10am-8pm Mon-Sat, to 7pm Sun; Ⓜ Charles de Gaulle–Étoile) Open racks of luscious totes fill this handbag designer's gleaming premises.

ERES — FASHION, ACCESSORIES

Map p386 (www.eresparis.com; 2 rue Tronchet, 8e; ⏱10am-7pm Mon-Sat; Ⓜ Madeleine) Anyone who has despaired of buying a swimsuit in the past will understand why the ones from this place have become a must-have item. The stunning suits are cut to suit all shapes and sizes, with bikini tops and bottoms sold separately.

HÔTEL DROUOT — ART, ANTIQUES

Map p386 (www.drouot.com; 7-9 rue Drouot, 9e; ⏱11am-6pm most days; Ⓜ Richelieu Drouot) Selling antiques and jewellery, rare books and art, Paris' most established auction house has been in business for more than a century. Viewings are from 11am to 6pm the day before and from 11am to noon the morning of the auction. Pick up the catalogue *Gazette de l'Hôtel Drouot,* published Fridays, in-house or at newsstands.

Louvre & Les Halles

LOUVRE | LES HALLES

Neighbourhood Top Five

❶ Getting lost in the mother of all museums, the palatial **Musée du Louvre** (p109).

❷ Contemplating contemporary art and architecture at the **Centre Pompidou** (p117).

❸ Meeting Monet and revelling in Paris at its symmetrical best in the **Jardin des Tuileries** (p119).

❹ Feasting on exquisite sacred art and soulful music in **Église St-Eustach** (p120).

❺ Browsing designer boutiques beneath the arcaded galleries of the **Jardin du Palais Royal** (p122).

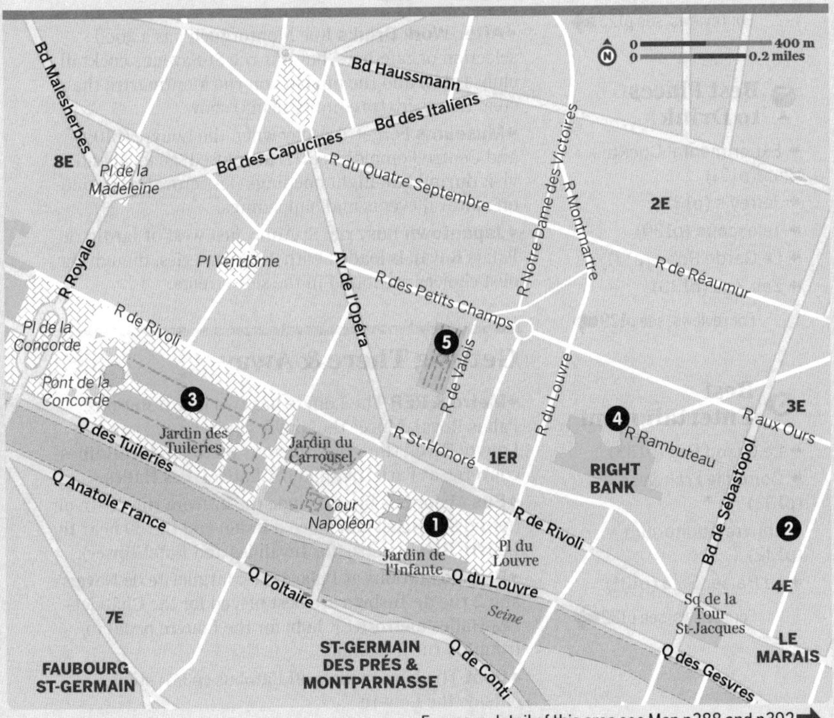

For more detail of this area see Map p388 and p392

Lonely Planet's Top Tip

Some of Paris' top tables are here, but you need to book in advance: plan two months ahead for a table at Frenchie (p127) or Yam'Tcha (p129) and up to a month ahead for Spring (p129) or Verjus (p127). Both Frenchie and Verjus have neighbouring wine bars where you simply rock up and wait for a stool to feast on lighter creations from the same talented chefs.

Best Places to Eat

- Frenchie (p127)
- Yam'Tcha (p129)
- Verjus (p127)
- Spring (p129)
- Pirouette (p128)

For reviews, see p123

Best Places to Drink

- Experimental Cocktail Club (p131)
- Jefrey's (p131)
- Telescope (p129)
- Le Garde Robe (p131)
- Zen Zoo (p130)

For reviews, see p129

Best Entertainment

- Le Grand Rex (p133)
- Comédie Française (p132)
- Louvre Auditorium (p132)
- Le Baiser Salé (p131)

For reviews, see p132

Explore: Louvre & Les Halles

The banks of the Seine make an enchanting starting point. A wonderful exploratory loop snakes westwards along quai des Tuileries, past the sculptures and green lawns, pools and fountains of Jardin des Tuileries, to the Musée de l'Orangerie and Jeu du Paume. Continue on foot north to ritzy place Vendôme, then loop back east along shop-chic rue St-Honoré to Palais Royal.

Set aside at least half a day for the Musée du Louvre. Avoid museum fatigue by combining the often-intimidating art gallery with a long lunch or a picnic and invigorating mooch around the designer galleries and manicured gardens of Jardin du Palais Royal. Serious art lovers will want to set aside another half-day minimum for the Centre Pompidou, for Europe's largest collection of modern art.

Once you cross rue du Louvre into Les Halles, the timeless sophistication of the Louvre area disappears. Instead, unwary passers-by are solicited with bright lights, jostling crowds, painted ladies and the swinging jazz clubs of rue des Lombards. Day and night the mainly pedestrian zone between the Centre Pompidou and Forum des Halles is packed with people, just as it was for the 850-odd years when Paris' main *halles* (marketplace) for foodstuffs was here.

Local Life

- **After-Work Drinks** Rue Montorgueil has a good selection of cafe-bars, but it is rue St-Saveur's cocktail clubs (p131) and the hip bars on rue Montmartre that steal the *apéro* (predinner drink) show.
- **Museums** Forget Tuesday when the Louvre (p109) and Centre Pompidou (p117) are closed; go local and visit during late-night openings (less crowded) or one-off cultural events and happenings.
- **Japantown** Busy rue St-Anne, just west of Jardin du Palais Royal, is loaded with Asian eateries, though the best choices are found in the side streets.

Getting There & Away

- **Metro & RER** The Louvre has two metro stations: Palais Royal–Musée du Louvre (lines 1 and 7) and Louvre Rivoli (line 1). Numerous metro and RER lines converge at Paris' main hub, Châtelet–Les Halles.
- **Bus** Major bus lines include the 27 from rue de Rivoli (for bd St-Michel and place d'Italie) and the 69 near the Louvre Rivoli metro (for Invalides and Eiffel Tower).
- **Bicycle** Stations at 1 place Ste-Marguerite de Navarre and 2 rue de Turbigo are best placed for the Châtelet–Les Halles metro/RER hub; for the Louvre pedal to/from 165 rue St-Honoré.
- **Boat** The hop-on, hop-off Batobus (p351) stops outside the Louvre.

NEALE CLARK / GETTY IMAGES ©

TOP SIGHT
THE LOUVRE

Few art galleries are as prized or daunting as the Musée du Louvre, Paris' pièce de résistance that no first-time visitor to the city can resist. This is, after all, one of the world's largest and most diverse museums. Showcasing 35,000 works of art, it would take nine months to glance at every piece, rendering advance planning essential.

Works of art from Europe form the permanent exhibition, alongside priceless collections of Mesopotamian, Egyptian, Greek, Roman and Islamic art and antiquities – a fascinating presentation of the evolution of Western art up through the mid-19th century.

Palais du Louvre

The Louvre today rambles over four floors and through three wings: the **Sully Wing** creates the four sides of the Cour Carrée (literally 'square courtyard') at the eastern end of the complex; the **Denon Wing** stretches 800m along the Seine to the south; and the northern **Richelieu Wing** skirts rue de Rivoli. The building started life as a fortress built by Philippe-Auguste in the 12th century – medieval remnants are still visible on the lower ground floor (Sully). In the 16th century it became a royal residence and after the Revolution, in 1793, it was turned into a national museum. Its booty was no more than 2500 paintings and objets d'art.

Over the centuries French governments amassed the paintings, sculptures and artefacts displayed today. The 'Grand Louvre' project inaugurated by the late President Mitterrand in 1989 doubled the museum's exhibition space, and both new and renovated galleries have since opened, including the state-of-the-art **Islamic art galleries** (lower ground floor, Denon) in the stunningly restored Cour Visconti.

DON'T MISS

- Mesopotamian and Egyptian collections
- 1st floor, Denon Wing
- *Mona Lisa*

PRACTICALITIES

- Map p388
- ☎01 40 20 53 17
- www.louvre.fr
- rue de Rivoli & quai des Tuileries, 1er
- adult/child €12/free
- 9am-6pm Mon, Thu, Sat & Sun, to 9.45pm Wed & Fri
- Ⓜ Palais Royal–Musée du Louvre

OUT TO LUNCH

Tickets to the Louvre are valid for the whole day, meaning you can nip out for lunch – the best way to avoid museum fatigue if you're there all day. For a quick and easy meal, grab a sandwich from the bakery Paul (Hall Napoléon) and picnic like a royal in the Jardin des Tuileries. Alternatively, stroll five minutes to enjoy fine wines and cuisine at Racines 2 (p129) or Garde Robe (p131), a Paris-perfect view at Saut du Loup (p130), or good value at Cojean (p128) and Sanukiya (p123).

You need to queue twice to get in: once for security and then again to buy tickets. The longest queues are outside the Grande Pyramide; use the Carrousel du Louvre entrance (99 rue de Rivoli or direct from the metro) or the Porte de Lions entrance (closed Wednesday and Friday) instead. A Museum Pass gives you priority; buying tickets in advance will also help expedite the process.

Priceless Antiquities

Whatever your plans are, don't rush by the Louvre's astonishing cache of treasures from antiquity: both **Mesopotamia** (ground floor, Richelieu) and **Egypt** (ground and 1st floors, Sully) are well represented, as seen in the *Code of Hammurabi* (Room 3, ground floor, Richelieu) and the *Seated Scribe* (Room 22, 1st floor, Sully). Room 12 (ground floor, Sackler Wing) holds impressive friezes and an enormous two-headed-bull column from the Darius Palace in ancient Iran, while an enormous seated statue of Pharaoh Ramesses II highlights the temple room (Room 12, Sully).

Also worth a look are the mosaics and figurines from the Byzantine empire (lower ground floor, Denon), and the Greek statuary collection, culminating with the world's most famous armless duo, the **Venus de Milo** (Room 16, ground floor, Sully) and the **Winged Victory of Samothrace** (top of Daru staircase, 1st floor, Denon, under renovation through 2015).

Mona Lisa

Easily the Louvre's most admired work (and the world's most famous painting) is Leonardo da Vinci's *La Joconde* (in French; *La Gioconda* in Italian), the lady with that enigmatic smile known as *Mona Lisa* (Room 6, 1st floor, Denon). For centuries admirers speculated on everything from the possibility that the subject was mourning the death of a loved one to the chance that she might have been in love or in bed with her portraitist.

Mona (*monna* in Italian) is a contraction of *madonna,* and Gioconda is the feminine form of the surname Giocondo. Canadian scientists used infrared technology to peer through paint layers and confirm *Mona Lisa's* identity as Lisa Gherardini (1479–1542), wife of Florentine merchant Francesco de Giocondo. Scientists also discovered that her dress was covered in a transparent gauze veil typically worn in early-16th-century Italy by pregnant women or new mothers; it's surmised that the work was painted to commemorate the birth of her second son around 1503, when she was aged about 24.

French & Italian Masterpieces

The 1st floor of the Denon Wing, where the *Mona Lisa* is found, is easily the most popular part of the Louvre – and with good reason. Rooms 75 through 77 are hung with monumental French paintings, many iconic: look for the *Consecration of the Emperor Napoleon I* (David), *The Raft of the Medusa* (Géricault) and *Grande Odalisque* (Ingres).

Rooms 1, 3, 5 and 8 are also must-visits. Filled with classic works by **Renaissance** masters – Raphael, Titian, Uccello, Botticini – this area culminates

LOUVRE

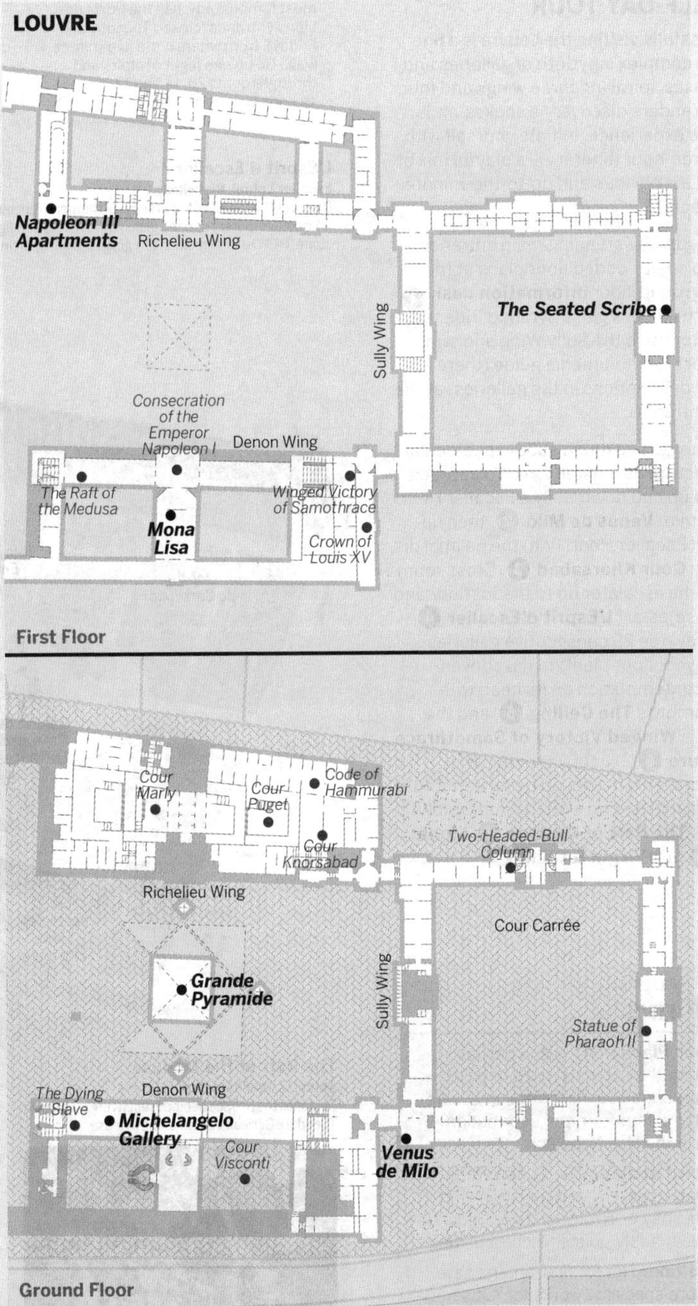
Napoleon III Apartments
Richelieu Wing
Sully Wing
The Seated Scribe
Consecration of the Emperor Napoleon I
Denon Wing
The Raft of the Medusa
Mona Lisa
Winged Victory of Samothrace
Crown of Louis XV
First Floor
Cour Marly
Cour Puget
Code of Hammurabi
Cour Khorsabad
Two-Headed-Bull Column
Richelieu Wing
Cour Carrée
Grande Pyramide
Sully Wing
Statue of Pharaoh II
The Dying Slave
Denon Wing
Michelangelo Gallery
Cour Visconti
Venus de Milo
Ground Floor

The Louvre

A HALF-DAY TOUR

Successfully visiting the Louvre is a fine art. Its complex labyrinth of galleries and staircases spiralling three wings and four floors renders discovery a snakes-and-ladders experience. Initiate yourself with this three-hour itinerary – a playful mix of Mona Lisa obvious and up-to-the-minute unexpected.

Arriving by the stunning main entrance, pick up colour-coded floor plans at the lower-ground-floor **information desk** ❶ beneath IM Pei's glass pyramid, ride the escalator up to the Sully Wing and swap passport for multimedia guide (there are limited descriptions in the galleries) at the wing entrance.

The Louvre is as much about spectacular architecture as masterly art. To appreciate this zip up and down Sully's Escalier Henri II to admire **Venus de Milo** ❷, then up parallel Escalier Henri IV to the palatial displays in **Cour Khorsabad** ❸. Cross room 1 to find the escalator up to the 1st floor and staircase-as-art **L'Esprit d'Escalier** ❹. Next traverse 25 consecutive galleries (thank you, floor plan!) to flip conventional contemplation on its head with Cy Twombly's **The Ceiling** ❺, and the hypnotic **Winged Victory of Samothrace sculpture** ❻ – just two rooms away – which brazenly insists on being admired from all angles. End with the impossibly famous **The Raft of Medusa** ❼, **Mona Lisa** ❽ and **Virgin & Child** ❾.

TOP TIPS

» **Floor Plans** Don't even consider entering the Louvre's maze of galleries without a Plan/Information Louvre brochure, free from the information desk in the Hall Napoléon

» **Crowd dodgers** The Denon Wing is always packed; visit on late nights Wednesday or Friday or trade Denon in for the notably quieter Richelieu Wing

» **2nd floor** Not for first-timers: save its more specialist works for subsequent visits

MISSION MONA LISA

If you just want to venerate the Louvre's most famous lady, use the Porte des Lions entrance (closed Tuesday and Friday), from where it's a five-minute walk. Go up one flight of stairs and through rooms 26, 14 and 13 to the Grande Galerie and adjoining room 6.

L'Esprit d'Escalier
Escalier Lefuel, Richelieu
Discover the 'Spirit of the Staircase' through François Morellet's contemporary stained glass, which casts new light on old stone. DETOUR» Napoleon III's gorgeous gilt apartments.

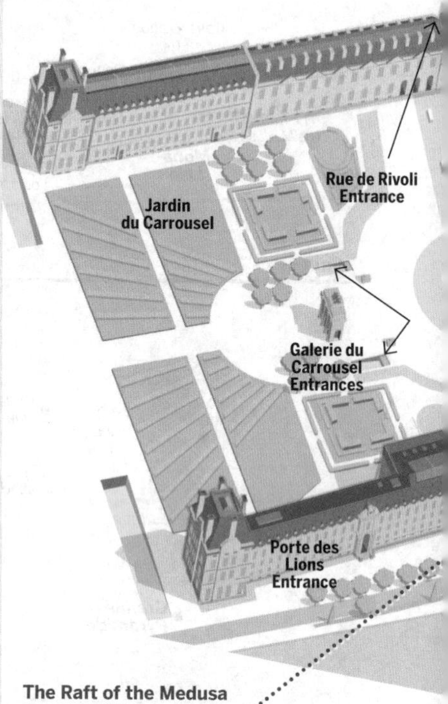

The Raft of the Medusa
Room 77, 1st Floor, Denon
Decipher the politics behind French romanticism in Théodore Géricault's *Raft of the Medusa.*

DEA/G.DAGLI ORTI/GETTY IMAGES ©

FRANCOIS GUILLOT/STAFF/GETTY IMAGES ©

The Ceiling

Room 32, 1st Floor, Sully

Admire the blue shock of Cy Twombly's 400-sq-metre contemporary ceiling fresco – the Louvre's latest, daring commission. **DETOUR»** *The Braque Ceiling*, room 33.

Cour Khorsabad

Ground Floor, Richelieu

Time travel with a pair of winged human-headed bulls to view some of the world's oldest Mesopotamian art. **DETOUR»** Night-lit statues in Cour Puget.

JOHN SONES SINGING BOWL MEDIA/ GETTY IMAGES ©

Venus de Milo

Room 16, Ground Floor, Sully

No one knows who sculpted this seductively realistic goddess from Greek antiquity. Naked to the hips, she is a Hellenistic masterpiece.

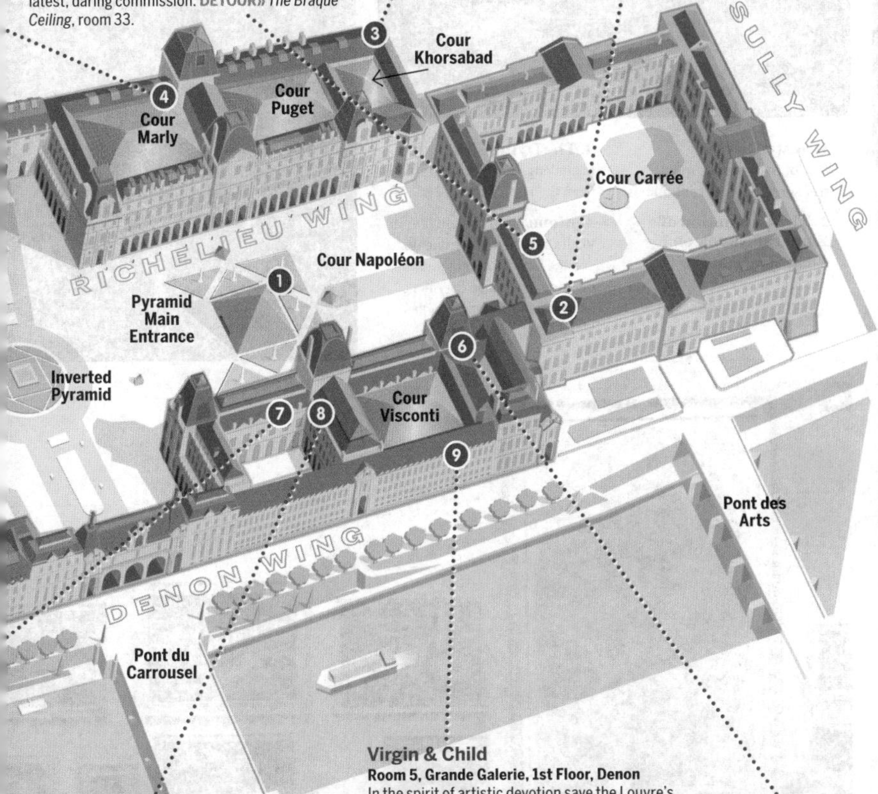

Virgin & Child

Room 5, Grande Galerie, 1st Floor, Denon

In the spirit of artistic devotion save the Louvre's most famous gallery for last: a feast of Virgin-and-child paintings by Raphael, Domenico Ghirlandaio, Giovanni Bellini and Francesco Botticini.

MITCH DIAMOND/GETTY IMAGES ©

Mona Lisa

Room 6, 1st Floor, Denon

No smile is as enigmatic or bewitching as hers. Da Vinci's diminutive *La Joconde* hangs opposite the largest painting in the Louvre – sumptuous, fellow Italian Renaissance artwork *The Wedding at Cana*.

Winged Victory of Samothrace

Escalier Daru, 1st Floor, Sully

Draw breath at the aggressive dynamism of this headless, handless Hellenistic goddess. **DETOUR»** The razzle-dazzle of the Apollo Gallery's crown jewels.

1. Seated Scribe
One of the Louvre's most treasured Egyptian antiquities.

2. The Coronation of Emperor Napoleon I
A magnificent painting by Jacques-Louis David depicting the crowning of Napoléon.

3. The Dying Slave
Michelangelo's marble statue from the Renaissance.

4. Mona Lisa
Visitors to the Louvre line up to see the world's most famous painting: Leonardo da Vinci's *La Joconde* (better known as *Mona Lisa*).

FINE ART IMAGES / GETTY IMAGES ©

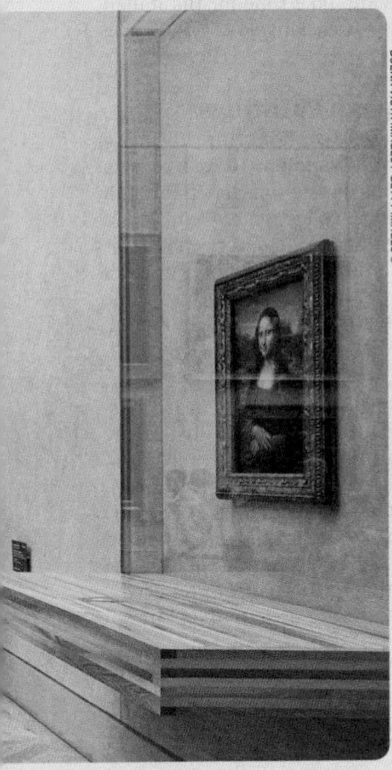

BUENA VISTA IMAGES / GETTY IMAGES ©

CORBIS ©

THE PYRAMID: INSIDE & OUT

Almost as stunning as the masterpieces inside is the 21m-high glass pyramid designed by Chinese-born American architect IM Pei that bedecks the main entrance to the Louvre in a dazzling crown. Beneath Pei's Grande Pyramide is the **Hall Napoléon**, the main entrance area, comprising an information booth, temporary exhibition hall, bookshop, souvenir store, cafe and auditoriums. To revel in another Pei pyramid of equally dramatic dimensions, head towards the **Carrousel du Louvre** (Map p388; www.carrouseldu-louvre.com; 99 rue de Rivoli; ⏲8am-11pm, shops 10am-8pm; ; MPalais Royal–Musée du Louvre), a busy shopping mall that loops underground from the Grande Pyramide to the Arc de Triomphe du Carrousel (p121) – its centrepiece is Pei's **Pyramide Inversée** (inverted glass pyramid).

French kings wore their crowns only once – at their coronation. Lined with embroidered satin and topped with openwork arches and a fleur-de-lis, Louis XV's 1722-crafted crown (Room 66, 1st floor, Denon) was originally adorned with pearls, sapphires, rubies, topazes, emeralds and diamonds.

Ancient Greek sculptures at the Louvre

with the crowds around the *Mona Lisa*. But you'll find plenty else to contemplate, from Botticelli's graceful frescoes (Room 1) to the superbly detailed *Wedding Feast at Cana* (Room 6). On the ground floor of the Denon Wing, take time for the Italian sculptures, including Michelangelo's *The Dying Slave* and Canova's *Psyche and Cupid* (Room 4).

Northern European Paintings

The 2nd floor of the Richelieu Wing, directly above the gilt and crystal of the **Napoleon III Apartments** (1st floor), allows for a quieter meander through the Louvre's inspirational collection of Flemish and Dutch paintings spearheaded by works by Peter Paul Rubens and Pieter Bruegel the Elder. Vermeer's *The Lacemaker* can be found in Room 38, while Room 31 is devoted chiefly to works by Rembrandt.

Trails & Tours

Self-guided thematic trails range from Louvre masterpieces and the art of eating to family-friendly topics. Download trail brochures in advance from the website. Another good option is to rent a **Nintendo 3DS multimedia guide** (adult/child €5/3; ID required). More formal, English-language **guided tours** (☎01 40 20 51 77; ⏲11am & 2pm except 1st Sun of month) depart from the Hall Napoléon. Reserve a spot up to 14 days in advance or sign up on arrival at the museum.

BRUNO DE HOGUES / GETTY IMAGES ©

TOP SIGHT
CENTRE POMPIDOU

The Pompidou Centre has amazed and delighted visitors ever since it opened in 1977, not just for its outstanding collection of modern art but also for its radical architectural statement, designed by architects Renzo Piano and Richard Rogers. The dynamic and vibrant arts centre delights and enthralls with its irresistible cocktail of galleries and exhibitions, hands-on workshops, dance performances, bookshop, design boutique, cinemas and other entertainment venues.

Musée National d'Art Moderne

Europe's largest collection of modern art fills the bright and airy, well-lit galleries of the National Museum of Modern Art, covering two complete floors of the Pompidou. For art lovers, this is one of the jewels of Paris. On a par with the permanent collection are the two **temporary exhibition halls** (on the ground floor/basement and the top floor), which showcase some memorable blockbuster exhibits. Also of note is the fabulous **children's gallery** on the 1st floor.

The permanent collection changes every two years, but the basic layout generally stays the same. The 5th floor showcases artists active between 1905 and 1970 (give or take a decade); the 4th floor focuses on more contemporary creations, roughly from the 1980s onward.

The most recent 5th-floor layout was a refreshing change from the old Eurocentric model. The dynamic presentation mixed up works by Picasso, Matisse, Chagall and Kandinsky with lesser-known contemporaries from as far afield as Brazil and China, as well as more famous cross-Atlantic names such as Rivera, Kahlo, Warhol, Pollock and Rothko.

DON'T MISS

- The Musée National d'Art Moderne
- Cutting-edge temporary exhibitions
- The 6th floor and its sweeping panorama of Paris

PRACTICALITIES

- Map p392
- 01 44 78 12 33
- www.centrepompidou.fr
- place Georges Pompidou, 4e
- museum, exhibitions & panorama adult/child €13/free
- 11am-9pm Wed-Mon
- Rambuteau

LUNCH OPTIONS

Georges' outdoor terrace on the 6th floor is a fabulous spot for a drink with a view, though it's not so great for dining. The inexpensive mezzanine cafe on the 1st floor is also unmemorable. Walk instead to Café La Fusée (p131) or Dame Tartine (p128) for an affordable lunch or well-deserved postmuseum aperitif.

The full-monty Pompidou experience is as much about hanging out in the busy streets and squares around it, packed with souvenir shops and people, as absorbing the centre's contents. West of the Centre Pompidou, fun-packed place Georges Pompidou and its nearby pedestrian streets attract bags of buskers, musicians, jugglers and mime artists. Don't miss place Igor Stravinsky with its fanciful mechanical fountains of skeletons, hearts, treble clefs and a big pair of ruby-red lips by Jean Tinguely and Niki de St-Phalle.

One floor down on the 4th, you'll find monumental paintings, installation pieces, sculpture and video take centre stage. The focus of the latest exhibition here is on art, architecture and design from the 1980s onward. The 4th floor also has an **Espace des Collections Nouveaux Médias et Film**, where visitors can discover 40 years of image and sound experimentation.

Architecture & Views

Former French President Georges Pompidou wanted an ultracontemporary artistic hub and he got it: competition-winning architects Renzo Piano and Richard Rogers designed the building inside out, with utilitarian features like plumbing, pipes, air vents and electrical cables forming part of the external facade. The building was completed in 1977.

Viewed from a distance (such as from Sacré-Cœur), the Centre Pompidou's primary-coloured, boxlike form amid a sea of muted grey Parisian rooftops makes it look like a child's Meccano set abandoned on someone's elegant living-room rug. Although the Centre Pompidou is just six storeys high, the city's low-rise cityscape means stupendous views extend from its roof (reached by external escalators enclosed in tubes). Rooftop prices is included in museum and exhibition admission – or buy a **panorama ticket** (admission €3; ⌚11am-10pm Wed-Mon) just for the roof.

Atelier Brancusi

West of the Centre Pompidou main building, this reconstruction of the **studio** (Map p392; 55 rue Rambuteau, 4e; ⌚2-6pm Wed-Mon; Ⓜ Rambuteau) FREE of Romanian-born sculptor Constantin Brancusi – known for works such as *The Kiss* and *Bird in Space* – contains over 100 sculptures in stone and wood. You'll also find drawings, pedestals and photographic plates from his original Paris studio.

Tours & Guides

Guided tours are only in French (the information desk in the central hall on the ground floor has details), but the gap is easily filled by the excellent **multimedia guide** (adult/under 13yr €5/3), which explains 62 works of art in the Musée National d'Art Moderne in detail on a 1½-hour trail. There is also a guide for each temporary exhibit; another covering the unique architecture of the Centre Pompidou; and one created with kids (ages eight to 12) in mind.

JULIAN ELLIOTT / GETTY IMAGES ©

TOP SIGHT
JARDIN DES TUILERIES

Filled with fountains, classical sculptures and magnificent panoramas every way you turn, this quintessentially Parisian park was laid out by André Le Nôtre, architect of the gardens at Versailles, in 1664.

The 16th-century Palais des Tuileries (home to Napoléon, among others) stood at the garden's western end until 1871, when it was razed during the upheaval of the Paris Commune. All that remains of the palace today are the former Orangerie and Jeu de Paume. If you're here in July or August with kids, don't miss the **Fête des Tuileries funfair**.

Musée de l'Orangerie

Set in a 19th-century orangery built to shelter the garden's orange trees in winter, the **Musée de l'Orangerie** (www.musee-orangerie.fr; adult/child €9/6.50; ⏲9am-6pm Wed-Mon) is a treat. The two oval rooms of the purpose-built top floor are the show-stealer; here you'll find eight of Monet's enormous, ethereal *Water Lilies* canvases bathed in natural light.

Downstairs is the private collection of art dealer Paul Guillaume (1891–1934), with works by all the big names of early modern art: Cézanne, Matisse, Picasso, Renoir, Modigliani, Soutine and Utrillo. Don't miss the haunting *Portrait of Lady Chanel* by Marie Laurencin or the disquieting *La Noce* by Rousseau.

There's always a queue, so arrive early. A combination ticket covering admission to the Musée d'Orsay costs €16.

Jeu de Paume

This wonderfully airy **gallery** (www.jeudepaume.org; adult/child €8.50/free; ⏲11am-9pm Tue, to 7pm Wed-Sun) is set in the Palais des Tuileries' erstwhile *jeu de paume* (real, or royal, tennis court). It stages innovative photography exhibitions.

DON'T MISS

- Monet's *Water Lilies*
- Paul Guillaume collection
- Picnic or stroll in the park

PRACTICALITIES

- Map p388
- gardens admission free
- ⏲7am-11pm Jun-Aug, shorter hours rest of year
- Ⓜ Tuileries or Concorde

ESCUDERO PATRICK / GETTY IMAGES ©

TOP SIGHT
ÉGLISE ST-EUSTACHE

Snuggling up to the city's old marketplace, now the soulless Forum des Halles, is one of the most beautiful churches in Paris. Majestic, architecturally magnificent and musically outstanding, St-Eustache has made spirits soar for centuries.

Tales of spiritual pomp and circumstance are plentiful. Richelieu and Molière were baptised here (Molière also got married here), Louis XIV celebrated his first Holy Communion here and Colbert was buried here. Mozart chose St-Eustache for the funeral mass of his mother and in 1855 Berlioz' *Te Deum* premiered here – the church's acoustics are extraordinary.

Art & Architecture

Built between 1532 and 1637, the church is primarily Gothic, although a neoclassical facade was added on the western side in the mid-18th century. Inside, contemplate the stained glass and paintings, many given by guilds and merchants from the nearby Les Halles. Highlights include a work by Rubens and the colourful bas-relief of Parisian market porters (1969) by British sculptor Raymond Mason in the side chapels. Outside the church is a **gigantic sculpture** of a head and hand entitled *L'Écoute* (Listen; 1986) by Henri de Miller.

The Organ

France's largest organ, above the church's western entrance, has 101 stops and 8000 pipes dating from 1854. **Organ recitals** at 5.30pm on Sunday are a must for music lovers, as is June's **Festival des 36 Heures de St-Eustache** – 36 hours of nonstop music embracing a symphony of genres, world music, choral and jazz included.

DON'T MISS

- *L'Écoute* sculpture
- Free Sunday afternoon organ recitals
- Artwork in the side chapels

PRACTICALITIES

- Map p392
- www.st-eustache.org
- 2 impasse St-Eustache, 1er
- 9.30am-7pm Mon-Fri, 9am-7pm Sat & Sun
- M Les Halles

SIGHTS

History and culture meet head on along the banks of the Seine in the 1er *arrondissement*, home to some of the most important sights for visitors to Paris, including the world-renowned Louvre and Centre Pompidou. It was in this same neighbourhood that Louis VI created *halles* (markets) in 1137 for the merchants who converged on the city centre to sell their wares, and for over 800 years they were, in the words of Émile Zola, the 'belly of Paris'. The wholesalers were moved lox, stock and cabbage out to the suburbs in 1971.

MUSÉE DU LOUVRE — MUSEUM

See p109.

CENTRE POMPIDOU — MUSEUM

See p117.

JARDIN DES TUILERIES — GARDEN

See p119.

ÉGLISE ST-EUSTACHE — CHURCH

See p120.

LES ARTS DÉCORATIFS — ART MUSEUM

Map p388 (www.lesartsdecoratifs.fr; 107 rue de Rivoli, 1er; aduld/child €11/free; ⏲11am-6pm Tue-Sun, to 9pm Thu; ⓂPalais Royal–Musée du Louvre) A trio of privately administered collections – Applied Arts, Advertising and Fashion & Textiles – sit in the Rohan Wing of the vast Palais du Louvre. They are collectively known as the Decorative Arts; admission includes entry to all three. For an extra €2, you can scoop up a combo ticket that also includes the Musée Nissim de Camondo (p141) in the 8e.

The **Arts Décoratifs** (Applied Arts) section takes up the majority of the space and displays furniture, jewellery and such objets d'art as ceramics and glassware from the Middle Ages and the Renaissance through the art-nouveau and art-deco periods to modern times. Its collections span from Europe to East Asia.

On the other side of the building is the smaller **Musée de la Publicité** (Advertising Museum), which has some 100,000 posters in its collection dating as far back as the 13th century and innumerable promotional materials. Most of the space is given over to special exhibitions.

Haute couture (high fashion) creations by the likes of Chanel and Jean-Paul Gaultier can be ogled in the **Musée de la Mode et du Textile** (Museum of Fashion & Textiles), home to some 16,000 costumes from the 16th century to the present day. Items are only on display during regularly scheduled themed exhibitions.

ÉGLISE ST-GERMAIN L'AUXERROIS — CHURCH

Map p392 (www.saintgermainauxerrois.cef.fr; 2 place du Louvre, 1er; ⏲8am-7pm Mon-Sat, 9am-8pm Sun; ⓂLouvre Rivoli or Pont Neuf) FREE Built between the 13th and 16th centuries in a mixture of Gothic and Renaissance styles and with similar dimensions and ground plans to those of Notre Dame, this once royal parish church stands on a site at the eastern end of the Louvre that has been used for Christian worship since about AD 500.

After being mutilated in the 18th century by clergy intent on 'modernisation' and damaged during the Revolution, the church was restored by the Gothic Revivalist architect Eugène Viollet-le-Duc in the mid-19th century. Peek inside at its fine Renaissance stained glass.

ARC DE TRIOMPHE DU CARROUSEL — MONUMENT

Map p388 (place du Carrousel, 1er; ⓂPalais Royal–Musée du Louvre) This triumphal arch, erected by Napoléon to celebrate his battlefield successes of 1805, sits with aplomb in the **Jardin du Carrousel**, the gardens immediately next to the Louvre. The eastern counterpoint to the other Arc de Triomphe (the more famous one), it is one of several monuments that comprise the *axe historique* (historical axis), which terminates with the statue of Louis XIV next to the Pyramide du Louvre.

PLACE VENDÔME — SQUARE

Map p388 (ⓂTuileries or Opéra) Octagonal place Vendôme and the arcaded and colonnaded buildings around it were constructed between 1687 and 1721. In March 1796 Napoléon married Josephine, Viscountess Beauharnais, in the building at No 3. Today the buildings surrounding the square house the posh Hôtel Ritz Paris and some of the city's most fashionable boutiques.

The 43.5m-tall **Colonne Vendôme** (Vendôme Column; Map p388) in the centre of the square consists of a stone core wrapped in a 160m-long bronze spiral made from

ART IN THE MAKING: 59 RUE DE RIVOLI

In such a classical part of Paris crammed with elegant historic architecture, **59 Rivoli** (Map p392; http://59rivoli-eng.org; 59 rue de Rivoli, 1er; ⏲1-8pm; Ⓜ Louvre-Rivoli) FREE is quite the bohemian breath of fresh air. Take time out to watch artists at work in the 30 *ateliers* (studios) strung on six floors of the long-abandoned bank building, now a legalised squat where some of Paris' most creative talent works (but doesn't live). The ground-floor gallery hosts a new exhibition every fortnight, and free gigs, concerts and shows pack the place out most weekends. Look for the sculpted façade festooned with catchy drapes, banners and unconventional recycled piping above the shop fronts.

hundreds of Austrian and Russian cannons captured by Napoléon at the Battle of Austerlitz in 1805. The statue on top depicts Napoléon in classical Roman dress.

JARDIN DU PALAIS ROYAL GARDEN

Map p388 (2 place Colette, 1er; ⏲7am-10.15pm Apr & May, to 11pm Jun-Aug, shorter hours rest of year; Ⓜ Palais Royal–Musée du Louvre) FREE The Jardin du Palais Royal is a perfect spot to sit, contemplate and picnic between boxed hedges or shop in the trio of arcades that frame the garden so beautifully: the Galerie de Valois (east), Galerie de Montpensier (west) and Galerie Beaujolais. However, it's the southern end of the complex, polka-dotted with sculptor Daniel Buren's 260 black-and-white striped columns, that has become the garden's signature feature.

This elegant urban space is fronted by the neoclassical **Palais Royal** (closed to the public), constructed in 1633 by Cardinal Richelieu but mostly dating to the late 18th century. Louis XIV hung out here in the 1640s; today it is home to the **Conseil d'État** (State Council; Map p388#).

The **Galerie de Valois** is the most upmarket arcade with designer boutiques like Stella McCartney, Pierre Hardy, Didier Ludot (p132) and coat-of-arms engraver Guillaumot, at work at Nos 151 to 154 since 1785. Across the garden, in the **Galerie de Montpensier**, the Revolution broke out in the Café du Foy on a warm mid-July day just three years after the galleries opened. The third arcade, tiny **Galerie Beaujolais**, is crossed by **Passage du Perron**, a passageway above which the writer Colette (1873–1954) lived out the last dozen years of her life.

FORUM DES HALLES SHOPPING MALL

Map p392 (www.forumdeshalles.com; 1 rue Pierre Lescot, 1er; ⏲shops 10am-8pm Mon-Sat; Ⓜ Châtelet–Les Halles) Paris' main wholesale food market stood here for nearly 800 years before being replaced by this underground shopping mall in 1971. Four floors of stores extend down to the city's busiest metro hub, while a massive renovation project – with an enormous golden-hued translucent canopy as centrepiece – is under way, with a target completion date of 2016.

Spilling out from the curvilinear, leaf-like rooftop will be new gardens designed by landscaper David Mangin, with pétanque and chess tables, a central patio and pedestrian walkways. The project will also open up the shopping centre, allowing for more natural light.

Renovation is being undertaken in stages; hence business should continue more or less as usual, with minimal disruption. Follow the project at www.parisleshalles.fr or pop into the information centre on **place Jean du Bellay**, a pretty square pierced by the Fontaine des Innocents (1549). The multi-tiered Renaissance fountain is named after the Cimetière des Innocents, a cemetery formerly on this site from which two million skeletons were disinterred after the Revolution and transferred to the Catacombes.

MUSÉE EN HERBE ART MUSEUM

Map p392 (☎01 40 67 97 66; www.musee-en-herbe.com; 21 rue Hérold, 1er; admission €6; ⏲10am-7pm Fri-Wed, to 9pm Thu; 👪; Ⓜ Les Halles) One of the city's great backstreet secrets, this children's museum is a surprise gem for art lovers of every age, not just kids. Its permanent exhibition changes every March and focuses on the work of one artist or theme through a series of interactive displays.

Captions are in English as well as French, children get a *jeu de piste* (activity sheet) to guide and entertain, and additional workshops and guided visits for kids and adults – think hands-on art workshops, afternoon tea, early-evening aperitifs and so on (€6 to €10, reserve in advance) – add to the playful experience.

BOURSE DE COMMERCE MONUMENT

Map p392 (2 rue de Viarmes, 1er; ⌚9am-6pm Mon-Fri; Ⓜ Les Halles) FREE At one time the city's grain market, the circular Trade Exchange was capped with a copper dome in 1811. The murals running along internal walls below the galleries were painted by five different artists in 1889 and restored in 1998. They represent French trade and industry through the ages.

TOUR JEAN SANS PEUR TOWER

Map p392 (Tower of John the Fearless; www.tourjeansanspeur.com; 20 rue Étienne Marcel, 2e; adult/7-18yr €5/3; ⌚1.30-6pm Wed-Sun Apr-early Nov, 1.30-6pm Wed, Sat & Sun early Nov-Mar; Ⓜ Étienne Marcel) This 29m-high Gothic tower was built during the Hundred Years' War by the Duke of Bourgogne so that he could take refuge from his enemies – such as the supporters of the Duke of Orléans, whom he had assassinated. Part of a splendid mansion in the early 15th century, it is one of the few examples of feudal military architecture extant in Paris. Climb 140 steps up the spiral staircase to the top turret (no views).

TOUR ST-JACQUES TOWER

Map p392 (39 rue de Rivoli, 4e; adult €6; Ⓜ Châtelet) Just north of place du Châtelet, the Flamboyant Gothic, 54m-high St James Tower is all that remains of the Église St-Jacques la Boucherie, built by the powerful butchers guild in 1523 as a starting point for pilgrims setting out for the shrine of St James at Santiago de Compostela in Spain. Recently restored, it should open to the public in the near future, allowing visitors to climb 300 stairs up to an expansive panorama.

EATING

Louvre

CLAUS BREAKFAST €

Map p392 (☎01 42 33 55 10; www.clausparis.com; 14 rue Jean-Jacques Rousseau, 1er; breakfasts €13-18, plats du jour €13; ⌚8am-5pm Mon-Fri, 9.30am-5pm Sat & Sun; Ⓜ Étienne Marcel) Dubbed the '*haute-couture* breakfast specialist' in Parisian foodie circles, this inspired *épicerie du petit-dej* (breakfast grocery shop) has everything you could possibly desire for the ultimate gourmet breakfast and brunch – organic mueslis and cereals, fresh juices, jams, honey and so on.

Breakfast or brunch on site, shop at Claus to create your own or ask for a luxury breakfast hamper to be delivered to your door. Its lunchtime salads, soups and tarts are equally tasty.

LE BOUGAINVILLE TRADITIONAL FRENCH €

Map p388 (5 Rue de la Banque, 2e; 2-course menus €17.50; ⌚to midnight Tue-Sat; Ⓜ Bourse) With floor-to-ceiling windows framing the faded grandeur of the Galerie Vivienne, the simple Bougainville overflows with regulars at lunchtime. The hearty French cooking – creamy *gratin dauphinois* (scalloped potatoes with cream cheese) roasted guinea-fowl – isn't the most sophisticated you'll ever taste, but you won't leave hungry.

CRÊPE DENTELLE CRÊPERIE €

Map p392 (☎01 40 41 04 23; 10 rue Léopold Bellan, 2e; crêpes €4.90-14.60, lunch menus €11.20; ⌚noon-3pm & 7.30-11pm Mon-Fri; 👪; Ⓜ Sentier) Named after a style of crêpe that's as delicate as fine lace (*dentelle*), this is probably not the place to go if you're starving. However, it is an excellent choice for a light and inexpensive lunch, and is certainly the best bet for crêpes near the Louvre. Arrive by 12.15pm or you may not get a seat.

KUNITORAYA 1 JAPANESE €

Map p388 (www.kunitoraya.com; 1 rue Villedo, 1er; noodles €10-22; ⌚noon-2.30pm & 7-10.30pm Thu-Tue; Ⓜ Pyramides) Some of Paris' best *udon* (thick Japanese noodles) is what this buzzing brick-walled address is all about. Grab a seat at one of the communal tables and watch the young chefs strut their stuff over steaming bowls laced with battered prawns, sweet duck and curry. Arrive well before 1pm (or 8pm) or risk leaving disappointed. Cash only, no reservations and no sign.

SANUKIYA JAPANESE €

Map p388 (9 rue d'Argenteuil, 1er; noodles €9-18; ⌚11.30am-10.30pm; Ⓜ Pyramides or Palais Royal–Musée du Louvre) Don't wear your favourite shirt to this popular Japanese eatery as you'll undoubtedly emerge with a few stains after slurping up a bowl of freshly made *udon* noodles. Dishes come in four styles: classic (served in broth), *bukkake* (with a hot broth added by the diner), *hiyashi* (with a cold broth added by the diner) and *zaru* (cold noodles with dipping sauce). *Itadakimasu!*

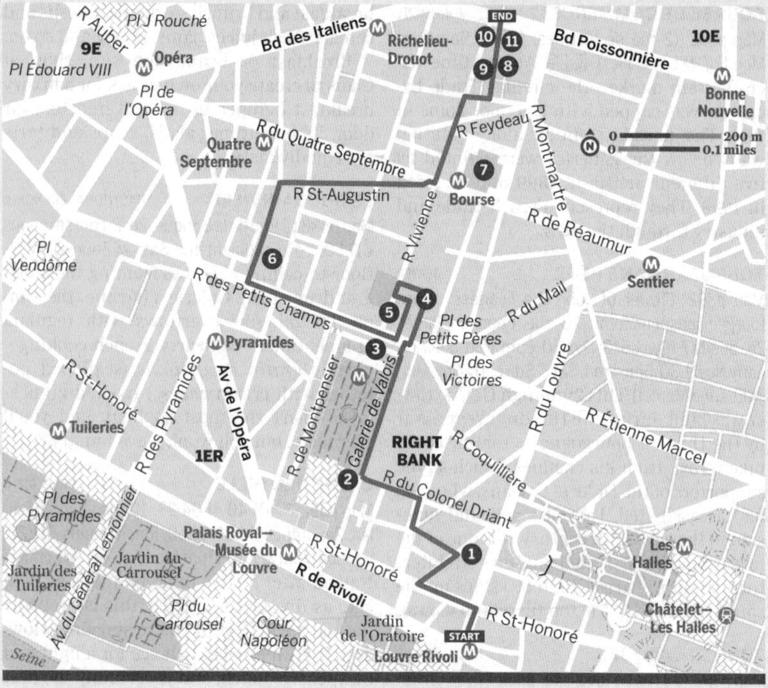

Neighbourhood Walk
Stepping Back into 19th-Century Paris

START METRO LOUVRE RIVOLI
END METRO LE PELETIER
LENGTH 3KM; TWO HOURS

The Right Bank's sumptuously decorated *passages couverts* (covered arcades) offer a walk through early-19th-century Paris. Avoid Sundays.

From the metro, cross rue de Rivoli, walk north along rue du Louvre, turn left onto rue St-Honoré then right onto rue Jean-Jacques Rousseau. At No 19 enter **1 Galerie Véro Dodat** (1823), fitted with skylights, ceiling murals, Corinthian columns and gas globe lamps (now electric). Bijou art galleries, boutiques and a music shop fill its quaint shop fronts.

The gallery's western exit leads to rue du Bouloi and rue Croix des Petits Champs. Head north to the corner of rue du Colonel Driant, turn left and walk to rue de Valois. At No 5 is an entrance to **2 Jardin du Palais Royal** (p122) and its arcades. Cut through **3 Passage des Deux Pavillons** and up the stairs to rue des Petits Champs. Turn right and duck into **4 Galerie Vivienne** at No 4. Decorated in 1826 with bas-reliefs of snakes (signifying prudence), scales (justice), anchors (hope), lutes (harmony) and cockerels (vigilance), this is Paris' poshest *passage*, with an old-fashioned bookshop much loved by Colette.

Exiting at 6 rue Vivienne, turn left and explore **5 Galerie Colbert** at No 2. Built in 1826 and now part of Paris University, the *passage* served as a car workshop-garage as recently as the 1980s. Follow the *passage* to its exit at 6 rue des Petits Champs, then head west for a few blocks and enter tatty **6 Passage Choiseul** (1824); Paul Verlaine (1844–96) drank absinthe here and Céline (1894–1961) grew up in his mother's lace shop at No 62.

Leave at 23 rue St-Augustin, and stroll east to rue du Quatre Septembre – the building across the square is the **7 Bourse de Commerce** (p123). Turn left up rue Vivienne, then right along rue St-Marc to **8 Passage des Panoramas** (p133). Lunch at **9 Coinstot Vino** (p125), **10 Racines** (p125) or **11 Noglu** (p125).

STUBE GERMAN €

Map p388 (www.lestube.fr; 31 rue de Richelieu, 1er; meals €11.50-16.50; ⏰10am-3.30pm Mon, to 10pm Tue-Sat; 👪; Ⓜ Pyramides) Specialising in *currywursts* (basically a chopped up hotdog covered in a curry sauce; €5), Stube does brisk business throughout the day, with lines out the door for beef sausages, savoury quiches, sauerkraut and a mouth-watering selection of freshly baked pies. Seating can be hard to find, but park benches in the Palais Royal are just across the street. Beck's on tap.

FRENCHIE TO GO FAST FOOD €

Map p392 (www.frenchietogo.com; 9 rue du Nil, 2e; sandwiches €8-14; ⏰8.30am-4.30pm Mon-Fri, 9.30am-5.30pm Sat & Sun; 📶; Ⓜ Sentier) Despite the drawbacks – limited seating, eye-poppingly expensive doughnuts – the fast-food outpost of the burgeoning Frenchie (p127) empire is a wildly popular destination. Bilingual staff transform choice ingredients (eg cuts of meat from the Ginger Pig in Yorkshire) into American classics like pulled-pork and pastrami sandwiches, accompanied by cornets of fries, coleslaw and pickled veggies.

RACINES WINE BAR €€

Map p388 (☎01 40 13 06 41; 8 Passage des Panoramas, 2e; mains €23-30; ⏰noon-2.30pm & 7.30-10.30pm Mon-Fri; Ⓜ Grands Boulevards or Richelieu-Drouot) Snug inside a former 19th-century *marchand de vin* (wine merchant's; look up to admire the lovely old gold lettering above the door), Racines (meaning 'Roots') is an address that shouts Paris at every turn. Shelves of wine bottles curtain the windows, the old patterned floor smacks of feasting and merriment, and the menu chalked on the blackboard is straightforward.

It's first and foremost a wine bar, though, notable for its excellent choice of organic and natural *vins*.

KUNITORAYA 2 JAPANESE €€

Map p388 (☎01 47 03 07 74; www.kunitoraya.com; 5 rue Villedo, 1er; lunch €21-46, dinner €70; ⏰noon-2.30pm & 7.30-10.30pm Tue-Sun; Ⓜ Pyramides) The fancy-pants version of Kunitoraya 1 (p123). The interior here conjures up belle époque France – antique mouldings and mirrors – providing a funky contrast to the wonderfully simple Japanese fare. At lunch, get your *udon* noodles served with *onigiri* (stuffed rice squares), sushi or as part of a *bento* (lunchbox).

Dinner is a pricier experience, with a single prix-fixe tasting menu featuring seven dishes chosen by the chef. Live gypsy jazz on Sunday afternoon.

JUVENILES WINE BAR €€

Map p388 (☎01 42 97 46 49; 47 rue de Richelieu, 1er; mains €17-18, lunch menus €16.50; ⏰7.30-10.30pm Mon, noon-2.30pm & 7.30-10.30pm Tue-Sat; Ⓜ Pyramides) Likely the only place in Paris where you'll find haggis 2.0 on the menu, this low-key wine bar is a hallowed retreat by the Palais Royal. Don't be deterred if sheep innards aren't your thing, though, as host Margaux and chef Romain offer a variety of other, more accessible dishes such as butternut-squash gnocchi or *magret de canard* (duck breast) and sweet potatoes. Unusual and varied wine list.

COINSTOT VINO TRADITIONAL FRENCH €€

Map p388 (☎01 44 82 08 54; http://coinstot-vino.com; 26bis Passage des Panoramas, 2e; mains €15-25, lunch menus €16; ⏰8.30am-midnight Mon-Fri, 6pm-midnight Sat; Ⓜ Richelieu-Drouot or Grands Boulevards) A simple bistro in the already crowded Passage des Panoramas, Coinstot Vino serves honest French fare (think veal ragout, and sea-urchin, tarama salata) and tasty pizzas, though it's the great selection of wines and friendly service that keep the regulars coming back to discuss life, love and the crippling lack of affordable real estate deep into the night.

NOGLU MODERN FRENCH €€

Map p388 (☎01 40 26 41 24; www.noglu.fr; 16 Passage des Panoramas, 2e; mains €16-20, menus €24; ⏰noon-2.30pm Mon-Sat, 7.30-10.30pm Tue-Sat; 🖉; Ⓜ Richelieu-Drouot or Grands Boulevards) Gluten-free kitchens are hard to find in France, but that's only one of the reasons that Noglu is such a jewel – this chic address builds on French tradition (*bœuf bourguignon*) while simultaneously drawing on newer culinary trends from across the Atlantic to create some devilishly good pastries, vegetarian plates and superb pizzas and salads. Don't skip the chocolate-passion tart. Reserve.

LA MAUVAISE RÉPUTATION MODERN FRENCH €€

Map p392 (☎01 42 36 92 44; www.lamauvaisereputation.fr; 28 rue Léopold-Bellan, 2e; 2-/3-course menus lunch €18/22, dinner €28/35;

LOCAL KNOWLEDGE

RUE MONTORGUEIL

A splinter of the historic Les Halles, rue Montorgueil was once the oyster market and the final stop for seafood merchants hailing from the coast. Immortalised by Balzac in *La Comédie humaine*, this compelling strip still draws Parisians to eat and shop – it's lined with *fromageries* (cheese shops), cafes, and street stalls selling fruit, veg and other foodstuffs.

➡ **Aux Tonneaux des Halles** (Map p392; 28 Rue Montorgueil, 1er; ⌚noon-11pm Mon-Sat; Ⓜ Les Halles) Originally a hotel, Aux Tonneaux only became a cafe in the 1920s – a relatively recent addition compared to some of the other addresses here. It boasts great wines and a fine outdoor terrace, as well as classic bistro fare such as *steak-frites*.

➡ **Charles Chocolatier** (Map p392; 15 Rue Montorgueil, 1er; ⌚10am-7.45pm Tue-Sat; Ⓜ Les Halles) Delectable artisan chocolates made with 100% cocoa butter (no milk, butter or cream). If the weather is chilly, pop in for a rich cup of hot chocolate to go.

➡ **Caldo Freddo** (Map p392; 34 Rue Montorgueil, 1er; pizza slices €4.90; ⌚noon-11pm; 👪; Ⓜ Les Halles) Pizzas by the pie and the slice (with a truffle topping!) along with *arancini* (fried rice balls), antipasti and panini.

➡ **Stohrer** (Map p392; www.stohrer.fr; 51 rue Montorgueil, 2e; ⌚7.30am-8.30pm; Ⓜ Les Halles) This bakery was opened in 1730 by the Polish pastry chef of queen consort Marie Leczinska (wife of Louis XV). Specialities include its very own *baba au rhum* (sponge cake soaked in rum-flavoured syrup) and *puits d'amour* (puff pasty with vanilla cream and caramel).

➡ **Au Rocher de Cancale** (Map p392; ☎01 42 33 50 29; www.aurocherdecancale.fr; 78 rue Montorgueil, 2e; mains €10.50-22; ⌚8am-2am; Ⓜ Sentier or Les Halles) This 19th-century timber-lined restaurant (first opened in 1804 at No 59) is the last remaining legacy of the old oyster market. You can feast on oysters and seafood from Cancale (in Brittany) as well as other *plats du jour*.

➡ **À La Mère de Famille** (Map p392; www.lameredefamille.com; 82 rue Montorgueil, 2e; ⌚10am-8pm Mon-Sat, to 1pm Sun; Ⓜ Sentier or Les Halles) The oldest confectionery house in Paris, with over 250 years of experience creating chocolates, *bonbons* and other sweet temptations.

➡ **La Fermette** (Map p392; www.lafermettemontorgueil.com; 86 rue Montorgueil, 2e; ⌚4-8pm Mon, 7.30am-8.30pm Tue-Sat, 7.30am-2pm Sun; Ⓜ Sentier or Les Halles) Not the most stylish *fromagerie* in town, but it always has great deals out front, where you can pick up a preselected assortment of cheese for under €10.

➡ **Nysa** (Map p392; www.nysa.fr; 94 rue de Montorgueil, 2e; ⌚10.30am-2pm & 4-9pm Wed-Mon, 4-9pm Tue; Ⓜ Sentier) This unpretentious wine store supports independent vineyards and has an interesting selection of bottles for under €15.

⌚noon-2.30pm Mon-Fri, 7.30-10.30pm Tue-Sat; Ⓜ Sentier) The name alone – Bad Reputation (yep, also a Georges Brassens album) – immediately makes you want to poke your nose in and see what's happening behind that bright-orange canopy and oyster-grey façade just footsteps from busy rue Montorgueil. Great bistro cooking and warm, engaging service in a catchy designer space with coloured spots on the wall and fresh flowers on each table is the answer.

L'ARDOISE BISTRO €€

Map p388 (☎01 42 96 28 18; www.lardoise-paris.com; 28 rue du Mont Thabor, 1er; menus €38; ⌚noon-2.30pm Mon-Sat, 7.30-10.30pm Mon-Sun; Ⓜ Concorde or Tuileries) This is a lovely little bistro with no menu as such (*ardoise* means 'blackboard', which is all there is), but who cares? The food – fricassee of corn-fed chicken with morels, pork cheeks in ginger, hare in black pepper, prepared dexterously by chef Pierre Jay (ex-Tour d'Argent) – is superb.

AUX LYONNAIS LYONNAIS €€

Map p388 (☎01 58 00 22 06; www.auxlyonnais.com; 32 rue St-Marc, 2e; lunch menus €32, mains €26-33; ⌚noon-2.30pm Tue-Fri, 7.30-10.30pm Tue-Sat; Ⓜ Richelieu-Drouot) This is where top

French chef Alain Ducasse and his followers 'slum' it. The venue is an art-nouveau masterpiece that feels more real than movie set; the food is perfectly restructured Lyonnais classics, such as quenelles (creamed fish or meat shaped like a dumpling) and blood sausage.

LE GRAND COLBERT TRADITIONAL FRENCH **€€**

Map p388 (☎01 42 86 87 88; www.legrandcolbert.fr; 2-4 rue Vivienne, 2e; 2-/3-course menus lunch €29/36, dinner €46/54; ⌚noon-1am; 📶; Ⓜ Pyramides) This former workers' *cafétéria* transformed into a fin de siècle showcase is more relaxed than many similarly restored restaurants and is a convenient spot for lunch after visiting the neighbouring covered shopping arcades – the daily *formule ardoise* (blackboard fixed menu; €17) is good value – or cruising the streets at night (last orders: midnight). Don't expect gastronomic miracles (despite Diane Keaton's claims in *Something's Gotta Give*), but portions are big and service is friendly. Sunday ushers in a pricier €42 menu.

★FRENCHIE BISTRO **€€€**

Map p392 (☎01 40 39 96 19; www.frenchie-restaurant.com; 5-6 rue du Nil, 2e; prix-fixe menus €48; ⌚7-11pm Mon-Fri; Ⓜ Sentier) Tucked down an alley you wouldn't venture down otherwise, this bijou bistro with wooden tables and old stone walls is iconic. Frenchie is always packed and for good reason: excellent-value dishes are modern, market-driven (the menu changes daily with a choice of two dishes) and prepared with just the right dose of unpretentious creative flair by French chef Gregory Marchand.

The only hiccup is snagging a table: reserve for one of two sittings (7pm or 9.30pm) two months in advance, arrive at 7pm and pray for a cancellation (it does happen) or – failing that – share tapas-style small plates with friends across the street at **Frenchie Bar à Vins** (⌚7-11pm Mon-Fri). No reservations at the latter – write your name on the sheet of paper strung outside, loiter in the alley and wait for your name to be called.

★VERJUS MODERN AMERICAN **€€€**

Map p388 (☎01 42 97 54 40; www.verjusparis.com; 52 rue de Richelieu, 1er; prix-fixe menu €60; ⌚7-10pm Mon-Fri; Ⓜ Bourse or Palais Royal–Musée du Louvre) Opened by American duo Braden Perkins and Laura Adrian, Verjus was born out of a wildly successful clandestine supper club known as the Hidden Kitchen. The restaurant builds on that tradition, offering a chance to sample some excellent, creative cuisine (gnocchi with shiitake relish and parmesan, wild-boar confit with cherry compote) in a casual space. The tasting menu is a series of small plates, using ingredients sourced straight from producers.

Reservations are advised, but walk-ins sometimes end up with a table, especially if you don't mind eating late. If you're just after an aperitif or a prelude to dinner, the **Verjus Bar à Vins** (47 rue de Montpensier, 1er; ⌚12.30-2pm Tue-Fri, 6-11pm Mon-Fri) cooks up what foodies rightfully claim to be the best buttermilk-fried chicken (€10) in the city, among other small plates. No reservations, so arrive early to snag one of 10 bar stools. It also serves gourmet sandwiches at lunch.

PASSAGE 53 MODERN FRENCH **€€€**

Map p388 (☎01 42 33 04 35; www.passage53.com; 53 Passage des Panoramas, 2e; lunch/dinner menus €60/130; ⌚noon-2.30pm & 7.30-10.30pm Tue-Sat; Ⓜ Grands Boulevards or Bourse) No address inside Passage des Panoramas contrasts more dramatically with the outside hustle and bustle than this elegant restaurant at No 53. An oasis of calm and tranquillity (with window blinds pulled firmly down when closed), this gastronomic address is an ode to the best French produce – worked to perfection in a series of tasting courses by Japanese chef Shinichi Sato. Reserve ahead.

LE GRAND VÉFOUR TRADITIONAL FRENCH **€€€**

Map p388 (☎01 42 96 56 27; www.grand-vefour.com; 17 rue de Beaujolais, 1er; lunch/dinner menu €98/298; ⌚noon-2.30pm & 7.30-10.30pm Mon-Fri; Ⓜ Pyramides) This 18th-century jewel on the northern edge of the Jardin du Palais Royal has been a dining favourite of the Parisian elite since 1784. Just look at who gets their names ascribed to each table – from Napoléon and Victor Hugo to Colette (who lived next door). The food is tip-top; expect a voyage of discovery in one of the most beautiful restaurants in the world.

RESTAURANT DU PALAIS ROYAL TRADITIONAL FRENCH **€€€**

Map p388 (☎01 40 20 00 27; www.restaurant-dupalaisroyal.com; 110 Galerie de Valois, 1er; mains €40-60; ⌚noon-2.30pm & 7-10.30pm mid-Apr–mid-Sep, Tue-Sat rest of year; Ⓜ Palais Royal–Musée du Louvre) The terrace of this Parisian classic overlooking the Palais Royal is certainly a coveted spot in fine weather. In colder months the traditional dining room is a cosy and stylish backdrop to classic French dishes by chef Eric Fontanini – think flounder *façon Richelieu* (that's a nod to the Palais Royal's origins) or veal with smoked endives and truffled mashed potatoes.

Les Halles

LE BIO D'ADAM ET EVE — VEGETARIAN €

Map p392 (www.lebiodadameteve.com; 41 rue St Honoré, 1er; meals from €7.60; ⏲11.30am-8pm Mon-Sat; 🖉; Ⓜ Châtelet) If you're having trouble finding dining options (eg gluten-free, dairy-free) that go beyond the rigidly circumscribed boundaries of traditional French cuisine, this vegan-friendly pit stop will do you right, with a creative selection of organic, feel-good smoothies, soups, salads and sandwiches. A buffet of just-cooked dishes (figure on €8) is also available for lunch and early dinner.

DAME TARTINE — CAFE €

Map p392 (2 Rue Brisemiche, 4e; tartines €8.90-11.20; ⏲9am-11.30pm; Ⓜ Hôtel de Ville) One of the few reasonable dining options near Centre Pompidou, Dame Tartine makes the most of its lively location across from the whimsical Stravinsky Fountain. Don't expect miracles on the culinary front, but its speciality – the *tartine*, or open-face sandwich – will hit the spot after a morning in the museum.

LA BAGUE DE KENZA — PATISSERIE €

Map p392 (www.labaguedekenza.com; 136 rue St-Honoré, 1er; tajines €15.30-18.90; ⏲11am-9pm Mon-Wed, to 10pm Thu-Sat, to 8pm Sun; Ⓜ Louvre Rivoli) Exquisite and seductively sweet Algerian pastries are what this speciality patisserie with tea room and restaurant up top does best. It serves *tajines* at lunch.

LINA'S BEAUTIFUL SANDWICH — SANDWICHES, SALADS €

Map p392 (www.linasparis.com; 50 rue Étienne Marcel, 2e; sandwiches €4.50-6.80; ⏲8.30am-6pm Mon-Fri, 9am-6.30pm Sat; 📶; Ⓜ Sentier or Bourse) For made-to-measure sandwiches built from five different bread types and countless fillings and dressings, there is no better address than this large, hip, contemporary space with bags of comfy seating. Free wi-fi is the icing on the cake.

COJEAN — SANDWICHES, SALADS €

Map p392 (www.cojean.fr; 3 place du Louvre, 1er; sandwiches €5.30-6.80; ⏲10am-4pm Mon-Fri, 11am-6pm Sat; 📶; Ⓜ Palais Royal–Musée du Louvre) Across the street from the Louvre, this stylish sandwich and salad bar promises a quick lunch for less than €10 beneath the splendour of an elegant moulded period ceiling.

SAVEURS VÉGÉT'HALLES — VEGETARIAN €

Map p392 (☎01 40 41 93 95; www.saveursvegethalles.fr; 41 rue des Bourdonnais, 1er; mains €13.10-13.90; ⏲noon-2.30pm & 7-10.30pm Mon-Sat; 🖉; Ⓜ Châtelet) This vegan eatery offers quite a few mock-meat dishes like *poulet végétal aux champignons* ('chicken' with mushrooms). No alcohol.

★PIROUETTE — NEOBISTRO €€

Map p392 (☎01 40 26 47 81; 5 rue Mondétour, 1er; lunch menus €18, 3-/6-course dinner menus €40/60; ⏲noon-2.30pm & 7.30-10.30pm Mon-Sat; Ⓜ Les Halles) In one of the best restaurants in the vicinity of the old 'belly of Paris', chef Tomy Gousset's kitchen crew is working wonders at this cool loft-like space, serving up tantalising creations that range from seared duck, asparagus and Buddha's hand fruit to rum baba with chantilly and lime. Some unique ingredients and a new spin for French cuisine.

LA TOUR DE MONTLHÉRY – CHEZ DENISE — TRADITIONAL FRENCH €€

Map p392 (☎01 42 36 21 82; 5 rue des Prouvaires, 1er; mains €23-28; ⏲noon-2.30pm & 7.30pm-5am Mon-Fri; Ⓜ Châtelet) The most traditional eatery near the former Les Halles marketplace, this boisterous old bistro with red-chequered tablecloths has been run by the same team for 30-some years. If you've just arrived and are ready to feast on all the French classics – snails in garlic sauce, veal liver, steak tartare, braised beef cheeks and housemade pâtés – reservations are in order. Open till dawn.

BEEF CLUB — STEAK €€

Map p392 (☎09 54 37 13 65; www.eccbeefclub.com; 58 rue Jean-Jacques Rousseau, 1er; mains €25-38; ⏲dinner; Ⓜ Les Halles) No steakhouse is more chic or hipper than this. Packed out ever since it threw its first T-bone on the grill in spring 2012, this beefy address is all about steak, dry aged and prepared to tender perfection. The vibe is hip New York and the downstairs cellar bar, the Ballroom,

THE CITY'S MOST FAMOUS HOT CHOCOLATE

Clink china with lunching ladies, their posturing poodles and half the students from Tokyo University at **Angelina** (226 rue de Rivoli, 1er; ⏰8am-7pm Mon-Fri, 9am-7pm Sat & Sun), a *grande dame* of a tearoom dating to 1903. Decadent pastries are served here, against a fresco backdrop of belle époque Nice, but it is the superthick, decadently sickening 'African' hot chocolate (€8.20), which comes with a pot of whipped cream and a carafe of water, that prompts the constant queue for a table at Angelina.

shakes a mean cocktail courtesy of the cool guys from the Experimental Cocktail Club (p131).

If seafood is more your thing, the impeccably chic **Fish Club** (Map p392; ☎01 40 26 68 75; 58 rue Jean-Jacques Rousseau, 1er; tapas €7-22; ⏰noon-3pm & 8-10.15pm Tue-Fri, 8-10.15pm Sat; Ⓜ Les Halles) conjures up a distinctly Peruvian vibe with its *ceviches* (marinated raw fish), *tiraditos* (thinly sliced raw fish) and pisco sours.

RACINES 2 MODERN FRENCH €€

Map p392 (☎01 42 60 77 34; 39 rue de l'Arbre Sec, 1er; 2-course lunch menus €18.50, mains €28-31; ⏰noon-2.30pm & 7.30-10.30pm Mon-Fri; Ⓜ Louvre Rivoli) R2 is a cousin of Racines in Passage des Panoramas, but that is about the extent of the family resemblance. No 2 is a thoroughly modern, urban bistro with a contemporary, Philippe Starck interior and an open stainless-steel kitchen where you can watch the hip, young, black-dressed chefs, tattoos and all, at work. What's cooking – just two or three choices for each course – is chalked on the board, and the Louvre, handily so, is just around the corner.

DJAKARTA BALI INDONESIAN €€

Map p392 (☎01 45 08 83 11; www.djakarta-bali.com; 9 rue Vauvilliers, 1er; lunch €14.50-18.50, dinner €25-55; ⏰noon-2.30pm Wed-Sun, 7.30-10.30pm Tue-Sun; Ⓜ Louvre Rivoli) OK, it might look like Hollywood's idea of an Indonesian restaurant with all those Balinese handicrafts adorning the walls, but this is the real thing, run by the progeny of an Indonesian diplomat exiled when former president Sukarno was overthrown in 1967. If you think you can handle it, order one of four *rijstafels* (Dutch for 'rice table') – a seemingly endless feast of seven to 10 courses. Those with nut allergies beware: peanuts appear in many dishes.

SPRING MODERN FRENCH €€€

Map p392 (☎01 45 96 05 72; www.springparis.fr; 6 rue Bailleul, 1er; prix-fixe menus €84; ⏰dinner Tue-Sat; Ⓜ Palais Royal–Musée du Louvre) One of the Right Bank's talk-of-the-town addresses, with Chicago-born Daniel Rose in the open kitchen and stunning food. It has no printed menu, meaning hungry gourmets put their appetites in the hands of the chefs and allow multilingual waiting staff to reveal what's cooking as each course is served. Reserve one month in advance.

YAM'TCHA FUSION €€€

Map p392 (☎01 40 26 08 07; www.yamtcha.com; 4 rue Sauval, 1er; prix-fixe menus €100; ⏰noon-2.30pm Wed-Sat, 7.30-10.30pm Tue-Sat; Ⓜ Louvre Rivoli) Chef Adeline Grattard's ingeniously fused French and Cantonese flavours (fried squid with sweet-potato noodles) have earned her no shortage of critical praise. Pair dishes on the frequently changing menu with wine or tea, or sample the special lunch menu (€60) offered Wednesday through Friday. Reserve up to two months in advance.

DRINKING & NIGHTLIFE

Louvre

TELESCOPE CAFE

Map p388 (www.telescopecafe.com; 5 rue Villedo, 1er; ⏰8.30am-5pm Mon-Fri, 9.30am-6.30pm Sat; Ⓜ Pyramides) The barista delivers at this minimalist coffee shop, which brews frothy cappuccinos and serves sweet pastries to boot.

LOCKWOOD CAFE

Map p392 (73 rue d'Aboukir, 2e; ⏰8am-2am Mon-Sat; Ⓜ Sentier) A handy address for hip coffee lovers. Savour beans from the Belleville Brûlerie during the day and well-mixed cocktails in the subterranean candle-lit *cave* (wine cellar) at night.

LOCAL KNOWLEDGE

RUE D'ARGOUT & RUE MONTMARTRE

Rue d'Argout is a slip of a street from the 13th century, but it's one of those short, stumble-upon strips where Paris' young bright things like to be, where you just know you'll walk down that same street tomorrow, or next week, or next month perhaps, and another trendsetter will have popped up.

Take **Blend** (Map p392; www.blendhamburger.com; 44 rue d'Argout, 2e; burger & fries €14; ⌚noon-11pm; Ⓜ Sentier), a gourmet burger bar the size of a pocket handkerchief that is still going strong following its 2012 opening. Easy to spot by the hungry crowd lingering outside waiting for a table, the sharp, smart, black and wood space cooks up bijou-sized burgers with homemade buns and meat from celebrity butcher Yves-Marie Le Bourdonnec.

Up the street is the colourful and always busy **Fée Nature** (Map p392; 67 rue d'Argout, 2e; plats du jour €8.50; ⌚noon-4pm Mon-Sat; 📶; Ⓜ Sentier), with its inventive, wholly *'bio et sain'* (organic and healthy) menu – there are even a few gluten-free options.

Just beyond is rue Montmartre, clad with numerous places to sip coffee and cocktails. Two of the longest running are the Crazy Heart, aka **Le Cœur Fou** (Map p392; 55 rue Montmartre, 2e; ⌚5pm-2am; Ⓜ Étienne Marcel), a tiny gallery-bar with candles nestled in whitewashed walls. A few doors down, **Le Tambour** (Map p392; ☎01 42 33 06 90; 41 rue Montmartre, 2e; ⌚8am-6am; Ⓜ Étienne Marcel or Sentier) is a vintage mecca for Parisian night owls with its long hours (food until 3.30am or 4am) and hip mix of recycled street furniture and old metro maps.

ZEN ZOO — TEAROOM

Map p388 (www.zen-zoo.com; 13 rue Chabanais, 2e; ⌚noon-7pm Mon-Sat; Ⓜ Quatre Septembre) Taiwan's fabulously addictive bubble tea (*zhēnzhū nǎichá*) has finally made it to Paris. If you're not familiar with the drink, which consists of sweet milk tea and chewy tapioca balls sucked up through an unusually large straw, then by all means pencil Zen Zoo into your Right Bank itinerary, either at tea time (dim sum served) or for a scrumptious Chinese lunch (€10).

LE SAUT DU LOUP — CAFE

Map p388 (☎01 42 25 49 55; 107 rue de Rivoli, 1er; ⌚10am-2pm; 📶; Ⓜ Louvre Rivoli) Given its location inside the Decorative Arts Museum, the interior design is, naturally, chic and impeccable. But it's the sweeping summer terrace with crunchy gravel underfoot and elegant tables overlooking the pea-green lawns of Jardin du Carrousel that really makes this a fine place to get off your feet.

LA CHAMPMESLÉ — BAR

Map p388 (www.lachampmesle.com; 4 rue Chabanais, 2e; ⌚4pm-dawn Mon-Sat; Ⓜ Pyramides) The *grande dame* of Parisian lesbian bars, around since 1979, is a cosy, relaxed spot that attracts an older crowd (about 75% are lesbians, the rest mostly gay men). Cabaret nights, tarot-card readings and fortune-telling sessions, and art exhibitions.

LE REX CLUB — CLUB

(www.rexclub.com; 5 bd Poissonnière, 2e; ⌚midnight-7am Thu-Sat; Ⓜ Bonne Nouvelle) Attached to the art-deco Grand Rex cinema, this is Paris' premier house and techno venue where some of the world's hottest DJs strut their stuff on a 70-speaker, multidiffusion sound system.

SOCIAL CLUB — CLUB

Map p388 (www.parissocialclub.com; 142 rue Montmartre, 2e; ⌚11pm-6am Tue-Sat; Ⓜ Grands Boulevards) These subterranean rooms showcasing electro, hip hop, funk and live acts are a magnet for clubbers who take their music seriously. Across the street at No 146 is the cafe where French socialist Jean Jaurès was assassinated in 1914.

SILENCIO — CLUB

Map p388 (http://silencio-club.com; 142 rue Montmartre, 2e; ⌚6pm-4am Tue-Sat; Ⓜ Bourse) A David Lynch–designed interior is what gives Silencio its aura of glamour and mystery. It's members only, although nonmembers who look like supermodels (or their dates) can, theoretically, breach the velvet rope after midnight.

Les Halles

EXPERIMENTAL COCKTAIL CLUB COCKTAIL BAR

Map p392 (www.experimentalcocktailclub.com; 37 rue St-Saveur, 2e; 7pm-2am; Réaumur-Sébastopol) Called ECC by trendies, this fabulous speakeasy with grey façade and old-beamed ceiling is effortlessly hip. Oozing spirit and soul, the cocktail bar – with retro-chic decor by American interior designer Cuoco Black and sister bars in London and New York – is a sophisticated flashback to those *années folles* (crazy years) of Prohibition New York.

Cocktails (€12 to €15) are individual and fabulous, and DJs set the space partying at weekends.

JEFREY'S COCKTAIL BAR

Map p392 (www.jefreys.fr; 14 rue St-Saveur, 2e; 7pm-2am Tue-Sat; Réaumur-Sébastopol) Oh how dandy this trendy drawing room with wooden façade, leather Chesterfields and old-fashioned gramophone is! It's a gentlemen's club in soul, yes, but creative cocktails are shaken for both him and her, and never more so than during happy hour (7pm to 10.30pm Tuesday and Thursday) when cocktails dip in price.

Favourites include I Wanna Be this Drink (rum, strawberry juice, fresh raspberries and balsamic-vinegar caramel) and the Grand Marnier–based Cucumber Cooler.

LE GARDE ROBE WINE BAR

Map p392 (41 rue de l'Arbre Sec, 1er; 12.30-2.30pm & 7.30-11pm Mon-Fri; Louvre Rivoli) The Garde Robe is possibly the only bar in the world to serve alcohol alongside a 'detox' menu. While you probably shouldn't come here for the full-on cleansing experience, you can definitely expect excellent, affordable natural wines, a casual atmosphere and a good selection of eats, ranging from the standard cheese and charcuterie plates to more adventurous veg-friendly options.

CAFÉ LA FUSÉE BAR

Map p392 (168 rue St-Martin, 3e; 8am-2am; Rambuteau or Étienne Marcel) A short walk from the Pompidou, the Rocket is a lively, laid-back indie hang-out with a red-and-white striped awning strung with fairy lights outside, and paint-peeling, tobacco-coloured walls indoors. You can grab simple meals here (€8 to €13), and it's got a decent wine selection by the glass.

DEPUR BAR

Map p392 (4bis rue St-Saveur, 2e; 9am-11pm; Étienne Marcel or Sentier) It's glitzy and chic, a definite after-dark dress-up spot. But what really gives this hybrid bar-restaurant wow factor is its courtyard terrace – covered in winter, open and star-topped in summer. Cocktails are shaken from 5pm.

KONG BAR

Map p392 (www.kong.fr; 1 rue du Pont Neuf, 1er; 12.15-11.30pm; Pont Neuf) Evenings at this Philippe Starck–designed riot of iridescent champagne-coloured vinyl booths, Japanese cartoon cut-outs and garden-gnome stools see Paris' glam young set guzzling Dom Pérignon, nibbling at tapas-style platters (mains €20 to €40) and shaking their designer-clad booty on the tables.

If you can, try to snag a table *à l'étage* (upstairs) in the part-glass-roofed terrace-gallery, where light floods across the giant geisha swooning horizontal across the ceiling, and stunning river views (particularly at sunset) make your head swim.

Ô CHATEAU WINE BAR

Map p392 (www.o-chateau.com; 68 rue Jean-Jacques Rousseau, 1er; 4pm-midnight Mon-Sat; ; Les Halles or Étienne Marcel) Wine aficionados can thank this young, fun, cosmopolitan *bar à vins* for bringing affordable tasting to Paris. Sit at the long, trendy bar and savour your pick of 40-odd *grands vins*

JAZZ DUO

Rue des Lombards is the street to swing by for live jazz.

➡ **Le Baiser Salé** (Map p392; www.lebaisersale.com; 58 rue des Lombards, 1er; daily; Châtelet) Known for its Afro and Latin jazz, and jazz fusion concerts, the Salty Kiss combines big names and unknown artists. The place has a relaxed vibe, with sets usually starting at 7.30pm or 9.30pm.

➡ **Sunset & Sunside** (Map p392; www.sunset-sunside.com; 60 rue des Lombards, 1er; daily; Châtelet) Two venues in one at this trendy, well-respected club: electric jazz, fusion and the odd salsa session downstairs; acoustics and concerts upstairs.

served by the glass (500-odd by the bottle!). Or sign up in advance for an intro to French wine (€30) or a guided cellar tasting in English over lunch (€75) or dinner (€100).

LE FUMOIR COCKTAIL BAR

Map p392 (www.lefumoir.com; 6 rue de l'Amiral de Coligny, 1er; ⏲11-2am; Ⓜ Louvre Rivoli) This colonial-style bar-restaurant is a fine spot to sip top-notch gin from quality glassware while nibbling olives from the vintage mahogany bar, or discover new cocktails with friends during happy hour (6pm to 8pm). A buoyant, corporate crowd packs out the place weekday evenings after work, while the restaurant revs into gear at mealtimes. The best seats in the house are in the 'library' and on the summer pavement terrace.

☆ ENTERTAINMENT

COMÉDIE FRANÇAISE THEATRE

Map p388 (www.comedie-francaise.fr; place Colette, 1er; Ⓜ Palais Royal–Musée du Louvre) Founded in 1680 under Louis XIV, this state-run theatre bases its repertoire around the works of classic French playwrights. The theatre has its roots in an earlier company directed by Molière at the Palais Royal – the French playwright and actor was seized by a convulsion on stage during the fourth performance of the *Imaginary Invalid* in 1673 and died later at his home on nearby rue de Richelieu.

THÉÂTRE DU CHÂTELET PERFORMING ARTS

Map p392 (www.chatelet-theatre.com; 1 place du Châtelet, 1er; Ⓜ Châtelet) This venue hosts concerts as well as operas, musical performances, theatre, ballet and popular Sunday-morning concerts.

LOUVRE AUDITORIUM MUSIC

Map p388 (☎01 40 20 55 00; www.louvre.fr/musiques; Hall Napoléon, Louvre, 1er; Ⓜ Palais Royal–Musée du Louvre) Excellent classical-music concerts are staged several times a week at the Louvre Auditorium (off the main entrance hall). Don't miss the Thursday lunchtime concerts, which cost a mere €6 to €12. The season runs from September to April or May, depending on the concert series.

THÉÂTRE DE LA VILLE DANCE

Map p392 (www.theatredelaville-paris.com; 2 place du Châtelet, 4e; Ⓜ Châtelet) It hosts theatre and music too, but this theatre is best known for its contemporary dance productions.

OPÉRA COMIQUE OPERA

Map p388 (www.opera-comique.com; 1 place Boïeldieu, 2e; Ⓜ Richelieu Drouot) This century-old hall has premiered many important French operas and continues to host classic and less-known works.

PARIS' FILM ARCHIVE

Cinemas showing films set in Paris are the centrepiece of the city's film archive, the **Forum des Images** (www.forumdesimages.fr; 1 Grande Galerie, Porte St-Eustache; ⏲1-10pm Tue-Fri, from 2pm Sat & Sun). Created in 1988 to establish 'an audiovisual memory bank of Paris', and renovated in dramatic shades of pink, grey and black, the five-screen complex has a new library and research centre with newsreels, documentaries and advertising. Check its program online for thematic series and frequent festivals and events.

SHOPPING

The 1e and 2e *arrondissements* are mostly about fashion. Indeed the Sentier district is something of a garment heaven, while rue Étienne Marcel, place des Victoires and rue du Jour flaunt prominent labels and shoe shops. Nearby rue Montmartre and rue Tiquetonne are the streets to shop for streetwear and avant-garde designs; the easternmost part of the 1e around Palais Royal, for fancy period and conservative label fashion.

★ DIDIER LUDOT FASHION

Map p388 (www.didierludot.fr; 19-20 & 23-24 Galerie de Montpensier, 1er; ⏲10.30am-7pm Mon-Sat; Ⓜ Palais Royal–Musée du Louvre) In the rag trade since 1975, collector Didier Ludot sells the city's finest couture creations of yesteryear in his exclusive twinset of boutiques, hosts exhibitions, and has published a book portraying the evolution of the little black dress, brilliantly brought to life in his shop that sells just that, **La Petite Robe Noire** (Map p388; 125 Galerie de Valois, 1er; ⏲11am-7pm Mon-Sat; Ⓜ Palais Royal–Musée du Louvre).

E DEHILLERIN HOMEWARES

Map p392 (www.dehillerin.com; 18-20 rue Coquillière, 1er; ⌚9am-12.30pm & 2-6pm Mon, 9am-6pm Tue-Sat; Ⓜ Les Halles) Founded in 1820, this extraordinary two-level store – think old-fashioned warehouse rather than shiny, chic boutique – carries an incredible selection of professional-quality *matériel de cuisine* (kitchenware). Poultry scissors, turbot poacher, professional copper cookware or Eiffel Tower–shaped cake tin – it's all here.

MORA HOMEWARES

Map p392 (13 Rue Montmartre, 1er; ⌚9am-6.15pm Mon-Fri, 10am-1pm & 1.45-6.30pm Sat; Ⓜ Les Halles) Both amateur and professional pastry chefs will want to stop by MORA to pick up all manner of specialist culinary items, from unique cake and pastry moulds to macaron mats, pasta makers, piping bags and cream chargers (in case you're considering some fresh-baked éclairs back home).

COLETTE CONCEPT STORE

Map p388 (www.colette.fr; 213 rue St-Honoré, 1er; ⌚11am-7pm Mon-Sat; Ⓜ Tuileries) Uber-hip is an understatement. Ogle designer fashion on the 1st floor, and streetwear, limited-edition sneakers, art books, music, gadgets and other high-tech, inventive and/or plain unusual items on the ground floor. End with a drink in the basement 'water bar' and pick up free design magazines and flyers for some of the city's hippest happenings by the door upon leaving.

PASSAGE DES PANORAMAS SHOPPING ARCADE

Map p388 (10 rue St-Marc, 2e; ⌚6am-midnight; Ⓜ Bourse) Built in 1800, this is the oldest covered arcade in Paris and the first to be lit by gas (1817). It's a bit faded around the edges now but retains a real 19th-century charm with several outstanding eateries, a theatre from where spectators would come out to shop during the interval, and autograph dealer Arnaud Magistry (at No 60).

ROOM SERVICE FASHION

Map p392 (www.roomservice.fr; 52 rue d'Argout, 2e; ⌚11am-7.30pm Mon-Sat; Ⓜ Les Halles) *'Atelier vintage'* (vintage workshop) is the thrust of this chic boutique that reinvents vintage pieces as new. Scarves, headpieces, sequins, bangles and beads casually strung up to be admired…the place oozes the femininity and refinement of an old-fashioned Parisian boudoir.

LOCAL KNOWLEDGE

BACKSTAGE AT THE FLICKS

A trip to 1932 art-deco cinematic icon **Le Grand Rex** (www.legrandrex.com; 1 bd Poissonnière, 2e; tours adult/child €11/9; ⌚tours 10am-7pm Wed-Sun; Ⓜ Bonne Nouvelle) is like no other trip to the flicks. Screenings aside, the cinema runs 50-minute behind-the-scenes tours (English soundtracks available) during which visitors – tracked by a sensor slung around their neck – are whisked right up (via a lift) behind the giant screen, tour a soundstage and get to have fun in a recording studio. Whiz-bang special effects along the way will stun adults and kids alike.

GALIGNANI BOOKS

Map p388 (http://galignani.com; 224 rue de Rivoli, 1er; ⌚10am-7pm Mon-Sat; Ⓜ Concorde) Proudly claiming to be the 'first English bookshop established on the continent', this ode to literature stocks French and English books and is the best spot in Paris for picking up just-published titles.

ANTOINE FASHION

Map p388 (10 av de l'Opéra, 1er; ⌚10.30am-1pm & 2-6.30pm Mon-Sat; Ⓜ Pyramides or Palais Royal–Musée du Louvre) Antoine has been the Parisian master of bespoke canes, umbrellas, fans and gloves since 1745.

JAMIN PUECH FASHION

Map p388 (www.jamin-puech.com; 26 rue Cambon, 1er; ⌚noon-7pm Tue, 11am-7pm Wed-Sat; Ⓜ Concorde) Among Paris' most creative handbag designers, Jamin Puech is known for its bold mix of colours, fabrics, leathers and textures – lots of beads, pompoms, shells, feathers and so on. Its Cocotte handbag starred in *Sex and the City 2*.

COMPTOIR DE LA GASTRONOMIE FOOD, DRINK

Map p392 (www.comptoirdelagastronomie.com; 34 rue Montmartre, 1er; ⌚6am-8pm Tue-Sat, 9am-8pm Mon; Ⓜ Les Halles) This elegant *épicerie fine* (specialist grocer) stocks a scrumptious array of gourmet goods to take away (particularly in the foie-gras department). It adjoins a striking art-nouveau dining room dating to 1894.

LIBRAIRIE GOURMANDE BOOKS

Map p392 (www.librairie-gourmande.fr; 92 rue Montmartre, 1er; ⊙11am-7pm Mon-Sat; MSentier) The city's leading bookshop dedicated to things culinary and gourmet.

WH SMITH BOOKS

Map p388 (www.whsmith.fr; 248 rue de Rivoli, 1er; ⊙9am-7pm Mon-Sat, 12.30-7pm Sun; MConcorde) This branch of the British-owned chain is supposedly Paris' largest English-language bookshop.

ALLSAINTS SPITALFIELDS FASHION

Map p392 (www.allsaints.com; 49 rue Étienne Marcel, 4e; ⊙10.30am-7.30pm Mon-Sat; MSentier) The industrial design of this British fashion house is eye-catching. Hundreds of vintage sewing machines fill its windows and garments inside are hung on old bits of hand-operated machinery.

AESOP COSMETICS

Map p388 (www.aesop.com; 256 rue St-Honoré, 1er; ⊙11am-7pm Mon-Thu, to 7.30pm Fri & Sat; MPalais Royal–Musée du Louvre) Browsing this Australian boutique is as much about admiring smart design as swooning over the lavender stems, camomile buds, roses, parsley seeds and other plants (or parts) that go into this sophisticated range of hair, skin and body-care products.

KABUKI FEMME FASHION

Map p392 (www.barbarabui.com; 25 rue Étienne Marcel, 2e; ⊙11am-7pm Mon-Sat; MÉtienne Marcel) Opened some 20 years ago, this is the shop that brought Barbara Bui to world attention. Her own eponymous store is next door and you'll find Kabuki for men two doors down. Judicious selections from other brands, too, including Prada, Balenciaga, Stella McCartney, Yves Saint Laurent and Dior.

KILIWATCH FASHION

Map p392 (http://espacekiliwatch.fr; 64 rue Tiquetonne, 2e; ⊙10.30am-7pm Mon, to 7.30pm Tue-Sat; MÉtienne Marcel) A Parisian institution, Kiliwatch gets jam-packed with hip guys and gals rummaging through racks of new and used streetwear. Startling vintage range of hats and boots plus art/photography books, eyewear and the latest sneakers.

LAVINIA FOOD, DRINK

Map p388 (www.lavinia.com; 3 bd de la Madeleine, 1er; ⊙10am-8pm Mon-Sat; MMadeleine) Among the largest and most exclusive drinks shops is this bastion of booze with a top collection of *eaux-de-vie* (fruit brandies).

LEGRAND FILLES & FILS FOOD, DRINK

Map p388 (www.caves-legrand.com; 1 rue de la Banque, 2e; ⊙noon-7.30pm Mon-Sat; MPyramides) Tucked inside Galerie Vivienne since 1880, Legrand sells fine wine and all the accoutrements: corkscrews, tasting glasses, decanters etc. It also has a fancy wine bar, *école du vin* (wine school) and *éspace dégustation* with several tastings a month; check its website for details.

BOÎTES À MUSIQUE ANNA JOLIET SOUVENIRS

Map p388 (Passage du Perron, 1er; ⊙noon-7pm Tue-Sat; MPyramides) This wonderful shop at the northern end of the Jardin du Palais Royal specialises in music boxes, new and old, from Switzerland.

Montmartre & Northern Paris

MONTMARTRE & PIGALLE | CLICHY | GARE DU NORD & CANAL ST-MARTIN

Neighbourhood Top Five

❶ Hiking up the steps to the **Basilique du Sacré-Cœur** (p137) for panoramic views from the outside and a glittering mosaic within.

❷ Catching a performance or exhibit at the **Parc de la Villette** (p139), the city's largest cultural playground.

❸ Stepping back into 19th-century opulence at the elegant **Musée Jaquemart André** (p143).

❹ Discovering the tombs of French royalty at the **Basilique de St-Denis** (p141).

❺ Treating the kids to a day at the **Cité des Sciences** (p142).

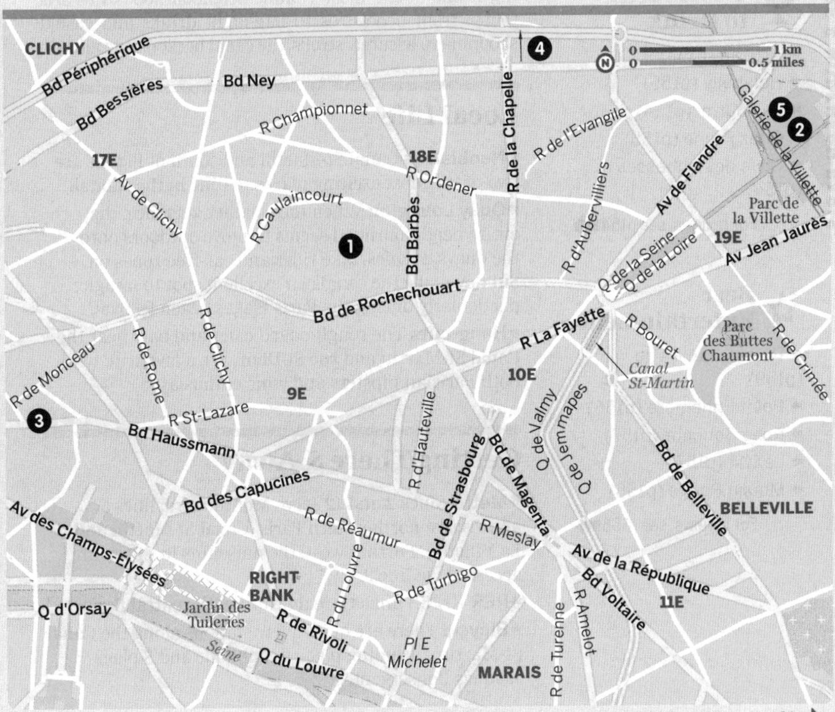

For more detail of this area see Map p394, p398, p400 and p401

Lonely Planet's Top Tip

Although gritty, the neighbourhoods in the north and northeast of Paris are fairly safe as far as big cities go. If there's one place you need to stay on your guard, it's at the foot of the hill that leads up to Sacré-Cœur. It's not unusual for pickpockets and con artists to work the crowds here.

Best Places to Eat

- Le Pantruche (p146)
- Chez Michel (p152)
- Abri (p152)
- Le Verre Volé (p152)
- Le Miroir (p146)

For reviews, see p144

Best Places to Drink

- Artisan (p154)
- Holybelly (p155)
- La Fourmi (p154)
- Chez Prune (p155)
- Cave des Abbesses (p154)

For reviews, see p154

Best Entertainment

- Parc de la Villette (p139)
- Point Éphémère (p156)
- Rosa Bonheur (p157)
- Le 104 (p157)
- Moulin Rouge (p155)

For reviews, see p155

Explore: Montmartre & Northern Paris

One of the wellsprings of Parisian myth, Montmartre has always stood apart. Bohemians, revolutionaries, artists, can-can girls and headless martyrs have all played a role in its story, and while it may belong to Paris today, vestiges of the original village – ivy-clad buildings, steep, narrow streets – remain. Crowned by the white domes of Sacré-Cœur, dragged back to earth by red-light Pigalle, it has forever encompassed contrast and conflict.

An ideal place to base yourself, Montmartre is fairly self-contained – it has plenty in the way of sights, cuisine, shopping and entertainment. Most visitors here spend half a day or more exploring the side streets that tumble from the summit in all directions, searching valiantly for that one perfect vista looking out over the city.

And while it's packed with crowds, there's still plenty of local life to enjoy – whether in the sizzling culinary hot spot south of Pigalle or the rarely visited streets on the backside of the Butte (as the hill is known).

Some excellent museums are located to the west, beyond place de Clichy, but for a taste of a more modern-day *bobo* (bourgeois bohemian) lifestyle, you'll need to head further east to the Canal St-Martin. The quays here have undergone an urban renaissance in the past decade, making it one of the most vibrant neighbourhoods in Paris today: from neobistros to late-night drinks and casual shopping to leisurely strolls, the canal beckons one and all.

Local Life

- **Neobistros** Canal St-Martin and south of Pigalle are two of the most exciting places to dine in the capital.
- **Quay Lounging** When the weather gets nice, the entire neighbourhood seems to move outdoors onto the quays. Picnics, bike rides and car-free zones on Sunday make the canals an excellent spot to mingle, particularly during the Paris Plages beach festival.
- **Hang-outs** The rough-edged cafes and bars near the Canal St-Martin and rue St-Denis are a favourite with both Parisian hipsters and wine enthusiasts.

Getting There & Away

- **Metro** Lines 2 and 12 serve Montmartre; lines 5 and 7 serve northeastern Paris (Canal St-Martin and La Villette). Further west, the museums in Clichy are accessed via line 2.
- **RER** RER B links Gare du Nord with central Paris.
- **Bicycle** There are quite a few stations along the Canal St-Martin, including place République and 8 place Jacques Bonsergent.

BRUNO DE HOGUES / GETTY IMAGES ©

TOP SIGHT
BASILIQUE DU SACRÉ-CŒUR

Although some may poke fun at Sacré-Cœur's unsubtle design, the view from in front of the church is one of those perfect Paris postcards. More than just a basilica, Sacré-Cœur is a veritable experience, from the musicians performing on the steps to the groups of friends picnicking on the hillside park. Touristy, yes. But beneath it all, Sacré-Cœur's heart still shines gold.

History

It may appear to be a place of peacefulness and worship today, but in truth Sacré-Cœur's foundations were laid amid bloodshed and controversy. Its construction began in 1875, in the wake of France's humiliating defeat by Prussia and the subsequent chaos of the Paris Commune. Following Napoléon III's surrender to von Bismarck in September 1870, angry Parisians, with the help of the National Guard, continued to hold out against Prussian forces – a harrowing siege that lasted four long winter months. By the time a ceasefire was negotiated in early 1871, the split between the radical working-class Parisians (supported by the National Guard) and the conservative national government (supported by the French army) had become insurmountable.

Over the next several months, the rebels, known as Communards, managed to overthrow the reactionary government and take over the city. It was a particularly chaotic and bloody moment in Parisian history, with mass executions on both sides and a wave of rampant destruction that spread throughout Paris. Montmartre was a key Communard stronghold – it was on the future site of Sacré-Cœur that the rebels won their first victory – and it was consequently the first neighbourhood to be targeted when the French army returned in full force in May 1871. Ultimately, many Communards were buried alive in the gypsum mines beneath the Butte.

DON'T MISS...

- The views from the parvis
- The apse mosaic *Christ in Majesty*
- The dome

PRACTICALITIES

- Map p394
- www.sacre-coeur-montmartre.com
- place du Parvis du Sacré-Cœur
- dome adult/child €6/4, cash only
- 6am-10.30pm, dome 9am-7pm Apr-Sep, to 5.30pm Oct-Mar
- M Anvers

A PLACE OF PILGRIMAGE

In a sense, atonement here has never stopped: a prayer 'cycle' that began in 1885 before the basilica's completion still continues around the clock, with perpetual adoration of the Blessed Sacrament continually on display above the high altar. The basilica's travertine stone exudes calcite, ensuring it remains white despite weathering and pollution.

In 1944, 13 Allied bombs were dropped on Montmartre, falling just next to Sacré-Cœur. Although the stained-glass windows all shattered from the force of the explosions, miraculously no one died and the basilica sustained no other damage.

The Basilica

In this context, the construction of an enormous basilica to expiate the city's sins seemed like a gesture of peace and forgiveness – indeed, the seven million French francs needed to construct the church's foundations came solely from the contributions of local Catholics. However, the Montmartre location was certainly no coincidence: the conservative old guard desperately wanted to assert its power in what was then a hotbed of revolution. The battle between the two camps – Catholic versus secular, royalists versus republican – raged on, and in 1882 the construction of the basilica was even voted down by the city council (on the grounds that it would continue to fan the flames of civil war), only to be overturned in the end by a technicality.

Six successive architects oversaw construction of the Romano-Byzantine–style basilica, and it wasn't until 1919 that Sacré-Cœur was finally consecrated, even then standing in utter contrast to the bohemian lifestyle that surrounded it. While criticism of its design and white travertine stone has continued throughout the decades (one poet called it a giant baby's bottle for angels), the interior is enlivened by the glittering apse mosaic *Christ in Majesty*, designed by Luc-Olivier Merson in 1922 and one of the largest in the world.

The Dome & Crypt

Outside, some 234 spiralling steps lead you to the basilica's dome, which affords one of Paris' most spectacular panoramas; they say you can see for 30km on a clear day. Weighing in at 19 tonnes, the bell called La Savoyarde in the tower above is the largest in France. The chapel-lined crypt, visited in conjunction with the dome (for an additional €2), is huge but not very interesting.

You can avoid most of the climb up to the basilica with the short but useful **funicular railway** (1 metro ticket; ⏲6am-midnight) or the **tourist train** (per person €6; ⏲10am-midnight Apr-Sep, to 6pm Oct-Mar), which leaves from place Pigalle.

CHICUREL ARNAUD / GETTY IMAGES ©

TOP SIGHT
PARC DE LA VILLETTE

The largest park in Paris, the Parc de la Villette is a cultural centre, kids' playground and landscaped urban space all rolled into one. The French love of geometric forms defines the layout – the colossal mirror-like sphere of the Géode cinema, an undulating strip of corrugated steel stretching for hundreds of metres, the bright-red cubical pavilions known as folies – but the intersection of two canals, the Ourcq and the St-Denis, brings the most natural and popular element: water. Although it's a fair hike from central Paris, consider the trip here for one of the many events (world, rock and classical music concerts; art exhibits; outdoor cinema; circuses; modern dance) or if you have children.

Events throughout the year are staged in the wonderful old Grande Halle, Le Zénith, the Cabaret Sauvage (p157) and the Cité de la Musique (p157). Additionally, the new Paris Philharmonic Hall is due to be completed here in 2015.

There's an information centre with maps at the park's southern edge.

When the weather's pleasant, children (and adults) will enjoy exploring the numerous themed gardens, the best of which double as playgrounds. These include the Jardin du Dragon (Dragon Garden), with an enormous dragon slide between the Géode and the nearest bridge, the Jardin des Dunes (Dunes Garden) and Jardin des Miroirs (Mirror Garden).

However, for the young ones, the star attraction is the Cité des Sciences and its attached cinemas. The brilliant Cité des Enfants is probably the most popular section, with a construction site, TV studio, robots and water-based physics experiments all designed for children.

DON'T MISS...

- Evening performances
- The themed gardens
- The Cité des Sciences (p142)

PRACTICALITIES

- Map p400
- www.villette.com
- Ⓜ Porte de la Villette or Porte de Pantin

SIGHTS

Montmartre & Pigalle

BASILIQUE DU SACRÉ-CŒUR BASILICA
See p137.

PLACE DU TERTRE SQUARE
Map p394 (MAbbesses) It would be hard to miss the place du Tertre, one of the most touristy spots in all of Paris. Although today it's filled with visitors, buskers and portrait artists, it was originally the main square of the village of Montmartre before it was incorporated into the city proper.

One of the more popular claims of Montmartre mythology is staked to La Mère Catherine at No 6: in 1814, so it's said, Cossack soldiers first introduced the term *bistro* (Russian for 'quickly') into the French lexicon. Another big moment came on Christmas eve 1898, when Louis Renault's first car was driven up the Butte to the place du Tertre, igniting the start of the French auto industry.

ÉGLISE ST-PIERRE DE MONTMARTRE CHURCH
Map p394 (MAbbesses) This church, all that remains of the former Benedictine Abbey of Montmartre, dates back to the 12th century and is one of the oldest in Paris, though it has been much restored. Built atop a Roman temple to Mars, it was witness to the founding of the Jesuits in 1534, who met in the crypt under the guidance of Ignatius of Loyola.

Some say that the name Montmartre is derived from 'Mons Martis' (Latin for Mount of Mars); others prefer the Christian 'Mont Martyr' (Mount of the Martyr), a reference to the 3rd-century St Denis, who, according to legend, walked across Montmartre and on to the site of today's Basilique St-Denis after having been beheaded by Roman priests.

MUSÉE DE MONTMARTRE MUSEUM
Map p394 (www.museedemontmartre.fr; 12 rue Cortot, 18e; adult/child €9/5; 10am-6pm; MLamarck–Caulaincourt) The Montmartre Museum displays paintings, lithographs and documents mostly relating to the area's rebellious and bohemian past. It's located in one of the oldest houses in Montmartre, a 17th-century manor home where over a dozen artists, including Renoir and Utrillo, once lived. Suzanne Valadon's restored studio was set to open here at the time of writing. The gift shop sells small bottles of the wine produced from grapes grown in the Clos Montmartre.

MUSÉE DE LA HALLE ST-PIERRE ART MUSEUM
Map p394 (www.hallesaintpierre.org; 2 rue Ronsard, 18e; adult/senior & under 26yr €8/6.50; 11am-6pm Mon-Fri, 11am-7pm Sat, noon-6pm Sun; MAnvers) Founded in 1986, this museum and gallery is in the lovely old covered St Peter's Market. It focuses on the primitive and Art Brut schools; there is no permanent collection, but the museum stages three temporary exhibitions a year. There's a lovely cafe on site.

DALÍ ESPACE MONTMARTRE ART MUSEUM
Map p394 (www.daliparis.com; 11 rue Poulbot, 18e; adult/8-25yr €11.50/6.50; 10am-6pm, to 8pm Jul & Aug; MAbbesses) More than 300 works by Salvador Dalí (1904–89), the flamboyant Catalan surrealist printmaker, painter, sculptor and self-promoter, are on display at this surrealist-style basement museum located just west of place du Tertre. The collection includes Dalí's strange sculptures (most in reproduction), lithographs, and many of his illustrations and furniture pieces, including the famous Mae West lips sofa.

MUSÉE DE LA VIE ROMANTIQUE MUSEUM
Map p394 (www.vie-romantique.paris.fr; 16 rue Chaptal, 9e; 10am-6pm Tue-Sun; MBlanche or St-Georges) FREE This small museum is dedicated to two artists active during the Romantic era: the writer George Sand and the painter Ary Scheffer. Located at the end of a film-worthy cobbled lane, the villa housing the museum originally belonged to Scheffer and was the setting for popular salons of the day, attended by such notable figures as Delacroix, Liszt and Chopin (Sand's lover).

The ground floor is devoted to Sand and is full of paintings, objets d'art and personal effects, while the 1st floor displays a selection of Scheffer's portraits.

CIMETIÈRE DE MONTMARTRE CEMETERY
Map p394 (8am-5.30pm Mon-Fri, from 8.30am Sat, from 9am Sun; MPlace de Clichy) Established in 1798, this 11-hectare cemetery is perhaps the most celebrated necropolis

in Paris after Père Lachaise. It contains the graves of writers Émile Zola (whose ashes are now in the Panthéon), Alexandre Dumas (fils) and Stendhal, composers Jacques Offenbach and Hector Berlioz, artist Edgar Degas, film director François Truffaut and dancer Vaslav Nijinsky, among others.

The entrance closest to the Butte de Montmartre is at the end of av Rachel, just off bd de Clichy, or down the stairs from 10 rue Caulaincourt. Maps showing the location of the tombs are available free from the **conservation office** (Map p394; 20 av Rachel, 18e) at the cemetery's entrance.

MUSÉE DE L'ÉROTISME ART MUSEUM

Map p394 (www.musee-erotisme.com; 72 bd de Clichy, 18e; admission €10; ⌚10am-2am; Ⓜ Blanche) The Museum of Erotic Art attempts to raise around 2000 titillating statuary, stimulating sexual aids and fetishist items to a loftier plane, with antique and modern erotic art from four continents spread out across several floors. Some of the exhibits are, well, breathtaking, to say the least.

Clichy

MUSÉE NISSIM DE CAMONDO MUSEUM

Map p401 (www.lesartsdecoratifs.fr; 63 rue de Monceau, 8e; adult/18-25yr/under 18yr €9/6.50/free; ⌚11am-6pm Tue, Wed & Fri-Sun, to 9pm Thu; Ⓜ Monceau or Villiers) The Nissim de Camondo Museum, housed in a sumptuous mansion modelled on the Petit Trianon at Versailles, displays 18th-century furniture, wood panelling, tapestries, porcelain and other objets d'art collected by Count Moïse de Camondo, a Sephardic Jewish banker who moved from Constantinople to Paris in the late 19th century. He bequeathed the mansion and his collection to the state on the proviso that it would be turned into a museum named in memory of his son Nissim (1892–1917), a pilot killed in action during WWI. It is part of Les Arts Décoratifs, the trio of museums in the Louvre's Rohan Wing.

MUSÉE CERNUSCHI ART MUSEUM

Map p401 (www.cernuschi.paris.fr; 7 av Vélasquez, 8e; ⌚10am-6pm Tue-Sun; Ⓜ Villiers) FREE The Cernuschi Museum comprises an excellent and rare collection of ancient

TOP SIGHT
BASILIQUE DE ST-DENIS

Once one of the most sacred sites in the country, the basilica was built atop the tomb of St Denis, the 3rd-century martyr and alleged first bishop of Paris who was beheaded by Roman priests. A popular pilgrimage site, by the 6th century it had become the royal necropolis: all but a handful of France's kings and queens from Dagobert I (r 629–39) to Louis XVIII (r 1814–24) were buried here (today it holds the remains of 42 kings and 32 queens).

The single-towered basilica, begun around 1136, was the first major structure in France to be built in the Gothic style, serving as a model for other 12th-century French cathedrals, including the one at Chartres. Features illustrating the transition from Romanesque to Gothic can be seen in the choir and double ambulatory, which are adorned with a number of 12th-century stained-glass windows.

The tombs in the crypt – Europe's largest collection of funerary art – are the real reason to make the trip out here, however. Adorned with *gisants* (recumbent figures), those made after 1285 were carved from death masks and are thus fairly lifelike; earlier sculptures are depictions of how earlier rulers might have looked.

DON'T MISS...

- The stained-glass windows
- The royal tombs

PRACTICALITIES

- www.monuments-nationaux.fr
- 1 rue de la Légion d'Honneur
- tombs adult/senior & 18-25yr €7.50/4.50, basilica free
- ⌚10am-6.15pm Mon-Sat, from noon Sun Apr-Sep, to 5pm Oct-Mar
- Ⓜ Basilique de St-Denis

WORTH A DETOUR

MUSÉE D'ART ET D'HISTOIRE

To the southwest of the Basilica de St-Denis is the **Museum of Art and History** (www.musee-saint-denis.fr; 22bis rue Gabriel Péri, St-Denis; adult/student & senior €5/3; ⏲10am-5.30pm Mon, Wed & Fri, to 8pm Thu, 2-6.30pm Sat & Sun; Ⓜ St-Denis-Porte de Paris), housed in a restored Carmelite convent founded in 1625 and later presided over by Louise de France, the youngest daughter of Louis XV. Displays include reconstructions of the Carmelites' cells, an 18th-century apothecary and, in the archaeology section, items found during excavations around the basilica.

There's a section on modern art, with a collection of work by a local son, the surrealist artist Paul Éluard (1895–1952), as well as an important collection of politically charged posters, cartoons, lithographs and paintings from the 1871 Paris Commune.

Chinese art (funerary statues, bronzes, ceramics), much of which predates the Tang dynasty (618–907), in addition to diverse pieces from Japan. Milan banker and philanthropist Henri Cernuschi (1821–96), who settled in Paris before the unification of Italy, assembled the collection during a world tour from 1871–73.

LE BAL GALLERY

Map p401 (www.le-bal.fr; 6 impasse de la Défense, 18e; adult/12-25yr €5/4; ⏲noon-8pm Wed-Sun, to 10pm Thu; Ⓜ Place de Clichy) Two-floor gallery specialising in contemporary photography exhibits, with ties to Magnum Photos. It's not central, but there's an excellent bookstore and cafe (p149) on site.

⊙ Gare du Nord & Canal St-Martin

PARC DE LA VILLETTE PARK

See p139.

CITÉ DES SCIENCES SCIENCE MUSEUM

Map p400 (☎01 56 43 20 20; www.cite-sciences.fr; Parc de la Villette, 19e; adult/under 26yr €9/6; ⏲10am-6pm Tue-Sat, to 7pm Sun; Ⓜ Porte de la Villette) This is the city's top museum for kids, with three floors of hands-on exhibits for children aged two and up, plus two special-effects cinemas, a planetarium and a retired submarine. The only drawback is that each exhibit has a separate admission fee (though some combined tickets do exist), so you'll have to do some pretrip research in order to figure out what's most appropriate. Make sure to reserve tickets in advance via the website if you plan on coming on a weekend or during school holidays. Packing a picnic is also a good idea. A new shopping centre, **Vill'up**, complete with a freefall simulator and cinema, also has several chain restaurants.

CITÉ DE LA MUSIQUE MUSEUM

Map p400 (www.cite-musique.fr; 221 av Jean Jaurès, 19e; ⏲noon-6pm Tue-Sat, 10am-6pm Sun; Ⓜ Porte de Pantin) The Cité de la Musique, on the southern edge of Parc de la Villette, is a striking, triangular-shaped concert hall whose mission is to introduce music from around the world to Parisians. The **Musée de la Musique** (Music Museum; Map p400; adult/child €7/free; Ⓜ Porte de Pantin) inside displays some 900 rare musical instruments; you can hear many of them being played on the audioguide.

Next door is the new Paris Philharmonic Hall (estimated opening 2015) as well as the prestigious Conservatoire National Supérieur de Musique et de Danse, a top school for classical musicians and dancers.

PARC DES BUTTES-CHAUMONT PARK

Map p400 (rue Manin & rue Botzaris, 19e; ⏲7am-10pm May-Sep, to 8pm Oct-Apr; Ⓜ Buttes-Chaumont or Botzaris) This quirky park is one of the city's largest green spaces; its landscaped slopes hide grottoes, waterfalls, a lake and even an island topped with a temple to Sybil. Once a gypsum quarry and rubbish dump, it was given its present form by Baron Haussmann in time for the opening of the 1867 Exposition Universelle.

It's a favourite with Parisians, who come here to practise tai chi, take the kids to a puppet show or simply to relax with a bottle of wine and a picnic dinner. The tracks of an abandoned 19th-century railway line (La Petite Ceinture, which once circled Paris) also run through the park.

LE 104 GALLERY

(www.104.fr; 104 rue d'Aubervilliers or 5 rue Curial, 19e; ⏲noon-7pm Tue-Fri, 11am-7pm Sat & Sun; Ⓜ Stalingrad or Crimée) FREE A former funeral parlour turned city-funded art space, Le

104 has provided a much-needed jolt of vitality to an otherwise neglected neighbourhood. Spread out over a massive 39,000 sq metres, the complex is a hive of activity: a random wander through the public areas will turn up breakdancers, wacky art installations and rehearsing actors.

Check the schedule for events to make the most of it: there's circus, theatre, music, monthly balls and even magic shows. Some things are free; others require an admission fee. Also on site are a pizza truck, a cafe and a restaurant-bar.

INSTITUT DES CULTURES D'ISLAM — CULTURAL CENTRE

Map p398 (www.institut-cultures-islam.org; 19 rue Léon, 18e; ⏲10am-8pm Tue-Sat; Ⓜ Château Rouge) FREE The Islam Cultural Institute, located in the heart of the Goutte d'Or neighbourhood, hosts concerts, poetry readings, film screenings and temporary art exhibits, generally related to North Africa or the Middle East. There's also a pleasant cafe on site. A nearby **branch** (56 rue Stephenson, 18e; ⏲10am-9pm Tue-Sat, from 4pm Fri, noon-7pm Sun), opened in 2013, holds more temporary exhibition space as well as a hammam (p158).

CANAL ST-MARTIN — PARK

Map p398 (Ⓜ République, Jaurès or Jacques Bonsergent) The tranquil, 4.5km-long Canal St-Martin was inaugurated in 1825 to provide a shipping link between the Seine and the northeastern Parisian suburbs. Emerging from below ground near place République, its shaded towpaths take you past locks, metal bridges and ordinary Parisian neighbourhoods. It's a great place for a romantic stroll or cycle. Note that some of the neighbourhood bistros here are closed or have limited hours on Sunday and Monday.

MUSÉE DE L'ÉVANTAIL — MUSEUM

Map p398 (www.annehoguet.fr; 2 bd de Strasbourg, 10e; adult €6.50; ⏲2-6pm Mon-Wed, closed Aug; Ⓜ Strasbourg–St-Denis) Around 900 handheld fans are on display here, dating as far back as the mid-18th century. The small museum is housed in what was once a well-known fan manufactory, and its original showroom, dating from 1893, is sublime.

PORTE ST-DENIS — LANDMARK

Map p398 (cnr rue du Faubourg St-Denis & bd St-Denis, 10e; Ⓜ Strasbourg–St-Denis) Porte St-Denis and nearby **Porte St-Martin**

TOP SIGHT
MUSÉE JACQUEMART-ANDRÉ

If you belonged to the cream of Parisian society in the late 19th century, chances are you would have been invited to one of the dazzling soirées held at this mansion. The home of art collectors Nélie Jacquemart and Édouard André, this opulent residence was designed in the then-fashionable eclectic style, which combined elements from different eras – seen here in the presence of Greek and Roman antiquities, Egyptian artefacts, period furnishings and portraits by Dutch masters.

A wander through the 16 rooms offers an absorbing glimpse of the lifestyle and tastes of Parisian high society: from the library, hung with canvases by Rembrandt and Van Dyck, to the marvelous Jardin d'Hiver – a glass-paned garden room backed by a magnificent double-helix staircase. Upstairs is an impressive collection of Italian Renaissance works by Botticelli, Donatello and Titian, among others.

The mansion's architect, Henri Parent, was nearly hired to work on the even more prestigious Paris opera house, the Palais Garnier – he was beat out only by the then-unknown Charles Garnier. After the tour, stop in at the **salon de thé** (open ⏲11.45am to 5.30pm), which serves pastries as extravagant as the decor.

DON'T MISS...

- The library
- The Jardin d'Hiver
- The Italian art collection on the 2nd floor
- The tearoom

PRACTICALITIES

- Map p401
- www.musee-jacquemart-andre.com
- 158 bd Haussmann, 8e
- adult/child €11/9.50
- ⏲10am-6pm, to 9.30pm Mon & Sat during temporary exhibits
- Ⓜ Miromesnil

(Map p398; Ⓜ Strasbourg-St-Denis) were both built in the late 17th century to commemorate victories by Louis XIV's armies. When these triumphal arches were constructed, they replaced medieval gates in the Paris city walls.

EATING

Not much changes in the staid western Paris culinary scene, but once you cross over that invisible border somewhere in the middle of the 9th arrondissement, it's a different world. Every year sees a flurry of new openings in the neighbourhoods south of Pigalle or along the Canal St-Martin, and the young chefs at work here boast some of the most exciting dining venues in Paris today.

Montmartre & Pigalle

LE PETIT TRIANON CAFE €

Map p394 (☎01 44 92 78 08; 80 bd de Rochechouart, 18e; mains €7.50-13.50; ⏰8am-2pm; Ⓜ Anvers) With its large windows and a few carefully chosen antiques, this recently revived belle époque cafe at the foot of Montmartre feels about as timeless as the Butte itself. Dating back to 1894 and attached to the century-old Le Trianon theatre, it's no stretch to imagine artists like Toulouse-Lautrec and crowds of show-goers once filling the place in the evening.

Well-prepared standards (steak tartare, grilled swordfish) are served throughout the day; you can also just stop in for a drink.

LE COQUELICOT BOULANGERIE €

Map p394 (www.coquelicot-montmartre.com; 24 rue des Abbesses, 18e; omelettes €6.80, quiche with salad €4.40; ⏰7.30am-8pm; 👪; Ⓜ Abbesses) Although nothing to blog about, the Coquelicot bakery is nonetheless a good spot for an easy meal, offering omelettes, quiches, sandwiches and yummy pastries. The outdoor tables occupy a prime location alongside rue des Abbesses. It also serves breakfast.

LE GRENIER À PAIN BOULANGERIE €

Map p394 (38 rue des Abbesses, 18e; ⏰7.30am-8pm Thu-Mon; Ⓜ Abbesses) The Grenier has won Paris' 'best baguette' prize, though you'd be forgiven for thinking that its real speciality lies in the savoury *fougasses* (like focaccias) and mini breads that come with a range of alluring toppings (fig and goat's cheese, bacon and olives).

ARNAUD DELMONTEL BOULANGERIE €

Map p394 (39 rue des Martyrs, 9e; ⏰7am-8.30pm Wed-Mon; Ⓜ Pigalle) One of several Montmartre bakeries to win Paris' 'best baguette' prize in the past decade, Delmontel specialises in gorgeous pastries, cakes and a variety of artisanal breads.

SOUL KITCHEN VEGETARIAN €

Map p394 (33 Rue Lamarck, 18e; menus €13.50; ⏰8.30am-6.30pm Tue-Fri, 10am-7pm Sat & Sun; 📶🌿; Ⓜ Lamarck Caulincourt) For a more typically residential Montmartre neighbourhood, head to the backside of the hill. There's plenty to discover here, such as this inviting vegetarian eatery housed in an old cafe, where you can pick up market-driven dishes that change daily, including scrumptious soups, quiches and lasagne.

AFGHANI AFGHAN €

Map p394 (☎01 42 51 08 72; 16 Rue Paul Albert, 18e; mains €11-14; ⏰noon-2.30pm Thu-Sat, 7-10.30pm Mon-Sat; Ⓜ Château Rouge or Anvers) When you need to escape the busy Paris streets and recharge the batteries over a quiet meal, consider this inviting Afghan restaurant. Expect succulent lamb kebabs and flatbread alongside several veggie options, including scallion dumplings with curry and yoghurt. Reserve for dinner.

CRÊPERIE PEN-TY CRÊPERIE €

Map p394 (☎01 48 74 18 49; 65 rue de Douai, 9e; galettes €3-9.80, crêpes €3.90-8.80; ⏰noon-2.30pm & 7.30-11pm Mon-Sat; Ⓜ Place de Clichy) Hailed as the best crêperie in northern Paris, Pen-Ty is worth the detour – but be sure to book ahead. Need to brush up on Breton Cuisine 101? A *galette* is a savoury crêpe made from buckwheat flour; a regular crêpe is sweet and made from white flour. Hit the takeaway window if you can't get a table.

LE RELAIS GASCON GASCON €

Map p394 (☎01 42 58 58 22; www.lerelaisgascon.fr; 6 rue des Abbesses, 18e; mains €11.50-16.50, lunch/dinner menus €17.50/27.50; ⏰10am-2am; Ⓜ Abbesses) Situated just a short stroll from the place des Abbesses, the Relais Gascon

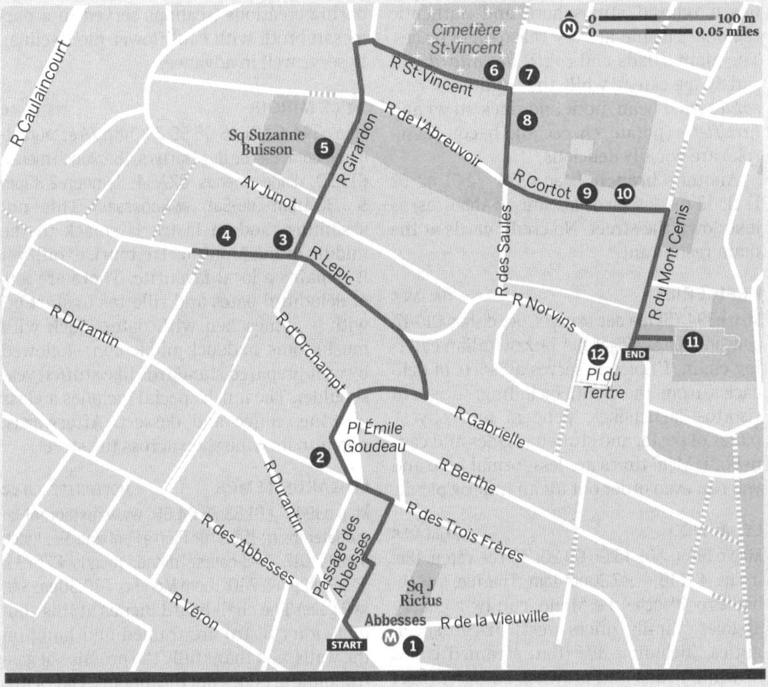

Neighbourhood Walk
Mythic Montmartre

START ABBESSES METRO STATION
END PLACE DU TERTRE
LENGTH 1KM; ONE HOUR

Begin at the 1 **place des Abbesses**, where Hector Guimard's iconic art-nouveau metro entrance (1900) still stands. Deep underground, beneath a maze of gypsum mines, is one of Paris' deepest metro stations.

Exit the square, heading up the passage des Abbesses to place Émile Goudeau. At No 11bis you'll find the 2 **Bateau Lavoir**, where Max Jacob, Amedeo Modigliani and Pablo Picasso – who painted his seminal *Les Demoiselles d'Avignon* (1907) here – once lived in great poverty.

Continue the climb up rue Lepic to Montmartre's two surviving windmills: the 3 **Moulin Radet** (now a restaurant) and, 100m west, the 4 **Moulin Blute-Fin**. In the 19th century, they were turned into the open-air dance hall Le Moulin de la Galette, immortalised by Renoir in his 1876 tableau *Le Bal du Moulin de la Galette* (displayed at the Musée d'Orsay). Just north of the windmills is Sq Suzanne Buisson, which holds a 5 **statue of St-Denis**, the 3rd-century martyr and patron saint of France who was beheaded by Roman priests.

After passing by the 6 **Cimetière St-Vincent**, where local painter Maurice Utrillo is buried, you'll come upon the celebrated cabaret 7 **Au Lapin Agile** (p156), which features a mural of a rabbit jumping out of a cooking pot by caricaturist André Gill. Just opposite is the 8 **Clos Montmartre**, a small vineyard dating from 1933, whose 2000 vines produce an average of 800 bottles of wine each October.

Up the hill is Montmartre's oldest building, a manor house built in the 17th century. The one-time home to painters Renoir, Utrillo and Raoul Dufy, it's now the 9 **Musée de Montmartre** (p140). Continue on past composer 10 **Eric Satie's former residence** (No 6) and then turn right onto rue du Mont Cenis; you'll soon come across the historic 11 **Église St-Pierre de Montmartre** (p140). End the tour at the busy 12 **place du Tertre** (p140), once the main square of the village.

has a relaxed atmosphere and authentic regional cuisine at very reasonable prices. The giant salads and *confit de canard* will satisfy big eaters, while the traditional *cassoulet* (rich bean, pork and duck stew) and *tartiflette* (potato, cheese and bacon casserole) are equally delicious.

Another **branch** (Map p394; ☎01 42 52 11 11; 13 rue Joseph de Maistre; Ⓜ Abbesses) is just down the street. No credit cards at the main restaurant.

L'ÉPICERIE — ITALIAN €

Map p394 (51 rue des Martyrs, 9e; dishes €10-17; ⏲noon-10pm; Ⓜ Pigalle) A buzzy Italian catering chain, L'Épicerie serves all sorts of delicacies from the Boot, including succulent risottos (artichokes, peppers and olives), plates of pasta, and stuffed veggies and cannelloni. Meal times are less formal here and you can even order out for an improv picnic.

LE MONO — AFRICAN €

Map p394 (☎01 46 06 99 20; 40 rue Véron, 18e; mains €11-18; ⏲7.30pm-1am Thu-Tue; Ⓜ Abbesses or Blanche) Le Mono, run by a cheery Togolese family, offers west African specialities, including *lélé* (flat, steamed cakes of white beans and prawns), *azidessi* (beef or chicken with peanut sauce), *gbekui* (goulash with spinach, onions, beef, fish and prawns) and *djenkoumé* (grilled chicken with semolina noodles). The rum-based punches are an excellent prelude.

L'ÉTÉ EN PENTE DOUCE — CAFE €

Map p394 (☎01 42 64 02 67; 23 rue Muller, 18e; mains €10.50-18.20; ⏲noon-midnight; Ⓜ Anvers) Parisian terraces don't get much better than this: a secret square wedged in between two flights of steep staircases on the backside of Montmartre, in a neighbourhood that's very much the real thing. Quiches, giant salads and classic dishes like Niçois-style stuffed veggies make up the menu.

★LE PANTRUCHE — BISTRO €€

Map p394 (☎01 48 78 55 60; www.lepantruche.com; 3 rue Victor Massé, 9e; lunch/dinner menus €19/35; ⏲12.30-2.30pm & 7.30-10.30pm Mon-Fri; Ⓜ Pigalle) Named after a nearby 19th-century theatre, classy Pantruche has been making waves in the already crowded dining hot spot of South Pigalle. No surprise, then, that it hits all the right notes: seasonal bistro fare, reasonable prices and an intimate setting. The menu runs from classics (steak with Béarnaise sauce) to more daring creations (scallops served in a parmesan broth with cauliflower mousseline). Reserve well in advance.

★LE MIROIR — BISTRO €€

Map p394 (☎01 46 06 50 73; http://restaurant-miroir.com; 94 rue des Martyrs, 18e; lunch menus €19.50, dinner menus €27-34; ⏲noon-2.30pm & 7.30-11pm Tue-Sat; Ⓜ Abbesses) This unassuming modern bistro is smack in the middle of the Montmartre tourist trail, yet it remains a local favourite. There are lots of delightful pâtés and rillettes to start off with – guinea hen with dates, duck with mushrooms, haddock and lemon – followed by well-prepared standards like stuffed veal shoulder. The lunch special includes a glass of wine, coffee and dessert. Afterwards, pop into its wine shop across the street.

LE GARDE TEMPS — MODERN FRENCH €€

Map p394 (☎01 83 76 04 66; www.restaurant-legardetemps.fr; 19bis rue Pierre Fontaine, 9e; lunch menus €17, 2-/3-course dinner menus €26/33; ⏲noon-2pm & 7-10.30pm Mon-Fri, 7-10.30pm Sat; Ⓜ Pigalle) The chalkboard menus at this contemporary bistro are framed and hung on the walls, and thankfully the promise of gastronomic art does not disappoint. Old bistro standards have been swept away in favour of more imaginative creations (fondant of red cabbage topped with quail confit) and – here's where the Garde Temps scores big points – the dinner prices aren't much more than that ho-hum cafe down the street.

BUVETTE GASTROTHÈQUE — NEOBISTRO €€

Map p394 (☎01 44 63 41 71; http://buvettegastrotheque.com; 28 rue Henry Monnier, 9e; small plates €5-10; ⏲8.30am-midnight Tue-Sun; 🖉; Ⓜ Pigalle) Parisians love anything that has to do with New York, and that includes French restaurants that hail from the West Village. But don't roll your eyes yet – owner Jody Williams has managed to combine the best of both worlds. There's nonstop service from breakfast (yes, breakfast!) to midnight, and a focus on flavour-filled small plates, meaning plenty of different dishes to sample. Think coq au vin, braised oxtails, roast bone marrow, honey-hazelnut *financiers* (tea cakes) and a good selection of veggie dishes, still something of a rarity in France. Tempting wine and cocktail list, but no reservations.

CHEZ TOINETTE — TRADITIONAL FRENCH €€

Map p394 (☎01 42 54 44 36; 20 rue Germain Pilon, 18e; mains €19-24; ⏲7-11.30pm Mon-Sat;

LOCAL KNOWLEDGE

BREAD & WINE BY THE GARE DU NORD

Yes, restaurant owners and chefs go out to eat, too. Charles Compagnon, owner of L'Office (p103), filled us in on his staff's top dining picks in Paris' burgeoning culinary hot spot, the 10e.

➡ **Le Grenier à Pain** (p144) They bake the bread we serve at L'Office. We really like *le pain de trois,* which is a kind of country bread that's made with three different types of flour. We also recommend their *gâteau basque* (a small round pastry filled with sweet almond paste).

➡ **Vivant** (p153) This is a great restaurant. The quality of the products is simply outstanding and the atmosphere is really *charmant* (charming). It's located in an old *oisellerie* (a place where exotic birds were raised and sold); the original faience tiling is still on the walls.

➡ **Albion** (p152) We really like this restaurant because of the quality of the cooking and the diverse wine selection.

MAbbesses) The atmosphere of this convivial restaurant is rivalled only by its fine cuisine (seared duck with honey, venison with foie gras). In the heart of one of the capital's most touristy neighbourhoods, Chez Toinette has kept alive the tradition of old Montmartre with its simplicity and culinary expertise. An excellent choice for a traditional French meal.

CUL DE POULE MODERN FRENCH €€

Map p394 (☎01 53 16 13 07; 53 rue des Martyrs, 9e; 2-/3-course menus lunch €16/19, dinner €24/29; ⏲noon-2.30pm & 8-11pm Mon-Sat; MPigalle) With plastic, orange cafeteria seats outside, you probably wouldn't wander into the Cul de Poule by accident. But the light-hearted spirit (yes, there is a mounted chicken's derrière on the wall) is deceiving; this is one of the most affordable quality kitchens in the Pigalle neighbourhood, with excellent neobistro fare that emphasises quality ingredients from the French countryside.

LE CAFÉ QUI PARLE MODERN FRENCH €€

Map p394 (☎01 46 06 06 88; 24 rue Caulaincourt, 18e; 2-/3-course lunch menus €12.50/17, mains €18-26; ⏲8.30am-11pm Mon-Sat, 9am-4.30pm Sun; 📶; MLamarck Caulaincourt or Blanche) The Café qui Parle is a fine example of where modern-day eateries are headed in Paris. It offers inventive, reasonably priced dishes prepared by owner-chef Damian Moeuf amid comfortable surroundings. Regulars love the art on the walls and ancient safes down below (the building was once a bank). A popular brunch is served on weekends, though it gets mixed reviews.

JEANNE B DELICATESSEN €€

Map p394 (61 rue Lepic, 18e; 2-/3-course menus lunch €19/23, dinner €23/27; ⏲9.30am-10.30pm; MAbbesses or Lamarck Caulincourt) Choose among the house-made terrines, stuffed veggies, salads, meat pies or roasted lamb and chicken at this gourmet sit-down deli. There's no overwrought buzz about the place, and even if the menu feels pricey, the dishes won't disappoint.

HÔTEL AMOUR BISTRO €€

Map p394 (☎01 48 78 31 80; www.hotelamour-paris.fr; 8 rue Navarin, 9e; mains €10-28; ⏲8am-midnight; 📶; MSt-Georges or Pigalle) Attached to the arty hotel of the same name, this buzzing hot spot is a cross between an American diner and a hip French bistro. The food is definitely not gourmet (*croque monsieur*, bacon cheeseburger), but it is served nonstop until midnight, making this a great after-hours stop. There is also fantastic garden seating – if you can get it.

CHEZ PLUMEAU FRENCH €€

Map p394 (☎01 46 06 26 29; 4 place du Calvaire, 18e; mains €15-26; ⏲11am-midnight Apr-Sep, noon-2.30pm & 7-10.30pm Thu-Mon Oct-Mar; 🖉; MAbbesses) Chez Plumeau caters to those who have just had their portraits done on place du Tertre. But for a tourist haunt it's not too bad (it even has veggie options), and the back terrace is great on a warm spring or summer afternoon.

LA MASCOTTE SEAFOOD, CAFE €€€

Map p394 (☎01 46 06 28 15; www.la-mascotte-montmartre.com; 52 rue des Abbesses, 18e; lunch/dinner menus €29/45, mains €23-39; ⏲8am-11.30pm; MAbbesses) Founded in

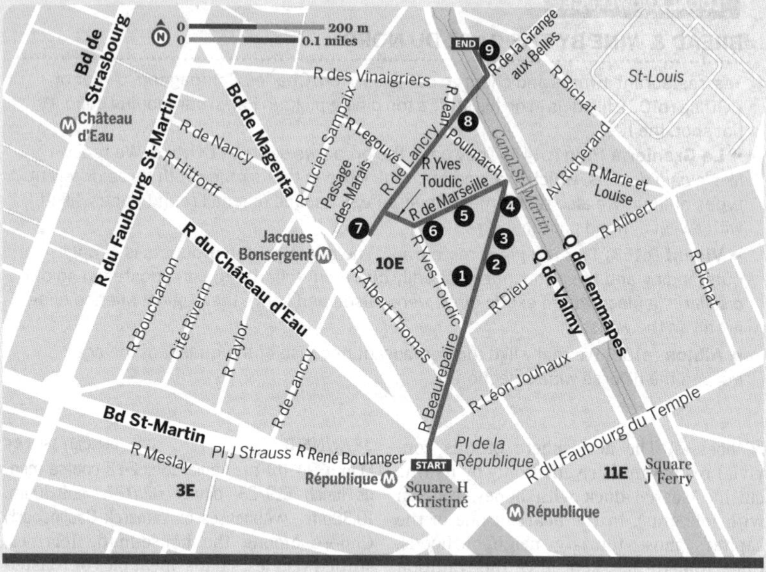

Local Life
Exploring the Canal St-Martin

Bordered by shaded towpaths and criss-crossed with iron footbridges, the Canal St-Martin wends through the city's northern neighbourhoods. Strolling among this rejuvenated *quartier*'s cool cafes, offbeat boutiques and hip restaurants lets you see why it's beloved by young Parisians.

❶ Rock 'n' Roll Fashion
Kick off on the boutique-lined rue Beaurepaire. One of the first designers to open up a store here was **Liza Korn** (Map p398; 19 rue Beaurepaire, 10e; ⏲11.30am-7.30pm Mon-Sat; Ⓜ Jacques Bonsergent), whose tiny store is a portal into a rich and playful imagination.

❷ Go Retro
Across the street, flip through racks of brand-name cast-offs at vintage boutique **Frivoli** (26 rue Beaurepaire, 10e; ⏲11am-7pm Mon-Fri, 2-7pm Sat & Sun) – among the best deals you'll find in the neighbourhood.

❸ Culture Vulture
Local artwork is often on display at **Espace Beaurepaire** (Map p398; www.espacebeaurepaire.com; 28 rue Beaurepaire, 10e; ⏲hours vary; Ⓜ Jacques Bonsergent) FREE, a gallery and cultural centre that also hosts events such as book signings, pop-up concept stores and dance performances.

❹ Canalside Cafes
Watch the passing boats from Chez Prune (p155), the rough-around-the-edges cafe that put Canal St-Martin on the map.

❺ Alternative Médecine
Around the corner is rue de Marseille, another great shopping street. You'll find a trio of famous Parisian brands here – Maje, Agnès B and APC – but don't overlook **Médecine Douce** (Map p398; www.bijouxmedecinedouce.com; 14 rue de Marseille, 10e; ⏲11am-7pm Tue-Sat, 2-7pm Mon; Ⓜ République or Jacques Bonsergent), a studio-showroom displaying gorgeous jewellery handmade on site.

❻ L'Heure du Gôuter
School kids pour into the belle époque bakery Du Pain et Des Ideés (p150) at *l'heure du gôuter* (snack time), seeking out the lemon and blackberry *escargots* ('snails', so called because of the shape of the pastry), croissants and bread.

Canal St-Martin (p143)

7 Say Cheese

If you're in need of supplies for a picnic on the canal quays, pop into local deli **La Crèmerie** (Map p398; 41 rue de Lancry, 10e; ⏲9.30am-1pm Mon, 9.30am-1.30pm & 4-8pm Tue-Sat; Ⓜ Jacques Bonsergent) for heavenly cheeses, cured hams, *saucisson* (dried cured sausage) and house-made jams.

8 Designer Books & Looks

Artazart (Map p398; www.artazart.com; 83 quai de Valmy, 10e; ⏲10.30am-7.30pm Mon-Sat, 1-7.30pm Sun; Ⓜ République or Jacques Bonsergent) is the leading design bookshop in Paris and, along with a fabulous collection of design and photography books in French and English, stocks quirky collector's items such as pinhole cameras, sleek kitchen utensils and sunflowers from a bag.

9 Historic Hotel & Cafe

The **Hôtel du Nord** (Map p398; www.hoteldunord.org; 102 quai de Jemmapes, 10e; ⏲9am-1.30am; 📶; Ⓜ Jacques Bonsergent) is the setting for Marcel Carné's 1938 film of the same name, which depicted the intersecting lives of those living in the hotel. Author Eugène Dabit, whose stories formed the film's basis, once lived here. It's now a book-lined cafe.

1889, this unassuming bar is about as authentic as it gets in Montmartre. It specialises in quality seafood – oysters, lobster, scallops – and regional dishes (Auvergne sausage), but you can also pull up a seat at the bar for a simple glass of wine and a plate of charcuterie.

LE COQ RICO FRENCH €€€

Map p394 (☎01 42 59 82 89; www.lecoqrico.com; 98 rue Lepic, 18e; mains €22-39, whole roast chicken €95; ⏲noon-2pm & 7-11pm; Ⓜ Abbesses) The first *haute cuisine* restaurant to open in Montmartre in years, Le Coq Rico specialises in poultry – and not just any poultry, but red-ribbon birds that have been raised in luxurious five-star chicken coops.

A selection of eggs, gizzards, bouillons, foie gras ravioli and other delicacies whet the appetite before the arrival of the pièce de résistance: an entire just-roasted chicken or guineafowl, which can be split up to four ways.

Clichy

MARCHÉ BATIGNOLLES-CLICHY MARKET €

Map p401 (bd des Batignolles, 8e & 17e; ⏲9am-2pm Sat; Ⓜ Place de Clichy) Near place de Clichy, this market is excellent for *produits biologiques* (organic produce).

LE BAL CAFÉ CAFE €€

Map p401 (☎01 44 70 75 51; www.le-bal.fr; 6 impasse de la Défense, 18e; 2-/3-course lunch menus €20/24; ⏲noon-8pm Wed-Sun, to 11pm Thu; 📶; Ⓜ Place de Clichy) Far off the beaten track, the Bal is an unlikely lunch destination in and of itself. But pair it with a photography exhibit at the adjacent gallery (p142), and you have an under-the-radar winner. Contemporary British fare is what's on the menu – think beef and Guinness pie and cheesecake with chutney. Good coffee too.

BISTRO DES DAMES BISTRO €€

Map p401 (☎01 45 22 13 42; 18 rue des Dames, 17e; mains €15-21; ⏲noon-2pm & 7-10.30pm; Ⓜ Place de Clichy) This charming little bistro will appeal to lovers of simple, authentic cuisine, with hearty salads, tortillas and glorious charcuterie platters of *pâté de campagne* and paper-thin Serrano ham. The dining room, which looks out onto the street, is lovely, but in summer it's the cool and tranquillity of the small back garden that pulls in the punters.

CHARLOT, ROI DES COQUILLAGES
FRENCH, SEAFOOD €€€

Map p401 (☎01 53 20 48 00; www.charlot-paris.com; 12 place de Clichy, 9e; lunch menus €22.50-€29.90, dinner menus €48; Ⓜ Place de Clichy) 'Charlot, the King of Shellfish' is an art-deco palace that is one of the best places in town for no-nonsense seafood. The platters and oysters are why everyone is here, but don't ignore the wonderful fish soup and mains, such as grilled sardines, *sole meunière* and bouillabaisse.

Gare du Nord & Canal St-Martin

LA POINTE DU GROIN
BRETON €

Map p398 (8 Rue de Belzunce, 10e; sandwiches & tapas from €4; ⏲8am-midnight Mon-Fri; Ⓜ Gare du Nord) This charmingly named eatery opened by chef Thierry Breton of Chez Michel (p152) specialises in top-quality tapas, Bretagne-style. Grab a gourmet sandwich to go – the bread is superb – or feast on oysters, chèvre-and-leek pie, *galette saucisse* (a hot dog wrapped in a crêpe) and *far Breton* (prune flan). Pints of Philomenn (Breton craft beer) and good wine are reasonably priced too.

There's a catch, of course, and in this case it's the bizarre payment system. You have to pay in, uh, groins, the local currency that you purchase from a coin dispenser (European credit cards and cash accepted) while waiting in line to order. There's a €10 minimum; one euro equals one groin.

DU PAIN ET DES IDÉES
BOULANGERIE €

Map p398 (34 rue Yves Toudic, 10e; ⏲7am-8pm Mon-Fri; Ⓜ Jacques Bonsergent) Fabulous traditional bakery with naturally leavened bread, orange-blossom brioche and *escargots* (similar to cinnamon rolls) in four decadent flavours – pistachio and chocolate, anyone? The bakery itself dates back to 1889.

LA CANTINE DE QUENTIN
TRADITIONAL FRENCH €

Map p398 (☎01 42 02 40 32; 52 rue Bichat, 10e; lunch menus €16.50; ⏲noon-2.30pm Tue-Sun, shop 10am-7.30pm; Ⓜ Jacques Bonsergent or Gare de l'Est) A bewitching combination of gourmet food shop and lunchtime bistro, La Cantine de Quentin stocks quality products from the countryside (*cassoulet*, charcuterie, wine, tapenade, vinegar, mushrooms), many of which find their way into the back-room kitchen. You won't leave empty handed.

KRISHNA BHAVAN
INDIAN, VEGETARIAN €

Map p398 (☎01 42 05 78 43; www.krishnabhavan.com; 24 rue Cail, 10e; thaali €10-12, dishes €4.50-6; ⏲11am-10.30pm; 🖉; Ⓜ La Chapelle) This is about as authentic an Indian vegetarian canteen as you'll find in Paris. If in doubt as to what to order, ask for a *thaali*, a circular steel tray with samosas, dosas and other wrapped goodies. Wash it all down with a yoghurt-based lassi, which comes in five flavours, including mango and rose. There's more seating across the street.

SÉSAME
CAFE €

Map p398 (☎01 42 49 03 21; www.au-sesame.com; 51 Quai de Valmy, 10e; dishes €8-13.50; ⏲9am-midnight Mon-Fri, from 10am Sat & Sun; 📶; Ⓜ République or Jacques Bonsergent) Whether you're in search of an artsy canal-side hangout or a picnic to go, this winning pink-hued cafe has all the goods, from psychedelic-coloured cupcakes and bagel sandwiches to salads (eg smoked duck), soups and death-by-chocolate upside-down brownie.

PINK FLAMINGO
PIZZERIA €

Map p398 (☎01 42 02 31 70; www.pinkflamingopizza.com; 67 rue Bichat, 10e; pizzas €11.50-17; ⏲7-11.30pm Mon-Thu, noon-3pm & 7-11.30pm Fri-Sun; 👪; Ⓜ Jacques Bonsergent) Not another pizza place? *Mais non, chérie!* Once the weather warms up, the Flamingo unveils its secret weapon – pink helium balloons that the delivery guy uses to locate you and your perfect canal-side picnic spot (GPS not needed). Order a Poulidor (duck, apple and chèvre) or a Basquiat (gorgonzola, figs and cured ham), pop into Le Verre Volé across the canal for the perfect bottle of vino and you're set.

BOB'S JUICE BAR
VEGETARIAN €

Map p398 (☎09 50 06 36 18; www.bobsjuicebar.com; 15 rue Lucien Sampaix, 10e; juices €4-6.50, sandwiches €6.50; ⏲7.30am-3pm Mon-Fri, 8.30am-4pm Sat; Ⓜ Jacques Bonsergent) In need of some vitamin C? Sweet-potato soup? This tiny outpost (and do note that it is tiny) with bags of rice flour and flaxseed lining the walls serves delicious smoothies, freshly squeezed organic juices, vegan breakfasts, hummus sandwiches...in short, all those things you might have trouble finding elsewhere in Paris.

LOCAL KNOWLEDGE

HÔTEL DU NORD

If you want a glimpse of life along the canal before it became cool, the movie to watch is Marcel Carné's *Hôtel du Nord* (1938). The story revolves around the residents of the hotel – including a canal worker, a prostitute, a drifting criminal and a lovesick girl – and is hardly short on drama; it begins with a botched double suicide and ends with a murder. The highlight, though, is the dialogue, delivered with an old-fashioned Parisian accent that, let's face it, is a lot more fun than the French you hear today. One of the most unforgettable lines in all French cinema belongs to Arletty's character (the prostitute). Accused of being a 'suffocating atmosphere' in a lovers' spat, she responds, *'Atmosphère? Atmosphère?! Est-ce que j'ai une gueule d'atmosphère?!'* (Atmosphere? Atmosphere?! Do I look like an atmosphere?!) Today the movie is referenced in the names of a local hotel, restaurant and cafe.

SUNKEN CHIP FAST FOOD €

Map p398 (www.thesunkenchip.com; 39 Rue des Vinaigriers, 10e; fish & chips €12-14; ⏲noon-2.30pm & 7-10.30pm Wed-Sun; 👪; Ⓜ Jacques Bonsergent) Although it's hard to believe anyone would come to Paris in search of fish 'n' chips, it's hard to argue with the battered, fried goodness at this ideally located takeaway. Nothing frozen here: it's all line-caught fish fresh from Brittany (three varieties per day), accompanied by thick-cut chips (peeled and chopped *sur place*), malt vinegar and mushy peas.

HELMUT NEWCAKE CAFE €

Map p398 (www.helmutnewcake.com; 36 rue Bichat, 10e; mains €7.80-9.80; ⏲noon-7.30pm Tue-Sat, to 6pm Sun; Ⓜ Goncourt) Combining the French genius for pastries with a 100% gluten-free kitchen, Helmut Newcake is one of those Parisian addresses that some will simply have to hang on to. Éclairs, fondants, cheesecake and tarts are some of the dessert options, while you can count on lunch (salads, quiches, soups, pizzas) to be scrumptious and market driven.

LE GRENIER À PAIN BOULANGERIE €

Map p386 (91 rue Faubourg Poissonnière, 9e; ⏲7.30am-8pm Thu-Tue, to 1.30pm Sun; Ⓜ Poissonnière) Michel Galloyer founded this string of artisan bakeries, which also includes an award-winning branch (p144) in Montmartre.

LE RÉVEIL DU XE TRADITIONAL FRENCH €

Map p398 (☎01 42 41 77 59; 35 rue du Château d'Eau, 10e; mains €11.50-18; ⏲noon-2.30pm & 7.30-10.30pm Mon-Fri, noon-2.30pm Sat; Ⓜ Château d'Eau) This corner bistro is slightly out of the way, but if you're in search of a locals' place you won't regret the trip. Plates of charcuterie (*saucisson*, rillettes, pâté) and Auvergne cheeses (cantal, St-Nectaire, *bleu*) supplement French standards, and there are even mixed salads for those hoping for a glimpse of the colour green.

LE CAMBODGE CAMBODIAN €

Map p398 (☎01 44 84 37 70; www.lecambodge.fr; 10 av Richerand, 10e; dishes €10-13.50; ⏲noon-2.30pm & 7-11pm Mon-Sat; Ⓜ Goncourt) Hidden in a quiet street between the gargantuan Hôpital St-Louis and Canal St-Martin, this long-standing favourite serves enormous spring rolls and the ever-popular *pique-nique Angkorien* (rice vermicelli and sautéed beef, which you wrap up in lettuce leaves). The food tastes homemade (if not especially authentic) and the vegetarian options are especially good.

If the wait to get a seat is long (often the case – there are no reservations), a hipper, more modern **branch** (Map p398; 20 Rue Alibert, 10e; dishes €10-13; ⏲noon-11pm; 📶; Ⓜ Goncourt) is located just down the street.

SOL SEMILLA VEGETARIAN €

Map p398 (www.sol-semilla.fr; 23 Rue des Vinaigriers, 10e; menus €14.50; ⏲noon-4pm Tue-Sun; 🌶; Ⓜ Jacques Bonsergent or Gare de l'Est) 🍃 The Parisian superfood specialist, Sol Semilla is both a boutique (get your spirulina here) and lunchtime canteen, where you'll find organic supersoups (vitality, detox), vegan-friendly seasonal salads and stir-fries, açaí berry smoothies and raw-cocoa desserts. The shop and smoothie station is open to 7pm.

MARCHÉ ST-QUENTIN MARKET €

Map p398 (85bis bd de Magenta, 10e; ⏲8am-8pm Tue-Sat, to 1.30pm Sun; Ⓜ Gare de l'Est) This iron-and-glass covered market, built in 1866, has the usual range of French specialities and produce, as well as affordable lunches at a variety of stalls (including African and Lebanese).

EL NOPAL MEXICAN €

Map p398 (3 Rue Eugène Varlin, 10e; 3 tacos €7.70; ⌚lunch & dinner Tue-Fri, 1-11pm Sat, 1-9pm Sun; Ⓜ Château Landon) For those in need of a *chicharrón* (fried pork crackling) and taco fix, this colourful hole in the wall with the line out the door is the place to be. You won't get a seat (there aren't any), but as long as the weather cooperates, you can't go wrong with an impromptu picnic on the canal.

LA MÔME NORTH AFRICAN €

Map p398 (☎01 42 23 35 64; 16 rue Stephenson, 18e; tajines €13-17; ⌚noon-3pm & 7-10.30pm Mon-Sat; Ⓜ La Chapelle or Barbès Rochechouart) For a mouth-watering selection of Moroccan *tajines* and *pastillas* (sweet and savoury meat pies), head up to the vibrant Goutte d'Or neighbourhood in northern Paris. An unassuming cafe with cracked tile floors and a cosy interior, La Môme's *tajine* menu runs from chicken and pears to duck with cherries and pistachios.

★LE VERRE VOLÉ BISTRO €€

Map p398 (☎01 48 03 17 34; 67 rue de Lancry, 10e; mains lunch €15-17, dinner €15-26; ⌚noon-2.30pm & 7-10.30pm; Ⓜ Jacques Bonsergent) The tiny 'Stolen Glass' – a wine shop with a few tables – is just about the most perfect wine bar–restaurant in Paris, with excellent wines and expert advice. Unpretentious and hearty *plats du jour* (dishes of the day) are excellent. Reserve well in advance for meals, or stop by to pick up a bottle.

★ABRI NEOBISTRO €€

Map p398 (☎01 83 97 00 00; 92 rue du Faubourg Poissonnière, 9e; lunch/dinner menus €25/43; ⌚noon-2.30pm Mon, noon-2.30pm & 7.30-10pm Tue-Sat; Ⓜ Poissonnière) It's no bigger than a shoebox and the decor is borderline nonexistent, but converts will tell you that's all part of the charm. The reason everyone's raving? Katsuaki Okiyama is a seriously talented chef with an artistic flair, and his tasting menus (three courses at lunch, six at dinner) are exceptionally good value.

On Monday and Saturday, a giant sandwich (€13, includes drink) is all that's served for lunch. Reserve well in advance.

★CHEZ MICHEL BRETON, SEAFOOD €€

Map p398 (☎01 44 53 06 20; 10 rue Belzunce, 10e; menus lunch/dinner €29/35; ⌚7pm-midnight Mon, noon-2.30pm & 7pm-midnight Tue-Fri; Ⓜ Gare du Nord) If all you know about Breton cuisine is crêpes and cider, a visit to Chez Michel is in order. The only option is to order the four-course *menu*, which features excellent seafood (scallop tartare, hake with Breton white beans) as well as numerous specialities like *kig ha farz* (Breton pot au feu), *keuz breizh* (Breton cheeses) and *kouign* (butter cake). An extra surcharge for certain dishes is common.

Two doors down is little brother **Chez Casimir** (6 rue Belzunce, 10e; menus €24-32; ⌚lunch & dinner Mon-Fri, 10am-7pm Sat & Sun; Ⓜ Gare du Nord), with decent bistro fare, while just next door is the endearingly quirky Pointe du Groin (p150).

PHILOU BISTRO €€

Map p398 (☎01 42 38 00 13; 12 av Richerand, 10e; 2-/3-course menus €27/34; ⌚noon-2.30pm & 8-10.30pm Mon-Fri; Ⓜ Jacques Bonsergent) The walls at this swanky bistro are nearly 100% chalkboard, with the day's temptations writ large. The brainchild of seasoned chef Philippe Damas – the man who founded Le Square Trousseau (p194) – Philou steers away from the latest trends, preferring instead succulent French comfort food prepared with top-of-the-line ingredients.

LES VINAIGRIERS MODERN FRENCH €€

Map p398 (☎01 46 07 97 12; 42 Rue des Vinaigriers, 10e; lunch menus €19, dinner mains €21-23; ⌚noon-3pm & 7.30-10.30pm Tue-Sat; Ⓜ Jacques Bonsergent or Gare de l'Est) This darling dining room, anchored by the vintage corkscrew staircase in the back and an open kitchen facing the street, offers one of the canal's best-value lunch deals. The modern French cuisine is excellent – think delicate pumpkin soup with mint and chèvre emulsion, or orecchiette pasta with a rich white-wine-based cream of chicken. Reserve.

ALBION NEOBISTRO €€

Map p398 (☎01 42 46 02 44; 80 rue du Faubourg Poissonnière, 10e; mains €21-28; ⌚noon-2pm & 7-10.30pm Tue-Sat; Ⓜ Poissonnière) Albion is the ancient Greek name for England and it's no coincidence that it's a mere five-minute jaunt from the Gare du Nord, and, what's more, run by two affable English speakers. But don't read into the name too much: this sleek new place is still very Paris, with bottles of wine lining one wall, waiting to be paired with the modern cuisine.

BISTRO BELLET NEOBISTRO €€

Map p398 (☎01 45 23 42 06; 84 Rue du Faubourg Saint-Denis, 10e; 2-/3-course menus €28/36; ⏰6.30pm-midnight Tue-Sat; MChâteau d'Eau) An energetic modern bistro, the Bellet doesn't stray far from the usual French standards on the culinary front (steak with Béarnaise sauce, roasted cod and asparagus), but the slight alterations to the usual template – excellent natural wines, a cocktail list, and both early and late-night service – have earned it plenty of praise among the out-and-about crowd.

LA MARINE CAFE €€

Map p398 (☎01 42 39 69 81; 55bis quai de Valmy, 10e; lunch menus €15, mains €16-22; ⏰7.30am-2am Mon-Fri, from 8.30am Sat & Sun; 📶; MRépublique) A large, airy hang-out overlooking Canal St-Martin, La Marine has been multitasking as a cafe, restaurant and bar for years now, and offers a good cross-section of the neighbourhood population.

LE CHANSONNIER TRADITIONAL FRENCH €€

Map p398 (☎01 42 09 40 58; www.lechansonnier.com; 14 rue Eugène Varlin, 10e; lunch/dinner menus €12.20/26; ⏰lunch & dinner Mon-Fri, dinner Sat & Sun; MChâteau Landon or Louis Blanc) The 'Singer' (named after the 19th-century Lyonnais socialist singer-songwriter Pierre Dupont) could be a film set, with its curved zinc bar and art-nouveau mouldings. Refreshingly unhip, the food is old-school French and very substantial with mains that range from *noix St-Jacques provençal* (scallops in herbed tomato sauce) and bouillabaisse to *daube de sanglier* (boar stew).

JAMBO AFRICAN €€

Map p398 (☎01 42 45 46 55; 23 rue Ste-Marthe, 10e; 3-course menus €28; ⏰7.30-10.30pm; MBelleville) This charming restaurant, decorated with shields and masks from different parts of Africa, was opened by a former aid worker and his Rwandan wife. The menu is inspired by central African cuisine; many of the ingredients are imported direct from Kigali, the Rwandan capital.

LA ROTONDE BRASSERIE €€

Map p398 (☎01 80 48 33 40; www.larotonde.com; 6-8 place de la Bataille de Stalingrad, 19e; mains €14-22, bar food from €3.50; ⏰10am-2am Mon-Sat, 11am-8pm Sun; 📶; MStalingrad) Overlooking the Bassin de la Villette, this striking 18th-century edifice went from customs station to police barracks to salt warehouse before its most recent conversion in late 2011 to hip new brasserie. The light-filled circular atrium is the show stealer, but the casual bar-cafe (opens 6pm) with inexpensive meals is what draws in the crowds.

WORTH A DETOUR

CHEZ LOUISETTE

Here since 1967, **Chez Louisette** (⏰8am-6pm Sat-Mon) is popular with tourists visiting Paris' largest flea market, the Marché aux Puces de St-Ouen. The food is as abysmal as the service; the real reason people come here is to hear old-time *chanteuses* and *chanteurs* belt out numbers by Piaf and other classic French singers.

TERMINUS NORD BRASSERIE €€

Map p398 (☎01 42 85 05 15; 23 rue de Dunkerque, 10e; mains €18.50-35.50, menus €28 & €34.50; ⏰7.30am-midnight; MGare du Nord) Directly across from the Gare du Nord, this landmark brasserie has a copper bar, waiters in white uniforms, brass fixtures and mirrored walls that look as they did when it opened in 1925. Breakfast is available from 7.30am to 10.30am.

VIVANT MODERN FRENCH €€€

Map p398 (☎01 42 46 43 55; http://vivantparis.com; 43 rue des Petites Écuries, 10e; mains €23-29; ⏰noon-2.30pm & 7-10.30pm Mon-Fri; MBonne Nouvelle) Pierre Jancou, the mind behind natural-wine bars like Racines (p125) and La Crèmerie, has moved on to his latest adventure set in a century-old exotic-bird shop. Here simple but elegant dishes – creamy burrata cheese, crispy duck leg with mashed potatoes, foie gras and roasted onion, an Italian cheese plate – are created to showcase the carefully sourced ingredients. Swiss-born Jancou is a natural-wine activist, so make sure you treat yourself to at least a glass: it's an essential part of the meal here (although be prepared: it's not cheap). Next door is the equally alluring wine bar, **Vivant Cave** (⏰5pm-midnight), where you can pop in for a glass, bottle or more casual meal. Reserve.

DRINKING & NIGHTLIFE

Crowded around place Pigalle (at the foot of Montmartre) you'll find an eclectic selection of nightlife options, from local cafes and hipster dives to dance clubs and hostess bars. In contrast, the trend around the Canal St-Martin is more barista-run cafes, though wonderful summer nights (and days) see everyone decamp to the canal-side quays with blankets, baguettes and bottles of wine.

Montmartre & Pigalle

ARTISAN — COCKTAIL BAR

Map p394 (14 rue Bochart de Saron, 9e; 7pm-2am Tue-Sat, noon-4pm Sun; M Anvers) Pigalle doesn't have many sophisticated drinking options, but the white-walled Artisan fits the bill nicely, with delicious small plates, wines by the glass and well-mixed cocktails.

LA FOURMI — BAR

Map p394 (74 rue des Martyrs, 18e; 8am-1am Mon-Thu, to 3am Fri & Sat, 10am-1am Sun; M Pigalle) A Pigalle institution, La Fourmi hits the mark with its high ceilings, long zinc bar and unpretentious vibe. Get up to speed on live music and club nights or sit down for a reasonably priced meal and drinks.

LE PROGRÈS — BAR

Map p394 (7 rue des Trois Frères, 18e; 9am-2am; M Abbesses) A real live *café du quartier* perched in the heart of Abbesses, the 'Progress' occupies a corner site with huge windows and simple seating and attracts a relaxed mix of local artists, shop staff, writers and hangers-on. It's great for convivial evenings, but it's also a good place to come for inexpensive meals and cups of coffee.

CAVE DES ABBESSES — WINE BAR

Map p394 (43 rue des Abbesses, 18e; cheese & charcuterie €7-13; 5-9.30pm Tue-Sun; M Abbesses) Pass through the door at the back of the Cave des Abbesses wine shop and you'll discover, no, not a storage room or a portal to another dimension, but instead a quirky little bar. It feels like one of those places only regulars know about, but don't be intimidated; sit down, order a plate of cheese and a glass of Corbières, and you'll blend right in.

KB CAFE — CAFE

Map p394 (53 ave Trudaine, 9e; 7.30am-6.30pm Mon-Fri, 9am-6.30pm Sat & Sun; wi-fi; M Pigalle) If you can't stomach another cup of carelessly brewed Parisian coffee, take note: KB (Kooka Boora) was probably opened just for you. The pros behind the counter can serve up the sacred bean in all of its myriad forms, along with freshly squeezed juices and baked nibbles for breakfast and lunch.

GLASS — BAR

Map p394 (7 rue Frochot, 9e; 7pm-2am; M Pigalle) Pop into this old girly bar, tinted windows and all, for Brooklyn Brewery and Demory beers on tap, beef hot dogs and punk rock on the stereo. With €4 half pints it's certainly no dive bar, however much it may look the part.

DIRTY DICK — BAR

Map p394 (10 rue Frochot, 9e; 6pm-2am; M Pigalle) Another former girly bar (as if you couldn't guess) that's been bought out and infused with hipster vibes, resulting in what is now the city's favourite tiki bar – except, of course, that, being in Paris, the Hawaiian smiles are a bit harder to come by.

LE SANCERRE — BAR

Map p394 (35 rue des Abbesses, 18e; 7am-2am; wi-fi; M Abbesses) Le Sancerre is a popular, rather brash bistro-bar that's often crowded to capacity in the evening, especially on Saturday. Scruffy yet attractive with its classic bistro decor and hip local mood, it has a prized terrace that gets the late-morning sun.

AU P'TIT DOUAI — BAR

Map p394 (92 rue Blanche, 9e; 8am-2am Sat, 11am-8pm Sun; wi-fi; M Blanche) This colourful neighbourhood cafe is just down the street from the Moulin Rouge, but it might as well be light years away. Trade in the mayhem for some tranquillity over coffee, wines by the glass or traditional French fare at mealtimes.

AU RENDEZ-VOUS DES AMIS — BAR

Map p394 (23 rue Gabrielle, 18e; 8am-2am; M Abbesses) If you need to ease your way up or down the steps of Montmartre, look no further than this kick-back cafe-bar, which serves inexpensive espresso and pitchers of beer. Sandwiches and snacks are prepared in Hell's Kitchen.

LE CARMEN CLUB

Map p394 (www.le-carmen.fr; 34 rue Duperré, 9e; ⌚midnight-6pm; Ⓜ Pigalle or Blanche) So named because this is where Bizet wrote the opera, the decor here is over-the-top opulent, with extravagant period details still intact and antique furnishings to boot. There's a bar on the ground floor (cocktails are just so-so) and a dance club in the basement.

LA MACHINE DU MOULIN ROUGE CLUB

Map p394 (90 bd de Clichy, 18e; ⌚hours vary; Ⓜ Blanche) Part of the original Moulin Rouge (well, the boiler room, anyway), this club packs 'em in on weekends with a dance floor, concert hall, champagne bar and terrace.

Gare du Nord & Canal St-Martin

★ HOLYBELLY CAFE

Map p398 (http://holybel.ly; 19 Rue Lucien Sampaix, 10e; ⌚9am-6pm Thu-Mon, from 10am Sat & Sun; Ⓜ Jacques Bonsergent) The largest and liveliest of Paris' new wave of barista-run coffee shops, this soulful hang-out features distressed decor and a serious kitchen serving up breakfast and lunch, with a list of seasonal fruits and veggies scrawled on the blackboard in the brick-walled back room. Bonus: pinball machine.

TUCK SHOP CAFE

Map p398 (13 rue Lucien Sampaix, 10e; ⌚10am-5pm Tue-Fri, 11am-6pm Sat & Sun; Ⓜ Jacques Bonsergent) Superb coffee at this Aussie-run vegetarian hang-out. Food is as affordable as it gets in Paris (€10 or under for a meal), though the space is small – getting a seat may require patience.

CHEZ PRUNE BAR

Map p398 (71 quai de Valmy, 10e; ⌚8am-2am Mon-Sat, 10am-2am Sun; Ⓜ République) This Soho-boho cafe put Canal St-Martin on the map a decade ago and its good vibes and rough-around-the-edges look show no sign of fading in the near future.

L'ATMOSPHÈRE BAR

Map p398 (49 rue Lucien Sampaix, 10e; ⌚9.30am-1.45am Mon-Sat, to midnight Sun; Ⓜ Jacques Bonsergent or Gare de l'Est) A nod to the 1938 flick *Hôtel du Nord,* this timber-and-tile cafe along the canal has an arty, spirited ambience, well-priced drinks and good food.

CHEZ JEANNETTE BAR

Map p398 (www.chezjeannette.com; 47 rue du Faubourg St-Denis, 10e; ⌚8am-2am; Ⓜ Château d'Eau) Cracked tile floors and original 1950s decor have turned Chez Jeannette into one of the 10e's most popular hot spots. Local hang-out by day, pints by night and reasonably priced meals around the clock.

CAFÉ CHÉRI(E) BAR

Map p398 (44 bd de la Villette, 19e; ⌚noon-1am; Ⓜ Belleville) An imaginative, colourful bar with its signature red lighting, infamous mojitos and *caipirinhas* and commitment to quality tunes, Chéri(e) is everyone's darling in this part of town. Gritty art-chic crowd and electro DJs Thursday to Saturday.

CORK & CAVAN PUB

Map p398 (70 Quai de Jemmapes, 10e; ⌚3pm-2am Mon-Fri, from 1pm Sat & Sun; 📶; Ⓜ République or Goncourt) It's the location that seals the deal for the Cork, with reasonably priced Guinness-to-go and an always busy scene that spills onto the quays in warm weather.

LE COQ COCKTAIL BAR

Map p398 (12 rue du Château d'Eau, 10e; ⌚6pm-2am; Ⓜ République or Jacques Bonsergent) 🍃 Pop art and concrete walls set the stage for the 10e's trendy cocktail bar, which serves up a short list of signature tipples incorporating French spirits – eg Les Fleurs du Mal (absinthe and rose-infused vodka) or Initials BB (Benedictine and bourbon).

DELAVILLE CAFÉ BAR

Map p398 (34 bd de Bonne Nouvelle, 10e; ⌚11am-2.30am; Ⓜ Bonne Nouvelle) This grand erstwhile brothel has an alluring mix of restored history and industrial chic. Between the high-ceilinged restaurant, one of the best terraces on the *grands boulevards* and the bar-lounge areas, you're sure to find your niche somewhere.

☆ ENTERTAINMENT

☆ Montmartre & Pigalle

MOULIN ROUGE CABARET

Map p394 (☎01 53 09 82 82; www.moulinrouge.fr; 82 bd de Clichy, 18e; Ⓜ Blanche) Immortalised in the posters of Toulouse-Lautrec and later on screen by Baz Luhrmann, the Moulin

Rouge twinkles beneath a 1925 replica of its original red windmill. Yes, it's rife with bus-tour crowds. But from the opening bars of music to the last high kick it's a whirl of fantastical costumes, sets, choreography and Champagne. Booking advised.

LE TRIANON LIVE MUSIC

Map p394 (☎01 44 92 78 00; www.letrianon.fr; 80 bd de Rochechouart, 18e; Ⓜ Anvers) This century-old music hall features two levels of balconies as well as a main floor area. An intimate spot to catch a quality show: think Dr John, John Butler and – flashback – Tower of Power.

LA CIGALE LIVE MUSIC

Map p394 (☎01 49 25 89 99; www.lacigale.fr; 120 bd de Rochechouart, 18e; admission €25-60; Ⓜ Anvers or Pigalle) Now classed as a historical monument, this music hall dates from 1887 but was redecorated 100 years later by Philippe Starck. Artists who have performed here recently include Rufus Wainwright, Ryan Adams and Ibrahim Maalouf.

LE DIVAN DU MONDE LIVE MUSIC

Map p394 (☎01 40 05 06 99; www.divandumonde.com; 75 rue des Martyrs, 18e; ⏲hours vary; Ⓜ Pigalle) Take some cinematographic events, gypsy gatherings, *nouvelles chansons françaises* (new French songs). Add in soul/funk fiestas, air-guitar face-offs and rock parties of the Arctic Monkeys/Killers/Libertines persuasion and stir with an Amy Winehouse swizzle stick. You may now be getting some idea of the inventive, open-minded approach at this excellent cross-cultural venue in Pigalle.

BUS PALLADIUM LIVE MUSIC

Map p394 (www.lebuspalladium.com; 6 rue Pierre Fontaine, 9e; ⏲hours vary; Ⓜ Blanche) Once the place to be back in the 1960s, the Bus is now back in business 50 years later, with funky DJs and a mixed bag of performances by indie and pop groups.

AU LAPIN AGILE CABARET

Map p394 (☎01 46 06 85 87; www.au-lapin-agile.com; 22 rue des Saules, 18e; adult €28, student except Sat €20; ⏲9pm-1am Tue-Sun; Ⓜ Lamarck-Caulaincourt) This rustic cabaret venue was favoured by artists and intellectuals in the early 20th century and traditional *chansons* are still performed here. The four-hour show starts at 9.30pm and includes singing and poetry. Some love it, others feel it's a bit of a trap. It's named after *Le Lapin à Gill*, a mural of a rabbit jumping out of a cooking pot by caricaturist André Gill, which can still be seen on the western exterior wall.

☆ Gare du Nord & Canal St-Martin

POINT ÉPHÉMÈRE LIVE MUSIC

Map p398 (www.pointephemere.org; 200 quai de Valmy, 10e; ⏲12.30pm-2am Mon-Sat, 12.30-11pm Sun; 📶; Ⓜ Louis Blanc) This arts and music venue by the Canal St-Martin attracts an underground crowd from noon till past midnight, for drinks, meals, concerts, dance nights and even art exhibitions. At the time of writing there were three different food trucks setting up shop here three days a week after 7pm.

CANAL CRUISES

Everyone takes the river boats down the Seine, but if you're up for something slightly different, why not try a canal cruise? Two companies run 2½-hour trips along the Canal St-Martin, chugging back and forth between central Paris and Parc de la Villette. Boats go at a leisurely pace, passing through four locks and an underground section (livened up somewhat by an art installation).

➔ **Canauxrama** (www.canauxrama.com; adult/student & senior/child 4-12yr €16/12/8.50) Departures are at 9.45am and 2.30pm from the Port de l'Arsenal at the Bastille and Parc de la Villette. There are also evening cruises on Friday and Saturday from May through September.

➔ **Paris Canal Croisières** (☎01 42 40 96 97; www.pariscanal.com; adult/senior & 12-25yr/ child 4-11yr €19/16/12; ⏲mid-Mar–mid-Nov) Cruises depart from near the Musée d'Orsay (quai Anatole France) at 9.30am and from Parc de la Villette at 2.30pm.

ROSA BONHEUR DANCE HALL

Map p400 (www.rosabonheur.fr; Parc des Buttes-Chaumont, 19e; ⌚noon-midnight Wed-Sun; Ⓜ Botzaris) This self-styled *guinguette* (old-fashioned dance hall) morphs from outdoor cafe by day into a jam-packed dance floor by night. Its setting inside the Parc des Buttes-Chaumont is surely the most bucolic getaway in the city, and even if the tapas aren't to die for, good vibes are virtually guaranteed. If the park is closed, you'll need to enter at 7 rue Botzaris.

LE 104 THEATRE

(www.le104.fr; 104 rue d'Aubervilliers or 5 rue Curial, 19e; ⌚noon-7pm Tue-Fri, 11am-7pm Sat & Sun; 📶; Ⓜ Stalingrad or Crimée) Circus, theatre, music, monthly balls, magic shows and even Paris' Maker Faire are held at this former funeral parlour turned city-funded art space (p142). Some shows are free; others charge an admission fee.

CABARET SAUVAGE WORLD MUSIC

Map p400 (www.cabaretsauvage.com; 221 av Jean Jaurès, 19e; ⌚hours vary; Ⓜ Porte de la Villette) This very cool space in the Parc de la Villette (it looks like a gigantic yurt) is host to African, reggae and raï concerts as well as DJ nights that last till dawn. Occasional hip-hop and indie acts also pass through.

CITÉ DE LA MUSIQUE WORLD MUSIC

Map p400 (www.citedelamusique.fr; 221 av Jean Jaurès, 19e; ⌚box office noon-6pm Tue-Sat, 10am-6pm Sun; Ⓜ Porte de Pantin) Every imaginable type of music and dance, from classical to North African to Japanese, is hosted at this venue's 1200-seat main auditorium. Smaller concerts are in the smaller Amphithéâtre du Musée de la Musique.

ALHAMBRA LIVE MUSIC

Map p398 (www.alhambra-paris.com; 21 rue Yves Toudic, 10e; ⌚hours vary; Ⓜ République or Jacques Bonsergent) The Subways and Tom Odell are among the artists who have played at this 1930s cinema-theatre, which now serves as a music hall for pop, rock and soul concerts.

NEW MORNING JAZZ, BLUES

Map p398 (www.newmorning.com; 7-9 rue des Petites Écuries, 10e; ⌚hours vary; Ⓜ Château d'Eau) New Morning is a highly regarded auditorium with excellent acoustics that hosts big-name jazz concerts (Ravi Coltrane, Lake Street Dive) as well as a variety of blues, rock, funk, salsa, Afro-Cuban and Brazilian music.

WORTH A DETOUR

MARCHÉ AUX PUCES DE ST-OUEN

A vast flea market, the **Marché aux Puces de St-Ouen** (⌚9am-6pm Sat, 10am-6pm Sun, 11am-5pm Sun) was founded in the late 19th century. It's said to be Europe's largest market, and has more than 2500 stalls grouped into a dozen *marchés* (market areas), each with its own speciality (eg Paul Bert for 17th-century furniture, Malik for clothing, Biron for Asian art). There are miles upon miles of 'freelance' stalls; come prepared to spend some time.

LE REGARD DU CYGNE DANCE

(www.leregarducygne.com; 210 rue de Belleville, 20e; Ⓜ Place des Fêtes) Le Regard du Cygne prides itself on being an independent, alternative performance space. Situated in the creative 20e, this is where many of Paris' young and daring talents in movement, music and theatre congregate to perform.

SHOPPING

There is a growing number of boutiques in the Pigalle area, but by far the best strips for fashion lovers are rue Beaurepaire and rue de Marseille, both by the Canal St-Martin.

Montmartre & Pigalle

LA CITADELLE FASHION, ACCESSORIES

Map p394 (1 rue des Trois Frères, 18e; ⌚10am-7pm; Ⓜ Abbesses) This designer discount shop hidden away in Montmartre has some real finds from new French, Italian and Japanese designers. Look out for such labels as Les Chemins Blancs and Yoshi Kondo.

ANTOINE ET LILI FASHION, HOMEWARES

Map p394 (90 rue des Martyrs, 18e; ⌚11am-8pm Mon-Sat, 10am-8pm Sun; Ⓜ Abbesses) Fashion from the Canal St-Martin label (p158).

TATI DEPARTMENT STORE

Map p394 (4 bd de Rochechouart, 18e; ⌚10am-7pm Mon-Fri, 9.30am-7pm Sat; Ⓜ Barbès Rochechouart) This bargain-filled, rough-and-tumble, frill-free department store is every fashionable Parisian's guilty secret.

Clichy

LES CAVES AUGÉ FOOD & WINE

Map p384 (www.cavesauge.com; 116 bd Haussmann, 8e; ⏰10am-7.30pm Mon-Sat; Ⓜ St-Augustin) Founded in 1850, this fantastic wine shop with bottles stacked in every conceivable nook and cranny should be your first choice if you trust the taste of Marcel Proust, who was a regular customer. The shop organises tastings every other Saturday (see website), where you can meet local winemakers from different regions.

FROMAGERIE ALLÉOSSE CHEESE

Map p401 (www.alleosse.com; 13 rue Poncelet, 17e; ⏰9am-1pm & 4-7pm Tue-Thu, 9am-1pm & 3.30-7pm Fri & Sat, 9am-1pm Sun; Ⓜ Ternes) Although there are cheese shops throughout the city, this one is actually worth a trip across town. Cheeses are sold as they should be, grouped into five main categories: *fromage de chèvre* (goat's-milk cheese), *fromage à pâte persillée* (veined or blue cheese), *fromage à pâte molle* (soft cheese), *fromage à pâte demi-dure* (semihard cheese) and *fromage à pâte dure* (hard cheese).

Gare du Nord & Canal St-Martin

ANTOINE ET LILI FASHION, HOMEWARES

Map p398 (95 quai de Valmy, 10e; ⏰11am-8pm Tue-Fri, to 7pm Sun & Mon; Ⓜ Jacques Bonsergent or Gare de l'Est) All the colours of the rainbow and all the patterns in the world congregate in this wonderful Parisian institution with designer clothing for women (pink store) and children (green store), and hip home decorations (yellow store).

IDÉCO HOMEWARES

Map p398 (19 rue Beaurepaire, 10e; ⏰11.30am-7.30pm Mon-Sat, 2-7pm Sun; Ⓜ République or Jacques Bonsergent) Pick up quirky knick-knacks and fun souvenirs at this idea-filled decor store. French recipe books, Eiffel Tower paper weights, Japanese trays, jewelery made from bonbons and all sorts of other weird and wonderful creations.

BAZAR ÉTHIC FASHION, HOMEWARES

Map p398 (25 rue Beaurepaire, 10e; ⏰11am-7.30pm Mon-Sat, 2.30-7pm Sun; Ⓜ République or Jacques Bonsergent) An excellent shop for a browse, Bazar Éthic specialises in chic fair-trade and ecofriendly products. It carries a range of clothing (organic-cotton jeans, children's wear) and home-design handicrafts, such as lacquered bamboo bowls.

MAJE FASHION, ACCESSORIES

Map p398 (6 rue de Marseille, 10e; ⏰11am-8pm Mon-Sat, 1.30-7.30pm Sun; Ⓜ Jacques Bonsergent) A Parisian prêt-à-porter brand featured regularly on the pages of *Elle, Glamour* and *Marie Claire,* Maje doesn't come cheaply – that is, unless you know about this outlet store, which sells most items at a 30% discount.

SPORTS & ACTIVITIES

HAMMAM MEDINA SPA

Map p400 (☎01 42 02 31 05; www.hammam-medina.com; 43-45 rue Petit, 19e; ⏰11am-10pm Mon-Fri, 10am-9pm Sat, 9am-7pm Sun; Ⓜ Laumière) The rhythmic release of eucalyptus-scented steam into this wonderful hammam will set mind and body at ease in minutes. Also included is an excruciating (but effective) exfoliation rub-down. The almond-oil massage and mint tea are extra, but they're an indulgent way to end any session. Saturdays are mixed (men and women), otherwise it's women only.

AZHAR HAMMAM SPA

Map p398 (☎01 42 58 02 02; www.azharspa.fr; 56 rue Stéphenson, 18e; ⏰women 10am-9pm Tue-Thu & Sat, men 4-9pm Fri & noon-7pm Sun; Ⓜ Marx Dormoy or Château Rouge) Part of the Institut des Cultures d'Islam (p143), this new hammam and spa is an excellent spot to decompress, with steam bath, exfoliation and massage.

STADE DE FRANCE STADIUM STADIUM

(www.stadefrance.com; rue Francis de Pressensé, St-Denis la Plaine; tours adult/child €15/10; ⏰11am-4pm; Ⓜ St-Denis-Porte de Paris or La Plaine Stade de France) This 80,000-seat stadium was built for the 1998 football World Cup, which France won by miraculously defeating Brazil 3-0. Today it hosts football and rugby matches, major gymnastic events and big-ticket music concerts.

Le Marais, Ménilmontant & Belleville

LE MARAIS | MÉNILMONTANT & BELLEVILLE

Neighbourhood Top Five

❶ Living the high life for free with a world-class art exhibition at Paris' neo-Renaissance **Hôtel de Ville** (p166) followed by a winter twirl on ice or a summer flop on a Seine-side beach.

❷ Walking through Parisian history at the atmospheric **Musée Carnavalet** (p164), secreted in two richly furnished 16th- and 17th-century mansions.

❸ Paying your respects to the rich, famous and infamous at **Cimetière du Père Lachaise** (p161).

❹ Being seduced by **place des Vosges** (p165), a square triumph of architectural symmetry and understated *bon goût*.

❺ Learning about German-occupied Paris and Holocaust horrors at the **Mémorial de la Shoah** (p166).

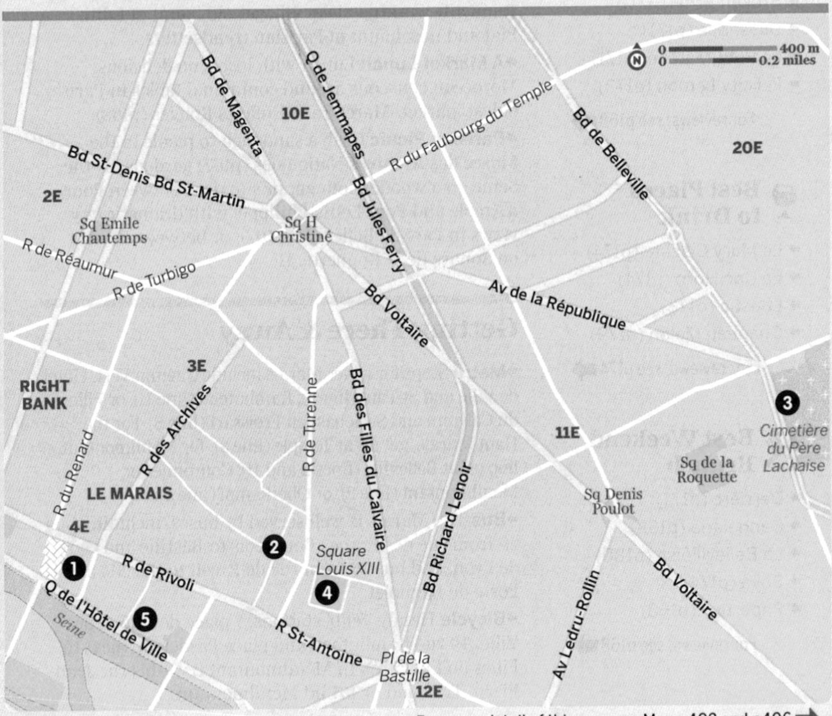

For more detail of this area see Map p402 and p406

Lonely Planet's Top Tip

The gentrification of the hip Haut Marais continues. Its western fringe – traditional home to wholesale handbag traders (slowly moving out to the northeastern suburb of Aubervilliers) – is the place to watch for achingly cool new openings, spear-headed by the brilliant 2014 Renaissance of mythical thermal-baths-turned-nightclub Les Bains (p301). Promising spots include rue Chapon and parallel streets; rue Reslay, rue Notre Dame de Nazareth and Rue du Verbois.

Best Places to Eat

- Candelaria (p168)
- Blue Valentine (p173)
- Broken Arm (p171)
- Dessance (p171)
- Le Petit Marché (p171)
- Felicity Lemon (p173)

For reviews, see p168

Best Places to Drink

- Le Mary Céleste (p174)
- Le Cap Horn (p174)
- Loustic (p178)
- Chapeau Melon (p179)

For reviews, see p174

Best Weekend Brunch

- Derrière (p171)
- Candelaria (p168)
- La Bellevilloise (p180)
- Soya (p174)
- Paperboy (p168)

For reviews, see p168

Explore: Le Marais, Ménilmontant & Belleville

Sublime place des Vosges is a perfect starting point. Head west along rue de Rivoli or rue du Roi de Sicile, a parallel twinset with shops, cafes and bars. Essential for history buffs is the Mémorial de la Shoah, a two-minute walk from some of the city's best coffee at La Caféothèque. Bearing north towards the Haut Marais, hipster strips laden with drinking and dining options include rue Vieille du Temple (near the revamped Musée Picasso), rue du Bourg Tibourg, and rue Rosiers in the heart of the historic Jewish quarter Pletzl. From the Haut Marais, bar-busy rue Oberkampf and rue Jean-Pierre Timbaud duck east into the solidly working-class districts of Ménilmontant and, further on, increasingly appealing and multicultural Belleville. Post-exploration, head to the river for a flop on the sand on the Seine-side quays immediately west of Pont de Sully – host to Paris Plages in July and August.

Local Life

- **Great Coffee** Join discerning coffee lovers in a bevy of coffee-driven cafe openings: Fondation Café (p178), Boot Cafe (p178), Belleville Brûlerie (p186).
- **Belleville** Explore this vibrant, multicultural and staunchly working-class 'village', old haunt of Edith Piaf and new haunt of Parisian trendsetters.
- **A Market Lunch** Lunch with locals on delicious Moroccan couscous around communal tables in Paris' oldest market, Marché aux Enfants Rouges (p168).
- **Parisian Picnic** Grab a sandwich to picnic in the Musée des Archives Nationales (p167) gardens, by the Seine on a wooden lounger or sun deck between Pont d'Arcole and Pont Louis-Philippe; with dramatic city views in Parc de Belleville (p167); or between flowers on Square de la Roquette, 11e.

Getting There & Away

- **Metro** Stops for lower Marais include Chemin Vert, Hôtel de Ville and St-Paul (line 1), Rambuteau (line 11), or Filles du Calvaire and St-Sébastien Froissart (line 8). For the Haut Marais, get off at Temple (line 3); for Ménilmontant, hop off at Belleville (lines 2 and 11), Couronnes or Ménilmontant (line 2), or Oberkampf (line 5).
- **Bus** The Marais is well served by buses, including bus 29 from rue des Francs Bourgeois to Bastille and Gare de Lyon, and bus 76 from rue de Rivoli to the 20e and Porte de Bagnolet.
- **Bicycle** Handy Vélib' stations: 7 place de l'Hôtel de Ville, 49 rue Rambuteau and place Pasdeloup (next to Filles du Calvaire). In Ménilmontant try 81bis rue Jean-Pierre Timbaud or 137 bd Ménilmontant.

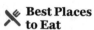

TOP SIGHT
CIMETIÈRE DU PÈRE LACHAISE

The world's most visited cemetery opened in 1804. Its 44 hectares hold more than 70,000 ornate tombs – a stroll here is akin to exploring a verdant sculpture garden. Père Lachaise was intended for Parisians, a response to local neighbourhood graveyards being full. It was ground-breaking for Parisians to be buried outside the *quartier* in which they'd lived.

Paris residency was the only criterion needed to be buried in Père Lachaise, hence the cemetery's cosmopolitan population. Among the 800,000-odd buried here are the composer Chopin; the playwright Molière; the poet Apollinaire; writers Balzac, Proust, Gertrude Stein and Colette; the actors Simone Signoret, Sarah Bernhardt and Yves Montand; the painters Pissarro, Seurat, Modigliani and Delacroix; the *chanteuse* Édith Piaf alongside her two-year-old daughter; and the dancer Isadora Duncan.

The grave of Irish playwright and humorist **Oscar Wilde** (1854–1900), division 89, is among the most visited (as the unfortunate glass barrier erected around his sculpted tomb attests). The other big hitter, likewise barricaded from overzealous fans, is 1960s rock star **Jim Morrison** (1943–71; he died in Le Marais; Map p402), division 6.

Up in division 92, protests saw the removal of a fence around the grave of **Monsieur Noir**, aka journalist Yvan Salman (1848–70), shot aged 22 by Pierre Bonaparte, great-nephew of Napoléon. Legend says women who stroke the amply filled crotch of Monsieur Noir's prostrate bronze effigy will enjoy a better sex life and fertility.

Commemorative memorials to victims of almost every war in modern history form a poignant alley alongside the **Mur des Fédérés**, an unmemorable plain brick wall against which Communard insurgents were lined up, shot and buried in a mass grave in 1871.

DON'T MISS

- Jim Morrison
- Édith Piaf
- Oscar Wilde
- Monsieur Noir
- Mur des Fédérés and commemorative war memorials

PRACTICALITIES

- ☎ 01 43 70 70 33
- www.pere-lachaise.com
- 16 rue du Repos & bd de Ménilmontant, 20e
- ⏲ 8am-6pm Mon-Fri, 8.30am-6pm Sat, 9am-6pm Sun
- Ⓜ Père Lachaise or Gambetta

Cimetière du Père Lachaise

A HALF-DAY TOUR

There is a certain romance to getting lost in Cimetière du Père Lachaise, a grave jungle spun from centuries of tales. But to search for one grave among 70,000 in this 44-hectare land of the dead is no joke – narrow the search with this itinerary.

From the main bd de Ménilmontant entrance (metro Père Lachaise or Philippe Auguste), head up av Principale, turn right onto av du Puits and collect a map from the **Bureaux de la Conservation** (1).

Backtrack along av du Puits, turn right onto av Latérale du Sud, scale the stairs and bear right along chemin Denon to New Realist artist **Arman** (2), film director **Claude Chabrol** (3) and **Chopin** (4).

Follow chemin Méhul downhill, cross av Casimir Périer and bear right onto chemin Serré. Take the second left (chemin Lebrun – unsigned), head uphill and near the top leave the footpath to weave through graves on your right to rock star **Jim Morrison** (5). Back on chemin Lauriston, continue uphill to roundabout **Rond-Point Casimir Périer** (6).

Admire the funerary art of contemporary photographer **André Chabot** (7), av de la Chapelle. Continue uphill for energising city views from the **chapel** (8) steps, then zig-zag to **Molière & La Fontaine** (9), on chemin Molière.

Cut between graves onto av Tranversale No 1 – spot potatoes atop **Parmentier's** (10) headstone. Continue straight onto av Greffülhe and left onto av Tranversale No 2 to rub **Monsieur Noir's** (11) shiny crotch.

Navigation to **Édith Piaf** (12) and the **Mur des Fédérés** (13) is straightforward. End with lipstick-kissed **Oscar Wilde** (14) near the Porte Gambetta entrance.

TOP TIPS

» **Say 'Cheese!'** Père Lachaise is photography paradise any time of day/year, but best are sunny autumn mornings after the rain.

» **Guided Tours** Cemetery lovers will appreciate themed guided tours (two hours) led by entertaining cemetery historian Thierry Le Roi (www.necro-romantiques.com).

Chopin, Division 11
Add a devotional note to the handwritten letters and flowers brightening the marble tomb of Polish composer/pianist Frédéric Chopin (1810–49), who spent his short adult life in Paris. His heart is buried in Warsaw.

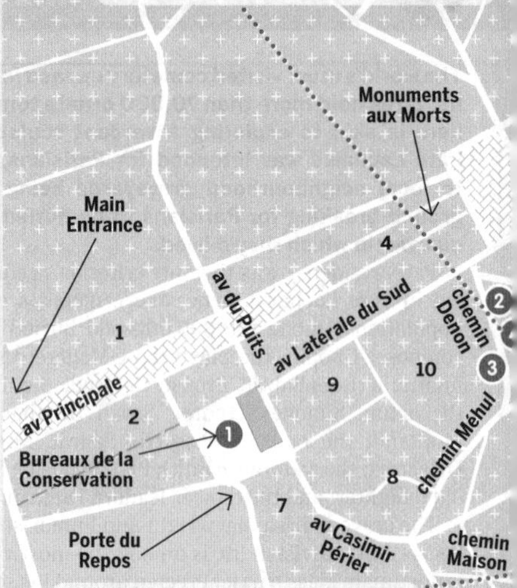

Jim Morrison, Division 6
The original bust adorning the disgracefully dishevelled grave of Jim Morrison (1943–71), lead singer of The Doors, was stolen. Pay your respects to rock's greatest legend – no chewing gum or padlocks please.

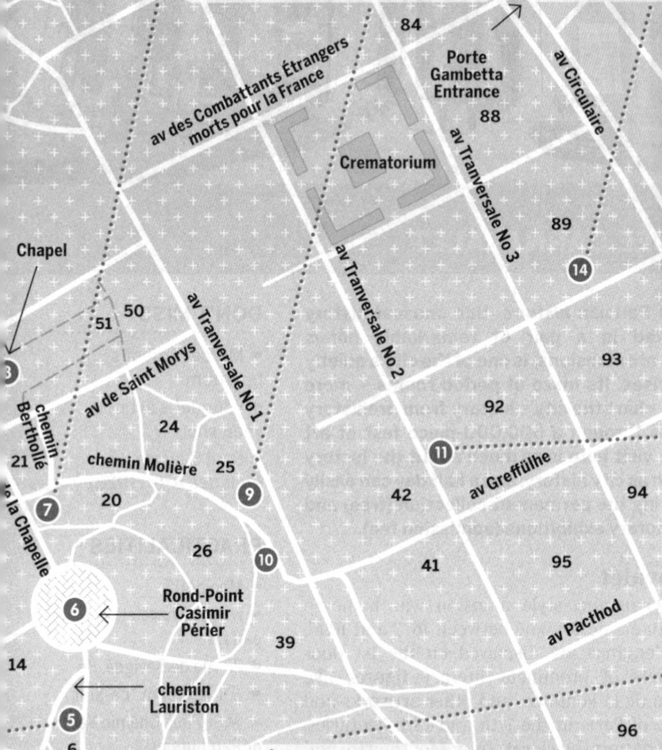

André Chabot, Division 20

Contemporary photographer André Chabot (b 1941) shoots funerary art, hence the bijou 19th-century chapel he's equipped with monumental granite camera in preparation for the day he departs – and a QR code.

BRUNO DE HOGUES / GETTY IMAGES ©

Molière & La Fontaine, Division 25

Parisians refused to leave their local *quartier* for Père Lachaise so in 1817 the authorities moved in popular playwright Molière (1622–73) and poet Jean de la Fontaine (1621–95). The marketing strategy worked.

BRUNO DE HOGUES / GETTY IMAGES ©

Oscar Wilde, Division 89

Homosexual Irish writer Oscar Wilde (1854–1900) was forever scandalous: check the enormous packet of the sphinx on his tomb, sculpted by British-American sculptor Jacob Epstein 11 years after he died.

BRUNO DE HOGUES / GETTY IMAGES ©

Monsieur Noir, Division 92

Cemetery sex stud Mr Black, alias 21-year-old journalist Victor Noir (1848–70), was shot by Napoleon III's nephew in a botched duel. Urban myth means women rub his crotch to boost fertility.

Édith Piaf, Division 97

The archbishop of Paris might have refused Parisian diva Édith Piaf (1915–63) the Catholic rite of burial, but that didn't stop more than 100,000 mourners attending her internment at Père Lachaise.

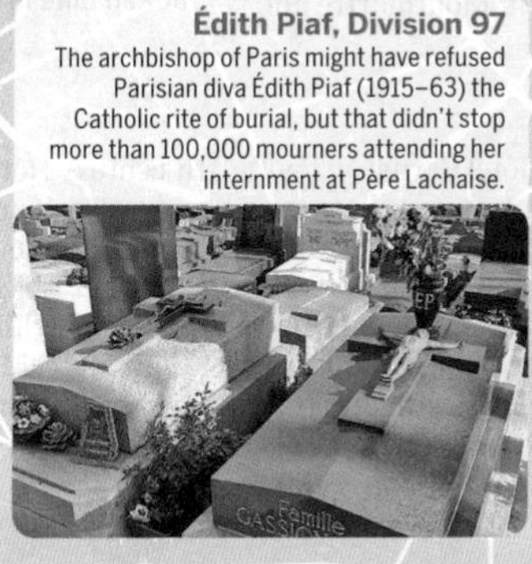

NICOLA WILLIAMS ©

Mur des Fédérés, Division 76

This plain brick wall was where 147 Communard insurgents were lined up and shot in 1871. Equally emotive is the sculpted walkway of commemorative war memorials surrounding the mass grave.

AA WORLD TRAVEL LIBRARY / ALAMY ©

TOP SIGHT
MUSÉE CARNAVALET

A poetic ode to Parisian *histoire*, this unusual history museum secreted in a pair of remarkable *hôtels particuliers* (private mansions) is one of the city's quietly wonderful surprises. Its maze of period rooms – more than 100 in all – chart the city's history from prehistory to modern times through a 600,000-piece fest of art and artefacts. A visit here is as much about the history of interior design as city history, and a half day can easily be spent savouring the permanent collection (free) and occasional temporary exhibitions (admission fee).

Hôtel Carnavalet

This sublime Renaissance-style mansion was home to letter-writer Madame de Sévigné between 1677 and 1696. Some of her belongings are displayed on the 1st floor alongside portraits of prominent literary figures like Molière and Jean de la Fontaine, and other artworks and objects evocative of Paris in the 17th and 18th centuries. Don't miss the *chat noir* (black cat) from Montmartre and various tools depicting shop trades.

DON'T MISS

- Marcel Proust's bedroom
- Fouquet's art nouveau shop
- Paul Signac's *Le Pont des Arts* (1928)

PRACTICALITIES

- Map p402
- www.carnavalet.paris.fr
- 23 rue de Sévigné, 3e
- 10am-6pm Tue-Sun
- M St-Paul, Chemin Vert or Rambuteau

Hôtel Le Peletier

A covered gallery on the 1st floor links Hôtel Carnavalet with 17th-century Hôtel Le Peletier de St-Fargeau. The lovely ground-floor orangery showcases the museum's archaeological collection from prehistory and the Gallo-Roman period, and is well worth seeking out. Some of the nation's most important documents, paintings and other objects from the French Revolution (rooms 100 to 113) are on the 2nd floor. First-floor highlights include Fouquet's stunning art nouveau jewellery shop from rue Royale and Marcel Proust's cork-tiled bedroom from his apartment on bd Haussmann (room 147), where he wrote most of the 7350-page literary cycle *À la Recherche du Temps Perdu* (Remembrance of Things Past).

SIGHTS

The Marais (meaning 'marsh' or 'swamp' in French) was exactly what its name implies right up until the 13th century, when it was converted to farmland. In the early 17th century Henri IV built place Royale (today's place des Vosges), turning the area into Paris' most fashionable residential address. When the aristocracy moved out of Paris to Versailles and Faubourg St-Germain, the Marais and its townhouses passed into the hands of ordinary Parisians. The 110-hectare area was given a major facelift in the late 1960s and early '70s, and today it is one of the city's most coveted addresses.

CIMETIÈRE DU PÈRE LACHAISE — CEMETERY

See p161.

MUSÉE CARNAVALET — MUSEUM

See p164.

MUSÉE PICASSO — ART MUSEUM

Map p402 (☎01 42 71 25 21; www.museepicassoparis.fr; 5 rue de Thorigny, 3e; admission €11; ⏲11.30am-6pm Tue-Sun, to 9pm 3rd Sat of month; Ⓜ St-Paul or Chemin Vert) One of Paris' most beloved art collections reopened its doors in late 2014 after a massive renovation and much controversy. Housed in the stunning, mid-17th-century Hôtel Salé, the Musée Picasso woos art lovers with 5000 drawings, engravings, paintings, ceramic works and sculptures by the *grand maître* (great master) Pablo Picasso (1881–1973). The extraordinary collection was donated to the French government by the artist's heirs in lieu of paying inheritance tax.

PLACE DES VOSGES — SQUARE

Map p402 (place des Vosges, 4e; Ⓜ St-Paul or Bastille) Inaugurated in 1612 as place Royale and thus Paris' oldest square, place des Vosges is a strikingly elegant ensemble of 36 symmetrical houses with ground-floor arcades, steep slate roofs and large dormer windows arranged around a leafy square with four symmetrical fountains and an 1829 copy of a mounted statue of Louis XIII. The square received its present name in 1800 to honour the Vosges *département* (administrative division) for being the first in France to pay its taxes. In Paris, only the earliest houses were built of brick; to save time, the rest were given timber frames and faced with plaster, later painted to resemble brick.

MAISON DE VICTOR HUGO — HOUSE MUSEUM

Map p402 (www.musee-hugo.paris.fr; 6 place des Vosges, 4e; ⏲10am-6pm Tue-Sun; Ⓜ St-Paul or Bastille) FREE Between 1832 and 1848 writer Victor Hugo lived in an apartment on the 3rd floor of Hôtel de Rohan-Guéménée, overlooking one of Paris' most elegant squares. He moved here a year after the publication of *Notre Dame de Paris* (The Hunchback of Notre Dame), completing *Ruy Blas* while living here. His house is now a small museum devoted to the life and times of the celebrated novelist and poet, with an impressive collection of his personal drawings and portraits.

HÔTEL DE SULLY — HISTORIC MANSION

Map p402 (62 rue St-Antoine, 4e; Ⓜ St-Paul or Bastille) In the southwestern corner of place des Vosges is the back entrance to this aristocratic mansion, built in 1625 and home to the headquarters of the Centre des Monuments Nationaux, responsible for many of France's historical monuments. From the square, duck beneath the arch and be instantly wooed by two beautifully decorated, late-Renaissance courtyards, both festooned with allegorical reliefs of the seasons and the elements. In the northern courtyard look to the southern side for spring (flowers and a bird in hand) and summer (wheat sheaves); in the southern courtyard turn to the northern side for autumn (grapes) and winter, with a symbol

LOCAL KNOWLEDGE

BELLEVILLE STREET ART

From Belleville metro station, walk east uphill along rue de Belleville and look for the red neon lights of **Aux Folies** (Map p406; 8 rue de Belleville, 19e; Ⓜ Belleville), the Belleville neighbourhood cafe where Edith Piaf used to sing. Turn right onto pedestrian **rue Dénoyez, 20e**, to be mesmerised by some of Paris' most dazzling street art. Everything on the small pedestrian street, from litter bins and flower pots to lamp posts and window shutters, is covered in colourful graffiti. Artists' workshops pepper the street where local kids kick footballs around and street art 'happenings' break out on sultry summer nights. Break for a drink at Le Barbouquin (p179) or lunch at Felicity Lemon (p173).

representing both the end of the year and the end of life. In the second courtyard are symbols for the elements: on the western side 'air' on the left and 'fire' on the right, and on the eastern side 'earth' on the left and 'water' on the right.

HÔTEL DE VILLE — CITY HALL

Map p402 (www.paris.fr; place de l'Hôtel de Ville, 4e; Ⓜ Hôtel de Ville) FREE Paris' beautiful neo-Renaissance town hall was gutted during the Paris Commune of 1871 and rebuilt in luxurious neo-Renaissance style between 1874 and 1882. The ornate façade is decorated with 108 statues of illustrious Parisians, and the outstanding temporary exhibitions (admission free) held inside in its **Salle St-Jean** almost always have a Parisian theme. From December to early March, an ice-skating rink sets up outside this beautiful building, creating a real picture-book experience.

MUSÉE COGNACQ-JAY — ART MUSEUM

Map p402 (www.cognacq-jay.paris.fr; 8 rue Elzévir, 3e; ⌚10am-6pm Tue-Sun; Ⓜ St-Paul or Chemin Vert) FREE This museum inside Hôtel de Donon displays oil paintings, pastels, sculpture, objets d'art, jewellery, porcelain and furniture from the 18th century assembled by Ernest Cognacq (1839–1928), founder of La Samaritaine department store, and his wife Louise Jay. Although Cognacq appreciated little of his collection, boasting that he had never visited the Louvre and was only acquiring collections for the status, the artwork and objets d'art give a good idea of upper-class tastes during the Age of Enlightenment.

★MUSÉE DES ARTS ET MÉTIERS — MUSEUM

Map p402 (www.arts-et-metiers.net; 60 rue de Réaumur, 3e; adult/child €6.50/free; ⌚10am-6pm Tue, Wed & Fri-Sun, to 9.30pm Thu; Ⓜ Arts et Métiers) The Arts & Crafts Museum, dating to 1794 and Europe's oldest science and technology museum, is a must for anyone with kids – or an interest in how things tick or work. Housed inside the sublime 18th-century priory of St-Martin des Champs, some 3000 instruments, machines and working models from the 18th to 20th centuries are displayed across three floors. In the attached church of St-Martin des Champs is Foucault's original pendulum, introduced to the world at the Universal Exhibition in Paris 1855. Louis Blériot's mono-

TOP SIGHT
MÉMORIAL DE LA SHOAH

No single sight in Paris is as exhaustive or emotionally exhausting as this. Secreted in what began in 1956 as a memorial to the unknown Jewish martyr, the Mémorial de la Shoah is now one of Europe's most important Holocaust museums and documentation centres. A vast permanent collection and well-thought-out temporary exhibits all pertain to the Holocaust and the German occupation of parts of France and Paris during WWII.

The entrance to the Mémorial de la Shoah remembers the victims of the Shoah – a Hebrew word meaning 'catastrophe' and synonymous in France with the Holocaust – with the **Mur des Noms** (Wall of Names; 2006), a wall inscribed with the names of 76,000 Jews, including 11,000 children, deported from France to Nazi extermination camps during WWII. Deep in the appropriately sombre, bunker-like building lies the **crypt and tomb to the unknown Jewish martyr** – all six million Jews with no grave of their own.

DON'T MISS

- Mur des Noms
- Crypt
- Guided tours in English, 3pm second Sunday of month

PRACTICALITIES

- Map p402
- www.memorialdelashoah.org
- 17 rue Geoffroy l'Asnier, 4e
- ⌚10am-6pm Sun-Wed & Fri, to 10pm Thu
- Ⓜ St-Paul

plane from 1909 is also here. Guided tours are in French only but the excellent English audioguide (€5) more than compensates.

MUSÉE DES ARCHIVES NATIONALES MUSEUM

Map p402 (60 rue des Francs Bourgeois, 3e; adult/child €3/free; ⏲10am-5.30pm Mon & Wed-Fri, 2-5.30pm Sat & Sun; Ⓜ Rambuteau or St-Paul) The greatest appeal of the National Archives and its small museum is the stunning twinset of *hôtels particuliers* they are squirreled away in – and the stunning gardens in which they languish. Dating from the early 18th century, Hôtel de Rohan and Hôtel de Soubise are extravagantly painted and gilded in the rococo style inside, with antique furniture and 18th-century paintings alongside a rather dry collection of documents on display (the most interesting and precious are hidden away in the archives).

MUSÉE DE LA CHASSE ET DE LA NATURE MUSEUM

Map p402 (www.chassenature.org; 62 rue des Archives, 3e; adult/child €8/free; ⏲11am-6pm Tue-Sun; Ⓜ Rambuteau or Hôtel de Ville) The Hunting and Nature Museum, inside the delightful Hôtel Guénégaud (1651), is crammed with weapons, paintings, sculpture and objets d'art related to hunting and, of course, lots and lots of trophies (horns, antlers, heads). Particularly appealing are its nature-themed workshops for children.

MUSÉE DE LA POUPÉE MUSEUM

Map p402 (www.museedelapoupeeparis.com; Impasse Berthaud, 3e; adult/child €8/4; ⏲1-6pm Tue-Sat; Ⓜ Rambuteau) Frightening to some – all those beady little eyes and silent screams – the Doll Museum is as much for adults as kids. Ogle at 500-odd dolls dating back to 1800, arranged in scenes representing the Parises of yesteryear. Well worth looking into are the creative, one-hour workshops it runs for children (€10 to €14).

MAISON EUROPÉENNE DE LA PHOTOGRAPHIE PHOTOGRAPHY MUSEUM

Map p402 (www.mep-fr.org; 5-7 rue de Fourcy, 4e; adult/child €8/4.50; ⏲11am-7.45pm Wed-Sun; Ⓜ St-Paul or Pont Marie) The European House of Photography, housed in the overly renovated Hôtel Hénault de Cantorbe (dating, believe it or not, from the early 18th century), has cutting-edge temporary exhibits (usually retrospectives on single photographers), as well as an enormous permanent collection on the history of photography and its connections with France. There are frequent showings of short films and documentaries on weekend afternoons. The Japanese garden at the entrance is a delight.

LOCAL KNOWLEDGE

SECRET CITY VIEWS

A few blocks east of bd de Belleville, the lovely but little-known **Parc de Belleville** (Map p406; Ⓜ Couronnes) ensnares a hill almost 200m above sea level amid 4.5 hectares of greenery. Climb to the top for some of the best views of the city – armed, if you're smart, with a bread-and-cheese picnic bought in Belleville from two of the finest in their field: Au 140 (p173) and Fromagerie Beaufils (p186).

MUSÉE ÉDITH PIAF MUSEUM

Map p406 (☎01 43 55 52 72; 5 rue Crespin du Gast, 11e; adult/child €4/free; ⏲by appt 1-6pm Mon-Wed; Ⓜ Ménilmontant) FREE This private museum in Ménilmontant, some 1.5km from the birthplace of the iconic singer Édith Piaf and closer to her final resting place in Cimetière du Père Lachaise, follows the life and career of the 'urchin sparrow' through memorabilia, recordings, personal objects, letters and other documentation. Admission by advance reservation, at least eight days in advance.

MUSÉE DE LA MAGIE MUSEUM

Map p402 (www.museedelamagie.com; 11 rue St-Paul, 4e; adult/child €9/7; ⏲2-7pm Wed, Sat & Sun; Ⓜ St-Paul) The ancient arts of magic, optical illusion and sleight of hand are explored in this museum, in the 16th-century *caves* (wine cellars) of the Marquis de Sade's former home. Admission includes a magic show, and a combination ticket covering admission to the adjoining **Musée des Automates** – a collection of antique wind-up toys – is also available (€12/9).

MUSÉE D'ART ET D'HISTOIRE DU JUDAÏSME MUSEUM

Map p402 (www.mahj.org; 71 rue du Temple, 4e; adult/child €8/free; ⏲11am-6pm Mon-Fri, 10am-6pm Sun; Ⓜ Rambuteau) To delve into the historic heart of the Marais' long-established Jewish community in Pletzl (from the Yiddish for 'little square'), visit this fascinating museum inside Hôtel de St-Aignan, dating from 1650. The museum traces the evolution of Jewish communities from the Middle Ages to the present, with particular emphasis on French Jewish history. Highlights include documents relating to the Dreyfus Affair; and works by Chagall, Modigliani and Soutine. Creative workshops for children, adults and families complement excellent temporary exhibitions.

ART NOUVEAU SYNAGOGUE SYNAGOGUE

Map p402 (10 rue Pavée, 4e) The colourful Jewish quarter of Pletzl starts in rue des Rosiers and continues along rue Ste-Croix de la Bretonnerie to rue du Temple. At its heart lies this art nouveau synagogue, designed in 1913 by Hector Guimard, also responsible for the city's famous metro entrances.

✗ EATING

Packed with restaurants and bistros of every imaginable type, Le Marais is one of Paris' premier dining neighbourhoods with many addresses requiring an advance reservation at weekends. Looking east, one of Paris' hippest addresses, Yard (p193), is next door to Cimitière du Père Lachaise – perfect for lunch or dinner post-grave walking.

✗ Le Marais

★CANDELARIA TAQUERIA €

Map p402 (www.candelariaparis.com; 52 rue Saintonge; tacos €3.20-3.75, quesadillas & tostadas €3.50, lunch menus €11.50; ⊘noon-midnight Thu-Sat, to 11pm Sun-Wed; ✷; MFilles du Calvaire) You need to know about this terribly cool *taqueria* (taco shop) to find it. Made of pure, unadulterated hipness in that brazenly nonchalant manner Paris does so well, clandestine Candelaria serves delicious homemade tacos, quesadillas and tostadas in a laid-back setting – squat at the bar in the front or lounge out back around a shared table with bar stools or at low coffee tables.

Come dark, the party kicks off with occasional DJ sets, tastings, post-gallery drinks and some of the best cocktails in town. Regulars swear by the Bloody Mary and cocktail-fuelled weekend brunches.

MARCHÉ AUX ENFANTS ROUGES MARKET €

Map p402 (39 rue de Bretagne, 3e; ⊘8.30am-1pm & 4-7.30pm Tue-Fri, 4-8pm Sat, 8.30am-2pm Sun; MFilles du Calvaire) Built in 1615, Paris' oldest covered market is secreted behind an inconspicuous green metal gate – and for good reason. A glorious maze of 20-odd food stalls selling ready-to-eat dishes from around the globe, it is a great place to come for a meander and munch with locals. Grab a Moroccan couscous or Caribbean platter and consume at communal tables.

PAPERBOY CAFE €

Map p402 (☑01 43 38 12 13; www.paper-boy.fr; 137 rue Amelot, 11e; sandwiches €10-13, brunch €23; ⊘9am-7.30pm Tue-Fri, 10am-7.30pm Sat & Sun; MOberkampf) The creation of Jeanne and James, this contemporary cafe is irresistible. From the crates of fruit and veg in the window to a menu that spells out the artisanal origin of the bread, bagels, pastrami, elderflower lemonade and so forth, Paperboy venerates local seasonal produce. Creative sandwiches come with a giant salad, and three types of brunch pack out the place on weekends.

NANASHI FUSION €

Map p402 (☑09 60 00 25 59; www.nanashi.fr; 57 rue Charlot, 3e; salads €6-7, bento boxes €14-16; ⊘noon-midnight Mon-Sat, to 6pm Sun; MFilles du Calvaire) An address that packs a punch in the Haut Marais, this hip industrial space with large street-facing windows and concrete floor is uber-cool, ultra-healthy and brilliant value. Pick from creative salads, soups and bento boxes – always one meat, one fish and one veggie option – chalked on the board. Don't miss the freshly squeezed, frothy-topped apple, carrot and ginger juice.

ROBERT ET LOUISE TRADITIONAL FRENCH €

Map p402 (☑01 42 78 55 89; http://robertetlouise.com; 64 rue Vieille du Temple, 4e; lunch menus €13, mains €12.50-20; ⊘noon-2pm Thu-Sun, 7.30-10.30pm Tue-Sun; MSt-Sébastien Froissart) This 'country inn' with red gingham curtains offers simple and inexpensive French food, including *côte de bœuf* (side of beef for two or three people) cooked on an open fire. Arrive early to snag the farmhouse table next to the fireplace – the makings of a real jolly Rabelaisian evening.

CANTINE MERCI SALADS, TARTS €

Map p402 (www.merci-merci.com; 111 bd Beaumarchais, 3e; soups €8, salads €10-15, tarts €16;

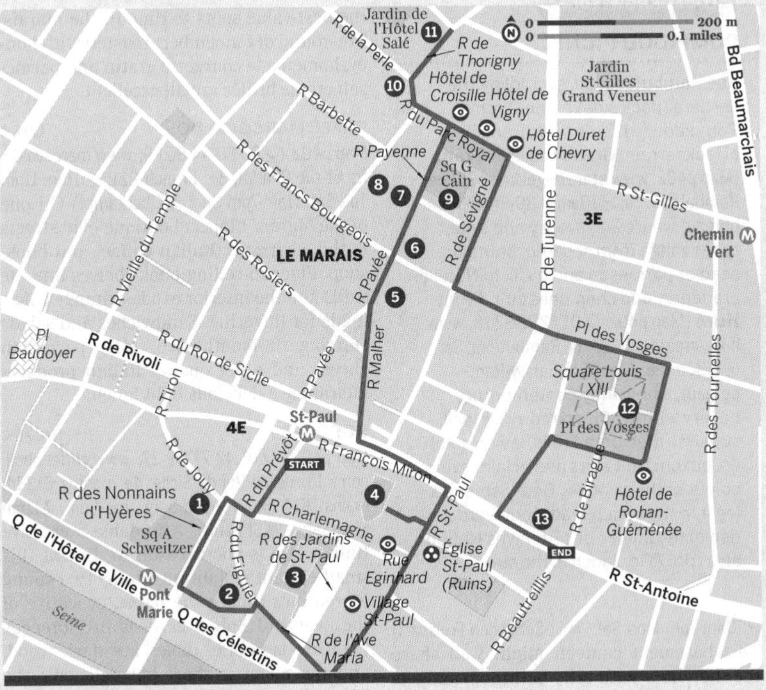

Neighbourhood Walk
Medieval Marais Meanderings

START METRO ST-PAUL
END HÔTEL DE SULLY
LENGTH 2KM; 1½ HOURS

While Henri IV was busy having place Royale (today's place des Vosges) built, aristocrats were commissioning gold-brick *hôtels particuliers* – the city's most beautiful Renaissance structures that lend the Marais a particular architectural harmony.

From rue François Miron, walk south on rue du Prévôt to rue Charlemagne. To the right at 7 rue de Jouy stands majestic **1 Hôtel d'Aumont**, built around 1650 for a financier. Continue south along rue des Nonnains d'Hyères and turn left onto rue de l'Hôtel de Ville. At 1 rue du Figuier is **2 Hôtel de Sens**, the oldest Marais mansion, with geometric gardens and a neo-Gothic turret. Begun around 1475, it was built as digs for the archbishops of Sens. It was restored in mock Gothic style in 1911.

Continue southeast along rue de l'Ave Maria, then northeast along rue des Jardins de St-Paul. To the left, two truncated towers are all that remain of Philippe-Auguste's **3 enceinte**, a fortified wall (1190) once guarded by 39 towers. Cross rue Charlemagne, duck into rue Eginhard and follow it to rue St-Paul and **4 Église St-Paul St-Louis** (1641). At the end of rue St-Paul, turn left, then walk north up rue Malher and rue Pavée, the first cobbled road in Paris. At No 24 is the late Renaissance **5 Hôtel Lamoignon**.

North along rue Payenne is the back of the **6 Musée Carnavalet** (p164); the Revolutionary-era 'Temple of Reason' **7 Chapelle de l'Humanité** at No 5; and the rear of **8 Musée Cognacq-Jay** (p166). From grassy **9 Sq George Cain** opposite 11 rue Payenne, walk northwest to more spectacular 17th-century *hôtels particuliers:* **10 Hôtel de Libéral Bruant** at 1 rue de la Perle, and **11 Hôtel Salé** crammed with Picassos at 5 rue de Thorigny.

Retrace your steps to rue du Parc Royal, walk south down rue de Sévigné and follow rue des Francs Bourgeois eastwards to end with sublime **12 place des Vosges** (p165) and **13 Hôtel de Sully** (p165).

LOCAL KNOWLEDGE

POMPIDOU PICNIC

Rue Rambuteau, 3e, straddling the *derrière* (back side) of the Centre Pompidou (p117), is tip-top snack-attack terrain. Grab a bagel at **Stanz** (Map p402; www.stanzbagel.com; 25 rue Rambuteau, 3e; ⌚10am-9.30pm; Ⓜ Rambuteau) where 24 savoury and sweet types range from sesame, pumpkin-seed or parmesan and basil, to Nutella, cranberry and choc-chestnut. Or hit **Huré** (Map p402; ☎01 42 72 32 18; www.hure-createur.fr; 18 rue Rambuteau, 3e; ⌚6.30am-8.30pm Tue-Sat; Ⓜ Rambuteau), a brilliantly contemporary bakery with graffitied red-brick wall, super-stuffed bread rolls, lavish quiches, buxom fruit tarts and éclairs every colour of the rainbow. Booty stashed, leg it to the bench-clad, courtyard garden of the Musée des Archives Nationales (p167) for lunch in the sun.

⌚10am-7pm Mon-Sat; Ⓜ St-Sébastien Froissart) This basement canteen might well share the shop floor with nifty bathroom gadgets and designer kitchen gear, but its gastronomic thrust is as inspired as the hip concept store (p182) in which it squats. Lunch, served noon to 3.30pm, is what girlfriends come here for (by the droves), to feast on zesty salads, soups and savoury tarts, all oozing bags of vegetable creativity.

CHEZ NÉNESSE — BISTRO €

Map p402 (☎01 42 78 46 49; 17 rue Saintonge, 3e; mains €19; ⌚lunch & dinner Mon-Fri; Ⓜ Filles du Calvaire) 'Old-world bistro' is the atmosphere at this tiny spot with lace curtains and a quality kitchen that cooks classic French dishes that have been around for centuries. Its *salade de canard au vinaigre d'hydromel* (duck salad in honey vinegar) and sweet *medallions de veau au miel* (veal medallions pan-fried in honey) are not to be scoffed at.

CAFÉ MARAIS — MODERN FRENCH €

Map p402 (☎01 42 71 61 46; 10 rue des Haudriettes, 3e; lunch/dinner menus €12.90/15.90; ⌚noon-3.30pm & 7-11pm Wed-Mon; Ⓜ Arts et Métiers) Exposed stone, beamed ceiling and silent B&W Charlie Chaplin movies screened on one wall create an appealing vintage feel in this small and excellent bistro – one of the best-value spots to dine in the Marais. The round of Camembert roasted with honey, homemade courgette gratin and parmesan crème brûlée are all excellent.

CAFFÈ MARCOVALDO — CAFE €

Map p402 (☎09 80 44 86 89; www.marcovaldo.fr; 61 rue Charlot, 3e; brunch €21; ⌚11am-11pm Tue-Sat, 11am-7pm Sun; Ⓜ Oberkampf) On one of the Marais' hippest boutique-clad streets is this charming Italian coffee- and bookshop. Floor to ceiling book shelves line the walls and the interior exudes vintage chic – made for lingering. Sandwiches and salads starring 18-month-aged AOP parmesan cheese and other quality Italian products guarantee a delicious light lunch.

BOBOLI — ITALIAN €

Map p402 (☎01 42 77 89 27; www.caffeboboli.com; 13 rue du Roi de Sicile, 4e; pastas €12-14, mains €14-16; ⌚noon-3pm Tue-Sun, 7-11pm Mon-Sat; Ⓜ St-Paul) Affordable, creative Italian fare is good reason to dine at this small elegant restaurant run by two young Florentines (hence the name, evocative of the beautiful Boboli gardens in Florence). Lighting is subtle, tables are dark wood, and the menu is short but delicious: the Parma ham and gooey mozzarella wrapped in grilled courgette strips are delicious.

100% BIO — ORGANIC €

Map p402 (6 rue du Farez, 3e; lunch menus €16.50 & €19.50, dish of the day €10-12; ⌚10am-10pm Mon-Sat; Ⓜ Filles du Calvaire) *'Cuisine bio and haute vitalité'* (organic and 'high vitality' cuisine) is what this small, cosy cafe across the street from Nanashi is all about – with outstanding success. Think sweet-potato felafel, pumpkin-spiked couscous, creative salads and a market-driven menu that changes daily. Arrive by noon to beat the trendy lunchtime crowd.

RACHEL'S CAKES — INTERNATIONAL, CAFE €

Map p402 (www.rachelscakes.fr; rue du Pont aux Choux, 3e; ⌚9am-11pm; Ⓜ St-Sébastien Froissart) Anyone familiar with Paris' burgeoning cafe scene will have heard about Rachel's Cakes, and probably eaten one of 'her' delicious cheesecakes, gateaux or tarts too, given it's Rachel and her partners, Maria and Birke, who make the cakes for stacks of Parisan cafes. Now the American-Bulgarian-Austrian female trio has branched out with its own space, designed to stunning effect by top interior designer Dorothée Meilichzon. Wow.

★BROKEN ARM CAFE €€

Map p402 (☎01 44 61 53 60; 2 rue Perrée, 3e; ⏲9am-6pm Tue-Sat, lunch noon-3.30pm; 📶; Ⓜ Temple or Arts & Metiers) Kick off with a freshly squeezed apple, kiwi and mint juice and congratulate yourself on scoring a table – inside or out – at this overpoweringly hipster address where the chic folk of Marais lunch after making an appearance in the adjoining concept store. The menu is limited but packed with goodness: excellent salads, cold platters and cakes.

★LE PETIT MARCHÉ BISTRO €€

Map p402 (☎01 42 72 06 67; 9 rue de Béarn, 3e; mains €18-26; ⏲noon-4pm & 7.30pm-midnight; Ⓜ Chemin Vert) A faintly fusion cuisine is what makes this cosy bistro, footsteps from place des Vosges, stand out. Dishes such as raw tuna wrapped in sesame seeds or caramelised duck breast served with roasted bananas lend a welcome Asian kick to a menu that otherwise reassures with old French bistro favourites that have been around for centuries. Also has a summer pavement terrace.

★DESSANCE DESSERTS €€

Map p402 (☎01 42 77 23 62; www.dessance.fr; 74 rue des Archives, 3e; desserts à la carte €19, 4-course dessert menus €36-44; ⏲3-11pm Wed-Fri, noon-midnight Sat & Sun; 👪; Ⓜ Arts et Métiers) Dining at Dessance is unique. Only desserts are served – with an astonishing eye for detail and creative zeal for marrying unexpected ingredients (yes, broccoli, beetroot and rocket with chocolate and caramel). Whether you opt for the four-dessert menu or à la carte, a sweet *amuse-bouche* kicks off the experience and a plate of mini *gourmandises* (sweet things) ends it.

To get the most out of this sweet dining experience, heed the chef's advice when it comes to drinks: the menu recommends alcoholic and non-alcoholic choices to accompany each dessert.

AU PASSAGE BISTRO €€

Map p402 (☎01 43 55 07 52; www.restaurant-aupassage.fr; 1bis passage de St-Sébastien, 11e; small plates €4-15; ⏲noon-3pm Thu & Fri, 7.30pm-1.30am Mon-Sat; Ⓜ St-Sébastien Froissart) Spawned by talented Australian chef James Henry, who went on to open Bones (p193), this *petit bar de quartier* (neighbourhood bar) remains raved about. Pick from a good-value, uncomplicated choice selection *of petites assiettes* (small plates designed to be shared) featuring various market produce – cold meats, raw or cooked fish, vegetables and so on. Advance reservations essential.

DERRIÈRE MODERN FRENCH €€

Map p402 (☎01 44 61 91 95; www.derriere-resto.com; 69 rue des Gravilliers, 3e; lunch menus €25, mains €17-24; ⏲noon-2.30pm & 8-11pm Mon-Sat, noon-4.30pm Sun; Ⓜ Arts et Métiers) Play table tennis, sit on the side of the bed, glass of champers in hand, or lounge between book cases – such is the nature of this restaurant with courtyard seating. Chilled vibe

CRÊPES, PANCAKES & TARTINES

The Marais ensnares some tip-top crêpe and pancake addresses – the perfect cheap lunch, sweet treat between meals or late-night munch.

➡ **Breizh Café** (Map p402; www.breizhcafe.com; 109 rue Vieille du Temple, 3e; crêpes & galettes €4-12; ⏲11.30am-11pm Wed-Sat, to 10pm Sun; Ⓜ St-Sébastien Froissart) Everything at the Breton Café (*breizh* is 'Breton' in Breton) is 100% authentic, be it the Cancale oysters, the 20 types of cider, or the organic-flour crêpes cooked to perfection.

➡ **Bob's Kitchen** (Map p402; 74 rue des Gravilliers, 11e; pancakes €5-10; ⏲11.30am-3pm Mon-Fri, 10.30am-4pm Sat & Sun; 🥬; Ⓜ Arts et Métiers) If it is pancakes US-style you're after, without a spot of cow's milk in sight, Bob's your man (although you might be hard pushed to even get into this tiny space, let alone snag a pew). Choose from sweet and savoury pancakes, milk- and gluten-free, alongside one of the most creative vegetarian lunch menus in town that changes daily and flits all over the globe.

➡ **Cuisine de Bar** (Map p402; 38 rue Debelleyme, 3e; tartines €9.80-12.50, sandwiches €6.40-14.40; ⏲10am-5.30pm Tue-Fri, 9am-4.30pm Sat & Sun; Ⓜ Filles du Calvaire) Paris' most famous bread-maker, Poilâne, cooks up savoury and sweet *tartines* (open sandwiches) in the Marais too. There is another branch (p241) in St-Germain.

FAST FOOD

If you want to grab a bite on the move, you won't do better than these:

➡ **Blend** (Map p402; www.blendhamburger.com; 1 bd des Filles du Calvaire, 3e; burgers €10, lunch menus €15; ❂noon-11pm; Ⓜ St-Sébastien Froissart) The gourmet burger bar born in the 2e now has a bar in the Marais and it's a roaring success. Easy to spot by the hungry crowd lingering outside waiting for a table or a takeaway in a brown paper bag, Blend is a small, smart, black-and-wood space serving the best bijou-sized burgers in town. Meat is by celebrity butcher Yves-Marie Le Bourdonnec.

➡ **L'As du Fallafel** (Map p402; 34 rue des Rosiers, 4e; takeaway dishes €5.50-8.50; ❂noon-midnight Sun-Thu, to 5pm Fri; Ⓜ St-Paul) A veteran Parisian favourite for lunch, this kosher address cooks up perfectly deep-fried chickpea balls and turkey or lamb shwarma sandwiches.

➡ **Pozzetto** (Map p402; www.pozzetto.biz; 16 rue Vieille du Temple, 4e; cones or pots €4-5.90; ❂11.30am-9pm Mon-Thu, to 11.30pm Fri-Sun; Ⓜ St-Paul) End with a gelato, in true Italian style spatula'd, not scooped. Twelve flavours include *gianduia* (hazelnut chocolate from Turin) and *zabaione*, made from egg yolks, sugar and sweet Marsala wine. Great Italian *caffè* too.

in a trendy 'shoes-off' style aside, Derrière (literally 'behind') is deadly serious in the kitchen. Classic French bistro dishes and more inventive creations are excellent, as is Sunday brunch.

CHEZ MARIANNE
JEWISH €€

Map p402 (2 rue des Hospitalières St-Gervais, 4e; mains €18-25; ❂noon-midnight; Ⓜ St-Paul) Heaving at lunchtime, Chez Marianne translates as elbow-to-elbow eating beneath age-old beams on copious portions of felafel, hummus, aubergine purée and 25-odd other *zakouski* (hors d'oeuvres; €14/16/18 for plates of four/five/six). Fare is Sephardic rather than Ashkenazi (the norm at most Pletzl eateries), not Beth Din kosher. A hole-in-the-wall window sells felafel in pitta (€7) to munch on the move.

PIERRE SANG BOYER
MODERN FRENCH €€

Map p406 (http://pierresangboyer.com; 55 rue Oberkamfp, 11e; 2-/3-/4-course lunch €20/25/35, 4-/6-course dinner €35/50; ❂noon-2.30pm & 7-10.30pm Tue-Sat; Ⓜ Oberkampf) *Top Chef* finalist Pierre Sang Boyer stars at his kitchen restaurant where foodies sit on bar stools and watch the French–South Korean chef perform. Cuisine is modern French with a strong fusion lilt, and the vibe is fun and casual – no reservations, no telephone and four or six courses for dinner depending on what time you arrive.

GLOU
MODERN FRENCH €€

Map p402 (☑ 01 42 74 44 32; www.glou-resto.com; 101 rue Vieille du Temple, 3e; lunch menus €17 &

€21, mains €20-25; ❂noon-2.30pm & 7.30-11pm Mon-Fri, noon-5pm & 7.30-11.30pm Sat & Sun; ⚛; Ⓜ St-Sébastien Froissart) A handy number for the Musée de Picasso and fashion boutiques of rue Vieille du Temple, Glou cooks up modern French cuisine with a welcome twist. Begin with lentil soup sprinkled with smoked haddock flakes perhaps, followed by the most succulent piece of roast veal you will ever eat. Despite its fashion-chic velour, Glou is super family-friendly – think colouring pens for the kids and an excellent value €15 *menu enfant* (children's menu).

LE TAXI JAUNE
TRADITIONAL FRENCH €€

Map p402 (☑ 01 42 76 00 40; 13 rue Chapon, 3e; lunch menus €19, mains €20; ❂noon-3pm & 8.30-10.30pm Mon-Fri; Ⓜ Rambuteau) Evening dining at the Yellow Taxi is not for the budget-conscious – but the excellent-value lunchtime *menu* is. Pick from a small but select choice of meat and fish dishes, and savour the grandeur of traditional French bistro cooking. Should you fall in love with the unusual wine you drank, nip into the restaurant's tiny shop across the street, L'Épicerie (p185).

CHEZ JANOU
PROVENÇAL €€

Map p402 (☑ 01 42 72 28 41; www.chezjanou.com; 2 rue Roger Verlomme, 3e; mains €15-25; ❂lunch & dinner; Ⓜ Chemin Vert) Push your way in, order a kir from the jam-packed bar while you wait for a table, and revel in the buzz of this busy spot. Cuisine is as close as you get to Provençal in Paris, with all the southern classics like *brandade de morue* (salt-cod purée with potatoes), ratatouille and lavender-scented crème brulée. It offers 80 different pastis types. Not recommended for the claustrophobic (unless it is summer and you succeed in nabbing a seat on the terrace).

✖ Ménilmontant & Belleville

MARCHÉ DE BELLEVILLE MARKET €
Map p406 (bd de Belleville, 11e & 20e; ⊘7am-2.30pm Tue & Fri; ⓂBelleville) Belleville Market has filled busy thoroughfare bd de Belleville with open-air fruit, veg and other fresh produce stalls since 1860. Shopping for food aside, it provides a fascinating entry into the large, vibrant community of this eastern neighbourhood, home to artists, students and immigrants from Africa, Asia and the Middle East.

AU 140 BOULANGERIE €
(www.au140.com; 140 rue de Belleville, 20e; ⊘7am-8pm Tue-Fri, 7.30am-8pm Sat, 7am-7pm Sun; ⓂJoudain) There is no finer picnic source than this world-class *boulangerie* (bakery), famed far and wide for its crunchy-to-perfection baguettes (€0.95) and gourmet, wood-fired oven breads laced with nuts, honey, almonds, cheese and all sorts else. Mini pizzas, quiches and filled baguette sandwiches stuffed to bursting (€3) make the perfect lunch: consume over sweeping city panoramas in nearby Parc de Belleville.

FELICITY LEMON NEOBISTRO €
Map p406 (☑01 71 32 71 11; www.felicitylemon.com; 4 rue Lemon, 20e; small plates €4-15; ⊘noon-2.30pm Wed-Sat, 7-10.30pm Tue-Sat; ⓂBelleville) Excellent music, a stylish interior with vintage tables and chairs, and contemporary art for sale give this small *'cantine de quartier'* in Belleville instant sex appeal. (Yes, it is named after the private secretary of Agatha Christie's Hercule Poirot.) The tapas-inspired menu features creative dishes to share: sweet duck breast with mango, pan-fried pears and asparagus, cucumber-feta salad etc. Watch Felicity Lemon's Facebook page for events and happenings.

DONG HUONG VIETNAMESE €
Map p406 (☑01 43 57 42 81; 14 rue Louis Bonnet, 11e; dishes €7-12; ⊘lunch & dinner Wed-Mon; ⓂBelleville) Despite a name that sounds like a Spanish Lothario, this no-frills Vietnamese canteen – a real Belleville institution – serves great bowls of *pho* (noodles) to rooms packed out with noisy, appreciative regulars. Food comes out fast, and extra kudos for the pictorial menu aimed at Dong Huong's adoring, non-Asian fans.

TAI YIEN CHINESE €
Map p406 (☑01 42 41 44 16; 5 rue de Belleville, 11e; noodles €5.80-9.20, mains €9.20-12.50; ⊘lunch & dinner; ⓂBelleville) Packed to the rafters at lunchtime, this wholly authentic Hong Kong–style 'steam restaurant' is the real McCoy – there is no better address for a rice or noodle fix, especially late in the evening. It's hard to imagine better *char siu* (barbecued pork) outside Chinatown.

★BLUE VALENTINE MODERN FRENCH €€
Map p406 (☑01 43 38 34 72; http://bluevalentine-restaurant.com; 13 rue de la Pierre Levée, 11e; 2-/3-course menus €29/36, 8-course tasting menus €54; ⊘noon-2.30pm & 7.30-11pm Wed-Sun, bar 7pm-2am; ⓂRépublique) This thoroughly modern bistro with retro decor in the increasingly gourmet 11e was a hit the moment it opened in late 2013. A hip crowd flocks here for well-crafted cocktails and Japanese chef Saito Terumitsu's exquisite dishes flavoured with edible flowers and a profusion of herbs. The menu is small – just three dishes to choose from per course – but memorable.

MON ONCLE LE VIGNERON FRENCH €€
(☑01 42 00 43 30; 71 rue de Rébeval, 19e; dinner with wine €30-40; ⊘8.30-11.30pm Mon-Sat; ⓂBelleville) The name alone enchants. My Uncle the Winemaker is a small, vintage-styled wine cellar and *épicerie fine* (upmarket grocer's) arranged like an old-fashioned kitchen – for good reason. Each evening this Pandora's box of gastronomic goodies in Belleville dons its *table d'hôte* apron. Dinner is around a shared table and advance reservations are essential.

LOCAL KNOWLEDGE

ASIAN EAT STREET
If it's a steaming bowl of noodles you fancy, make a beeline for **rue au Maire, 3e** (metro Arts et Métiers), a small restaurant- and shop-lined street known for cooking authentic Chinese food and saving the trek to the larger Chinatown in the 13e.

LE DAUPHIN BISTRO €€

Map p406 (☎01 55 28 78 88; 131 av Parmentier, 11e; 2-/3-course lunch menus €23/27, mains €15-20; ⏰12.30-2.30pm Tue-Fri, 7.30-11.30pm Tue-Sat; Ⓜ Goncourt) Advance reservations are essential at this buzzing bistro. Run by the same team as nearby Le Chateaubriand, the stark white space with marble floor, bar, ceiling and walls (and the odd mirror) is a temple to taste. Lunch is a choice of two starters and two mains (one fish, one meat), presented like a work of art on white china. Dinner is strictly à la carte.

CHATOMAT MODERN FRENCH €€

Map p406 (☎01 47 97 25 77; 6 rue Victor Letalle, 20e; mains €15-20; ⏰7.30-10.30pm Tue-Sat & 1st Sun of month; Ⓜ Ménilmontant, Couronnes or Père Lachaise) No dinner address is worth the trek to Belleville more than this contemporary bistro with plain white walls, post-industrial flavour and bags of foodie buzz. In the kitchen of the old shop-turned-restaurant, Alice and Victor cook up just three starters, three mains and three desserts each night – and none disappoint. Book in advance.

SOYA VEGETARIAN €€

Map p406 (☎01 48 06 33 02; 20 rue de la Pierre Levée, 11e; lunch menus €16-20, brunch €25; ⏰noon-3.30pm & 7-11pm Mon-Fri, 11.30am-11pm Sat, 11.30am-4pm Sun; 🖉; Ⓜ Goncourt or République) A favourite for its ubercool location in an industrial *atelier* (with bare cement, metal columns and big windows), Soya is a full-on *cantine bio* (organic eatery) in what was once a staunchly working-class district. Dishes, many tofu-based, are vegetarian and the weekend brunch buffet is deliciously lazy and languid.

LE BARATIN BISTRO €€

Map p406 (☎01 43 49 39 70; 3 rue Jouye-Rouve, 20e; mains €20-30, lunch menus €19, dinner menus €35-52; ⏰noon-2.30pm Tue-Fri, 7.30-11.15pm Tue-Sat; Ⓜ Pyrénées or Belleville) *Baratin* (chatter) rhymes with *bar à vin* (wine bar) in French and this animated venue just steps from the lively Belleville quarter does both awfully well. In addition it offers some of the best (and very affordable) French food in the 20e on its ever-changing blackboard. The selection of wine (some organic) by the glass or carafe is excellent.

LE CHATEAUBRIAND NEOBISTRO €€€

Map p406 (☎01 43 57 45 95; 129 av Parmentier, 11e; menus €60-120; ⏰7.30-10.30pm Tue-Sat; Ⓜ Goncourt) Le Chateaubriand is an elegantly tiled, art deco dining room with strikingly imaginative cuisine. Basque chef Iñaki Aizpitarte is well travelled and his dishes show that global exposure again and again in their odd combinations (watermelon and mackerel, milk-fed veal with langoustines and truffles). Advance reservations absolutely essential; if you don't have one, try your luck, but only after 9.30pm.

DRINKING & NIGHTLIFE

Le Marais is a spot par excellence when it comes to a good night out, the lively scene embracing everything from gay-friendly and gay-only to bourgeois arty cafes, eclectic bars and raucous pubs. Rue Oberkampf and parallel rue Jean-Pierre Timbaud are hubs of the Ménilmontant bar crawl, a scene that is edging out steadily through cosmopolitan Belleville.

Le Marais

★LE MARY CÉLESTE COCKTAIL BAR

Map p402 (www.lemaryceleste.com; 1 rue Commines, 3e; cocktails €12-13, tapas €8-12; ⏰6pm-2am; Ⓜ Filles du Calvaire) Predictably there's a distinct nautical feel to this fashionable, ubercool cocktail bar in the Marais. Snag a stool at the central circular bar or play savvy and reserve one of a handful of tables (in advance online). Cocktails are creative and the perfect partner to a dozen oysters or your pick of a dozen-odd, tapas-style 'small plates' designed to be shared.

★LE CAP HORN BAR

Map p402 (8 rue de Birague, 4e; ⏰10-1am; Ⓜ St-Paul or Chemin Vert) On summer evenings the ambience at this laid-back, Chilean bar is electric. The crowd spills onto the pavement, parked cars doubling as tabletops for well-shaken pina coladas, punch cocos and cocktails made with pisco, a fiery Chilean grape eau-de-vie. Find it steps from place des Vosges.

LE PETIT FER À CHEVAL CAFE, BAR

Map p402 (30 rue Vieille du Temple, 4e; ⏰daily; Ⓜ Hôtel de Ville or St-Paul) A Marais institution, the Little Horseshoe is a pocket-size cafe-

HISTORIC INTERIORS

Depending where you eat, Parisian dining can be more about feasting on a breathtaking vintage interior than food.

➡ **Bofinger** (Map p402; 5-7 rue de la Bastille, 4e; ⏲noon-3pm & 6.30pm-midnight) Scoff *choucroute* (sauerkraut), seafood dishes and other brasserie fare between art nouveau brass, glass and mirrors in Paris' oldest brasserie dating to 1864. Ask for a table downstairs beneath the *coupole* (stained-glass dome).

➡ **Le Dôme du Marais** (Map p402; ☎01 42 74 54 17; www.ledomedumarais.fr; 53bis rue des Francs Bourgeois, 4e; 2-/3-course lunch menus €25/29, mains €21-33; ⏲noon-1am; ⓂRambuteau) Classic French dishes in a sublime, pre-Revolution building and former auction room with a glassed-in courtyard and knock-out, octagonal-shaped dining room. At brunch, help yourself to as much as you can eat for €30.

➡ **Chez Jenny** (Map p402; ☎01 44 54 39 00; www.chezjenny.com; 39 bd du Temple, 3e; lunch menus €19.80, mains €20-30; ⏲noon-midnight Sun-Thu, to 1am Fri & Sat; ⓂRépublique) Feast on huge Alsatian *choucroute garnie* (sauerkraut with smoked or salted pork, frankfurters and potatoes), *baeckeoffe* (Alsatian meat and veg stew) and stunning marquetry of Alsatian scenes by Charles Spindler on the 1st floor at this cavernous brasserie from 1932.

bar with an original horseshoe-shaped zinc bar from 1903. The place overflows with regulars from dawn to dark. Great *apéro* (predinner drink) spot and great WC – stainless-steel toilet stalls straight out of a Flash Gordon film (actually inspired by the interior of the *Nautilus* submarine in Jules Verne's *20,000 Leagues under the Sea*).

L'EBOUILLANTÉ CAFE

Map p402 (http://ebouillante.pagesperso-orange.fr; 6 rue des Barres, 4e; ⏲noon-10pm summer, to 7pm winter; ⓂHôtel de Ville) On sunny days there is no prettier cafe terrace. Enjoying a privileged position on a pedestrian, stone-flagged street just footsteps from the Seine, L'Ebouillanté buzzes with savvy Parisians sipping refreshing glasses of homemade *citronnade* (ginger lemonade), hibiscus flower cordial and herbal teas. Delicious cakes, jumbo salads, savoury crêpes and Sunday brunch (€21) complement the long drinks menu.

CAFÉ CHARLOT CAFE

Map p402 (www.cafecharlotparis.com; 38 rue de Bretagne, 3e; ⏲7am-2am; ⓂFilles du Calvaire) Across the street from the Marché aux Enfants Rouges, Café Charlot is a buzzing neighbourhood cafe in a former bakery with retro white tiles. The pavement terrace is perfect for lapping up the authentic Haut Marais vibe.

CINÉMA CAFÉ MERCI CAFE

Map p402 (www.merci-merci.com; 111 bd Beaumarchais, 3e; ⏲10am-6.30pm Mon-Sat; ⓂSt-Sébastien Froissart) A retro interior dresses this cafe dedicated to the seventh art. Black-and-white snaps of movie stars grace the walls; seating is a hip mix of banquet, low coffee table etc; and its retro *citronnade maison* – extra tart and tongue-tickling, home-made lemonade – and freshly squeezed fruit juices are worth every cent. Excellent lunchtime salads (€8 to €10) and cheese/cold meat platters (€16).

LE BARAV WINE BAR

Map p402 (☎01 48 04 57 59; www.lebarav.fr; 6 rue Charles-François Dupuis, 3e; ⏲noon-3pm Mon-Fri, 6pm-12.30am Tue-Sat; ⓂTemple) This hipster *bar à vin,* smart in the trendy Haut Marais, oozes atmosphere – and has one of the city's loveliest pavement terraces. Its extensive wine list is complemented by tasty food.

PANIC ROOM BAR

Map p402 (www.panicroomparis.com; 101 rue Amelot, 11e; ⏲6.30pm-2am Mon-Sat; ⓂSt-Sébastien Froissart) This brazenly wild bar is not quite as terrifying as its name suggests. A wildly flavoured cocktail – such as gin shaken with strawberries and basil, or a cognac-based creation mixing cucumber, coriander and ginger – is the thing to sip here, especially during happy hour (6.30pm to 9pm). Check its website for DJ sets, gigs and happenings.

LE TRINQUETTE WINE BAR

Map p402 (67 rue des Gravilliers, 3e; ⏲7pm-midnight Mon-Wed, 7pm-2am Thu-Sat; ⓂArts et Metiers) Find this atmospheric *bar à vins*

PIZZA PICK

➡ **Pink Flamingo** (Map p402; ☎01 42 71 28 20; www.pinkflamingopizza.com; 105 rue Vieille du Temple, 3e; pizzas €11.50-17; ⊙noon-3pm & 7-11.30pm; Ⓜ St-Sébastien-Froissart) The capital's most inventive, dare we say romantic, pizza joint on the Canal St-Martin (p150) has spawned a base in the Marais too. Yes!

➡ **Al Taglio** (Map p406; 2bis rue Neuve Popincourt, 11e; pizzas per kg €26.30-36.40; ⊙noon-11pm Mon-Fri, to midnight Sat & Sun; Ⓜ St-Sébastien-Froissart) Pizza *au poids* (by weight) as in Rome is the trademark of this contemporary space with a trio of shared high tables with bar stools and a couple of regular tables spilling onto a side alley. Its **second branch** (Map p402; ☎09 50 48 84 06; 27 rue de Saintonge, 3e; pizzas per kg €26.30-36.40; ⊙noon-11pm Mon-Fri, to midnight Sat & Sun; Ⓜ Filles-du-Calvaire) in the 3e gets more crowded.

➡ **La Briciola** (Map p402; ☎01 42 77 34 10; 64 rue Charlot, 3e; pizzas €9.50-15; ⊙noon-2.30pm & 7.30pm-midnight Mon-Sat; Ⓜ Oberkampf) Excellent pizza, salads and wine at this friendly Italian eatery in the northern Marais.

➡ **Grazie** (Map p402; ☎01 42 78 11 96; 91 bd Beaumarchais, 3e; pizzas €10-20; ⊙12.30-3pm & 7.30-11.30pm; Ⓜ Filles du Calvaire) Pizza chic is what this oh-so *bobo* Italian pizzeria and cocktail bar is all about. The place is designed like a New York loft and beautiful people are a constant.

and *cave* in a former cane and umbrella factory, compete with dandy racing-green façade and vintage gold lettering above the door. But step inside and it is pure 21st-century chic in that distressed, 'peeling paint on the walls', 'wine barrels as tables' kinda way.

LA MANGERIE — TAPAS BAR

Map p402 (☎01 42 77 49 35; http://la-mangerie.com; 7 rue de Jarente, 4e; ⊙6-11pm Mon-Fri, 6-11.30pm Sat; Ⓜ St-Paul) A heaving 'after work' drinks venue in winter particularly, La Mangerie cooks a colourful choice of Spanish-inspired tapas (grab a pencil and paper and tick the boxes to order; €9 to €16) and has a good choice of wine by the glass. But it's the buoyant vibe and buzzing atmosphere, orchestrated to perfection by charismatic front-of-houser Serge, that are the real reasons to come.

ZÉRO ZÉRO — BAR

Map p402 (www.radiozerozero.com; 89 rue Amelot, 11e; ⊙7.30pm-midnight Mon-Sat; Ⓜ St-Sébastien Froissart) Zéro Zéro screams Berlin with its banquette seating and tag-covered walls (and ceiling, and windows, and bar...). Electro and house is the sound and the house cocktail, a potent rum-and-ginger concoction, ensures a wild party spirit.

LA BELLE HORTENSE — WINE BAR

Map p402 (www.cafeine.com; 31 rue Vieille du Temple, 4e; ⊙5pm-2am; Ⓜ Hôtel de Ville or St-Paul) This creative wine bar named after a Jacques Roubaud novel fuses shelf after shelf of good books to read with an excellent wine list and enriching weekly agenda of book readings, signings and art events. A zinc bar and original 19th-century ceiling set the mood perfectly.

ANDY WAHLOO — COCKTAIL BAR

Map p402 (http://andywahloo-bar.com; 69 rue des Gravilliers, 3e; ⊙7pm-1.45am Tue-Sat; Ⓜ Arts et Métiers) Casablanca meets pop-artist Andy Warhol in this cool cocktail lounge at home in a former *fabrique de chemises* (shirt factory). Its clever name means 'I have nothing' in Arabic and is a major misnomer: think acid-yellow coloured decor, sweet cocktails, pushy staff and loud house music. Its courtyard is paradise for smokers and pullers.

LE PICK-CLOPS — BAR

Map p402 (16 rue Vieille du Temple, 4e; ⊙8am-2am Mon-Sun; 📶; Ⓜ Hôtel de Ville or St-Paul) This buzzy bar-cafe – all shades of yellow and lit by neon – has formica tables, ancient bar stools and plenty of mirrors. Attracting a friendly flow of locals and passersby, it's a great place for morning or afternoon coffee, or that last drink alone or with friends.

LA PERLE — CAFE, BAR

Map p402 (http://cafelaperle.com; 78 rue Vieille du Temple, 3e; ⊙9am-2am; Ⓜ St-Paul or Chemin Vert) This party bar is where *bobos* (bohemian bourgeois) come to slum it over *un rouge* (glass of red wine) in the Marais until the

DJ arrives to liven things up. Unique trademarks: the (for real) distressed look of the place and the model locomotive over the bar.

LE CLOWN BAR WINE BAR

Map p402 (☎01 43 55 87 35; 114 rue Amelot, 11e; Ⓜ Filles du Calvaire) A historic monument next to the city's winter circus, the Cirque d'Hiver (1852), this unique address is practically a museum with its painted ceilings, mosaics on the wall, zinc bar and purist art-deco style. A restaurant for decades, the mythical address was taken over in early 2014 by chef-sommelier duo Sven Chartier and Ewen Lemoigne.

LES ÉTAGES BAR

Map p402 (35 rue Vieille du Temple, 4e; ⏲2pm-2am; ; Ⓜ Hôtel de Ville or St-Paul) Students and expats find the 'Storeys' (all three floors), with its faded sage-green façade, a viable alternative to the standard Marais fare, and happily appropriate the upgraded lounge rooms upstairs.

POP IN BAR

Map p402 (http://popin.fr; 105 rue Amelot, 4e; ⏲6.30pm-1.30am; Ⓜ St-Sébastien Froissart) All skinny jeans and cultivated pop-rock nonchalance, the Pop In somehow got itself on the in-crowd map but maintains a relaxed regulars' vibe. It's popular with expats and Parisian students starting their evenings, and the drinks are reasonably priced. Whisper sweet nothings as you leave; it's had a lot of problems with noise-sensitive neighbours.

CAFÉ SUÉDOIS CAFE

Map p402 (https://paris.si.se; 11 rue Payenne, 3e; ⏲noon-6pm Tue-Sun; ; Ⓜ Chemin Vert) Housed in the beautiful 16th-century Hôtel de Marle, this gorgeous cafe in the Swedish Cultural Institute lures Parisians like bees to a honey pot with its tranquil paved courtyard. Delicious soups, sandwiches and cakes too.

CAFÉ MARTINI BAR

Map p402 (www.cafemartini.fr; 9 rue du Pas de la Mule, 4e; ⏲6pm-midnight; Ⓜ Chemin Vert) Skip the unmemorable cafe-bars on place des Vosges and nip around the corner to this cosy den with wood-panelling, beams and a buzzing after-work crowd – the saggy sofa is the hot spot! Spoil yourself with smoothies, thick-enough-to-spoon *chocolat chaud à l'ancienne,* copious cheese/cold-meat platters and happy-hour cocktails.

(A)PPAREMMENT CAFÉ CAFE

Map p402 (18 rue des Coutures St-Gervais, 3e; ⏲11am-midnight; Ⓜ St-Sébastien Froissart) This tasteful haven, tucked behind the Musée Picasso, is just like home with its wood panelling, leather sofas, scattered parlour games to play and dog-eared books to read. Build-your-own salads and Sunday brunch (mains €13 to €15).

LA TARTINE WINE BAR

Map p402 (24 rue de Rivoli & 17 rue du Roi de Sicile, 11e; ⏲7.30am-2am; Ⓜ St-Paul) A wine bar where little has changed since the days of gas lighting, this busy place offers 15 selected reds, whites and rosés by the *pot* (46cL). Its fabulous choice of *tartines* (open-faced sandwiches, €5.80 to €9.90) served on Poilâne bread make it a hot choice for lunch.

BESPOKE COCKTAIL BAR

Map p402 (3 rue Oberkampf, 11e; ⏲noon-2am Tue-Sun; Ⓜ Filles du Calvaire) Particularly handy for guests staying at Hôtel Beaumarchais next door, this design-driven space is a sweet, late-night drink call. In keeping with the image its name evokes, cocktails are its thing – sipped over shared small plates (€6 to €9) and excellent sweet-potato fries (€3.50) perhaps. Check out the leather-belt wall!

L'ÉTOILE MANQUANTE CAFE, BAR

Map p402 (34 rue Vieille du Temple, 4e; ⏲9am-2am; Ⓜ Hôtel de Ville or St-Paul) With its fabulous pavement terrace, spilling onto rue Ste-Croix de la Bretonnerie, the Missing Star is a trendy, gay-friendly bar with a retro interior topped by star-lit vaults.

OPEN CAFÉ CAFE

Map p402 (www.opencafe.fr; 17 rue des Archives, 4e; ⏲11am-2am; Ⓜ Hôtel de Ville) A gay venue for all types at all hours, this spacious bar-cafe with twinkling disco balls strung from the starry ceiling has bags of appeal – not least, a big buzzing pavement terrace, a kitchen serving breakfast (€8.70), all-day *tartines* (€6.70), and a four-hour happy hour kicking in daily at 6pm.

LE COX GAY BAR

Map p402 (www.coxbar.fr; 15 rue des Archives, 4e; ⏲5pm-2am; Ⓜ Hôtel de Ville) This small gay bar with decor that changes every quarter is *the* meeting place for an interesting (and interested) cruisy crowd throughout the evening from dusk on. OK, we don't like the in-your-face name either, but what's a boy to do? Happy hour runs 6pm to 10pm daily.

COFFEE & TEA

For die-hard connoisseurs craving a genuine cup of proper tea or coffee, Paris savours a handful of memorable addresses, a couple of which run fascinating *ateliers de dégustation* (tasting workshops).

➡ **Belleville Brûlerie** (p186) The roastery opens Saturday for coffee sales and one-hour 'cupping' sessions (€20; book online) during which you taste different coffees, compare tasting notes and get a bag of beans to take home.

➡ **La Caféothèque** (Map p402; www.lacafeotheque.com; 52 rue de l'Hôtel de Ville, 4e; ◎9.30am-7.30pm; ☎; ⓜSt-Paul or Hôtel de Ville) From the industrial grinder to the elaborate tasting notes, this maze of a coffee house is serious. Grab a pew, pick your bean and get it served just the way you like it (espresso, ristretto, latte etc). The coffee of the day (€3) keeps well-travelled taste buds on their toes, as does the €10 *dégustation* (tasting) of three different coffees.

➡ **Fondation Café** (Map p402; 16 rue Dupetit Thoars, 3e; ◎8am-6pm Mon-Fri, 9am-6pm Sat & Sun; ⓜTemple) It is easily one of the city's smallest cafes – just three teeny tables inside, four outside and no toilet. Yet that doesn't stop Paris' international set flocking here for excellent coffee brewed from Belleville-roasted beans. Pair with a sublime slice of warm, buttered banana bread for a match made in heaven.

➡ **Boot Café** (Map p402; 19 rue du Pont aux Choux, 3e; ◎8.30am-7.30pm Tue-Fri, 10am-6pm Sat; ⓜFilles du Calvaire) The charm of this three-table cafe is its façade. The original washed-blue exterior and 'Cordonnerie' lettering of the old cobbler's shop have been beautifully preserved, as has the fantastic red boot sign above. Excellent coffee, roasted in Paris, to boot – to drink in or take out.

➡ **Loustic** (Map p402; 40 rue Chapon, 3e; ◎8am-6pm Mon-Fri, 10am-5pm Sat, 11am-6pm Sun; ☎; ⓜArts et Metiers or Rambuteau) This pocket-sized espresso bar with Londoner Channa at its helm has been cleverly designed (by Parisian hotshot Dorothée Meilichzon, no less) for lounging over excellent coffee (roasted in Belgium and ground to coffee-lover perfection in situ on a Florentine Marzocco machine), a lazy breakfast (€10.50 to €12) or a revitalising cup of chai tea latté. 'Loustic', incidentally, is old Breton for a 'smart Alec'.

➡ **Le Loir dans La Théière** (Map p402; 3 rue des Rosiers, 4e; ◎9am-7.30pm; ⓜSt-Paul) Cutesy name (Dormouse in the Teapot) notwithstanding, this is a wonderful old space filled with retro toys, comfy couches and scenes of *Through the Looking Glass* on the walls. Its dozen different types of tea poured in the company of tip-top savoury tarts and crumble-type desserts ensure a constant queue on the street. Breakfast (€12) and brunch (€19.50) too.

➡ **Mariage Frères** (Map p402; www.mariagefreres.com; 30, 32 & 35 rue du Bourg Tibourg, 4e; pot of tea €10, brunch €32-55, mains €24-27; ◎daily; ⓜHôtel de Ville) Founded in 1854, this is Paris' first and arguably finest tearoom with a shop and a Saturday-morning Tea Club that runs 1½ hour tasting workshops (€65). Choose from more than 500 varieties of tea sourced from some 35 countries. The tearoom also serves brunch (€32 to €55), lunch (mains €24 to €27) and sandwich and cake afternoon teas (€23 to €38).

QUETZAL GAY BAR

Map p402 (10 rue de la Verrerie, 4e; ◎5pm-2am; ⓜHôtel de Ville) This perennial favourite gay bar is opposite rue des Mauvais Garçons (Bad Boys' Street), a road named after the brigands who congregated here in 1540. It's always busy, with house and dance music playing at night, and cruisy at all hours; plate-glass windows allow you to check out the talent before it arrives.

3W KAFÉ GAY BAR

Map p402 (8 rue des Écouffes, 4e; ◎8pm-3am Wed & Thu, to 5.30am Fri & Sat; ⓜSt-Paul) The name of this flagship cocktail bar-pub on a street with several lesbian bars means 'women with women'. It's relaxed and there's no ban on men (they must be accompanied by a woman). On weekends there's dancing downstairs with a DJ and themed evenings take place regularly. Check its Facebook page for events.

LES JACASSES GAY BAR

Map p402 (5 rue des Écouffes, 4e; 5pm-2am Wed-Sun; M St-Paul) Girls will love this sister bar to 3W (p178) – it looks like it's been transplanted directly from Normandy. It has softer music, hard-core evenings and a happy 'hour' that happily lasts for four (from 5pm).

LE TANGO CLUB

Map p402 (www.boiteafrissons.fr; 13 rue au Maire, 3e; admission €6-9; 10.30pm-5am Fri & Sat, 6-11pm Sun; M Arts et Métiers) Billing itself as a *boîte à frissons* (club of thrills), Le Tango hosts a mixed and cosmopolitan, gay and lesbian crowd in a historic 1930s dancehall. Its atmosphere and style is retro and festive, with waltzing, salsa and tango getting going from the moment it opens. From about 12.30am onwards DJs play. Sunday's gay tea dance is legendary.

Ménilmontant & Belleville

★LE BARBOUQUIN CAFE

Map p406 (www.lebarbouquin.fr; 3 rue Ramponeau, 20e; 10.30am-6pm Tue-Sat; M Belleville) There is no lovelier spot to relax in a vintage armchair over a cup of organic tea or freshly juiced carrot-and-apple cocktail after a hectic morning at Belleville market. Secondhand books – to be borrowed, exchanged or bought – line one wall and the twinset of pavement-terrace tables outside sit on magnificently graffitied rue Dénoyez. Breakfast and weekend brunch.

CHAPEAU MELON WINE BAR

(01 42 02 68 60; 92 rue Rébeval, 19e; 8.30-10.30pm Wed-Sun; M Pyrénées) Very much a Belleville 'in-the-know' address, this stylish wine cellar – a spellbinding maze of bottles – is the best place around for a glass of natural French wine accompanied by a perfectly ripened cheese, mixed charcuterie platter or small plate of delicious home cooking. Reservations recommended.

AUX DEUX AMIS CAFE, BAR

Map p406 (01 58 30 38 13; 45 rue Oberkampf, 11e; 8am-2am Tue-Sat; M Oberkampf) From the well-worn, tiled floor to the day's menu scrawled in marker on the vintage mirror behind the bar (two-/three-course lunch menu €18/22), Aux Deux Amis is the quintessential Parisian neighbourhood bar. It's perfect for a coffee any time and come dusk it serves tapas-style dishes. Friday brings the house speciality – *tartare de cheval* (hand-chopped horsemeat seasoned with a secret mix of herbs).

LA CARAVANE BAR

Map p406 (www.lacaravane.eu; 35 rue de la Fontaine au Roi, 11e; 11am-2am; ; M Goncourt) This funky, animated bar is a little jewel tucked away between République and Oberkampf; look for the tiny campervan above the pavement. The bar is surrounded by colourful kitsch furnishings, and the people around it and behind it are amiable and relaxed.

CAFÉ CHARBON BAR

Map p406 (www.lecafecharbon.com; 109 rue Oberkampf, 11e; 9am-2am; ; M Parmentier) With its post-industrial belle époque ambience, the Charbon was the first of the hip cafes and bars to catch on in Ménilmontant. It's always crowded and worth heading to for the distressed decor with high ceilings, chandeliers and perched DJ booth.

BLOODIES WINE BAR

Map p406 (52 av de la République, 11e; M St-Maur) Despite its somewhat unappealing name in English, Bloodies is a cavernous and airy space with high ceiling, huge street-facing windows and large pavement terrace. Its backside peeps out on a green-filled courtyard, and a meaty menu complements the extensive wine list.

SCREAM CLUB CLUB

Map p402 (www.scream-paris.com; 18 rue du Faubourg du Temple, 11e; admission €15; midnight-7am Sat; M Belleville or Goncourt) What started out as a summer party is now a permanent fixture on the city's gay scene (marketed

> **LOCAL KNOWLEDGE**
>
> **AT DUSK**
>
> As the bewitching hour for that all-essential early evening *apéro* beckons, there is no lovelier city square in which to sit beneath fairy lights and lap up local life than pedestrian **place du Marché Ste-Catherine, 4e** (metro St-Paul). Clad with benches and trees, it is framed on three sides by atmospheric cafe pavement terraces – perfect for a simple *pression* (glass of draft beer) or kir (white wine and cassis) at dusk.

as Paris' biggest gay party). The Saturday-night *soirée gay* brings clubbers together on two dance floors – one dedicated to pop, the other to sets by an international DJ – and an ooh la la! *espace cruising*.

☆ ENTERTAINMENT

GAÎTÉ LYRIQUE CULTURAL CENTRE
Map p402 (☎01 53 01 52 00; www.gaite-lyrique.net; 3bis rue Papin, 3e; exhibitions €5-7, concerts variable; ⊙2-8pm Tue-Sat, noon-6pm Sun; Ⓜ Arts et Metiers or Réaumur-Sébastopol) Unique and fascinating exhibitions – usually art or installation-art orientated – are the mainstay of this vibrant cultural centre in the Marais. Families with teens will find it particularly appealing; post-exhibition, don't miss the video-game room and library.

LE CARREAU DU TEMPLE CULTURAL CENTRE
Map p402 (☎01 83 81 93 30; www.lecarreaudutemple.eu; 4 rue Eugène Spuller, 3e; ⊙ticket office 2-6pm Mon-Sat; Ⓜ Temple) The quarter's old covered market with drop-dead-gorgeous art-nouveau ironwork is now the city's most architecturally appealing cultural centre and entertainment venue. The place where silks, lace, leather and other materials were sold in the 19th century is now a vast stage for exhibitions, concerts, sports classes and theatre. Check the program online.

LA BELLEVILLOISE CULTURAL CENTRE
(☎01 46 36 07 07; www.labellevilloise.com; 19-21 rue Boyer, 20e; ⊙7pm-1am Wed & Thu, 7pm-2am Fri, 6pm-2am Sat, 11.30am-midnight Sun; Ⓜ Ménilmontant) Gigs, concerts, theatrical performances, exhibitions, readings, dance classes and workshops: this arts centre is where it all happens after dark in Ménilmontant. Sunday brunch (adult/child €29/13) accompanied by live jazz in the trendy cafe-restaurant – gorgeous in summer with its sunlit tables beneath 100-year-old olive trees – packs out the place. Advance reservations recommended.

LA MAROQUINERIE LIVE MUSIC
(☎01 40 33 64 85; http://lamaroquinerie.fr; 23 rue Boyer, 20e; ⊙7.30-11.30pm; Ⓜ Ménilmontant) This tiny but trendy venue in Ménilmontant entices a staunchly local, in-the-know set with real cutting-edge gigs – many bands kick off their European tour here. The alfresco courtyard and restaurant renders La Maroquinerie an address impossible to resist; to see for yourself head east along rue Ménilmontant and take the second right after place de Ménilmontant.

LE NOUVEAU CASINO LIVE MUSIC
Map p406 (www.nouveaucasino.net; 109 rue Oberkampf, 11e; ⊙Tue-Sun; Ⓜ Parmentier) This club-concert annexe of Café Charbon (p179) has made a name for itself amid the bars of Oberkampf with its live-music concerts (usually Tuesday, Thursday and Friday) and lively club nights on weekends. Electro, pop, deep house, rock – the program is eclectic, underground and always up to the minute. Check the website for listings.

THÉÂTRE LE POINT VIRGULE COMEDY
Map p402 (www.lepointvirgule.com; 7 rue Ste-Croix de la Bretonnerie, 4e; Ⓜ Hôtel de Ville) This tiny and convivial comedy spot in the Marais has been going strong for well over five decades. It offers cafe-theatre at its best – stand-up comics, performance artists, musical acts. The quality is variable, but it's great fun and the place has a reputation for discovering new talent.

LA FAVELA CHIC WORLD MUSIC
Map p402 (☎01 40 21 38 14; www.favelachic.com; 18 rue du Faubourg du Temple, 11e; ⊙from 7.30pm Tue-Sat; Ⓜ République) It starts as a chic, convivial restaurant and gives way to caipirinha- and mojito-fuelled bumping, grinding, flirting and dancing (mostly on the long tables). The music is traditionally bossa nova, samba, *baile* (dance), funk and Brazilian pop, and it can get very crowded and hot.

LA JAVA WORLD MUSIC
Map p406 (www.la-java.fr; 105 rue du Faubourg du Temple, 11e; Ⓜ Goncourt) Built in 1922, this is the dance hall where Édith Piaf got her first break, and it now reverberates to the sound of live salsa, rock and world music. Live concerts usually take place during the week at 8pm or 9pm. Afterwards a festive crowd gets dancing to electro, house, disco and Latino DJs.

LE BATACLAN LIVE MUSIC
Map p402 (www.bataclan.fr; 50 bd Voltaire, 11e; Ⓜ Oberkampf or St-Ambroise) Built in 1864 and Maurice Chevalier's debut venue in 1910, this excellent little concert hall – a symphony of lively red, yellow and green hues – draws big-ticket French (and some international) rock and pop legends. Le

Bataclan also masquerades as a theatre and dance hall.

SATELLIT CAFÉ WORLD MUSIC

Map p406 (☎01 47 00 48 87; www.satellit-cafe.com; 44 rue de la Folie Méricourt, 11e; ⊙Tue-Sun; Ⓜ Oberkampf or St-Ambroise) A great venue for world music and not as painfully trendy as some others in Paris – come to hear everything from blues and flamenco to African and Bollywood. Sunday is salsa. Check its Facebook page for events and opening times.

LE VIEUX BELLEVILLE LIVE MUSIC

Map p406 (www.le-vieux-belleville.com; 12 rue des Envierges, 20e; ⊙11am-3pm Mon-Fri, 8pm-2am Thu-Sat; Ⓜ Pyrénées) This old-fashioned bistro and *musette* at the top of Parc de Belleville is an atmospheric venue for performances of *chansons* featuring accordions and an organ grinder three times a week. It's a lively favourite with locals, so booking ahead is advised.

L'ALIMENTATION GÉNÉRALE LIVE MUSIC

Map p406 (☎01 43 55 42 50; http://alimentation-generale.net; 64 rue Jean-Pierre Timbaud, 11e; admission Fri & Sat €10; ⊙7pm-2am Wed, Thu & Sun, 7pm-5am Fri & Sat; Ⓜ Parmentier) A rue JPT stalwart, the 'Grocery Store' is a massive space, with crazy retro decor and some outrageous toilets. Music is a very big deal here. DJs rock the joint on weekends.

CAFÉ DE LA GARE THEATRE, COMEDY

Map p402 (☎01 42 78 52 51; www.cafe-de-la-gare.fr.st; 41 rue du Temple, 4e; Ⓜ Hôtel de Ville) The 'Station Cafe', in the erstwhile mews of a Marais *hôtel particulier* (private mansion) with fabulous interior courtyard, is one of the best and most innovative cafe-theatres in Paris. Acts range from comic theatre and stand-up to reinterpreted classics.

SHOPPING

The Marais boasts excellent speciality stores and an ever-expanding fashion presence. Hip young designers have colonised the upper reaches of the 3e towards rue Charlot as well as rue de Turenne. Meanwhile, rue des Francs Bourgeois and, towards the other side of rue de Rivoli, rue François Mirron in the 4e have well-established boutique shopping for clothing, hats, home furnishings and stationery. Place des Vosges is lined with very high-end art and antique galleries with some amazing sculptures for sale.

Le Marais

★PARIS RENDEZ-VOUS CONCEPT STORE

Map p402 (29 rue de Rivoli, 4e; ⊙10am-7pm Mon-Sat; Ⓜ Hôtel de Ville) Only the city of Paris could be so chic as to have its own designer line of souvenirs, sold in its own ubercool concept store inside the Hôtel de Ville. Shop here for everything from clothing and homewares to Paris-themed books, toy sailing boats and signature Jardin du Luxembourg's Fermob chairs. *Quel style!*

★FLEUX DESIGN, HOMEWARES

Map p402 (www.fleux.com; 39 & 52 rue Sainte Croix de la Bretonnerie, 4e; ⊙10.45am-7.30pm Mon-Fri, 10.30am-8pm Sat, 1.30-7.30pm Sun; Ⓜ Hôtel de Ville) Innovative designs for the home by European designers fill this twin-set of big white mazes. Products range from super chic to kitsch, clever and plain crazy. Its e-boutique stocks about 10% of what you see on the shop floor, but Fleux can post most Paris purchases home for you (at a price, *bien sûr*).

★L'ÉCLAIR DE GÉNIE CAKES

Map p402 (www.leclairdegenie.com; 14 rue Pavée, 4e; ⊙11am-7pm Mon-Fri, 10am-7.30pm Sat & Sun; Ⓜ St-Paul) A thrill to visit, this luminous boutique is an ode to sweet éclairs and chocolate truffles. Éclairs created by *pâtissier* Christophe Adam are displayed like art beneath glass, with dazzling effect. Pick your flavours, pay at the back of the boutique, pick up your goodie bag and pinch yourself that you've just paid between €5 and €7 for one tiny éclair. It's worth it.

★CHEZ HÉLÈNE CONFECTIONERY

Map p402 (www.chezhelene-paris.com; 28 rue Saint-Gilles, 3e; ⊙11.30am-7.30pm Mon-Sat, 11am-1pm & 3-7pm Sun; Ⓜ Rambuteau) Pure indulgence is what this irresistible *bonbon* (sweet) boutique – a child's dream come true – is about. Old-fashioned toffees and caramels, fudge, liquorice, Eiffel Tower sugar cubes, designer lollipops, artisanal marshmallows, Provençal *calissons*...the choice of quality, well-made *bonbons* and *gourmandises* (sweet treats) is outstanding.

LOCAL KNOWLEDGE

SECRET SHOPPING

Some of the Marais' sweetest boutique shopping is secreted down peaceful alleyways and courtyards, free of cars, as they were centuries ago. Take **rue du Trésor** (Map p402; Ⓜ Hôtel de Ville or St-Paul) for example, a pedestrian dead-end passage off rue du Vieille du Temple, encrusted with an exclusive handful of hip boutiques like **Trésor** (Map p402; 5 rue du Trésor, 4e; Ⓜ Hôtel de Ville or St-Paul) by Brigitte Masson, a bohemian boutique with catchy salmon-orange façade strung with old-fashioned fairy lights and fresh, individual women's fashion inside. End with a drink or lunch on the buzzing pavement terrace of **La Chaise au Plafond** (Map p402; 10 rue du Trésor, 4e; ⏲9am-2am; Ⓜ Hôtel de Ville or St-Paul).

From Monday to Friday its cobbled alleys are mostly mouse quiet, but come the weekend savvy trendsetters mingle at **Village St-Paul** (Map p402; rue St-Paul, des rue Jardins St-Paul & rue Charlemagne, 4e; Ⓜ St-Paul), a designer set of five vintage courtyards, refashioned in the 1970s from the 14th-century walled gardens of King Charles V. Meander away Saturday afternoon with a courtyard-to-courtyard stroll, paved in old stone, pierced with ancient fountains and riddled with tiny artisan boutiques, galleries and antique shops.

MERCI — CONCEPT STORE

Map p402 (www.merci-merci.com; 111 bd Beaumarchais, 3e; ⏲10am-7pm Mon-Sat; Ⓜ St-Sébastien Froissart) A Fiat Cinquecento marks the entrance to this unique concept store, which donates all its profits to a children's charity in Madagascar. Shop for fashion, accessories, linens, lamps and nifty designs for the home. Complete the experience with a coffee in its hybrid used-book-shop-cafe or lunch in its stylish basement.

BONTON — CHILDREN'S FASHION

Map p402 (www.bonton.fr; 5 bd des Filles du Calvaire, 3e; ⏲10am-7pm Mon-Sat; Ⓜ Filles du Calvaire) Chic and stylish, this concept store stocks vintage-inspired fashion, furnishings and knick-knacks for babies, toddlers and children. Don't leave without donning an old-fashioned, floppy sunhat or pair of oversized sunglasses and getting your photo snapped in its retro photo booth. Parents note: loo with changing mat in the basement.

JAMIN PUECH — ACCESSORIES

Map p402 (www.jamin-puech.com; 68 rue Vieille du Temple, 4e; ⏲11am-7pm Mon & Wed-Sat, noon-7pm Tue; Ⓜ St-Sébastian Froissart) A girl's best friend in *bobo* circles, this Parisian design house creates beautiful handbags in all manner of bold colours, textures and textiles. Isabelle Puech and Benoît Jamin are the duo behind the catchy, ethno-urban look. For vintage pieces from the 1990s, head to the couple's first boutique at 61 rue d'Hauteville, 10e.

SAMUEL CORAUX — JEWELLERY

Map p402 (www.coraux.book.fr; 18 rue Ste-Anastase, 3e; ⏲10am-6pm Mon-Fri) The stark black façade at this hybrid boutique-workshop provides a dramatic contrast to the brilliantly coloured, contemporary creations crafted inside by jewellery designer Samuel Coraux. Every material stars here, shiny plastic appearing a hot favourite.

NATHALIE SEVIKÏAN — JEWELLERY

Map p402 (www.nathaliesevikian.com; 13 rue Froissart, 3e; ⏲10am-7pm Mon-Sat; Ⓜ St-Sébastien Froissart) Much thought goes into each individual piece of jewellery crafted by Provençal gemologist Nathalie Sevikïan. Her pieces are bold, contemporary and loaded with spiritual meaning.

VIRGINIE MONROE — ACCESSORIES, JEWELLERY

Map p402 (www.virginiemonroe.com; 24 rue de Poitou, 3e; ⏲11am-7pm Mon-Sat; Ⓜ St-Sébastien Froissart) Delicate rows of beads, lace-fine bracelets and other colourfully beaded pieces are the mainstay of this chic jewellery designer whose creative life was born in Brazil. She now has boutiques in Paris, Marseille and Lille.

ÉTAT LIBRE D'ORANGE — PERFUME

Map p402 (www.etatlibredorange.com; 69 rue des Archives, 3e; ⏲noon-7.30pm Tue-Sat; Ⓜ Arts et Métiers) This perfumery screams Marais hipster. And with scents bearing names such as Fat Electrician, Jasmin et Cigarette, Malaise of the 1970s and Delicious Closet Queen, there really is something for everyone.

LE LABO
PERFUME

Map p402 (www.lelabofragrances.com; 7 rue Froissart, 3e; ⏲11am-7pm Mon-Sat; Ⓜ St-Sébastien Froissart) Sniff your way through 14 scents, each carefully crafted by a *nez* (nose) in Grasse in southern France, then place your order.

FRAGONARD
PERFUME, HOMEWARES

Map p402 (www.fragonard.com; 51 rue des Francs Bourgeois, 4e; ⏲10.30am-7.30pm Mon-Fri, noon-7pm Sat; Ⓜ St-Paul) This Parisian perfume maker has alluring natural scents in elegant bottles as well as candles, essential oils and soaps. In addition to the splendid smells, there's a small, expensive and very tasteful selection of clothing, hand-stitched linen tablecloths and napkins.

ANDREA CREWS
FASHION

Map p402 (www.andreacrews.com; 83 rue de Turenne, 3e; ⏲11am-7pm Mon-Fri, 12.30-7.30pm Sat; Ⓜ St-Sébastien Froissart) Using everything from discarded clothing to electrical fittings and household bric-a-brac, this bold art and fashion collective sews, recycles and reinvents to create the most extraordinary pieces. Watch out for 'happenings' in this Marais boutique.

OFR LIBRAIRIE
BOOKS

Map p402 (20 rue Dupetit Thouars, 3e; ⏲10am-8pm Mon-Fri, 8am-7pm Sat & Sun; Ⓜ Temple) Art, design and history books and mags – many about Paris – are the mainstay of this trendy Marais store with a one-room gallery out back. The latest hip bags, Kasia Dietz totes, T-shirts and other items can also be found here.

LOSCO
ACCESSORIES

Map p402 (www.losco.fr; 20 rue de Sévigné, 4e; ⏲11am-1pm Wed-Fri, 2-7pm Sun-Fri, 11am-7pm Sat; Ⓜ St-Paul) This artisan *ceinturier* epitomises the main draw of shopping in Paris – stumbling upon tiny boutique-workshops selling 101 quality variations of one single item, in this case *ceintures* (belts). Pick leather type (lizard, python, croc etc), length and buckle to suit just you. Expect to pay anything upwards of €160.

LA BOUTIQUE EXTRAORDINAIRE
FASHION

Map p402 (67 rue Charlot, 3e; ⏲11am-8pm Tue-Sat, 3-7pm Sun; Ⓜ Filles du Calvaire) Mohair, silk and other natural, organic and ethical materials are hand-knitted into exquisite garments, almost too precious to wear, at this unusual and captivating Haut Marais boutique.

SOLE DESIGN

The real joy of mooching around the Marais is stumbling across tiny *ateliers* (workshops) and boutiques to watch just-established or rising designers at work.

➡ **Moon Young Hee** (Map p402; 62 rue Charlot, 3e; ⏲11am-7pm Mon-Sat; Ⓜ Filles du Calvaire) Watch fanciful 'origami' creations being cut by hand in the studio of Korean designer Moon Young Hee. Ancient beams, exposed stone walls and huge street-facing windows form the perfect stage.

➡ **Valentine Gauthier** (Map p402; www.valentinegauthier.com; 58 rue Charlot, 3e; ⏲9.30am-7.30pm Mon-Sat; Ⓜ Filles du Calvaire) Go green with jackets, mules, cowboy boots and other romantic, natural and urban designs by one of Paris' most talented ecoconscious designers.

➡ **Anne Elisabeth** (Map p402; www.anne-elisabeth.com; 50 rue des Francs Bourgeois, 4e; ⏲11am-7.30pm Mon-Sat, 1.30-7pm Sun; Ⓜ St-Paul) Every creation of Anne Elisabeth is named after a river, town, character in a novel or simply something that happens to inspire this well-travelled Parisian designer of the moment. Bold colours, printed housecoats and wide trousers are among her signature 'arty-couture' garments inspired by 1950s and 1960s fashion.

➡ **Kate Mack** (Map p402; www.kate-mack.com; 15 rue Oberkampf, 11e; ⏲noon-2pm & 3-8pm Tue-Sat; Ⓜ Oberkampf) A hard-core address for getting to the core of Parisian trends, this studio-boutique of Kate Mack is a real delight. Ogle silver-skinned mannequins modelling overtly feminine but funky, femme-fatale designs.

➡ **Le Boudoir 26** (Map p402; www.johannabraitbart.com; 26 rue des Blancs Manteaux, 4e; ⏲11am-8pm Mon-Sat; Ⓜ St-Sébastian Froissart) Extraordinary handmade hat pieces, almost too exquisite to wear, are made with much love and creative talent by Johanna Braitbart in her small Marais *atelier*.

LOCAL KNOWLEDGE

VINTAGE JACKPOT

Fashionistas keen to save a bob will be in heaven in the Marais where a small but highly select choice of boutiques sell top-quality vintage.

➜ **Violette et Léonie** (Map p402; www.violetteleonie.com; 114 rue de Turenne, 3e; ⏱1-7.30pm Mon, 11am-7.30pm Tue-Sat, 2-7pm Sun; Ⓜ Filles du Calvaire) So chic and of such high quality that it really does not seem like secondhand, Violette et Léonie is a first-class *dépôt-vente* boutique specialising in vintage. Shop in its wonderfully spacious concept store or online.

➜ **Odetta Vintage** (Map p402; www.odettavintage.com; 76 rue des Tournelles, 3e; ⏱2-7.30pm Tue-Sat, 3-7pm Sun; Ⓜ Chemin Vert) Odetta specialises in luxury vintage from the 1960s to 1980s. If you're going to find a runway sample, it's here. Think women's shoes, accessories and clothing fashion, as well as the odd piece of remarkable vintage furniture.

➜ **Vintage Désir** (Map p402; 32 rue des Rosiers, 4e; ⏱11am-7pm; Ⓜ St-Paul) Always stuffed to the gills with clothing and customers, this tiny shop on busy rue Rosiers is a top spot to pick up quality pieces without breaking the bank. No credit cards and, yes, the name above the shop reads 'Coiffeur' ('hairdresser') because that is what this charming old space used to be.

ISABEL MARANT — FASHION

Map p402 (www.isabelmarant.fr; 47 rue Saintonge, 3e; ⏱11am-7pm Mon, 10.30am-7.30pm Tue-Sat; Ⓜ Filles du Calvaire) The historic setting – an old *atelier de rémoulage* (remoulding workshop) complete with faded gold lettering above the shop front – makes the shopping experience at this Haut Marais boutique filled with Isabel Marant designs all the more pleasurable.

PAULINE PIN — ACCESSORIES

Map p402 (www.paulinepin.com; 51 rue Charlot, 3e; ⏱11am-7.30pm Tue-Sat; Ⓜ Filles du Calvaire) Invest in a super-soft and stylish handbag made by designer Clarisse at her workshop in the Marais. She now has a handful of boutiques in France and beyond.

K JACQUES — SHOES

Map p402 (www.kjacques.fr; 6 rue Pavée, 4e; ⏱11am-7pm Mon-Sat; Ⓜ St-Paul) Traditional strappy sandals, supposedly inspired by a simple leather pair brought by writer Colette from Greece to show her cobbler, is the speciality of this shoemaker from St-Tropez. Celebrity clients included Picasso, Brigitte Bardot and the Baba Cool Generation.

ROUGIER & PLÉ — FINE ARTS

Map p402 (www.rougier-ple.fr; 13 bd des Filles du Calvaire, 3e; ⏱11am-7pm Tue-Sat, 2.30-7pm Sun & Mon; Ⓜ Filles du Calvaire) The city's oldest *beaux arts* (fine arts) shop, in business since 1854, sells paper, pens, arts and crafts materials – everything imaginable, in fact, for *le plaisir de crée* (the pleasure of creation).

TUMBLEWEED — TOYS, FASHION

Map p402 (www.tumbleweedparis.com; 19 rue de Turenne, 4e; ⏱11am-7pm; Ⓜ St-Paul or Chemin Vert) This little shop specialises in leather slippers for kids and *l'artisanat d'art ludique* (crafts of the playing art): think handmade wooden toys and exquisitely made brain teasers and puzzles for adults, such as Japanese 'spin' and 'secret' boxes that defy entry.

PETIT PAN — HOMEWARES, FASHION

Map p402 (www.petitpan.com; 76 rue François Miron, 4e; ⏱10.30am-7.30pm; Ⓜ St-Paul) Few boutiques are as enchanting or dazzling as Petit Pan, a wonderful Pandora's box of beautiful fabrics, buttons and threads in every colour of the rainbow. A second space across the street, **Petit Pan Bébé** (Map p402; 39 rue François Miron, 4e; Ⓜ St-Paul), homes in on baby and children's wear, exquisitely stitched in the same mesmerising array of colours and patterns.

AZAG — HOMEWARES

Map p402 (www.azag.fr; 9 rue François Miron, 4e; ⏱11am-7pm Mon-Fri, 10.30am-7.30pm Sat, 2.30-6.30pm Sun; Ⓜ St-Paul) 'Style and accessories, home and design' – often with a Paris slant – is the strapline of this delightful little boutique, a perfect one-stop shop for discovering unique and unusual gifts and souvenirs.

CSAO SOUVENIRS

Map p402 (www.csao.fr; 9 & 9bis rue Elzévir, 4e; ⌚11am-7pm Tue-Fri, 11am-7.30pm Sat, noon-7pm Sun; ⓂSt-Paul or Chemin Vert) This wonderful shop and gallery, owned and operated by the charitable Compagnie du Sénégal et de l'Afrique de l'Ouest (CSAO; Senegal and West Africa Company), distributes the work of African craftspeople and artists. Many of the colourful fabrics and weavings are exquisite. Included are items handmade from recycled handbags, aluminium cans and tomato-paste tins.

CHOCOLATERIE JOSÉPHINE VANNIER CHOCOLATE

Map p402 (www.chocolats-vannier.com; 4 rue du Pas de la Mule, 4e; ⌚11am-1pm & 2-7pm Tue-Sat, 2.30-7pm Sun; ⓂChemin Vert) Miniature piano keyboards, violins, chic ballerina slippers or a pair of jogging shoes...you name it, *chocolatier* Joséphine Vannier creates it out of chocolate in her shop steps from place des Vosges.

MAISON GEORGES LARNICOL CHOCOLATE

Map p402 (www.chocolaterielarnicol.fr; 14 rue de Rivoli, 4e; ⌚10am-10pm; ⓂChemin Vert) Coco-ginger bites, caramels and chocolate sculptures are among the sweet treats created by this master chocolate maker from Brittany. But it's his syrupy, chewy *kouignettes* (Breton butter cakes unusually made in mini dimensions and different flavours; €2.50 per 100g) that steal the show. Oh, and the glass jars of *caramel au beurre salé* (butter caramel) sold with a small spoon...

L'ÉPICERIE WINE, DRINK

Map p402 (opposite 13 rue Chapon, 3e; ⌚8.30am-10pm Mon-Fri; ⓂArts et Métiers) This bijou space teases taste buds. From the carefully chosen artwork on the ceiling (look up!) to the discerning selection of wine produced by interesting small French growers, the Grocer's is made for browsing and tasting. Shop here for wine, liqueurs, fruit juices and syrups you'll be hard-pressed to find elsewhere.

VERT D'ABSINTHE DRINK

Map p402 (www.vertdabsinthe.com; 11 rue d'Ormesson, 4e; ⌚noon-7pm Tue-Sat; ⓂSt-Paul) Fans of the *fée verte* (green fairy), as absinthe was known during the belle époque, will think they've died and gone to heaven. Here, you can buy not only bottles of the best-quality hooch but all the paraphernalia as well: glasses, water jugs and tiny slotted spoons for the all-important sugar cube.

BHV DEPARTMENT STORE

Map p402 (www.bhv.fr; 52 rue de Rivoli, 4e; ⌚9.30am-8pm Mon, Tue & Thu-Sat, to 9pm Wed; ⓂHôtel de Ville) BHV (bay-ash-vay) is a straightforward – and vast, thanks to its recent extension – department store where you can buy everything from guidebooks on Paris to every imaginable type of hammer, power tool, nail, plug and hinge.

L'ÉCLAIREUR CONCEPT STORE

Map p402 (www.leclaireur.com; 40 rue de Sévigné, 4e; ⌚11am-7pm Mon-Sat; ⓂSt-Paul) Part art space, part lounge and part deconstructionist fashion statement, this shop for women is known for having the next big thing first. The nearby **menswear store** (Map p402; www.leclaireur.com; 12 rue Malher, 4e; ⓂSt-Paul) fills an equally stunning, old warehouse-turned-art space.

L'HABILLEUR FASHION, ACCESSORIES

Map p402 (www.lhabilleur.fr; 44 rue de Poitou, 4e; ⌚noon-7.30pm Mon-Sat; ⓂSt-Sébastien Froissart) Discount designer wear – 50% to 70% off original prices – is the lure of this veteran boutique. It generally stocks last season's collections.

SHINE FASHION

Map p402 (15 rue de Poitou, 3e; ⌚11am-7.30pm Mon-Sat; ⓂFilles du Calvaire) A limited but discerning collection of designer gear: women's clothing, excellent shoes and handbags with plenty of Marc Jacobs, See by Chloé and K by Karl Lagerfeld, as well as jewellery by Bijoux de Sophie.

SIC AMOR FASHION, ACCESSORIES

Map p402 (www.french-jewellery.fr; 20 rue du Pont Louis-Philippe, 4e; ⌚2-7pm Mon, 11am-7pm Tue-Sat; ⓂPont Marie) Bright and colourful, contemporary jewellery by local designers from a shop opposite the headquarters of the all-but-moribund Partie Communiste Française is what this address is all about. For bold, frilly, gorgeous and oftentimes out-of-this-world hats and scarves, walk south along the same street to its sister boutique **Mi Amor** (Map p402; 10 rue du Pont Louis-Philippe, 4e; ⓂPont Marie).

SURFACE TO AIR FASHION, ACCESSORIES

Map p402 (www.surfacetoair.com; 108 rue Vieille du Temple, 3e; ⌚11.30am-7.30pm Mon-Sat, 1.30-7.30pm Sun; ⓂSt-Sébastien Froissart or Filles du Calvaire) This shop has very edgy clothing as well as arty books and accessories. With an exceedingly up-to-date collection of daring local and international designs, the space also welcomes regular installations and collaborative events with artists.

Ménilmontant & Belleville

★BELLEVILLE BRÛLERIE COFFEE

(☎09 83 75 60 80; http://cafesbelleville.com; 10 rue Pradier, 19e; 300g packet €13-16; ⏲11.30am-6.30pm Sat; Ⓜ Belleville) With its understated steel-grey façade, this ground-breaking roastery in Belleville is easy to miss. Don't! These are the guys who brought good coffee to Paris and their beans go into some of the best espressos and cappuccinos in town. Taste the week's selection, compare tasting notes, and buy a bag to take home. Online shop too.

★FROMAGERIE GONCOURT FOOD

Map p406 (1 rue Abel Rabaud, 11e; ⏲9am-1pm & 4-8.30pm Tue-Fri, 9am-8pm Sat; Ⓜ Goncourt) Styled like a boutique, this contemporary *fromagerie* (cheese shop) is a must-discover. Clément Brossault ditched a career in banking to become a *fromager* and his cheese selection – 70-odd types – is superb. Cheeses flagged with a bicycle symbol are varieties he discovered in situ during a two-month French cheese tour he embarked on as part of his training.

★FROMAGERIE BEAUFILS FOOD

(www.fromagerie-beaufils.com; 118 rue de Belleville, 20e; ⏲8am-1pm & 3.30-7.45pm Tue-Sat, 8.30am-1pm Sun; Ⓜ Jourdain) The queue outside the door, especially at weekends, says it all. This family-run *fromagerie* and *affineur* (ripener) in Belleville is among the best in Paris, with dozens of French cheeses you're unlikely to see elsewhere.

BY SOPHIE CHILDREN'S FASHION

Map p406 (www.bysophie.fr; 50 rue Jean-Pierre Timbaud, 11e; ⏲11am-7pm Tue-Fri; Ⓜ Parmentier) Stylish parents keen to don their kids in chic, retro fashion should make a beeline for this vintage-style boutique with clothes and accessories for babies, toddlers and young children. Sophie also hosts hip knitting workshops.

MADE BY MOI FASHION

Map p406 (☎01 58 30 95 78; www.madebymoi.fr; 86 rue Oberkampf, 11e; ⏲2.30-8pm Mon, 11am-8pm Tue-Sat; Ⓜ Parmentier) 'Made by Me', aka handmade, is the driver of this appealing boutique on trendy rue Oberkampf. Mooch here for women's fashion, homewares and so on.

PUZZLE MICHÈLE WILSON GAMES, HOBBIES

Map p406 (www.puzzles-et-jeux.com; 39 rue de la Folie Méricourt, 11e; ⏲10am-7pm Tue-Sat; Ⓜ St-Ambroise) *Puzzleurs* and *puzzleuses* will love the selection of hand-cut wooden jigsaws available in this shop. Ranging in size (and degree of difficulty) from 80 to 5000 pieces, the puzzles depict for the most part major works of art. The ones of medieval stained glass and 18th-century fans are particularly fine. There are two other outlets in Paris.

BOUTIQUE OBUT GAMES, HOBBIES

Map p406 (www.labouleobut.com; 60 av de la République, 11e; ⏲10am-noon & 12.30-6.30pm Tue-Sat; Ⓜ Parmentier) This is the Parisian mecca for fans of *pétanque* or the similar (though more formal) game of boules, a form of bowls played with heavy steel balls wherever a bit of flat and shady ground can be found. It will kit you out with all the equipment necessary to get a game going and even has team uniforms.

SPORTS & ACTIVITIES

LES BAINS DU MARAIS SPA

Map p402 (☎01 44 61 02 02; www.lesbainsdumarais.com; 31-33 rue des Blancs Manteaux, 4e; ⏲10am-11pm Tue-Thu & Sun, 10am-8pm Fri & Sat; Ⓜ Rambuteau or Hôtel de Ville) Luxury personified, this hammam combines the classical with modern – mint tea and Levantine decor with as many pampering treatments as you'd care to name. The hammam is reserved for men and for women on certain days; 'mixed days', when bathing suits are obligatory, are Wednesday evening and all day Saturday and Sunday.

NOMADESHOP SKATING

Map p402 (☎01 44 54 07 44; www.nomadeshop.com; 37 bd Bourdon, 4e; half/full day from €5/8; ⏲11am-1.30pm & 2.30-7.30pm Tue-Fri, 10am-7pm Sat, noon-6pm Sun; Ⓜ Bastille) Paris' 'Harrods for roller-heads' rents and sells equipment and accessories, including wheels, helmets, and elbow and knee guards. The shop is also the departure point for Sunday's 'Randonnée en Rollers' around Paris, kicking off at 2.30pm (and lasting three hours), organised by skating club **Rollers & Coquillages** (Map p402; www.rollers-coquillages.org) FREE.

Bastille & Eastern Paris

Neighbourhood Top Five

❶ Taking in a performance at the modern monolith **Opéra Bastille** (p198).

❷ Catching timeless cinematic classics at the **Cinémathèque Française** (p198).

❸ Strolling the elevated **Promenade Plantée** (p189).

❹ Exploring Paris' only medieval castle, **Château de Vincennes** (p190).

❺ Meeting lions, white rhinos, giraffes and wolverines at the newly reopened **Parc Zoologique de Paris** (p190).

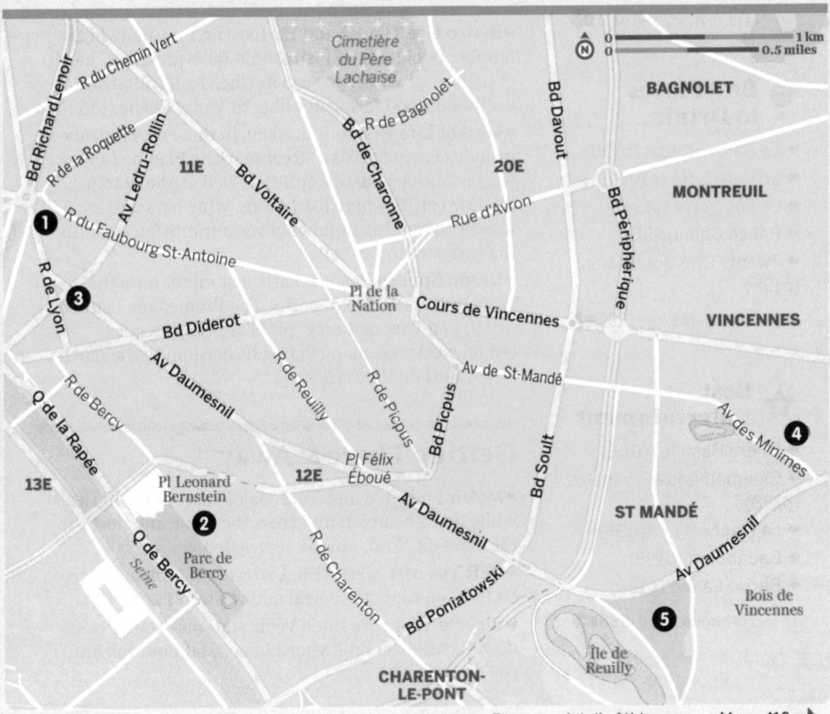

For more detail of this area see Map p410

Lonely Planet's Top Tip

While the area immediately surrounding the Bastille has spawned a clutch of faceless bars and restaurant chains, walking a little bit further north on rue de Charonne or east to Ledru-Rollin and Faidherbe-Chaligny will bring you to a much more interesting neighbourhood, filled with exciting restaurants, modest cafes and all the quirky, unusual shops that make a city great.

Best Places to Eat

- Le 6 Paul Bert (p192)
- Bones (p193)
- Septime (p195)
- CheZaline (p191)
- À la Biche au Bois (p193)

For reviews, see p191

Best Places to Drink

- Le Baron Rouge (p196)
- Le Pure Café (p196)
- La Fée Verte (p196)
- Pause Café (p196)
- Twenty One Sound Bar (p196)

For reviews, see p196

Best Entertainment

- Opéra Bastille (p198)
- Cinémathèque Française (p198)
- La Flèche d'Or (p198)
- Badaboum (p198)
- Barrio Latino (p198)

For reviews, see p198

Explore: Bastille & Eastern Paris

Bastille isn't known for its sights, but it's nonetheless a fascinating area to explore on foot. As it's still authentically residential in most parts, a wander will give you a taste of everyday life in one of Paris' most dynamic neighbourhoods. For a more voyeuristic glimpse, ascend to elevated park the Promenade Plantée, which looks down on the streets around you and offers the occasional peek through an apartment window.

Bastille's main attraction is not aimless *flâneurie* (urban strolling), however: this former working-class district doesn't exactly have the same visual knockout factor as central Paris. It's best for dipping your toes into a vibrant restaurant scene dominated by young, creative chefs; its scores of popular, inexpensive bars and cafes; and the profusion of evening entertainment, from avant-garde opera to indie rock.

You may be reluctant to leave the city behind with so much to explore, but an easy trip to the Bois de Vincennes, the city's largest park, never disappoints. From a castle and zoo to outdoor concerts, bike excursions, pickup football matches and picnics, it's one of the most-loved spots in the capital to unwind.

Local Life

- **Bistro Life** The 11e and 12e have an unusually high number of old-school bistros that have preserved much of their original decor, such as Chez Paul (p193) and neighbourhood favourites like Au Vieux Chêne (p193).
- **Market Life** Fabulous markets in this neighbourhood include classic Parisian street markets like the twice-weekly Marché Bastille (p191) as well as the Marché d'Aligre (p191), where food shops, wine bars and a rapidly increasing number of restaurants fan out into the surrounding streets.
- **Green Spaces** Eastern Paris just might have the city's best collection of parks. The Promenade Plantée (p189) and Parc de Bercy (p189) are easy escapes, but on weekends many Parisians decamp to the much larger Bois de Vincennes.

Getting There & Away

- **Metro** Lines 1, 8 and 9 are major east–west arteries, while line 5 heads south across the Seine and north to the Gare du Nord. Line 14 serves Bercy.
- **RER** The east–west RER A stops at Nation and Gare de Lyon en route to central and western Paris.
- **Bicycle** There are three Vélib' stations around place de la Bastille: on bd Richard Lenoir, bd Bourdon and rue de Lyon.

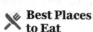

⊙ SIGHTS

PLACE DE LA BASTILLE — SQUARE

Map p410 (ⓂBastille) The Bastille, a 14th-century fortress built to protect the city gates, is the most famous monument in Paris that no longer exists. Nothing remains of the prison it became under Cardinal Richelieu, which was mobbed on 14 July 1789, igniting the French Revolution, but you can't miss the 52m-high green-bronze column topped by a gilded, winged Liberty. Revolutionaries from the uprising of 1830 are buried beneath. Now a skirmishly busy roundabout, it's still Paris' most symbolic destination for political protests. If you're interested in finding the Bastille's one-time foundations, look for a triple row of paving stones that traces the building's outline on the ground between bd Henri IV and rue St-Antoine. The foundations are also marked below ground in the Bastille metro station, on the platform of line 5.

CINÉMATHÈQUE FRANÇAISE — MUSEUM

Map p410 (www.cinematheque.fr; 51 rue de Bercy, 12e; exhibits adult/child €6/3; ⊙noon-7pm Mon & Wed-Sat, to 8pm Sun; ⓂBercy) A little-known gem near the Parc de Bercy, the Cinémathèque Française was originally created in 1936 by film archivist Henri Langlois. On site are two museums, one presenting temporary exhibitions (usually taking a behind-the-scenes look at a particular film) and the other devoted to the history of cinema, with props (including some from Méliès' classic *A Trip to the Moon*, featured in *Hugo*), early equipment and short clips of a few classics. Enter via place Léonard-Bernstein by the park. Also here is a vast film library for researchers and a theatre (p198) screening up to 10 films daily.

PROMENADE PLANTÉE — PARK

Map p410 (12e; ⊙8am-9.30pm May-Aug, to 5.30pm Sep-Apr; ⓂBastille or Gare de Lyon) The disused 19th-century Vincennes railway viaduct was successfully reborn as the world's first elevated park, planted with a fragrant profusion of cherry trees, maples, rose trellises, bamboo corridors and lavender. Three storeys above ground, it provides a unique aerial vantage point on the surrounding architecture. Access is via staircase – usually at least one per city block – and lift (elevator; although they're invariably out of service). At street level, the Viaduc des Arts (p199) gallery-workshops run along av Daumesnil.

En route, look out for the spectacular art-deco police station at the start of rue de Rambouillet, which is topped with a dozen huge, identical marble caryatids.

The viaduct drops back to street level at the Jardin de Reuilly (1.5km), but it's possible to follow the line to the Bois de Vincennes. This latter section, known as the Coulée Verte (3km), can also be done on a bike or in-line skates. At square Charles Péguy, behind the ping-pong tables, you can access a 200m section of another abandoned Parisian railway-turned-park, the Petite Ceinture, here known as the **Petite Ceinture du 12e** (PC 12; www.paris.fr; square Charles Péguy, 21 rue Rottembourg, 12e; ⊙9am-8.30pm May-Aug, to 7.30pm Apr & Sep, to 6pm Mar, reduced hours Oct-Feb; ⓂMichel Bizot), which also has a *jardin partagé* (community garden).

OPÉRA BASTILLE — OPERA HOUSE

Map p410 (www.operadeparis.fr; 2-6 place de la Bastille, 12e; guided tours adult/child €12/6; ⓂBastille) One of the late President Mitterand's pet projects, this 3400-seat venue was intended to strip opera of its elitist airs – hence the notable inauguration date of 13 July 1989, the eve of the 200th anniversary of the storming of the Bastille.

There are 75-minute **guided tours** of the building, which depart at wildly different times depending on the date – you'll need to check in at the **box office** (Map p410; ☑01 40 01 19 70; 130 rue de Lyon, 12e; ⊙2.30-6.30pm Mon-Sat; ⓂBastille). Tickets go on sale 10 minutes before tours begin.

MAISON ROUGE — GALLERY

Map p410 (www.lamaisonrouge.org; 10 bd de la Bastille; adult/child €8/5.50; ⊙11am-7pm Wed-Sun, to 9pm Thu; ⓂQuai de la Rapée) Subtitled 'Fondation Antoine de Galbert' after the man who endowed it, this cutting-edge gallery shows contemporary artists and seldom-seen works from private collections. Note that everything closes between exhibits.

PARC DE BERCY — PARK

(rue Paul Belmondo; ⊙8am-sunset Mon-Fri, from 9am Sat & Sun; ⓂCour St-Émilion or Bercy) Built atop the site of a former wine depot, this large, well-landscaped park is a great place to break for a picnic and let the kids run free. Bercy reached its height as the 'world's

WORTH A DETOUR

BOIS DE VINCENNES

Paris is flanked by two large woodlands, the Bois de Boulogne in the west and the Bois de Vincennes in the east. Originally royal hunting grounds, the Bois de Vincennes was annexed by the army following the Revolution and then donated to the city in 1860 by Napoléon III. A fabulous place to escape the endless stretches of Parisian concrete, the Bois de Vincennes also contains a handful of notable sights, and is close to the Cité Nationale de l'Histoire de l'Immigration and Aquarium Tropical. Metro lines 1 (St-Mandé, Château de Vincennes) and 8 (Porte Dorée, Porte de Charenton) will get you to the eastern edges of the park. Pick up picnic supplies on rue de Midi, Vincennes' main shopping street.

➡ **Château de Vincennes** (www.chateau-vincennes.fr; av de Paris, Vincennes; adult/child €8.50/free; ⌚10am-6pm mid-May–mid-Sep, to 5pm mid-Sep–mid-May; Ⓜ Château de Vincennes) Originally a meagre 12th-century hunting lodge, the castle here was expanded several times throughout the centuries until it reached its present size under Louis XIV. Notable features include the beautiful 52m-high keep (1370) and the royal chapel (1552), both of which are open to visits. Note that the chapel is only open between 11am and noon, and 2.30pm and 4pm.

➡ **Parc Zoologique de Paris** (Zoo de Vincennes; http://parczoologiquedeparis.fr; cnr Daumesnil & rte de la Ceinture du Lac, 12e; adult/child €22/16.50; ⌚10am-6pm Mon-Fri, 9.30am-7.30pm Sat & Sun mid-Mar–mid-Oct, 10am-5pm daily mid-Oct–mid-Mar; Ⓜ Porte Dorée) Reopened in 2014 after years of renovations, Paris' largest, now state-of-the-art zoo focuses on the conservation of species and habitats, with camouflaged vantage points (no peering through fences). Its biozones include Patagonia, with sea lions to cougars; the savannah of Sahel-Sudan, with lions, white rhinos and giraffes; forested Europe, with wolves, lynxes and wolverines; a Guiana rainforest with jaguars, monkeys and anacondas; and Madagascar, home to lemurs. Other highlights include Australian marsupials and manatees (sea cows).

➡ **Parc Floral de Paris** (adult/child €5.50/2.75; ⌚9.30am-8pm Apr-Sep, shorter hours rest of year) This magnificent botanical park is one of the highlights of the Bois de Vincennes. Natural landscaping and a magnificent collection of plants will keep amateur gardeners happy, while Paris' largest play area (giant climbing webs and slides, jungle gyms, sandboxes) will absolutely thrill families. Open-air concerts are staged throughout summer, making it a first-rate picnic destination.

➡ **Lac Daumesnil** (Ⓜ Porte Dorée) Like something out of a Renoir painting, the largest lake in the Bois de Vincennes is a popular destination for walks and rowboat excursions in warmer months (from €12 per half-hour). A Buddhist temple is located nearby.

wine cellar' in the 19th century: it was right on the Seine, close to Paris yet outside the city walls, meaning that shipping was convenient and commerce tax-free.

Vestiges of its former incarnation are spread across the park and the Cour St-Émilion, where the warehouses were located. In some spots you'll see the old railroad tracks; in others you'll find grape vines.

CITÉ NATIONALE DE L'HISTOIRE DE L'IMMIGRATION — IMMIGRATION MUSEUM

(www.histoire-immigration.fr; 293 av Daumesnil, 12e; admission €4.50, with Aquarium Tropical €8; ⌚10am-5.30pm Tue-Fri, to 7pm Sat & Sun; Ⓜ Porte Dorée) This heavyweight museum documents the hot-potato topic of immigration through a series of informative historical displays that cover groups as diverse as the Vietnamese, Portuguese, Jews and Russians. The multimedia permanent collection called Repères (Landmarks) and the gallery of personal items donated by members of the public are emotive and informative. It's housed in the lavish 1931 Palais de la Porte Dorée along with the Aquarium Tropical. Admission prices rise during temporary exhibitions.

AQUARIUM TROPICAL — AQUARIUM

(www.aquarium-portedoree.fr; 293 av Daumesnil, 12e; admission €5, with Cité Nationale de l'Histoire de l'Immigration €8; ⏲10am-5.30pm Tue-Fri, to 7pm Sat & Sun; Ⓜ Porte Dorée) Although this aquarium is a bit dated, the inexpensive admission makes it a popular choice with many a Parisian family. It's located in the basement of the Palais de la Porte Dorée, beneath the Cité Nationale de l'Histoire de l'Immigration.

LA MANUFACTURE 111 — CULTURAL CENTRE

(111 rue des Pyrénées, 20e; ⏲6-10pm Fri, noon-10pm Sat, noon-8pm Sun, but variable; Ⓜ Maraîchers) A massive 1500-sq-metre former garage now houses this edgy new urban cultural centre. Street art and hip-hop are at the heart of its exhibitions; you can also catch a food truck, concerts and various events here. Check its Facebook page or Twitter feed for updates.

EATING

Bastille dining tends to swing between a highly lauded group of up-and-coming chefs, who run the hip new neobistros that have reinspired Parisian cooking, and the die-hard traditionalists, who rarely venture beyond the much-loved standards of French cuisine.

CHEZALINE — DELICATESSEN €

Map p410 (85 rue de la Roquette, 11e; dishes €6.50-9; ⏲11am-5.30pm Mon-Fri; Ⓜ Voltaire) A former horse-meat butcher's shop (*chevaline,* hence the spin on the name) is now a fabulous deli creating seasonally changing baguettes filled with ingredients like ham and house-made pesto. Other delicacies include salads and homemade terrines. There's a handful of seats (and plenty of parks nearby). Prepare to queue.

LE SIFFLEUR DE BALLONS — WINE BAR €

Map p410 (www.lesiffleurdeballons.net; 34 rue de Citeaux, 12e; lunch menus €14, mains €7-16; ⏲10.30am-3pm & 5.30-11pm Tue-Fri, 10.30am-11pm Sat; Ⓜ Faidherbe-Chaligny) With Tom Waits on the stereo and cacti atop the register, this contemporary wine bar has a dash of California in its soul. The wines, though, are all French – and all natural – and paired with a quality selection of simple but delicious offerings: tartines, soups, lentil salad with truffle oil, cheeses and Iberian charcuterie plates. Look out for the weekly tastings with winemakers. No reservations, so don't waltz in too late.

MARCHÉ BASTILLE — MARKET €

Map p410 (bd Richard Lenoir, 11e; ⏲7am-2.30pm Thu & Sun; Ⓜ Bastille or Richard Lenoir) If you only get to one open-air street market in Paris, this one – stretching between the Bastille and Richard Lenoir metro stations – is among the very best.

MARCHÉ D'ALIGRE — MARKET €

Map p410 (http://marchedaligre.free.fr; rue d'Aligre, 12e; ⏲8am-1pm & 4-7.30pm Tue-Sat, 8am-1.30pm Sun; Ⓜ Ledru-Rollin) All the staples of French cuisine can be found in this chaotic marketplace: cheese, coffee, chocolate, wine, charcuterie, even Tunisian pastries. It's a fantastic place to put together a DIY lunch. Offerings in the covered **Marché Beauvau**, in the centre of place d'Aligre, are a bit more gourmet. The morning **Marché aux Puces d'Aligre** (Map p410; place d'Aligre, 12e; ⏲8am-1pm Tue-Sun; Ⓜ Ledru-Rollin) flea market takes place here.

Other places to look out for here include **Pink Flamingo** (Map p410; www.pinkflamingopizza.com; 23 rue de l'Aligre, 12e; pizzas €11.50-17; ⏲noon-3pm & 7-11.30pm Tue-Sun; Ⓜ Ledru-Rollin) and the boulangerie **Moisan** (Map p410; 5 place d'Aligre, 12e; ⏲6.30am-8.30pm Tue-Sat, to 2pm Sun; Ⓜ Ledru-Rollin).

GENTLE GOURMET CAFÉ — CAFE, VEGAN €

Map p410 (☎01 43 43 48 49; www.gentlegourmet-cafe.com; 24 bd de la Bastille, 12e; mains €14-19; ⏲11.30am-3pm & 6-11pm Tue-Sun; 📶📝; Ⓜ Bastille) 🌿 If you've been overdoing the *steak-frites* in Paris, head here for a reprieve. All of its dishes are vegan and most are organic (tofu ricotta cannelloni, portobello-mushroom burger in sesame brioche buns, raw lasagne); there are also detox juices and teas. Large windows fill the cafe with natural light, but the best seats are on the terrace.

MISS LUNCH AT PREMIÈRE PRESSION PROVENCE — CAFE €

Map p410 (☎01 53 33 03 59; www.lunchintheloft.com; 3 rue Antoine Vollon, 12e; 2-course menus €15, mains €12; ⏲noon-2.30pm & 7-10.30pm Thu & Fri, noon-2.30pm Wed & Sat; Ⓜ Ledru-Rollin) What started as a clandestine supper club (or rather lunch club) by cook-visual artist Claude Cabri, aka Miss Lunch, is now a unique cafe with the backing of Première Pression Provence founder Olivier Baussan, whose AOC-rated cold-pressed *huile d'olive* (olive oil) stars in dishes like cottage-cheese salad with cucumbers, peppers and mint on piombi pasta. You can buy the light, fruity oils here, or take a cooking class (from €120 for 2½ hours including a meal and wine). Cabri still hosts a multicourse Lunch in the Loft one Sunday a month (€70).

PARIS HANOÏ
VIETNAMESE €

Map p410 (☎01 47 00 47 59; www.parishanoi.fr; 74 rue de Charonne, 11e; mains €9.80-11; ⏰noon-2.30pm & 7-10.30pm; MCharonne) This upbeat restaurant is an excellent place to come for *pho* (soup noodles with beef) and other classic Vietnamese dishes. It doesn't take reservations and the place is a veritable legend, so be prepared to join the queue. You can also learn to make the dishes yourself at cooking courses (from €33 for one hour).

40/60
PIZZERIA €

Map p410 (www.40x60.fr; 44 rue Trousseau, 11e; pizza slices from €10; ⏰noon-3pm Mon, noon-3pm & 6-10.30pm Tue-Thu, noon-3pm & 6-11pm Fri & Sat; MLedru-Rollin) You'd be hard-pressed to find a hipper pizzeria than 40/60, which features black-and-white Qbert-style floor tiles (imported from Spain) and Genovese pizza baked on large trays and cut by the rectangle. The pricing system is a bit complex if you're not a maths whiz, but hey, the thick-crust gourmet slices are worth the mental workout. Also does takeaway.

CRÊPERIE BRETONNE
BRETON, CRÊPERIE €

Map p410 (☎01 43 55 02 29; 67 rue de Charonne, 12e; crêpes €3.40-10.20; ⏰noon-2.15pm & 7-11pm Mon-Sat, 7-10pm Sun; MCharonne) Authentic down to its buckwheat *galettes* and perfectly buttered sweet crêpes, this charmer is filled with emotive black-and-white photos of Brittany and – joy of joys! – serves brut Val de Rance cider. *Yec'hed mat* (cheers)!

L'ENCRIER
BISTRO €

Map p410 (☎01 44 68 08 16; www.restaurant-encrier-paris.fr; 55 rue Traversière, 12e; 2-/3-course menus lunch €13.50/15.50, dinner €17.50/20.90; ⏰noon-2.15pm & 7.30-11pm Mon-Fri, 7.30-11pm Sat; MLedru-Rollin or Gare de Lyon) Always heaving but especially at lunch, the 'Inkwell' draws them in with generously sized dishes, ranging from steak with Roquefort sauce or delicate pig's cheeks with spices to simple veggie lasagne. The open kitchen, large picture window and great-value prices make it a winner.

AGUA LIMÓN
TAPAS €

Map p410 (☎01 43 44 92 24; www.restaurant-agualimon.com; 12 rue Théophile Roussel, 12e; tapas €5-13, 2-/3-course lunch menus €12/16.50; ⏰noon-2pm & 7.30-11pm Tue-Sat; 📶; MLedru-Rollin) Head to this lemon-coloured tapas place for a shot of Mediterranean sunlight. The menu includes standards such as Catalan-style octopus, goat cheese in olive oil and, of course, *patatas bravas*. There's a selection of Spanish wines and sangria.

BAR À SOUPES
SOUP €

Map p410 (www.lebarasoupes.com; 33 rue de Charonne, 11e; soups €5.50-6, lunch menus €11.30; ⏰noon-3pm & 6.30-10.30pm Mon-Wed, noon-3pm & 6.30-11pm Thu-Sat; MLedru-Rollin) With 36 varieties of soup served per week (six daily), chances are you'll always find something here to warm you up and please your palate. Stalwarts include pumpkin-chestnut borscht, creamed red lentils and coconut milk, cauliflower and bleu d'Auvergne cheese, and the vodka-laced Bloody Mary.

À LA BANANE IVOIRIENNE
AFRICAN €

Map p410 (☎01 43 70 49 90; 10 rue de la Forge Royale, 11e; 3-course menu €28.50, mains €10.50-15.50; ⏰7-11pm Tue-Thu, to 11pm Fri & Sat; 🖉; MLedru-Rollin) An institution in Paris for over two decades, À La Banane Ivoirienne dishes up the best Ivorian food in the capital. West African specialities (including a generous vegetarian platter) are served in a relaxed and friendly setting, with lots of gewgaws on display.

BISTROT MÉLAC
TRADITIONAL FRENCH €

Map p410 (☎01 43 70 59 27; http://bistrot-melac.fr; 42 rue Léon Frot, 11e; lunch menus €15, mains €12-22; ⏰kitchen noon-11pm Tue-Sat; MCharonne) Fringed with its very own venerable grape vine (Château Charonne), this quintessential neighbourhood wine bar has been defending French culinary traditions since 1938. Cash only.

★LE 6 PAUL BERT
BISTRO €€

Map p410 (☎01 43 79 14 32; 6 rue Paul Bert, 12e; 2-/3-course lunch menus €15/19, 4-course dinner menus €44; ⏰noon-2pm Tue, noon-2pm & 7.30-11pm Wed-Sat; MFaidherbe-Chaligny) Opened by Bertrand Auboyneau of neighbouring Bistrot Paul Bert and Québecois chef Louis-Philippe Riel, Le 6 serves mindblowing multicourse menus of small(ish) plates. The exquisitely prepared and presented creations from Riel's open kitchen change daily but invariably involve unexpected flavour combinations (quail/turnip, asparagus/monkfish, artichoke/white chocolate).

★**BONES** BISTRO €€

Map p410 (☎09 80 75 32 08; www.bonesparis.com; 43 rue Godefroy Cavaignac, 11e; bar dishes €4-16, 4-/5-course menus €47/55; ⏱kitchen 7-11pm Tue-Sat; Ⓜ Voltaire) Even if you don't score a first-service (7pm to 7.30pm) reservation for red-hot Australian chef James Henry's stripped-back new premises, you have a couple of back-up options. The second service (9.30pm to 10.30pm) is walk-in only. Or you can order Henry's signature small plates (smoked oyster, beef heart, seabass carpaccio, house-cured charcuterie) at the lively bar.

À LA BICHE AU BOIS TRADITIONAL FRENCH €€

Map p410 (☎01 43 43 34 38; 45 av Ledru-Rollin, 12e; 7-10.45pm Mon, noon-2.30pm & 7-10.45pm Tue-Sat; ⏱3-course lunch menus €29.80, mains €17-22.50; Ⓜ Gare de Lyon) Game, especially *la biche,* is the speciality of the convivial 'doe in the woods', but dishes like foie gras and *coq au vin* also add to the ambience of being out in the countryside, as do the green awning and potted plants out front. The cheeses and wines are excellent, but top honours, game aside, go to the sensational *frites*.

CLAMATO SEAFOOD €€

Map p410 (www.septime-charonne.fr; 80 rue de Charonne, 11e; tapas €6-19; ⏱7-11pm Mon-Fri, noon-11pm Sat & Sun; Ⓜ Charonne) Arrive early: unlike its raved-about sister restaurant and next-door neighbour Septime (p195), Clamato doesn't take reservations and you seriously don't want to miss out on Bertrand Grébaut and Théo Pourriat's seafood tapas. The menu changes daily but might include mussels with onion confit and saffron, baked razor clams with crushed peanuts and herb butter or octopus carpaccio with grapefruit pulp.

BISTROT PAUL BERT BISTRO €€

Map p410 (☎01 43 72 24 01; 18 rue Paul Bert, 11e; 3-course lunch/dinner menus €19/38; ⏱noon-2pm & 7.30-11pm Tue-Sat; Ⓜ Faidherbe-Chaligny) When food writers list Paris' best bistros, one of the names that consistently pops up is Paul Bert. The timeless vintage decor and perfectly executed classic dishes like *steak-frites* and hazelnut-cream Paris-Brest pastry merit booking ahead. Look out for its siblings L'Écailler du Bistrot (p195; seafood) and Le 6 Paul Bert (p192; small plates) in the same street.

LE COTTE RÔTI NEOBISTRO €€

Map p410 (☎01 43 45 06 37; 1 rue de Cotte, 12e; 2-/3-course lunch menus, 3-course dinner menus €39; ⏱noon-2.30pm & 8-11pm Tue-Fri, 8-11pm Sat; Ⓜ Ledru-Rollin) Contemporary cooking by Nicolas Michel and a chic charcoal-hued dining space ensure this under-the-radar restaurant won't remain so for long. *Menu* choices are explained to you in detail; mainstays include Michel's signature *épaule d'agneau confite* (shoulder of lamb cooked slowly in its own fat) and stunning desserts like pistachio soufflé. Be sure to book.

AU VIEUX CHÊNE BISTRO €€

Map p410 (☎01 43 71 67 69; www.vieuxchene.fr; 7 rue du Dahomey, 11e; 2-/3-course menus lunch €15/19, dinner €28/33; ⏱noon-2pm & 8-10.30pm Mon-Fri; Ⓜ Faidherbe-Chaligny) Along a quiet side street in a neighbourhood full of traditional woodworking studios, this retro bistro offers an excellent seasonal menu, with specialities like rabbit stuffed with foie gras, and some well-chosen wines. Three of the cast-iron columns holding the place up are registered monuments.

CHEZ PAUL BISTRO €€

Map p410 (☎01 47 00 34 57; www.chezpaul.com; 13 rue de Charonne, 11e; 2-/3-course lunch menus €18/21, mains €16-26; ⏱noon-3pm & 7pm-12.30am Mon-Fri, noon-12.30am Sat & Sun; Ⓜ Ledru-Rollin) This is Paris as your grandmother would have known it: chequered red-and-white napkins, faded photographs on the walls, old red banquettes and traditional French dishes handwritten on a yellowing menu. Stick with the simplest of dishes and make sure you've booked ahead.

YARD MODERN FRENCH €€

Map p410 (☎01 40 09 70 30; 6 rue de Mont Louis, 11e; 3-course lunch menus €18, mains €15-18; ⏱noon-2.30pm Mon, noon-2.30pm & 8-10.30pm Tue-Fri; Ⓜ Philippe Auguste) Opening to an atmospheric terrace near Père Lachaise cemetery, this bistro built on a former construction yard has been resurrected by chefs Shaun Kelly (previously of Au Passage) and Elenie Sapera (of Bones) working the open kitchen and tapas bar. Daily changing menus incorporate seasonal dishes such as spring lamb with leeks. Book ahead for dinner.

À LA RENAISSANCE CAFE €€

Map p410 (☎01 43 79 83 09; 87 rue de la Roquette, 11e; lunch/dinner menus €22/30, mains €10.50-22; ⊙kitchen noon-2.30pm & 7.30-11pm; MVoltaire) This popular locals' cafe is certainly out of the way, but if you're looking for an authentic meal in a neighbourhood setting, it's a good bet. Along with wine and plates of cheese, it serves mackerel *rillettes,* steak tartare and that all-time favourite, *œufs à la coq aux tartines* (soft-boiled eggs with toast).

LE SQUARE TROUSSEAU CAFE €€

Map p410 (☎01 43 43 06 00; www.squaretrousseau.com; 1 rue Antoine Vollon, 12e; mains €18-26; ⊙kitchen noon-2.30pm & 7-10pm; 📶; MLedru-Rollin) With etched glass, zinc bar and polished wood panelling, this vintage (c 1900) bistro has become a Parisian landmark of sorts – come here for a classic French meal or simply coffee and a croissant on the terrace.

UNICO ARGENTINE €€

Map p410 (☎01 43 67 68 08; www.resto-unico.com; 15 rue Paul Bert, 11e; mains €27-43; ⊙12.30-2.30pm & 8-11pm Tue-Sat, 8-11pm Mon; MFaidherbe-Chaligny) This very trendy, very orange Argentine *parrillada* (steakhouse) took over an old butcher's shop and put a retro 1970s spin on it. Unico is all about meat – especially the barbecued *entrecôte* (rib steak) with chunky *frites.* To order, study the diagram of the steer and choose your territory.

Pick up Argentine wines at its neighbouring bodega, El Galpon (p199).

COCOTTE ET CANOU BISTRO €€

Map p410 (☎01 43 70 81 77; 3 Cité de Phalsbourg, 11e; 2-/3-course menus €24/29.50; ⊙noon-2pm & 6-10.30pm Mon-Thu, noon-2pm & 6-11pm Fri; MCharonne) Paris mayor Anne Hidalgo gave this bistro tucked down a small alleyway her stamp of approval, but it's still off tourists' (and even many local foodies') radars. The red-splashed dining room is a vivifying spot for daily changing dishes like roasted scallops with caramelised endives and saffron made from fresh-as-it-gets seasonal ingredients. Good wines, great all-round value.

LES AMIS DES MESSINA SICILIAN €€

Map p410 (☎01 43 67 96 01; www.lesamisdesmessina.com; 204 rue du Faubourg St-Antoine, 12e; pastas €12.40-22, mains €18-25; ⊙noon-2.30pm & 7.30-11pm Mon-Fri, 7.30-11pm Sat; MFaidherbe-Chaligny) At this stone-walled restaurant, chef Ignazio Messina prepares gorgeous pasta dishes alongside the fresh *pesci* (fish) and *carni* (meat), not to mention all the other decadent Sicilian specialties. Do it right and start off with the two-person platter of house antipasti.

LE VIADUC CAFÉ INTERNATIONAL, CAFE €€

Map p410 (☎01 44 74 70 70; www.leviaduc-cafe.com; 43 av Daumesnil, 12e; 2-course menu $15.50, mains €12-21.50, jazz brunch €25; ⊙kitchen noon-11pm; 👪; MGare de Lyon) In one of the glassed-in arches of the Viaduc des Arts (p199), this cavernous cafe is always a great spot to while away the hours or people-watch from the terrace, but the best time to head here is for Sunday's jazz brunch (noon to 4pm).

CHALET SAVOYARD FONDUE €€

Map p410 (☎01 48 05 13 13; www.chalet-savoyard.fr; 58 rue de Charonne, 11e; 3-course menus €29, mains €13-21; ⊙noon-2.30pm & 7-11pm Sun-Thu, to midnight Fri & Sat; 👪; MLedru-Rollin) Fondue restaurants are a fairly rare breed in Paris,

LES PASSAGES DE LA BASTILLE

The area east of the Bastille was originally outside city limits and under the control of the nearby Abbey de Saint-Antoine (now the St-Antoine Hospital). In 1471, King Louis XI granted the abbey an unusual privilege: craftsmen living on the abbey's land were granted exemption from city taxes, and more importantly, from the stringent guild regulations that stifled innovation. Cabinetmakers, gilders, varnishers and others flocked here, and the result was a flurry of creativity that resulted in the introduction of prized new furniture styles over the centuries, such as Louis XIV, Louis XV and Louis XVI.

The imaginatively named passages and courtyards once inhabited by artisans still exist – you'll find plenty if you look closely while walking down rue du Faubourg St-Antoine – but the sounds of hammer and saw have since been replaced by the secluded live-work spaces of architects and graphic designers, as well as perennially popular restaurants.

which probably accounts for the incredible popularity of the hearty cuisine here. Fill up on alpine specialities like *tartiflette* (melted reblochon cheese and bacon baked with potatoes), 12 types of cheese fondue (served with bread and potatoes) or *raclette* (another type of melted cheese that's served over – surprise! – potatoes).

L'ÉBAUCHOIR BISTRO €€

Map p410 (☎01 43 42 49 31; www.lebauchoir.com; 45 rue de Cîteaux, 12e; mains €18-24; ⊙8-11pm Mon, noon-2.30pm & 8-11pm Tue-Thu, noon-2.30pm & 7.30-11pm Fri & Sat; MFaidherbe-Chaligny) This one-time workers' eatery has been upgraded to a convivial gourmet bistro, where regulars drop in for personal creations from chef Thomas Dufour, like lentils with Beaufort cheese or veal liver with honey and ginger.

LES DOMAINES QUI MONTENT WINE BAR €€

Map p410 (☎01 43 56 89 15; www.lesdomainesquimontent.com; 136 bd Voltaire, 11e; menus €15.50; ⊙kitchen noon-2pm Mon-Sat; MVoltaire) Les Domaines Qui Montent has been around since before the *cave à manger* (wine shop/restaurant) trend began, and although it's not quite as trendy as most newcomers, it is very much the real thing. Above all a wine shop, it offers simple two-course menus at lunch that you can pair with any of its available bottles.

CHEZ RAMULAUD BRASSERIE €€

Map p410 (☎01 43 72 23 29; 269 rue du Faubourg St-Antoine, 11e; menus lunch €12-15, dinner €29; ⊙noon-2.30pm & 7.30-10.30pm Mon-Fri, 7.30-10.30pm Sat; MFaidherbe-Chaligny) With its peaceful, retro atmosphere, this old-school brasserie is reminiscent of an established provincial restaurant. The blackboard offerings are both comforting and substantial: daily soups, terrines, coddled eggs with seasonal mushrooms and other French classics.

SWANN ET VINCENT ITALIAN €€

Map p410 (☎01 43 43 49 40; www.swann-vincent.fr; 7 rue St-Nicolas, 12e; mains €13-19, lunch menus €17.50; ⊙noon-2.30pm & 7.45-11.30pm; MLedru-Rollin) Paris meets Italy in this elegant, old-fashioned restaurant. Unpretentious staff will help you select from the huge blackboard, whose offerings include temptations such as saffron risotto with speck and veal cutlets drizzled with lemon. Go easy on the olive-and-herb bread – you need to leave room for the tiramisu.

LE SOUK NORTH AFRICAN €€

Map p410 (☎01 49 29 05 08; www.le-souk-paris.com; 1 rue Keller, 11e; menus €18.50-24.50; ⊙noon-2.30pm & 7pm-midnight Tue-Sun; ✎; MLedru-Rollin) You'll enjoy this place almost as much for the decor as the food – from the clay pots overflowing with spices on the outside to the exuberant Moroccan interior. The food is just as authentic, notably the duck *tajine,* the pigeon *pastilla* (pie) and the vegetarian couscous.

SEPTIME MODERN FRENCH €€€

Map p410 (☎01 43 67 38 29; 80 rue de Charonne, 11e; menus lunch €28-55, dinner €58; ⊙7-10pm Mon, 12.15-2pm & 7-10pm Tue-Fri; MCharonne) Reading the menu at newly Michelin-starred Septime won't get you far, as it looks mostly like an obscure shopping list (hanger steak/chicory/roots, chicken's egg/foie gras/*lardo*). And that's if you even get a menu – if you order the excellent five-course meal (available for both lunch and dinner), you won't even know what's being served until it arrives. Reserve in advance.

The alchemists in Bertrand Grébaut's kitchen are capable of producing some truly beautiful creations, and the blue-smocked waitstaff go out of their way to ensure that the culinary surprises are all pleasant ones.

For a pre- or post-meal drink, drop by its wine bar Septime La Cave (p196). And for stunning seafood tapas, try its sister restaurant Clamato (p193).

L'ÉCAILLER DU BISTROT SEAFOOD €€€

Map p410 (☎01 43 72 76 77; 22 rue Paul Bert, 11e; mains €17-34, seafood platters €65; ⊙noon-2.30pm & 7.30-11pm Tue-Sat; MFaidherbe-Chaligny) Oyster lovers should make a beeline for the famous seafood annexe of Bistrot Paul Bert (p193), a rustic maritime spot serving a dozen varieties of fresh bivalves, freshly shucked and accompanied by a little lemon juice. Other delights are platters of seafood, a half-dozen *oursins* (sea urchins), minute-cooked tuna steak with sesame oil and the *très* extravagant lobster *menu.*

TABLE MODERN FRENCH €€€

Map p410 (☎01 43 43 12 26; www.tablerestaurant.fr; 3 rue de Prague, 12e; lunch menus €29, mains €32-49; ⊙noon-3pm & 7.45-10.30pm Mon-Fri; MLedru-Rollin) You have to be confident of word-of-mouth to open a restaurant in Paris simply named 'table', but that's not a problem for acclaimed food critic Bruno Verjus, who runs the open kitchen in this glossy black restaurant framed by a retractable glass wall. The star dishes on each day's short menu come from the rotisserie and incorporate artisan-produced ingredients.

LE TRAIN BLEU
BRASSERIE €€€

Map p410 (☐01 43 43 09 06; www.le-train-bleu.com; 1st fl, Gare de Lyon, 26 place Louis Armand, 12e; menus €60-102, mains €27-46; ⊙kitchen 11.30am-3pm & 7-11pm, bar 7.30am-11pm Mon-Sat, 9am-11pm Sun; 🗟🚻; MGare de Lyon) In all probability you've never – ever – seen a railway-station restaurant as sumptuous as this heritage-listed belle époque showpiece. This is a top-end spot to dine on such fare as foie gras with a confiture of red onions, grapes and hazelnuts, Charolais beef tartare, prepared at your table, and the house-made *baba au rhum* (rum baba).

Otherwise, enjoy a tea or pastry in the regal Big Ben Bar before boarding your train to the sunny south.

DRINKING & NIGHTLIFE

Place de la Bastille has become increasingly crass over the years, but it invariably draws a crowd, particularly along rue de Lappe just east. Continue east and the options become much more appealing.

⭐LE BARON ROUGE
WINE BAR

Map p410 (1 rue Théophile Roussel, 12e; ⊙10am-2pm & 5-10pm Tue-Fri, 10am-10pm Sat, 10am-4pm Sun; MLedru-Rollin) Just about the ultimate Parisian wine-bar experience, this place has barrels stacked against the bottle-lined walls. As unpretentious as you'll find, it's a local meeting place where everyone is welcome and it's especially busy on Sunday after the Marché d'Aligre (p191) wraps up. All the usual suspects – cheese, charcuterie and oysters – will keep your belly full.

For a small deposit, you can fill up 1L bottles straight from the barrel for under €5.

LE PURE CAFÉ
CAFE

Map p410 (www.purecafe.fr; 14 rue Jean Macé, 11e; ⊙7am-2am Mon-Fri, 8am-2am Sat, 9am-midnight Sun; MCharonne) A classic Parisian haunt, this rustic, cherry-red corner cafe featured in the art-house film *Before Sunset*, but it's still a refreshingly unpretentious spot for a

drink, cheese or chacuterie platters, fusion cuisine or Sunday brunch.

LA FÉE VERTE
BAR

Map p410 (108 rue de la Roquette, 11e; ⊙8am-2am Mon-Sat, 9am-2am Sun; 🗟; MVoltaire) You guessed it: the 'Green Fairy' specialises in absinthe (served traditionally with spoons and sugar cubes), but this fabulously old-fashioned neighbourhood cafe and bar also serves terrific food.

PAUSE CAFÉ
BAR

Map p410 (41 rue de Charonne, 11e; ⊙8am-2am Mon-Sat, 9am-8pm Sun; MLedru-Rollin) Well situated away from the fray of Bastille, this happening cafe does it all: drinks, meals, coffee and brunch. Its generous terrace, covered in winter, fills up with fashionable locals and the almost famous. French film buffs may recognise it from the gen-X hit *Chacun cherche son chat* (When the Cat's Away; 1996).

TWENTY ONE SOUND BAR
CLUB

Map p410 (20 rue de la Forge Royale, 11e; ⊙8pm-2am Tue-Thu, from 9pm Fri & Sat; MFaidherbe-Chaligny) Stark steel and concrete amp up the acoustics at this hip-hop haven, with renowned (sometimes legendary) DJs mixing on the decks and regular drinks specials.

SEPTIME LA CAVE
WINE BAR

Map p410 (www.septime-charonne.fr; 3 rue Basfroi, 11e; ⊙4-11pm Tue-Sat; MCharonne) Star restaurant Septime's wine bar is an ideal spot for a pre- or post-meal glass or two, with chacuterie and other tantalising snacks costing €10 to €15. Or pick up a bottle to take away.

CAFÉ TITON
CAFE

Map p410 (www.cafetiton.com; 34 rue Titon, 11e; ⊙8am-2am Mon-Sat, 10am-7pm Sun Sep-Jul; MRue des Boulets) Every day feels like Oktoberfest (or at least a rocking *biergarten*) at this fun-loving German bar, but never more so than when it's screening German football (soccer) matches. Needless to say the selection of beers is superb; it also serves *glühwein* (mulled wine) and cocktails, including that German-adopted favourite, caipirinhas. Soak them up with *currywurst*, pretzels, sauerkraut and schnitzel.

MOJITO LAB
COCKTAIL BAR

Map p410 (www.mojitolab.com; 28 rue Keller, 11e; ⊙11am-2am Mon-Sat, 5pm-2am Sun; 🗟;

LOCAL KNOWLEDGE

RUE DE LAPPE

Although at night it's one of the rowdiest bar-hopping streets in Paris, rue de Lappe is actually quite peaceful during the day and worth a quick wander. Like most streets in the area, it dates back to the 17th century and was originally home to cabinetmakers, who first moved in to escape the taxes and restrictions imposed by guilds operating within city limits.

In the centuries that followed, the street was gradually taken over by metalworkers, who equipped the city with its zinc bars, copper piping and the like. At the same time, immigrants from the central French region of Auvergne also moved in, opening up *cafés-charbons*, places where you could go for a drink and buy coal at the same time. In this way the street eventually became a popular drinking strip, and its accordion-driven dance halls, which hosted *bals-musettes*, were to become famous throughout Paris. The dance hall Le Balajo (p198) dates back to 1936 and continues to host a weekly *bal-musette*.

You can still find an Auvergne speciality shop here, Chez Teil, at No 6, as well as a beautiful old bistro, Les Sans-Culottes, at No 27.

MBastille) A good deal classier than pretty much any bar in the Bastille area, the Lab is a study in mojito mixology – some 20 versions, such as jelly mojito, made with French banana mint are available for connoisseurs. Ninety-minute mixing classes (with/without canapés €45/35) are also held here, beginning at 6pm and 8pm (except Wednesday and Sunday).

LES FUNAMBULES BAR

Map p410 (12 rue Faidherbe, 11e; 7.30am-2am; ; MFaidherbe-Chaligny) Like so many small cafes in Paris, Les Funambules turns into a fashionable bar as evening approaches. While the original architecture provides character (check out the frescoes, birdcages and a stunning coffered ceiling with chandelier), nowadays the terrace is crammed with beautiful people on warm summer evenings.

TROLL CAFÉ BAR

Map p410 (www.trollcafe.fr; 27 rue de Cotte, 12e; 5pm-2am; MLedru-Rollin) This fun-loving music and beer bar just up from the Marché d'Aligre takes Brittany as its theme (at least the eponymous Troll is supposedly from there), but its beer selection (over 100 bottled varieties plus many on tap) is primarily Belgian.

LE BISTROT DU PEINTRE BAR

Map p410 (www.bistrotdupeintre.com; 116 av Ledru-Rollin, 11e; 7am-2am; ; MLedru-Rollin) This lovely belle époque bistro and wine bar could just as easily count as a restaurant rather than a drinking place; after all, the Auvergne-inspired dishes are great. But it's the 1902 art nouveau bar, elegant terrace and spot-on service that have put it on the apéritif A-list of local artists, bobos (bourgeois bohemians) and local celebs.

LE CHINA COCKTAIL BAR

Map p410 (www.lechina.eu; 50 rue de Charenton, 12e; noon-2am Mon-Thu, noon-4am Fri & Sat, 5pm-2am Sun; MLedru-Rollin or Bastille) Deep leather couches and a 1930s Shanghai decor make this a wonderfully plush place to meet for drinks. Live concerts often take place in the basement.

LA LIBERTÉ BAR

Map p410 (196 rue de Faubourg St-Antoine, 11e; 9am-2am Mon-Fri, 11am-2am Sat & Sun; ; MFaidherbe-Chaligny) Infused with the spirit of the '68 revolution, local institution the Liberty does simple meals and wine by day, and is a heaving mix of regulars and drop-ins, raspy-voiced arguments and glasses going clink by night. It's the kind of place where bobos, artists and old rockers find their common point: a passionate love of drink and talk.

TAPE BAR BAR

Map p410 (21 rue de la Roquette, 11e; 6pm-2am; MBastille) Graffiti tags are scrawled on every possible surface inside the Tape Bar, marking this as the only underground hang-out within a minute's walk of the Bastille. Cheap drinks (even cheaper during happy hour from 6pm to 9pm) and decent music.

BARRIO LATINO CLUB

Map p410 (www.barrio-latino.com; 46-48 rue du Faubourg St-Antoine, 11e; ⏲noon-2am Sun-Thu, to 2.30am Fri, to 3am Sat; Ⓜ Bastille) Still squeezing the salsa theme for all it's worth, this enormous bar-restaurant with serious dancing is spread over three highly impressive floors. It attracts Latinos, Latino wannabes, Latino wannahaves and a gay crowd. Don't arrive too late; the queue to get in can be formidably long.

SANZ BY BIZZ'ART CLUB

Map p410 (☎01 44 75 78 78; http://sanzbybizzart.com; 49 rue du Faubourg St-Antoine, 11e; ⏲6pm-5am Tue-Sat; 📶; Ⓜ Bastille) A little cheesy, a little sleazy, this lively bar clad in red velvet and zebra stripes continues to hold out as a busy drinking venue on the Bastille beat. DJs spin everything from electronic to funk and soul, and the crowd is similarly unpredictable.

☆ ENTERTAINMENT

OPÉRA BASTILLE OPERA, BALLET

Map p410 (☎08 92 89 90 90; www.operadeparis.fr; 2-6 place de la Bastille, 12e; Ⓜ Bastille) This 3400-seat venue is the city's main opera hall; it also occasionally stages ballet and classical concerts. Tickets go on sale online up to two weeks before they're available by telephone or at the box office (p189). Standing-only tickets (*places débouts*; €5) are available 90 minutes before performances begin.

CINÉMATHÈQUE FRANÇAISE CINEMA

(www.cinemathequefrancaise.com; 51 rue Bercy, 12e; ⏲noon-7pm Mon & Wed-Sat, 10am-5pm Sun; Ⓜ Bercy) This national institution is a temple to the 'seventh art' and always screens its foreign offerings in their original versions. Up to 10 movies a day are shown, usually retrospectives (Spielberg, Altman, Eastwood) mixed in with related but more obscure films. Tickets €6 to €8.

LA FLÈCHE D'OR LIVE MUSIC

(www.flechedor.fr; 102bis rue de Bagnolet, 20e; ⏲vary; Ⓜ Alexandre Dumas or Gambetta) Just over 1km northeast of place de la Nation in a former railway station on central Paris' outer edge, this awesome music venue hosts both indie rock concerts and house/electro DJ nights. The Golden Arrow – named for the train to Calais in the 1930s – has a solid reputation for promoting new talent.

Kick off the evening with pizzas and beer on the summertime rooftop terrace at **Mama Shelter** (☎01 43 48 48 48; www.mamashelter.com; 109 rue de Bagnolet, 20e; pizzas €9-16; ⏲noon-1am; 📶🍷; 🚌76, Ⓜ Alexandre Dumas or Gambetta) across the street.

BADABOUM LIVE MUSIC

Map p410 (www.badaboum-paris.com; 2bis rue des Taillandiers, 11e; ⏲cocktail bar 7pm-2am Wed-Sat, club & concerts vary; Ⓜ Bastille or Ledru-Rollin) Formerly La Scène Bastille and freshly refitted, the onomatopoeically named Badaboum hosts a mixed bag of concerts on its up-close-and-personal stage but focusses on electro, funk and hip-hop. Great atmosphere, super cocktails and a secret room upstairs.

LE BALAJO LIVE MUSIC

Map p410 (www.balajo.fr; 9 rue de Lappe, 11e; ⏲vary; Ⓜ Bastille) A mainstay of Parisian nightlife since 1936, this ancient ballroom is devoted to salsa classes and Latino music during the week, with an R&B slant on weekends. But the best time to visit is for its old-fashioned *musette* (accordion music) gigs on Monday afternoon from 2pm to 7pm.

LE MOTEL LIVE MUSIC

Map p410 (www.lemotel.fr; 8 passage Josset, 11e; ⏲6pm-1.45am Tue-Sun; Ⓜ Ledru-Rollin) This hole-in-the-wall venue in the hot-to-boiling-point 11e has become the go-to indie bar around Bastille. It's particularly well loved for its comfy sofas, inexpensive but quality drinks (Belgian beers on tap) and excellent music. Live bands and DJs throughout the week.

LA CHAPELLE DES LOMBARDS LIVE MUSIC

Map p410 (www.la-chapelle-des-lombards.com; 19 rue de Lappe, 11e; ⏲11pm-5am Sun, Wed & Thu, to 6am Fri & Sat; Ⓜ Bastille) World music dominates this perennially popular Bastille dance club, with happening Latino DJs and reggae, funk and Afro jazz concerts. Concerts usually take place on Friday and Saturday.

SHOPPING

LA MANUFACTURE DE CHOCOLAT FOOD, DRINK

Map p410 (www.lechocolat-alainducasse.com; 40 rue de la Roquette, 11e; ⏲10.30am-7pm Tue-

Sat; Ⓜ Bastille) If you dine at superstar chef Alain Ducasse's restaurants, the chocolate will have been made here at Ducasse's own chocolate factory – the first in Paris to produce 'bean-to-bar' chocolate – which he set up with his former executive pastry chef Nicolas Berger. Deliberate over ganaches, pralines and truffles and no fewer than 44 flavours of chocolate bar. You can also buy Ducasse's chocolates at his Left Bank boutique, Le Chocolat Alain Ducasse (p252).

BERCY VILLAGE — MALL

(www.bercyvillage.com; cour St-Émilion, 12e; shops 11am-9pm Mon-Sat, restaurants & bars 11am-2am daily; Ⓜ Cour St-Émilion) Set in the former Bercy wine warehouses, this popular outdoor mall has an 18-screen cinema, restaurants, bars and a string of stores catering to the needs of Parisian families: home design, clever kitchen supplies, quality toy stores and more.

VIADUC DES ARTS — ARTS & CRAFTS

Map p410 (www.viaducdesarts.fr; 1-129 av Daumesnil, 12e; vary; Ⓜ Bastille or Gare de Lyon) Located beneath the red-brick arches of the Promenade Plantée (p189) is the Viaduc des Arts, where traditional artisans and contemporary designers carry out antique renovations and create new items using traditional methods. Artisans include furniture and tapestry restorers, interior designers, cabinet makers, violin- and flute-makers, embroiderers and jewellers.

MY CRAZY POP — FOOD

Map p410 (15 rue Trousseau, 11e; 11am-7pm Tue-Fri, to 8pm Sat; Ⓜ Ledru-Rollin) Wasabi, parmesan, barbecue and olive tapenade are among the amazing savoury flavours at this popcorn shop (a French first); sweet styles include gingerbread praline, salted-butter caramel and orange and cinnamon. Wander through to the viewing window at the back to watch the kernels being popped using heat and pressure only (no oil).

EL GALPON — WINE

Map p410 (www.elgalpon.fr; 12 rue Paul Bert, 11e; 3-11pm Mon-Sat; Ⓜ Faidherbe-Chaligny) Across the street from its restaurant, Unico (p194), this is Europe's largest Argentine wine cellar, with over 100 varieties. Drop in for an *apéro* between 5pm and 9pm.

FROMAGERIE LEFÈBVRE — FOOD

Map p410 (229 rue de Charenton, 12e; 8am-1pm & 4-8pm Tue-Sat, 8am-1pm Sun; Ⓜ Dugommier) Worth crossing town for, this small *fromagerie* is welcoming, well priced and sumptuously stocked with exceptional and often hard-to-find cheeses.

LA COCOTTE — HOMEWARES

Map p410 (www.lacocotte.net; 5 rue Paul Bert, 11e; 12.30-7pm Tue-Sat; Ⓜ Faidherbe-Chaligny) If the slew of gourmet restaurants along rue Paul Bert have inspired you to get into the kitchen, stop by this cute boutique for stylish, often Paris- and/or French-themed accoutrements such as tea towels, oven mitts, aprons, cookware, shopping bags and more.

FERMOB — HOMEWARES

Map p410 (www.paris.fermob.com; 81-83 av Ledru-Rollin, 12e; 10am-7pm Mon-Sat; Ⓜ Ledru-Rollin) If you want to create the 'Jardin du Luxembourg' look in your own garden, head for Fermob. It makes French park-style benches and folding chairs in a range of yummy colours – from carrot and lemon to fuchsia and aubergine.

The Islands

ÎLE DE LA CITÉ | ÎLE ST-LOUIS

Neighbourhood Top Five

❶ Revelling in the crowning glory of medieval Gothic architecture and its brilliantly bestial rooftop walk: **Cathédrale Notre Dame de Paris** (p202).

❷ Reading richly coloured biblical tales, exquisitely told with a stained-glass grace and beauty impossible to find elsewhere at **Sainte-Chapelle** (p207).

❸ Learning how Marie-Antoinette and thousands of others lived out their final days before being beheaded at the **Conciergerie** (p208).

❹ Skipping across **Pont Neuf** (p208) and imagining it Christo-wrapped.

❺ Savouring the sweetness of a famous Parisian **Berthillon** (p208) ice-cream.

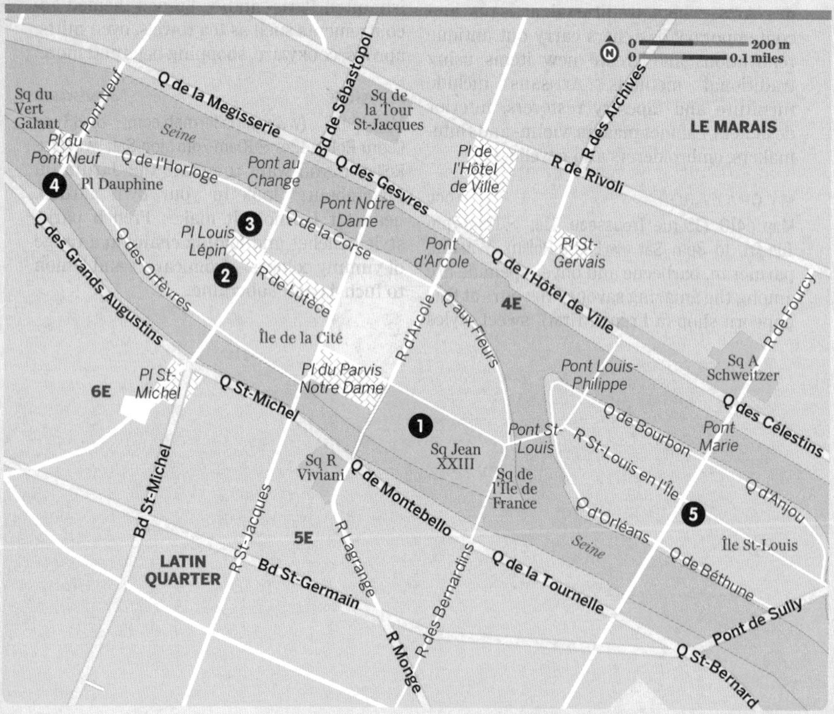

For more detail of this area see Map p412

Explore: the Islands

Paris' island duo could not be more different – or more enchanting to meander on foot. Start the day on Île de la Cité, where the Conciergerie, Sainte-Chapelle and Pont Neuf fill the morning with historical drama and intrigue. Indulge in a light lunch and a glass of wine at Les Voyelles, then stroll east, cutting through the flower and bird markets to get to Cathédrale Notre Dame. Scale the cathedral towers, tour the cathedral interior and end with a serious flop in the grassy gardens of square Jean XXIII.

Or squirrel away the finer details of Notre Dame for day two and splurge the afternoon on exploring the delicious car-free lanes on neighbouring Île St-Louis – the islet with ample eating and boutique-shopping opportunities but not a sight in sight. End the day near Pont St-Louis and Pont Louis-Philippe, a romantic spot where lovers mingle with cello-playing buskers and teenage skateboarders. Come nightfall, the Seine dances with the watery reflections of streetlights, stop signals and the dim glow of curtained windows, brightened from time to time by the lamps of tourist boats cruising by.

Local Life

➡ **Art Exhibitions** Viewing one of the cutting-edge, contemporary art exhibitions hosted by the Conciergerie (p208) is the most exciting way to experience Europe's largest surviving medieval hall.

➡ **Markets** Île de la Cité's daily flower market, Marché aux Fleurs (p210), has brightened up place Louis Lépin since 1808 and on Sunday it becomes a bird market, atmospheric to meander.

➡ **Free Entertainment** Pont au Double (linking Notre Dame with the Left Bank) and Pont St-Louis (linking the two islands) buzz with street performers in summer.

➡ **A Parisian Picnic** Find yourself a bench in the grassy gardens behind Cathédrale Notre Dame (p202) to admire its flying buttresses between sandwich bites; Huré (p208) is the gourmet takeaway-sandwich spot.

Getting There & Away

➡ **Metro** The closest stations are Cité (line 4) and Pont Marie (line 7).

➡ **Bus** Bus 47 links Île de la Cité with the Marais and Gare de l'Est; bus 21 with Opéra and Gare St-Lazare. On Île St-Louis it's bus 67 to Jardin des Plantes and place d'Italie, and bus 87 through the Latin Quarter to École Militaire and Champ de Mars.

➡ **Bicycle** Île de la Cité has a trio of handy Vélib' stations: place Louis Lépine by the Cité metro station, and also at 1 quai aux Fleurs and 5 rue d'Arcole, both by Cathédrale Notre Dame.

Lonely Planet's Top Tip

Queues to see the sunlight stream through spectacular stained-glass at Sainte-Chapelle are staggeringly long. To dodge the line and sail through with little or no waiting, first visit the Conciergerie and buy a combination ticket covering admission to both the old prison and the chapel. With this *billet jumelé* firmly in hand, you skip the ticket queue at Sainte-Chapelle and enter via the line for museum-pass holders and combination tickets.

Best Places to Eat

➡ Berthillon (p208)
➡ Les Voyelles (p209)
➡ Huré (p208)
➡ Le Tastevin (p209)
➡ Mon Vieil Ami (p209)

For reviews, see p208 ➡

Best Places to Drink

➡ Café Saint Régis (p209)
➡ Taverne Henri IV (p209)
➡ La Charlotte de l'Isle (p209)

For reviews, see p209 ➡

Best Places to Romance

➡ Hidden corners, stairwells and the rooftop of Notre Dame bell towers (p202)
➡ Pont St-Louis and Pont Louis-Philippe
➡ Pont Neuf (p208)
➡ Square du Vert Galant
➡ Square Jean XXIII

For reviews, see p208 ➡

TOP SIGHT
CATHÉDRALE NOTRE DAME DE PARIS

Notre Dame, the most visited unticketed site in Paris with upwards of 14 million people crossing its threshold annually, is a masterpiece of French Gothic architecture and the focus of Catholic Paris for seven centuries. Its vast stained-glass-lit interior has wow factor aplenty, but it is the sky-high meander around its gargoyle-guarded rooftop and extraordinary sculpted façade – best photographed in the afternoon sun – that most visitors swoon over.

Architecture

Built on a site occupied by earlier churches and, a millennium prior, a Gallo-Roman temple, Notre Dame was begun in 1163 and largely completed by the early 14th century. The cathedral was badly damaged during the Revolution, prompting architect Eugène Emmanuel Viollet-le-Duc to oversee extensive renovations between 1845 and 1864. Enter the magnificent forest of ornate **flying buttresses** that encircle the cathedral chancel and support its walls and roof.

Notre Dame is known for its sublime balance, though if you look closely you'll see all sorts of minor asymmetrical elements introduced to avoid monotony, in accordance with standard Gothic practice. These include the slightly different shapes of each of the three main **portals**, whose statues were once brightly coloured to make them more effective as a *Biblia pauperum* – a 'Bible of the poor' to help the illiterate faithful understand Old Testament stories, the Passion of the Christ and the lives of the saints.

Learn more with an audioguide (€5), available at the front desk upon entering the cathedral.

DON'T MISS...

- Rose windows
- Treasury
- Bell towers
- Square Jean XXIII
- Flying buttresses

PRACTICALITIES

- Map p412
- ☎01 53 10 07 00
- www.cathedraledeparis.com
- 6 place du Parvis Notre Dame, 4e
- cathedral free, towers adult/child €8.50/free, treasury €2/1
- cathedral 7.45am-6.45pm Mon-Sat, to 7.15pm Sun, towers 10am-6.30pm, to 11pm Fri & Sat Jul & Aug
- M Cité

Rose Windows

The cathedral's grand dimensions are immediately evident when you first enter: the interior alone is 130m long, 48m wide and 35m high and can accommodate more than 6000 worshippers.

The most spectacular interior features are three rose windows. The most renowned are the 10m-wide window over the western facade above the 7800-pipe organ, and the window on the northern side of the transept (virtually unchanged since the 13th century).

Towers

A constant queue marks the entrance to the **Tours de Notre Dame**, the cathedral's bell towers. Climb the 400-odd spiralling steps to the top of the western facade of the North Tower, where you'll find yourself on the rooftop **Galerie des Chimères** (Gargoyles Gallery), face-to-face with frightening and fantastic gargoyles, and a spectacular view of Paris. In the South Tower, under renovation at the time of writing, hangs Emmanuel, the cathedral's original 13-tonne bell. In 2013, to celebrate Notre Dame's 850th anniversary, the cathedral was kitted out with nine new bells – each named, of course – to complement Emmanuel. At the same time, the four less-tuneful bells added in 1856 were taken down and displayed for posterity in **square Jean XXIII**, the grassy park behind the cathedral.

Treasury

In the southeastern transept, the **trésor** (treasury) contains artwork, liturgical objects and first-class relics; pay a small fee to enter. Among its religious jewels and gems is the **Ste-Couronne** (Holy Crown), purportedly the wreath of thorns placed on Jesus' head before he was crucified. It is exhibited between 3pm and 4pm on the first Friday of each month, 3pm to 4pm every Friday during Lent, and 10am to 5pm on Good Friday.

Easier to admire is the treasury's wonderful collection, **Les Camées des Papes** (Papal cameos). Sculpted with incredible finesse in shell and framed in silver, the 268-piece collection depicts every pope in miniature from St Pierre to the present day, ending with Pope Francis. Note the different posture, hand gestures and clothes of each pope.

The Mays

Walk past the **choir**, with its carved wooden stalls and statues representing the Passion of the Christ, to admire the cathedral's wonderful collection of paintings in its nave side chapels. From 1449 onwards, city goldsmiths offered to the cathedral each year on 1 May a tree strung with devotional ribbons and banners to honour the Virgin Mary – to whom Notre Dame (Our Lady) is dedicated. Fifty years later the goldsmiths' annual gift, known as a **May**, had become a tabernacle decorated with scenes from the Old Testament, and, from 1630, a large canvas – 3m tall – commemorating one of the Acts of the Apostles, accompanied by a poem or literary explanation. By the early 18th century, when the brotherhood of goldsmiths was dissolved, the cathedral had received 76 such monumental paintings – just 13 can be admired today.

Crypt

Under the square in front of Notre Dame lies the **Crypte Archéologique** (Archaeological Crypt; Map p412; 1 place du Parvis Notre Dame, 1er; adult/child €6/4.50; ⏲10am-6pm; Ⓜ Cité), a 117m-long and 28m-wide area displaying in situ the remains of structures built on this site during the Gallo-Roman period, a 4th-century enclosure wall, the foundations of the medieval foundlings hospice and a few of the original sewers sunk by Haussmann.

THE HEART OF PARIS

Notre Dame is the heart of the city, so much so that distances from Paris to every part of metropolitan France are measured from **place du Parvis Notre Dame**, the vast square in front of the cathedral across which Charlemagne (AD 742–814), emperor of the Franks, rides his steed through the tourist crowds. Indeed, on summer afternoons when the sun floods onto the cathedral's exquisitely sculpted front facade, the square is packed with people admiring Notre Dame, taking 'selfies' with it as a backdrop, and generally hanging out – making it a challenge to locate the bronze star on the street that marks the exact location of **Point Zéro des Routes de France** (Map p412).

Music has been a sacred part of Notre Dame's soul since birth and there's no better day to revel in the cathedral's rousing musical heritage than on Sunday at a Gregorian or polyphonic Mass (10am and 6.30pm respectively) or a free organ recital (4.30pm). October to June, the cathedral stages evening concerts; find the program online at www.musique-sacree-notredamedeparis.fr.

Notre Dame

TIMELINE

1160 Maurice de Sully becomes bishop of Paris. Mission: to grace growing Paris with a lofty new cathedral.

1182–90 The **choir with double ambulatory** ❶ is finished and work starts on the nave and side chapels.

1200–50 The **west facade** ❷, with rose window, three portals and two soaring towers, goes up. Everyone is stunned.

1345 Some 180 years after the foundation stone was laid, the Cathédrale de Notre Dame is complete. It is dedicated to notre dame (our lady), the Virgin Mary.

1789 Revolutionaries smash the original **Gallery of Kings** ❸, pillage the cathedral and melt all its bells except the great bell Emmanuel. The cathedral becomes a Temple of Reason then a warehouse.

1831 Victor Hugo's novel The Hunchback of Notre Dame inspires new interest in the half-ruined Gothic cathedral.

1845–50 Architect Viollet-le-Duc undertakes its restoration. Twenty-eight new kings are sculpted for the west facade. The heavily decorated **portals** ❹ and **spire** ❺ are reconstructed. The neo-Gothic **treasury** ❻ is built.

1860 The area in front of Notre Dame is cleared to create the parvis, an alfresco classroom where Parisians can learn a catechism illustrated on sculpted stone portals.

1935 A rooster bearing part of the relics of the Crown of Thorns, St Denis and St Geneviève is put on top of the cathedral spire to protect those who pray inside.

1991 The architectural masterpiece of Notre Dame and its Seine-side riverbanks become a Unesco World Heritage Site.

2013 Notre Dame celebrates 850 years since construction began with a bevy of new bells and restoration works.

JOHN SONES SINGING BOWL MEDIA/GETTY IMAGES ©

Virgin & Child
Spot all 37 artworks representing the Virgin Mary. Pilgrims have revered the pearly-cream sculpture of her in the sanctuary since the 14th century. Light a devotional candle and write some words to the *Livre de Vie* (Book of Life).

North Rose Window
See prophets, judges, kings and priests venerate Mary in vivid blue and violet glass, one of three beautiful rose blooms (1225–70), each almost 10m in diameter.

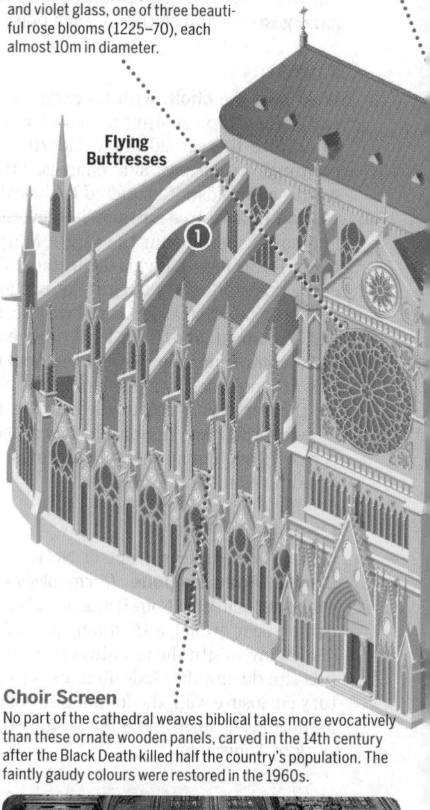

Choir Screen
No part of the cathedral weaves biblical tales more evocatively than these ornate wooden panels, carved in the 14th century after the Black Death killed half the country's population. The faintly gaudy colours were restored in the 1960s.

JULIAN ELLIOTT/GETTY IMAGES ©

JOHN SONES SINGING BOWL MEDIA/GETTY IMAGES ©

Treasury

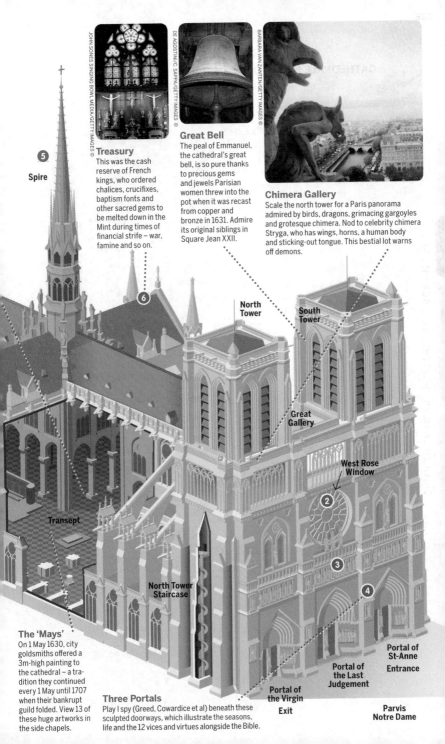

This was the cash reserve of French kings, who ordered chalices, crucifixes, baptism fonts and other sacred gems to be melted down in the Mint during times of financial strife – war, famine and so on.

DE AGOSTINI/C. SAPPA/GETTY IMAGES ©

Great Bell

The peal of Emmanuel, the cathedral's great bell, is so pure thanks to precious gems and jewels Parisian women threw into the pot when it was recast from copper and bronze in 1631. Admire its original siblings in Square Jean XXII.

BARBARA VAN ZANTEN/GETTY IMAGES ©

Chimera Gallery

Scale the north tower for a Paris panorama admired by birds, dragons, grimacing gargoyles and grotesque chimera. Nod to celebrity chimera Stryga, who has wings, horns, a human body and sticking-out tongue. This bestial lot warns off demons.

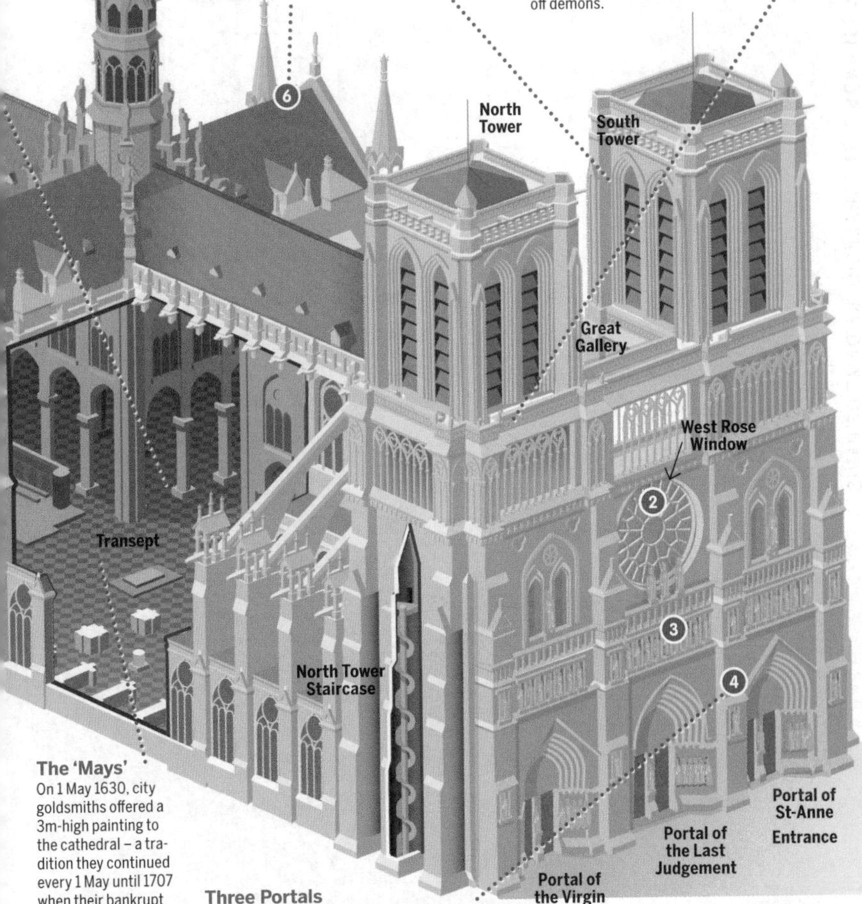

The 'Mays'

On 1 May 1630, city goldsmiths offered a 3m-high painting to the cathedral – a tradition they continued every 1 May until 1707 when their bankrupt guild folded. View 13 of these huge artworks in the side chapels.

Three Portals

Play I spy (Greed, Cowardice et al) beneath these sculpted doorways, which illustrate the seasons, life and the 12 vices and virtues alongside the Bible.

CATHÉDRALE NOTRE DAME DE PARIS

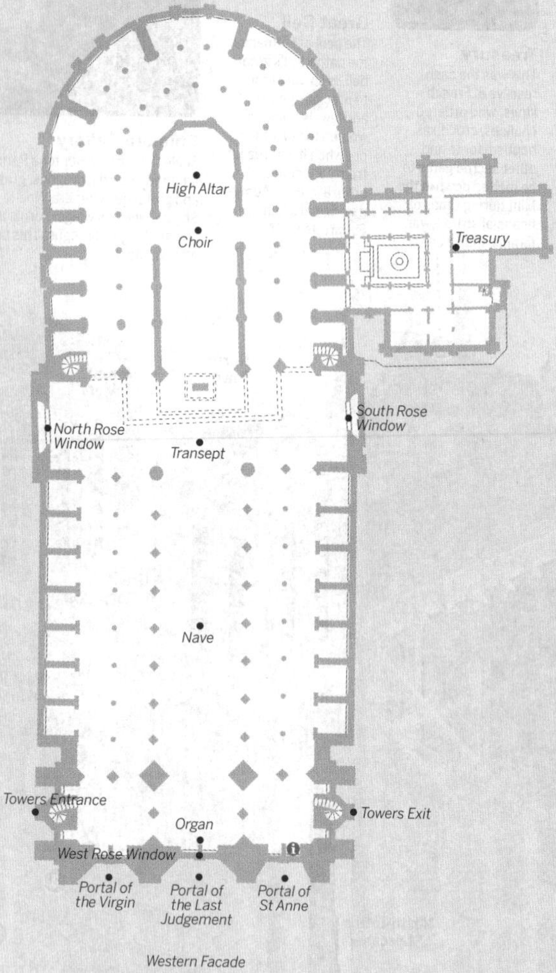

TOP SIGHT
SAINTE-CHAPELLE

Try to save Sainte-Chapelle for a sunny day, when Paris' oldest, finest stained glass is at its dazzling, sun-lit best – the colours and glass-cut detail are both extraordinary. Enshrined within the Palais de Justice (Law Courts), this gemlike Holy Chapel is Paris' most exquisite Gothic monument. Peek at its exterior (not a patch on its interior) from across the street, by the law courts' magnificently gilded 18th-century gate facing rue de Lutèce.

Sainte-Chapelle was built in just six years (compared with nearly 200 years for Notre Dame) and was consecrated in 1248. The chapel was conceived by Louis IX to house his personal collection of holy relics, including the famous Ste-Couronne (Holy Crown), acquired by the French king in 1239 from the emperors of Constantinople for a sum of money easily exceeding the amount it cost to build the chapel! The wreath of thorns is safeguarded today in the treasury at Cathédrale Notre Dame.

Statues, foliage-decorated capitals, angels and so on decorate this sumptuous, bijou chapel. But it is the 1113 scenes depicted in its 15 floor-to-ceiling stained-glass windows – 15.5m high in the nave, 13.5m in the apse – that stun visitors. From the bookshop in the former ground-floor chapel reserved for palace staff, spiral up the staircase to the upper chapel, where only the king and his close friends were allowed. Grab a storyboard in English to 'read' the 15-window biblical story – from Genesis through to the resurrection of Christ. To learn more rent an audioguide (€4.50/6 for one/two people) or join a 1½-hour guided tour in English at 11am, 3pm or 4pm; no reservations necessary. Occasional classical- and sacred-music concerts are also held here – a soul-stirring experience really not to be missed.

DON'T MISS...

- Stained glass

PRACTICALITIES

- Map p412
- ☎01 53 40 60 80, concerts 01 42 77 65 65
- http://sainte-chapelle.monuments-nationaux.fr
- 8 bd du Palais, 1er
- adult/child €8.50/free, joint ticket with Conciergerie €12.50
- ⏲9.30am-6pm Mar-Oct, to 9pm Wed mid-May–mid-Sep
- Ⓜ Cité

SIGHTS

Île de la Cité was the site of the first settlement in Paris (c 3rd century BC) and later the centre of Roman Lutetia. The island remained the hub of royal and ecclesiastical power, even after the city spread to both banks of the Seine in the Middle Ages. Smaller Île St-Louis was actually two uninhabited islets called Île Notre Dame (Our Lady Isle) and Île aux Vaches (Cows Island) in the early 17th century – until a building contractor and two financiers worked out a deal with Louis XIII to create one island and build two stone bridges to the mainland.

CATHÉDRALE NOTRE DAME DE PARIS — CATHEDRAL

See p202.

CONCIERGERIE — MONUMENT

Map p412 (www.monuments-nationaux.fr; 2 bd du Palais, 1er; adult/child €8.50/free, joint ticket with Sainte-Chapelle €12.50; ⏲9.30am-6pm; Ⓜ Cité) A royal palace in the 14th century, the Conciergerie later became a prison. During the Reign of Terror (1793–94) alleged enemies of the Revolution were incarcerated here before being brought before the Revolutionary Tribunal next door in the **Palais de Justice**. Top-billing exhibitions take place in the beautiful, Rayonnant Gothic **Salle des Gens d'Armes**, Europe's largest surviving medieval hall.

Of the almost 2800 prisoners held in the dungeons during the Reign of Terror (in various 'classes' of cells, no less) before being sent in tumbrels to the guillotine, star prisoner was Queen Marie-Antoinette – see a reproduction of her cell. As the Revolution began to turn on its own, radicals Danton and Robespierre made an appearance at the Conciergerie and, finally, the judges of the tribunal themselves.

PONT NEUF — BRIDGE

Map p412 (Ⓜ Pont Neuf) Paris' oldest bridge has linked the western end of Île de la Cité with both river banks since 1607, when the king inaugurated it by crossing the bridge on a white stallion. The occasion is commemorated by an equestrian **statue of Henry IV**, known to his subjects as the Vert Galant ('jolly rogue' or 'dirty old man', perspective depending).

View the bridge's seven arches, decorated with humorous and grotesque figures of barbers, dentists, pickpockets, loiterers etc, from a spot along the river or afloat.

Pont Neuf and nearby place Dauphine were used for public exhibitions in the 18th century. In the last century the bridge became an objet d'art: in 1963 School of Paris artist Nonda built, exhibited and lived in a huge Trojan horse of steel and wood on the bridge; in 1984 Japanese designer Kenzo covered it with flowers; and in 1985 Bulgarian-born 'environmental sculptor' Christo famously wrapped the bridge in beige fabric.

MÉMORIAL DES MARTYRS DE LA DÉPORTATION — MONUMENT

Map p412 (square de l'Île de France, 4e; ⏲10am-noon & 2-7pm Apr-Sep, to 5pm Oct-Mar; RER St-Michel–Notre Dame) The Memorial to the Victims of the Deportation, erected in 1962, remembers the 160,000 residents of France (including 76,000 Jews, of whom 11,000 were children) deported to and murdered in Nazi concentration camps during WWII. A single barred 'window' separates the bleak, rough-concrete courtyard from the waters of the Seine. Inside lies the **Tomb of the Unknown Deportee**.

EATING

Île St-Louis is a pleasant if pricey and overly touristy place to eat. Otherwise barren of decent eating places, Île de la Cité squirrels away a couple of lovely addresses on its western tip.

★HURÉ — BOULANGERIE €

Map p412 (www.hure-createur.fr; 1 rue d'Arcole, 4e; takeaway lunch menus €8.50-9.30, sandwiches €4-6; ⏲6.30am-8pm Mon-Sat; Ⓜ St-Michel Notre Dame or Châtelet) Feisty savoury tarts and quiches, jumbo salads bursting with fresh veggies, giant cookies and cakes every colour and flavour of the rainbow: assuming it's a light lunch alfresco you're after, you'll be hard-pressed to find a better *boulangerie* in spitting distance of Notre Dame than this. Simply look for the mountains of giant meringues piled high on the counter and queue stretching halfway down the street.

BERTHILLON — ICE CREAM €

Map p412 (31 rue St-Louis en l'Île, 4e; 2-/3-/4-ball cone or tub €2.50/5.50/7; ⏲10am-8pm Wed-Sun; Ⓜ Pont Marie) Berthillon is to ice cream what

Château Lafite Rothschild is to wine and Valrhona is to chocolate. Among its 70-odd flavours, the fruit sorbets are renowned, as are its rich chocolate, coffee, *marrons glacés* (candied chestnuts) and Agenaise (Armagnac and prunes). Watch for seasonal flavours such as roasted pineapple and basil, or ginger and caramel. Eat in or take away.

★LES VOYELLES MODERN FRENCH €€

Map p412 (☎01 46 33 69 75; www.les-voyelles.com; 74 quai des Orfèvres, 4e; plats du jour €12, 2-/3-course menus €17/22.50; ⏰8am-midnight Tue-Sat; Ⓜ Pont Neuf) This new kid on the block is worth the short walk from Notre Dame. The Vowels – spot the letters casually scattered between books and beautiful objects on the shelves lining the intimate 'library' dining room – is thoroughly contemporary, with a menu ranging from finger food to full-blown dinner to match. Its pavement terrace is Paris gold.

LES FOUS DE L'ÎLE BRASSERIE €€

Map p412 (☎01 43 25 76 67; www.lesfousdelile.com; 33 rue des Deux Ponts, 4e; 2-/3-course menus lunch €19/25, dinner €23/28; ⏰10am-2am; Ⓜ Pont Marie) This typical brasserie is a popular family address with a lovely open kitchen and an unusual cockerel theme (we don't know either) throughout. Hearty fare like *cassoulet* (traditional Languedoc stew with beans and meat) and lighter Spanish-inspired tapas dishes are served continuously between noon and 11pm. Sunday brunch (€24, €29 with a cocktail), served noon to 4pm, buzzes.

LE TASTEVIN TRADITIONAL FRENCH €€€

Map p412 (☎01 43 54 17 31; www.letastevin-paris.com; 46 rue St-Louis en l'Île, 4e; mains €27-34.50, menus from €33; ⏰noon-2pm & 7-11.15pm Tue-Sun; Ⓜ Pont Marie) With its old-fashioned lace curtains, wood panelling and beamed ceiling, this posh old-style address in a 17th-century building smacks of charm. Its excellent cuisine is equally traditional: think escargot, foie gras, sole, or *ris de veau* (calf sweetbreads) with morels and tagliatelle.

MON VIEIL AMI TRADITIONAL FRENCH €€€

Map p412 (☎01 40 46 01 35; www.mon-vieil-ami.com; 69 rue St-Louis en l'Île, 4e; plats du jour €15.50, menus €47.50; ⏰noon-2.30pm & 7-11pm; Ⓜ Pont Marie) Alsatian chef Antoine Westermann is the creative talent behind this sleek black neobistro where guests are treated like old friends (hence the name) and vegetables get royal treatment. The good-value lunchtime *plat du jour* (dish of the day) is a perfect reflection of the season. Dinner is served from around 7pm – handy for those seeking an early-ish meal.

LOCAL KNOWLEDGE

CAFÉ SAINT RÉGIS

Hip and historical with an effortless dose of retro vintage thrown in for good measure, **Le Saint Regis** (Map p412; http://cafesaintregisparis.com; 6 rue du Jean de Bellay, 4e; salads & mains €14.50-28; ⏰7am-2am; 📶; Ⓜ Pont Marie) – as those in the know call it – is a deliciously Parisian hang-out any time of day. From pastries for breakfast to a mid-morning pancake, brasserie lunch or early-evening oyster platter, Café Saint Regis hits the spot just right. Sunday brunch jostles with happy hour (7pm to 9pm) for best crowd-packed moment. Magazines and newspapers to read, charismatic waiters in long white aprons, and a lovely white ceramic-tiled interior top off the appealing ensemble.

DRINKING & NIGHTLIFE

Drinking venues on the islands are as scarce as hens' teeth. They do exist, but use them as a starting point as very few places stay open after the bewitching hour of midnight.

TAVERNE HENRI IV WINE BAR

Map p412 (13 place du Pont Neuf, 1er; ⏰11.30am-11pm Mon-Sat, closed Aug; Ⓜ Pont Neuf) One of the few places to drink on Île de la Cité, this wine bar dates to 1885 and lures a fair few legal types from the nearby Palais de Justice (not to mention celeb writers and actors, as the autographed snaps testify). A tasty choice of *tartines* (open sandwiches), charcuterie and cheese platters complement its extensive wine list.

LA CHARLOTTE DE L'ISLE TEAROOM

Map p412 (www.lacharlottedelisle.fr; 24 rue St-Louis en l'Île, 4e; ⏰11am-7pm Wed-Sun; Ⓜ Pont Marie) This tiny place is a particularly lovely *salon de thé* (tearoom) with a quaint fairy-tale theme, old-fashioned glass sweet jars on the shelf and a fine collection of tea to taste in situ or buy to sip at home. Hot chocolate, chocolate sculptures, cakes and pastries are other sweet reasons to come here.

LE FLORE EN L'ÎLE CAFE

Map p412 (42 quai d'Orléans, 4e; 8am-1am; M Pont Marie) A tourist crowd piles into this excellent and elegant old-world people-watching spot with prime views of the buskers on Pont St-Louis.

SHOPPING

Île St-Louis is a shopper's delight with crafty boutiques and tiny charm-rich specialist stores, while Île de la Cité is good for souvenirs and tourist kitsch.

★ 38 SAINT LOUIS CHEESE

Map p412 (38 rue St-Louis en l'Île, 4e; 9am-9.30pm Tue-Sat, to 7pm Sun & Mon; M Pont Marie) Saturday wine tastings, artisan fruit chutneys, grape juice and prepared dishes to go: there is far more to this thoroughly modern *fromagerie* than its old-fashioned facade and absolutely superb selection of first-class French cheese. The shop is run by a young, dynamic duo, driven by food. Buy a wooden box filled with vacuum-packed cheese to take home.

MARCHÉ AUX FLEURS REINE ELIZABETH II MARKET

Map p412 (place Louis Lépin, 4e; 8am-7.30pm Mon-Sat; M Cité) Blooms have been sold at this flower market since 1808, making it the oldest market of any kind in Paris. On Sunday it transforms into a twittering bird market, **Marché aux Oiseaux** (9am-7pm Sun).

IL CAMPIELLO CRAFTS

Map p412 (www.ilcampiello.com; 88 rue St-Louis en l'Île, 4e; 11am-7pm; M Pont Marie) Venetian carnival masks – intricately crafted from papier mâché, ceramics and leather – are the speciality of this exquisite shop, which also sells jewellery made from Murano glass beads. It was established by a native of Venice, to which the Île St-Louis bears more than a passing resemblance.

LIBRAIRIE ULYSSE BOOKS

Map p412 (www.ulysse.fr; 26 rue St-Louis en l'Île, 4e; 2-8pm Tue-Fri; M Pont Marie) You can barely move in between this shop's antiquarian and new travel guides, *National Geographic* back editions and maps. Opened in 1971 by the intrepid Catherine Domaine, this was the world's first travel bookshop. Hours vary, but ring the bell and Catherine will open up if she's around.

CLAIR DE RÊVE TOYS

Map p412 (www.clairdereve.com; 35 rue St-Louis en l'Île, 4e; 11am-1pm & 2-7pm Mon-Sat; M Pont Marie) This shop is all about wind-up toys, music boxes and puppets – mostly marionettes, which sway and bob suspended from the ceiling.

PREMIÈRE PRESSION PROVENCE FOOD

Map p412 (51 rue St-Louis en l'Île, 4e; 11am-1pm & 2-7pm Mon-Sat; M Pont Marie) Its name evokes the first pressing of olives to make olive oil in the south of France and that is precisely what this gourmet boutique sells – be it as oil or in any number of spreads and sauces (pesto, tapenade etc).

Latin Quarter

Neighbourhood Top Five

❶ Time travelling back to the Middle Ages at the **Musée National du Moyen Âge** (p213).

❷ Visiting the new-look exhibits inside the gorgeous **Institut du Monde Arabe** (p216) – don't miss the view from the roof!

❸ Strolling around Paris' sprawling botanic gardens, the **Jardin des Plantes** (p214), and visit the Natural History Museum.

❹ Curling up with a volume of poetry in the magical bookshop **Shakespeare & Company** (p225).

❺ Paying homage to France's greatest thinkers buried beneath the neoclassical **Panthéon** (p215).

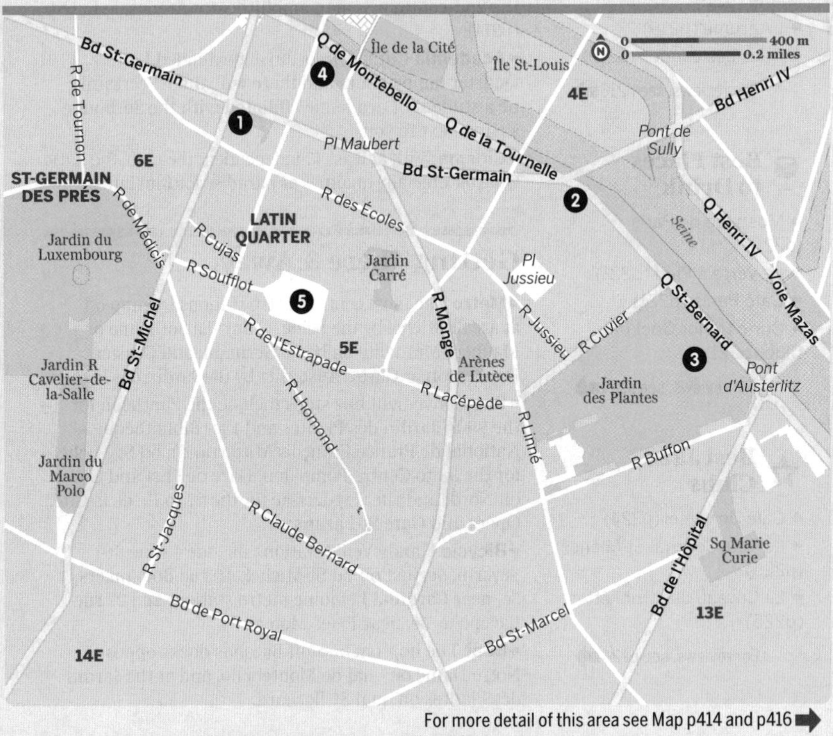

For more detail of this area see Map p414 and p416 ➡

Lonely Planet's Top Tip

While hungry first-time visitors are often sucked into the maze of tiny streets between the Seine, rue St-Jacques and bd St-Germain, you'd be wise to simply avoid this area altogether. Instead, consider grabbing some bread, cheese, charcuterie and wine from local speciality shops and enjoy some multimillion dollar views with lunch or dinner. Best bets? The quays along the Seine, the place du Panthéon (a fave with students), and the leafy Jardin des Plantes.

Best Places to Eat

- Les Pipos (p219)
- Sola (p220)
- Café de la Nouvelle Mairie (p219)
- L'Agrume (p219)
- Dans Les Landes (p219)

For reviews, see p216

Best Places to Drink

- Mosquée de Paris (p220)
- Le Verre à Pied (p221)
- Café Panis (p221)
- Curio Parlor Cocktail Club (p221)

For reviews, see p221

Best Jazz Clubs

- Café Universel (p224)
- Le Petit Journal St-Michel (p225)
- Le Caveau des Oubliettes (p225)

For reviews, see p224

Explore: Latin Quarter

The centre of Parisian higher education since the Middle Ages, the Latin Quarter takes its name from the classical language spoken here by students and professors until the French Revolution. A serene spot to begin the day is in the botanic gardens, the Jardin des Plantes, before sipping sweet mint tea in the Mosquée de Paris or strolling through the engaging Arab World Institute.

But there's no better strip to see, smell and taste the Latin Quarter than the thriving rue Mouffetard, so it's worth combining a flit from food stall to fabulous food shop with lunch at one of the restaurants utilising its produce (skip it on Mondays, when the market stalls are shut).

After admiring the Panthéon's vast interior, the hollow of the afternoon is a contemplative time to meander through the Musée National du Moyen Âge for the ultimate medieval history lesson.

After dinner at a local bistro, head down into a medieval cellar (many used as Revolutionary prisons) for live jazz and jam sessions, or join the area's students in the quarter's lively pubs.

Local Life

- **Sports** Join the locals playing boules and football in the 2nd-century Roman amphitheatre Arènes de Lutèce (p214).
- **Academia** Clink drinks during extended Latin Quarter happy hours and there will almost certainly be a student or academic affiliated with the Sorbonne sitting next to you.
- **Cinema** With at least 13 independent theatres, the Latin Quarter officially qualifies as paradise for film buffs.

Getting There & Away

- **Metro** The most central metro stations to jump off at are St-Michel by the Seine; Cluny–La Sorbonne or Maubert-Mutualité on bd St-Germain; and Censier Daubenton or Gare d'Austerlitz by the Jardin des Plantes.
- **Bus** Convenient bus stops include the Panthéon for the 89 to Jardin des Plantes and 13e (Bibliothèque National de France François Mitterrand); bd St-Michel for the 38 to Centre Pompidou, Gare de l'Est and Gare du Nord; and rue Gay Lussac for the 27 to Île de la Cité, Opéra and Gare St-Lazare.
- **Bicycle** Handy Vélib' stations include 42 rue St-Severin, 5e, just off bd St-Michel; 40 rue Boulangers, 5e, near Cardinal Lemoine metro station; and 27 rue Lacépède, 5e, near Place Monge.
- **Boat** The hop-on, hop-off Batobus docks opposite Notre Dame on quai de Montebello, and at the Jardin des Plantes on quai St-Bernard.

TOP SIGHT
MUSÉE NATIONAL DU MOYEN ÂGE

CRAIG PERSHOUSE / GETTY IMAGES ©

The National Museum of the Middle Ages holds a series of sublime treasures, from medieval statuary, stained glass and objets d'art to its celebrated series of tapestries, *The Lady and the Unicorn*. Throw in the extant architecture – an ornate 15th-century mansion (the Hôtel de Cluny), and the much older frigidarium (cold room) of an enormous Roman-era bathhouse – and you have one of Paris' top small museums.

Initially the residential quarters of the Cluny Abbots, the **Hôtel de Cluny** today holds some fascinating relics, not least of which is an entire room (No 8) dedicated to **statuary** from Notre Dame's facade, removed during the Revolution and later used to support the foundations of a private mansion.

The museum's northwestern corner is where you'll find the remains of the Gallo-Roman **bathhouse**, built around AD 200. Look for the display of the fragment of mosaic *Love Riding a Dolphin,* as well as a gorgeous marble bathtub from Rome. Outside the museum, remnants of the other rooms – a palaestra (exercise room), tepidarium (warm bath) and caldarium (hot bath) – are visible.

Upstairs on the 1st floor (room 13) are the unicorn **tapestries**, representing the five senses and an enigmatic sixth, perhaps the heart. It's believed that they were originally commissioned around 1500 by the Le Viste family in Paris. Discovered in 1814 in the Chateau de Boussac, they were acquired by the museum in 1882 and have since provided inspiration to many, from Prosper Mérimée and George Sand to, most recently, Tracy Chevalier.

Small **gardens** to the museum's northeast, including the Jardin Céleste (Celestial Garden) and the Jardin d'Amour (Garden of Love), are planted with flowers, herbs and shrubs that appear in works hanging throughout the museum.

DON'T MISS

- Tapestries
- Hôtel de Cluny
- Frigidarium
- Notre Dame statuary

PRACTICALITIES

- Map p414
- www.musee-moyenage.fr
- 6 place Paul Painlevé, 5e
- adult/child €8/free
- 9.15am-5.45pm Wed-Mon
- M Cluny-La Sorbonne

SIGHTS

MUSÉE NATIONAL DU MOYEN ÂGE MUSEUM

See p213.

SORBONNE UNIVERSITY

Map p414 (12 rue de la Sorbonne, 5e; MCluny-La Sorbonne or RER Luxembourg) The crème de la crème of academia flock to this distinguished university, one of the world's most famous. Today, 'La Sorbonne' embraces most of the 13 autonomous universities – 35,500-odd students in all – created when the University of Paris was reorganised after the student protests of 1968. Until 2015, when an ambitious, 10-year modernisation program costing €45 million reaches completion, parts of the complex will be under renovation. Visitors are not permitted to enter.

The original Sorbonne was founded in 1253 by Robert de Sorbon, confessor to Louis IX, as a college for 16 impoverished theology students; soon after it grew into a powerful body with its own government and laws.

The **Chapelle de la Sorbonne** (Map p414), the university's distinctive domed church, was built between 1635 and 1642. The remains of Cardinal Richelieu (1585–1642) lie in a tomb with an effigy of a cardinal's hat suspended above.

ÉGLISE ST ÉTIENNE DU MONT CHURCH

Map p416 (www.saintetiennedumont.fr; 1 place Ste-Geneviève, 5e; 8.45am-7.30pm Tue-Fri, 8.45am-noon & 2-7.45pm Sat & Sun; MCardinal Lemoine) FREE The Church of Mount St Stephen, built between 1492 and 1655, contains Paris' only surviving rood screen (1535), separating the chancel from the nave; the others were removed during the late Renaissance because they prevented the faithful in the nave from seeing the priest celebrate Mass.

In the nave's southeastern corner, the tomb of Ste Geneviève lies in a chapel. The patron of Paris, Ste Geneviève was born at Nanterre in AD 422 and turned away Attila the Hun from Paris in AD 451. A highly decorated reliquary near her tomb contains all that is left of her earthly remains – a finger bone.

ARÈNES DE LUTÈCE RUINS

Map p416 (www.arenesdelutece.com; 49 rue Monge, 5e; 9am-9.30pm Apr-Oct, 8am-5.30pm Nov-Mar; MPlace Monge) FREE The 2nd-century Roman amphitheatre Lutetia Arena once sat 10,000 people for gladiatorial combats and other events. Found by accident in 1869 when rue Monge was under construction, it's now used by locals playing football and, especially, boules.

MOSQUÉE DE PARIS MOSQUE

Map p416 (01 45 35 97 33; www.la-mosquee.com; 2bis place du Puits de l'Ermite, 5e; adult/child €3/2; mosque 9am-noon & 2-6pm Sat-Thu; MCensier Daubenton or Place Monge) Paris' central mosque, with striking 26m-high minaret, was completed in 1926 in an ornate art deco–Moorish style. You can visit the interior to admire the intricate tile work and calligraphy. A separate entrance leads to the wonderful North African–style *hammam* (p227), restaurant (p220) and *salon de thé* (tearoom), and a small *souk* (actually more of a gift shop). Visitors must be modestly dressed.

JARDIN DES PLANTES GARDEN

Map p416 (www.jardindesplantes.net; place Valhubert & 36 rue Geoffroy-Saint-Hilaire, 5e; 7.30am-7.45pm Apr-Oct, 8am-5.15pm Nov-Mar; MGare d'Austerlitz, Censier Daubenton or Jussieu) FREE Founded in 1626 as a medicinal herb garden for Louis XIII, Paris' 24-hectare botanic gardens – visually defined by the double alley of plane trees that run the length of the park – are an idyllic spot to stroll around, break for a picnic (watch out for the automatic sprinklers!) and escape the city concrete for a spell. Upping its appeal are three museums from the Muséum National d'Histoire Naturelle and a small zoo, Menagerie du Jardin des Plantes.

Other attractions include peony and rose gardens, an alpine garden, and the gardens of the École de Botanique, used by students of the school and green-fingered Parisians. The beautiful glass-and-metal **Grandes Serres** (Map p416; adult/child €6/4; 10am-6pm) (a series of four greenhouses) have been in use since 1714, and several of Henri Rousseau's jungle paintings (sometimes on display in the Musée d'Orsay (p230) were inspired by his frequent visits here.

MUSÉUM NATIONAL D'HISTOIRE NATURELLE NATURAL HISTORY MUSEUM

Map p416 (www.mnhn.fr; place Valhubert & 36 rue Geoffroy St-Hilaire, 5e; MGare d'Austerlitz, Censier Daubenton or Jussieu) Despite the name, the Natural History Museum is not a single building, but a collection of sites through-

TOP SIGHT
PANTHÉON

Overlooking the city from its Left Bank perch, the Panthéon's stately **neoclassical dome** stands out as one of the most recognisable icons in the Parisian skyline. Louis XV originally commissioned the vast architectural masterpiece around 1750 as an abbey dedicated to Ste Geneviève in thanksgiving for his recovery from an illness. However, due to financial and structural problems, it wasn't completed until 1789 – not a good year for church openings in Paris.

It reverted to religious duties twice after the Revolution but has played a secular role ever since 1885, and the **crypt** now serves as the resting place of some of France's greatest thinkers, including Voltaire, Rousseau, Braille and Hugo. The first woman to be interred in the Panthéon based on achievement was two-time Nobel Prize winner Marie Curie (1867–1934), reburied here, along with her husband, Pierre, in 1995.

The dome is closed for renovations through 2015 (other structural work will continue through to 2022). A copy of **Foucault's pendulum**, originally hung from the dome in 1851 to demonstrate the rotation of the earth, should return to its display following the dome's renovation.

DON'T MISS

- The architecture
- Foucault's Pendulum
- Crypt

PRACTICALITIES

- Map p416
- www.monum.fr
- place du Panthéon, 5e
- adult/child €7.50/free
- 10am-6.30pm Apr-Sep, to 6pm Oct-Mar
- Maubert-Mutualité, Cardinal Lemoine or RER Luxembourg

out France. Its historic home is in the Jardin des Plantes, and it's here you'll find the greatest number of branches: taxidermied animals in the excellent **Grande Galerie de l'Évolution** (Map p416; adult/child €7/free; 10am-6pm Wed-Mon), fossils and dinosaur skeletons in the **Galeries d'Anatomie Comparée et de Paléontologie** (Map p416; adult/child €7/free; 10am-5pm Wed-Mon) and meteorites and crystals in the **Galerie de Minéralogie et de Géologie** (Map p416).

Created in 1793, the National Museum of Natural History became a site of significant scientific research in the 19th century. Of the three museums here, the four-floor Grande Galerie de l'Évolution is a particular winner if you're travelling with kids: life-sized elephants, tigers and rhinos play safari, and imaginative exhibits on evolution, extinction and global warming fill 6000 sq metres. The temporary exhibits are generally excellent. Within this building is a separate attraction – the **Galerie des Enfants** (Map p416; adult/child €9/7) – which is a hands-on science museum tailored to children from ages six to 12.

MÉNAGERIE DU JARDIN DES PLANTES — ZOO

Map p416 (www.mnhn.fr; 57 rue Cuvier, 5e; adult/child €11/9; 9am-6.30pm Apr-Oct, shorter hours rest of year; M Gare d'Austerlitz, Censier Daubenton or Jussieu) Like the Jardin des Plantes in which it's located, this 1000-animal zoo is more than a tourist attraction, also doubling as a research centre for the reproduction of rare and endangered species. During the Prussian siege of 1870, the animals of the day were themselves endangered, when almost all were eaten by starving Parisians. Do note that the recently renovated zoo (p190) in Vincennes is considerably larger.

MUSÉE DE LA SCULPTURE EN PLEIN AIR — MUSEUM

Map p414 (quai St-Bernard, 5e; M Gare d'Austerlitz) FREE Along quai St-Bernard, this open-air sculpture museum (also known as the Jardin Tino Rossi) has more than 50 late-20th-century unfenced sculptures, and makes a great picnic spot. A salad beneath a César or a baguette beside a Brancusi is a pretty classy way to see the Seine up close.

TOP SIGHT
INSTITUT DU MONDE ARABE

The Arab World Institute was jointly founded by France and 18 Middle Eastern and North African nations in 1980, with the aim of promoting cross-cultural dialogue. In addition to hosting concerts, film screenings and a research centre, the stunning landmark is also home to a new museum and temporary exhibition space.

You certainly can't miss the building: architect Jean Nouvel took his inspiration from traditional latticed wood windows, creating thousands of modern *mashrabiya,* photoelectrically sensitive apertures built into the glass walls that allow you to see out without being seen. The apertures are opened and closed by electric motors in order to regulate the amount of light and heat that reach the institute's interior.

The overhauled **museum** (7th to 4th floors) introduces elements from disparate time periods and cultures, focusing on art, artisanship and science. You'll find everything from pre-Islamic ceramics to ancient astronomical instruments.

From the top (9th) floor **observation terrace**, incredible views stretch across the Seine as far as Sacré-Cœur. There's a panoramic restaurant here, as well as a cafeteria/tearoom (no views) and decent cafe (ground floor).

DON'T MISS

- Museum
- Observation terrace

PRACTICALITIES

- Arab World Institute
- Map p414
- www.imarabe.org
- 1 place Mohammed V, 5e
- adult/child €8/4
- ⏲10am-6pm Tue-Thu, to 9.30pm Fri, to 7pm Sat & Sun
- Ⓜ Jussieu

COLLÈGE DES BERNARDINS HISTORIC BUILDING

Map p414 (www.collegedesbernardins.fr; 18-24 rue de Poissy, 5e; ⏲10am-6pm Mon-Sat, 2-6pm Sun; ⓂMaubert-Mutualité or Cardinal Lemoine) FREE Dating back to 1248, this former Cistercian college originally served as living quarters and place of study for novice monks. Following a decade of renovations, it reopened in 2008 as an art gallery and centre for Christian culture with events ranging from lectures to film screenings and music performances.

EATING

From chandelier-lit palaces loaded with history to cheap-eat student haunts, the 5e *arrondissement* (city district) has something to suit every budget and culinary taste. Rue Mouffetard is famed for its food market and food shops, though you'll have to trek down some less touristy side streets for the neighbourhood's best meals.

LE POT O'LAIT CRÊPERIE €

Map p416 (www.lepotolait.com; 41 rue Censier, 5e; lunch menus €10 & 12.90, crêpes €3-11.50; ⏲noon-2.30pm & 7.30-10.30pm Tue-Sat; 👪; ⓂCensier Daubenton) A bright, contemporary spot, the Milk Can is the business when it comes to *galettes* (savoury buckwheat crêpes) – try smoked salmon or goat's cheese and bacon – and sweet crêpes (pistachio ice cream, zesty orange, hot chocolate and whipped cream). Salads are spectacular; kids will love the ice-cream sundaes.

LE JARDIN DES PÂTES ORGANIC, PASTA €

Map p416 (☎01 43 31 50 71; 4 rue Lacépède, 5e; pasta €10.50-14; ⏲noon-2.30pm & 7.30-10.30pm; 👪; ⓂPlace Monge) 🍃 A crisp white-and-green facade handily placed next to a Vélib' station flags the Pasta Garden, a simple, smart 100% *bio* (organic) place where pasta comes in every guise imaginable – barley, buckwheat, rye, wheat, rice, chestnut and so on. Try the *pâtes de chataignes* (chestnut pasta) with duck breast, nutmeg, crème fraîche and mushrooms.

BOULANGERIE ERIC KAYSER
BOULANGERIE €

Map p414 (www.maison-kayser.com; 8 rue Monge, 5e; 6.45am-8.30pm Wed-Mon; M Maubert-Mutualité) The original branch of Eric Kayser, which has now become a household name in Paris. It's one of the best bakeries that's reasonably close to the Seine and the islands. A few doors down (at No 12) is a second shop, with seating, coffee and light, flaky pastries.

LE COMPTOIR DU PANTHÉON
CAFE, BRASSERIE €

Map p416 (01 43 54 75 56; 5 rue Soufflot, 5e; salads €11-13, mains €12.40-15.40; 7am-1.45am; ; M Cardinal Lemoine or RER Luxembourg) Enormous, creative meal-size salads are the reason to pick this as a dining spot. Magnificently placed across from the domed Panthéon on the shady side of the street, its pavement terrace is big, busy and oh so Parisian – turn your head away from Voltaire's burial place and the Eiffel Tower pops into view. Service is superspeedy and food is handily served all day.

58 QUALITÉ STREET
DELICATESSEN €

Map p414 (58 rue de la Montagne Ste-Geneviève, 5e; sandwiches €4.90, mains €8.50-18; noon-11pm Mon-Sat; M Maubert-Mutualité or Cardinal Lemoine) An inviting red-walled deli, this is a handy address if you're after a light meal or an off-hours pick-me-up. There's a handful of main courses (*tartiflette*, pot au feu) prepared in the open 'kitchen' – although truthfully the cooking equipment is pretty limited – along with simple but quality sandwiches to take away and charcuterie and cheese plates to savour over a glass of wine. Cash only.

PETITS PLATS DE MARC
CAFE €

Map p416 (6 Rue de l'Arbalète, 5e; quiches €7, lunch menus €10-14; 9.30am-3.30pm Tue & Wed, 9am-7pm Thu-Sun; ; M Censier Daubenton) This tiny pit stop off rue Mouffetard is wonderfully cosy and a change from the usual humdrum tourist stops; the homemade soups, quiches, pastries and salads are delicious and easy on the wallet. Tea and coffee is served throughout the day.

LE PUITS DE LÉGUMES
VEGETARIAN €

Map p414 (01 43 25 50 95; www.lepuitsdelegumesbio.fr; 18 rue du Cardinal Lemoine, 5e; mains €9.50-16; noon-4pm & 7-10pm Mon-Sat; ; M Cardinal Lemoine) Homemade tarts, quiches and rice dishes loaded with fresh seasonal vegetables are the draw of the 'Vegetable Well', a vegetarian (plus fish) student favourite. From the tiny kitchen out back a comforting waft of homemade cooking pervades the simple dining room, filled with a handful of condiment-laden tables. Specials are chalked on the board outside.

BOULANGERIE BRUNO SOLQUES
BOULANGERIE, PATISSERIE €

Map p416 (243 rue St-Jacques, 5e; 6.30am-1:30pm & 3:30-8pm Mon-Fri; ; M Place Monge or RER Luxembourg) Inventive *pâtissier* Bruno Solques crafts oddly shaped flat tarts with mashed fruit, fruit-filled brioches and subtly spiced gingerbread. This small, bare-boards shop is also filled with wonderfully rustic breads. It's on the pricey side but worth it – kids from the school across the way can't get enough.

CAVE MAVROMMATIS
GREEK €

Map p416 (www.mavrommatis.com; 49 rue Censier, 5e; meze €2.50-7.80, sandwiches €6.70; 9.30am-10pm; M Censier Daubenton) Gourmet meze (*tarama*-drenched toast, eggplant caviar), pita sandwiches and Greek wines make this casual eatery perfect for a quick bite or drink at any time of day. Seating is limited, but it also does takeaway.

LOVE LOCKS

Stretching from the Latin Quarter's quai de la Tournelle to the eastern tip of the Île de la Cité, the **Pont de l'Archevêché** footbridge is one of many Parisian bridges covered in padlocks. Inscribed with initials and sometimes adorned with ribbons, the locks are attached by couples who then throw the key into the Seine as a symbol of eternal love. Although it sounds romantic, there are now so many padlocks that several bridge railings and grates have been permanently damaged by the sheer weight. One of Mme Hidalgo's first high-profile acts as Paris mayor was to remove the locks on the adorned **Pont des Arts** (west of the Île de la Cité), but just weeks after the initial clean-up the locks were back, causing a section of railing to collapse – a signal to couples that it may be time to find a new way to express their love. Flowers, perhaps?

LATIN QUARTER LITERARY ADDRESSES

Like its Left Bank neighbours, the Latin Quarter is steeped in literary history.

James Joyce's flat (Map p416; MCardinal Lemoine) Peer down the passageway at 71 rue du Cardinal Lemoine: Irish writer James Joyce (1882–1941) lived in the courtyard flat at the back marked 'E' when he arrived in Paris in 1921; he finished editing *Ulysses* here.

Ernest Hemingway's apartment (Map p416; MCardinal Lemoine) At 74 rue du Cardinal Lemoine is the apartment where Ernest Hemingway (1899–1961) lived with his first wife, Hadley, from January 1922 until August 1923. Just below was Bal au Printemps, a popular *bal musette* (dancing club) that served as the model for the one where Jake Barnes meets Brett Ashley in Hemingway's *The Sun Also Rises*.

Paul Verlaine's garret (Map p416; MCardinal Lemoine) Hemingway wrote in a top-floor garret of a hotel (round the corner from his apartment) at 39 rue Descartes, the very hotel where the poet Paul Verlaine (1844–96) died. Ignore the incorrect plaque.

Place de la Contrescarpe Rue Descartes runs south into place de la Contrescarpe (Place Monge), now a well-scrubbed square with four Judas trees and a fountain, but once a 'cesspool' (said Hemingway), especially Café des Amateurs at 2–4 place de la Contrescarpe, now Café Delmas (p222).

George Orwell's boarding house (Map p416; MPlace Monge) In 1928 George Orwell (1903–50) stayed in a cheap boarding house above 6 rue du Pot de Fer while working as a dishwasher. Read about it and the street, which he called 'rue du Coq d'Or' (Street of the Golden Rooster), in *Down and Out in Paris and London* (1933).

BONJOUR VIETNAM — VIETNAMESE €

Map p416 (01 43 54 78 04; 6 rue Thouin, 5e; mains €10-14; noon-3pm & 7-11pm Wed-Mon; MCardinal Lemoine) Stop by this lauded Vietnamese eatery for a bowl of *pho* (noodle soup with thin slices of rare beef, mint, anise and lime) or *bobun* (cold rice-noodle salad with marinated beef). There are only a handful of tables, so best to reserve.

CIEL — PATISSERIE €

Map p414 (www.patisserie-ciel.com; 3 rue Monge, 5e; cakes from €6; 10:30am-11pm Tue-Thu, to 1am Fri & Sat, to 5pm Sun; MMaubert-Mutualité) The minimalist wooden bar at this modern Japanese tearoom seats just eight, but the delicate teas and light and airy sponge cakes – cherry blossom, raspberry, vanilla – will take you right up to a high-end designer clad heaven. Evening brings savoury snacks from Sola (p220) and cocktails.

LA SALLE À MANGER — TRADITIONAL FRENCH €

Map p416 (01 55 43 91 99; 138 rue Mouffetard, 5e; mains €10-14; 8.30am-6.30pm; MCensier Daubenton) With a sunny pavement terrace beneath trees enviably placed at the foot of foodie street rue Mouffetard, the 'Dining Room' is prime real estate. Its 360-degree outlook – market stalls, fountain, church and garden with playground for tots – couldn't be prettier, and its salads, *tartines* (open-faced sandwiches), tarts and pastries ensure packed tables at breakfast, lunch and weekend brunch.

MACHU PICCHU — SOUTH AMERICAN €

Map p416 (01 43 26 13 13; 9 rue Royer-Collard, 5e; 3-course lunch menu €11.50, mains €10.80-15; noon-2.30pm & 7.30-10.30pm Mon-Sat; MCluny-La Sorbonne or RER Luxembourg) Locals adore this place. Going strong since the 1980s, it serves excellent Peruvian meat and seafood dishes as well as a bargain-basement lunch *menu* (set menu) and *plats du jour* (dishes of the day). Cash only.

TASHI DELEK — TIBETAN €

Map p416 (01 43 26 55 55; 4 rue des Fossés St-Jacques, 5e; menus from €11, mains €7.35-14; noon-2.30pm & 7.30-10.30pm Mon-Sat; MCardinal Lemoine or RER Luxembourg) Cheap, tasty Tibetan fare from *tsampa* (a roasted barley staple) to delicious *daril seu* (meatballs with garlic, ginger and rice) or *tselmok* (cheese and vegetable ravioli). Wash it down with traditional or salted-butter tea. Don't forget to say *tashi delek* upon entering – it means *bonjour* in Tibetan.

KOOTCHI — AFGHAN €

Map p414 (01 44 07 20 56; 40 rue du Cardinal Lemoine, 5e; lunch/dinner menus €9.50/16; noon-2.30pm & 7.30-10.30pm Mon-Sat; MCardinal Lemoine) Behind a sky-blue facade, carpets, traditional instruments and other jumble lend this Afghan restaurant a central-Asian caravanserai air. Specialities include *qhaboli palawo* (veal stew with nuts and spices); *dogh*, a drink similar to salted Indian lassi; and traditional *halwa* (sweet cake) perfumed with rose and cardamom.

Vegetarians keen to spice up their culinary life should go for the *borani palawo* (spicy vegetable stew) as a main course.

★LES PIPOS BISTRO €€

Map p414 (☎01 43 54 11 40; www.les-pipos.com; 2 rue de l'École Polytechnique, 5e; mains €13.90-26.90; ⊙8am-2am Mon-Sat; Ⓜ Maubert-Mutualité) A feast for the eyes and the senses, this *bar à vins* is above all worth a visit for its food. The bistro standards (boeuf bourguignon) and *charcuteries de terroir* (regional cold meats and sausages) are mouth-watering, as is the cheese board, which includes all the gourmet names (bleu d'Auvergne, St-Félicien, St-Marcellin). No credit cards.

★CAFÉ DE LA NOUVELLE MAIRIE BISTRO €€

Map p416 (19 rue des Fossés St-Jacques, 5e; mains €14-16; ⊙8am-midnight Mon-Fri; Ⓜ Cardinal-Lemoine) Shhhh…just around the corner from the Panthéon but hidden away on a small, fountained square, the narrow wine bar Café de la Nouvelle is a neighbourhood secret, serving blackboard-chalked natural wines by the glass and delicious seasonal bistro fare from oysters and ribs *(à la française)* to grilled lamb sausage over lentils.

★L'AGRUME NEOBISTRO €€

Map p416 (☎01 43 31 86 48; www.restaurant-lagrume.fr; 15 rue des Fossés St-Marcel, 5e; 2-/3-course lunch menus €22/25, dinner menu €45; ⊙noon-2.30pm & 7.30-10.30pm Tue-Sat; Ⓜ Censier Daubenton) Snagging a table at L'Agrume (meaning 'Citrus Fruit') can be tough; reserve several days ahead. The reward is watching chefs work with seasonal products in the open kitchen while you dine – at a table, bar stool or *comptoir* (counter) – at this pocket-size contemporary bistro on a little-known street on the Latin Quarter's southern fringe. Lunch is magnificent value and a real gourmet experience. Evening dining is an exquisite, no-choice *dégustation* (tasting) melody of five courses, different every day.

★DANS LES LANDES GASCOGNE €€

Map p416 (☎01 45 87 06 00; www.danslesiandes-maisaparis.com; 119bis rue Monge, 5e; tapas €8-16; ⊙noon-11pm; Ⓜ Censier Daubenton) Treat yourself to a trip to the Basque Country: Gascogne chef Julien Duboué presents his artful, tapas-size take on southwestern cuisine, with whimsical dishes that range from smoked duck with polenta and chili-smothered *xistoria* (Basque sausages) to truffled artichoke dip, duck neck confit and jars of foie gras. One of the few places in Paris to carry Basque wines.

L'AOC TRADITIONAL FRENCH €€

Map p414 (☎01 43 54 22 52; www.restoaoc.com; 14 rue des Fossés St-Bernard, 5e; 2-/3-course lunch menus €21/29, mains €19-36; ⊙noon-2.30pm & 7.30-10.30pm Tue-Sat; Ⓜ Cardinal Lemoine) *'Bistrot carnivore'* is the strapline of this ingenious restaurant concocted around France's most respected culinary products. The concept is Appellation d'Origine Contrôlée (AOC), meaning everything has been reared or produced according to strict guidelines. The result? Only the best! Choose between meaty favourites (steak tartare) or the rotisserie menu, ranging from roast chicken to suckling pig.

LES PAPILLES BISTRO €€

Map p416 (☎01 43 25 20 79; www.lespapillesparis.com; 30 rue Gay Lussac, 5e; 2-/3-course menus from €22/31; ⊙noon-2.30pm & 7-10pm Tue-Sat; Ⓜ Raspail or RER Luxembourg) This hybrid bistro, wine cellar and *épicerie* (specialist grocer) with sunflower-yellow facade is one of those fabulous Parisian dining experiences. Meals are served at simply dressed tables wedged beneath bottle-lined walls, and fare is market-driven: each weekday there's a different *marmite du marché* (market casserole). But what really sets it apart is its exceptional wine list.

It only seats around 15 people; reserve a few days in advance to guarantee a table. After your meal, stock your own *cave* (wine cellar) at Les Papilles' *cave à vin*.

LE PETIT PONTOISE BISTRO €€

Map p414 (☎01 43 29 25 20; 9 rue de Pontoise, 5e; mains €21-30; ⊙noon-2.30pm & 7.30-10.30pm; Ⓜ Maubert-Mutualité) Sit at a wooden table behind the lace curtains hiding you from the world and indulge in fantastic old-fashioned classics like *rognons de veau à l'ancienne* (calf kidneys), *boudin campagnard* (black pudding) and sweet apple purée or roast quail with dates. Dishes – like the decor – might seem simple, but you'll leave pledging to return.

MOSQUÉE DE PARIS NORTH AFRICAN €€
Map p416 (☎01 43 31 38 20; www.la-mosquee.com; 39 rue Geoffroy St-Hilaire, 5e; mains €15-26; ⏰noon-2.30pm & 7.30-10.30pm; Ⓜ Censier Daubenton or Place Monge) Dig into one of nine types of couscous, or choose a heaping *tajine* or meaty grill at this richly decorated, authentic-as-it-gets North African restaurant tucked within the walls of the city's art deco–Moorish mosque, or sip a sweet mint tea and nibble on a *pâtisserie orientale* between trees and chirping birds in the courtyard of the **tearoom** (⏰9am-11.30pm).

Feeling decadent? Book a *formule orientale* (€63), which includes a body scrub, 10-minute massage and a lounge in the *hammam* (p227) as well as lunch, mint tea and sweet pastry.

LE PRÉ VERRE BISTRO €€
Map p414 (☎01 43 54 59 47; www.lepreverre.com; 25 rue Thénard, 5e; lunch menu €14.50, mains €20; ⏰noon-2.30pm & 7.30-10.30pm Tue-Sat; 👶; Ⓜ Maubert-Mutualité) Noisy, busy and buzzing, the Delacourcelle brothers' jovial bistro plunges diners into the heart of a Parisian's Paris. At lunchtime join the flock and go for the fabulous-value *formule dejeuner* (lunch menu), which might be curried chickpea soup, guinea-fowl thigh spiced with ginger on a bed of red and green cabbage, a glass of wine and loads of ultracrusty, ultrachewy baguette (the best).

Desserts mix Asian spices with traditional French equally well, thanks to chef Philippe's extended sojourns in China, Malaysia, Japan and India. Marc is the man behind the interesting wine list, which features France's small independent *vignerons* (wine producers).

TERROIR PARISIEN BISTRO €€
Map p414 (☎01 44 31 54 54; www.yannick-alleno.com; 20 rue Saint-Victor, 5e; mains €19-25; ⏰noon-2.30pm & 7-10.30pm; Ⓜ Maubert-Mutualité or Cardinal Lemoine) A good concept (a focus on local dishes and ingredients) and an airy, modern interior give Terroir Parisien a nice one-two punch. You can expect contemporary interpretations of typically Parisian fare, such as deconstructed onion soup or a perfect disk of blood sausage over creamy puréed potatoes. A few quick bites (eg croque monsieur) are also served. Do note, portions are small.

LENGUÉ JAPANESE €€
Map p414 (☎01 46 33 75 10; http://lengue.fr; 31 rue de la Parcheminerie, 5e; lunch/dinner €18/40; ⏰noon-3pm Tue-Sat, 7-11pm Tue-Sun; Ⓜ Cluny-La Sorbonne) This modish Japanese *izakaya* bar is incongruously set in medieval French surrounds, with exposed wooden rafters, old stone walls and a downstairs cellar. In the evening, expect communal tapas-style dishes (vegetable dumplings, prawn tempura) accompanied by wine and sake; for lunch, it's one hot main and several cold sides, served bento (lunchbox) style. Despite the touristy location, it's very hip. Reserve.

ANAHUACALLI MEXICAN €€
Map p414 (☎01 43 26 10 20; www.anahuacalli.fr; 30 rue des Bernardins, 5e; mains €17-22; ⏰7.30-10.30pm daily, noon-2.30pm Sun; Ⓜ Maubert-Mutualité) Mexican food is riding a wave of popularity in Paris and this upmarket restaurant – behind a discreet rosemary-coloured facade, with a sparingly decorated interior lined with mirrors and statuettes – offers some of the best. Authentic enchiladas, tamales and mole poblano are all elegantly presented; fish aficionados should try the *pescado à la veracruzana* (fish of the day flambéed with tequila).

LE COUPE-CHOU TRADITIONAL FRENCH €€
Map p414 (☎01 46 33 68 69; www.lecoupechou.com; 9 & 11 rue de Lanneau, 5e; 2-/3-course menus €27/33; ⏰noon-2.30pm & 7.30-10.30pm; Ⓜ Maubert-Mutualité) This maze of candlelit rooms inside a vine-clad 17th-century townhouse is overwhelmingly romantic. Ceilings are beamed, furnishings are antique, and background classical music mingles with the intimate chatter of diners. As in the days when Marlene Dietrich dined here, advance reservations are essential.

Timeless French dishes include Burgundy snails, steak tartare and bœuf bourguignon, finished off with fabulous cheeses sourced from *fromagerie* (cheese shop) Quatrehomme and a silken crème brûlée.

Le Coupe-Chou, incidentally, has nothing to do with *chou* (cabbage); rather it's named after the barber's razor once wielded with a deft hand in one of its seven rooms.

★SOLA FUSION €€€
Map p414 (☎dinner 01 43 29 59 04, lunch 09 65 01 73 68; www.restaurant-sola.com; 12 rue de l'Hôtel

Colbert, 5e; lunch/dinner €48/98; ⌚noon-2pm & 7-10pm Tue-Sat; Ⓜ St-Michel) For serious gourmands, Sola is arguably the Latin Quarter's proverbial brass ring. Pedigreed chef Hiroki Yoshitake combines French technique with Japanese sensibility, resulting in gorgeous signature creations (such as miso-marinated foie gras on *feuille de brick* served on a slice of tree trunk). The artful presentations and attentive service make this a great choice for a romantic meal – go for the full experience and reserve a table in the Japanese dining room downstairs.

LE BUISSON ARDENT MODERN FRENCH €€€

Map p416 (☎01 43 54 93 02; www.lebuissonardent.fr; 25 rue Jussieu, 5e; lunch/dinner menu €28/41; ⌚noon-2.30pm & 7.30-10.30pm; Ⓜ Jussieu) Housed in a former coach house, this time-worn bistro (murals in the front room date to the 1920s) serves classy, exciting French fare, from sea bass with grilled fennel and chorizo to spare ribs with olive paste, polenta and onion jam.

MOISSONNIER LYONNAIS €€€

Map p414 (☎01 43 29 87 65; 28 rue des Fossés St-Bernard, 5e; lunch mains €17-26, 4-/6-course dinner menus €75/115; ⌚noon-2.30pm & 7.30-10.30pm Tue-Sat; Ⓜ Cardinal Lemoine) It's Lyon, not Paris, that French gourmets venerate as the French food capital. Take one bite of a big, fat *andouillette* (pig-intestine sausage), *tablier de sapeur* (breaded, fried stomach), traditional *quenelles* (dumplings) or *boudin noir aux pommes* (black pudding with apples) and you'll realise why. A perfect reflection of one of France's most unforgettable regional cuisines.

LA TOUR D'ARGENT GASTRONOMIC €€€

Map p414 (☎01 43 54 23 31; www.latourdargent.com; 15 quai de la Tournelle, 5e; lunch menus €65, dinner menus €170-190; ⌚noon-2.30pm & 7.30-10.30pm Tue-Sat; Ⓜ Cardinal Lemoine or Pont Marie) The venerable 'Silver Tower' is famous for its *caneton* (duckling), rooftop garden with glimmering Notre Dame views and a fabulous history harking back to 1582 – from Henry III's inauguration of the first fork in France to inspiration for the winsome animated film *Ratatouille*. Its wine cellar is one of Paris' best; dining is dressy and exceedingly fine.

Reserve eight to 10 days ahead for lunch, three weeks ahead for dinner – and don't miss its chocolate and coconut sphere with banana and lime sorbet for dessert. Buy fine food and accessories in its **boutique** (Map p414; ⌚11:15am-7:15pm Tue-Sat) directly across the street.

DRINKING & NIGHTLIFE

Rive Gauche romantics, well-heeled cafe society types and students by the gallon drink in the 5e *arrondissement*, where old-but-good recipes, nostalgic formulas and a deluge of early-evening happy hours ensure a quintessential Parisian soirée. It's not ground-breaking but it's all good fun.

★LE VERRE À PIED CAFE

Map p416 (http://leverreapied.fr; 118bis rue Mouffetard, 5e; ⌚9am-9pm Tue-Sat, 9.30am-4pm Sun; Ⓜ Censier Daubenton) This *café-tabac* is a pearl of a place where little has changed since 1870. Its nicotine-hued mirrored wall, moulded cornices and original bar make it part of a dying breed, but the place oozes the charm, glamour and romance of an old Paris everyone loves, including stall holders from the rue Mouffetard market who yo-yo in and out. Contemporary photography and art adorn one wall. Lunch is a busy, lively affair, and live music quickens the pulse a couple of evenings a week.

★CAFÉ PANIS CAFE

Map p414 (21 quai de Montebello, 5e; ⌚7am-midnight; 📶; Ⓜ St-Michel) Snag a sunlit table to write your postcards home at this busy, timeless cafe facing Notre Dame. Coffee, tea and inexpensive French comfort food – croque monsieur, *magret de canard* – make it an excellent place to linger and refuel.

★CURIO PARLOR COCKTAIL CLUB COCKTAIL BAR

Map p414 (www.curioparlor.com; 16 rue des Bernardins, 5e; ⌚7pm-2am Mon-Thu, to 4am Fri-Sun; Ⓜ Maubert-Mutualité) Run by the same switched-on, chilled-out team as the Experimental Cocktail Club, this hybrid bar-club looks to the interwar *années folles* (crazy years) of 1920s Paris, London and New York for inspiration. Its racing -green facade with a simple brass plaque on the door is the height of discretion. Go to its Facebook page to find out which party is happening when.

LE PUB ST-HILAIRE PUB

Map p414 (2 rue Valette, 5e; ⏲3pm-2am Mon-Thu, 3pm-4am Fri, 4pm-4am Sat, 4pm-midnight Sun; Ⓜ Maubert-Mutualité) 'Buzzing' fails to do justice to the pulsating vibe inside this student-loved pub. Generous happy hours last several hours and the place is kept packed with a trio of pool tables, board games, music on two floors, hearty bar food and various gimmicks to rev up the party crowd (a metre of cocktails, 'be your own barman' etc).

L'ACADÉMIE DE LA BIÈRE PUB

Map p416 (www.academie-biere.com; 88bis bd de Port Royal, 5e; ⏲10am-2am Sun-Thu, to 3am Fri & Sat; Ⓜ Vavin or RER Pont Royal) Serious students of Belgian beer should head to this 'beer academy' to try its 12 on tap or choose from more than 300 bottled varieties, including Trappist (monk-made) beers like prized Westmalle, abbey beers including Grimbergen and Leffe, fruit beers, and Cantillon *gueuze* (double-fermented Lambic beer made in Brussels).

In true Belgian tradition, it also serves *moules* (mussels), delivered and cleaned each morning, cooked in creative ways including with mustard, curry or roquefort, and served continuously.

LE VIEUX CHÊNE BAR

Map p416 (69 rue Mouffetard, 5e; ⏲4pm-2am Sun-Thu, to 5am Fri & Sat; Ⓜ Place Monge) This rue Mouffetard institution is reckoned to be Paris' oldest bar. Indeed, a revolutionary circle met here in 1848 and it was a popular *bal musette* (dancing club) in the late 19th and early 20th centuries. These days it's a student favourite, especially during happy hour (4pm to 9pm Tuesday to Sunday, and from 4pm until closing on Monday). Resident DJs mix it up on Friday and Saturday nights.

CAFÉ DELMAS CAFE

Map p416 (www.cafedelmasparis.com; 2 place de la Contrescarpe, 5e; ⏲8am-2am Sun-Thu, to 4am Fri & Sat; 📶; Ⓜ Place Monge) Enviably situated on tree-studded place de la Contrescarpe, the Delmas is a hot spot for chilling over *un café*/cappuccino or all-day breakfast. Cosy up beneath overhead heaters outside to soak up the street atmosphere or snuggle up between books in the library-style interior – awash with students from the nearby universities. If you're looking for the bathrooms, note that Jacqueline is for women, Jacques for men.

Local Life
A Stroll Along Rue Mouffetard

Originally a Roman road, the sloping, cobbled rue Mouffetard acquired its name in the 18th century, when the now underground River Bièvre became the communal waste disposal for local tanners and wood pulpers. The odours gave rise to the name Mouffette (skunk), which evolved into Mouffetard. The street is now filled with market stalls, cheap eateries and lively bars.

1 Market Shopping

Today the aromas on 'La Mouffe', as it's nicknamed by locals, are infinitely more enticing. Grocers, butchers, fishmongers and other food purveyors set their goods out on street stalls during the **Marché Mouffetard** (Map p416; ⏲8am-7.30pm Tue-Sat, to noon Sun; Ⓜ Censier Daubenton).

2 Fine Cheeses

You won't even have to worry about the aromas if you're taking home the scrumptious cheeses from fromagerie **Androuet** (Map p416; http://androuet.com; 134 rue Mouffetard, 5e; ⏲9.30am-1pm & 4-7.30pm Tue-Fri, 9.30am-7.30pm Sat, to 1.30pm Sun; Ⓜ Censier Daubenton) – all of its cheeses can be vacuum-packed for free. (Be sure to look up to see the beautiful murals on the building's façade!)

3 Delicious Deli

Stuffed olives, capsicums and marinated eggplant are among the picnic goodies at gourmet Italian deli **Delizius** (Map p416; 134 rue Mouffetard, 5e; ⏲9.30am-8pm Tue-Sat, 9am-2pm Sun; Ⓜ Censier Daubenton), which also sells ready-to-eat hot meals and fresh and dried pasta.

4 Movie Time

Even locals find it easy to miss the small doorway leading to cinema **L'Epée de Bois** (Map p416; 100 rue Mouffetard, 5e; Ⓜ Censier Daubenton), which screens both art-house flicks and big-budget blockbusters.

The food market on Rue Mouffetard

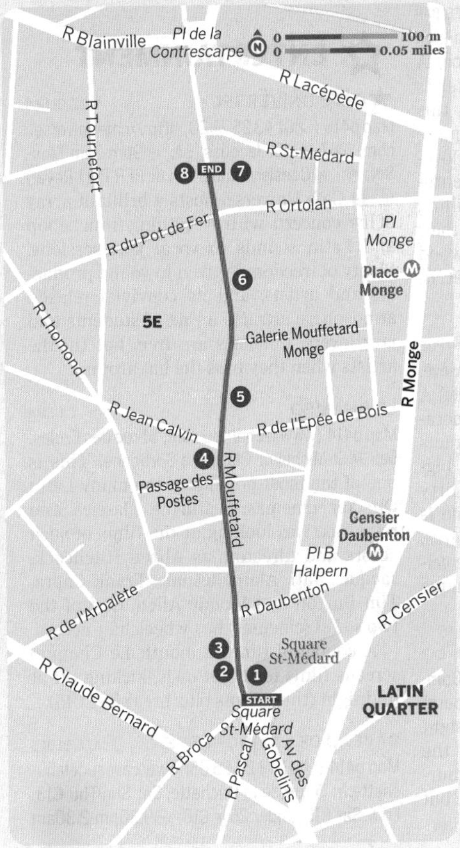

❺ Sweet Treats

Light, luscious macaroons in flavours like jasmine, raspberry and blackcurrant, and a mouth-watering range of chocolates by three *maîtres chocolatiers* (master chocolate-makers) – Fabrice Gillotte, Jacques Bellanger and Patrice Chapoare – are laid out like jewels at **Chocolats Mococha** (Map p416; www.chocolatsmococha.com; 89 rue Mouffetard, 5e; ⏲11am-8pm; Ⓜ Censier Daubenton).

❻ Apéro at Le Vieux Chêne

Host to revolutionary meetings in 1848, these days Le Vieux Chêne is a student favourite, especially during happy hour (4pm to 9pm Tuesday to Sunday, and from 4pm until closing on Monday).

❼ Ice Cream

All that walking and peering in at gourmet food shops will no doubt leave you hungry, which means it's time for a stop at **Gelati d'Alberto** (Map p416; 45 rue Mouffetard, 5e; ⏲noon-midnight; Ⓜ Place Monge), where Italian ice-cream wizards shape your cone into a two-flavour (or more!) flower.

❽ Crêpes at Chez Nicos

If you prefer savoury to sweet or hot to cold, check the signboard outside crêpe artist Nicos' unassuming little shop **Chez Nicos** (Map p416; 44 rue Mouffetard, 5e; crêpes €3-6; ⏲noon-2am; 👪; Ⓜ Place Monge) – it chalks up dozens of fillings. Ask for his masterpiece, *la crêpe du chef*, stuffed with eggplant, feta, mozzarella, lettuce, tomatoes and onions. There's a handful of tables inside; otherwise head to a nearby park.

LE CROCODILE BAR

Map p416 (6 rue Royer-Collard, 5e; ⏲6pm-2am Mon-Sat; Ⓜ Odén or RER Luxembourg) This green-shuttered bar has been dispensing affordable cocktails (more than 200 on the list) since 1966. The '70s were 'epic' here, and the dream kicks on well into the new millennium. Arrive late for a truly eclectic crowd, including lots of students, and an atmosphere that can go from quiet tippling to raucous revelry. Hours can vary.

LE PIANO VACHE BAR

Map p414 (www.lepianovache.com; 8 rue Laplace, 5e; ⏲noon-4pm Mon-Fri, 7pm-2am Mon-Sat; Ⓜ Maubert-Mutualité) Down the hill from the Panthéon, this bar is covered in old posters above old couches and drenched in 1970s and '80s rock ambience. Effortlessly underground and a real student fave, it has bands and DJs playing mainly rock, plus some goth, reggae and pop.

CAVE LA BOURGOGNE CAFE, BAR

Map p416 (144 rue Mouffetard, 5e; ⏲7am-2am Mon-Sat, to 11pm Sun; Ⓜ Censier Daubenton) A prime spot for lapping up rue Mouffetard's contagious 'saunter-all-day' spirit, this neighbourhood hang-out sits on square St-Médard, one of the Latin Quarter's loveliest, with flower-bedecked fountain, centuries-old church and market stalls spilling across one side. Inside, old ladies and their pet dogs meet for coffee around dark wood tables alongside a local wine-sipping set. In summer everything spills outside.

LE VIOLON DINGUE PUB

Map p414 (46 rue de la Montagne Ste-Geneviève, 5e; ⏲7pm-5am Tue-Sat; Ⓜ Maubert-Mutualité) A loud, lively bar adopted by revolving generations of students, the 'Crazy Violin' attracts lots of young English-speakers with big-screen sports shown upstairs and the flirty 'Dingue Lounge' downstairs. The name is a pun on the expression *le violon d'Ingres*, meaning 'hobby' in French because the celebrated painter Jean-Auguste-Dominique Ingres played fiddle in his spare time.

LE PANTALON BAR

Map p416 (7 rue Royer-Collard, 5e; ⏲5.30pm-2am; Ⓜ Cluny-La Sorbonne or RER Luxembourg) Ripped vinyl seats, coloured-glass light fittings and old stickers plastered on the walls make this rockin' little bar a favourite hang-out for those with little change but lots of heart.

LE MAUZAC WINE BAR

Map p416 (7 rue de l'Abbé de l'Epée, 5e; ⏲noon-2.30pm & 7.30-10.30pm Mon-Sat; Ⓜ Place Monge or RER Luxembourg) Fronted by a leafy garden terrace, this wine bar has street lamps and stone floors indoors, giving it the atmosphere of a Parisian street – although the wine bottles lining the walls are a greater indication of its raison d'être. Some 60 varieties of red, white and rosé wines are available by the glass; food includes Landes foie gras and Breton oysters.

TEA CADDY TEAROOM

Map p414 (14 rue St-Julien le Pauvre, 5e; ⏲11am-7pm Sat-Wed, to 11pm Thu & Fri; Ⓜ St-Michel) Arguably the most English of the 'English' tearooms in Paris, this institution, founded in 1928, is a fine place to break for a slice of quiche (€10) or a nice genteel tea (€6) with a Devon scone after a tour of nearby Notre Dame, Ste-Chapelle or the Conciergerie.

☆ ENTERTAINMENT

★CAFÉ UNIVERSEL JAZZ, BLUES

Map p416 (☎01 43 25 74 20; http://cafeuniversel.com; 267 rue St-Jacques, 5e; ⏲9pm-2am Mon-Sat; 📶; Ⓜ Censier Daubenton or RER Port Royal) FREE Café Universel hosts a brilliant array of live concerts with everything from bebop and Latin sounds to vocal jazz sessions. Plenty of freedom is given to young producers and artists, and its convivial relaxed atmosphere attracts a mix of students and jazz lovers. Concerts are free, but tip the artists when they pass the hat around.

LE CHAMPO CINEMA

Map p414 (www.lechampo.com; 51 rue des Écoles, 5e; Ⓜ St-Michel or Cluny–La Sorbonne) This is one of the most popular of the many Latin Quarter cinemas, featuring classics and retrospectives looking at the films of such actors and directors as Alfred Hitchcock, Jacques Tati, Alain Resnais, Frank Capra, Tim Burton and Woody Allen. One of the two *salles* (cinemas) has wheelchair access.

A couple of times a month Le Champo screens films for night owls, kicking off at midnight (three films plus breakfast €15).

CAVEAU DE LA HUCHETTE JAZZ, BLUES

Map p414 (☎01 43 26 65 05; www.caveaudelahuchette.fr; 5 rue de la Huchette, 5e; Sun-Thu €13, Fri & Sat €15, under 25yr €10; ⏲9.30pm-2.30am

Sun-Wed, to 4am Thu-Sat; Ⓜ St-Michel) Housed in a medieval *caveau* (cellar) used as a courtroom and torture chamber during the Revolution, this club is where virtually all the jazz greats have played since the end of WWII. It attracts its fair share of tourists, but the atmosphere can be more electric than at the more serious jazz clubs. Sessions start at 10pm.

LE PETIT JOURNAL ST-MICHEL JAZZ, BLUES

Map p416 (☎01 43 26 28 59; www.petitjournal-saintmichel.com; 71 bd St-Michel, 5e; admission incl 1 drink €20, with dinner €49-53; ⏲Mon-Sat; Ⓜ Cluny-La Sorbonne or RER Luxembourg) Classic jazz concerts kick off at 9.15pm in the atmospheric downstairs cellar of this sophisticated jazz venue across from the Jardin du Luxembourg. Everything ranging from Dixieland and vocals to big band and swing sets patrons' toes tapping. Dinner is served at 8pm.

LE CAVEAU DES OUBLIETTES JAZZ, BLUES

Map p414 (☎01 46 34 24 09; www.caveaudesoubliettes.fr; 52 rue Galande, 5e; ⏲5pm-4am; Ⓜ St-Michel) From the 16th-century ground-floor pub, descend to the 12th-century dungeon for jazz, blues and funk concerts and jam sessions (from 10pm).

ÉGLISE ST-JULIEN LE PAUVRE CLASSICAL

Map p414 (☎01 42 26 00 00; www.concertinparis.com; 1 rue St-Julien le Pauvre, 5e; Ⓜ St-Michel) Piano recitals (Chopin, Liszt) are staged two evenings a week in one of the oldest churches in Paris.

SHOPPING

Bookworms in particular will love this part of the Left Bank, which is home to some wonderful bookshops. Other student-frequented shops include camping stores, comic shops, old-school music shops where collectors browse for hours, and cheap, colourful homewares stores, interspersed with the occasional *droguerie-quincaillerie* (hardware store) – easily spotted by the jumble of laundry baskets, buckets etc piled on the pavement in front.

★SHAKESPEARE & COMPANY BOOKS

Map p414 (www.shakespeareandcompany.com; 37 rue de la Bûcherie, 5e; ⏲10am-11pm Mon-Fri, from 11am Sat & Sun; Ⓜ St-Michel) This bookshop is the stuff of legends. A kind of spell descends as you enter, weaving between nooks and crannies overflowing with new and secondhand English-language books. The original shop (12 rue l'Odéon, 6e; closed by the Nazis in 1941) was run by Sylvia Beach and became the meeting point for Hemingway's 'Lost Generation'. Readings by emerging and illustrious authors take place at 7pm most Mondays; it also hosts workshops and festivals.

American-born George Whitman opened the present incarnation in 1951, attracting a beat-poet clientele, and scores of authors have since passed through its doors. In 2006 Whitman was awarded the Officier des Arts et Lettres by the French Minister of Culture, recognising 'significant contribution to the enrichment of the French cultural inheritance'. Whitman died in 2011, aged 98; he is buried in division 73 of Cimetière du Père Lachaise. Today his daughter, Sylvia Beach Whitman, maintains Shakespeare & Company's serendipitous magic. It's fabled for nurturing writers, and at night its couches turn into beds where writers stay in exchange for stacking shelves.

CROCODISC MUSIC

Map p414 (www.crocodisc.com; 40 & 42 rue des Écoles, 5e; ⏲11am-7pm Tue-Sat; Ⓜ Maubert-Mutualité) Music might be more accessible than ever before thanks to iPods, iPads and phones, but for many it will never replace rummaging through racks for treasures. New and secondhand CDs and vinyl discs at 40 rue des Écoles span world music, rap, reggae, salsa, soul and disco, while No 42 has pop, rock, punk, new wave, Electro and soundtracks.

Its nearby sister shop **Crocojazz** (Map p414; 64 rue de la Montagne Ste-Geneviève, 5e; ⏲11am-1pm & 2-7pm Tue-Sat; Ⓜ Maubert-Mutualité) specialises in jazz, blues, gospel and timeless crooners, with books and DVDs as well as recordings.

ALBUM COMICS

Map p414 (www.album.fr; 67 bd St-Germain, 5e; ⏲10am-8pm Mon-Sat, noon-7pm Sun; Ⓜ Cluny-La Sorbonne) Album specialises in *bandes dessinées* (comics and graphic novels), which have an enormous following in France, with everything from Tintin and Babar to erotic comics and the latest Japanese manga. Serious comic collectors – and anyone excited by Harry Potter

LOCAL KNOWLEDGE

LES BOUQUINISTES

With some 3km of wagon-green boxes lining the Seine, more than 300,000 used books and a handful of rare Van Gogh masterpieces (yours for only €4!), Paris' **bouquinistes** (Map p414; ⌚11.30am-sunset), or used-book sellers, are as integral to the cityscape as Notre Dame. The *bouquinistes* have been in business since the 16th century, when they were itinerant peddlers selling their wares on Parisian bridges – back then their sometimes subversive (eg Protestant) materials would get them in trouble with the authorities. By 1859 the city had finally wised up: official licenses were issued, space was rented (10m of railing) and eventually the permanent green boxes were installed.

Today, *bouquinistes* (the official count ranges from 217 to 240) are allowed to have four boxes, only one of which can be used to sell souvenirs. You'll find them on the Left Bank from quai Voltaire to quai de la Tournelle, and on the Right Bank from Pont Marie to Quai du Louvre. Look hard enough and you just might find some real treasures: old comic books, forgotten first editions, maps, stamps, erotica and prewar newspapers – as in centuries past, it's all there, waiting to be rediscovered.

wands, Star Wars, Superman and other superhero figurines and T-shirts (you know who you are!) – shouldn't miss it.

FROMAGERIE LAURENT DUBOIS FOOD, DRINK
Map p414 (www.fromageslaurentdubois.fr; 47ter bd St-Germain, 5e; ⌚8.30am-7.30pm Tue-Sat, to 1pm Sun; Ⓜ Maubert-Mutualité) One of the best *fromageries* in Paris, this cheese-lover's nirvana is filled with to-die-for delicacies such as St-Félicien with Périgord truffles. Rare, limited-production cheeses include blue Termignon and Tarentaise goat's cheese. All are appropriately cellared in warm, humid or cold environments. There's also a 15e branch (p271).

AU VIEUX CAMPEUR OUTDOOR EQUIPMENT
Map p414 (www.auvieuxcampeur.fr; 48 rue des Écoles, 5e; ⌚11am-7.30pm Mon-Wed, Fri & Sat, to 9pm Thu; Ⓜ Maubert-Mutualité or Cluny-La Sorbonne) This outdoor store seems to have colonised the Latin Quarter, with some 25 different outlets scattered about, each devoted to your favourite sport: climbing, skiing, diving, camping, biking and so on. While it's a great resource if you need any gear, the many boutiques make shopping something of a treasure hunt – especially as many outlets change what they sell with the seasons.

Ask for directions to other branches at this flagship store (or any other that you come across), which generally sells mountaineering equipment.

Paris' most complete range of maps and guides is at 2 rue de Latran.

ABBEY BOOKSHOP BOOKS
Map p414 (☎01 46 33 16 24; 29 rue de la Parcheminerie, 5e; ⌚10am-7pm Mon-Sat; Ⓜ St-Michel or Cluny-La Sorbonne) In a heritage-listed townhouse, this welcoming Canadian-run bookshop serves free coffee (sweetened with maple syrup) to sip while you browse tens of thousands of new and used books, and organises literary events and countryside hikes.

MAGIE GAMES, HOBBIES
Map p414 (☎01 43 54 13 63; www.mayette.com; 8 rue des Carmes, 5e; ⌚1-8pm Mon-Sat; Ⓜ Maubert-Mutualité) One of a kind, this 1808-established magic shop is said to be the world's oldest. Since 1991 it's been in the hands of world-famous magic pro Dominique Duvivier. Professional and hobbyist magicians flock here to discuss king sandwiches, reverse assemblies, false cuts and other card tricks with him and his daughter, Alexandra. Should you want to learn the tricks of the trade, Duvivier has magic courses up his sleeve.

LIBRAIRIE EYROLLES BOOKS
Map p414 (www.eyrolles.com; 61 bd St-Germain, 5e; ⌚9.30am-7.30pm Mon-Fri, to 8pm Sat; Ⓜ Maubert-Mutualité) Art, design, architecture, dictionaries and kids' books are the mainstay of this large bookshop with titles in English and stacks of browsing space.

For maps, guides and travel lit hop across the street to its **Librairie de Voyage** (Map p414; 63 bd St-Germain, 5e; ⌚9.30am-7.30pm Mon-Fri, to 8pm Sat; Ⓜ Maubert Mutualité).

MARCHÉ MAUBERT — MARKET

Map p414 (place Maubert, 5e; ⏲7am-2.30pm Tue, Thu & Sat; Ⓜ Maubert-Mutualité) The Left Bank's bourgeois bohemian soul lives on at this colourful street market. Expect the usual line of tempting market fare, though it doesn't come cheap.

MARCHÉ MONGE — MARKET

Map p416 (place Monge, 5e; ⏲7am-2pm Wed, Fri & Sun; Ⓜ Place Monge) The open-air Marché Monge is laden with wonderful cheeses, baked goods and a host of other temptations.

SPORTS & ACTIVITIES

HAMMAM DE LA MOSQUÉE DE PARIS — SPA

Map p416 (☎01 43 31 38 20; www.la-mosquee.com; 39 rue Geoffroy St-Hilaire, 5e; admission/spa package €18/from €43; ⏲10am-9pm Wed-Mon; Ⓜ Censier Daubenton or Place Monge) Massages at this atmospheric *hammam* (Turkish steambath) cost a little over €1 a minute and come in 10-, 20- or 30-minute bookings. The exfoliating body scrub is generally regarded as an integral part of the experience, so you may as well opt for one of the spa packages. There are also lunch deals at the restaurant (p220). Bring a swimsuit but hire a towel/dressing gown (€4/5). Women only, and no children under 12.

BOWLING MOUFFETARD — BOWLING

Map p416 (☎01 43 31 09 35; www.bowling-mouffetard.abcsalles.com; 73 rue Mouffetard, 5e; games €4.90, shoes €2; ⏲3pm-2am Mon-Fri, 10am-2am Sat & Sun; Ⓜ Place Monge) Intimate, friendly alley with eight lanes. There's a separate entrance off rue Gracieuse, though it was reserved for deliveries at last check.

PISCINE PONTOISE — SWIMMING

Map p414 (☎01 55 42 77 88; http://piscine.equipement.paris.fr; 19 rue de Pontoise, 5e; adult/concession €4.80/2.90; ⏲hours vary; Ⓜ Maubert-Mutualité) A beautiful art deco–style indoor pool in the heart of the Latin Quarter. An €11.10 evening ticket (from 8pm) covers entry to the pool, gym and sauna. It has shorter hours during term time check times online.

St-Germain & Les Invalides

ST-GERMAIN | LES INVALIDES

Neighbourhood Top Five

❶ Revelling in a wealth of world-famous impressionist masterpieces and art-nouveau architecture at the glorious **Musée d'Orsay** (p230).

❷ Sprinting, skating, cycling, bar-hopping or just Zenning out along the riverside promenade **Les Berges de Seine** (p240).

❸ Indulging in an exquisitely Parisian moment in the sculpture-filled gardens of the **Musée Rodin** (p236).

❹ Feasting your eyes on the fantastical food displays at **La Grande Épicerie de Paris** (p252).

❺ Visiting Napoléon's elaborate tomb in the monumental **Hôtel des Invalides** (p237) complex.

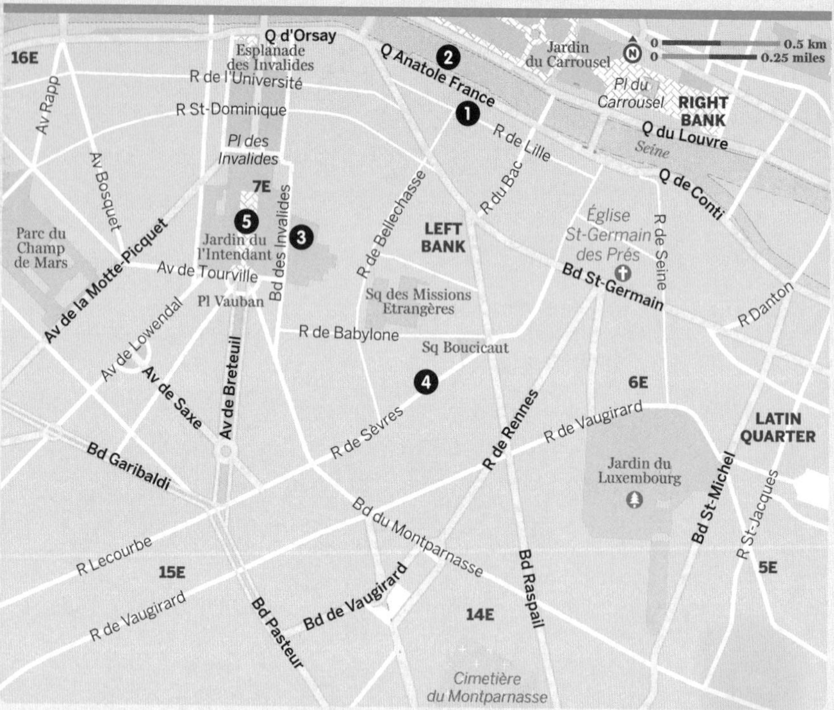

For more detail of this area see Map p418 and p422

Explore: St-Germain & Les Invalides

Despite gentrification since its early-20th-century bohemian days, there remains a startling cinematic quality to this soulful part of the Left Bank where artists, writers, actors and musicians cross paths and *la vie germanopratine* (St-Germain life) is *belle*.

This is one of those neighbourhoods whose very fabric is an attraction in itself, so allow plenty of time to stroll its side streets and stop at its fabled literary cafes, prêt-à-porter stores, gourmet shops, grand department store Le Bon Marché, and its vast white spaces showcasing interior design. In between, view Delacroix' works at the Église St-Sulpice and his former studio, the Musée National Eugène Delacroix, linger in the masterpiece-filled sculpture garden of the Musée Rodin, and be moved by the handwritten letters and annotations of renowned scientists, musicians, artists, authors and other historical figures at the Musée des Lettres et Manuscrits.

Entry to the Musée d'Orsay is cheaper in the late afternoon, so it's an ideal time to check out its breathtaking collections, before dining in the area's stylish restaurants and swizzling cocktails at its bars.

Local Life

➡ **Park Life** To see Parisians at play, visit the city's most popular park, the beautiful Jardin du Luxembourg (p234), a must-stroll, particularly at weekends.

➡ **Market Life** Street markets where locals stock up on bountiful fresh produce include Marché Raspail (p247) and rue Cler (p247).

➡ **Fashion Finds** Scour the racks for designer cast-offs at St-Germain's secondhand boutiques.

Getting There & Away

➡ **Metro** This area is well served by metro and RER. Get off at metro stations St-Germain des Prés, Mabillon or Odéon for its busy bd St-Germain heart. RER line C shadows the Seine along the Left Bank and is a fast way to get from St-Michel to the Musée d'Orsay.

➡ **Bicycle** Handy Vélib' stations include 141 bd St-Germain, 6e; opposite 2 bd Raspail, 6e; and 62 rue de Lille, 7e.

➡ **Boat** Batobus boats dock by quai Malaquais for St-Germain des Prés and quai de Solférino for the Musée d'Orsay.

Lonely Planet's Top Tip

Particularly around the Seine, in an unfortunately all-too-common ruse, scammers pretend to 'find' a gold ring (after subtly dropping it on the ground) and offer it to you as a diversionary tactic while they surreptitiously reach into your pockets or bags. Variations include offering to sell you the ring for an outrageous price, or having the ring's 'owner' arrive and demand compensation. Don't fall for it!

Best Places to Eat

➡ Restaurant David Toutain (p248)

➡ Bouillon Racine (p243)

➡ Semilla (p244)

➡ JSFP Traiteur (p241)

➡ Cuisine de Bar (p241)

For reviews, see p241 ➡

Best Places to Drink

➡ Les Deux Magots (p249)

➡ Au Sauvignon (p249)

➡ Coutume (p251)

➡ Castor Club (p249)

For reviews, see p248 ➡

Best Churches

➡ Église St-Germain des Prés (p238)

➡ Église St-Sulpice (p238)

➡ Basilique Ste-Clotilde (p240)

➡ Chapelle Notre Dame de la Medaille Miraculeuse (p239)

For reviews, see p238 ➡

TOP SIGHT
MUSÉE D'ORSAY

The home of France's national collection from the impressionist, postimpressionist and art-nouveau movements is, appropriately, the glorious former Gare d'Orsay. The railway station is itself an art-nouveau masterpiece designed by competition-winning architect Victor Laloux. Transforming the languishing building into the country's premier showcase for art from 1848 to 1914 was the grand project of former president Valéry Giscard d'Estaing, who signed off on it in 1977. The museum opened its doors in 1986, with a roll call of instantly recognisable works from French and international masters.

Far from resting on its laurels, the Musée d'Orsay's recent renovations incorporate a re-energised layout and increased exhibition space. Rather than being lost in a sea of white, prized paintings now gleam from richly coloured walls that create an intimate, stately-home-like atmosphere, with high-tech illumination literally casting the masterpieces in a new light.

For a thorough introduction to the museum, 90-minute 'Masterpieces of the Musée d'Orsay' guided tours (€6) in English generally run at least once a day from Tuesday to Saturday; 90-minute 'Nineteenth-Century Art' tours (€6) are also available. Check the website for seasonal departure times. Kids under 13 aren't permitted on tours.

DON'T MISS...

- The building
- Painting collections
- Decorative-arts collections
- Sculptures
- Graphic-arts collections

PRACTICALITIES

- Map p422
- www.musee-orsay.fr
- 62 rue de Lille, 7e
- adult/child €11/free
- 9.30am-6pm Tue, Wed & Fri-Sun, to 9.45pm Thu
- M Assemblée Nationale or RER Musée d'Orsay

Photography of all kinds (including from mobile phones) is forbidden to avoid crowd bottlenecks. If you want something more tangible than memories to take with you, there's an excellent book- and gift shop.

Even on its completion, just in time for the 1900 Exposition Universelle, painter Edouard Detaille declared that the new station looked like a Palais des Beaux Arts. But although it had all the mod-cons of the day – including luggage lifts and passenger elevators – by 1939 the increasing electrification of the rail network meant the platforms were too short for mainline trains, and within a few years all rail services ceased.

The station was used as a mailing centre during WWII, and in 1962 Orson Welles filmed Kafka's *The Trial* in the then-abandoned building. Fortunately, it was saved from being demolished and replaced with a hotel complex by a Historical Monument listing in 1973, before the government set about establishing the palatial museum.

Paintings

Top of every visitor's must-see list is the world's largest collection of impressionist and post-impressionist art. Just some of its highlights include Manet's *On the Beach* and *Woman with Fans;* Monet's gardens at Giverny and *Rue Montorgueil, Paris, Festival of June 30, 1878;* Cézanne's card players, *Green Apples* and *Blue Vase;* Renoir's *Ball at the Moulin de la Galette* and *Young Girls at the Piano;* Degas' ballerinas; Toulouse-Lautrec's cabaret dancers; Pissarro's *The Harvest;* Sisley's *View of the Canal St-Martin;* and Van Gogh's self-portraits, *Bedroom in Arles* and *Starry Night over the Rhône*. One of the museum's newer acquisitions is James Tissot's 1868 painting *The Circle of the Rue Royale,* classified a National Treasure.

Decorative & Graphic Arts

Household items such as hat and coat stands, candlesticks, desks, chairs, bookcases, vases, pot-plant holders, freestanding screens, wall mirrors, water pitchers, plates, goblets and bowls become works of art in the hands of their creators from the era, incorporating exquisite design elements.

Drawings, pastels and sketches from major artists are another of the d'Orsay's lesser-known highlights. Look for Georges Seurat's *The Black Bow* (c 1882), which uses crayon on paper to define forms by contrasting between black and white, and Paul Gaugin's poignant self-portrait (c 1902–03), drawn near the end of his life.

Sculptures

The cavernous former station is a magnificent setting for sculptures, including works by Degas, Gaugin, Camille Claudel, Renoir and Rodin.

SAVINGS TIPS

A combined ticket with the Musée de l'Orangerie is €16 (visit both museums within four days); one with the Musée Rodin is €15 (visit both on the same day). Musée d'Orsay admission drops to €8.50 after 4.30pm (6pm Thursday).

The museum is busiest Tuesday and Sunday, followed by Thursday and Saturday. Save time by buying tickets online and head directly to entrance C.

DINING TIPS

Designed like a fantasy underwater world, **Café Campana** (Map p422; dishes €9-18; ⏰10am-5pm Tue, Wed & Fri-Sun, to 9pm Thu) serves a short, stylish menu. Time has scarcely changed the museum's sumptuous **Restaurant Musée d'Orsay** (Map p422; ☎01 45 49 47 03; 2-/3-course lunch menus €22/32, mains €16-25; ⏰9.30am-5.45pm Tue, Wed & Fri-Sun, to 9.30pm Thu).

Don't miss the Parisian panorama through the giant glass clockface and from the adjacent terrace.

CUBO IMAGES / ROBERT HARDING ©

1. La Toilette
Henri de Toulouse-Lautrec's provocative masterpiece.

2. The Siesta
Vincent van Gogh's depiction of the afternoon rest.

3. Woman with a Parasol Turned to the Right
Claude Monet's 1886 oil-on-canvas painting is on show at the museum.

4. Pathway Through the High Grass
Pierre-Auguste Renoir's work is a highlight of the collection.

DEA / G. DAGLI ORTI / GETTY IMAGES ©

DEA / G. DAGLI ORTI / GETTY IMAGES ©

3

DEA / G. DAGLI ORTI / GETTY IMAGES ©

ELFI KLUCK / GETTY IMAGES ©

TOP SIGHT
JARDIN DU LUXEMBOURG

This inner-city oasis of formal terraces, chestnut groves and lush lawns has a special place in Parisians' hearts. Napoléon dedicated the 23 gracefully laid-out hectares of the Luxembourg Gardens to the children of Paris, and many residents spent their childhood prodding little wooden sailboats with long sticks on the octagonal pond, watching puppet shows, and riding the carousel or ponies.

All those activities are still here today, as well as modern play equipment, tennis and other sporting and games venues.

The Jardin du Luxembourg's history stretches further back than Napoléon. The gardens are a backdrop to the Palais du Luxembourg, built in the 1620s for Marie de Médici, Henri IV's consort, to assuage her longing for the Pitti Palace in Florence. The Palais is now home to the French Senate, which, in addition to parliamentary-assembly activities like voting on legislation, is charged with promoting the palace and its gardens.

Numerous overhauls over the centuries have given the Jardin du Luxembourg a blend of traditional French- and English-style gardens that is unique in Paris.

DON'T MISS...

- Grand Bassin
- Puppet shows
- Orchards
- Palais du Luxembourg
- Musée du Luxembourg

PRACTICALITIES

- Map p418
- numerous entrances
- hours vary
- M St-Sulpice, Rennes or Notre Dame des Champs, or RER Luxembourg

Grand Bassin

All ages love the octagonal Grand Bassin (Map p418), a serene ornamental pond where adults can lounge and kids can play with 1920s **toy sailboats** (Apr-Oct; per 30min €3). Nearby, littlies can take **pony rides** (rides €3.50; Apr-Oct) or romp around the **playgrounds** (Map p418; adult/child €1.20/2.50) – the green half is for kids aged seven to 12 years, the blue half for under-sevens.

Puppet Shows

You don't have to be a kid or speak French to be delighted by marionette shows, which have entertained audiences in France since the Middle Ages. The lively puppets perform in the Jardin du Luxembourg's little **Théâtre du Luxembourg** (www.marionnettesduluxembourg.fr; tickets €4.80). Show times can vary; check the program online and arrive half an hour ahead.

Orchards

Dozens of apple varieties grow in the orchards in the gardens' south. Bees have produced honey in the nearby apiary, the **Rucher du Luxembourg**, since the 19th century. The annual Fête du Miel (Honey Festival) offers two days of tasting and buying its sweet harvest around late September in the ornate **Pavillon Davioud** (Map p418; 55bis rue d'Assas).

Palais du Luxembourg

The **Palais du Luxembourg** (rue de Vaugirard) was built in the 1620s and has been home to the Sénat (French Senate) since 1958. It's occasionally visitable by guided tour.

East of the palace is the ornate, Italianate **Fontaine des Médici**, built in 1630. During Baron Haussmann's 19th-century reshaping of the roads, the fountain was moved 30m and the pond and dramatic statues of the giant bronze Polyphemus discovering the white-marble lovers Acis and Galatea were added.

Musée du Luxembourg

Prestigious temporary art exhibitions, such as 'Cézanne et Paris', take place in the beautiful **Musée du Luxembourg** (19 rue de Vaugirard, 6e; exhibitions adult/child from €13.50/9; ⏲10am-7.30pm Tue-Thu & Sat-Sun, to 10pm Fri & Mon).

Around the back of the museum, lemon and orange trees, palms, grenadiers and oleanders shelter from the cold in the palace's **orangery** (Map p418). Nearby, the heavily guarded **Hôtel du Petit Luxembourg** was where Marie de Médici lived while the Palais du Luxembourg was being built. The president of the Senate has called it home since 1825.

PICNICKING

Kiosks and cafes are dotted throughout the park, including places selling fairy (candy) floss. If you're planning on picnicking, forget bringing a blanket – the elegantly manicured lawns are off-limits apart from a small wedge on the southern boundary. Instead, do as Parisians do, and corral one of the iconic 1923-designed green metal chairs and find your own favourite part of the park.

The Jardin du Luxembourg plays a pivotal role in Victor Hugo's *Les Misérables:* the book's lovers Marius and Cosette meet here.

DINING

For decadent-and-then-some hot chocolate and delicious dining, head to the excellent *salon de thé* cafe-restaurant **Angelina** (Map p418; www.angelina-paris.fr; rue de Vaugirard; ⏲10am-7.30pm Tue-Thu, Sat & Sun, from 9am Mon & Fri; Ⓜ Rennes) adjacent to the Musée du Luxembourg.

The gardens are studded with over 100 sculptures. Look out for statues of Stendhal, Chopin, Baudelaire and Delacroix.

LUGRIS / ALAMY ©

TOP SIGHT
MUSÉE RODIN

Sculptor, painter, sketcher, engraver and collector Auguste Rodin donated his entire collection to the French state in 1908 on the proviso they dedicate his former workshop and showroom, the beautiful Hôtel Biron (1730), to displaying his works. The collection, including Rodin's prized collection of works by artists including Van Gogh and Renoir, is now installed not only in the mansion itself but in its rose-filled garden – one of the most peaceful places in central Paris. The museum also features many sculptures by Camille Claudel, Rodin's protégé.

The first large-scale cast of Rodin's famous sculpture **The Thinker** *(Le Penseur)*, made in 1902, resides in the garden – the perfect place to contemplate this heroic naked figure conceived by Rodin to represent intellect and poetry (it was originally titled *The Poet*).

The Gates of Hell *(La Porte de l'Enfer)* was commissioned in 1880 as the entrance for a never-built museum, and Rodin worked on his sculptural masterwork up until his death in 1917. Standing 6m high by 4m wide, its 180 figures comprise an intricate scene from Dante's *Inferno.*

Marble monument to love **The Kiss** *(Le Baiser)* was originally part of *The Gates of Hell*. The sculpture's entwined lovers caused controversy on its completion due to Rodin's then-radical approach of depicting women as equal partners in ardour.

DON'T MISS...

- *The Thinker*
- *The Gates of Hell*
- *The Kiss*
- Camille Claudel sculptures
- Collections

PRACTICALITIES

- Map p422
- www.musee-rodin.fr
- 79 rue de Varenne, 7e
- adult/child museum incl garden €6/free, garden only €2/free
- 10am-5.45pm Tue & Thu-Sun, to 8.45pm Wed
- M Varenne

JOHN HARPER / GETTY IMAGES ©

TOP SIGHT
HÔTEL DES INVALIDES

The Hôtel des Invalides was built in the 1670s by Louis XIV to provide housing for 4000 *invalides* (disabled war veterans). On 14 July 1789, a mob forced its way into the building and, after fierce fighting, seized 32,000 rifles before heading on to storm the prison at Bastille and starting the French Revolution. At the southern end of the esplanade, laid out between 1704 and 1720, is the final resting place of Napoléon.

North of the main courtyard is the **Musée de l'Armée** – the nation's largest collection on French military history. Sobering wartime footage screens at this army museum, which also has weaponry, flag and medal displays as well as a multimedia area dedicated to Charles de Gaulle.

South of the main courtyard is the **Église du Dôme**, which, with its sparkling golden dome (1677–1735), is one of the finest religious edifices erected under Louis XIV, and was the inspiration for the United States' Capitol building.

The very extravagant **Tombeau de Napoléon 1er** (Napoléon's Tomb), in the centre of the Église du Dôme, comprises six coffins fitting into one another like a Russian doll.

Also south of the main courtyard is the **Église St-Louis des Invalides**, once used by soldiers.

Within the Hôtel des Invalides itself, the esoteric **Musée des Plans-Reliefs** is full of scale models of towns, fortresses and châteaux across France.

Hours for some of the Hôtel des Invalides' individual sites can vary – check the website for updates. Regular classical concerts (some free, others costing up to €9) take place here year-round.

DON'T MISS...

- Musée de l'Armée
- Église du Dôme
- Tombeau de Napoléon 1er
- Église St-Louis des Invalides
- Musée des Plans-Reliefs

PRACTICALITIES

- Map p422
- www.musee-armee.fr
- 129 rue de Grenelle, 7e
- adult/child €9.50/free
- 7.30am-7pm daily, to 9pm Tue Apr-Sep, hours can vary
- M Invalides

SIGHTS

St-Germain

JARDIN DU LUXEMBOURG PARK

See p234.

MUSÉE DES LETTRES ET MANUSCRITS LETTERS & MANUSCRIPTS MUSEUM

Map p418 (MLM; www.museedeslettres.fr; 222 bd St-Germain, 7e; adult/child €7/5; ⏲10am-7pm Tue, Wed & Fri-Sun, to 9.30pm Thu; MRue du Bac) Grouped into five themes – history, science, music, art and literature – the handwritten and annotated letters and works on display at this captivating museum provide a powerful emotional connection to their authors. They include Napoléon, Charles de Gaulle, Marie Curie, Albert Einstein, Mozart, Beethoven, Piaf, Monet, Toulouse-Lautrec, Van Gogh, Victor Hugo, Hemingway and F Scott Fitzgerald; there are many, many more. It's thoroughly absorbing – allow at least a couple of hours. Temporary exhibitions also take place regularly.

MUSÉE NATIONAL EUGÈNE DELACROIX MUSEUM

Map p418 (www.musee-delacroix.fr; 6 rue de Furstemberg, 6e; adult/child €6/free; ⏲9.30am-5pm Wed-Mon; MMabillon or St-Germain des Prés) In a courtyard off a magnolia-shaded square, this was the romantic artist's home and studio at the time of his death in 1863, and contains a collection of his oil paintings, watercolours, pastels and drawings, including many of his more intimate works, such as *An Unmade Bed* (1828) and his paintings of Morocco.

A Musée du Louvre ticket allows entry to the museum on the same day (you can also buy tickets here and skip the Louvre's queues).

As well as the Musée du Louvre, you can see Delacroix' works at the Musée d'Orsay and frescoes at Église St-Sulpice.

ÉGLISE ST-SULPICE CHURCH

Map p418 (http://pss75.fr/saint-sulpice-paris; place St-Sulpice, 6e; ⏲7.30am-7.30pm; MSt-Sulpice) In 1646 work started on the twin-towered Church of St Sulpicius, lined inside with 21 side chapels, and it took six architects 150 years to finish. What draws most visitors isn't its striking Italianate façade

TOP SIGHT
ÉGLISE ST-GERMAIN DES PRÉS

Paris' oldest standing church, the Romanesque St Germanus of the Fields was built in the 11th century on the site of a 6th-century abbey and was the dominant place of worship in Paris until the arrival of Notre Dame. It's undergone numerous alterations since, but the **Chapelle de St-Symphorien** (to the right as you enter) was part of the original abbey.

The Chapelle de St-Symphorien is believed to be the resting place of St Germanus (496–576), the first bishop of Paris. The Merovingian kings were buried here during the 6th and 7th centuries, but their tombs disappeared during the Revolution.

Over the western entrance, the **bell tower** has changed little since 990, although the spire dates only from the 19th century.

Until the late 17th century the abbey owned most of the land in the Left Bank west of what's now bd St-Michel, and donated some of its lands along the Seine – the Pré aux Clercs (Fields of the Scholars) – to house the University of Paris (hence the names of the nearby streets, rues du Pré aux Clercs and de l'Université).

DON'T MISS...

- Chapelle de St-Symphorien
- Bell tower

PRACTICALITIES

- Map p418
- www.eglise-sgp.org
- 3 place St-Germain des Prés, 6e
- ⏲8am-7.45pm Mon-Sat, 9am-8pm Sun
- MSt-Germain des Prés

with two rows of superimposed columns, its Counter-Reformation-influenced neoclassical decor or even its frescoes by Eugène Delecroix, but its setting for a murderous scene in Dan Brown's *The Da Vinci Code*.

You can hear the monumental, 1781-built organ during 10.30am Mass on Sunday or the occasional Sunday-afternoon concert.

The frescoes in the Chapelle des Sts-Anges (Chapel of the Holy Angels), first to the right as you enter the chapel, depict Jacob wrestling with the angel (to the left) and Michael the Archangel doing battle with Satan (to the right) and were painted by Delacroix between 1855 and 1861.

MUSÉE ATELIER ZADKINE — MUSEUM

Map p418 (www.zadkine.paris.fr; 100bis rue d'Assas, 6e; ⏲10am-6pm Tue-Sun; Ⓜ Vavin) FREE Russian cubist sculptor Ossip Zadkine (1890–1967) arrived in Paris in 1908 and lived and worked in this cottage for almost 40 years. Zadkine produced an enormous catalogue of sculptures made from clay, stone, bronze and wood. The museum covers his life and work; one room displays figures he sculpted in contrasting walnut, pear, ebony, acacia, elm and oak.

MUSÉE DE LA MONNAIE DE PARIS — MUSEUM

Map p418 (☎01 40 46 56 66; www.monnaiedeparis.fr; 11 quai de Conti, 6e; Ⓜ Pont Neuf) Due to have reopened after extensive renovations by the time you're reading this, the Parisian Mint Museum traces the history of French coinage from antiquity onwards, with displays that help to bring to life this otherwise niche subject. It's housed in the 18th-century royal mint, the Monnaie de Paris, which is still used by the Ministry of Finance to produce commemorative medals and coins.

The overhaul of this sumptuous neoclassical building with one of the longest façades on the Seine will incorporate interior streets, the restoration of an aristocratic town house built by Jules Hardouin Mansart in 1690, and triple-Michelin-starred chef Guy Savoy's flagship restaurant as well as his casual courtyard brasserie, the Métal cafe.

INSTITUT DE FRANCE — HISTORIC BUILDING

Map p418 (www.institut-de-france.fr; 23 quai de Conti, 6e; Ⓜ Mabillon or Pont Neuf) The French Institute, created in 1795, brought together five of France's academies of arts and sciences. The most famous of these is the **Académie Française** (French Academy; Map p418), founded in 1635 by Cardinal Richelieu. Its 40 members, known as the Immortels (Immortals), have the Herculean (some say impossible) task of safeguarding the purity of the French language.

The domed building housing the institute, across the Seine from the Louvre's eastern end, is a masterpiece of French neoclassical architecture.

BIBLIOTHÈQUE MAZARINE — LIBRARY

Map p418 (☎01 44 41 44 06; www.bibliothequemazarine.fr; 23 quai de Conti, 6e; 5-day admission pass free; ⏲10am-6pm Mon-Fri; Ⓜ Mabillon or Pont Neuf) Within the Institut de France, the Mazarine Library is France's oldest public library, founded in 1643. You can visit the bust-lined, late-17th-century reading room or consult the library's collection of 500,000 volumes, using a pass valid for five consecutive days obtained by providing ID.

⊙ Les Invalides

MUSÉE D'ORSAY — MUSEUM

See p230.

MUSÉE RODIN — GARDEN, MUSEUM

See p236.

HÔTEL DES INVALIDES — MONUMENT, MUSEUM

See p237.

MUSÉE MAILLOL-FONDATION DINA VIERNY — MUSEUM

Map p422 (www.museemaillol.com; 61 rue de Grenelle, 7e; adult/child €13/11; ⏲10.30am-7pm Sat-Thu, to 9.30pm Fri; Ⓜ Rue du Bac) This splendid little museum focuses on the work of sculptor Aristide Maillol (1861–1944) and also includes works by Matisse, Gauguin, Kandinsky, Cézanne and Picasso. All are from the private collection of Odessa-born Dina Vierny (b 1915), Maillol's principal model for 10 years from the age of 15. The museum is located in the stunning 18th-century Hôtel Bouchardon.

CHAPELLE NOTRE DAME DE LA MEDAILLE MIRACULEUSE — CHURCH

Map p422 (☎01 49 54 78 88; www.chapellenotredamedelamedaillemiraculeuse.com; 140 rue du Bac, 7e; ⏲7.45am-1pm & 2.30-7pm Mon & Wed-Sun, 7.45am-7pm Tue; Ⓜ Rue du Bac or Vaneau) Tucked away at the end of a courtyard

FAUBOURG ST-GERMAIN

In the 18th century, Faubourg St-Germain – a formal world of exquisite ironwork, gold leaf and conventional manners west of St-Germain des Prés – was Paris' most fashionable neighbourhood. French nobility moved across the river from the more crowded, polluted Marais and built magnificent *hôtels particuliers* (private mansions), particularly around rue de Lille, rue de Grenelle and rue de Varenne. Balzac captured its aristocratic way of life in his novel *La Duchesse de Langeais*.

After the Revolution, many of these mansions were turned into national institutions, and there's now an overdose of embassies and government ministries; **Hôtel Matignon** (Map p422; 57 rue de Varenne, 7e; MSolférino) has been the official residence of the French prime minister since the start of the Fifth Republic (1958). Rodin worked and exhibited in the palatial 1730-built Hôtel Biron, now the Musée Rodin (p236), and it was to the stylish pad at **53 rue de Varenne** that Edith Wharton moved in 1910 to write *Le Temps de l'Innocence (The Age of Innocence)*.

But the area's finest example of timeless extravagance is **5bis rue Verneuil** (Map p418) – the house where Parisian singer, sexpot and provocateur Serge Gainsbourg lived from 1969 until his death in 1991. It's still owned by his daughter, actor-singer Charlotte Gainsbourg; tours have been mooted but as yet haven't happened due to the logistics of accommodating legions of fans in the space. Meanwhile, neighbours have long since given up scrubbing off admirers' reappearing graffiti and messages.

across from Le Bon Marché department store, this extraordinary and beautiful chapel is a place of pilgrimage. In 1830, the Virgin Mary spoke to 24-year-old Catherine Labouré (1806–76). In a series of three miraculous apparitions that took place here, the young novice seminary sister was told to have a medal made that would protect and grace those who wore it. The first Miraculous Medals were made in 1832.

The same year a cholera epidemic plagued Paris and the medals' popularity spread rapidly as wearers of the medal found themselves miraculously cured or protected from the deadly disease. Devout Roman Catholics around the world still wear the medal today.

Catherine Labouré, the eighth child of a Burgundian farmer, was beatified in 1933 and her body moved to a reliquary beneath the altar of Our Lady of the Globe (to the right as you face the main altar) inside the Chapel of Our Lady of the Miraculous Medal.

FONDATION DUBUFFET — ART MUSEUM

Map p422 (www.dubuffetfondation.com; 137 rue de Sèvres, 6e; adult/child €6/4; 2-6pm Mon-Fri Sep-Jul; MDuroc) Situated in a lovely 19th-century *hôtel particulier* (private mansion) at the end of a courtyard, the foundation houses the collection of Jean Dubuffet (1901–85), chief of the Art Brut school (a term he himself coined to describe all works of artistic expression not officially recognised). Much of his work is incredibly modern and expressive.

BASILIQUE STE-CLOTILDE — CHURCH

Map p422 (01 44 18 62 63; www.sainte-clotilde.com; 23bis rue las Cases, 7e; 9am-7.30pm Mon-Fri, 10am-8pm Sat & Sun; MSolférino) Resembling a mini-Notre Dame, with twin conical steeples, this delightful basilica presides over a pretty park. Dating from 1856, its sculptures, paintings and stained glass are the handiwork of some of the 19th century's finest artists, including Pradier, Préault, Guillaume, Lenepveu and Thibaut. The organ is magnificent.

ASSEMBLÉE NATIONALE — HISTORIC BUILDING

Map p422 (www.assemblee-nationale.fr; 33 quai d'Orsay & 126 rue de l'Université, 7e; MAssemblée Nationale or Invalides) The lower house of the French parliament, known as the National Assembly, meets in the 18th-century Palais Bourbon, which fronts the Seine. Tours are available through local deputies, making citizens and residents the only eligible visitors. Next door is the Second Empire–style **Ministère des Affaires Étrangères** (Ministry of Foreign Affairs; Map p422; www.diplomatie.gouv.fr; 37 quai d'Orsay, 7e), built between 1845 and 1855.

LES BERGES DE SEINE — PROMENADE

Map p422 (http://lesberges.paris.fr; btwn Musée d'Orsay & Pont de l'Alma, 7e; information point noon-7pm Sun-Thu, 10am-10pm Fri & Sat; Ⓜ Solférino, Assemblée Nationale or Invalides) A breath of fresh air, this 2.3km-long riverside promenade is Parisians' latest spot to run, cycle, skate, play board games or take part in a packed program of events. Equally it's simply a great place to hang out – in a Zzz shipping-container hut (free by reservation at the information point just west of the Musée d'Orsay), on the archipelago of floating gardens, or at the burgeoning restaurants and bars (some floating too aboard boats and barges).

MUSÉE DES ÉGOUTS DE PARIS MUSEUM

Map p422 (place de la Résistance, 7e; adult/child €4.40/3.60; ⏲11am-5pm Sat-Wed May-Sep, 11am-4pm Sat-Wed Oct-Dec & Feb-Apr; Ⓜ Alma Marceau or RER Pont de l'Alma) Raw sewage flows beneath your feet as you walk through 480m of odoriferous tunnels in this working sewer museum. Exhibitions cover the development of Paris' waste-water-disposal system, including its resident rats (there's an estimated one sewer rat for every Parisian above ground). Enter via a rectangular maintenance hole topped with a kiosk across the street from 93 quai d'Orsay, 7e. The sewers keep regular hours except when rain floods the tunnels. Toy rats are sold at its gift shop.

EATING

The picnicking turf of the Jardin de Luxembourg is complemented by some fabulous places to buy picnic ingredients. Even if it's not picnic weather, the neighbourhood's streets are lined with everything from quintessential Parisian bistros to chic designer restaurants. You'll find some charming places inside Cour du Commerce St-André, a glass-covered passageway built in 1735 to link two *jeu de paume* (old-style tennis) courts.

St-Germain

★JSFP TRAITEUR DELICATESSEN €

Map p418 (http://jsfp-traiteur.com; 8 rue de Buci, 6e; dishes €3.40-5.70; ⏲9.30am-8.30pm; ✎; Ⓜ Mabillon) Brimming with big bowls of salad, terrines, pâté and other prepared delicacies, this deli is a brilliant bet for quality Parisian 'fast food' such as quiches in a variety of flavour combinations (courgette and chive, mozzarella and basil, salmon and spinach…) to take to a nearby park, square or stretch of riverfront.

L'AVANT COMPTOIR FRENCH TAPAS €

Map p418 (www.hotel-paris-relais-saint-germain.com; 3 Carrefour de l'Odéon, 6e; tapas €3-7; ⏲noon-midnight; Ⓜ Odéon) Squeeze in around the zinc bar (there are no seats and it's tiny) and order off the menu suspended from the ceiling to feast on amazing tapas dishes like Iberian ham or salmon tartare croquettes, duck-sausage hot dogs, blood-sausage macarons, and prosciutto and artichoke waffles with wines by the glass in a chaotically sociable atmosphere.

AU PIED DE FOUET BISTRO €

Map p418 (☎01 43 54 87 83; www.aupieddefouet.com; 50 rue St-Benoît, 6e; mains €9-12.50; ⏲noon-2.30pm & 7-11pm Mon-Sat; Ⓜ St-Germain des Prés) Wholly classic bistro dishes such as *entrecôte* (steak), *confit de canard* (duck cooked slowly in its own fat) and *foie de volailles sauté* (pan-fried chicken livers) at this busy bistro are astonishingly good value. Round off your meal with a *tarte Tatin*, wine-soaked prunes or bowl of *fromage blanc* (a cross between yoghurt, sour cream and cream cheese).

LITTLE BREIZH CRÊPERIE €

Map p418 (☎01 43 54 60 74; www.littlebreizh.fr; 11 rue Grégoire de Tours, 6e; crêpes €4.50-12; ⏲noon-2.30pm & 7-10pm; ✎ 👪; Ⓜ Odéon) As authentic as you'd find in Brittany, but with some innovative twists (such as Breton sardines, olive oil and sundried tomatoes; goat's cheese, stewed apple, hazelnuts, rosemary and honey; smoked salmon, dill cream, pink peppercorns and lemon), the crêpes at this sweet spot are infinitely more enticing than those sold on nearby street corners. Hours can fluctuate; book ahead.

CUISINE DE BAR SANDWICHES €

Map p418 (www.cuisinedebar.fr; 8 rue du Cherche Midi, 6e; dishes €9.20-13.50; ⏲8.30am-7pm Tue-Sat, 9.30am-3.30pm Sun; 📶; Ⓜ Sèvres-Babylone) As next-door neighbour to one of Paris' most famous bakers, this isn't your average sandwich bar. Instead, it's an ultrachic spot to lunch between designer boutiques on open sandwiches cut from that celebrated Poilâne (p243) bread and fabulously topped with gourmet goodies such as foie gras,

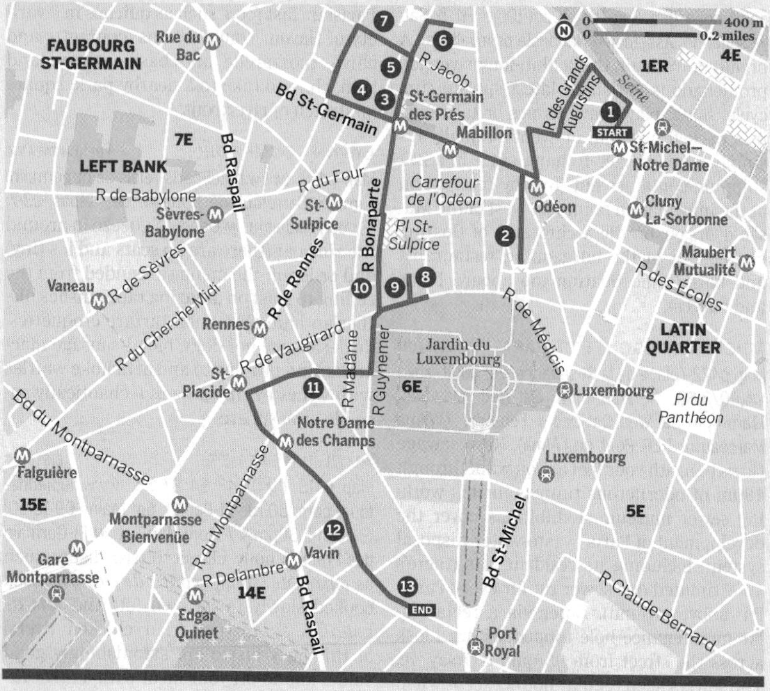

Neighbourhood Walk Left Bank Literary Loop

START QUAI DES GRANDS AUGUSTINS
END 113 RUE NOTRE DAMES DES CHAMPS
LENGTH 5KM; ONE TO TWO HOURS

To retrace the footsteps of Left Bank literary luminaries, begin by following the Seine west past the *bouquinistes* (secondhand booksellers) that Ernest Hemingway loved.

South is the 'Beat Hotel', now the **1 Relais Hôtel du Vieux Paris**, where Allen Ginsberg, Jack Kerouac, William S Burroughs and others holed up in the 1950s.

At **2 12 rue de l'Odéon** stood the original Shakespeare & Company bookshop where owner Sylvia Beach lent books to Hemingway, and edited, retyped and published *Ulysses* for James Joyce in 1922. It was closed during the occupation when Beach refused to sell her last copy of Joyce's *Finnegans Wake* to a Nazi officer.

Bd St-Germain's **3 Les Deux Magots** (p249) and **4 Café de Flore** (p250) were favourite cafes of postwar intellectuals Jean-Paul Sartre and Simone de Beauvoir.

At **5 36 rue Bonaparte** Henry Miller stayed in a 5th-floor mansard room in 1930, which he later wrote about in *Letters to Emil* (1989). **6 L'Hôtel** (p304), the former Hôtel d'Alsace, is where Oscar Wilde died in 1900. Hemingway spent his first night in Paris in room 14 of the **7 Hôtel d'Angleterre** (p304) in 1921.

In 1925 William Faulkner stayed several months at what's now the posh **8 Hôtel Luxembourg Parc**, and Hemingway's last years in Paris were at **9 6 rue Férou**. F Scott and Zelda Fitzgerald lived at **10 58 rue de Vaugirard** in 1928, near **11 27 rue de Fleurus**, where Gertrude Stein lived and entertained artists and writers including Matisse, Picasso, Braque, Gauguin, Fitzgerald, Hemingway and Ezra Pound.

Pound lived at **12 70bis rue Notre Dame des Champs** in a flat filled with Japanese paintings and packing crates, while Hemingway's first apartment in this area was above a sawmill at **13 113 rue Notre Dames des Champs**.

smoked duck, gooey St-Marcellin cheese and Bayonne ham.

LA BOTTEGA DI PASTAVINO ITALIAN €

Map p418 (☎01 44 07 09 56; 18 rue de Buci, 6e; deli dishes €5.30-6, restaurant mains €18-35; ⏰deli 9.30am-8.15pm Mon-Sat, restaurant 8-11.30pm Mon-Sat; Ⓜ St-Germain des Prés) Crammed with imported Italian groceries – marinated capsicums, artichokes and olives, dozens of varieties of dried and fresh pasta, white-truffle cream and bottles of Italian *vino* – this Aladdin's-cave deli also dishes up freshly cooked pasta, salads, and piping-hot panini for lunch on the run. At the back, up a spiral staircase, is its 20-seat restaurant, L'Étage.

TREIZE CAFE €

Map p418 (Thirteen – A Baker's Dozen; ☎01 73 77 27 89; 16 rue des Sts-Pères, 7e; lunch menus €13-17, brunch menus €10-23, mains €13-15; ⏰10am-6pm Tue-Sat; 🖉; Ⓜ Rue du Bac or St-Germain des Prés) Pass through a passageway, cross a cobbled courtyard and at the very end you'll find the latticed doors of Treize, a charming contemporary cafe turning out savoury pies, creative salads and sweet cakes (the carrot cake has a local following), along with unique tea blends, and coffee by Parisian roaster Coutume (p251). Perfect for whiling away an afternoon.

PAIN & CHOCOLAT CAFE €

Map p422 (16 av de la Motte-Picquet, 7e; mains €10-22, brunch menus €7-22; ⏰9am-7pm Tue-Fri, 10am-7pm Sat & Sun; Ⓜ La Tour Maubourg) You'll be glad you forewent that overpriced, underdelivering hotel breakfast when you start the day in proper Parisian style at this delightfully retro cafe. Everything is made on the premises, salads, tartines, egg dishes and cakes, pastries and quiches included. Don't miss the hot chocolate, made from an old family recipe.

COSI SANDWICHES €

Map p418 (54 rue de Seine, 6e; sandwich menus €10-15; ⏰noon-11pm; 📶🖉👪; Ⓜ Odéon or Mabillon) An institution in the 6e for a quick, cheap sandwich fix – like tandoori turkey and coleslaw, black-olive tapenade and roast tomato, or blue cheese and walnuts – to eat in its upstairs dining room or take to a park. Classical music plays in the background and the homemade focaccia is still warm from the oven.

GÉRARD MULOT PATISSERIE €

Map p418 (www.gerard-mulot.com; 76 rue de Seine, 6e; ⏰6.45am-8pm Thu-Tue; Ⓜ Odéon or Mabillon) Fruit tarts (peach, lemon, apple), *tarte normande* (apple cake) and *clafoutis* (cherry flan) are among this celebrated patisserie's specialities.

POILÂNE BOULANGERIE €

Map p418 (www.poilane.fr; 8 rue du Cherche Midi, 6e; ⏰7.15am-8.15pm Mon-Sat; Ⓜ Sèvres-Babylone) Pierre Poilâne opened his *boulangerie* upon arriving from Normandy in 1932. Today his granddaughter Apollonia runs the company, which still turns out wood-fired, rounded sourdough loaves made with stone-milled flour and Guérande sea salt.

GIRAUDET BOUTIQUE LYONNAIS €

Map p418 (www.giraudet.fr; 16 rue Mabillon, 6e; dishes from €2.70; ⏰2-7pm Mon, 10am-7.30pm Tue-Sat; Ⓜ Mabillon) In Lyon, Giraudet is synonymous with contemporary takes on Lyonnais staples. This sleek outpost specialises in soups and *quenelles* (feather-light flour, egg and cream dumplings) to take away.

LADURÉE PATISSERIE €

Map p418 (www.laduree.com; 21 rue Bonaparte, 6e; ⏰8.30am-7.30pm Mon-Fri, 8.30am-8.30pm Sat, 10am-7.30pm Sun; Ⓜ St-Germain des Prés) Queues stretch around the block from the St-Germain branch of famous patisserie Ladurée for its picture-perfect delicacies, including its rainbow of macarons and *le baiser Ladurée* (layered almond cake with strawberries and cream). Its flagship store is on the Champs-Élysées.

GROM ICE CREAM €

Map p418 (www.grom.it; 81 rue de Seine, 6e; ice creams from €3.70; ⏰1-10.30pm Mon-Wed, 1pm-midnight Thu-Sat, noon-10.30pm Sun; 👪; Ⓜ Mabillon) 🍃 Flavours change monthly at France's only outlet of prestigious Turin gelato-maker Grom. All include sustainably sourced, high-grade ingredients like Madagascan vanilla and Venezuelan chocolate chips.

★BOUILLON RACINE BRASSERIE €€

Map p418 (☎01 44 32 15 60; www.bouillonracine.com; 3 rue Racine, 6e; weekday lunch menus €16, menus €31-42; ⏰noon-11pm; 👪; Ⓜ Cluny–La Sorbonne) Inconspicuously situated in a quiet street, this heritage-listed 1906 art-nouveau 'soup kitchen', with mirrored walls, floral motifs and ceramic tiling, was built in 1906 to feed market workers. Despite the magnificent interior, the food – inspired by age-old recipes – is by no means an afterthought.

Superbly executed dishes include stuffed, spit-roasted suckling pig, pork shank in Rodenbach red beer, and scallops and shrimps with lobster coulis. Finish off your foray into gastronomic history with an old-fashioned sherbet.

★SEMILLA NEOBISTRO €€

Map p418 (☎01 43 54 34 50; 54 rue de Seine, 6e; lunch menus €24, mains €20-50; ⌚12.30-2.30pm & 7-10.45pm; MOdéon or Mabillon) Stark concrete, exposed pipes and an open kitchen (in front of which you can book front-row 'chef seats') set the factory-style scene for edgy, modern, daily changing dishes like pork spare ribs with sweet potato and cinnamon, mushrooms in hazelnut butter and trout with passionfruit and ginger. Desserts are outstanding. Be sure to book.

HUÎTRERIE REGIS SEAFOOD €€

Map p418 (☎01 44 41 10 07; http://huitrerieregis.com; 3 rue de Montfaucon, 6e; dozen oysters from €16; ⌚noon-2.30pm & 6.30-10.30pm Tue-Sun; MMabillon) Trendy, tiny and white, this is *the* spot for slurping oysters on crisp winter days. They come only by the dozen, along with fresh bread and butter, but wash them down with a glass of chilled Muscadet and voila, one perfect lunch. A twinset of tables loiters on the pavement; otherwise it's all inside.

LA GRANDE CRÈMERIE WINE BAR €€

Map p418 (☎01 43 26 09 09; www.lagrandecremerie.fr; 8 rue Grégoire de Tours, 6e; mains €14-23; ⌚noon-2pm & 7.30-11pm Tue-Sat; MOdéon) The success of Serge Mathieu's tiny *cave gourmande* (gourmet wine cellar), La Crèmerie (p254), prompted the opening of this larger rustic space serving the earthy flavours of the French countryside on cold platters designed for sharing, along with splendid wines.

UN DIMANCHE À PARIS FUSION €€

Map p418 (☎01 56 81 18 18; www.un-dimanche-a-paris.com; 4-8 Cour du Commerce St-André, 6e; lunch/dinner/brunch menus from €25/32/38; ⌚restaurant 7-10pm Tue, noon-2pm & 7-10pm Wed-Sat, 11am-2.30pm Sun; MOdéon) Inside the beautiful covered passageway Cour du Commerce St-André, this 'chocolate concept store' incorporates a boutique (where you can order a decadently rich hot chocolate), patisserie classes (from €55), a tearoom and a restaurant serving chocaholic dishes like ricotta-filled pasta in hazelnut and white-chocolate broth, prawns with cocoa and candied pineapple, and seared beef with Brazilian-chocolate jus.

PÈRES ET FILLES MODERN FRENCH €€

Map p418 (☎01 43 25 00 28; 81 rue de Seine, 6e; mains €17-31; ⌚kitchen noon-2.30pm & 7.30-11pm Mon-Wed, noon-2.30pm & 7.30-11.30pm Thu-Sat, 7.30-11pm Sun; MMabillon) Retractable timber-framed glass doors opening onto the street make this locals' favourite a top spot for people-watching while dining on French fare with fusion elements like Thai veggies, and bantering with the fun-loving staff. Inside, black-and-white photos and books line the walls of the spacious ground floor and mezzanine.

BRASSERIE LIPP BRASSERIE €€

Map p418 (☎01 45 48 53 91; 151 bd St-Germain, 6e; mains €22-38; ⌚11.45am-12.45am; MSt-Germain des Prés) Waiters in black waistcoats, bow ties and long white aprons serve brasserie favourites like *choucroute garnie* (sauerkraut with smoked or salted pork, frankfurters and potatoes) and *jarret de porc aux lentilles* (pork knuckle with lentils) at this illustrious wood-panelled establishment. (Arrive hungry: salads aren't allowed as meals.) Opened by Léonard Lipp in 1880, the brasserie achieved immortality when Hemingway sang its praises in *A Moveable Feast*.

LE PARC AUX CERFS MODERN FRENCH €€

Map p418 (☎01 43 54 87 83; 50 rue Vavin, 6e; lunch menus €19.50, menus €27-32; ⌚noon-2pm & 7-11.15pm; MNotre Dame des Champs) Evening reservations are essential at this small, stylish restaurant named for the clearings used as French aristocracy hunting fields prior to the French Revolution. Creative dishes span two-cabbage salad, *tartare de saumon* (raw chopped salmon) with pink peppercorns and grapefruit, and goat's cheese and almonds, but the pièce de résistance is the delightful patio garden out back.

FISH LA BOISSONNERIE BISTRO €€

Map p418 (☎01 43 54 34 69; 69 rue de Seine, 6e; lunch/dinner menus from €28.50/35, mains €17; ⌚12.30-2.30pm & 7-10.45pm; MMabillon) This former fish shop, with its wonderful old mosaic on the front façade, rustic commu-

PARIS' OLDEST RESTAURANT & CAFE

St-Germain claims both the city's oldest restaurant and its oldest cafe.

➡ **À la Petite Chaise** (Map p418; ☎01 42 22 13 35; www.alapetitechaise.fr; 36 rue de Grenelle, 6e; lunch/dinner menus from €23/36; ⏲noon-2pm & 7-11pm; Ⓜ Sèvres-Babylone) Paris' oldest restaurant hides behind an iron gate that's been here since the restaurant opened in 1680, when wine merchant Georges Rameau served food to the public to accompany his wares. Classical decor and cuisine (onion soup, foie gras, duck, lamb and unexpected delights like truffled asparagus) make it worth a visit above and beyond its history.

➡ **Le Procope** (Map p418; www.procope.com; 13 rue de l'Ancienne Comédie, 6e; 2-/3-course menus from €29/36; ⏲11.30am-midnight Sun-Wed, to 1am Thu-Sat; 👪; Ⓜ Odéon) The city's oldest cafe welcomed its first patrons in 1686, and was frequented by Voltaire, Molière and Balzac. Its chandeliered interior also has an entrance onto the 1735-built glass-roofed passageway Cour du Commerce St-André. Along with house specialities like coq au vin, calf's-head casserole in veal stock, and calf kidneys with violet mustard, it serves its own sorbets and ice creams, which have been made here since 1686 too.

nal seating and multilingual bonhomie, is almost as much a wine bar as a restaurant. Dishes like pork tenderloin with fennel risotto are complemented by outstanding wines.

POLIDOR — TRADITIONAL FRENCH €€

Map p418 (☎01 43 26 95 34; www.polidor.com; 41 rue Monsieur le Prince, 6e; menus €22-35; ⏲noon-2.30pm & 7pm-12.30am Mon-Sat, noon-2.30pm & 7-11pm Sun; 👪; Ⓜ Odéon) A meal at this quintessentially Parisian *crèmerie-restaurant* is like a trip to Victor Hugo's Paris: the restaurant and its decor date from 1845. *Menus* of tasty, family-style French cuisine ensure a stream of diners eager to sample bœuf bourguignon, *blanquette de veau à l'ancienne* (veal in white sauce) and Polidor's famous *tarte Tatin*. Expect to wait. No credit cards.

Midnight in Paris fans might recognise it as the place Owen Wilson's character meets Hemingway (who dined here in his day).

ROGER LA GRENOUILLE — TRADITIONAL FRENCH €€

Map p418 (☎01 56 24 24 34; 26-28 rue des Grands Augins, 6e; lunch/dinner menus from €22/27; ⏲7-11pm Mon, noon-2pm & 7-11pm Tue-Sat; Ⓜ St-Michel) Scattered with frog sculptures, B&W pictures of 1920s Paris and an array of old lamps, time-worn, sepia-coloured institution 'Roger the Frog' serves nine varieties of frogs' legs such as à la Provençale (with tomato) and Normande (cooked in cider and served with apple). If you're squeamish about devouring Roger, alternatives include dishes like roast sea bass with braised fennel.

LES ÉDITEURS — CAFE €€

Map p418 (☎01 43 26 67 76; www.lesediteurs.fr; 4 Carrefour de l'Odéon, 6e; 2-/3-course menus €20.50/25.50; ⏲8am-midnight; Ⓜ Odéon) A hybrid cafe, restaurant, library (there are more than 5000 books on hand), bar and *salon de thé,* Les Éditeurs' floor-to-ceiling windows make it a great place to watch the Germanopratin (yes, there is an adjective for St-Germain des Prés) goings-on. Weekend brunch (11am to 5pm; €26), with fresh-squeezed juices and bourbon-vanilla panna cotta, is big here.

Outside, a statue of **Georges Danton** (Map p418), a leader of the Revolution and later one of its guillotined victims, stands, head intact.

CASA BINI — ITALIAN €€

Map p418 (☎01 46 34 05 60; www.casabini.fr; 36 rue Gregoire de Tours, 6e; 2-/3-course lunch menus €23/27, mains €23-39; ⏲12.30-2.30pm & 7.30-11pm; 👪; Ⓜ Odéon) At this highly recommended Italian restaurant, homemade pasta is cooked to al dente perfection and children are treated like gods. Dishes span squid and creamed courgette soup, *tagliolini* studded with white summer truffles or a classic veal saltimbocca (veal escalope flavoured with ham, thyme and sage).

LE PETIT ZINC — BRASSERIE €€

Map p418 (☎01 42 86 61 00; www.petit-zinc.com; 11 rue St-Benoît, 6e; 2-/3-course menus €22.20/29.50; ⏲noon-midnight; 👪; Ⓜ St-Germain des Prés) Not a 'little bar', as its name would suggest, but a large, wonderful

LOCAL KNOWLEDGE

STARS OF THE FUTURE

Founded in 1920 by Paris' chamber of commerce and industry, **Restaurants d'Application de Ferrandi** (Map p422; www.ferrandi-paris.fr; 28 rue de l'Abbé Grégoire, 6e; lunch/dinner menus Le Premier €25/40, Le 28 €30/45; ⌚by reservation Le Premier 12.30pm Tue-Fri, dinner Thu, Le 28 12.30pm Wed-Fri, 7.30pm Mon & Tue, both closed school holidays; Ⓜ St-Placide) is arguably France's most prestigious culinary school, turning out a who's who of industry professionals. You can taste these future Michelin-starred chefs' creations at bargain prices at the school's two training restaurants, **Le Premier** (focusing on classical French cookery) and **Le 28** (high-level gastronomy), overseen by Ferrandi's esteemed professors.

brasserie serving mountains of fresh seafood and other traditional brasserie specialities in art-nouveau splendour (book ahead and dress accordingly).

PIZZA CHIC PIZZERIA €€

Map p418 (☎01 45 48 30 38; www.pizzachic.fr; 13 rue Mézières, 6e; pizzas €17-22; ⌚12.30-2.30pm & 7.30-11pm Mon-Thu, to 11.30pm Fri, 12.30-3pm & 7.30-11.30pm Sat, noon-3pm & 7.30-10pm Sun; 👪; Ⓜ St-Sulpice) The antithesis of chains-that-shall-not-be-mentioned, Pizza Chic's cast-iron walls and crisp white tablecloths set the scene for rarefied pizzas like artichoke with parmesan aged for two years, accompanied by a lush wine list. *Aperitivi* and antipasti choices are many; desserts include a rich panna cotta and even richer tiramisu.

LE MÂCHON D'HENRI BISTRO €€

Map p418 (☎01 43 29 08 70; 8 rue Guisarde, 6e; menus €35, mains €15-29; ⌚noon-2.30pm & 7-11pm; Ⓜ St-Sulpice or Mabillon) Feisty French staples at this tiny, jam-packed bistro might include Lyonnais *boudin noir aux pommes* (black pudding with apples), Jura *saucisse de Morteau* (a type of sausage) and lentils or tripe cooked Caen-style.

LA JACOBINE TEAROOM €€

Map p418 (☎01 46 34 15 95; 59-61 rue St-André des Arts, 6e; 2-/3-course menus €27/34; ⌚5-11.30pm Mon, from noon Tue-Sun; Ⓜ Odéon) Popular for its homemade tarts, giant-size salads and crêpes, olde-worlde tearoom La Jacobine is packed to the rafters by noon. Its lovely location inside the glass-covered passageway Cour du Commerce St-André makes it all the more romantic.

LE CHERCHE MIDI ITALIAN €€

Map p418 (☎01 45 48 27 44; www.lecherchemidi.fr; 22 rue du Cherche Midi, 6e; mains €12-17; ⌚noon-3pm & 7.30-11.15pm; Ⓜ Sèvres-Babylone) This popular restaurant with red awning and classic interior buzzes all the more at weekends when Saturday shoppers and Sunday strollers make a beeline for its small, sunlit pavement terrace. Cuisine is classic and elegant. Get here by 12.30pm and 8pm respectively to be sure of getting a table.

LE COMPTOIR DU RELAIS BISTRO €€€

Map p418 (☎01 44 27 07 97; www.hotel-paris-relais-saint-germain.com; 9 Carrefour de l'Odéon, 6e; mains €14-45, dinner menus €60; ⌚noon-6pm & 8.30-11pm Mon-Fri, noon-11pm Sat & Sun; Ⓜ Odéon) Simply known as Le Comptoir (the Counter) among foodies, top chef Yves Camdeborde's gourmet bistro cooks up seriously creative seasonal dishes like asparagus and foie gras salad. Arrive early to bag a table at lunchtime (no reservations), but forget gastronomic evening dining unless you've booked months in advance. Or pop next door for tapas at its annexe, L'Avant Comptoir (p241).

ZE KITCHEN GALERIE GASTRONOMIC €€€

Map p418 (☎01 44 32 00 32; www.zekitchen-galerie.fr; 4 rue des Grands Augustins, 6e; lunch/dinner menus from €41/85; ⌚noon-2.30pm & 7-11pm Tue-Fri, 7-11pm Sat; Ⓜ St-Michel) William Ledeuil's passion for Southeast Asia shows in the vibrant dishes he creates in his Michelin-starred glass-box kitchen. Hosting several art exhibitions a year, the restaurant-gallery's menu includes broths loaded with Thai herbs and coconut milk, meat and fish cooked *à la plancha* (on a griddle) and inventive desserts like white-chocolate and wasabi ice cream. Alternatively, try offshoot **KGB** (Kitchen Galerie Bis; Map p418; ☎01 46 33 00 85; http://zekitchen-galerie.fr; 25 rue des Grands Augustins, 6e; lunch menus €29-36, dinner menus €55-62; ⌚noon-2.30pm & 7.30-11pm Tue-Fri, 7.30-11pm Sat; Ⓜ St-Michel).

RESTAURANT HÉLÈNE DARROZE MODERN FRENCH €€€

Map p418 (☎01 42 22 00 11; www.helenedarroze.com; 4 rue d'Assas, 6e; lunch/dinner menus from €39/92; ⌚12.30-2.30pm & 7.30-10.30pm Tue-Sat; ⓂSèvres-Babylone) Female star chefs are a rarity in Paris, but Hélène Darroze is a stellar exception (and the inspiration for the character Colette in the winsome animated film *Ratatouille*). These premises house both her elegant Michelin-starred Salle à Manger restaurant upstairs and relaxed downstairs Salon d'Hélène, where multicourse tasting menus, including dishes such as wood-grilled foie gras, reflect Darroze's native southwestern France.

L'ATELIER DE JOËL ROBUCHON GASTRONOMIC €€€

Map p418 (☎01 42 22 56 52; www.joel-robuchon.com; 5 rue de Montalembert, 7e; mains €38-79; ⌚11.30am-3.30pm & 6.30pm-midnight; ⓂRue du Bac) Celebrity chef Joël Robuchon takes diners on a mind-blowing culinary tour of French gastronomy's finer ingredients, lobster, sardines, foie gras and milk-fed lamb included. Dining is stool-style around a communal U-shaped black-lacquer bar (ideal for solo diners) in a Japanese-accented dining room with bamboo in glass vases. Robuchon recently opened another *atelier* inside the Champs-Élysées' Publicis Drugstore.

Les Invalides

LE BAC À GLACES ICE CREAM €

Map p422 (www.bacaglaces.com; 109 rue du Bac, 7e; ice creams from €3.50; ⌚10.30am-7.30pm Mon-Sat; 👪; ⓂSèvres-Babylone) Apricot and thyme, lemon and basil, strawberry and rose, and orange and sauvignon blanc are among the 60 flavours of all-natural ice creams at this luscious *glacier* (ice-cream maker).

BESNIER BOULANGERIE €

Map p422 (40 rue de Bourgogne, 7e; ⌚7am-8pm Mon-Fri Sep-Jul; ⓂVarenne) You can watch baguettes being made through the viewing window of this award-winning *boulangerie*.

LA PÂTISSERIE DES RÊVES PATISSERIE €

Map p422 (www.lapatisseriedesreves.com; 93 rue du Bac, 7e; ⌚9am-8pm Tue-Sat, to 6pm Sun; ⓂRue du Bac) The most extraordinary cakes, far too beautiful to eat, are showcased beneath glass domes at this contemporary 'patisserie of dreams' of big-name *pâtissier* Philippe Conticini. Each season sees different fruit tarts, such as citrus and quince in winter, rhubarb and berries in spring and summer.

MARCHÉ RASPAIL MARKET €

Map p422 (bd Raspail btwn rue de Rennes & rue du Cherche Midi, 6e; ⌚regular market 7am-2.30pm Tue & Fri, organic market 9am-3pm Sun; ⓂRennes) A traditional open-air market on Tuesday and Friday, Marché Raspail is especially popular on Sunday, when it's filled with *biologique* (organic) produce.

POISSONNERIE DU BAC SEAFOOD €

Map p422 (www.poissonnerie-paris.fr; 69 rue du Bac, 7e; ⌚9am-1pm & 4-7.30pm Tue-Sat, 9.30am-1pm Sun; ⓂRue du Bac) Self-caterers shouldn't miss this superb aquamarine- and cobalt-tiled fishmonger. Even if you don't have access to a kitchen in Paris, the fish, scallops, prawns, crabs and other crustaceans laid out on beds of crushed ice are a visual feast.

CAFÉ TRAMA MODERN FRENCH €€

Map p422 (☎01 45 48 33 71; 83 rue du Cherche Midi, 6e; mains €15-22; ⌚kitchen noon-2.45pm & 7.30-10pm Tue-Sat; ⓂVaneau or St-Placide) Cafe classics come with a contemporary twist at this black-awning-framed local with mellow lighting, chequered tiles, vintage furniture and pavement tables. Try the pan-fried squid with rocket and orange segments, *croque monsieur* with truffle salt on premium Poujauran bread, or ginger and basil beef tartare with meat from famed Parisian butcher Hugo Desnoyer, along with all-natural wines.

LOCAL KNOWLEDGE

RUE CLER

Pick up fresh bread, sandwich fillings, pastries and wine for a picnic along the typically Parisian market street **rue Cler** (Map p422; rue Cler, 7e; ⌚most shops 8am-7pm Tue-Sat, to noon Sun; ⓂÉcole Militaire), which buzzes with local shoppers, especially on weekends.

Interspersed between the *boulangeries, fromageries*, grocers, butchers, delis and other food shops, including a wonderful *glacier* (ice-cream maker; Martine Lambert, at No 39), many with pavement stalls, lively cafe terraces overflow with locals too.

LE SQUARE REGIONAL CUISINE €€

Map p422 (☎01 45 51 09 03; www.restaurant-lesquare.com; 31 rue St-Dominique, 7e; lunch/dinner menus from €19.50/26; ⏲kitchen noon-2.30pm & 7-10pm Mon-Sat; 📶; Ⓜ Solférino) The terrace tables along rue Casimir Périer are the best seats in the house for views of the neighbouring Basilique Ste-Clotilde. Inside, autumnal-hued banquettes and wood panelling make this an elegant spot to dine on classical dishes with a southwestern accent such as beef with Béarnaise sauce and potato gratin. The bar opens from 8am to 11pm.

LES COCOTTES MODERN FRENCH €€

Map p422 (www.maisonconstant.com; 135 rue Ste-Dominique, 7e; mains €15-29; ⏲noon-3.30pm & 6.30-10.30pm Sun-Thu, noon-3.30pm & 6.30-11.30pm Fri & Sat; Ⓜ École Militaire or RER Port de l'Alma) Christian Constant's chic concept space is devoted to *cocottes* (casseroles), with a buoyant crowd feasting on inventive seasonal creations cooked to perfection in little black-enamel, oven-to-table casserole dishes. Seating is on bar stools around high tables and there are no reservations: arrive by noon or 7.15pm.

If the queue's out the door, nip a couple of doors down for a drink at **Café Constant** (Map p422; www.maisonconstant.com; 139 rue Ste-Dominique, 7e; mains €16-24; ⏲kitchen noon-3pm & 7-11pm; Ⓜ École Militaire or RER Port de l'Alma).

BRASSERIE THOUMIEUX TRADITIONAL FRENCH €€

Map p422 (☎01 47 05 49 75; www.thoumieux.com; 79 rue St-Dominique, 7e; mains €21-45; ⏲noon-midnight; Ⓜ La Tour Maubourg) Founded in 1923, Thoumieux has been worshipped by generations of diners ever since for its menu of duck, veal and snails and its smooth-as-silk service. It's now run by Thierry Costes and multi-award-winning chef Jean-François Piège, who has his twin-Michelin-starred restaurant upstairs, adjacent to the boutique Hôtel Thoumieux (doubles from €200).

★**RESTAURANT DAVID TOUTAIN** GASTRONOMIC €€€

Map p422 (☎01 45 51 11 10; http://davidtoutain.com; 29 rue Surcouf, 7e; lunch menus €42, lunch & dinner menus €68-98; ⏲noon-2.30pm & 8-10pm Mon-Fri; Ⓜ Invalides) Prepare to be wowed: David Toutain pushes the envelope at his eponymous new restaurant with some of the most creative high-end cooking in Paris today. Mystery degustation courses include unlikely combinations such as smoked eel in green-apple and black-sesame mousse, or candied celery and truffled rice pudding with artichoke praline (stunning wine pairings available).

The best seats in the Scandinavian-style mint-green, muted-blue and burnt-orange dining room with blond-wood tables and textured walls are on the mezzanine, though once the food arrives, you won't be thinking about anything else.

CHEZ FRANÇOISE TRADITIONAL FRENCH €€€

Map p422 (☎01 47 05 49 03; http://chezfrancoise.com; Aérogare des Invalides; 2-/3-course menus from €28/33, oysters per half-dozen €15.50-29; ⏲noon-3pm & 7pm-midnight; Ⓜ Invalides) Buried beneath the enormous Air France building but opening to a retractable-roofed terrace, this old-school 1949-opened restaurant – a favourite with parliamentary workers from the Assemblée Nationale – recalls the early glamour of air travel. Specialities include *entrecôte de bœuf* and sublime oysters.

LES CLIMATS TRADITIONAL FRENCH €€€

Map p422 (http://lesclimats.fr; 41 rue de Lille, 7e; 2-/3-course lunch menus €36/42, mains €32-44, bar snacks €7-22; ⏲restaurant noon-2.30pm & 7-10.30pm Tue-Sat, bar noon-2.30pm & 6-11pm; Ⓜ Solférino) Like the neighbouring Musée d'Orsay, this is a magnficent art-nouveau treasure – a 1905-built former home for female telephone, telegram and postal workers – featuring soaring vaulted ceilings and original stained glass, as well as a garden for summer lunches and a glassed-in winter garden. Exquisite dishes complement its 150-page list of wines, sparkling wines and whiskies purely from Burgundy.

DRINKING & NIGHTLIFE

St-Germain's Carrefour de l'Odéon has a cluster of lively bars and cafes. Rues de Buci, St-André des Arts and de l'Odéon enjoy a fair slice of night action with arty cafes and busy pubs, while place St-Germain des Prés buzzes with the pavement terraces of fabled literary cafes. Les Invalides is a day rather than night venue, with government ministries and embassies outweighing drinking

venues, but, particularly in summer, look out for bars along Les Berges de Seine (p240).

St-Germain

★LES DEUX MAGOTS — CAFE

Map p418 (www.lesdeuxmagots.fr; 170 bd St-Germain, 6e; ⏲7.30am-1am; Ⓜ St-Germain des Prés) If ever there were a cafe that summed up St-Germain des Prés' early-20th-century literary scene, it's this former hang-out of anyone who was anyone. You will spend *beaucoup* to sip a coffee in a wicker chair on the terrace shaded by dark-green awnings and geraniums spilling from window boxes, but it's an undeniable piece of Parisian history.

If you're feeling decadent, order its famous shop-made hot chocolate, served in porcelain jugs. The name refers to the two *magots* (grotesque figurines) of Chinese dignitaries at the entrance.

★AU SAUVIGNON — WINE BAR

Map p418 (80 rue des St-Pères, 7e; ⏲8.30am-10pm Mon-Sat, to 9pm Sun; Ⓜ Sèvres-Babylone) Grab a table in the evening sun at this wonderfully authentic *bar à vin* or head to the quintessential bistro interior, with an original zinc bar, tightly packed tables and hand-painted ceiling celebrating French viticultural tradition. A plate of *casse-croûtes au pain Poilâne* – toast with ham, pâté, terrine, smoked salmon and foie gras – is the perfect accompaniment.

CASTOR CLUB — COCKTAIL BAR

Map p418 (14 rue Hautefeuille, 6e; ⏲7pm-4am Wed-Sat; Ⓜ Odéon) Discreetly signed, this underground cocktail bar has an intimate upstairs bar and 18th-century cellar with hole-in-the-wall booths where you can sip superb-value cocktails (custom-made, if you like) and groove to smooth '50s, '60s and '70s tracks. Very cool.

BRASSERIE O'NEIL — MICROBREWERY

Map p418 (www.oneilbar.fr; 20 rue des Canettes, 6e; ⏲noon-2am; Ⓜ St-Sulpice or Mabillon) Paris'

LOCAL KNOWLEDGE

PATRICIA WELLS' CULINARY SHOPPING SECRETS

Cookery teacher and author of *The Food Lover's Guide to Paris*, American Patricia Wells (www.patriciawells.com) has lived, cooked and shopped in Paris since 1980, and is considered to have truly captured the soul of French cuisine.

What is it that makes Paris so wonderful for culinary shopping? The tradition, the quality, the quantity, the atmosphere and the physical beauty!

Where do you buy your weekly groceries? All over: the Sunday organic market at Rennes (Marché Raspail; p247) – I love the dried fruits and nuts; Poilâne (p243) for bread; Quatrehomme (p254) for cheese; and Poissonnerie du Bac (p247) for fish.

What about for an extra-special gourmet meal? I shop regularly at Le Bon Marché's La Grande Épicerie de Paris (p252) because it is right down the street from me. But for special meals I always order things in advance and go from shop to shop – La Maison du Chocolat (p255) and Pierre Hermé (p255) for chocolate and cakes, and La Dernière Goutte (p254) for wine. That is the fun of Paris, and of France.

Your top food-shopping tip? If you live in Paris, become a *client fidèle* so they reach in the back and give you the best stuff. If you only go once in a while, just smile and be friendly.

A perfect souvenir from Paris? Fragonard (p255), the perfume maker, has a great shop on bd St-Germain. It has a changing litany of *great* things for the home, such as fabulous vases with an Eiffel Tower theme, lovely embroidered napkins with a fish or vegetable theme, and great little spoons with a cake or pastry theme. Nothing is very expensive and the offerings change every few months, so you have to pounce when you find something you love. The gift wrapping in gorgeous Fragonard bags is worth it alone!

Interviewed by Nicola Williams

first microbrewery was opened by a French restaurateur and French brewer over two decades ago, and still brews four fabulous beers (blond, amber, bitter brown and citrusy white) on the premises. Soak them up with thin-crusted *flammekueches* (Alsatian pizzas).

BISTRO DES AUGUSTINS BAR, BISTRO

Map p418 (39 quai des Grands Augins, 6e; ⌚10am-2am; Ⓜ St-Michel) Plastered with old advertising posters from the *bouquiniste* (booksellers) stalls opposite, this bistro and bar manages to remain authentic and down-to-earth despite its epicentral Seine-side location. It's a cosy spot for a glass of red or a light meal like *gratin dauphinois* (potato bake). A handful of pavement-set tables overlook the river.

CAFÉ DE FLORE CAFE

Map p418 (www.cafedeflore.fr; 172 bd St-Germain, 6e; ⌚7am-2am; Ⓜ St-Germain des Prés) The red upholstered benches, mirrors and marble walls at this art-deco landmark haven't changed much since the days when Jean-Paul Sartre and Simone de Beauvoir essentially set up office here, writing in its warmth during the Nazi occupation. It also hosts a monthly English-language philo-café (p36) session.

LE PRÉ BAR

Map p418 (www.cafelepreparis.com; 4-6 rue du Four, 6e; ⌚7.30am-5am; Ⓜ Mabillon) Vivid indigo-coloured wicker chairs line the terrace of this hip drinking spot, while inside the chrome-and-laminex bar resembles a 1950s Airstream trailer. The food (macaroni gratin with foie gras) takes a walk on the wild side too.

CUBANA CAFÉ COCKTAIL BAR

Map p418 (www.cubanacafe.com; 47 rue Vavin, 6e; ⌚10am-3am Sun-Thu, to dawn Fri & Sat; Ⓜ Vavin) A post-work crowd sinks into leather armchairs beneath oil paintings of daily life in Cuba for a huge range of Cuban cocktails made with Havana rum, DJs, salsa and regular free live Cuban music (check the program online).

CAFÉ LA PALETTE CAFE

Map p418 (www.cafelapaletteparis.com; 43 rue de Seine, 6e; ⌚8am-2am; 📶; Ⓜ Mabillon) In the heart of gallery land, this fin-de-siècle cafe and erstwhile stomping ground of Paul Cézanne and Georges Braque attracts a grown-up set of fashion-industry professionals and local art dealers. Its summer terrace is beautiful.

PRESCRIPTION COCKTAIL CLUB COCKTAIL BAR

Map p418 (www.prescriptioncocktailclub.com; 23 rue Mazarine, 6e; ⌚7pm-2am Mon-Thu, 7pm-4am Fri & Sat, 8pm-2am Sun; Ⓜ Odéon) With bowler and flat-top hats as lampshades and a 1930s speakeasy New York air to the place, this cocktail club – run by the same mega-successful team as at Curio Parlor and Experimental – is very Parisian-cool. Getting past the doorman can be tough, but, once in, it's friendliness and old-fashioned cocktails all round.

LE ZÉRO DE CONDUITE BAR

Map p418 (☎01 46 34 26 35; www.zerodeconduite.fr; 14 rue Jacob, 6e; ⌚8.30pm-1.30am Mon-Thu, 6pm-2am Fri & Sat, 9pm-1am Sun; Ⓜ Odéon or Mabillon) In the house where Richard Wagner lived briefly in the 1840s, Le Zéro De Conduite goes all out to rekindle your infancy, serving cocktails in *biberons* (baby bottles), throwing *concours de grimaces* (face-pulling competitions), and offering cards, dice and board games. Advance table reservations are recommended.

L'URGENCE BAR BAR

Map p418 (www.urgencebar.com; 45 rue Monsieur-le-Prince, 6e; ⌚9pm-4am Tue-Sat; Ⓜ Odéon or RER Luxembourg) At this medical-themed 'emergency room' just south of the École de Médecine, the future doctors of France imbibe luridly coloured liquor from babies' bottles and test tubes, loosen their stethoscopes and point to the 'X-ray art' – making comments like '*Mais non!* Clarisse, that's so not the tibia!'

LA MEZZANINE COCKTAIL BAR

Map p418 (www.alcazar.fr; 62 rue Mazarine, 6e; ⌚7.30pm-2am; Ⓜ Odéon) Overlooking the sleek restaurant Alcazar, this hip white-and-glass mezzanine bar is narcissistic but alluring, with fancy cocktails and a fashionable clientele. Thursday to Saturday, DJs 'pass records' in the corner – this place is famous for its excellent trip-hop/house/lounge music compilations.

LE 10 PUB

Map p418 (http://10bar.pagesperso-orange.fr; 10 rue de l'Odéon, 6e; ⌚6pm-2am; Ⓜ Odéon) Plastered with posters, cellar pub 'Le Dix' is a student favourite, not least for its cheap sangria. An eclectic selection emerges from the jukebox – everything from jazz and the Doors to traditional French *chansons* (à la Édith Piaf). It's the ideal spot for plotting the next revolution or conquering a lonely heart.

JANE CLUB CLUB

Map p418 (www.wagg.fr; 62 rue Mazarine, 6e; ⏲10.30pm-6am Fri & Sat, 3.30pm-2am Sun; 📶; Ⓜ Odéon) Formerly Le Wagg and kitted out with a kickin' new sound system, Jane Club is a temple to golden '80s, golden '90s and timeless rock and roll. You can also catch live concerts here (Pete Doherty, for example). Salsa takes place every Sunday. Hours can vary.

Les Invalides

★COUTUME CAFE

Map p422 (http://coutumecafe.com; 47 rue Babylone, 7e; ⏲8am-7pm Mon-Fri, from 10am Sat & Sun; 📶; Ⓜ St-François Xavier or Vaneau) If you've noticed the coffee in Paris getting better lately, it's thanks in no small part to Coutume, artisan roaster of premium beans for scores of establishments around town. Its flagship cafe – a bright, light-filled, post-industrial space – is ground zero for innovative preparation methods including cold extraction and siphon brews. Fabulous organic fare and pastries too.

NATUR'ELLE CAFÉ CAFE

Map p422 (67 av de la Bourdonnais, 7e; ⏲9am-6.30pm Mon-Sat, to 2pm Sun; Ⓜ École Militaire) Poppy-red chairs and tables propagate on the pavement out the front of this welcoming spot serving coffee from Ethiopia, Peru, Colombia, Brazil and the Dominican Republic. In warm weather, go for a frappé, iced tea or freshly squeezed juice, along with light dishes like sandwiches, salads, pastries and cakes.

ALAIN MILLIAT JUICE BAR

Map p422 (☎01 45 55 63 86; www.alain-milliat.com; 159 rue de Grenelle, 7e; ⏲11am-3pm & 6pm-midnight Tue-Fri, 9am-midnight Sat, 10am-6pm Sun; Ⓜ La Tour Maubourg) Alain Milliat's fruit juices, bottled in the south of France, were once reserved for ultra-exclusive hotels and restaurants. But you can pop into his Parisian juice bar–bistro to buy one of the 33 varieties of juice and nectar, or sip them in house. Stunning flavours include rosé-grape or green-tomato juice and white-peach nectar.

Milliat's jams and compotes are equally lush; try them during the bountiful weekend brunch (noon to 3pm Saturday, noon to 4pm Sun; €38).

★ ENTERTAINMENT

St-Germain and especially Les Invalides aren't major nightlife destinations – eating, drinking and, above all, shopping are the main entertainment here. For live music, check for events in bars along Les Berges de Seine (p240), or head to the Latin Quarter or the floating nightclubs in Montparnasse and southern Paris. Cinemagoers are well catered for, with multiplexes concentrated around the Odéon metro station on bd St-Germain.

LE LUCERNAIRE CULTURAL CENTRE

Map p418 (☎reservations 01 45 44 57 34; www.lucernaire.fr; 53 rue Notre Dame des Champs, 6e; ⏲bar 11am-10pm Mon, 11am-12.30am Fri, 4pm-12.30am Sat, 4-10pm Sun; Ⓜ Notre Dame des Champs) Sunday-evening concerts are a fixture on the impressive repertoire of this dynamic Centre National d'Art et d'Essai (National Arts Centre). Be it classical guitar, baroque, French *chansons* or oriental music, these weekly concerts starting at 7.30pm are a real treat. Art and photography exhibitions, cinema, theatre, lectures, debates and guided walks round off the packed cultural agenda.

CINÉMA LA PAGODE CINEMA

Map p422 (☎01 45 55 48 48; www.etoile-cinema.com; 57bis rue de Babylone, 7e; Ⓜ St-François Xavier) This 19th-century Japanese pagoda was converted into a cinema in the 1930s and remains the most atmospheric spot in Paris to catch art-house and classic films. Don't miss a moment or two in its bamboo-enshrined garden.

A classified historical monument, the pagoda was shipped to France, piece by piece, in 1895 by Monsieur Morin (the then proprietor of Le Bon Marché), who had it rebuilt in his garden on rue de Babylone as a present for his wife. The wife clearly wasn't too impressed – she left him a year later. But Parisian cinephiles who flock here to revel in its eclectic program are.

COMÉDIE FRANÇAISE THÉÂTRE DU VIEUX COLOMBIER THEATRE

Map p418 (☎01 44 58 15 15; www.comedie-francaise.fr; 21 rue du Vieux Colombier, 6e; ⏲Sep-Jul; Ⓜ St-Sulpice) One of three Comédie Française venues, along with the Right Bank's main Salle Richelieu and Studio Théâtre. Founded in 1680, it presents works by classic French playwrights such as Molière.

SHOPPING

The northern wedge of the 6e between Église St-Germain des Prés and the Seine is a dream to mooch with its bijou art galleries, antique shops, stylish vintage clothes and designer boutiques (Vanessa Bruno, Isabel Marant et al). St-Germain's style continues along the western half of bd St-Germain and rue du Bac with a striking collection of contemporary furniture, kitchen and design shops. Gourmet food and wine shops galore make it a foodie paradise.

★GAB & JO CONCEPT STORE

Map p418 (www.gabjo.fr; 28 rue Jacob, 6e; ⏲11am-7pm Mon-Sat; Ⓜ St-Germain des Prés) Forget mass-produced, imported souvenirs: for quality local gifts to take home, browse the shelves of Gab & Jo, the country's first-ever concept store stocking only made-in-France items. Designers include Marie-Jeanne de Grasse (scented candles), Marius Fabre (Marseille soaps), Germaine-des-Prés (lingerie), MILF (sunglasses) and Monsieur Marcel (T-shirts).

CIRE TRUDON CANDLES

Map p418 (www.ciretrudon.com; 78 rue de Seine, 6e; ⏲10am-7pm Tue-Sat; Ⓜ Odéon) Claude Trudon began selling candles here in 1643, and the company – which officially supplied Versailles and Napoléon with light – is now the world's oldest candle-maker (look for the plaque to the left of the shop's awning). A rainbow of candles and candlesticks fill the shelves inside.

LE BON MARCHÉ DEPARTMENT STORE

Map p422 (www.bonmarche.fr; 24 rue de Sèvres, 7e; ⏲10am-8pm Mon-Wed & Sat, to 9pm Thu & Fri; Ⓜ Sèvres Babylone) Built by Gustave Eiffel as Paris' first department store in 1852, Le Bon Marché is the epitome of style, with a superb concentration of men's and women's fashions, beautiful homewares, stationery, books and toys as well as chic dining options. The icing on the cake is its glorious food hall, La Grande Épicerie de Paris.

LA GRANDE ÉPICERIE DE PARIS FOOD, DRINK

Map p422 (www.lagrandeepicerie.fr; 36 rue de Sèvres, 7e; ⏲8.30am-9pm Mon-Sat; Ⓜ Sèvres Babylone) Among other edibles, the magnificent food hall of Le Bon Marché department store sells vodka-flavoured lollipops with detoxified ants inside and fist-sized Himalayan salt crystals to grate over food. Its fantastical displays of chocolates, pastries, biscuits, cheeses, fresh fruit and vegetables and deli goods are a sight in themselves.

AU PLAT D'ÉTAIN GAMES

Map p418 (www.auplatdetain.sitew.com; 16 rue Guisarde, 6e; ⏲10.30am-6.30pm Tue-Sat; Ⓜ Odéon or Mabillon) Tiny tin *(étain)* and lead soldiers, snipers, cavaliers, military drummers and musicians (great for chessboard pieces) cram this fascinating boutique. In business since 1775, the shop itself is practically a collectable.

LA MAISON DE POUPÉE ANTIQUES

Map p418 (☎06 09 65 58 68; 40 rue de Vaugirard, 6e; ⏲2.30-7pm Mon-Sat, by appointment Sun; Ⓜ Odéon or RER Luxembourg) Opposite the residence of the French Senate's president, this delightful little shop sells its namesake dolls' houses as well as *poupées anciennes* (antique dolls).

LE CHOCOLAT ALAIN DUCASSE CHOCOLATE

Map p418 (www.lechocolat-alainducasse.com; 26 rue St-Benoît, 6e; ⏲10.30am-7.30pm Tue-Sat; Ⓜ St-Germain des Prés) A mouth-watering range of chocolates made from bean to bar by legendary French chef Alain Ducasse at his new Bastille factory La Manufacture de Chocolat is available for purchase in this glass-fronted Left Bank boutique.

FRÉDÉRIC MALLE PERFUME

Map p418 (www.fredericmalle.com; 37 rue de Grenelle, 7e; ⏲noon-7pm Mon, 11am-7pm Tue-Sat; Ⓜ Rue du Bac) Taking the approach of an 'editor', Malle works with his perfume 'authors' to produce unique fragrance 'editions' (all are refrigerated until sold). These apartment-style premises were his first Paris shop; there are now a couple of others, plus one in New York.

ART & ANTIQUE STREETS

St-Germain's narrow streets are filled with art and antique shops.

Meander along rue Mazarine, rue Jacques Callot, rue des Beaux Arts and rue de Seine for art galleries. Edgier galleries include:

➡ **Galerie Loft** (Map p418; www.galerieloft.com; 3bis rue des Beaux Arts, 6e; ⏲10.30am-6.30pm Tue-Sat; Ⓜ St-Germain des Prés) All forms of art (digital video and performance photography included) by contemporary Chinese artists are on show at this courtyard gallery.

➡ **La Galerie Moderne** (Map p418; www.lagaleriemoderne.com; 52 rue Mazarine, 6e; ⏲2-7pm Tue-Sat; Ⓜ St-Germain des Prés) Original designer furniture and lights from the 1950s, '60s and '70s.

For antiques, try the following:

➡ **Carré Rive Gauche** (Map p418; www.carrerivegauche.com; Ⓜ Rue du Bac or Solférino) Bounded by quai Voltaire and rues de l'Université, des Sts-Pères and du Bac, this 'Left Bank square' is home to more than 120 specialised merchants. Antiques fairs are usually held in spring, while exhibitions take place during the year.

➡ **Hapart** (Map p418; 72 rue Mazarine, 6e; ⏲2-7pm Tue-Sun; Ⓜ Odéon) A collector's delight the size of a pocket handkerchief, Hapart recalls lost childhood with its romantic selection of old and antique toys.

THEATR'HALL FASHION

Map p418 (www.theatrhall.com; 3 Carrefour de l'Odéon, 6e; ⏲11am-7.30pm Mon-Sat; Ⓜ Odéon) Should you have an upcoming masquerade ball, this wonderful old space selling theatrical garb – shirts in medieval, Revolution and belle époque styles, capes, top hats and Venetian masks – is the place to come to look the part.

HERMÈS CONCEPT STORE

Map p418 (www.hermes.com; 17 rue de Sèvres, 6e; ⏲10.30am-7pm Mon-Sat; Ⓜ Sèvres-Babylone) A stunning art-deco swimming pool now houses luxury label Hermès' inaugural concept store. Retaining its original mosaic tiles and iron balustrades and adding enormous timber pod-like 'huts', the vast, tiered space showcases new directions in home furnishings such as fabrics and wallpaper, as well as classic lines including its signature scarves. There's also an appropriately chic cafe, Le Plongeoir.

DEYROLLE ANTIQUES, HOMEWARES

Map p418 (www.deyrolle.com; 46 rue du Bac, 7e; ⏲10am-1pm & 2-7pm Mon, 10am-7pm Tue-Sat; Ⓜ Rue du Bac) Overrun with creatures including lions, tigers, zebras and storks, taxidermist Deyrolle opened in 1831. In addition to stuffed animals (for rent and sale), it stocks minerals, shells, corals and crustaceans, stand-mounted ostrich eggs and pedagogical storyboards. There are also rare and unusual seeds (including many old types of tomato), gardening tools and accessories.

ALEXANDRA SOJFER ACCESSORIES

Map p418 (www.alexandrasojfer.com; 218 bd St-Germain, 7e; ⏲10am-7pm Mon-Sat; Ⓜ Rue du Bac) Become Parisian chic with a frivolous, frilly, fantastical or frightfully fashionable *parapluie* (umbrella), parasol or walking cane handcrafted by Alexandra Sojfer at this St-Germain boutique, in the trade since 1834.

BARTHÉLÉMY FOOD

Map p422 (51 rue de Grenelle, 7e; ⏲8.30am-1pm & 3.30-7.15pm Tue-Thu, 8.30am-7pm Fri & Sat; Ⓜ Rue du Bac) You'll be tempted to whip out your camera at this jewel box of an old-fashioned *fromagerie*, with its marble cupboards, beautiful blue-tiled floors, sheep figurines and, of course, incredible cheeses (it supplies the palais de l'Élysée, no less). However, as photos are resolutely forbidden, you'll have to content yourself with stocking up instead.

LE BAIN ROSE HOMEWARES

Map p418 (www.le-bain-rose.fr; 11 rue d'Assas, 6e; ⏲11.30am-7pm Mon-Sat, closed Aug; Ⓜ Rennes) The antique and retro mirrors (hand-held and on stands), perfume spritzers, soap dishes and even basins and tapware at this long-established shop can transform your bathroom into a belle époque sanctum.

SECONDHAND CHIC

When St-Germain's well-heeled residents spring-clean their wardrobes, they take their designer and vintage cast-offs to *dépôt-vente* (secondhand) boutiques, where savvy locals snap up serious bargains. Try your luck at the following addresses:

➡ **Chercheminippes** (102, 109-11, 114 & 124 rue du Cherche Midi, 6e; ⏲11am-7pm Mon-Sat) Six beautifully presented boutiques on one street selling secondhand pieces by current designers. Each specialises in a different genre (*haute couture*, kids, menswear etc), perfectly ordered by size and designer. There are even changing rooms.

➡ **Le Dépôt-Vente de Buci** (Map p418; 4 rue Bourbon le Château, 6e; ⏲9am-noon & 2-6pm Tue-Sat; Ⓜ Mabillon) Fronted by a black wooden façade, this stylish 'boutique of curiosities' stocks hand-me-downs mainly from the 1960s on consignment, returning anything that hasn't sold after three months.

➡ **Ragtime** (Map p418; 23 rue de l'Échaudé, 6e; ⏲2.30-7pm Mon-Sat; Ⓜ Mabillon) Madame Auguet's boutique sells *vêtements anciens* (vintage clothes) from 1870 to 1970.

➡ **L'Embellie** (Map p422; 2 rue du Regard, 6e; ⏲10.30am-1.30pm & 2.30-7pm Tue-Sat, by appointment Mon; Ⓜ Sèvres-Babylone) Superb selection of vintage fashion.

QUATREHOMME — FOOD

Map p422 (www.quatrehomme.fr; 62 rue de Sèvres, 6e; ⏲9am-7.45pm Tue-Sat; Ⓜ Vanneau) Buy the best of French cheeses, many with an original take (eg Epoisses boxed in chestnut leaves, Mont d'Or flavoured with black truffles, spiced honey and Roquefort bread etc), at this king of *fromageries*. The smell alone as you enter is heavenly.

A LA RECHERCHE DE JANE — ACCESSORIES

Map p418 (http://alarecherchedejane.wordpress.com; 41 rue Dauphine, 6e; ⏲11.30am-7pm Wed-Sat, 1-7pm Sun; Ⓜ Odéon) This welcoming *chapelier* (milliner) has literally thousands of handcrafted hats on hand for both men and women, and can also make them to order.

LA CRÈMERIE — FOOD, DRINK

Map p418 (www.lacremerie.fr; 9 rue des 4 Vents, 6e; ⏲shop 3.30-8.30pm Mon, 10.30am-10pm Tue-Sat; Ⓜ Odéon) Beneath its glass-covered ceiling, this 19th-century marble-walled boutique stocks over 400 wines and exquisite gourmet goods. Although dining primarily now takes place at its new, nearby premises La Grande Crèmerie (p244), it's still a delightful spot for an early-evening *apéro* accompanied by tapas-style dishes (smoked-trout terrine, goat's cheese and olives, black-pudding-topped toast; dishes €12). Hours fluctuate.

JB GUANTI — ACCESSORIES

Map p418 (www.jbguanti.fr; 59 rue de Rennes, 6e; ⏲10am-7pm Mon-Sat; Ⓜ St-Sulpice or Mabillon) For the ultimate finishing touch, the men's and women's gloves at this boutique, which specialises solely in gloves, are the epitome of both style and comfort, whether unlined, silk lined, cashmere lined, lambskin lined or trimmed with rabbit fur.

Buying for someone else? To get their glove size, measure the length in centimetres of their middle finger from the top to where it joins their hand – the number of centimetres equals the size (eg 5cm is a size 5).

CAVE ST-SULPICE — DRINK

Map p418 (www.cavesaintsulpice.com; 3 rue St-Sulpice, 6e; ⏲10am-noon & 3-7pm Tue-Thu, to 7.30pm Fri & Sat, 10am-1pm Sun; Ⓜ Odéon) Champagne is the speciality of this lovely little boutique, by the half-bottle, bottle or magnum; pink, white or designer. You can also splash out on champagne flutes and ice buckets.

LA DERNIÈRE GOUTTE — WINE

Map p418 (www.ladernieregoutte.net; 6 rue du Bourbon le Château, 6e; ⏲3-8pm Mon, 10.30am-1.30pm & 3-8pm Tue-Fri, 11am-7pm Sat; Ⓜ Mabillon) 'The Last Drop' is the brainchild of Cuban-American sommelier Juan Sánchez, whose tiny wine shop is packed with exciting French *vins de propriétaires* (estate-bottled wines) made by small independent producers.

PÂTISSERIE SADAHARU AOKI — FOOD

Map p418 (www.sadaharuaoki.com; 35 rue de Vaugirard, 6e; ⏲11am-7pm Tue-Sat, 10am-6pm Sun; Ⓜ Rennes or St-Sulpice) 'Exquisite' fails to describe the creations of one of Paris' top pastry chefs, Tokyo-born Sadaharu Aoki. His gourmet works include boxes of 72 different flavoured macaroons and green-tea chocolate.

PIERRE HERMÉ FOOD

Map p418 (www.pierreherme.com; 72 rue Bonaparte, 6e; ⌚10am-7pm Sun-Wed, to 7.30pm Thu & Fri, to 8pm Sat; Ⓜ Odéon or RER Luxembourg) It's the size of a chocolate box, but once you're in, your taste buds will go wild. Pierre Hermé is one of Paris' top chocolatiers and this boutique is a veritable feast of perfectly presented petits fours, cakes, chocolates, nougats, macarons and jam.

ROUGE ET NOIR GAMES

Map p418 (www.rouge-et-noir.fr; 26 rue Vavin, 6e; ⌚11am-7pm Tue-Sat; Ⓜ Vavin) FREE Trivial Pursuit Paris, Rubik's cubes, juggling balls, backgammon, chess, tarot and playing cards… This small family-run boutique specialising in traditional and not-so-traditional games offers bags of fun.

MICHEL CHAUDUN CHOCOLATE

Map p422 (Michel; 149 rue de l'Université, 7e; ⌚9.30am-12.30pm & 1-6pm Mon, 9.15am-noon & 1-7pm Tue-Sat; Ⓜ La Tour-Maubourg) Ganache *pavés* ('cobblestones' torn up and thrown during Paris' May 1968 student uprisings) are the standouts at Michel Chaudun's entrancing chocolate shop, which resembles a toy shop thanks to creations like chocolate horses and chess pieces.

FLAMANT HOME INTERIORS HOMEWARES

Map p418 (www.flamant.com; 8 place de Furstenberg, 6e; ⌚10.30am-7pm Mon-Sat; Ⓜ Mabillon) Silverware, curtains, cutlery, tableware, linen and other quality home furnishings: this maze of a store with two entrances (you can also enter via 8 rue de l'Abbaye) is the place where moneyed Parisians shop for the household.

PLASTIQUES HOMEWARES

Map p418 (www.plastiques-paris.fr; 103 rue de Rennes, 6e; ⌚10.15am-7pm Mon-Sat; Ⓜ Rennes) Lollypop-coloured tableware (trays, serving bowls, dinner settings etc) and cookware (whisks, mixing bowls and much more) fill this original, inexpensive boutique.

LA CLEF DES MARQUES FASHION

Map p418 (www.laclefdesmarques.com; 122-126 bd Raspail, 6e; ⌚12.30-7pm Mon, 10.30am-7pm Tue-Sat; Ⓜ Vavin) This designer outlet specialises in *grandes marques* (big names) at knock-down prices for men, women and kids, with labels like Emilio Pucci, Ralph Lauren, Calvin Klein, Le Petit Bateau, Diesel and stacks of sportswear.

GÉRARD DURAND ACCESSORIES

Map p422 (www.accessoires-mode.com; 75-77 rue du Bac, 7e; ⌚9am-7pm Mon-Sat; Ⓜ Rue du Bac) Brightly coloured, boldly printed *collants* and *bas* (tights and stockings) are the speciality of this boutique, which also stocks equally vibrant socks, scarves and gloves.

SONIA RYKIEL FASHION

Map p418 (www.soniarykiel.com; 175 bd St-Germain, 6e; ⌚10.30am-7pm Mon-Sat; Ⓜ St-Germain des Prés) In the heady days of May 1968 amid Paris' student uprisings, Sonia Rykiel opened her inaugural Left Bank boutique here, and went on to revolutionise garments with inverted seams, 'no hems' and 'no lining'. Her diffusion labels (including children's wear) are housed in separate boutiques nearby, with other outlets around Paris.

LA MAISON DU CHOCOLAT CHOCOLATE

Map p418 (www.lamaisonduchocolat.fr; 19 rue de Sèvres, 6e; ⌚10am-7.30pm Mon-Sat, to 1pm Sun; Ⓜ Sèvres-Babylone) Pralines, ganaches and fruit chocolates are the hallmark of this exquisite chocolatier. Other treats include macarons inspired by its signature chocolates, such as Rigoletto (chocolate and salted caramel) and Salvador (chocolate and raspberry), as well as decadent éclairs.

FRAGONARD BOUTIQUE PERFUME, SOUVENIRS

Map p418 (☎01 42 84 12 12; www.fragonard.com; 196 bd St-Germain, 6e; ⌚10am-7pm Mon-Sat; Ⓜ Rue du Bac or St-Germain des Prés) The bd St-Germain boutique of perfume maker Fragonard (which runs Paris' perfume museum; p100) stocks a heady range of souvenirs – from scarves to cookbooks – evoking the sights, scents and flavours of France.

SAN FRANCISCO BOOK COMPANY BOOKS

Map p418 (www.sanfranciscobooksparis.com; 17 rue Monsieur le Prince, 6e; ⌚11am-9pm Mon-Sat, 2-7.30pm Sun; Ⓜ Odéon) Art, architecture, literary criticism, politics and science are among the non-fiction titles at this haven of a little secondhand English-language bookshop. You could easily lose hours browsing its shelves brimming with classic and contemporary novels.

CENTRALE DU FUSIL D'OCCASION ANTIQUES

Map p422 (69 rue de Grenelle, 7e; ⌚10am-12.30pm & 2.30-6.30pm Tue-Sun; Ⓜ Rue du Bac) If antique pistols and rifles fire your interest, this musty gunsmith is one not to miss.

Montparnasse & Southern Paris

MONTPARNASSE & 15E | PLACE D'ITALIE & CHINATOWN

Neighbourhood Top Five

❶ Ignoring the '70s smoked-glass exterior of **Tour Montparnasse** (p259) and zipping to the top for a glass of Champagne on the terrace, taking in one of the finest panoramas of Paris.

❷ Prowling the spine-prickling, skull-and-bone-packed tunnels of Paris' creepy ossuary, **Les Catacombes** (p258).

❸ Visiting Jean-Paul Sartre, Simone de Beauvoir and Serge Gainsbourg at **Cimetière du Montparnasse** (p260).

❹ Strolling the tree-lined **Île aux Cygnes** (p260) from the Statue of Liberty replica towards the Eiffel Tower.

❺ Catching superb exhibitions at France's national library, the book-shaped **Bibliothèque Nationale de France** (p261).

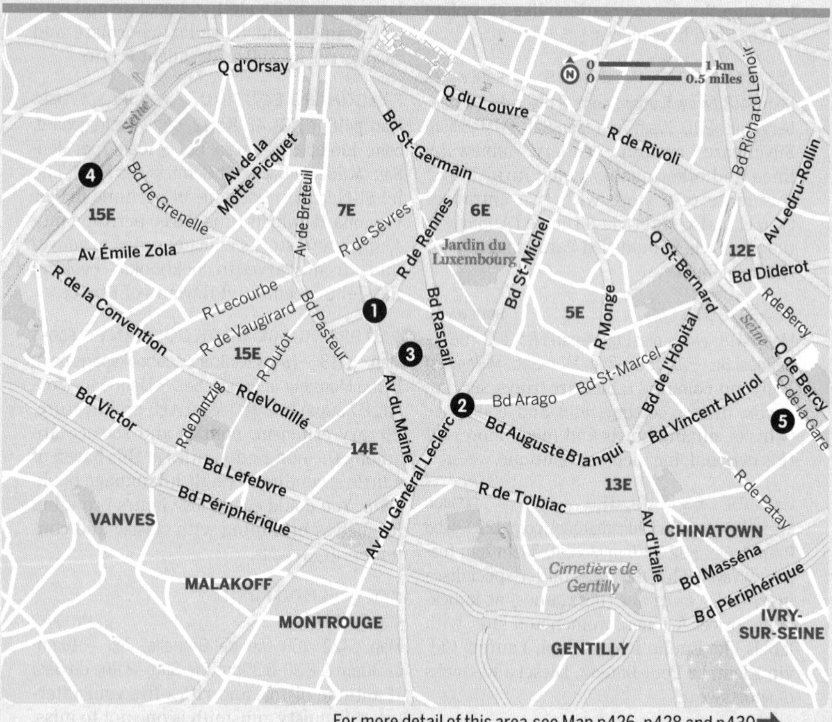

For more detail of this area, see Map p426, p428 and p430 ➡

Explore: Montparnasse & Southern Paris

Tour Montparnasse is an unavoidable sight, but its observation deck offers an unrivalled spot for getting to grips with the lay of the land. At its feet are the cafes, brasseries and backstreets where some of the early 20th century's most seminal artists and writers hung out – albeit now swathed by urban grit. The area's tree-filled cemetery is a peaceful spot to escape to – and to visit the graves of many of those same visionaries.

West in the gentrified 15e, take in more great views by strolling the Île aux Cygnes or boarding a balloon 'flight' in the Parc André-Citroën, one of the capital's most innovative open spaces.

To Montparnasse's east, the ever-regenerating 13e is home to the country's national library as well as Paris' largest Chinatown. No matter where you end up for dinner in this sprawling southern sector of Paris, head back to the river to dance until dawn on the floating bars/nightclubs moored on the Seine's quays.

Local Life

- **Street life** Join locals shopping for flowers, cheese, charcuterie and more along rue Daguerre.
- **Track life** Explore Paris' former steam railway line on the newly reopened Petite Ceinture du 15e.
- **Breton life** Take a crêperie crawl through Montparnasse's 'Little Brittany'.
- **Fashion life** Find bargain designer seconds, samples and last season's stock on the 14e's rue d'Alésia.

Getting There & Away

- **Metro** Montparnasse Bienvenüe is the transport hub for Montparnasse and the 15e. Bibliothèque and Place d'Italie are convenient stops in place d'Italie and Chinatown.
- **Bus** Buses help fill the gap in areas lacking comprehensive metro coverage. From Gare Montparnasse, bus 91 goes to Gare d'Austerlitz, Gare de Lyon and Bastille; bus 92 to Charles de Gaulle-Étoile; and bus 94 to Sèvres Babylone. Pick up bus 82 on bd du Montparnasse for Invalides and the Eiffel Tower. Bus 62 from the Bibliothèque Nationale de France crosses the 13e to rue d'Alésia and rue de la Convention. At place d'Italie, take bus 67 to Mosquée de Paris, Jardin des Plantes, Île de St-Louis, Hôtel de Ville and Pigalle, and bus 83 to the Jardin de Luxembourg and Les Invalides.
- **Bicycle** Handy Vélib' stations include 5-7 rue d'Odessa, 14e; 13 bd Edgar Quinet, 14e; 2 av René Coty, 14e; and two facing place d'Italie, 13e.

Lonely Planet's Top Tip

The metro is tailor-made for cross-town trips, but to whiz around Paris' perimeter, hop on the T3 tram. From the Pont du Garigliano, 15e, it currently skims the city's edge as far as Porte de la Chapelle, 18e. An extension to Porte d'Asnières, 17e, is due for completion in 2017, encircling some three-quarters of the city. Passengers use standard t+ tickets. For updates on Paris' trams, visit www.tramway.paris.fr.

Best Places to Eat

- Le Casse Noix (p263)
- Jeu de Quilles (p263)
- La Véraison (p263)
- Pho 14 (p265)
- Restaurant Variations (p266)

For reviews, see p262

Best Places to Drink

- Félicie (p268)
- Le Rosebud (p268)
- Le Select (p268)
- Tandem (p268)

For reviews, see p268

Best Floating Clubs

- Le Batofar (p268)
- Bateau El Alamein (p269)
- Petit Bain (p270)
- Péniche l'Improviste (p270)
- La Dame de Canton (p269)

For reviews, see p268

OSSEMENS DE L'EGLISE
ET DU CLOITRE
DU PETIT S^T ANTOINE,
LE 17 JUILLET 1804

PETE SEAWARD / GETTY IMAGES ©

TOP SIGHT
LES CATACOMBES

Paris' most macabre sight is its series of underground tunnels lined with skulls and bones. In 1785 it was decided that in order to rectify the hygiene problems of Paris' overflowing cemeteries the bones would be exhumed and stored in disused quarry tunnels. Thus, the Catacombes were created in 1810.

The route through the Catacombes begins at a small, dark-green belle époque building in the centre of a grassy area of av Colonel Henri Roi-Tanguy, adjacent to place Denfert Rochereau. After descending 20m (via 130 narrow, dizzying spiral steps) below street level, you follow the dark, subterranean passages to reach the ossuary itself, with a mind-boggling amount of bones and skulls of millions of Parisians neatly packed along the walls.

You'll traverse 2km of tunnels in all. The surface is uneven and often slippery due to loose stones and mud – sturdy shoes are essential. In the tunnels the temperature is a cool 14°C, there are no toilets and flash photography isn't permitted. A maximum of 200 people are allowed in the tunnels at a time and queues can be huge – arrive early in the morning to beat the worst of the crowds. Last entry is at 4pm. Bear in mind that it's not suitable for young children (nor anyone faint-hearted).

Renting an audioguide (€3) greatly enhances the experience; 90-minute guided tours in English (€4.50) take place at noon on Tuesday and Wednesday.

The exit is back up 83 steps onto rue Remy Dumoncel, 14e (metro Mouton-Duvernet), 700m southwest of av Colonel Henri Roi-Tanguy. Bag searches are carried out to prevent visitors 'souveniring' bones. A gift shop selling quirky skull-and-bone-themed items (Jenga, candles, shot glasses) is across the street from the exit.

DID YOU KNOW?

- During WWII these tunnels were used as a headquarters by the Resistance.
- Thrill-seeking cataphiles are often caught (and fined) roaming the tunnels at night.

PRACTICALITIES

- Map p428
- www.catacombes.paris.fr
- 1 av Colonel Henri Roi-Tanguy, 14e
- adult/child €8/free
- 10am-5pm Tue-Sun
- M Denfert Rochereau

SIGHTS

Montparnasse & 15e

LES CATACOMBES CEMETERY

See p258.

TOUR MONTPARNASSE VIEWPOINT

Map p428 (www.tourmontparnasse56.com; rue de l'Arrivée, 15e; adult/child €14.50/9; 9.30am-11.30pm daily Apr-Sep, to 10.30pm Sun-Thu, to 11pm Fri & Sat Oct-Mar; MMontparnasse Bienvenüe) Spectacular views unfold from this 210m-high smoked-glass and steel office block, built in 1973. (Bonus: it's about the only spot in the city you can't see this startlingly ugly skyscraper, which dwarfs low-rise Paris.) Europe's fastest lift (elevator) whisks visitors up in 38 seconds to the indoor observatory on the 56th floor, with multimedia displays. Finish with a hike up the stairs to the 59th-floor open-air terrace (with a sheltered walkway) and bubbly at the terrace's Champagne bar.

The tower also houses the city's highest restaurant, Le Ciel de Paris (p265).

GARE MONTPARNASSE TRAIN STATION

Map p428 (place Raoul Dautry, 14e; MMontparnasse Bienvenüe) Several unusual attractions hide on the rooftop of this sprawling train station, reached by the metal staircase next to platform 1 or lifts on rue du Commandant Rene Mouchotte. The **Jardin de l'Atlantique** (Map p428; place des Cinq Martyr du Lycée Buffon, 14e; 8am-5.30pm Mon-Fri, 9am-5.30pm Sat & Sun), whose 3.5 hectares carpets the station's roof, offers greenery and tranquillity in the heart of the urban tumult. Its futuristic **Observatoire Météorologique** 'sculpture' measures precipitation, temperature and wind speed.

Next to the garden is the Resistance museum, the **Musée Jean Moulin** (Map p428; 01 40 64 39 44; www.ml-leclerc-moulin.paris.fr; 23 allée de la 2e DB, 14e; 10am-6pm Tue-Sun) FREE. Devoted to the WWII German occupation of Paris, the small museum focuses on the Resistance and its leader, Jean Moulin (1899–1943). The attached **Mémorial du Maréchal Leclerc de Hauteclocque et de la Libération de Paris** (Map p428) shows a panoramic film on the eponymous general (1902–47), who led the Free French units during the war and helped to liberate the city in 1944.

MUSÉE BOURDELLE MUSEUM

Map p428 (www.bourdelle.paris.fr; 18 rue Antoine Bourdelle, 15e; 10am-6pm Tue-Sun; MFalguière) FREE Monumental bronzes fill the house and workshop where sculptor Antoine Bourdelle (1861–1929), a pupil of Rodin, lived and worked. The three sculpture gardens are particularly lovely, with a flavour of belle époque and post-WWI Montparnasse. The museum usually has a temporary exhibition (attracting an admission fee) going on alongside its free permanent collection.

FONDATION CARTIER POUR L'ART CONTEMPORAIN GALLERY

Map p428 (www.fondation.cartier.com; 261 bd Raspail, 14e; adult/11-26yr €10.50/7; 11am-10pm Tue, to 8pm Wed-Sun; MRaspail) Designed by Jean Nouvel, this stunning glass-and-steel building is a work of art in itself. It hosts temporary exhibits on contemporary art (from the 1980s to today) in a diverse variety of media – from painting and photography to video and fashion, as well as performance art. Artist Lothar Baumgarten created the wonderfully rambling garden.

L'ADRESSE MUSEUM

Map p428 (Musée de la Poste; www.ladressemuseedelaposte.fr; 34 bd de Vaugirard, 15e; MMontparnasse Bienvenüe or Pasteur) Anyone who enjoys travel, exploration and communication will enjoy this contemporary postal museum, which offers a fascinating overview of the history of the French postal service, with exhibits spanning several floors. Imaginative temporary exhibitions might be anything from artist-designed letterboxes to wartime postal services or postcards. The permanent collection was closed for renovation at the time of writing; contact the museum for updates.

Don't miss the shop selling every imaginable French stamp, from Harry Potter designs to romantic red heart-shaped stamps, as well as stamps from overseas French territories including New Caledonia and French Polynesia.

MUSÉE PASTEUR MUSEUM

Map p428 (Institut Pasteur; www.pasteur.fr; 25 rue du Docteur Roux, 15e; adult/student €7/3; 2pm, 3pm & 4pm Mon-Fri Sep-Jul; MPasteur) Tours of the apartment where the famous chemist and bacteriologist spent the last seven years of his life (1888–95) take you through Pasteur's private rooms, with odds

TOP SIGHT
CIMETIÈRE DU MONTPARNASSE

Opened in 1824, Montparnasse Cemetery, Paris' second-largest after Père Lachaise (p161), sprawls over 19 hectares shaded by 1200 trees including maples, ash, limes and conifers. Although it doesn't have the sheer scale of celebrities laid to rest as its bigger and better-known counterpart, there are still numerous famous graves.

Some of the illustrious 'residents' at Cimetière du Montparnasse include poet **Charles Baudelaire**, writer Guy de Maupassant, playwright **Samuel Beckett**, sculptor Constantin Brancusi, painter Chaim Soutine, photographer Man Ray, industrialist André Citroën, actress Jean Seberg, and **Jean-Paul Sartre** and **Simone de Beauvoir**, who are buried together.

Like Père Lachaise, Cimetière du Montparnasse has its time-honoured tomb traditions. One of the most popular is fans leaving metro tickets atop the grave of crooner **Serge Gainsbourg** (in division 1, just off av Transversale), in reference to his 1958 song 'Le Poinçonneur des Lilas' (The Ticket Puncher of Lilas), depicting workaday monotony through the eyes of a metro ticket-puncher. Gainsbourg enacted the soul-destroying job (since eclipsed by machines) on film when recording the song in the Porte des Lilas station.

DON'T MISS

- Charles Baudelaire's grave
- Samuel Beckett's grave
- Jean-Paul Sartre and Simone de Beauvoir's graves
- Serge Gainsbourg's grave

PRACTICALITIES

- Map p428
- bd Edgar Quinet & rue Froidevaux, 14e
- 8am-6pm Mon-Fri, 8.30am-6pm Sat, 9am-6pm Sun
- M Edgar Quinet or Raspail

and ends including gifts presented to him by heads of state and drawings he did as a young man.

You'll need to show a passport or ID card to gain entrance. Tours lasting 45 minutes to one hour are in French; printed English guides are available.

After Pasteur's death, the French government wanted to entomb his remains in the Panthéon, but his family, acting in accordance with his wishes, obtained permission to have him buried at his institute. The great savant lies in the basement crypt.

PARC ANDRÉ-CITROËN PARK

Map p430 (quai André-Citroën, 15e; 8am-9.30pm May-Aug, shorter hrs rest of yr; M Balard)

In 1915 automotive entrepreneur André Citroën built a vast car-manufacturing plant here in the 15e. After it closed in the 1970s, the vacated site was eventually turned into this forward-looking 14-hectare urban park. Its central lawn is flanked by greenhouses, dancing fountains, an elevated reflecting pool, and smaller gardens themed around movement and the (six) senses. Opening hours vary depending on the season – check signs posted at the entrances.

LE BALLON AIR DE PARIS SCENIC BALLOON

Map p430 (01 44 26 20 00; www.ballondeparis.com; Parc André Citroën, 2 rue de la Montagne de la Fage, 15e; adult/child €12/6; 9am-9.30pm, closes earlier Sep-Apr; M Balard or Lourmel)

Drift up and up but not away – this helium-filled balloon remains tethered to the ground as it lifts you 150m into the air for spectacular panoramas over Paris. The balloon plays an active environmental role, changing colour depending on the air quality and pollution levels. Confirm ahead; the balloon doesn't ascend in windy conditions.

ÎLE AUX CYGNES ISLAND

Map p430 (Isle of Swans; btwn Pont de Grenelle & Pont de Bir Hakeim, 15e; M Javel or Bir Hakeim)

Paris' little-known third island, the artificially created Île aux Cygnes (Isle of Swans), was formed in 1827 to protect the river port and measures just 850m by 11m. On the western side of the Pont de Grenelle is a soaring one-quarter scale **Statue of Liberty replica** (Map p430), inaugurated in 1889. Walk east along the Allée des Cygnes – the tree-lined walkway that runs the length of the island – for knock-out Eiffel Tower views.

Place d'Italie & Chinatown

BIBLIOTHÈQUE NATIONALE DE FRANCE — LIBRARY

Map p426 (01 53 79 59 59; www.bnf.fr; 11 quai François Mauriac, 13e; temporary exhibitions adult/child from €9/free; exhibitions 10am-7pm Tue-Sat, 1-7pm Sun, closed early-late Sep; M Bibliothèque) With four glass towers shaped like half-open books, the 1995-opened National Library of France was one of President Mitterand's most ambitious and costliest *grands projets* (huge public edifices). Some 12 million tomes are stored on 420km of shelves and the library can accommodate 2000 readers and 2000 researchers. Excellent temporary exhibitions (entrance E) revolve around 'the word' – from storytelling to bookbinding and French heroes. Exhibition admission includes free same-day access to the reference library.

No expense was spared to carry out the library's grand design, which many claimed defied logic. Books and historical documents are shelved in the sunny, 23-storey and 79m-high towers, while patrons sit in artificially lit basement halls built around a 'forest courtyard' of 140 50-year-old pines, trucked in from the countryside. The towers have since been fitted with a complex (and expensive) shutter system but the basement is prone to flooding from the Seine.

GALERIE ITINERRANCE — GALLERY

Map p426 (www.itinerrance.fr; 7bis, rue René Goscinny, 13e; 2-7pm Wed-Sat; M Bibliothèque) Testament to the 13e's ongoing creative renaissance, this very funky gallery showcases graffiti and street art. Artists and events vary.

DOCKS EN SEINE — CULTURAL CENTRE

Map p426 (Cité de la Mode et du Design; www.paris-docks-en-seine.fr; 36 quai d'Austerlitz, 13e; 10am-midnight; M Gare d'Austerlitz) Framed by a lurid-lime wavelike glass façade, a transformed Seine-side warehouse now houses the French fashion institute, the **Institut Français de la Mode** (hence the docks' alternative name, Cité de la Mode et du Design), mounting fashion and design exhibitions and events throughout the year. Other draws include an entertainment-themed contemporary-art museum, Art Ludique-Le Musée (p262), along with ultrahip bars, clubs and restaurants and huge riverside terraces.

LOCAL KNOWLEDGE

PETITE CEINTURE

Long before the tramway or even the metro, the 35km Petite Ceinture (Little Belt) steam railway encircled the city of Paris. Constructed during the reign of Napoléon III between 1852 and 1869 as a way to move troops and goods around the city's fortifications, it became a thriving passenger service until the metro arrived in 1900. Most passenger services ceased in 1934 and goods services in 1993, and the line became an overgrown wilderness. Until recently, access was forbidden (although that didn't stop maverick urban explorers scrambling along its tracks and tunnels). Of the line's original 29 stations, 17 survive (in various states of disrepair).

Plans for regenerating the Petite Ceinture railway corridor have progressed with the recent opening of three sections with walkways alongside the tracks. Other areas remain off limits.

In southern Paris, the **Petite Ceinture du 15e (PC 15)** (Map p430; www.paris.fr; btwn rue Olivier de Serres & rue St-Charles, 15e; 9am-8.30pm May-Aug, to 7.30pm Apr & Sep, to 6pm Mar, reduced hrs Nov-Feb; M Balard or Porte de Versailles) FREE stretches for 1.3km, with biodiverse habitats including forest, grassland and prairies supporting 220 species of flora and fauna. In addition to the end points, there are three lift/elevator-enabled access points along its route: 397ter rue de Vaugirard; opposite 82 rue Desnouettes; and place Robert Guillemard. Ultimately the goal is to open the entire section of track between parcs Georges-Brassens and André-Citroën, around 3km in all.

Sections in eastern Paris, **Petite Ceinture du 12e (PC 12)**, near the Bois de Vincennes, and western Paris, **Petite Ceinture du 16e (PC 16)**, near the Bois de Boulogne are also open to the public.

The docks occupy a 20,000-sq-metre riverside warehouse built in 1907 (the first industrial complex in Paris to use reinforced concrete), where goods were delivered by barge. For the best view of the water-facing facade, cross the Seine over Pont Charles de Gaulle.

ART LUDIQUE-LE MUSÉE MUSEUM

Map p426 (http://artludique.com; 34 quai d'Austerlitz, 13e, Docks en Seine; adult/child €15/9.50; ⌚11am-7pm Mon, 11am-10pm Wed-Fri, 10am-10pm Sat & Sun; Ⓜ Gare d'Austerlitz) Comics, mangas, video games and animated and live-action cinema are treated as seriously as any other art form at this contemporary-art museum in the cutting-edge Docks en Seine complex. Chronologically arranged exhibits showing the evolution of the genre form the core of the permanent collection, but the real crowd pleasers are the blockbuster temporary exhibitions such as a Pixar retrospective or Marvel superheros. Online bookings cost a euro extra but allow you to skip the queues. Hours can vary.

MANUFACTURE DES GOBELINS FACTORY, GALLERY

Map p426 (☎01 44 08 52 00; www.mobiliernational.culture.gouv.fr; 42 av des Gobelins, 13e; gallery adult/child €6/4, tour & gallery €10/4; ⌚gallery 11-6pm Tue-Sun, guided tours 4pm Tue-Fri & Sun, 2.30pm & 4pm Sat; Ⓜ Les Gobelins) The Gobelins Factory has been weaving *haute lisse* (high relief) tapestries on specialised looms since the 18th century along with Beauvais-style *basse lisse* (low relief) ones and Savonnerie rugs. Superb examples are showcased in its gallery; factory visits (1½ hours), by guided tour, take you through the *ateliers* (workshops) and exhibits of the thousands of carpets and tapestries woven here.

Buy tickets in advance from Fnac or turn up well ahead of time for same-day tour tickets.

PARC MONTSOURIS PARK

Map p426 (av Reille, 14e; ⌚8am-9.30pm summer, shorter hrs rest of yr; Ⓜ Porte d'Orléans or RER Cité-Universitaire) The name of this sprawling lakeside park – planted with horse-chestnut, yew, cedar, weeping beech and buttonwood trees – derives from *moque souris* (mice mockery) because the area was once overrun with rodents. Today it's a delightful spot for a picnic, and has endearing playground areas such as a concrete 'road system' where litties can trundle matchbox cars (BYO cars).

The park neighbours the groundbreaking 1920s-built Cité Universitaire (student halls of residence).

EATING

Since the 1920s, bd du Montparnasse has been one of the city's premier avenues for enjoying Parisian cafe life, with legendary brasseries and cafes. The down-to-earth 15e cooks up fabulous bistro fare – key streets are rues de la Convention, de Vaugirard, St-Charles and du Commerce, and south of bd de Grenelle. For Asian food, try Chinatown's avs de Choisy and d'Ivry and rue Baudricourt. The villagey Butte aux Cailles, 13e, south of Corvisart metro station, is chock-a-block with interesting addresses. Uberhip restaurants hide inside the Docks en Seine (p261).

Montparnasse & 15e

LA CABANE À HUÎTRES SEAFOOD €

Map p428 (☎01 45 49 47 27; 4 rue Antoine Bourdelle, 14e; dozen oysters €17, menu €21.90; ⌚noon-2.15pm & 7-10.15pm Wed-Sat; Ⓜ Montparnasse Bienvenüe) Wonderfully rustic, this wooden-styled *cabane* (cabin) with just nine tables is the pride and joy of fifth-generation oyster farmer Françis Dubourg, who splits his time between the capital and his oyster farm in Arcachon on the Atlantic coast. The fixed menu includes a dozen oysters, foie gras, *magret de canard fumé* (smoked duck breast) or smoked salmon.

POILÂNE BOULANGERIE €

Map p430 (www.poilane.fr; 49 bd de Grenelle, 15e; ⌚7.15am-8.15pm Tue-Sun; Ⓜ Dupleix) Pick up handcrafted sourdough bread from this branch of one of Paris' most famous bakeries (p243), as well as its delicious *punitions* (crispy butter biscuits).

DES GÂTEAUX ET DU PAIN BOULANGERIE, PATISSERIE €

Map p428 (www.desgateauxetdupain.com; 63 bd Pasteur, 15e; ⌚9am-8pm Mon & Wed-Sat, to 6pm Sun; Ⓜ Pasteur) Looking more like an exclusive boutique, the dramatic black walls at this ultracontemporary boulangerie/patisserie showcase the jewel-like cakes, tarts and artisan breads created by David Granger and Claire Damon – one of France's leading female pastry chefs.

MARCHÉ EDGAR QUINET MARKET €

Map p428 (bd Edgar Quinet, 14e; 7am-2.30pm Wed, to 3pm Sat; M Edgar Quinet or Montparnasse Bienvenüe) Opposite Tour Montparnasse, this open-air street market teems with neighbourhood shoppers. There's always a great range of cheeses, as well as stalls sizzling up snacks to eat on the run, from crêpes to spicy felafels.

MARCHÉ BRANCUSI MARKET €

Map p428 (place Constantin Brancusi, 14e; 9am-3pm Sat; M Gaîté) Overdose on *biologique* (organic) produce at this weekly open-air market.

★LE CASSE NOIX MODERN FRENCH €€

Map p430 (01 45 66 09 01; www.le-cassenoix.fr; 56 rue de la Fédération, 15e; 2-/3-course lunch menus €21/26, 3-course dinner menu €33; noon-2.30pm & 7-10.30pm Mon-Fri; M Bir Hakeim) Proving that a location footsteps from the Eiffel Tower doesn't mean compromising on quality, quantity or authenticity, 'the nutcracker' is a neighbourhood gem with a cosy retro interior, affordable prices and exceptional cuisine that changes by season and by the inspiration of owner-chef Pierre Olivier Lenormand, who has honed his skills in some of Paris' most fêted kitchens. Book ahead.

★JEU DE QUILLES BISTRO €€

Map p428 (01 53 90 76 22; www.jdequilles.fr; 45 rue Boulard, 14e; mains €25-40; noon-2pm Wed-Sat, 8-10pm Tue-Sat; M Mouton-Duvernet) When your next-door neighbour is the original premises of celebrated butcher Hugo Desnoyer, you have an inside track to serve exceptional meat-based dishes, and chef Benoît Reix does at this brilliant bistro. Creations such as artichoke-paste-encrusted pork or veal carpaccio pair with an extensive selection of natural wines. Reserve ahead: there are just 18 seats and locals love it.

★LA VÉRAISON MODERN FRENCH €€

Map p430 (01 45 32 39 39; www.laveraison.com; 64 rue de la Croix Nivert, 15e; 2-/3-course lunch menus €15/18, mains €19-24; 12.30-2pm & 8-10pm Tue-Fri, 7.30-10pm Sat; M Commerce) The elegant simplicity of owner-chef Ulla Bosse's welcoming neighbourhood bistro belies the outstanding cuisine she creates in her open kitchen. The starters alone – truffled chestnut velouté, foie gras ravioli in cognac sauce, *burrata* cheese with orange, crispy 'Peking duck' morsels, Thai crab cakes with mango dip – are reason enough to return.

PARIS RIVE GAUCHE

Paris' largest urban redevelopment since Haussmann's 19th-century reformation is gathering pace in the 13e *arrondissement* (city district). Centred on a once nondescript area south of the Latin Quarter spiralling out from big busy traffic hub place d'Italie, the renaissance of the area known as Paris Rive Gauche was heralded in the 1990s by the controversial Bibliothèque Nationale de France and the arrival of the high-speed Météor metro line. They were followed, among other additions, by the MK2 entertainment complex, the Piscine Joséphine Baker swimming pool floating on the Seine, and Paris' most recent bridge, the Passerelle Simone de Beauvoir (2006), providing a cycle and pedestrian link to the Right Bank. And work isn't slated to stop until the Paris Rive Gauche project ends in 2020.

Pivotal to this 130-hectare redevelopment zone is the Paris 7 university campus hosting some 30,000 students. Other institutions to have moved in include the French fashion institute, the Institut Français de la Mode (p261) in the stylised former warehouse Docks en Seine.

The area's mainline train station, the Gare d'Austerlitz, is getting a €600 million makeover from celebrated architect Jean Nouvel. Not only will the station itself be overhauled (including €200 million alone on the grand hall's glass roof, beneath which hot-air balloons were manufactured during the 1870 siege of Paris), but shops, cafes and green spaces will fill the surrounding streets. The renovation is also due to wrap up in 2020.

Track updates on the area at www.parisrivegauche.com.

LOCAL KNOWLEDGE

RUE DAGUERRE

Paris' traditional village atmosphere thrives along rue Daguerre, 14e.

Tucked just southwest of the Denfert-Rochereau metro and RER stations, this narrow street – pedestrianised between av du Général-Leclerc and rue Boulard – is lined with florists, *fromageries*, *boulangeries*, patisseries, greengrocers, delis (including Greek, Asian and Italian) and classic cafes where you can watch the local goings on.

Shops set up market stalls on the pavement; Sunday mornings are especially lively. It's a great option for lunch before or after visiting Les Catacombes, or for packing a picnic to take to one of the area's parks and squares.

LA CERISAIE
REGIONAL CUISINE €€

Map p428 (☎01 43 20 98 98; www.restaurantlacerisaie.com; 70 bd Edgar Quinet, 14e; mains €16-25; ⊗noon-2pm & 7-10pm Mon-Fri; Ⓜ Edgar Quinet) Chef Cyril Lalanne shows how inventive southwestern cuisine can be at this snug 22-seat restaurant behind a cherry-coloured facade. Starters such as snail cassoulet are followed by rich, often game-based mains (partridge, pheasant) and amazing desserts like blue-cheese ice cream with fig purée. The wine list is extensive and extremely well priced. Be sure to book.

LE SÉVÉRO
BISTRO €€

Map p428 (☎01 45 40 40 91; 8 rue des Plantes, 14e; mains €15-36; ⊗noon-2pm & 7.30-10pm Mon-Fri; Ⓜ Mouton Duvernet) Steaks served with sensational fries are the mainstay of this upmarket bistro (it's run by ex-butcher William Bernet); other meat specialities include black pudding and pigs' trotters. Wash them down with any number of excellent wines, which are chalked on an entire wall. With just 30 seats, reconfirming advance reservations by noon is essential.

LA ROTONDE MONTPARNASSE
BRASSERIE €€

Map p418 (☎01 43 26 48 26; www.rotondemontparnasse.com; 105 bd du Montparnasse, 6e; 3-course menu €42, mains €14.50-42; ⊗6am-2am, menus noon-3pm & 7-11pm; Ⓜ Vavin) Opened in 1911 and recently restored to its former glory, La Rotonde may be awash with the same Les Montparnos history as its famous neighbours like Le Select et al, but the real reason to come is for the superior food. Meat comes from Parisian butcher extraordinaire Hugo Desnoyer, salmon and chicken are organic and brasserie classics are cooked to perfection.

JADIS
NEOBISTRO €€

Map p430 (☎01 45 57 73 20; www.bistrotjadisparis.com; 208 rue de la Croix Nivert, 15e; lunch/dinner menus from €26.50/38; ⊗12.15-2pm & 7.15-11pm Mon-Fri; Ⓜ Boucicaut) This classy, crimson-fronted neobistro on the corner of a very unassuming street remains one of Paris' most revered (ie reserve in advance). Traditional French dishes pack a modern punch thanks to risk-taking young chef Guillaume Delage. The lunch *menu* (set menu) is extraordinarily good value and the chocolate soufflé – order it at the start of your meal – is divine.

LA CLOSERIE DES LILAS
BRASSERIE €€

Map p428 (☎01 40 51 34 50; www.closeriedeslilas.fr; 171 bd du Montparnasse, 6e; brasserie mains €25-33, restaurant mains €27.50-56.50; ⊗restaurant noon-2.15pm & 7-11.30pm, brasserie noon-12.30am, piano bar 11am-1.30am; Ⓜ Vavin or RER Port Royal) Brass plaques tell you exactly where Hemingway (who wrote much of *The Sun Also Rises* here) and luminaries like Picasso, Apollinaire, Man Ray, Jean-Paul Sartre and Samuel Beckett stood, sat or fell. The 'Lilac Enclosure' is split into a late-night piano bar, upmarket restaurant and more lovable (and cheaper) brasserie with a hedged-in pavement terrace.

LA GAULOISE
TRADITIONAL FRENCH €€

Map p430 (☎01 47 34 11 64; 59 av de la Motte-Picquet, 15e; 2-/3-course lunch menus €24.50/29.50, mains €25-36; ⊗noon-2.30pm & 7-11pm; Ⓜ La Motte Picquet Grenelle) With a name like La Gauloise, you wouldn't expect this venerable, terrace-fronted restaurant to serve anything other than traditional fare, which it does, very well. From the onion soup to the braised stuffed cabbage and duckling with old-fashioned mashed potato, *îles flottantes* for dessert, and Madeleine cakes with coffee, it refines but doesn't reinvent the classics that make French cuisine iconic.

LE BANYAN
THAI €€

Map p430 (☎01 40 60 09 20; 24 place Étienne Pernet, 15e; lunch/dinner menus from €20/35;

⊘noon-2.30pm daily, 7-10.30pm Sun-Thu, 7-11pm Fri & Sat; 🖼; MFélix Faure) Timeless Thai dishes are artfully presented and utterly delicious at this airy, uncluttered space in a very local neighbourhood. Desserts like mango and coconut rice are especially good; kids are warmly welcomed.

LA COUPOLE
BRASSERIE €€
Map p428 (☑01 43 20 14 20; www.lacoupole-paris.com; 102 bd du Montparnasse, 14e; lunch menus €29.50-36.50, mains €22.50-46; ⊘kitchen 8am-midnight Tue-Sat, to 11pm Sun & Mon; 🖼; MVavin) The reason for visiting this enormous, 450-seat brasserie, designed by the Solvet brothers and opened in 1927, is more history than gastronomy. Its famous mural-covered columns (painted by such artists as Brancusi and Chagall), dark wood panelling and soft lighting have hardly changed an iota since the days of Sartre, Soutine, Man Ray, the dancer Josephine Baker and other regulars.

LE CRISTAL DE SEL
NEOBISTRO €€
Map p430 (☑01 42 50 35 29; www.lecristaldesel.fr; 13 rue Mademoiselle, 15e; mains €23-26; ⊘12.15-2pm & 7.30-10pm Tue-Sat; MCommerce) Chef Karil Lopez' modern bistro has a distinct kitchen feel with its small brightly lit white walls and white-painted beams. The only decorative feature is a candlelit crystal of rose-tinted salt on each table – signalling that food (free-range chicken stuffed with dried fruit, beef cooked in duck fat, langoustine ravioli...) is the Salt Crystal's raison d'être.

LES TROIS GARÇONS
BISTRO €€
Map p430 (☑01 40 60 14 35; 165 rue de Javel, 15e; mains €15-19; ⊘kitchen noon-3pm & 7-10.45pm; MFélix Faure) Service can be hit-and-miss but the blackboard-chalked menu – crab and avocado millefeuille, tartare, cod with tapenade – is more hit than miss, and the sundrenched terrace (heated in winter), with wicker chairs spilling onto a paved square, is an absolute winner. There's a terrific wine list with plenty of by-the-glass options; the bar stays open all day.

LE DÔME
HISTORIC BRASSERIE €€€
Map p428 (☑01 43 35 25 81; 108 bd du Montparnasse, 14e; mains €43-66.50, seafood platters €66; ⊘noon-3pm & 7-11pm; MVavin) A 1930s art deco extravaganza of the formal white-tablecloth and bow-tied-waiter variety, monumental Le Dôme is one of the swishest places around for shellfish platters piled high with fresh oysters, king prawns, crab claws and much more, followed by traditional creamy homemade millefeuille for dessert, wheeled in on a trolley and cut in front of you. Its cheaper bistro and *poissonnerie* (fishmonger) are around the corner.

LE CIEL DE PARIS
TRADITIONAL FRENCH €€€
Map p428 (☑01 40 64 77 64; www.cieldeparis.com; level 56, Tour Montparnasse, 33 av du Maine, 14e; lunch/dinner menus from €30/45; ⊘7.30am-11pm; MMontparnasse Bienvenüe) Views don't get much better than 'the sky of Paris', the Tour Montparnasse's 56th-floor restaurant, accessed by private lift/elevator. Starters include Burgundy snails and pigs' trotters; seafood is a speciality. The gastronomic Grand Écran menu (€128), available at dinner daily and Sunday lunch, includes a guaranteed window table and bottle of Champagne per person. The bar stays open until 1am.

🍴 Place d'Italie & Chinatown

⭐ PHO 14
VIETNAMESE €
Map p426 (129 av de Choisy, 13e; mains €6.50-9.80; ⊘9am-11pm; MTolbiac) Expect a wait at this small, simple restaurant (also known as Pho Banh Cuon 14) – it doesn't take bookings and is popular with in-the-know locals for its authentic and astonishingly cheap *pho*. The steaming Vietnamese broth is flavoured with cinnamon and incorporates noodles and traditional beef or chicken.

LAURENT DUCHÊNE
BOULANGERIE, PATISSERIE €
Map p426 (http://laurent-duchene.com; 2 rue Wurtz, 13e; ⊘7.30am-8pm Mon-Sat; MGlacière) Prize-winning croissants made with *beurre Charentes-Poitou* AOC butter are the speciality of this lauded *boulangerie*/patisserie, and its tantalising rainbow of macarons, tarts and intricately layered cakes taste even more luscious than they look.

LA TROPICALE
ICE CREAM €
Map p426 (www.latropicaleglacier.com; 180 bd Vincent Auriol, 13e; ice cream from €2.50, lunch menus €8-12; ⊘noon-4pm Mon, Tue & Thu, noon-6pm Wed, noon-8pm Fri, 3-7pm Sat; 🖼; MPlace d'Italie) 🍃 All-natural flavours like lychee, guava, mango and papaya, honey and pine nut, as well as a pina-colada-like coconut, rum and pineapple, transport you to the

'LITTLE BRITTANY'

Trains leave from Gare Montparnasse for the windswept region of Brittany, a couple of hours west, but you don't have to leave the capital for authentic Breton crêpes. Due to the Breton population congregating in this area, the surrounding streets – especially rue du Montparnasse, 14e, and rue Odessa, 14e, one block west – are lined with dozens of crêperies.

Unlike the rolled-up crêpes sold on street corners, Breton crêpes are folded envelope style at the edges, served flat on a plate and eaten using cutlery – and are best washed down with bowls of brut Breton cider. Savoury *galettes* use *blé noir* (buckwheat flour; *sarrasin* in Breton), while both *galettes* and sweet crêpes made from white flour use salted Breton butter. Traditional toppings include *andouille* (Breton sausage), and *caramel au beurre salé* (salted caramel sauce; *salidou* in Breton).

Top picks:

➜ **Crêperie Josselin** (Map p428; ☎01 43 20 93 50; 67 rue du Montparnasse, 14e; crêpes €7-10; ⏰11.30am-3pm & 5-11pm Tue-Fri, 11.30am-11pm Sat & Sun; 👪; Ⓜ Edgar Quinet) Filled with dark timber furniture, painted plates and screened by lace curtains, Josselin takes its name from the eastern Breton village crowned by a 14th-century castle. Locals crowd around the open kitchen waiting for a table. Delicious *galettes* include Roquefort with walnuts.

➜ **Crêperie Plougastel** (Map p428; ☎01 42 79 90 63; www.creperie-plougastel.com; 47 rue du Montparnasse, 14e; crêpes €3.10-10.90; ⏰noon-midnight; 👪; Ⓜ Edgar Quinet) Named for the Breton commune near Brest, Plougastel's decor might be spartan, but its *galettes* and crêpes are anything but, with generous toppings including St-Jacques scallops.

tropics at this mint-coloured *glacier-salon de thé*. It also serves seasonally changing lunchtime quiches, flans and a *plat du jour* (dish of the day).

LE TEMPS DES CÉRISES — TRADITIONAL FRENCH €

Map p426 (☎01 45 89 69 48; www.letemps-descerisescoop.com; 18-20 rue de la Butte aux Cailles, 13e; mains €11.50-20.50; ⏰11.45am-2.30pm & 7-11.45pm Mon-Sat; Ⓜ Corvisart or Place d'Italie) Run by a workers' cooperative for nearly four decades, the 'Time of Cherries' (ie 'days of wine and roses') is an easygoing restaurant (provided you switch off your phone!) serving faithfully solid fare in a quintessentially Parisian atmosphere.

CHEZ GLADINES — FRENCH BASQUE €

Map p426 (☎01 45 80 70 10; www.gladines.com; 30 rue des Cinq Diamants, 13e; mains €8.50-13; ⏰noon-3pm Mon-Fri, noon-4pm Sat & Sun, 7pm-midnight Sun-Tue, 7pm-1am Wed-Sat; 📶; Ⓜ Corvisart) Colossal 'meal-in-a-metal-bowl' salads are the prime draw of this down-to-earth bistro with red-checked tablecloths in the Buttes aux Cailles (the original of five Paris locations). It buzzes with students and spendthrift diners and is always a hoot. Traditional Basque specialities include *pipérade* and *poulet basque* (chicken cooked with tomatoes, onions, peppers and white wine). Arrive early to grab a seat.

HAO HAO — CHINESE €

Map p426 (23 av de Choisy, 13e; mains €7.50-12; ⏰9am-2am; Ⓜ Porte de Choisy) Clattering with diners until late in the night, Hao Hao cooks up cheap, filling and delicious Chinese dishes, such as Sichuan chicken, in its open kitchen. If you want to push the boat out, there are pricier seafood dishes.

LA CHINE MASSÉNA — CHINESE €

Map p426 (☎01 45 83 98 88; www.chinemassena.fr; 18 av de Choisy, 13e; lunch/dinner menus from €11/16; ⏰noon-3pm & 7-11pm; Ⓜ Porte de Choisy) Set back off the street adjoining a shopping mall, this enormous restaurant specialising in Cantonese and Chiu Chow cuisine is a real favourite in Chinatown, particularly with large groups (it has plenty of room to accommodate them). The live-tank seafood and traditional dim sum are especially good. Dancing accompanied by a live orchestra takes place on Friday and Saturday nights.

★ RESTAURANT VARIATIONS — BISTRO €€

Map p426 (☎01 43 31 36 04; www.restaurantvariations.com; 18 rue des Wallons, 13e; lunch menus

€16.50-19, dinner menus €24-44; noon-2pm Mon-Fri, 7-10pm Mon-Sat; MSt-Marcel) In a pin-drop-quiet backstreet you'd never stumble on by chance, this light-filled restaurant is a diamond find. It's framed by huge glass windows and artfully decorated with large-scale photographs; square white plates showcase the colours and textures of brothers Philippe and Pierre Tondetta's Italian-accented offerings, such as rack of lamb accompanied by polenta with olives and aged parmesan.

AU PETIT MARGUERY TRADITIONAL FRENCH €€

Map p426 (01 43 31 58 59; http://petitmarguery.com; 9 bd de Port Royal, 13e; lunch menus €24-29, dinner menus €31-37; noon-2.15pm & 7.15-10.15pm; MLes Gobelins) This wonderfully traditional restaurant is a perfect choice for honest-to-goodness, heartily proportioned dishes like pan-fried veal in black truffle sauce and Grand Marnier soufflé. It's popular with locals (so popular that it's not only extended its hours but opened a Right Bank restaurant too), so book ahead to avoid a lengthy wait.

ENTOTO ETHIOPIAN €€

Map p426 (01 45 87 08 51; www.restaurant-entoto.com; 145 rue Léon-Maurice Nordmann, 13e; mains €14.50-16.50; 7pm-midnight; MGlacière) Tear off an *injera* (Ethiopian pancake) and scoop up delectable vegetable and spicy meat accompaniments at France's first Ethiopian restaurant, opened in 1983 and filled with redolent photos of the country's people and landscapes. A potent pot of Ethiopian coffee is the traditional way to finish the meal – prepare to be wired all night.

AU MOULIN VERT TRADITIONAL FRENCH €€

Map p428 (01 45 39 31 31; www.aumoulinvert.com; 34bis Rue des Plantes, 14e; lunch/dinner menus from €19.50/30; noon-2.30pm daily, 7-10.30pm Mon-Thu, 7-11pm Fri & Sat, 7-10pm Sun; ; MAlésia) The Moulin Rouge ('red windmill') might be more famous but at the opposite end of town, the 19th-century 'green windmill' is a delightful, relaxed neighbourhood restaurant opening to a glass-paned winter garden and sunlit terrace. Chef Gérard Chagot's seasonal creations like duck in cherries, cod in cider and snails in garlic are served by aproned waiters at white-clothed tables.

L'OURCINE NEOBISTRO €€

Map p426 (01 47 07 13 65; www.restaurant-lourcine.fr; 92 rue Broca, 13e; menus €35; noon-2.30pm & 7-11pm Tue-Sat; MLes Gobelins) With wine corks in the window, this intimate place may be casual (no dress code) and affordable but it takes its food seriously. The superb menu spans starters like fish velouté or pig's head with mesclun to mains such as wild sea bream with semolina or free-range chicken with foie gras, and desserts like poached rhubarb with almond sorbet.

CHEZ NATHALIE MODERN FRENCH €€

Map p426 (01 45 80 20 42; www.cheznathalie.fr; 41 rue Vandrezanne, 13e; mains €21-28; noon-2.30pm Tue-Fri, 7-11pm Tue-Sat; MCorvisart or Place d'Italie) On a quiet street with summertime terrace tables, this pocket-size restaurant is a lovely spot to dine tête à tête. Transparent Kartell chairs and deep-purple table tops complement the stylised menu, which fuses traditional French with world food such as rabbit *tajine* with dates, oranges and almonds, creamy tomato, prawn and ginger risotto, or squid pan-fried with Espelette peppers.

L'AUBERGE DU 15 GASTRONOMIC €€€

Map p426 (01 47 07 07 45; www.laubergedu15.com; 15 Rue de la Santé, 13e; 4-course lunch menu €39, 7-/9-course menus €65/85, mains €35-45; noon-2.30pm Tue-Sat, 7.30-11pm Tue-Thu, 7-11pm Fri & Sat; MSt-Jacques or RER Port Royal) With rough-hewn stone walls, chocolate-toned decor and classic French dishes, Nicolas Castelet's charming 'inn' evokes a country retreat. Choose dining companions who share your culinary tastes – many of the mains must be ordered by a minimum of two people and the *dégustation* (tasting) menus by the entire table.

L'AUBERGE DU ROI GRADLON BRETON, GASTRONOMIC €€€

Map p426 (01 45 35 48 71; http://roigradlon.fr; 36 bd Arago, 13e; lunch menu €24, 5-course menu €68, mains €22-52; noon-2pm & 7-11.30pm Fri-Tue; MLes Gobelins) Nicolas Castelet, whose inaugural restaurant L'Auberge du 15 continues its unabated success, is the mastermind behind this fine-dining gem partially set in a stone cellar. Castelet has teamed up with two Bretons, sommelier Geoffreoy Damville and chef Antoine Bertho, giving traditional dishes like *kig ha farz* (meats simmered in broth with buckwheat-flour pudding) an ultragourmet twist.

Other Breton specialities include lobster and as well as desserts like *kouign amann* (butter cake, served with salted caramel).

DRINKING & NIGHTLIFE

The comings and goings of the Gare Montparnasse train station and a dynamic cultural centre keep things lively. Southwest of place d'Italie, rue de la Butte aux Cailles and the surrounding Butte aux Cailles molehill have a plethora of options popular with students and local residents; places here tend to have die-hard regulars.

Montparnasse & 15e

★FÉLICIE
CAFE, BAR

Map p428 (www.felicie.info; 174 ave du Maine, 14e; 7am-2am; ; MLourmel) Chances are your first visit won't be your last at this unpretentious neighbourhood cafe with a big heated pavement terrace, fun-loving staff and a laid-back vibe. It's a quintessentially Parisian spot to hang out any time of day, but especially during Sunday brunch, lunches built around bistro classics like steak tartare, and late at night.

★LE ROSEBUD
COCKTAIL BAR

Map p428 (11bis rue Delambre, 14e; 7pm-2am; MEdgar Quinet or Vavin) Like the sleigh of that name in *Citizen Kane,* Rosebud harks back to the past. In this case it's to Montparnasse's early-20th-century heyday (the decor has scarcely changed since Sartre drank here). Enjoy a Champagne cocktail amid the quiet elegance of polished wood and aged leather.

★LE SELECT
CAFE

Map p428 (99 bd du Montparnasse, 6e; 7am-3am; MVavin) Dating from 1923, this Montparnasse institution was the first of the area's grand cafes to stay open late into the night, and it still draws everyone from beer-swigging students to whisky-swilling politicians. *Tartines* (open-faced sandwiches) made with Poilâne bread are a speciality.

AUTO PASSION CAFÉ
CAFE

(www.autopassioncafe.fr; 197 bd Brune, 14e; 10am-2am; ; MPorte d'Orléans) This motor-enthusiast-run cafe is filled with racing memorabilia, including engines, petrol pumps and some very cool cars, and features many excellent cocktails with auto themes, such as *injecteur* (vodka, guava, strawberries, passionfruit and grenadine). Nonalcoholic options include *autostoppeuse* (orange juice, pineapple, banana and strawberries). Even its menu, *'la kart'*, reflects the race track.

LE REDLIGHT
CLUB

Map p428 (www.leredlight.com; 34 rue du Départ, 14e; midnight to 6am Fri & Sat; MMontparnasse Bienvenüe) Beneath Tour Montparnasse, this huge, laser-lit venue – fittingly called *l'enfer* (hell) in a previous life and sharing space with Brazilian cabaret Brasil Tropical – is up there among Paris' busiest house, techno and electro clubs. Its podiums get packed out with a young, dance-mad crowd. Hours often vary depending on the soirée. Enter down the stairs across the street from Monoprix.

LA RUCHE
CAFE

Map p428 (73 bd du Montparnasse, 14e; 6am-2am; MMontparnasse Bienvenüe) Even when other cafes in the Montparnasse area are quiet, this strawberry-red, split-level cafe hung with funky light fittings buzzes with a young, fun crowd.

Place d'Italie & Chinatown

★LE BATOFAR
CLUB

Map p426 (www.batofar.org; opposite 11 quai François Mauriac, 13e; bar 12.30pm-midnight Tue, to 6am Wed-Fri, 6pm-6am Sat; MQuai de la Gare or Bibliothèque) This much-loved, red-metal tugboat has a rooftop bar that's terrific in summer, and a respected restaurant, while the club underneath provides memorable underwater acoustics between its metal walls and portholes. Le Batofar is known for its edgy, experimental music policy and live performances, mostly electro-oriented but also incorporating hip hop, new wave, rock, punk or jazz.

★TANDEM
WINE BAR

Map p426 (10 rue de la Butte aux Cailles, 13e; noon-3pm & 7.30-11pm Tue-Sat; MCorvisart or Place d'Italie) Crammed with regulars, this old-fashioned *bar à vins* is run by two brothers with a fierce oenological passion who home in on 'boutique' *(vins de propriétés)* and organic wines as well as those produced by new vignerons (winemakers). A traditional bistro menu complements the wine list.

LES MONTPARNOS

Peer long and hard (and long and hard again) around the unfortunate 1960s Gare Montparnasse complex and glimmers of the area's bohemian past occasionally emerge: after WWI, writers, poets and artists of the avant-garde abandoned Montmartre on the Right Bank and crossed the Seine, shifting the centre of Paris' artistic ferment to the area around bd du Montparnasse.

It was known as les Montparnos, and artists Chagall, Modigliani, Léger, Soutine, Miró, Matisse, Kandinsky and Picasso, composer Stravinsky, and writers Hemingway, Ezra Pound and Cocteau were among those who hung out here, talking endlessly in the cafes and restaurants for which the quarter became famous. It remained a creative hub until the mid-1930s.

Historic brasseries that recall les Montparnos' legacy include La Rotonde Montparnasse (p264); Le Select (p268); La Coupole (p265), with muraled columns painted by artists including Chagall; Hemingway's favourite, the hedged La Closerie des Lilas (p264); and Le Dôme (p265), where Gertrude Stein is said to have encouraged Matisse to open his artist academy (only for Matisse to later add his voice to the 1935 'Testimony Against Gertrude Stein' pamphlet, condemning Stein's interpretation of how cubism emerged in her 1933 *Autobiography of Alice B Toklas*).

BATEAU EL ALAMEIN — CLUB

Map p426 (http://elalamein.free.fr; opposite 11 quai François Mauriac, 13e; ⌚terrace from 6pm Mon-Fri, from 3.30pm Sat & Sun; Ⓜ Quai de la Gare or Bibliothèque) Strung with terracotta pots of flowers, this deep-purple boat is a lovely spot on the Seine to sit amid tulips and enjoy live bands (flyers are stuck on the lamppost out front). Less hectic than Paris' other floating clubs moored here, hence the older crowd, it plays sounds spanning jazz, world and Piaf-style *chansons*. Hours vary.

FROG & BRITISH LIBRARY — MICROBREWERY, PUB

Map p426 (www.frogpubs.com; 114 av de France, 13e; ⌚7.30am-2am Mon-Fri, noon-2am Sat & Sun; 📶; Ⓜ Bibliothèque) A hybrid English pub–French brasserie, this spacious drinking venue around the corner from the Bibliothèque Nationale is propped up by expats and French students who flock here between library visits. The pick of the drinks list is its half-dozen beers brewed on the premises with inspired names like 'Dark de Triomphe', 'Inseine' and 'Parislytic'.

LA DAME DE CANTON — CLUB

Map p426 (www.damedecanton.com; opposite 11 quai François Mauriac, 13e; ⌚7pm-2am Tue-Thu, to dawn Fri & Sat; Ⓜ Quai de la Gare or Bibliothèque) This floating *boîte* (club) aboard a three-masted Chinese junk with a couple of world voyages under its belt bobs beneath the Bibliothèque Nationale de France. Concerts range from pop and indie to electro, hip hop, reggae and rock; afterwards DJs keep the young crowd moving. There's also a popular restaurant and bar.

LA FÛT GUEUZE — BAR

Map p426 (24 rue Dumeril, 13e; ⌚4pm-2am; Ⓜ Campo-Formio) You won't find big-name, mass-market beers at this corner neighbourhood bar but you will find 74 bottled brews, mainly French, Belgian and German, and another 12 on tap, as well as a good-time atmosphere. Happy 'hour' runs from 4pm to 9pm.

LE DJOON — CLUB

Map p426 (www.djoon.com; 22-24 bd Vincent Auriol, 13e; ⌚bar 10am-3.30pm Mon & Tue, to 12.30am Wed, to 1.30am Thu, to 5am Fri, 7.30pm-5am Sat; Ⓜ Quai de la Gare) In the regenerating Paris Rive Gauche area, increasingly known for its cutting-edge venues, this urbanite glass-and-steel loft club and restaurant has carved out a name for itself as a stylish weekend venue for soul, funk, deep house, garage and disco, courtesy of visiting DJs. Thursday and Sunday evenings are tamer but still DJ-fed dance.

LE MERLE MOQUEUR — BAR

Map p426 (11 rue de la Butte aux Cailles, 13e; ⌚5pm-2am; Ⓜ Corvisart) Friendly and convivial, the tiny, retro Mocking Magpie serves a huge selection of rum punches (more than 20 at last count) and unearths long-forgotten '80s tracks from the musical vaults.

LA FOLIE EN TÊTE BAR

Map p426 (http://lafolieentete.wix.com/lesite; 33 rue de la Butte aux Cailles, 13e; ⏲5pm-2am Mon-Sat, some Sun; Ⓜ Corvisart) Guitars and brass instruments strung on the walls attest to this jammed little bar's musical roots. Although it no longer features the profusion of acts it did in decades past, it still hosts occasional live *chansons,* world music, jazz and rock; check the line-up online. Already-cheap drinks are even cheaper during happy hour (5pm to 8pm).

SPUTNIK BAR

Map p426 (www.sputnik.fr; 14 rue de la Butte aux Cailles, 13e; ⏲2pm-2am Mon-Sat, 4pm-midnight Sun; 📶; Ⓜ Corvisart or Place d'Italie) Sputnik began life as an internet cafe (remember those?) and these days its large bar, buzzing pavement terrace on one of Paris' funkiest streets and a pool table and foosball make it a chilled-right-out student haven.

☆ ENTERTAINMENT

Many of the 13e's floating nightclubs have live music. Events regularly take place at Docks en Seine (p261).

PETIT BAIN LIVE MUSIC

Map p426 (☎01 80 48 49 81; www.petitbain.org; 7 Port de la Gare, 13e; Ⓜ Quai de la Gare) 'Floating cultural centre' Petit Bain has a packed program of DJs, club events and concerts – from soul, funk, punk, pop, rock and hip hop to headbanging metal.

L'ENTREPÔT CULTURAL CENTRE

Map p428 (☎01 45 40 07 50; www.lentrepot.fr; 7-9 rue Francis de Pressensé, 14e; Ⓜ Pernety or Plaisance) Everything from film screenings to jazz and world-music concerts, poetry slams, photography, painting and sculpture exhibitions, art installations and much more take place at this dynamic cultural space near Gare Montparnasse. It happens to be a fantastic place to eat too, with dozens of tables beneath the trees in its leafy back garden.

PÉNICHE L'IMPROVISTE LIVE MUSIC

Map p426 (☎06 52 82 28 54; www.improviste.fr; 36 Quai d'Austerlitz, 13e; Ⓜ Quai de la Gare or Gare d'Austerlitz) Many of the jazz concerts aboard the barge containing this floating jazz club are free, including regular jam sessions.

DANCING LA COUPOLE DANCING

Map p428 (☎01 43 27 56 00; www.lacoupole-paris.com; 102 bd du Montparnasse, 14e; ⏲2.30-7pm Sun; Ⓜ Vavin) Swing, rumba, cha-cha, foxtrot, tango and more at roaring 1920s-style tea dances held in the ballroom of the historic brasserie of the same name. Check the website's *actualités* (current events) section for dates.

LE PETIT JOURNAL MONTPARNASSE JAZZ, BLUES

Map p428 (☎01 43 21 56 70; http://petitjournal-montparnasse.com; 13 rue du Commandant René Mouchotte, 14e; admission incl 1 drink €20, with dinner €60; ⏲concerts from 9.30pm Mon-Sat; Ⓜ Gaîté) Like its sister club Le Petit Journal St-Michel (p225), this jazz and blues club near Gare Montparnasse serves meals followed by a fabulous range of jazz and blues concerts.

MK2 BIBLIOTHÈQUE CINEMA, PHOTOGRAPHY

Map p426 (www.mk2.com; 128-162 av de France, 13e; Ⓜ Bibliothèque) This branch of the ever-growing chain next to the Bibliothèque Nationale is the most ambitious yet, with 14 screens showing a variety of blockbusters and studio films, a trendy cafe, brasserie, restaurant, late-night bar, and shops specialising in DVDs, books, comics and graphic novels. Get glamorous black-and-white portraits, shot using continuous light, at Studio Harcourt's booth (four for €10).

SHOPPING

The concrete-block shopping mall opposite Gare Montparnasse includes a branch of department store Galeries Lafayette. Savvy fashion shoppers head to the southern 14e to shop for discount designer wear, while the 15e is filled with specialist addresses. In the 13e you'll find Asian grocery stores and supermarkets in Chinatown, and an enormous state-of-the-art shopping mall at place d'Italie.

★ADAM MONTPARNASSE ART SUPPLIES

Map p428 (www.adamparis.com; 11 bd Edgar Quinet, 14e; ⏲9.30am-7pm Mon-Sat; Ⓜ Edgar Quinet) If Paris' art galleries have inspired you, pick up paintbrushes, charcoals, pastels, sketchpads, watercolours, oils, acryl-

DISCOUNT DESIGNER OUTLETS

Save up to 70% off men's, women's and kids' fashions from previous seasons' collections, surpluses, prototypes and seconds by name-brand designers at the discounted outlet stores along rue d'Alésia, 14e, west of the Alésia metro station (particularly between av de Maine and rue Raymond-Losserand).

Shops pop up regularly and close just as often, so you can never be sure what you'll find. Familiar labels to look out for include:

- **Sonia Rykiel** (Map p428; 64 & 110-112 rue d'Alésia, 14e; ⏲noon-7pm Mon, 11am-7pm Tue-Sat; Ⓜ Alésia) Two shops stocking Sonia Rykiel designs. No 64 has lower-priced, more casual clothes, while No 110–112 has Sonia Rykiel's classic lines.
- **Naf Naf Stock** (Map p428; 143 rue d'Alésia, 14e; ⏲11am-7pm Mon-Sat; Ⓜ Alésia) Fun, flirty female fashions.

For slashed prices on *grandes marques* (big names) under one roof, head to the 15e's **Mistigriff** (Map p430; www.mistigriff.fr; 83-85 rue St-Charles, 15e; ⏲10.30am-7.30pm Mon-Sat; Ⓜ Charles Michels).

ics, canvases and more at this historic shop. Picasso, Brancusi and Giacometti were among Édouard Adam's clients. Another seminal client was Yves Klein, with whom Adam developed the ultramarine 'Klein blue' – the VLB25 'Klein Blue' varnish is sold exclusively here.

MARCHÉ GEORGES BRASSENS — BOOKS

(104 rue Brancion, 15e; ⏲9am-6pm Sat & Sun; Ⓜ Porte de Vanves) If you like the *bouquiniste* (used-book sellers) stalls along the Seine, you'll adore this enormous secondhand and antiquarian book market adjacent to beautiful Parc Georges Brassens. More than 60 vendors sell their wares beneath the pavilions of this former abattoir. Most (but not all) books are in French, ranging from €1 euro paperbacks all the way to coveted collectors' editions.

FROMAGERIE LAURENT DUBOIS — FOOD

Map p430 (www.fromageslaurentdubois.fr; 2 rue de Lourmel, 15e; ⏲9am-1pm & 4-7.45pm Tue-Fri, 8.30am-7.45pm Sat, 9am-1pm Sun; Ⓜ Dupleix) The finest French cheeses are tantalisingly displayed at this branch of fêted Fromagerie Laurent Dubois and can be vacuum-packed. There are two other shops in Paris, including a Latin Quarter premises.

TANG FRÈRES — FOOD, DRINK

Map p426 (48 av d'Ivry, 13e; ⏲9am-8pm Tue-Sat, to 1pm Sun; Ⓜ Porte d'Ivry) Chinatown's beating heart centres on this enormous Asian supermarket, where you'd be forgiven for thinking you'd been transported to another continent. Spices, sauces, freezers full of frozen dumplings, and kitchen utensils are imported from Asia along with beverages including Chinese beer. Ready-to-eat snacks are sold opposite the entrance.

LA PETITE CHALOUPE — FOOD, DRINK

Map p426 (7 bd Port-Royal, 13e; ⏲10am-1.45pm & 3.30-8.30pm Tue-Sat, 10am-1.30pm Sun; Ⓜ Les Gobelins) Named for a type of historic fishing boat, this adorable marine-blue-painted shop sells authentic Breton products. Sardines in exquisite tins are a speciality; other delicacies include smoked salmon, salted butter caramels and ciders. Three tiny tables amid the shelves are a convivial spot to dine on sardines on bread or oysters in season.

PIERRE HERMÉ — FOOD

Map p428 (www.pierreherme.com; 185 rue Vaugirard, 15e; ⏲10am-7pm Mon-Thu, to 8pm Fri & Sat, 9am-5pm Sun; Ⓜ Pasteur) Petits fours, cakes, chocolate, nougat, jam and, of course, *macarons* from maestro Pierre Hermé. There is also a branch in St-Germain.

LE PETIT BAZAR — TOYS

Map p430 (www.lepetitbazar.com; 10 rue Gramme, 15e; ⏲10am-7pm Tue-Sat; Ⓜ Av Émile Zola) 🍃 A real *quartier* (neighbourhood) boutique with a distinctly 'green' philosophy, this mini-emporium for tots has it all: imaginative games and toys, clothes, bedroom furnishings and accessories, stuff for school and babycare products – all organic, recycled or made by local artisans.

MARCHÉ AUX PUCES DE LA PORTE DE VANVES — MARKET

(http://pucesdevanves.typepad.com; av Georges Lafenestre & av Marc Sangnier, 14e; ⏲7am-2pm

Sat & Sun; ⓂPorte de Vanves) The Porte de Vanves flea market is the smallest and one of the friendliest of the lot. Av Georges Lafenestre has lots of 'curios' that don't quite qualify as antiques. Av Marc Sangnier is lined with stalls of new clothes, shoes, handbags and household items for sale.

BEAUGRENELLE
MALL

Map p430 (☑01 53 95 24 00; www.beaugrenelle-paris.com; rue Linois, 15e; ⏰shops 10am-9pm Mon-Wed, Fri & Sat, 10am-10pm Thu, cinema & restaurants 10am-midnight daily; ⓂBir Hakeim or Charles Michel) A free *navette fluviale* (water bus) shuttles between the Eiffel Tower and this spiffing new riverfront shopping mall spanning three buildings (two linked by a scenic air bridge). Beaugrenelle's 100 shops range from chains like H&M and Zara to Marks & Spencer (with a British food hall) and a large Fnac. There's also a 10-screen cinema and 10 restaurants.

SPORTS & ACTIVITIES

PISCINE JOSÉPHINE BAKER
SWIMMING

Map p426 (☑01 56 61 96 50; quai François Mauriac, 13e; pool adult/child €3/1.70, sauna €10/5; ⏰7-8.30am & 1-9pm Mon, Wed & Fri, 1-11pm Tue & Thu, 11am-8pm Sat, 10am-8pm Sun; ⓂBibliothèque or Quai de la Gare) Floating on the Seine, this striking swimming pool is style indeed (named after the sensual 1920s American singer, what else could it be?). More of a spot to be seen than to thrash laps, the two 25m-by-10m pools lure Parisians like bees to a honey pot in summer when the roof slides back.

PARI ROLLER
ROLLERBLADING

Map p428 (www.pari-roller.com; place Raoul Dautry, 14e; ⏰10pm-1am Fri, arrive 9.30pm; ⓂMontparnasse Bienvenüe) The world's larg-

est inline mass skate, Pari Roller regularly attracts more than 10,000 bladers. Dubbed 'Friday Night Fever', this fast-paced skate covers a different 30km-odd route each week. Most incorporate cobblestones and downhill stretches, and are geared for experienced bladers only (for your safety and everyone else's). It takes place year-round except when wet weather makes conditions treacherous.

Like its gentler counterpart, the Marais-based Rollers & Coquillages (p186), it's accompanied by yellow-jersey-clad volunteer marshals, along with police (some on inline skates) and ambulances. Wear bright clothes to make yourself visible to drivers and other skaters.

FOREST HILL AQUABOULEVARD
SWIMMING

Map p430 (☑01 40 60 10 00; www.aquaboulevard.fr; 4-6 rue Louis Armand, 15e; adult weekday/weekend €22/28, child €15; ⏰9am-midnight Mon-Fri, 8am-midnight Sat, 8am-11pm Sun; ⓂBalard) Just outside the Périphérique (ring road), this huge tropical 'beach' and aquatic park is well worth a visit, particularly if you're travelling with kids (over three years – under threes aren't allowed), with water slides, waterfalls and wave pools. Don't want to get wet? Play tennis, squash, golf, use the gym or take dance classes. Last admission is 9pm.

PISCINE DE LA BUTTE AUX CAILLES
SWIMMING

Map p426 (☑01 45 89 60 05; http://piscine.equipement.paris.fr; 5 place Paul Verlaine, 13e; adult/child €3/1.70; ⏰7am-8.30am Tue & Thu-Sat, 11.30am-1.30pm & 4.30-9pm Tue, 7am-7pm Wed, 11.30am-6.30pm Thu & Fri, 10am-6.30pm Sat, 8am-6pm Sun; ⓂPlace d'Italie) This stunning pool, built in 1924, takes advantage of the lovely warm water issuing from a nearby artesian well. Come summer, its two outdoor pools buzz with swimmers frolicking in the sun. Hours can vary.

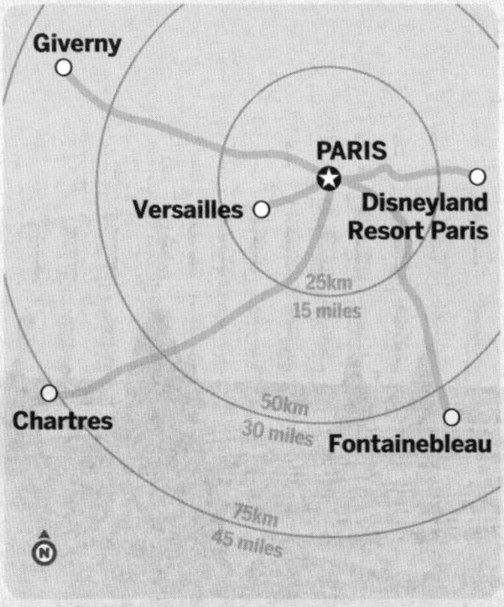

Day Trips from Paris

Versailles p274

When it comes to over-the-top opulence, the colossal Château de Versailles (shut Monday) is in a class of its own, even for France.

Disneyland Resort Paris p280

The 'party never stops' at Europe's Disneyland theme park, Disney Village's hotels, shops, restaurants and clubs, and Walt Disney Studios Park, bringing film, animation and TV production to life.

Fontainebleau p281

A lavish château (shut Tuesday) and rambling forest grace the elegant town of Fontainebleau, and its international business school gives it a vibrant edge.

Chartres p284

Rising from fertile farmland, Chartres' Cathédrale Notre Dame, famed for its beautiful stained glass, dominates the charming medieval town of Chartres.

Giverny p287

Art and/or garden lovers shouldn't miss Giverny's Maison et Jardins de Claude Monet (closed from November to March), the former home and flower-filled gardens of the impressionist master.

CHRISTOPHE LEHENAFF / GETTY IMAGES ©

TOP SIGHT
VERSAILLES

Louis XIV transformed his father's hunting lodge into the monumental Château de Versailles in the mid-17th century, and it remains France's most famous, grandest palace. Situated 22km southwest of Paris, the baroque château was the kingdom's political capital and the seat of the royal court from 1682 until the French Revolution in 1789.

Intending the château to house his court of 6000 people, Louis XIV hired four talented men to take on the gargantuan task: architect Louis Le Vau; Jules Hardouin-Mansart, who took over from Le Vau in the mid-1670s; painter and interior designer Charles Le Brun; and landscape designer André Le Nôtre, under whom entire hills were flattened, marshes drained and forests moved to create the seemingly endless gardens, ponds and fountains for which Versailles is so well known. It has been on Unesco's World Heritage list since 1979.

Sprawling over 900 hectares, the estate is divided into four main sections: the 580m-long palace; the gardens, canals and pools to the west of the palace; two smaller palaces, the Grand Trianon and the Petit Trianon, to the northwest; and the Hameau de la Reine (Queen's Hamlet) north of the Petit Trianon.

Tickets include an English-language audioguide. For an offbeat insight, check out the independent app **Happy Versailles** (www.happy-visit-versailles.com; €2.69).

Versailles is easy to reach from Paris. The most convenient option is to take RER C5 (€3.25, 45 minutes, frequent), which goes from Paris' Left Bank RER stations to Versailles-Château–Rive Gauche station. There are also other rail connections, buses and organised tours.

DON'T MISS...

- Château de Versailles
- Gardens
- Marie Antoinette's estate
- Trianon palaces

PRACTICALITIES

- ☎01 30 83 78 00
- www.chateauversailles.fr
- passport ticket incl estatewide access adult/child €18/free, with musical events €25/free, palace €15/free
- ⏰9am-6.30pm Tue-Sat, to 6pm Sun Apr-Oct, to 5.30pm Tue-Sun Nov-Mar
- Ⓜ RER Versailles-Château–Rive Gauche

Château de Versailles

Few alterations have been made to the château since its construction, apart from most of the interior furnishings disappearing during the Revolution and many of the rooms being rebuilt by Louis-Philippe (r 1830–48), who opened part of the château to the public in 1837. The current €400-million restoration program is the most ambitious yet and until it's completed in 2020 a part of the palace is likely to be clad in scaffolding when you visit.

To access areas that are otherwise off limits and to learn more about Versailles' history, take a 90-minute **guided tour** (☎01 30 83 77 88; www.chateauversailles.fr; tours €7 plus palace admission; ⏰English-language tours Tue-Sun, tour times vary) of the Private Apartments of Louis XV and Louis XVI and the Opera House or Royal Chapel. Tour tickets include access to the most famous parts of the palace, such as the Hall of Mirrors and the King's and Queen's State Apartments; prebook online.

Prams/buggies and metal-frame baby carriers aren't allowed inside the palace.

Hall of Mirrors

The palace's opulence peaks in its shimmering Galerie des Glaces (Hall of Mirrors). This 75m-long ballroom has 17 sparkling mirrors on one side and an equal number of windows on the other.

King's & Queen's State Apartments

Luxurious, ostentatious appointments – frescos, marble, gilt and woodcarvings, with themes and symbols drawn from Greek and Roman mythology – adorn every moulding, cornice, ceiling and door in the palace's Grands Appartements du Roi et de la Reine (King's and Queen's State Apartments).

Gardens

Don't miss a stroll through the château's magnificent **gardens** (except during musical events admission free; ⏰gardens 9am-8.30pm Apr-Oct, 8am-6pm Nov-Mar, park 7am-8.30pm Apr-Oct, 8am-6pm Nov-Mar). The best view over the rectangular pools is from the Hall of Mirrors. Pathways include the Royal Walk's verdant 'green carpet', with smaller paths leading to leafy groves.

The gardens' largest **fountains** are the 17th-century **Bassin de Neptune** (Neptune's Fountain), a dazzling mirage of 99 spouting fountains 300m north of the palace, and the **Bassin d'Apollon** (Apollo's Fountain), built in 1668 at the eastern end of the Grand Canal.

Canals

The **Grand Canal**, 1.6km long and 62m wide, is oriented to reflect the setting sun. It's traversed by the 1km-long **Petit Canal**, forming a cross-shaped body of water with a perimeter of more than 5.5km.

PLANNING FOR VERSAILLES

By noon queues spiral out of control: arrive early and avoid Tuesday and Sunday, the busiest days. Prepurchase tickets on the château's website or at Fnac branches and go straight to Entrance A.

The estate is so vast that the only way to see it all is to hire a four-person electric car (☎01 39 66 97 66; per hr €32) or hop aboard the shuttle train (www.train-versailles.com; adult/child €7.50/5.80); you can also rent a bike (☎01 39 66 97 66; per hour €6.50) or boat (☎01 39 66 97 66; per hour €15).

DINING AT VERSAILLES

Eateries include tearoom **Angelina** (www.angelina-versailles.fr; snacks €14-25; ⏰10am-6pm Tue-Sat Apr-Oct, to 5pm Tue-Sat Nov-Mar), with branches inside the palace and by the Petit Trianon. In the Louis XIV–created town of Versailles, rue de Satory is lined with restaurants; try **À la Ferme** (☎01 39 53 10 81; www.alaferme-versailles.com; 3 rue du Maréchal Joffre; menus €15.50-26.20; ⏰noon-2pm & 7-10pm Wed-Sun).

Versailles

A DAY IN COURT

Visiting Versailles – even just the State Apartments – may seem overwhelming at first, but think of it as a house where people ate, drank, worked, slept and conspired and you'll be on the right path.

Some two decades into his long reign, Louis XIV began turning his father's hunting lodge into a palace large enough to house his entire court (to keep closer tabs on the 6000-strong army of courtiers). Sparing no expense, the Sun King employed the greatest artists and craftspeople of the day and by 1682 he'd created the most extravagant dormitory in history.

The royal schedule was as accurate and predictable as a Swiss watch. By following this itinerary of rooms you can recreate the king's day, starting with the **King's Bedchamber** ❶ and the **Queen's Bedchamber** ❷, where the royal couple was roused at about the same time. The royal procession then leads through the **Hall of Mirrors** ❸ to the **Royal Chapel** ❹ for morning Mass and returns to the **Council Chamber** ❺ for late-morning meetings with ministers. After lunch the king might ride or hunt or visit the **King's Library** ❻. Later he could join courtesans for an 'apartment evening' starting from the **Hercules Drawing Room** ❼ or play billiards in the **Diana Drawing Room** ❽ before supping at 10pm.

CHRISTOPHE LEHENAFF/GETTY IMAGES ©

Queen's Bedchamber
Chambre de la Reine
The queen's life was on constant public display and even the births of her children were watched by crowds of spectators in her own bedchamber. **DETOUR »** The Guardroom, with a dozen armed men at the ready.

LUNCH BREAK

Diner-style food at Sister's Café, crêpes at Le Phare St-Louis or picnic in the park.

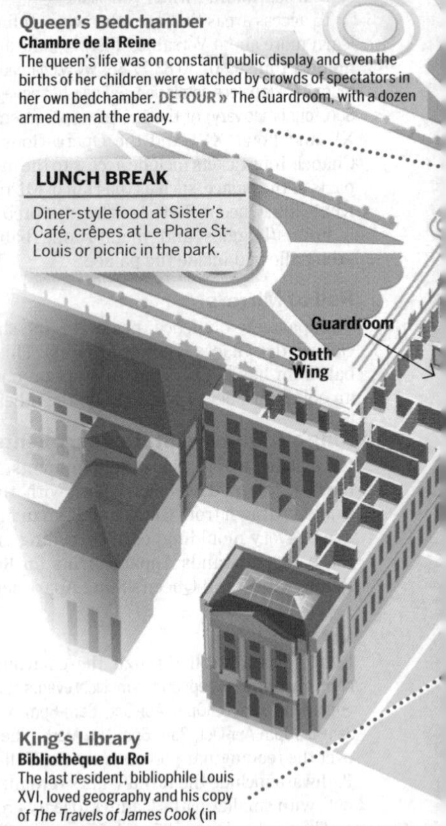

King's Library
Bibliothèque du Roi
The last resident, bibliophile Louis XVI, loved geography and his copy of *The Travels of James Cook* (in English, which he read fluently) is still on the shelf here.

DEA/G. DAGLI ORTI/GETTY IMAGES ©

SAVVY SIGHTSEEING

Avoid Versailles on Monday (closed), Tuesday (many Paris museums close, so visitors flock here) and Sunday, the busiest day. Also, book tickets online so you don't have to queue.

VERSAILLES BY NUMBERS

- » **Rooms** 700 (11 hectares of roof)
- » **Windows** 2153
- » **Staircases** 67
- » **Gardens and parks** 800 hectares
- » **Trees** 200,000
- » **Fountains** 50 (with 620 nozzles)
- » **Paintings** 6300 (measuring 11km laid end to end)
- » **Statues and sculptures** 2100
- » **Objets d'art and furnishings** 5000
- » **Visitors** 5.3 million per year

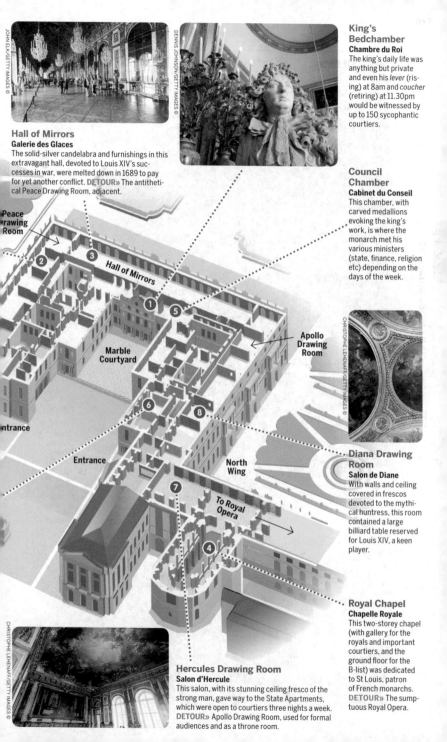

JOHN ELK/GETTY IMAGES ©

Hall of Mirrors

Galerie des Glaces

The solid-silver candelabra and furnishings in this extravagant hall, devoted to Louis XIV's successes in war, were melted down in 1689 to pay for yet another conflict. **DETOUR»** The antithetical Peace Drawing Room, adjacent.

DENNIS JOHNSON/GETTY IMAGES ©

King's Bedchamber

Chambre du Roi

The king's daily life was anything but private and even his *lever* (rising) at 8am and *coucher* (retiring) at 11.30pm would be witnessed by up to 150 sycophantic courtiers.

Council Chamber

Cabinet du Conseil

This chamber, with carved medallions evoking the king's work, is where the monarch met his various ministers (state, finance, religion etc) depending on the days of the week.

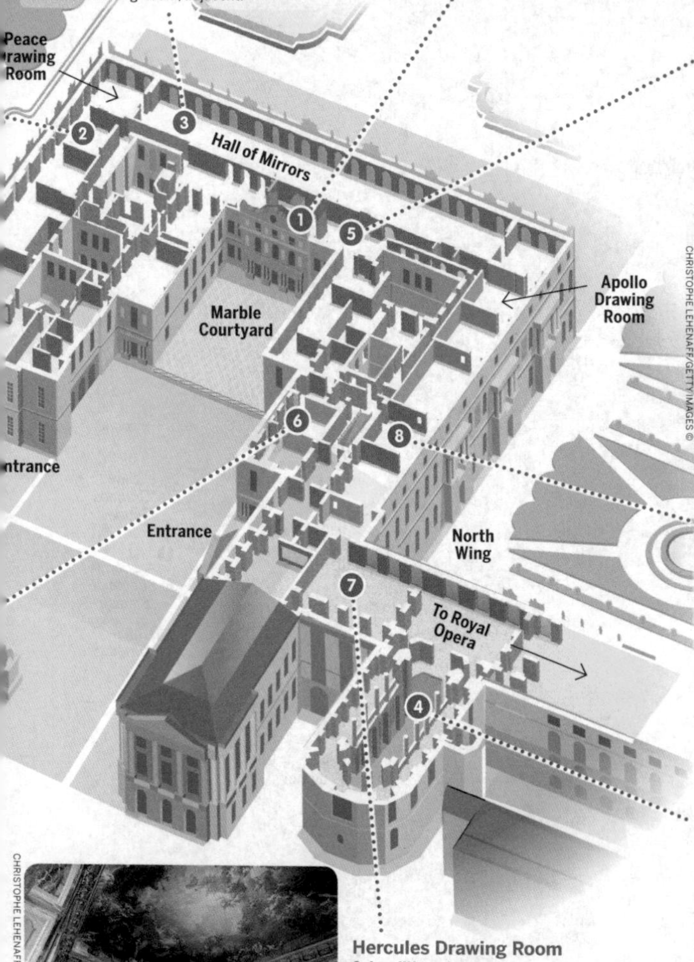

CHRISTOPHE LEHENAFF/GETTY IMAGES ©

Diana Drawing Room

Salon de Diane

With walls and ceiling covered in frescos devoted to the mythical huntress, this room contained a large billiard table reserved for Louis XIV, a keen player.

Royal Chapel

Chapelle Royale

This two-storey chapel (with gallery for the royals and important courtiers, and the ground floor for the B-list) was dedicated to St Louis, patron of French monarchs. **DETOUR»** The sumptuous Royal Opera.

CHRISTOPHE LEHENAFF/GETTY IMAGES ©

Hercules Drawing Room

Salon d'Hercule

This salon, with its stunning ceiling fresco of the strong man, gave way to the State Apartments, which were open to courtiers three nights a week. **DETOUR»** Apollo Drawing Room, used for formal audiences and as a throne room.

VERSAILLES

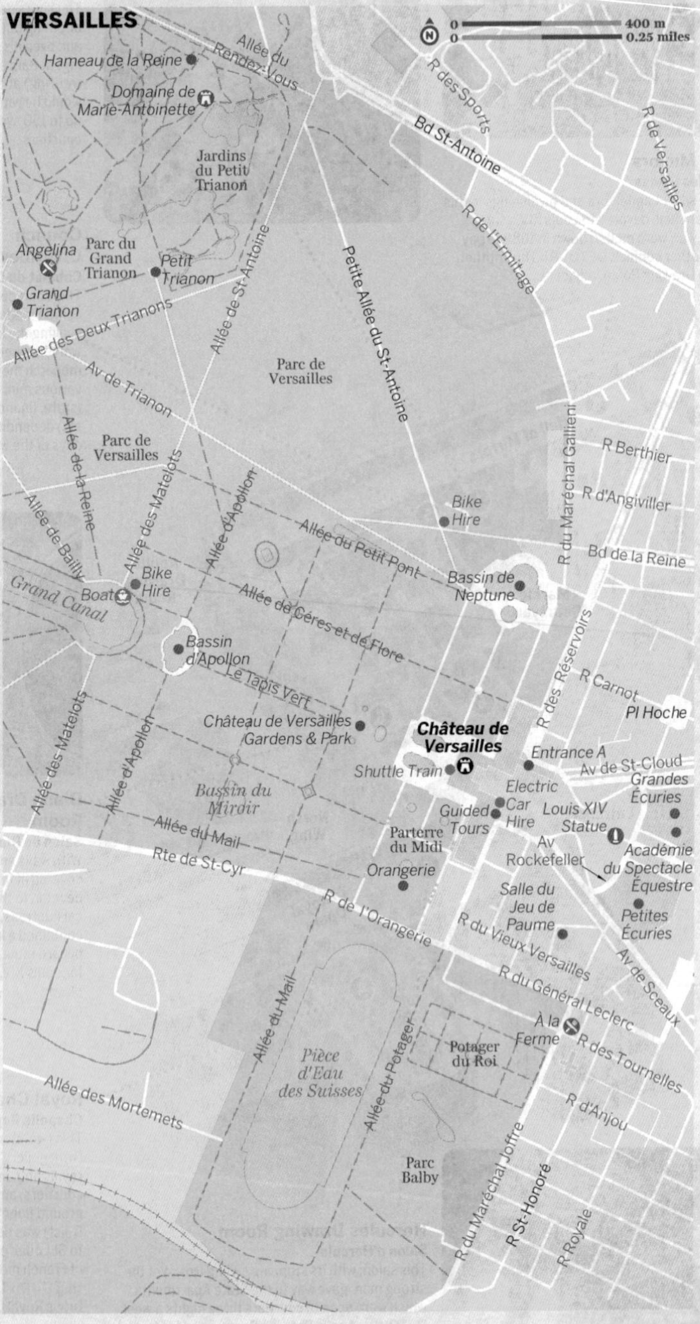

0 400 m
0 0.25 miles
Hameau de la Reine
Domaine de Marie-Antoinette
Allée du Rendez-Vous
Jardins du Petit Trianon
R des Sports
Bd St-Antoine
R de Versailles
R de l'Ermitage
Angelina
Parc du Grand Trianon
Petit Trianon
Grand Trianon
Allée des Deux Trianons
Allée de St-Antoine
Petite Allée du St-Antoine
Parc de Versailles
Av de Trianon
Parc de Versailles
Allée de la Reine
Allée des Matelots
Allée d'Apollon
Allée de Bailly
R Berthier
R d'Angiviller
R du Maréchal Gallieni
Bike Hire
Allée du Petit Pont
Bd de la Reine
Bassin de Neptune
Bike Hire
Boat
Grand Canal
Allée de Céres et de Flore
Bassin d'Apollon
Le Tapis Vert
R des Réservoirs
R Carnot
Pl Hoche
Château de Versailles Gardens & Park
Château de Versailles
Entrance A
Av de St-Cloud
Shuttle Train
Grandes Écuries
Allée des Matelots
Allée d'Apollon
Bassin du Miroir
Electric Car Hire
Guided Tours
Louis XIV Statue
Allée du Mail
Parterre du Midi
Av Rockefeller
Académie du Spectacle Équestre
Rte de St-Cyr
Orangerie
Salle du Jeu de Paume
Petites Écuries
R de l'Orangerie
R du Vieux Versailles
Av de Sceaux
R du Général Leclerc
À la Ferme
R des Tournelles
Allée du Mail
Allée du Potager
Potager du Roi
Pièce d'Eau des Suisses
R d'Anjou
Allée des Mortemets
Parc Balby
R du Maréchal Joffre
R St-Honoré
R Royale

Carved column at the Temple of Love in the garden of Petit Trianon

Marie Antoinette's Estate

Northwest of the main palace is the **Domaine de Marie-Antoinette** (Marie-Antoinette's Estate; adult/child €10/free, with passport ticket free; ⏲noon-6.30pm Tue-Sun Apr-Oct, to 5.30pm Tue-Sat Nov-Mar). Tickets include the Grand and Petit Trianon palaces, and the **Hameau de la Reine** (Queen's Hamlet), a mock village of thatched cottages completed in 1784, where Marie Antoinette played milkmaid.

Trianon Palaces

The pink-colonnaded **Grand Trianon** was built in 1687 for Louis XIV and his family as a place of escape from the rigid etiquette of the court, and renovated under Napoléon I in the Empire style. The ochre-coloured, 1760s **Petit Trianon** was redecorated in 1867 by the consort of Napoleon III, Empress Eugénie, who added Louis XVI–style furnishings.

Musical Fountain Shows

Try to time your visit for the **Grandes Eaux Musicales** (adult/child €9/7.50; ⏲11am-noon & 3.30-5pm Tue, Sat & Sun mid-May–late Jun, 11am-noon & 3.30-5pm Sat & Sun Apr–mid-May & Jul-Oct) or the after-dark **Grandes Eaux Nocturnes** (adult/child €24/20; ⏲from 8.30pm Sat mid-Jun–mid-Sep), truly magical 'dancing water' displays – set to music composed by baroque- and classical-era composers – throughout the grounds in summer.

THE STABLES

Today Versailles' school of architecture and restoration workshops fill the Petites Écuries (Little Stables), while the Grandes Écuries (Big Stables) house the **Académie du Spectacle Équestre** (www.acadequestre.fr; 1 av Rockefeller; 45min training session 11.15am last Sat & Sun of month; adult child €12/6.50). In addition to its 45-minute Les Matinales the academy presents spectacular Reprises Musicales, which sell out weeks in advance.

Louis XVI convened the États-Généraux, made up of more than 1118 deputies representing the nobility, the clergy and the Third Estate ('common people') in May 1789 to moderate dissent. Denied entry, the Third Estate's reps met separately on the 1686-built royal tennis court, formed a National Assembly and took the Serment du Jeu de Paume (Tennis Court Oath), swearing not to dissolve it until Louis XVI accepted a new constitution.

TOP SIGHT
DISNEYLAND RESORT PARIS

It took almost €4.6 billion to turn the beet fields 32km east of Paris into Europe's first Disney theme park. What started out as Euro-Disney in 1992 today comprises the traditional Disneyland Park theme park, the film-oriented Walt Disney Studios Park, and hotel-, shop- and restaurant-filled Disney Village. And kids – and kids-at-heart – can't seem to get enough.

One-day admission includes unlimited access to attractions in *either* Disneyland Park or Walt Disney Studios Park. The latter includes entry to Disneyland Park three hours before it closes. A multitude of multiday passes, special offers and packages are always available.

No picnic hampers/coolers are allowed, but you can bring snacks, sandwiches, bottled water (refillable at water fountains) and the like. The resort has numerous themed restaurants of varying quality and value; tables can be reserved online up to two months in advance. Its seven American-styled hotels are linked by free shuttle bus to the parks. Rates vary hugely. There are also plenty of chain-style hotels in the vicinity.

Disneyland is easily reached by RER A4 (€7.50, 40 minutes to one hour, frequent), which runs from central Paris to Marne-la-Vallée/Chessy, Disneyland's RER station.

Top tips:

➡ Preplan your day on Disney's website, working out which rides, shows etc you really want to see.

➡ Buy tickets in advance to avoid the queue.

➡ The free Disney app provides real-time waiting time for attractions, but note that free wi-fi is only available in limited areas within the park.

➡ Once in, reserve your time slot on the busiest rides using FastPass, the park's ride-reservation system (limited to one reservation at a time).

➡ Disney hotel guests are often entitled to two 'Magic hours' in Disneyland Park (usually from 8am May to October) before it opens to the public; however, not all rides run during these hours.

DON'T MISS...

➡ Disneyland Park

➡ Walt Disney Studios Park

PRACTICALITIES

➡ ☎hotel bookings 01 60 30 60 30, restaurant reservations 01 60 30 40 50

➡ www.disneylandparis.com

➡ one day adult/child €64/58

➡ ⏲hours vary

➡ Ⓜ RER Marne-la-Vallée/Chessy

Disneyland Park (⏲10am-11pm May-Aug, to 10pm Sep, to 6pm Oct-Apr, hours can vary) has five themed *pays* (lands): the 1900s-styled **Main Street USA**; **Frontierland**, home to the legendary Big Thunder Mountain ride; **Adventureland**, which evokes exotic locales in rides like Pirates of the Caribbean and Indiana Jones and the Temple of Peril; **Fantasyland**, crowned by Sleeping Beauty's castle; and the high-tech **Discoveryland**, with massive-queue rides such as Space Mountain: Mission 2, Star Wars and Buzz Lightyear Laser Blast.

The sound stage, production back lot and animation studios at **Walt Disney Studios Park** (⏲10am-7pm May-Sep, to 6pm Oct-Apr, hours can vary) provide an up-close illustration of how films, TV programs and cartoons are produced, with behind-the-scenes tours, larger-than-life characters and spine-tingling rides like the Twilight Zone Tower of Terror. Its latest addition is the outsized Ratatouille ride, based on the winsome 2007 film about a rat who dreams of becoming a top Parisian chef and offering a multisensory rat's perspective of Paris' rooftops and restaurant kitchens aboard a trackless 'ratmobile'.

Fontainebleau

Explore

Fresh air fills your lungs on arriving in the smart town of Fontainebleau (population 16,302), which is enveloped by the 200-sq-km Forêt de Fontainebleau, one of France's loveliest woods.

The town grew up around its magnificent château, which has a list of former tenants and visitors that reads like a who's who of French royalty. Although it's less crowded and pressured than Versailles, exploring it can still take the best part of a day.

Rich in game, and walking, cycling, rock-climbing and horse-riding opportunities, the surrounding forest is as big a playground today as it was in the 16th century, so it's worth prolonging your stay if you can. Fontainebleau also has a cosmopolitan drinking and dining scene, thanks to the town's lifeblood, the international graduate business school Insead.

The Best...

- ➡ **Sight** Château de Fontainebleau
- ➡ **Place to Eat** Dardonville (p282)
- ➡ **Place to Drink** Le Ferrare (p282)

Top Tip

Train tickets to Fontainebleau Avon are sold at Gare de Lyon's SNCF Transilien counter/Billet Ile-de-France machines, *not* SNCF mainline counters/machines. On returning, tickets include travel to any Paris metro station.

Getting There & Around

➡ **Train** Up to 40 daily SNCF Transilien commuter trains link Paris' Gare de Lyon with Fontainebleau Avon station (€8.75, 35 to 60 minutes).

➡ **Bus** Local bus line A links the train station with Château de Fontainebleau (€2), 2km southwest, every 10 minutes; the stop is opposite the main entrance.

➡ **Bike** A la Petite Reine (☎01 60 74 57 57; www.alapetitereine.com; 14 rue de la Paroisse; bike hire per hr/day €8/15; ⏰9am-7.30pm Tue-Sat, to 6pm Sun) rents bikes.

TOP SIGHT
CHÂTEAU DE FONTAINEBLEAU

The resplendent, 1900-room Château de Fontainebleau once housed tenants and guests who were the crème de la crème of French royalty and aristocracy. Every square centimetre of wall and ceiling space is richly adorned with wood panelling, gilded carvings, frescos, tapestries and paintings, with furniture including Renaissance originals.

The first château was built here in the early 12th century, but only a single medieval tower survived the reconstruction undertaken by François I (r 1515–47). It was further enlarged and reworked by successive heads of state including Napoléon Bonaparte.

Among the château's many highlights are the **Grands Appartements**, which embrace several outstanding rooms, including the Second Empire salon and Musée Chinois de l'Impératice Eugénie (Chinese Museum of Empress Eugénie). The **Galerie François 1er** (François I Gallery) is a jewel of Renaissance architecture.

The château's stately **gardens** (⏰9am-6.30pm May-Sep, to 5.30pm Mar, Apr & Oct, to 4.30pm Nov-Feb, palace park 24hr) FREE and courtyards include André Le Nôtre's formal, 17th-century Jardin Français (French Garden), also known as the Grand Parterre, and informal Jardin Anglais (English Garden).

Don't Miss...

- ➡ Grands Appartements
- ➡ Galerie François 1er
- ➡ Gardens and courtyards

Practicalities

- ➡ ☎01 60 71 50 70
- ➡ www.musee-chateau-fontainebleau.fr
- ➡ place Général de Gaulle
- ➡ adult/child €11/free
- ➡ ⏰9.30am-6pm Wed-Mon Apr-Sep, to 5pm Wed-Mon Oct-Mar

Need to Know

➡**Location** 69km southeast of Paris

➡**Tourist Office** (☎01 60 74 99 99; www.fontainebleau-tourisme.com; 4 rue Royale; ⊙10am-6pm Mon-Sat, 10am-1pm & 2-5pm Sun May-Oct, 10am-6pm Mon-Sat, 10am-1pm Sun Nov-Apr; 📶)

SIGHTS

Aside from its monumental château, Fontainebleau's other big draw is the **Forêt de Fontainebleau** (Fontainebleau Forest).

EATING & DRINKING

There are lovely cafe terraces on place Napoléon Bonaparte and some appealing drinking options on rue de la Corne. For fabulous *fromageries* (cheese shops), head to rue des Sablons and rue Grande.

★**DARDONVILLE** PATISSERIE, BOULANGERIE €

(24 rue des Sablons; ⊙7am-1.30pm & 3.15-7.30pm Tue-Sat, 7am-1.30pm Sun) Melt-in-your-mouth macarons, in flavours like poppy seed and gingerbread, cost just €4.80 per dozen (per *dozen!*) at this exceptional pâtisserie-*boulangerie* (bakery). Queues also form out the door for its amazing breads and savoury petits fours such as tiny pastry-wrapped sausages and teensy coin-size quiches that make perfect picnic fare.

CRÊPERIE TY KOZ CRÊPERIE €

(☎01 64 22 00 55; www.creperiety-koz.com; 18 rue de la Cloche; crêpes & galettes €3-12.80; ⊙noon-2pm & 7-10pm Tue-Wed, noon-2pm & 7-10.30pm Thu-Sun) Tucked away in an attractive courtyard, this Breton hidey-hole cooks up authentic sweet crêpes and *simple* (single thickness) and *pourleth* (double thickness) *galettes* (savoury buckwheat crêpes). Wash them down with traditional Val de Rance cider.

LE FERRARE BRASSERIE €

(☎01 60 72 37 04; 23 rue de France; 2-/3-course menus €12.30/13.90; ⊙7.30am-4pm Mon, to 10.30pm Tue-Thu, to 1am Fri & Sat; 📶) Locals pile into this quintessential bar-brasserie, which has a blackboard full of Auvergne specialities and bargain-priced *plats du jour* (daily specials; €10.80).

LE BISTROT 9 BISTRO €€

(☎01 64 22 87 84; www.lebistrot9.com; 9 rue de Montebello; mains €16-29; ⊙noon-2pm & 7-10pm Mon-Thu, noon-2pm & 7-11pm Fri & Sat, noon-2.30pm Sun) Fronted by an awning-covered, timber-decked terrace (heated in winter), this locals' favourite has a cheerful red- and yellow-painted, bare-boards interior and delicious specialities including beef tartare, poached salmon in *beurre blanc* (white sauce), *sole meunière* (floured, fried sole served with butter sauce with lemon) and profiteroles for dessert as well as oysters in season. Great value and lively vibe.

LE FRANKLIN ROOSEVELT BRASSERIE €€

(☎01 64 22 28 73; 20 rue Grande; mains €13.50-24.50; ⊙10am-1am Mon-Sat) With wooden panelling, red banquette seating and atmosphere to spare, the Franklin keeps locals well fed: the *salades composées* (salads with meat or fish) are healthy and huge.

SPORTS & ACTIVITIES

Beginning just 500m south of the château is the lush Forêt de Fontainebleau. Its national walking trails, the GR1 and GR11, are excellent for jogging, walking, cycling and horse riding, and for climbers the forest is a veritable paradise. Rock-climbing enthusiasts have long come to its sandstone ridges, cliffs and overhangs to hone their skills before setting off for the Alps. There are different grades marked by colours, with white representing easy climbs (suitable for children) and black representing climbs up and over death-defying boulders. The website Bleau has stacks of information on climbing in the forest.

To give it a go, contact **Top Loisirs** (☎01 60 74 08 50; www.toploisirs.fr) about equipment hire and instruction. Two gorges worth visiting are the **Gorges d'Apremont**, 7km northwest near Barbizon, and the **Gorges de Franchard**, a few kilometres south of Gorges d'Apremont.

Fontainebleau

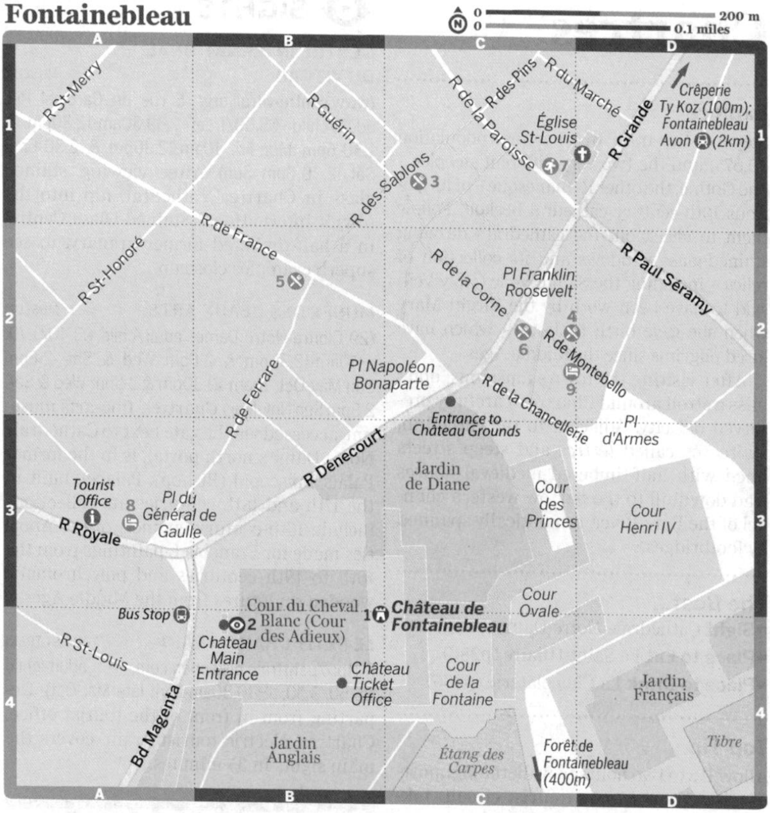

SLEEPING

LA GUÉRINIÈRE B&B €

(☎06 13 50 50 37; balestier.gerard@wanadoo.fr; 10 rue de Montebello; d incl breakfast €70; @ 📶) This charming B&B provides some of the best-value accommodation in town. Owner Monsieur Balestier speaks English and has five rooms, each named after a different flower and dressed in white linens and period furniture; some have wooden beams. Breakfast includes homemade jam and zesty marmalade.

HÔTEL DE LONDRES HOTEL €€

(☎01 64 22 20 21; www.hoteldelondres.com; 1 place Général de Gaulle; d €95-185; ❄ @ 📶) Classy, cosy and beautifully kept, the 16-room 'Hotel London' is furnished in warm reds and royal blues. The priciest rooms (eg room 5) have balconies with dreamy château views.

Fontainebleau

Top Sights
1 Château de Fontainebleau B4

Sights
2 Château de Fontainebleau Gardens & Park B4

Eating
3 Dardonville C1
4 Le Bistrot 9 .... C2
5 Le Ferrare B2
6 Le Franklin Roosevelt C2

Sports & Activities
7 A la Petite Reine C1

Sleeping
8 Hôtel de Londres A3
9 La Guérinière C2

Chartres

Explore

Step off the train in Chartres (population 40,675) and the two very different steeples – one Gothic, the other Romanesque – of its glorious 13th-century cathedral beckon. Follow them to check out the cathedral's dazzling stained-glass windows and its collection of relics – including the Sainte Voile (Holy Veil) said to have been worn by the Virgin Mary when she gave birth to Jesus – which have lured pilgrims since the Middle Ages.

After visiting the town's museums, don't miss a stroll around Chartres' carefully preserved old city. Adjacent to the cathedral, staircases called *tertres* and steep streets lined with half-timbered medieval houses lead downhill to the narrow western channel of the Eure River, romantically spanned by footbridges.

The Best...

➡**Sight** Cathédrale Notre Dame (p286)

➡**Place to Eat** Le Saint-Hilaire (p286)

➡**Place to Drink** La Chocolaterie (p286)

Top Tip

Allow 1½ to two hours to walk the signposted *circuit touristique* (tourist circuit) taking in Chartres' key sights. Free town maps from the tourist office also mark the route.

Getting There & Away

➡**Train** Frequent SNCF trains link Paris' Gare Montparnasse with Chartres (€15.60, 55 to 70 minutes), some of which stop at Versailles-Chantiers (€13.20, 45 to 60 minutes).

Need to Know

➡**Location** 91km southwest of Paris

➡**Tourist Office** (☎02 37 18 26 26; www.chartres-tourisme.com; 8-10 rue de la Poissonnerie; ⏲10am-6pm Mon-Sat, to 5pm Sun) Housed in the historic Maison du Saumon, with an exhibition on Chartres' history. Rents 1½-hour English-language audioguide tours (€5.50/8.50 for one/two) of the medieval city as well as binoculars (€2), fabulous for seeing details of the cathedral close up.

SIGHTS

CENTRE INTERNATIONAL DU VITRAIL MUSEUM

(www.centre-vitrail.org; 5 rue du Cardinal Pie; adult/child €5.50/free; ⏲9.30am-12.30pm & 1.30-6pm Mon-Fri, 10am-12.30pm & 2.30-6pm Sat, 2.30-6pm Sun) After viewing stained glass in Chartres' cathedral, nip into the town's International Stained-Glass Centre, in a half-timbered former granary, to see superb examples close up.

MUSÉE DES BEAUX-ARTS MUSEUM

(29 Cloître Notre Dame; adult/child €3.40/1.70; ⏲10am-12.30pm & 2-6pm Wed & Sat, 2-6pm Sun May-Oct, 10am-12.30pm & 2-5pm Wed & Sat, 2-5pm Sun Nov-Mar) Chartres' fine-arts museum, accessed via the gate next to Cathédrale Notre Dame's north portal, is in the former Palais Épiscopal (Bishop's Palace), built in the 17th and 18th centuries. Its collections include 16th-century enamels of the Apostles made for François I, paintings from the 16th to 19th centuries and polychromatic wooden sculptures from the Middle Ages.

LE PETIT CHART' TRAIN TOURIST TRAIN

(http://petittrain.olikeopen.com; adult/child €6.50/3.50; ⏲10.30am-2pm late Mar-Oct) Departing from in front of the tourist office, Chartres' electric tourist 'train' covers the main sights in 35 minutes.

Old City

Chartres' beautiful medieval old city is northeast and east of the cathedral. Highlights include the 12th-century **Collégiale St-André** (place St-André), a Romanesque church that's now an exhibition centre; **rue de la Tannerie** and its extension **rue de la Foulerie**, lined with flower gardens, millraces and the restored remnants of riverside trades: wash houses, tanneries and the like; and **rue des Écuyers**, with many structures dating from around the 16th century.

Flying buttresses hold up the 12th- and 13th-century **Église St-Pierre** (place St-Pierre; ⏲10am-5pm). Once part of a Benedictine monastery founded in the 7th century, it was outside the city walls and thus vulnerable to attack; the fortresslike, pre-Romanesque bell tower attached to it was used as a refuge by monks, and dates from around 1000. The fine, brightly coloured clerestory windows in

Chartres

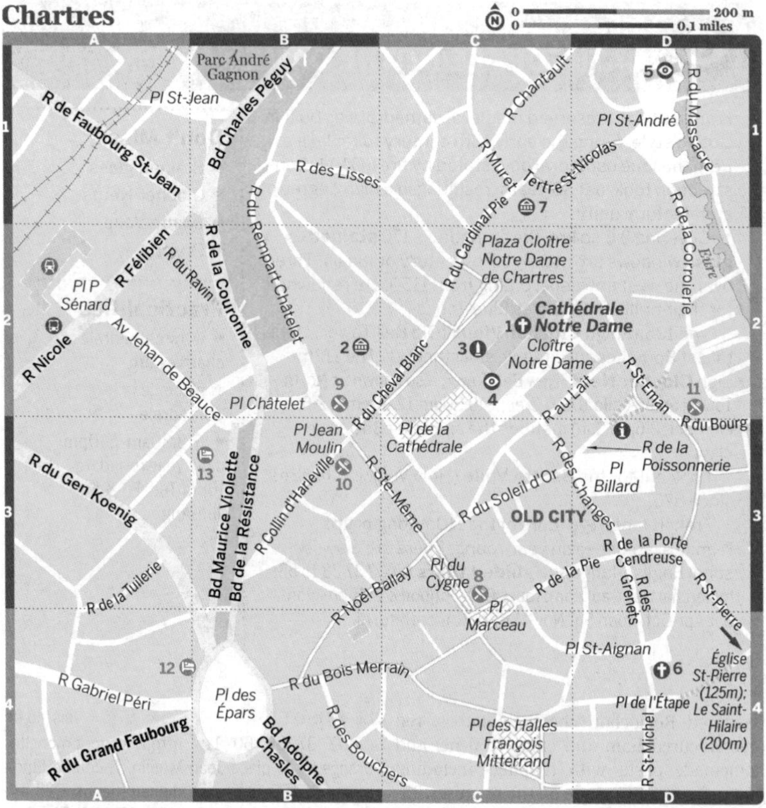

Chartres

Top Sights
1 Cathédrale Notre Dame C2

Sights
2 Centre International du Vitrail B2
3 Clocher Neuf C2
4 Clocher Vieux C2
5 Collégiale St-André D1
6 Église St-Aignan D4
7 Musée des Beaux-Arts C1

Eating
8 La Chocolaterie C3
9 La Passacaille B2
10 Le Tripot B3
11 L'Escalier D2

Sleeping
12 Best Western Le Grand Monarque A4
13 Hôtel du Bœuf Couronné B3

Église St-Pierre's nave, choir and apse date from the early 14th century.

Église St-Aignan (place St-Aignan; ⌚8.30am-6pm) is interesting for its wooden barrel-vault roof (1625), arcaded nave and painted interior of faded blue and gold floral motifs (c 1870). The stained glass and the Renaissance Chapelle de St-Michel date from the 16th and 17th centuries.

EATING & DRINKING

LA PASSACAILLE ITALIAN €

(☎02 37 21 52 10; www.lapassacaille.fr; 30 rue Ste-Même; 2-/3-course menus €16/19, pizzas €10.30-14.90, pasta €10.90-15.60; ⌚11.45am-2pm & 6.45-10pm Thu & Sun-Tue, 11.45am-2pm & 6.45-10.30pm Fri & Sat; 👪) This welcoming spot has particularly good pizzas (try the Montagnarde with tomato, mozzarella, soft, nutty-

TOP SIGHT
CATHÉDRALE NOTRE DAME

France's best-preserved medieval cathedral was built in Gothic style during the early 13th century to replace a Romanesque cathedral devastated by fire in 1194. Construction took just 30 years, resulting in a high degree of architectural unity.

Covering 2.6 sq km, the cathedral's 176 **stained-glass** windows are mostly 13th-century originals. Three over the west entrance, dating from 1150, are renowned for their brilliant 'Chartres blue' tones.

The 105m-high **Clocher Vieux** (Old Bell Tower) is the tallest Romanesque steeple still standing. The 112m-high **Clocher Neuf** (New Bell Tower, also known as North Tower; adult/child €7.50/free; ⏲9.30am-12.30pm & 2-6pm Mon-Sat, 2-6pm Sun) justifies the spiralling 350-step climb.

Look out for the **Sainte Voile** (Holy Veil), in Chartres since 876.

French-language tours of the 110m-long **crypt** – France's largest – run year-round. There are also seasonal English-language **guided tours** (☎02 37 28 15 58; millerchartres@aol.com; tours €10; ⏲noon & 2.45pm Mon-Sat Apr-Oct, noon Sat Nov-Mar) of the cathedral.

Don't Miss...

- Stained glass
- Clocher Neuf
- Sainte Voile
- Crypt

Practicalities

- www.cathedrale-chartres.org
- place de la Cathédrale
- ⏲8.30am-7.30pm daily year-round, to 10pm Tue, Fri & Sun Jun-Aug

flavoured Reblochon cheese, potatoes, red onions, cured ham and crème fraîche) and homemade pasta with toppings including *pistou* (pesto) also made on the premises. Tables spill onto the square out front in summer.

LA CHOCOLATERIE PATISSERIE, TEAROOM **€**

(2 place du Cygne; dishes €3.80-5.50; ⏲8am-7.30pm Tue-Sat, 10am-7.30pm Sun & Mon) Soak up local life overlooking the open-air flower market. This tearoom/patisserie's hot chocolate and macarons (flavoured with orange, apricot, peanut, pineapple and so on) are sublime, as are its sweet homemade crêpes and miniature madeleine cakes.

★LE SAINT-HILAIRE REGIONAL CUISINE **€€**

(☎02 37 30 97 57; www.restaurant-saint-hilaire.fr; 11 rue du Pont St-Hilaire; 3-course menus from €29; ⏲noon-2pm & 7-9.30pm Tue-Sat) At this pistachio-painted, wood-beamed charmer, local products are ingeniously used in to-die-for dishes like bacon-wrapped prawns with leek fondue, honey-roasted duck, and escalope of veal in hazelnut and foie gras sauce. Don't miss its lobster menu in season, or the aromatic cheese platters.

LE TRIPOT BISTRO **€€**

(☎02 37 36 60 11; http://letripot.monsite-orange.fr; 11 place Jean Moulin; 3-course lunch menu €15.50, 3-course dinner menus €28-44; ⏲noon-1.45pm & 7.30-9.15pm Tue & Thu-Sat, noon-1.45pm Sun) Tucked off the tourist trail and easy to miss, even if you do chance down its narrow street, this atmospheric space with low beamed ceilings is a winner for authentic and adventurous French fare like saddle of rabbit stuffed with snails, and grilled turbot in truffled hollandaise sauce. Locals are onto it, so booking ahead's advised.

L'ESCALIER BISTRO **€€**

(☎02 37 33 05 45; www.lescalier-chartres.com; 1 rue du Bourg; 2-/3-course menus €18/22; ⏲noon-3pm & 7-10pm) On a steep corner near its namesake staircase in Chartres' hilly Old City, this deceptively large, very local restaurant has a wonderful terrace for summertime dining and is worth the pre- or postmeal climb for its short but superb menu (foie gras platters, succulent steaks and classic desserts like crème caramel). Look out for live jazz performances.

SLEEPING

HÔTEL DU BŒUF COURONNÉ HOTEL €€
(☎02 37 18 06 06; www.leboeufcouronne.com; 15 place Châtelet; s €57-96, d €67-121; @ 📶) The red-curtained entrance lends a vaguely theatrical air to this two-star Logis guesthouse in the centre of everything. Its summertime terrace restaurant has cathedral-view dining and the XV bar mixes great cocktails.

BEST WESTERN LE GRAND MONARQUE HOTEL €€€
(☎02 37 18 15 15; www.bw-grand-monarque.com; 22 place des Épars; d €139-206, f €206; ❄ @ 📶) With its teal blue shutters gracing its 1779 facade, lovely stained-glass ceiling and treasure trove of period furnishings, old B&W photos and knick-knacks, the refurbished Grand Monarque (with air-con in some rooms) is a historical gem and very central. A host of hydrotherapy treatments are available at its decadent spa; its elegant restaurant, Georges (three-course menus from €51; ⊙noon-2pm & 7.30-10pm Tue-Sat, noon-2pm Sun), has a Michelin star. Staff are charming.

Giverny

Explore

The village's two main draws, impressionist museum the Musée des Impressionnismes Giverny and, especially, Monet's former home and gardens, the Maison et Jardins de Claude Monet, are only open from April to October (as are most places to eat, drink and sleep). Alas, if you're visiting Paris outside these times, there's no reason to make the trip to Giverny (population 516). If you are here during these months, however, the gardens surrounding Monet's home are magnificent, so factor in plenty of time to enjoy them. From early to late spring, daffodils, tulips, rhododendrons, wisteria and irises appear, followed by poppies and lilies. By June, nasturtiums, roses and sweet peas are in blossom. And around September there are dahlias, sunflowers and hollyhocks.

The Best...

➜**Sight** Maison et Jardins de Claude Monet (p288)

➜**Place to Paint** Musée des Impressionnismes Giverny (p287)

➜**Place to Eat** Le Jardin des Plumes (p288)

Top Tip

Be aware that the village has no public toilets, ATMs or bureaux de change.

Getting There & Around

➜**Train** From Paris Gare St-Lazare there are up to 15 daily trains to Vernon (€14.30, 50 minutes), 7km to the west of Giverny.

➜**Bus** Shuttle buses (€8 return, 20 minutes, four daily April to October) meet most trains to and from Paris.

➜**Taxi** Usually waiting outside the train station in Vernon, **taxis** (☎06 07 01 83 50, 06 81 09 00 43) charge around €15 for the one-way trip to Giverny.

➜**Bike** Rent bikes at the **Café L'Arrivée de Giverny** (☎02 32 21 16 01; 1 place de la Gare; per day €14; ⊙7am-11pm), opposite the train station in Vernon, from where Giverny is a signposted 5km along a direct (and flat) cycling-walking track.

Need to Know

➜**Location** 74km northwest of Paris

➜**Tourist Office** (☎02 32 64 45 01; www.cape-tourisme.fr; 80 rue Claude Monet; ⊙10am-6pm Apr-Oct)

SIGHTS

MUSÉE DES IMPRESSIONNISMES GIVERNY ART MUSEUM
(☎02 32 51 94 65; www.mdig.fr; 99 rue Claude Monet; adult/child €7/4.50, incl Maison et Jardins de Claude Monet €16.50/8; ⊙10am-6pm Apr-Oct) About 100m northwest of the Maison de Claude Monet is the Giverny Museum of Impressionisms. Set up in partnership with the Musée d'Orsay, among others, the pluralised name reinforces its coverage of all aspects of impressionism and related movements in its permanent collection and temporary exhibitions. Reserve ahead for two-hour **art workshops** (€12.50 including materials) offering an introduction to watercolour, drawing, sketching or pastels. Lectures, readings, concerts and documentaries also take place regularly.

TOP SIGHT
MAISON ET JARDINS DE CLAUDE MONET

The prized drawcard of tiny Giverny is the home and flower-filled garden of the seminal impressionist painter and his family from 1883 to 1926. Here Monet painted some of his most famous series, including *Décorations des Nymphéas* (Water Lilies).

Monet's hectare of land encompasses two distinct areas, cut by the Chemin du Roy, a small railway line that has been converted into the D5 road, but linked by a foot tunnel.

The artist's pastel pink house and Water Lily studio stand on the periphery of the **Clos Normand**, with its symmetrically laid-out gardens bursting with flowers. Monet bought the **Jardin d'Eau** (Water Garden) in 1895 and set about creating his trademark lily pond, as well as the famous Japanese bridge (since rebuilt). Draped with purple wisteria, the bridge blends into the asymmetrical foreground and background, creating the intimate atmosphere for which the 'painter of light' was renowned.

The charmingly preserved house and beautiful bloom-filled gardens are the attractions here.

Combined tickets with Paris' Musée Marmottan Monet per adult/child cost €18.50/9, and combined adult tickets with Paris' Musée de l'Orangerie cost €18.50.

Don't Miss...

- Clos Normand
- Jardin d'Eau

Practicalities

- 02 32 51 28 21
- www.fondation-monet.com
- 84 rue Claude Monet
- adult/child €9.50/5, incl Musée des Impressionnismes Giverny €16.50/8
- 9.30am-6pm Apr-Oct

EATING & DRINKING

★LE JARDIN DES PLUMES MODERN FRENCH €€
(02 32 54 26 35; www.lejardindesplumes.fr; 1 rue du Milieu; 2-course lunch menu €29, 3-/5-/7-course dinner menus €39/62/82; 12.15-1.45pm & 7.15-9pm Wed-Sun;) Opened in 2012, this gorgeous sky-blue-trimmed property's airy white dining room sets the stage for chef Eric Guerin's exquisite, inventive cuisine, which justifies the trip from Paris alone. Its four rooms (€160 to €200) and four suites (€250 to €290) combine vintage and contemporary furnishings. It's less than 10 minutes' walk to the Maison et Jardins de Claude Monet.

SLEEPING

LE CLOS FLEURI B&B €€
(02 32 21 36 51; www.giverny-leclosfleuri.fr; 5 rue de la Dîme; s/d €93/98; Apr-Oct; PW) Big rooms with king-size beds and exposed wood beams overlook the hedged gardens of this delightful B&B within strolling distance of the Maison et Jardins de Claude Monet. Each of its three rooms is named after a different flower; green-thumbed host Danielle speaks fluent English.

LA PLUIE DE ROSES B&B €€
(02 32 51 10 67; www.givernylapluiederoses.fr; 14 rue Claude Monet; s/d/tr/f €120/130/175/220; PW) You'll be won over by this adorable private home cocooned in a dreamy, peaceful garden. Inside, the three rooms are so comfy it's hard to wake up. Superb breakfast in a verandah awash with sunlight. Payment is by cash only.

LA MUSARDIÈRE HOTEL €€
(02 32 21 03 18; www.lamusardiere.fr; 123 rue Claude Monet; d €84-99, tr €123-136, f €146, 3-course menus €26-36; hotel Feb–mid-Dec; PW) This two-star 10-room hotel dating back to 1880 and evocatively called the 'Idler' is set amid a lovely garden less than 100m northeast of the Maison et Jardins de Claude Monet. Savouring a crêpe in its restaurant (open noon to 10pm April to October) is a pleasure.

Sleeping

Paris has a huge choice of accommodation, from hostels through to deluxe hotels, some of which rank among the world's finest. Yet, although the city has in excess of 1500 establishments, you'll still need to book well ahead during the warmer months (April to October) and all public and school holidays.

Hotels

Hotels in Paris are inspected by government authorities and classified into six categories, from no star to five stars. The vast majority are two- and three-star hotels, which are generally well equipped. All hotels must display their rates, including TVA (*taxe sur la valeur ajoutée;* valued-added tax).

Rooms tend to be small by international standards. Families will probably need connecting rooms but if children are too young to stay in their own room, it's possible to make do with triples, quads or suites in some places.

Cheaper hotels may not have lifts/elevators and/or air-conditioning. Some don't accept credit cards. Breakfast is rarely included in hotel rates; heading to a cafe often works out to be better value.

Hostels

Paris is awash with hostels, and standards are consistently improving. A wave of state-of-the-art hostels have recently opened their doors, with more in the works, including a 950-bed 'megahostel' by leading hostel chain **Generator** (www.generatorhostels.com) near Canal St-Martin, 10e.

More institutional hostels have daytime lockouts and curfews; some have a maximum three-night stay. Places that have upper age limits tend not to enforce them except at the busiest of times. Only the official *auberges de jeunesse* (youth hostels) require guests to present Hostelling International (HI) cards or their equivalent.

Hostel rates often include basic breakfast.

B&Bs & Homestays

B&B accommodation (*chambres d'hôte* in French) is increasingly popular. **Paris Quality Hosts** (Hôtes Qualité Paris; www.hotesqualiteparis.fr) fosters B&Bs, in part to ease the isolation of Parisians, half of whom live alone. There's often a minimum stay of three nights.

Apartments

Families, and anyone wanting to self-cater, should consider a short-stay apartment. Paris has a number of excellent apartment hotels, such as the international chain **Apart'hotels Citadines** (www.citadines.com).

For an even more authentic Parisian experience, sites such as Airbnb offer entire private apartments, some in unique locations like houseboats. Agencies also list furnished residential apartments for stays of a few days to several months. Beware of direct-rental scams.

Websites

➡**Lonely Planet** (www.lonelyplanet.com/france/paris/hotels) Our top choices.

➡**Paris Hotel Service** (www.parishotelservice.com) Boutique hotel gems.

➡**Paris Hotel** (www.hotels-paris.fr) Well-organised booking site with lots of reviews.

➡**Guest Apartment Services** (www.guestapartment.com) Romantic apartment rentals on and around Paris' islands.

➡**Room Sélection** (www.room-selection.com) Select apartment rentals centred on Le Marais.

➡**Paris Attitude** (www.parisattitude.com) Thousands of apartment rentals, professional service, reasonable fees.

NEED TO KNOW

Price Ranges

In our reviews, the following price ranges apply for a double room with en suite bathroom in high season (breakfast not included).

€	less than €130
€€	€130 to €250
€€€	over €250

Taxe de Séjour

The city of Paris levies a *taxe de séjour* (tourist tax) of between €0.20 (campgrounds, 'NN' or unclassified hotels) and €1.50 (four- and five-star hotels) per person per night on all forms of accommodation.

Internet Access

Wi-fi (pronounced *wee-fee* in French) is increasingly free of charge at hotels and hostels. You may find that in many hotels, especially older ones, the higher the floor, the less reliable the wi-fi connection.

Smoking

Smoking is now officially banned in all Paris hotels.

Lonely Planet's Top Choices

Edgar (p293) Twelve individually themed rooms, each by a different artist or designer.

Hôtel Emile (p298) Pure unadulterated design steals hearts at this Marais trendsetter.

L'Hôtel (p304) The stuff of romance, Parisian myths and urban legends.

Le Citizen Hotel (p296) Modern and tech-savvy, with a warm minimalist design.

Best by Budget

€

Cosmos Hôtel (p297) Cheap, brilliant value and footsteps from the nightlife of Le Marais' rue JPT.

Hôtel du Nord – Le Pari Vélo (p294) Bric-a-brac charm and bikes on loan.

Mama Shelter (p300) Philippe Starck–designed hipster haven with in-house pizzeria.

Hôtel de la Porte Dorée (p300) Family-friendly country-manor-style elegance.

Hôtel Vic Eiffel (p305) Contemporary rooms a short walk from the Eiffel Tower.

€€

Hôtel Amour (p296) Stylish choice for a romantic getaway.

Familia Hôtel (p302) Sepia murals and flower-bedecked balconies in the Latin Quarter.

Hôtel Jeanne d'Arc (p298) Gorgeous, like a family home, in a quiet Marais backstreet.

Hôtel Saint Charles (p306) Peaceful local living in the villagey Butte aux Cailles.

€€€

Hôtel Fabric (p299) Stylish ode to the 19th-century textile industry in the Oberkampf area.

Hôtel Molitor (p292) Stunningly restored art deco swimming pool with gallery-style poolside rooms.

Hotel Crayon (p294) Line drawings, retro furnishings and coloured-glass shower doors.

Best Boutique Hotels

Sublim Eiffel (p305) Amazing interior design inspired by the City of Light.

Hôtel Félicien (p292) Boutique chic squirrelled away in a 1930s building in the 16e.

Hôtel du Petit Moulin (p300) A bakery at the time of Henri IV redesigned from head to toe by Christian Lacroix.

Best Historic Hotels

Hôtel St-Merry (p294) Medieval charm in a former presbytery.

La Maison Favart (p294) Art nouveau elegance taking you back to the belle époque.

Hôtel d'Angleterre (p304) Exquisite former embassy hosting seminal guests.

Best Hostels

St Christopher's (p295) Modern hostel amenities in two convenient locations.

BVJ Monceau (p295) Brand-new hostel in a former *hôtel particulier* (private mansion) steps from the Champs Élysées.

Plug-Inn Hostel (p295) Idyllic Montmartre setting and friendly staff.

Auberge de Jeunesse Yves Robert (p295) Snazzy design and ecofriendly construction.

MIJE Fourcy (p297) In a historic *hôtel particulier*; one of a trio in Le Marais.

Where to Stay

Neighbourhood	For	Against
Eiffel Tower & Western Paris	Close to Paris' iconic tower and museums. Upmarket area with quiet residential streets.	Short on budget and midrange accommodation. Limited nightlife.
Champs-Élysées & Grands Boulevards	Luxury hotels, famous boutiques and department stores, gastronomic restaurants, great nightlife.	Some areas extremely pricey. Nightlife hot spots can be noisy.
Louvre & Les Halles	Epicentral location, excellent transport links, major museums, shopping galore.	Not many bargains. Ongoing Forum des Halles construction work may be noisy/inconvenient.
Montmartre & Northern Paris	Village atmosphere and some lively multicultural areas. Many places have views across Paris.	Hilly streets, further out than some areas, some parts very touristy. The red-light district around Pigalle, although well lit and safe, won't appeal to some travellers.
Le Marais, Ménilmontant & Belleville	Buzzing nightlife, hip shopping, great range of eating options in all price ranges. Excellent museums. Lively gay and lesbian scene. Busier on Sundays than most areas. Very central.	Can be seriously noisy in areas where bars and clubs are concentrated.
Bastille & Eastern Paris	Few tourists, allowing you to see the 'real' Paris up close. Excellent markets, loads of nightlife options.	Some areas slightly out of the way.
The Islands	As geographically central as it gets. Almost all accommodation situated on the peaceful, romantic Île St-Louis.	No metro station on the Île St-Louis. Limited self-catering shops, zero nightlife.
Latin Quarter	Energetic student area, stacks of eating and drinking options, late-opening bookshops.	Popularity with students and visiting academics makes rooms hardest to find during conferences and seminars from March to June and in October.
St-Germain & Les Invalides	Stylish, central location, superb shopping, sophisticated dining, proximity to the Jardin du Luxembourg.	Budget accommodation is seriously short-changed.
Montparnasse & Southern Paris	Good value, few tourists, excellent links to both major airports.	Some areas slightly out of the way.

Eiffel Tower & Western Paris

★**HÔTEL DU BOIS** HOTEL €€
Map p382 (01 45 00 31 96; www.hoteldubois.com; 11 rue du Dôme, 16e; d €230-270, tr €370; ; Champs-Élysées) In an area with few midrange hotels, this fresh, homely and effortlessly stylish address charms. The pretty reception doubles as a lounge, with an eye-catching collection of terracotta pots. The 39 rooms mix soft hues with Pierre Frey fabrics and well-thought-out touches: top marks for the tea, coffee and kettle in each room.

★**HÔTEL FÉLICIEN** BOUTIQUE HOTEL €€
Map p382 (01 83 76 02 45; www.hotelfelicienparis.com; 21 rue Félicien David, 16e; d €120-280; @; Mirabeau) The price–quality ratio at this chic boutique hotel, squirrelled away in a 1930s building, is outstanding. Exquisitely designed rooms feel more five-star than four, with 'White' and 'Silver' suites on the hotel's top 'Sky floor' more than satisfying their promise of indulgent cocooning. Romantics, eat your heart out.

★**HÔTEL MOLITOR** BOUTIQUE HOTEL €€€
Map p382 (01 56 07 08 50; www.mltr.fr; 2 av de la porte Molitor, 16e; d from €270; @; Michel Ange Molitor) Famed as Paris' swishest swimming pool in the 1930s (where the bikini made its first appearance, no less) and hot spot for graffiti art in the 1990s, the Molitor is one seriously legedendary address. The art deco complex, built in 1929 and abandoned from 1989, has been restored to stunning effect. All 124 hotel rooms are arranged gallery-style in a U overlooking the pool. The rooftop cocktail bar, restaurant by Yannick Alléno, and original changing cabins transformed into contemporary artworks sign off the dramatic ensemble.

HÔTEL SEZZ BOUTIQUE HOTEL €€€
Map p382 (01 56 75 26 26; www.hotelsezz.com; 6 av Frémiet, 16e; d €290-587, ste €556-1236; @; Passy) Punning on the number of the posh *arrondissement* – 16 (*seize* in French) – in which it finds itself, this 27-room boutique bonanza is heavy on design, technology and Zen spirit. A *hammam* (Turkish steambath), jacuzzi and massage room, Champagne bar, and personal assistant for each guest goes some way towards justifying the price.

Champs-Élysées & Grands Boulevards

HÔTEL FRANCE ALBION HOTEL €
Map p386 (01 45 26 00 81; www.albion-paris-hotel.com; 11 rue Notre Dame de Lorette, 9e; s €77-103, d €97-123, f €163; ; St-Georges) For the quietest night's sleep, go for a room facing the courtyard of this neat-as-a-pin budget hotel. Its rooms all have en suite bathrooms and, for Paris, are decently sized (doubles from 14 sq metres), and staff are eager to please. The location, near Opéra, is fabulous.

HÔTEL MONTE CARLO HOTEL €
Map p386 (01 47 70 36 75; www.hotelmontecarlo.fr; 44 rue du Faubourg Montmartre, 9e; s without en suite €59-88, with en suite €79-117, d without en suite €69-98, with en suite €89-147, tr with en suite €125-167; ; Le Peletier) A unique budget hotel, the Monte Carlo is a steal, with colourful, personalised rooms and a great neighbourhood location. The owners go the extra mile and even provide a partly organic breakfast. The cheaper rooms don't have private bathroom facilities, but overall it outclasses many of the other choices in its price range.

HÔTEL CHOPIN HISTORIC HOTEL €
Map p386 (01 47 70 58 10; www.hotelchopin.fr; 46 passage Jouffroy, 9e; d €85-145; @; Grands Boulevards) Dating from 1846, the 36-room Chopin is inside one of Paris' most delightful 19th-century *passages couverts* (covered shopping arcades). The rooms don't have much in the way of personality (and the cheaper rooms are small and dark), but the belle époque location is beautiful.

BVJ OPÉRA HOSTEL €
Map p386 (01 42 36 88 18; www.bvjhotel.com; 1 rue de la Tour des Dames, 9e; dm/s/d incl breakfast €30/49/70; ; Trinité) Clean rooms at this Bureau des Voyages de la Jeunesse (BVJ) hostel might be monastic but that's negated by its fantastic location near the Palais Garnier and Grands Boulevards department stores, and its 19th-century building opening to a cobbled courtyard. Wi-fi is €5 per four hours. Cash only.

HÔTEL LANGLOIS HISTORIC HOTEL €€
Map p386 (01 48 74 78 24; www.hotel-langlois.com; 63 rue St-Lazare, 9e; s €150-160, d €180-190; @; Trinité) Built in 1870, this

27-room hotel has kept its charm, from the tiny caged elevator to sandstone fireplaces (sadly decommissioned) in many rooms as well as original bathroom fixtures and tiles. Room 64 has wonderful views of Montmartre's rooftops.

HÔTEL AMARANTE BEAU MANOIR — HOTEL €€€

Map p386 (☎01 53 43 28 28; www.amarante-beaumanoir.com; 6 rue de l'Arcade, 8e; d €228-266; ❄@📶; Ⓜ Madeleine) Among the cosier hotels in the 8e, the 18th-century Amarante has traditional-style rooms, with exposed rafters, wooden furniture and oak panelling. It has a prime location just around the corner from place Madeleine, and free w-fi. The breakfast room is in a beautiful cross-vaulted stone cellar.

HIDDEN HOTEL — BOUTIQUE HOTEL €€€

Map p384 (☎01 40 55 03 57; www.hidden-hotel.com; 28 rue de l'Arc de Triomphe, 17e; d €389-454; ❄@📶; Ⓜ Charles de Gaulle-Étoile) 🍃 The Hidden is one of the Champs-Élysées' best secrets. It's serene, stylish, reasonably spacious, and it even sports green credentials: the earth-coloured tones are the result of natural pigments (no paint), and all rooms feature handmade wooden furniture, stone basins, and linen curtains surrounding the beds. The queen-size Emotion rooms are among the most popular.

HÔTEL JOYCE — DESIGN HOTEL €€€

Map p386 (☎01 55 07 00 01; www.astotel.com; 29 rue la Bruyère, 9e; d from €320; ❄@📶; Ⓜ St-Georges) 🍃 Located in a lovely residential area between Montmartre and Opéra, this place has all the modern design touches (iPod docks, individually styled rooms, a skylit breakfast room fitted out with old Range Rover seats) and makes some eco-friendly claims – it relies on 50% renewable energy and uses organic products. Rates start from €230 outside high season.

🛏 Louvre & Les Halles

HÔTEL TIQUETONNE — HOTEL €

Map p392 (☎01 42 36 94 58; www.hoteltiquetonne.fr; 6 rue Tiquetonne, 2e; d €65, with shared shower €50; 📶; Ⓜ Étienne Marcel) What heart-warmingly good value this 45-room cheapie is. This serious, well-tended address has been in the hotel biz since the 1900s and is much loved by a loyal clientele of all ages. Rooms range across seven floors, are spick and span, and sport an inoffensive mix of vintage decor – roughly 1930s to 1980s, with brand-new bathrooms and parquet flooring in recently renovated rooms.

Ask for a room in the rooftops with a view of the Sacré-Cœur (701, 702 or 703) or Eiffel Tower (704 and 705)! Shared-shower *jetons* (tokens) cost €5; ask at reception.

HÔTEL VIVIENNE — HOTEL €

Map p388 (☎01 42 33 13 26; www.hotel-vivienne.com; 40 rue Vivienne, 2e; d €108-150, tr & q €160; @📶; Ⓜ Grands Boulevards) This stylish two-star hotel is amazingly good value for Paris. While the 45 rooms are not huge, they have all the mod cons; some even boast little balconies. Family rooms accommodate up to two children on a sofa bed.

★EDGAR — BOUTIQUE HOTEL €€

Map p392 (☎01 40 41 05 19; www.edgarparis.com; 31 rue d'Alexandrie, 2e; d €235-295; ❄📶; Ⓜ Strasbourg St-Denis) Twelve playful rooms, each decorated by a different team of artists or designers, await the lucky few who secure a reservation at this former convent/seamstress workshop. Milagros conjures up all the magic of the Far West, while Dream echoes the rich imagination of childhood with surrealist installations. Breakfast is served in the popular downstairs restaurant, and the hidden tree-shaded square is a fabulous location.

HÔTEL O — BOUTIQUE HOTEL €€

Map p392 (☎01 42 36 04 02; www.hotel-o-paris.com; 19 rue Hérold, 1er; d €229-299; ❄📶; Ⓜ Sentier or Bourse) A futuristic refuge from the busy Paris streets, Hôtel O makes use of clever design to maximise small spaces. French designer Ora-Ito echoes the natural world with elegant curves and simple, eco-friendly materials such as felt, oak and cork. Choose from one of three styles of room: Cocoon, Odyssey or the deluxe Galileo.

HÔTEL DE LA PLACE DU LOUVRE — BOUTIQUE HOTEL €€

Map p392 (☎01 42 33 78 68; www.paris-hotel-place-du-louvre.com; 21 rue des Prêtres St-Germain l'Auxerrois, 1er; d €135-205; ❄📶; Ⓜ Pont Neuf) Not to be confused with the Relais du Louvre (p294) next door, this fairly recent addition to the Parisian hotel scene is warmly welcomed. It has just 20 rooms split across five floors – a couple on each floor are lucky enough to ogle the majestic Louvre across the street.

Decor is contemporary and stylish – lots of white and oyster grey to show off those enviable views to perfection – and the kettle with tea and coffee in each room is an appreciated, atypical-for-Paris perk. Check the hotel website for last-minute deals and special offers.

HÔTEL ST-MERRY HISTORIC HOTEL €€

Map p392 (☎01 42 78 14 15; www.hotelsaintmerryparis.com; 78 rue de la Verrerie, 4e; d €170-240, tr €295; ❄📶; Ⓜ Châtelet) The interior of this 12-room hostelry, with beamed ceilings, church pews and wrought-iron candelabra, is a neo-Goth's wet dream; you have to see the architectural elements of room 9 (flying buttress over the bed) and the furnishings of room 12 (choir-stall bed board) to believe them. On the downside there is no lift connecting the postage-stamp lobby with the four upper floors, and not all rooms have air-con.

LE RELAIS DU LOUVRE BOUTIQUE HOTEL €€

Map p392 (☎01 40 41 96 42; www.relaisdulouvre.com; 19 rue des Prêtres St-Germain l'Auxerrois, 1er; s €135-180, d €175-263, tr €235-263; ❄📶; Ⓜ Pont Neuf) If you like style in a traditional sense, choose this lovely 21-room hotel just west of the Louvre and across the street from Église St-Germain l'Auxerrois with its melodious chime of bells. The nine rooms facing the street and church are petite, while room 2 has access to the garden.

HÔTEL THÉRÈSE HOTEL €€

Map p388 (☎01 42 96 10 01; www.hoteltherese.com; 5-7 rue Thérèse, 1er; s & d €180-310; ❄📶; Ⓜ Pyramides) From the same people who brought you the Left Bank's lovely Hotel Verneuil, the Thérèse is ideal for those with a fetish for Japanese food – this chic address is steps from rue Ste-Anne and Japantown. Rooms are individually decorated, classical yet eclectic in design.

In nicer rooms, expect stylish linen panels on the windows and tubs in the bathroom. The cheaper, smaller rooms – and they are small – have showers. Highlight: the clubby library lounge.

★ **HÔTEL CRAYON** BOUTIQUE HOTEL €€€

Map p392 (☎01 42 36 54 19; www.hotelcrayon.com; 25 rue du Bouloi, 1er; s/d €311/347; ❄📶; Ⓜ Les Halles or Sentier) Line drawings by French artist Julie Gauthron bedeck walls and doors at this creative boutique hotel. *Le crayon* (the pencil) is the theme, with 26 rooms sporting a different shade of each floor's chosen colour – we love the coloured-glass shower doors and the books on the bedside table guests can swap and take home.

Beautiful pieces of 1950s and 1960s flea-market furniture add a dash of retro, and doodling on the walls is a unique perk for guests sleeping in the dazzling white-and-silver suite. Pick which fragrance you'd like your room perfumed with, help yourself to coffee or grab a drink from the fridge, and make yourself at home. *Quel bonheur!* Online deals often slash rates by over 50%.

LA MAISON FAVART HISTORIC HOTEL €€€

Map p388 (☎01 42 97 59 83; www.lamaisonfavart.fr; 5 rue de Marivaux, 2e; d €200-390; ❄📶; Ⓜ Richelieu Drouot) This stylish art nouveau hotel facing the Opéra Comique feels like it never let go of the belle époque. It's an excellent choice if you're interested in shopping, and is within easy walking distance of the *grands magasins* (department stores) on bd Haussmann. Goya slept here in 1824.

LE PRADEY DESIGN HOTEL €€€

Map p388 (☎01 42 60 31 70; www.lepradey.com; 5 rue St-Roch, 1er; d €390-460; ❄@📶; Ⓜ Tuileries) Enviably secreted behind the Louvre and Jardin des Tuileries on boutique-smart rue St-Honoré, this exclusive address is the last word in luxury hotel design. Guests linger over glossy art books in the understatedly chic mezzanine lounge – if they can drag themselves away from whichever individually themed suite they are staying in.

Exuberant Cabaret evokes the theatrical glamour of the Moulin Rouge with its frilly-skirt bedspread, deep red walls and heart-shaped door frame; while Opéra, elegantly dressed in pretty pinks and greys, treats guests to a magical night at the ballet.

Montmartre & Northern Paris

HÔTEL DU NORD – LE PARI VÉLO HOTEL €

Map p398 (☎01 42 01 66 00; www.hoteldunord-leparivelo.com; 47 rue Albert Thomas, 10e; d €73-86, tr/q €96/125; 📶; Ⓜ République) This particularly charming place has 24 personalised rooms decorated with flea-market antiques. Beyond the bric-a-brac charm (and the ever-popular dog, Pluto), Hôtel du

Nord's other winning attribute is its prized location near place République. Bikes are available for guests to loan.

A ROOM IN PARIS
B&B €

Map p398 (☎06 33 10 25 78; www.aroominparis.com; 130 rue La Fayette, 10e; r €80-155; 📶; Ⓜ Gare du Nord) Stay in a Parisian apartment at this cosy B&B near the Gare du Nord. Five rooms (three of which sleep up to four people) are available in a Haussmann-era building with herringbone parquet floors, period moulding and a fireplace. Three rooms share two bathrooms, the other two have private bathrooms. Thierry and Peet can also provide home-cooked dinners.

ST CHRISTOPHER'S GARE DU NORD
HOSTEL €

Map p398 (☎01 70 08 52 22; www.st-christophers.co.uk/paris-hostels; 5 rue de Dunkerque, 10e; incl breakfast dm €20-44, d €90-170; @📶; Ⓜ Gare du Nord) Just steps from the Gare du Nord, this newer St Christopher's, opened in 2013, has brought more modern hostel accommodation to the city, with six floors of light-filled rooms (600 total). Dorms sleep four, six, eight and 10 people but there is a catch – unless you reserve months in advance, they won't come cheap. Facilities include a bar, restaurant, cafe, laundry and female-only floor. Bring a towel and padlock. No kitchen.

ST CHRISTOPHER'S CANAL
HOSTEL €

Map p400 (☎01 40 34 34 40; www.st-christophers.co.uk/paris-hostels; 159 rue de Crimée, 19e; dm €20-52, d from €85; @📶; Ⓜ Riquet or Jaurès) Opened in 2008, this is certainly one of Paris' best, biggest (300 beds) and most up-to-date hostels. It features modern design, four types of dorms (12, 10, eight and six bed) and doubles with or without bathrooms. Other perks include a canal-side cafe, a bar, a female-only floor, bike rental and organised day trips. Daily prices vary wildly; check the website for an accurate quote and reserve as far in advance as possible to secure reasonable prices. No kitchen.

BVJ MONCEAU
HOSTEL €

Map p401 (☎01 43 29 34 80; www.bvjhotel.com; 12 rue Léon Jost, 17e; dm/d per person incl breakfast €30/35; 📶; Ⓜ Courcelles) Set in the former studio and *hôtel particulier* of painter Henri Gervex (1852–1929), this new hostel near the Champs Élysées has 24 spacious rooms, sleeping two to 10 people each. Bathrooms are shared. Unlike more recent additions to the Paris hostel scene, the BVJ has retained a period feel, with original moulding, a secluded courtyard and parquet floors throughout. Sheets are included, though you do need to make your own bed. Wi-fi is on the ground floor only.

PLUG-INN HOSTEL
HOSTEL €

Map p394 (☎01 42 58 42 58; www.plug-inn.fr; 7 rue Aristide Bruant, 18e; incl breakfast dm €25-37, d €90-105; @📶; Ⓜ Abbesses or Blanche) This 2010 hostel has several things going for it, the first of which is its central Montmartre location. The four- to six-person rooms all have their own showers, there's a kitchen, and the staff are even friendly (a rarity among Parisian hostels). One drawback is that communal areas are small. No curfew at night.

AUBERGE DE JEUNESSE YVES ROBERT
HOSTEL €

Map p398 (☎01 40 38 87 90; www.fuaj.org; 20 rue Pajol, 18e; dm/d per person incl breakfast €31/60; Ⓜ Marx Dormoy) 🍃 Overlooking the railway tracks behind the Gare de l'Est is this snazzy new solar-powered hostel. The spacious ground-floor area houses a cafe and communal area; rooms sleep one to six people. On the down side, it can be a hike to get anywhere else in the city, and wi-fi is only in the reception area.

WOODSTOCK HOSTEL
HOSTEL €

Map p394 (☎01 48 78 87 76; www.woodstock.fr; 48 rue Rodier, 9e; dm/d incl breakfast €25/54; @📶; Ⓜ Anvers) This hostel is just down the hill from place Pigalle in a quiet residential quarter. Dorm beds are bunks in rooms sleeping four to six people. Each room has washbasin only; showers and toilets are off the corridor. The eat-in kitchen, down the steps from the patio, has everything. Curfew is 2am.

HÔTEL REGYN'S MONTMARTRE
HOTEL €

Map p394 (☎01 42 54 45 21; www.hotel-regynsparis.com; 18 place des Abbesses, 18e; s €65-155, d & tw €115-175; @📶; Ⓜ Abbesses) This 22-room hotel is a good choice if you want to stay in Montmartre and not break the bank. Although the rooms are nothing to crow about, its location is unbeatable – just opposite the Abbesses metro station. Some rooms have views over Paris.

HOTEL CAULAINCOURT SQUARE — HOSTEL €

Map p394 (01 46 06 46 06; www.caulaincourt.com; 2 square Caulaincourt, 18e; dm €25-30, s €60-70, d €70-86; @; Lamarck-Caulaincourt) This hotel with dorm rooms is perched on the backside of Montmartre, beyond the tourist hoopla in a real Parisian neighbourhood. The rooms are in decent condition, with parquet floors and a funky design, though there is no lift. Wi-fi in the reception area only. Single travellers should also note there are no communal hang-out areas, meaning you won't meet others easily.

HÔTEL ELDORADO — HOTEL €

Map p401 (01 45 22 35 21; www.eldoradohotel.fr; 18 rue des Dames, 17e; s €43-71, d €65-94, tr €82-102; Place de Clichy) This bohemian place is one of Paris' greatest finds: a welcoming, reasonably well-run hotel with 23 colourfully decorated and (often) ethnically themed rooms, with a private garden at the back. Unfortunately rooms facing the garden will probably be quite noisy as they look out onto the restaurant – earplugs may be a good idea. Cheaper-category singles have washbasin only.

RÉPUBLIQUE HÔTEL — HOTEL €

Map p398 (01 42 39 19 03; www.republique-hotel.com; 31 rue Albert Thomas, 10e; s €55-87, d €60-100, tr €135; République) This hip spot is heavy on pop art – local street artists did some of the paintings – and features what is possibly the narrowest elevator in Paris, if not the world. Regardless of what you think about the garden gnomes in the breakfast room or the poor soundproofing (bring earplugs), you won't be able to fault the inexpensive rates and fantastic location off place République.

★LE CITIZEN HOTEL — BOUTIQUE HOTEL €€

Map p398 (01 83 62 55 50; www.lecitizenhotel.com; 96 quai de Jemmapes, 10e; d €199 & €269; Gare de l'Est or Jacques Bonsergent) Opened in 2011, the Citizen is a sign the times are a changin' on the Canal St-Martin. A team of forward-thinking creative types put their heads together for this one, and the result is 12 alluring rooms equipped with niceties such as iPads, filtered water and warm minimalist design. Artwork is from Oakland's Creative Growth Art Center for disabled artists.

★LOFT — APARTMENT €€

Map p394 (06 14 48 47 48; www.loft-paris.fr; 7 cité Véron, 18e; apt €100-270; Blanche) Book months in advance to secure one of the stylish apartments in this gem, which offers an intimacy that simply cannot be replicated in a hotel. Just around the corner from the Moulin Rouge, this apartment block offers choices ranging from a two-person studio to a loft that can fit a large family or group. The owner, a culture journalist, is a great resource.

★HÔTEL AMOUR — BOUTIQUE HOTEL €€

Map p394 (01 48 78 31 80; www.hotelamourparis.fr; 8 rue Navarin, 9e; s €145, d €170-225; St-Georges or Pigalle) Planning a romantic escapade to Paris? Say no more. The inimitable black-clad Amour (formerly a love hotel by the hour) features original design and artwork in each of the rooms – you won't find a more unique place to lay your head in Paris at these prices. You have to be willing to forgo television – but who needs TV when you're in love?

ROBINET D'OR — BOUTIQUE HOTEL €€

Map p398 (01 44 65 14 50; www.lerobinetdor.com; 7 rue Robert Blache, 10e; d €187-352, q from €363; Château Landon) A former faucet factory (hence the name 'The Golden Faucet'), this relatively new boutique hotel has a stylish, modern feel: parquet floors and tasteful flea-market furnishings mix well with the modern amenities and inviting rain showers. Family suites are available, and breakfast is served in the very popular brasserie downstairs.

AU SOURIRE DE MONTMARTRE — B&B €€

(06 64 64 72 86; www.sourire-de-montmartre.com; 64 rue du Mont Cenis, 18e; r €125-170; Jules Joffrin) This charming family-run B&B on the backside of Montmartre has four rooms and one studio, each individually decorated with either French antiques or Moroccan motifs. The surrounding neighbourhood is delightful though slightly out of the way (directions are available upon confirmation of booking). Note there is no lift.

HÔTEL DES ARTS — HOTEL €€

Map p394 (01 46 06 30 52; www.arts-hotel-paris.com; 5 rue Tholozé, 18e; s/d from €145/160; Abbesses or Blanche) The Hôtel des Arts is a friendly, attractive 50-room hotel, convenient to both place Pigalle and Montmartre. It has comfortable midrange rooms that are excellent value; consider spending an extra €20 for the superior rooms, which have nicer views. Just up the street is the old-style windmill Moulin de la Galette. Better rates are often available online.

NEW ORIENT HÔTEL HOTEL €€

Map p401 (☎01 45 22 21 64; www.hotelneworient.com; 16 rue de Constantinople, 8e; s €128, d €158-185, q €195; ❄📶; MEurope) This delightful place has lots of personality – several rooms have Second Empire furnishings and decorative busts – and its tasteful decor makes this one of the nicest midrange choices in western Paris. The only drawback is its location, which is somewhat off the beaten track.

MANOIR DE BEAUREGARD B&B €€

Map p400 (☎01 42 03 10 20; manoir-de-beauregard-paris.com; 43 rue des Lilas, 19e; r €185-265; 📶; MDanube) If you ever dreamt of staying in an 18th-century French townhouse, this would certainly be your pick. Rooms (sleeping two to four people) are luxurious and done up in period style, with beautiful linens, floral wallpaper and original parquet floors – and there's even a garden, a true rarity in Parisian homes. Breakfast comes with homemade jam.

ERMITAGE HÔTEL HISTORIC HOTEL €€

Map p394 (☎01 42 64 79 22; www.ermitagesacrecoeur.fr; 24 rue Lamarck, 18e; s €95, d €115-120, tr/q €150/170; @; MLamarck-Caulaincourt) Located in a 19th-century townhouse, the family-run Ermitage is a quaint 12-room bed and breakfast in the shadow of Sacré-Cœur. The traditional-style rooms are simple but attractive, with floral-patterned fabric on the walls and antique furnishings that convey a yesteryear charm. Like many hotels in this area, the upper floors have good views.

RELAIS MONTMARTRE HOTEL €€

Map p394 (☎01 70 64 25 25; www.relaismontmartre.fr; 6 rue Constance, 18e; d €199-259; ❄📶; MAbbesses or Blanche) This popular choice has an excellent location and country-style decor, with matching floral prints and exposed rafters painted to match the colour scheme in each room. The service is excellent.

TERRASS HÔTEL HOTEL €€€

Map p394 (☎01 46 06 72 85; www.terrass-hotel.com; 12 rue Joseph de Maistre, 18e; s & d €345-450; ❄📶; MBlanche) This very sedate, stylish hotel has 98 spacious, well-designed rooms and some of the best views in town. For the ultimate Parisian experience, choose room 608 (a double) for stunning views of the Eiffel Tower and Panthéon, or room 802, which boasts its own private terrace. Some of the rooms on floors four, five and six were designed by Kenzo. Online deals can drop rates by over 50%, making this a very good choice.

Le Marais, Ménilmontant & Belleville

★COSMOS HÔTEL HOTEL €

Map p406 (☎01 43 57 25 88; www.cosmos-hotel-paris.com; 35 rue Jean-Pierre Timbaud, 11e; s €62-75, d €68-75, tr/q €85/94; 📶; MRépublique) Cheap, brilliant value and just footsteps from the nightlife of rue JPT, Cosmos is a shiny star with retro style on the budget-hotel scene. It has been around for 30-odd years but, unlike most other hotels in the same price bracket, Cosmos has been treated to a thoroughly modern makeover this century. Breakfast €8.

HÔTEL BEAUMARCHAIS DESIGN HOTEL €

Map p402 (☎01 53 36 86 86; www.hotelbeaumarchais.com; 3 rue Oberkampf, 11e; s €75-100, d €90-145; 📶; MFilles du Calvaire) This brighter-than-bright 31-room design hotel, with its emphasis on sunbursts and bold primary colours, is just this side of kitsch. But it makes for a bright Paris experience. There are monthly art exhibitions and guests are invited to the *vernissage* (opening night). The boutiques and bars of the Marais are a two-minute walk away.

MIJE FOURCY HOSTEL €

Map p402 (☎01 42 74 23 45; www.mije.com; 6 rue de Fourcy, 4e; dm incl breakfast €33.50, s/d/tr €55/82/100.50; 📶; MSt-Paul or Pont Marie) Sweep through this *hôtel particulier's* elegant front door and pride yourself on scoring such magnificent digs. Fourcy welcomes guests with clean rooms and a summer garden to breakfast/hang out in. Rooms (closed noon to 3pm) have a shower but share toilets in the corridor. Curfew 1am to 7am; no children under six years. One of three Marais hostels run by the Maison Internationale de la Jeunesse et des Étudiants; the others are **MIJE Le Fauconnier** (Map p402; 11 rue du Fauconnier, 4e; MSt-Paul or Pont Marie) and **MIJE**

Maubuisson (Map p402; 12 rue des Barres, 4e; Ⓜ Hôtel de Ville or Pont Marie).

HÔTEL RIVOLI HOTEL €

Map p402 (☎01 42 72 08 41; www.hotel-rivoli.fr; 2 rue des Mauvais Garçons, 4e; s/d with washbasin €38/47, s/d/tr with shower €50/61/76; Ⓜ Hôtel de Ville) The Rivoli remains forever dirt cheap and cheery, with 20 basic if noisy rooms. The cheapest share a bathroom, but use of the shower room in the hallway is free. Annoyingly – given that it is in the heart of the Marais nightlife area – the front door is locked from 2am to 7am. Find reception on the 1st floor. Breakfast €5.

HÔTEL DE NICE HOTEL €

Map p402 (☎01 42 78 55 29; www.hoteldenice.com; 42bis rue de Rivoli, 4e; s €80-100, d €100-220, tr €135-240; ; Ⓜ Hôtel de Ville) This is an especially warm, family-run place with 23 comfy rooms full of Second Empire–style furniture, Oriental carpets and lamps with fringed shades. Some have balconies high above busy rue de Rivoli. Breakfast €8.

HÔTEL DU LOIRET HOTEL €

Map p402 (☎01 48 87 77 00; www.hotel-du-loiret.fr; 8 rue des Mauvais Garçons, 4e; d/tr €100/150; Ⓜ Hôtel de Ville or St-Paul) This 27-room budget hotel on the 'Street of the Bad Boys' in the heart of gay Marais is popular with young male travellers.

★ **HÔTEL JEANNE D'ARC** HOTEL €€

Map p402 (☎01 48 87 62 11; www.hoteljeannedarc.com; 3 rue de Jarente, 4e; s €72, d €98-120, q €250; ; Ⓜ St-Paul) About the only thing wrong with this gorgeous address is everyone knows about it; book well in advance. Games to play, a painted rocking chair for tots in the bijou lounge, knick-knacks everywhere and the most extraordinary mirror in the breakfast room create a real 'family home' air in this 35-room house. The pièce de résistance: the 6th-floor attic room with sweeping Paris rooftop view.

★ **HÔTEL EMILE** DESIGN HOTEL €€

Map p402 (☎01 42 72 76 17; www.hotelemile.com; 2 rue Malher, 4e; incl breakfast s €170, d €180-230, ste €350; ; Ⓜ St-Paul) Prepare to be dazzled – literally. Retro B&W, geometrically patterned carpets, curtains, wallpapers and drapes dress this chic hotel, wedged between boutiques and restaurants in the Marais. Pricier 'top floor' doubles are just that, complete with breathtaking outlook over Parisian roofs and chimney pots. Breakfast is eaten on bar stools in the lobby; open the cupboard to find the 'kitchen'.

HÔTEL DE LA HERSE D'OR HOTEL €€

Map p402 (☎01 48 87 84 09; www.hotel-hersedor.com; 20 rue St-Antoine, 4e; s €99, d €129-189, tr €159-209; ; Ⓜ Bastille) This friendly, down-to-earth address on a busy shopping street has 30-odd serviceable rooms, some with original old stone fireplace and a couple with alfresco terrace. If you're looking to pay less, go for a cheaper 'older' room with carpet and dated furnishings; pricier rooms have been renovated and are crisp white and modern. Breakfast is a bargain at €6. And no, *herse* is not 'hearse' in French but rather 'portcullis'. So let's call it the 'Golden Gate Hotel'.

HÔTEL GEORGETTE DESIGN HOTEL €€

Map p402 (☎01 44 61 10 10; www.hotelgeorgette.com; 36 rue du Grenier St-Lazare, 3e; d €153-216; ; Ⓜ Rambuteau) Clearly seeking inspiration from the Centre Pompidou around the corner, this sweet little neighbourhood hotel is a steal. The lobby is bright and appealing, and rooms are a decorative ode to either Pop Art, Op Art, Dada or New Realism with lots of bold colours and funky touches like Warhol-inspired Campbell-soup-can lamp shades.

HÔTEL DE LA PLACE DES VOSGES HOTEL €€

Map p402 (☎01 42 72 60 46; www.hotelplacedesvosges.com; 12 rue de Birague, 4e; d €95-160, q €200-250; ; Ⓜ St-Paul) This superbly situated 17-room hotel – stables to the nearby Bastille in the 16th century – is a hop and a skip from sublime place des Vosges. Ancient wood beams and exposed stone inject heaps of character into the hotel, which has 16 rooms and a loft suite (with a couple of pull-out beds for families) piled up on six floors. Breakfast €8.

HÔTEL DU HAUT MARAIS B&B €€

Map p402 (☎01 42 77 65 52; www.hotelhautmarais.com; 7 rue des Vertus, 3e; d/ste/apt incl breakfast €125/185/198; ; Ⓜ Arts et Métiers) Otherwise called Chez Didier et Marc, this 15th-century town house is perfect for those seeking a stylish 'home away from home' experience. Didier, Marc and their pet dog live at this boutique address with eight rooms, each different in design and comfortably spread across five floors. Breakfast is taken around a shared table in the cellar.

HÔTEL CARON DE BEAUMARCHAIS BOUTIQUE HOTEL €€

Map p402 (☎01 42 72 34 12; www.carondebeaumarchais.com; 12 rue Vieille du Temple, 4e; d €160-198; @ 📶; Ⓜ St-Paul) The attention to detail at this unique themed hotel, decorated like an 18th-century private house, is impressive. From the period card table set as if time stopped halfway through a game, to the harp and well-worn sheet music propped on the music stand, the decor evokes the life and times of the 18th-century playwright after whom the hotel is named.

GRAND HÔTEL MALHER HOTEL €€

Map p402 (☎01 42 72 60 92; www.grandhotelmalher.com; 5 rue Malher, 4e; s €130-160, d €160-200, tr €250; 📶; Ⓜ St-Paul) Rooms are not quite as stylish as the design-driven lobby and lounge would have you believe. But this welcoming establishment is comfortable nonetheless. Road-facing rooms come with cute wrought-iron balcony, and the ground-floor room with courtyard garden is designed especially for travellers in wheelchairs.

HÔTEL CARON HOTEL €€

Map p402 (☎01 40 29 02 94; www.hotelcaron.com; 3 rue Caron, 4e; d €249-259; ❄ 📶; Ⓜ St-Paul) Footsteps from delightful place du Marché Ste-Catherine, this is a solid mid-range hotel with convivial cosmopolitan neighbours (Scottish pub, Italian grocery and so on). Soft natural hues give its 18 double rooms instant appeal and the L'Occitane bathroom products are a sweet-smelling touch. Breakfast (€14) in the cream-stone, vaulted cellar is a highlight.

HÔTEL BASTILLE DE LAUNAY HOTEL €€

Map p402 (☎01 47 00 88 11; www.bastilledelaunay-hotel-paris.com; 42 rue Amelot, 3e; s/d €150/180; Ⓜ Chemin Vert) Glitzy and glam, this smart hotel with 36 rooms in two buildings separated by a small courtyard is good value. Large windows and a judicious use of mirrors create a bright (and very quiet) environment just steps from busy bd Beaumarchais and place de la Bastille. Breakfast €12.

HÔTEL DES MÉTALLOS HOTEL €€

Map p406 (☎01 43 38 73 63; www.hoteldesmetallos.com; 50 rue de la Folie Méricourt, 11e; s €75-159, d €79-189; ❄ @ 📶; Ⓜ St-Ambroise or Parmentier) A short stroll from Marché Popincourt, this modern hotel is a bright space with 32 well-equipped rooms and spacious communal areas. Breakfast costs €10 and, rather cleverly, there's a *petit dej 'sur la pouce'* ('on the run') – pastries and a hot drink to take away – served from 6am for early birds.

HÔTEL DU VIEUX SAULE HOTEL €€

Map p402 (☎01 42 72 01 14; www.hotelvieuxsaule.com; 6 rue de Picardie, 3e; s €95-125, d €110-165; 📶; Ⓜ Filles du Calvaire) This flower-bedecked 27-room hostelry, just around the corner from the Marché aux Rouges Enfants, is something of a find because of its slightly off-the-beaten-track location. Breakfast (€12) is served in a 16th-century vaulted cellar.

CASTEX HÔTEL HOTEL €€

Map p402 (☎01 42 72 31 52; www.castexhotel.com; 5 rue Castex, 4e; s/d €169/199; Ⓜ Bastille) Equidistant from the Bastille and the Marais, 30-room Castex retains a certain 17th-century charm with its vaulted stone cellar used as a breakfast room, terracotta floor tiles and toile de Jouy wallpaper. Try to get one of the independent rooms (1 and 2) off the lovely patio; no 3 is a two-room suite or family room. Breakfast €11.

HÔTEL DU 7E ART HOTEL €€

Map p402 (☎01 44 54 85 00; www.paris-hotel-7art.com; 20 rue St-Paul, 4e; s €85, d €120-180, tr €180-200, q €220; 📶; Ⓜ St-Paul) Just across the road from the Village St-Paul, *le septième art* (or 'seventh art', as the French know cinema) is a fun place for film buffs, with its jaunty 1950s and '60s movie posters and cinematic black-and-white bathroom tiling. The ground-floor reception doubles as a cosy cafe-bar selling postcards and figurines. Breakfast €8.

★HÔTEL FABRIC DESIGN HOTEL €€€

Map p406 (☎01 43 57 27 00; www.hotelfabric.com; 31 rue de la Folie Méricourt, 11e; d €240-360; ❄ 📶; Ⓜ Oberkampf) Four-star Hôtel Fabric is a stylish ode to its industrial heritage as a 19th-century textile factory. Steely pillars prop up the red-brick lounge area with *table d'hôte* (set menu at a fixed price) dining table and vintage touches including a Singer sewing machine. Darkly carpeted corridors open onto crisp, bright rooms with beautiful textiles and uber-cool cupboards (upcycled packing crates!). Breakfast €15.

HÔTEL SAINT PAUL DE MARAIS HOTEL €€€
Map p402 (01 48 04 97 27; www.saint-paul-marais.fr; 8 rue de Sévigné, 4e; s/d/tr €220/280/350; ; St-Paul) From its soft sage green facade to the endearing maze of family-friendly mezzanine rooms in the attic, Saint Paul charms. The hotel is perfect for really getting one's teeth into the Marais' superb dining, and its 28 traditional rooms are warm and cosy. Each comes with a kettle, and breakfast (€12) is delightfully served in the cellar 'kitchen' or summer courtyard garden.

LE PAVILLON DE LA REINE HISTORIC HOTEL €€€
Map p402 (01 44 59 80 40; www.pavillondelareine.com; 28 place des Vosges, 3e; d €385-550; ; Chemin Vert) Discretely set in a cobblestone courtyard off beautiful place des Vosges, this is a sumptuous address loaded with history – the hotel is named after former guest Anne of Austria, queen to Louis XIII from 1615. A bijou garden and revitalising spa render it a real country retreat from the hubbub of urban Paris.

HÔTEL DU PETIT MOULIN BOUTIQUE HOTEL €€€
Map p402 (01 42 74 10 10; www.hoteldupetitmoulin.com; 29-31 rue du Poitou, 3e; d €220-350; ; Filles du Calvaire) This scrumptious 17-room hotel, a bakery at the time of Henri IV, was designed from head to toe by Christian Lacroix. Pick from medieval and rococo Marais (rooms sporting exposed beams and dressed in toile de Jouy wallpaper), or more modern surrounds with contemporary murals and heart-shaped mirrors just this side of kitsch.

Bastille & Eastern Paris

★MAMA SHELTER DESIGN HOTEL €
(01 43 48 48 48; www.mamashelter.com; 109 rue de Bagnolet, 20e; s/d from €79/89; ; 76, Alexandre Dumas or Gambetta) Coaxed into its zany new incarnation by uber-designer Philippe Starck, this former car park offers what is surely the best-value accommodation in the city. Its 170 supercomfortable rooms feature iMacs, trademark Starck details like a chocolate-and-fuchsia colour scheme, concrete walls and even microwave ovens, while a rooftop terrace and cool pizzeria add to the hotel's street cred.

The only drawback? Mama Shelter is a hike from both central Paris and the nearest metro stop, but bus 76 from the centre via place de la Bastille drops you at the door.

HÔTEL DE LA PORTE DORÉE HOTEL €
(01 43 07 56 97; www.hoteldelaportedoree.com; 273 av Daumesnil, 12e; s €66-78, d €91-105, tr €133; ; Porte Dorée) A few blocks inside the bd Périphérique ring road and footsteps from the Porte Dorée metro station, this country-manor-style hotel is as family friendly as you'll find, with crayons and paper at reception, toy boxes in the rooms and the beautiful Bois de Vincennes right nearby. Some of the 43 hardwood-floored rooms have period fireplaces.

HÔTEL DU PRINTEMPS HOTEL €
(01 43 43 62 31; www.hotel-paris-printemps.com; 80 bd de Picpus, 12e; s €79-104, d €89-136, tr €116-157; ; Picpus) It may not be in the centre of the action, but the 38-room Spring Hotel offers excellent value for its standard of comfort. Located just off place de la Nation, central Paris is less than 10 minutes away via the RER A.

HÔTEL DAVAL HOTEL €
Map p410 (01 47 00 51 23; www.hoteldaval.com; 21 rue Daval, 11e; s/d/tr/q €98/109/149/169; ; Bastille) This 23-room hotel with lift/elevator is a very central option if you're looking for budget accommodation just off place de la Bastille. Rooms and bathrooms are on the small side; to ensure peace and quiet, choose a back room (eg room 13).

HÔTEL PARIS BASTILLE HOTEL €€
Map p410 (01 40 01 07 17; www.hotelparisbastille.com; 67 rue de Lyon, 12e; s/d/tr/q €200/214/265/288; ; Bastille) A haven of serenity near busy Bastille and Le Marais, this comfortable midrange hotel has a range of modern rooms. Although it feels slightly chainlike, it's nonetheless one of the nicest and most dependable options in the neighbourhood.

HI MATIC HOTEL €€
Map p410 (01 43 67 56 56; www.hi-matic.net; 71 rue de Charonne, 11e; d €156-176, f €196; ; Bastille) The upside of this 'urban hotel of the future' is its eco-cred (LED energy-saving lights, natural pigments instead of paint) and colourful, imaginative space-saving design (mattresses rolled out onto

WATCH THIS SPACE

Set to open sometime in 2015, **Les Bains** (www.lesbains-paris.com; 7 rue du Bourg-l'Abbé, 3e) promises to be an amazing place to stay. Its past, after all, is mythical. Built in 1885 as thermal baths, it was a place where Marcel Proust et al hung out over a Turkish, Russian or sulphur bath. In 1978 the baths shut and the Bains-Douches nightclub opened, much to the joy of David Bowie, Mick Jagger and a host of other world rock stars and celebs who frequented the iconic joint. In 2011 the nightclub shut, paving the way for its magnificent renaissance as a 'chic, inventive, transcultural, historical' and absolutely amazing place to stay.

tatamis at night) that some will find kind of fun. The drawback is that service is minimal, with computerised check-in and vending-machine-dispensed organic breakfasts, but there's an on-site manager.

STANDARD DESIGN HÔTEL DESIGN HOTEL €€€
Map p410 (01 48 05 30 97; www.standard-design-hotel-paris.com; 29 rue des Taillandiers, 11e; d €300-350; ; Bastille) Monochrome black-on-white or white-on-black stripes rule at this sharp, contemporary hotel, broken up by splashes of colour. It's brilliantly located close to Bastille and Le Marais, but not so close that you can't sleep at night (rooms are well soundproofed; ask for a room back from the street if you want even more tranquility).

The Islands

HÔTEL SAINT-LOUIS EN L'ISLE BOUTIQUE HOTEL €€
Map p412 (01 46 34 04 80; www.saintlouisenlisle.com; 75 rue St-Louis en l'Île, 4e; d €159-249, tr €289; ; Pont Marie) This elegant abode brandishes a pristine taupe facade and perfectly polished interior. Spot-on home comforts like a kettle with complimentary tea and coffee in each room or the iPod docking station next to the bed make Saint-Louis stand out. Room 52 on the 5th floor with beams and balcony is dreamy, and the stone-cellar breakfast room is a 17th-century gem. Breakfast €13.

HÔTEL DE LUTÈCE HOTEL €€
Map p412 (01 43 26 23 52; www.paris-hotel-lutece.com; 65 rue St-Louis en l'Île, 4e; s €210, d €210-285; ; Pont Marie) A lobby salon with ancient fireplace, wood panelling, antique furnishings and terracotta tiles set the inviting tone of the lovely Lutèce, an exquisite hotel with tastefully decorated rooms and one of the city's most desirable locations. Breakfast €14.

HÔTEL DU JEU DE PAUME BOUTIQUE HOTEL €€€
Map p412 (01 43 26 14 18; www.hotel-saint-louis.com; 54 rue St-Louis en l'Île, 4e; s €185-255, d €285-360; ; Pont Marie) Romantically set in a courtyard off the main street on Île St-Louis, this four-star hotel languishes in a 17th-century royal tennis court. Contemporary chic is its vibe and each of its 30 rooms is inspired by a different modern artist. Panton chairs add a design edge to the historic beamed house, and its leafy patio garden is simply divine, darling. Breakfast €18.

Latin Quarter

HÔTEL ESMERALDA HOTEL €
Map p414 (01 43 54 19 20; www.hotel-esmeralda.fr; 4 rue St-Julien le Pauvre, 5e; s €80-100, d €115-130, tr €140; ; St-Michel) Tucked away in a quiet street with million-dollar views of Notre Dame (choose room 12!), this no-frills place is about as central to the Latin Quarter as it gets. At these prices, the 19 rooms are no great shakes (the cheapest singles have washbasin only) but they're popular. Book well ahead by phone (no online bookings). Wi-fi in reception area only.

YOUNG & HAPPY HOSTEL €
Map p416 (01 47 07 47 07; www.youngandhappy.fr; 80 rue Mouffetard, 5e; incl breakfast dm €22-33, d €60-90; ; Place Monge) This friendly if frayed Latin Quarter favourite was Paris' first independent hostel. Breakfast is served in the dark stone-vaulted cellar, and the self-catering kitchen gets a workout from guests trawling rue Mouffetard's markets and food shops. Beds are in cramped rooms with washbasins, but women are in luck with an en suite female

dorm (€28 to €38). Wi-fi in the reception area only. Book well ahead.

HÔTEL DE L'ESPÉRANCE HOTEL €

Map p416 (☎01 47 07 10 99; www.hoteldelesperance.fr; 15 rue Pascal, 5e; s €85-96, d €95-98; ❄@📶; Ⓜ Censier Daubenton) Although this place stakes its claim as a 'hôtel de charme', the dated floral decor won't be to everyone's taste. No, the real reason to book a bed here is take advantage of the rates – under €100 – and a prime location at the bottom of rue Mouffetard.

★**FAMILIA HÔTEL** HOTEL €€

Map p414 (☎01 43 54 55 27; www.familiahotel.com; 11 rue des Écoles, 5e; s €96-105, d €129-147, tr €175-186; ❄@📶; Ⓜ Cardinal Lemoine) Sepia murals of Parisian landmarks, flower bedecked windows and exposed rafters and stone walls make this friendly family-run hotel (in business for three generations) one of the most attractive 'almost budget' options on this side of the Seine. Eight rooms have little balconies, from which you can catch a glimpse of Notre Dame.

HÔTEL DES GRANDES ÉCOLES HOTEL €€

Map p416 (☎01 43 26 79 23; www.hotel-grandes-ecoles.com; 75 rue du Cardinal Lemoine, 5e; d €130-160; @📶; Ⓜ Cardinal Lemoine or Place Monge) Spanning three two-storey buildings, this welcoming hotel just north of place de la Contrescarpe has one of the loveliest situations in the Latin Quarter, set around its own private garden courtyard off a medieval street. Rooms are simple but not without charm.

HÔTEL MINERVE HOTEL €€

Map p414 (☎01 43 26 26 04; www.parishotel-minerve.com; 13 rue des Écoles, 5e; s €125, d €146-202, tr €202; ❄@📶; Ⓜ Cardinal Lemoine) Oriental carpets, antique books, frescos of French monuments and wall tapestries make this family-run hotel a lovely and reasonably priced place to stay. Room styles are a mix of traditional and modern (renovated 2014); some have small balconies with views of Notre Dame, while the 1st-floor rooms all have parquet floors.

HÔTEL ST-JACQUES HOTEL €€

Map p414 (☎01 44 07 45 45; www.hotel-saint-jacques.com; 35 rue des Écoles, 5e; s €179, d €200-260, tr €312; ❄📶; Ⓜ Maubert-Mutualité) Audrey Hepburn and Cary Grant filmed some scenes of *Charade* here in the 1960s, and it still retains original 19th-century details such as trompe l'œil ceilings that look like cloud-filled skies, an iron staircase and balconies overlooking the Panthéon (but alas no lift). Welcome touches include a cabaret-themed breakfast room and bowl of jelly beans in the lobby.

HÔTEL HENRI IV RIVE GAUCHE HOTEL €€

Map p414 (☎01 46 33 20 20; www.henri-paris-hotel.com; 9-11 rue St-Jacques, 5e; s/d/tr €210/230/255; ❄📶; Ⓜ Cluny-La Sorbonne or RER St-Michel Notre Dame) Reminiscent of a Normandy manor house (18th-century fireplace, terracotta tiles and portraits in the lobby), this three-star hotel is a Latin Quarter oasis just steps from Notre Dame and the Seine. Rooms are comfortable if somewhat lacking in charm, though front rooms have nice views of the Église St-Séverin and its buttresses. Online rates drop significantly out of season.

HÔTEL LES DEGRÉS DE NOTRE DAME HOTEL €€

Map p414 (☎01 55 42 88 88; www.lesdegreshotel.com; 10 rue des Grands Degrés, 5e; d incl breakfast €120-170; 📶; Ⓜ Maubert-Mutualité) Wonderfully old-school, with a winding timber staircase (no lift) and charming staff, this hotel a block from the Seine is good value. Breakfast comes with fresh-squeezed OJ. Rooms 47 and the spacious 501 have romantic views of Notre Dame. Rooms have not been renovated for some time, however.

SELECT HÔTEL BOUTIQUE HOTEL €€€

Map p414 (☎01 46 34 14 80; www.selecthotel.fr; 1 place de la Sorbonne, 5e; d €195-332, tr €275-340; ❄@📶; Ⓜ Cluny-La Sorbonne) In the heart of the studenty Sorbonne area, the Select is a very Parisian art deco minipalace, with an atrium and cactus-strewn winter garden, an 18th-century vaulted breakfast room and 67 small but stylish bedrooms with ingenious design solutions to maximise their limited space. The 1920s-style cocktail bar with an attached 'library' just off the lobby is a delight.

FIVE HOTEL BOUTIQUE HOTEL €€€

Map p416 (☎01 43 31 74 21; www.thefivehotel.com; 3 rue Flatters, 5e; s €255, d €285-305; ❄📶; Ⓜ Les Gobelins) Choose from one of five perfumes to fragrance your (small) room at this contemporary romantic sanctum. Its private apartment, One by the Five, has a phenomenal 'levitating' bed. Rates are often discounted by up to 50% online, making it a better deal than it first appears.

HÔTEL RÉSIDENCE HENRI IV HOTEL €€€

Map p414 (☑01 44 41 31 81; www.residencehenri4. com; 50 rue des Bernadins, 5e; d €285, ste €365-395; ❋❈; MMaubert-Mutualité) This exquisite late-19th-century cul-de-sac hotel has eight generously sized rooms (minimum 17 sq metres) and five two-room apartments (minimum 25 sq metres), done up with medieval-style touches. All are equipped with kitchenettes (induction cooktops, fridge, microwave and dishes), making them particularly handy for families and market goers.

🛏 St-Germain & Les Invalides

HÔTEL ST-ANDRÉ DES ARTS HOTEL €

Map p418 (☑01 43 26 96 16; 66 rue St-André des Arts, 6e; s/d/tr/q incl breakfast €81/101/129/144; ❈; MOdéon) Located on a lively, restaurant-lined thoroughfare, this 31-room hotel is a veritable bargain in the centre of the action. The rooms are basic and there's no lift, but the public areas are very evocative of *vieux Paris* (old Paris), with beamed ceilings and ancient stone walls.

HÔTEL DE NESLE HOTEL €

Map p418 (☑01 43 54 62 41; www.hotelde-nesleparis.com; 7 rue de Nesle, 6e; s/d without toilet €75/85, with toilet €85/120; ❈; MOdéon or Mabillon) Most of the Nesle's 20 rooms – all with shower but not all with toilet – are painted with brightly coloured naïve murals inspired by French literature. But its greatest asset is the huge (by Parisian standards) garden – a backyard really – accessible from the 1st floor, with pathways, trellis and even a small fountain. Phone reservations only.

HÔTEL DU CHAMP-DE-MARS HOTEL €

Map p422 (☑01 45 51 52 30; www.hotelduchamp-demars.com; 7 rue du Champ de Mars, 7e; s/d €105/130; @❈; MÉcole Militaire) This charming 25-room cheapie (relatively speaking) in the shadow of the Eiffel Tower is on everyone's wish list – book a month or two ahead. Two ground-floor rooms overlook a flowered courtyard.

HÔTEL PERREYVE HOTEL €€

Map p418 (☑01 45 48 35 01; www.hotel-perreyve. com; 63 rue Madame, 6e; s €140, d €175-200; ❋❈; MRennes) A hop, skip and a jump from the Jardin du Luxembourg, this welcoming 1920s hotel is superb value given its coveted location. Cosy, carpeted rooms have enormous frescos; on the ground floor, start the day in the pretty breakfast room with herringbone floors and fire-engine-red tables and chairs.

LE BELLECHASSE DESIGN HOTEL €€

Map p422 (☑01 45 50 22 31; www.lebellechasse. com; 8 rue de Bellechasse, 7e; s/d from €183/192; ❋❈; MSolférino) Fashion (and, increasingly, interior) designer Christian Lacroix' entrancing room themes – including St-Germain, with brocades, zebra striping and faux-gold leafing; Tuileries, with trompe l'œil and palms; and Jeu de Paume, with giant playing-card motifs – give the impression you've stepped into a larger-than-life oil painting. Mod cons include iPod docks and 200 TV channels. Rates include a glass of Champagne.

HÔTEL DANEMARK BOUTIQUE HOTEL €€

Map p418 (☑01 43 26 93 78; www.hotel danemark.com; 21 rue Vavin, 6e; d €185-205; ❋@❈; MVavin) In a peaceful location near the Jardin du Luxembourg, this stone-walled hotel has 15 scrumptious, eclectically furnished rooms. All are well soundproofed and at least 20 sq metres, which is bigger than many Parisians' apartments. Also unlike many residential apartments, all have bath tubs.

HÔTEL DES MARRONNIERS HOTEL €€

Map p418 (☑01 43 25 30 60; www.hotel-marron niers.com; 21 rue Jacob, 6e; s from €100, d €145-155, tr/q €215/260; ❋@❈; MSt-Germain des Prés) At the end of a small courtyard 30m from the main street, this 37-room hotel has a delightful conservatory leading on to a magical garden. From the 3rd floor up, rooms ending in 1, 2 or 3 look on to the garden; the rooms on the 5th and 6th floors have views over Paris' rooftops.

HÔTEL LE CLÉMENT HOTEL €€

Map p418 (☑01 43 26 53 60; www.hotelclement-paris.com; 6 rue Clément, 6e; d €119-165; ❋@❈; MSt-Germain des Prés) Excellent value for the style and tranquillity it offers, the Clément has 28 stylish rooms, some of which overlook the Marché St-Germain (eg room 100).

Rooms on the very top floor have sloping ceilings. The proprietors know what they're doing – this place has been in the same family for over a century.

GRAND HÔTEL LÉVÈQUE HOTEL €€

Map p422 (☎01 47 05 49 15; www.hotel-leveque.com; 29 rue Cler, 7e; s/d/tr €85/170/190; ❄📶; Ⓜ École Militaire) Quieter rooms are dark and small, and singles miniscule, but this 50-room hotel is recommended less for its charms than its *bon rapport qualité prix* (good value for money) and excellent location. Choose any room ending in 1, 2 or 3, all of which have two windows overlooking rue Cler's market.

★L'HÔTEL BOUTIQUE HOTEL €€€

Map p418 (☎01 44 41 99 00; www.l-hotel.com; 13 rue des Beaux Arts, 6e; d €275-495; ❄@📶🏊; Ⓜ St-Germain des Prés) In a quiet quayside street, this award-winning hostelry is the stuff of romance, Parisian myths and urban legends. Rock- and film-star patrons fight to sleep in room 16, where Oscar Wilde died in 1900 and which is now decorated with a peacock motif, or in the art deco room 36 (which entertainer Mistinguett once stayed in), with its huge mirrored bed. A stunning, modern swimming pool occupies the ancient cellar. Guests and nonguests can soak up the atmosphere of the fantastic bar (often with live music by up-and-coming new talent) and Michelin-starred restaurant (called, what else, Le Restaurant) under a glass canopy.

L'APOSTROPHE DESIGN HOTEL €€€

Map p418 (☎01 56 54 31 31; www.apostrophe-hotel.com; 3 rue de Chevreuse, 6e; d €299-353; ❄@📶; Ⓜ Vavin) A street work-of-art with its stencilled façade, this art hotel's 16 dramatically different rooms pay homage to the written word. Spray-painted graffiti tags cover one wall of room U (for *urbain*), which has a ceiling shaped like a skateboard ramp. Room P (for Paris parody) sits in the clouds overlooking Paris' rooftops. Other inspired design features include double sets of imprinted curtains (one for day, one for night) and a 'bar table' on wheels that slots over the bed. Rates tumble to midrange territory outside high season.

HÔTEL D'ANGLETERRE HISTORIC HOTEL €€€

Map p418 (☎01 42 60 34 72; www.hotel-dangleterre.com; 44 rue Jacob, 6e; incl breakfast s €175, d €250-275; @📶; Ⓜ St-Germain des Prés) If the walls could talk...this former garden of the British embassy is where the Treaty of Paris ending the American Revolution was prepared in 1783. Hemingway lodged here in 1921, as did Charles Lindbergh in 1927 after completing the world's first solo nonstop flight from New York to Paris. Its 27 exquisite rooms are individually decorated.

HÔTEL DES ACADÉMIES ET DES ARTS DESIGN HOTEL €€€

Map p418 (☎01 43 26 66 44; www.hotel-des-academies.com; 15 rue de la Grande Chaumiére, 6e; d €242-322; ❄@📶; Ⓜ Vavin) Inspired by 1920s Montparnasse, a five-minute walk away, this avant-garde address features the distinctive signature of French street artist Jérôme Mesnager whose impish white figures backflip up walls, scale stairs and dance above fireplaces – ride the lift to the 5th floor for the ultimate acrobatic performance. Midrange prices outside high season.

HÔTEL DE L'ABBAYE SAINT GERMAIN HOTEL €€€

Map p418 (☎01 45 44 38 11; www.hotelabbayeparis.com; 10 rue Cassette, 6e; d €273-450; ❄@📶; Ⓜ St-Sulpice) It's the delightfully romantic outside areas that set this hotel apart from the four-star crowd. Swing through the wrought-iron gates and enjoy a moment in the plant- and flower-filled front courtyard, and linger over breakfast served beneath ivy-clad walls on one of the city's prettiest patios.

LE SIX BOUTIQUE HOTEL €€€

Map p418 (☎01 42 22 00 75; www.hotel-le-six.com; 14 rue Stanislas, 6e; d €300-450; ❄@📶; Ⓜ Notre Dame des Champs) From the funky red-leather reception bar to rotating art exhibitions, glass-topped courtyard salon and ultracool spa, this four-star hotel defines contemporary design. Beds are queen or king size and kids are warmly welcomed. But the biggest asset is the outstanding service on every level.

HÔTEL ST-GERMAIN DES PRÉS HOTEL €€€

Map p418 (☎01 43 26 00 19; www.hotel-paris-saint-germain.com; 36 rue Bonaparte, 6e; s €185, d €205-400, tr €450; ❄@📶; Ⓜ St-Germain des Prés) Many guests come to lay their head where Henry Miller did at this tapestry-adorned, period-furnished hotel. Its location, just up from the cafes and hubbub of place St-Germain des Prés, couldn't be handier.

Montparnasse & Southern Paris

★**HÔTEL VIC EIFFEL** BOUTIQUE HOTEL €

(www.hotelviceiffel.com; 92 bd Garibaldi, 15e; s/d from €99/109; ; MSèvres-Lecourbe) Outstanding value for money, this pristine hotel with chic orange and oyster grey rooms (two are wheelchair accessible) is a short walk from the Eiffel Tower, with the metro on the doorstep. Budget-priced Classic rooms are small but perfectly functional; midrange Superior and Privilege rooms offer increased space. Friendly staff go out of their way to help.

LA MAISON BOUTIQUE HOTEL €

Map p428 (01 45 42 11 39; www.lamaison-montparnasse.com; 53 rue de Gergovie, 14e; s €95-110, d €115-130, tr €135-160, f €165-205; @; MPernety) The House goes all out to re-create home, with homemade cakes and jams for breakfast in the open-plan kitchen-lounge or little courtyard garden. A candy-striped staircase leads to its 36 rooms (there's a box-sized lift too) with bold pinks, violets and soft neutral tones. Ask for an Eiffel Tower–view room.

ARTY PARIS HOSTEL €

Map p430 (01 40 34 40 34; www.artyparis.fr; 62 rue des Morillons, 15e; dm €22-35, s €65-100, d €75-120, tr €80-135, q €100-180; ; MPorte de Vanves) Freebies at this fun, all-en-suite hostel/budget hotel include lockers, croissant breakfasts and wi-fi. Private rooms come with plasma TVs, but since that's not why you came to Paris, you'll be more interested in the hotel's authentic local neighbourhood location by Parc Georges Brassens, moments from the T3 tram, and buses that can zip you to St-Germain, the Louvre and Montmartre.

HÔTEL CARLADEZ CAMBRONNE HOTEL €

Map p430 (01 47 34 07 12; www.hotelcarladez.com; 3 place du Général Beuret, 15e; d €97-155, f €170-235; ; MVaugirard) On a quintessentially Parisian cafe-clad square, this freshly renovated hotel has comfortable rooms. Higher-priced superior rooms come with bath tubs, more space and tend to be quieter. Communal coffee- and tea-making facilities let you make yourself at home. Very good value.

OOPS HOSTEL €

Map p426 (01 47 07 47 00; www.oops-paris.com; 50 av des Gobelins, 13e; dm/d incl breakfast €42/115; @; MGobelins) A candy-floss-pink elevator scales the six colourful floors of Paris' first 'design hostel'. Good-size four- to six-bed dorms and doubles (from €27 and €70, respectively, outside high season) are all en suite and accessible all day. Some have Eiffel Tower views. There's no kitchen. No credit cards, no alcohol allowed.

HÔTEL DE LA LOIRE HOTEL €

Map p428 (01 45 40 66 88; www.hoteldelaloire-paris.com; 39bis rue du Moulin Vert, 14e; s €75, d €80-85, tr/apt €100/140; P; MAlésia) Obviously at this price don't expect luxury but do expect a warm welcome and clean, colourful en suite rooms at this budget hotel of old. The lovely villagey location near Denfert-Rochereau makes it easy to reach both major airports and Gare du Nord and there's a pretty table-set garden. The kitchen-equipped apartment sleeps four.

ALOHA HOSTEL HOSTEL €

Map p430 (01 42 73 03 03; www.aloha.fr; 1 rue Borromée, 15e; per person incl breakfast dm €30-32, d €35; @; MVolontaires) Avocado-coloured walls are among the rainbow of colours brightening this laid-back crash pad, with a hybrid reception-lounge and stone-walled self-catering kitchen. Cheaper dorms sleep six to 10, higher-priced dorms just four. Bonus: there's no longer a daytime lockout or a curfew. You'll need a credit card to reserve but must pay cash on arrival.

CELTIC HÔTEL HOTEL €

Map p428 (01 43 20 93 53; hotelceltic@wanadoo.fr; 15 rue d'Odessa, 14e; s €75-96, d €96-110, tr €130; ; MEdgar Quinet) A cheapie of the old school, this 29-room hotel has a small but handy lift/elevator. The cheaper singles are pretty bare and even the en suite doubles and triples are not exactly *tout confort* (with all the mod cons), but Gare Montparnasse is only 200m away.

★**SUBLIM EIFFEL** DESIGN HOTEL €€

(01 40 65 95 95; www.sublimeiffel.com; 94 bd Garibaldi, 15e; d from €140; ; MSèvres-Lecourbe) There's no forgetting what city you're in with the Eiffel Tower motifs in reception and rooms (along with Parisian street-map carpets and metro-tunnel-shaped bedheads) plus glittering tower views from upper-floor windows. Edgy design elements also include cobblestone staircase carpeting (there's also an elevator) and, fittingly in *la ville lumière,* technicoloured

in-room fibre-optic lighting. The small wellness centre/*hammam* offers massages.

★HÔTEL SAINT CHARLES HOTEL €€

Map p426 (☎01 45 89 56 54; www.hotel-saint-charles.com; 6 rue de l'Espérance, 13e; d/tr/q €170/210/280; ❄📶; Ⓜ Corvisart) Live like a local at this Butte aux Cailles hotel, located on a quiet, villagelike street yet close to the area's lively bars and restaurants. Some of its 57 streamlined, contemporary rooms with aubergine tones have balconies; communal outdoor areas include a timber-decked terrace and fern- and conifer-filled garden.

HÔTEL DE LA PAIX DESIGN HOTEL €€

Map p428 (☎01 43 20 35 82; www.hoteldelapaix.com; 225 bd Raspail, 14e; d €110-240; ❄@📶; Ⓜ Montparnasse Bienvenüe) Stacked on seven floors of a 1970s building, this chic hotel's 39 light-filled modern rooms have at least one vintage feature – old pegs to hang coats on, an old-fashioned school desk, or wooden-slat house shutters recycled as a bed head. Cheaper rooms are simply smaller than dearer ones.

HÔTEL DELAMBRE HOTEL €€

Map p428 (☎01 43 20 66 31; www.delambre-paris-hotel.com; 35 rue Delambre, 14e; d €145-165; ❄@📶; Ⓜ Montparnasse Bienvenüe) Wrought iron is used functionally (bed frames, lamps, shelving) and decoratively throughout this 30-room hotel, where writer André Breton (1896–1966) lived in the 1920s. Room 7 has its own little terrace while rooms 1 and 2 look onto a small private courtyard. Prices start from €90 outside high season.

HÔTEL LA DEMEURE BOUTIQUE HOTEL €€

Map p426 (☎01 43 37 81 25; www.hotel-paris-lademeure.com; 51 bd St-Marcel, 13e; d €180-250; ❄@📶; Ⓜ Gobelins) Jet showers, wine glasses for guests who like to BYO, and art on the walls that can be bought are just some of the touches that make this small family-run hotel a pleasure.

HÔTEL LA MANUFACTURE BOUTIQUE HOTEL €€

Map p426 (☎01 45 35 45 25; www.hotel-la-manufacture.com; 8 rue Philippe de Champagne, 13e; d €200-260, f €265; ❄@📶; Ⓜ Place d'Italie) On the fringe of the Latin Quarter, minimalist La Manufacture has 57 individually decorated rooms. Those on the top (7th) floor are the most spacious and coveted; room 71 has a view of the Panthéon while room 74 glimpses the Eiffel Tower. A handful of rooms have balconies.

Understand Paris

Paris Today

While the elegance, depth and extraordinary spirit of the Paris of Haussmann, Hugo and Toulouse-Lautrec will never disappear, Europe's mythical 'City of Light' is on the brink of redefinition, with a long-awaited expansion into the suburbs beginning to take shape. Parisians themselves, moreover, are in the mood for change: the 2014 municipal elections ushered in the city's first-ever female mayor.

Best on Film

Les 400 Coups (400 Blows; 1959) Moving portrayal of the magic and disillusionment of childhood.
La Haine (Hate; 1995) Mathieu Kassovitz's prescient take on social tensions in modern Paris.
Le Fabuleux Destin d'Amélie Poulain (Amélie; 2001) Endearing story of a winsome young Parisian.
La Môme (La Vie en Rose; 2007) Édith Piaf, from street urchin to international superstar.
Hugo (2011) A tribute to cinema and the legendary Georges Méliès.

Best in Print

Notre Dame de Paris (Victor Hugo; 1831) The classic tale of the hunchback of Notre Dame.
A Moveable Feast (Ernest Hemingway; 1964) Memoirs of the aspiring writer's life in Paris.
Paris to the Moon (Adam Gopnick; 2000) Illuminating essays from the *New Yorker* correspondent.
The Elegance of the Hedgehog (Muriel Barbery; 2008) French bestseller that unveils the world behind a Parisian façade.
Parisians: An Adventure History of Paris (Robb Graham; 2010) Both history tome and unexpected page turner, filled with little-known gems.

Madame la Maire

Paris has a history of political subversiveness, and while it's no longer the radical hotbed it once was, it continues to reveal an independent streak that runs counter to nationwide sentiment. This was most recently on display during the April 2014 municipal elections. While the vast majority of the country swung decisively to the right – political payback for President François Hollande's seemingly ineffectual policies – the capital remained resolutely left. But the big story was not that Parisians stuck with the eco-leaning Socialists for a third straight term, but rather that the election's two leading candidates were women: the Spanish-born deputy mayor Anne Hidalgo, and the former minister of ecology, Nathalie Kosciusko-Morizet. Hidalgo won with a substantial 55% of the vote, becoming the first-ever female mayor of Paris.

Greater Paris

Most visitors to Paris – and, in fact, many French – continue to think of the city as a self-contained whole, with limits that are both physically and conceptually defined by the traffic-snarled boulevard Périphérique – the ring road that stands on the site of the former city walls. This vision, however, is a far cry from reality: the vast majority of Parisians (8.2 million) now live in the adjacent suburbs, compared with only 2.2 million residents who live in the city proper. The steadily growing suburban population – indeed, the real-estate boom of the past decade has pushed most middle-class residents and large companies outside the Périphérique – has created a real need to redefine Paris, on both an administrative and infrastructural scale.

Enter the Grand Paris (Greater Paris) redevelopment project, a Sarkozy-era initiative. The crux of Grand Paris is a massive decentralised metro expansion, with

72 new stations and six suburban lines, with a target completion date of 2025. The principal goal is to connect the suburbs with one another, instead of relying on a central inner-city hub from which all lines radiate outwards (the current model).

In terms of administration, it is expected that the surrounding suburbs – Vincennes, Neuilly, Issy, St-Denis etc – will eventually lose their autonomy and become part of a much larger Grand Paris, all governed by the Hôtel de Ville (City Hall). It is no done deal, however, as uniting the wildly diverse municipalities will be no easy feat.

Green Transportation

Fundamentally interconnected with Grand Paris is the issue of transportation. Former mayor Bertrand Delanoë introduced several controversial but ultimately popular green initiatives during his tenure to help improve – or hinder, for those driving cars – transportation in Paris. These included the now famous Vélib' bike-share program, the Autolib' electric-car-share program, and the creation of hundreds of kilometres of new bus and bike lanes. Delanoë's outgoing project was to close the riverside roads along the Left Bank and reinvent a new pedestrian-friendly public area, known as the Berges de Seine. Other recent developments include several new tram lines that serve the city outskirts, with more on the way.

Renovation & Reclamation

Urban renovation in France never comes easy, as restrictive building codes and a conservative-minded public often join forces to delay the creation of pretty much anything that threatens the country's treasured architectural harmony. Give credit to Paris, then, that it has not been content to rest on its laurels. From community actions, like turning an art nouveau covered market to a sports centre in the Haut-Marais, to gargantuan projects affecting thousands of commuters every day, such as the complete overhaul of the Forum des Halles, urban planners have been busy. The French capital is an architectural reference accustomed to looking good, and faded grandeur or a glamorous history is simply not sufficient.

Other big projects include reclaiming old industrial zones and turning them into green space. The abandoned Petite Ceniture railway line – which over the years has become a wildlife corridor – was recently opened to the public in three separate areas, the longest being a 1.3km stretch in the 15e. Another inventive reclamation project is Île Seguin, in Boulogne-Billancourt on Paris' western fringe, which may see Jean Nouvel morph an abandoned Renault car factory on an island into a visionary eco-city with a cultural centre, artists residences, waterside gardens, walkways, tree-lined esplanades, restaurants and play spaces.

if Paris were 100 people

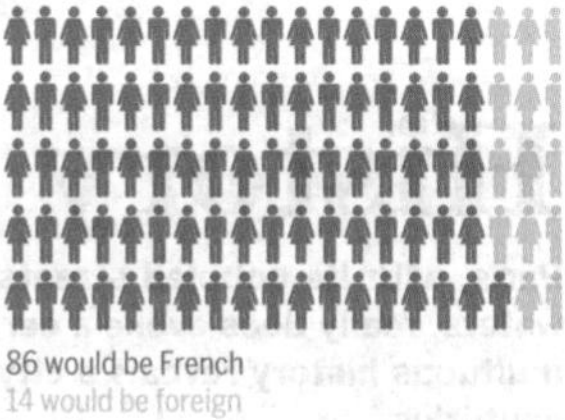

living in Paris

(% of population by area)

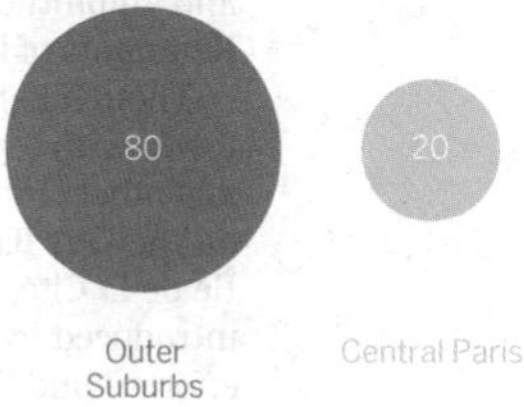

population per sq km

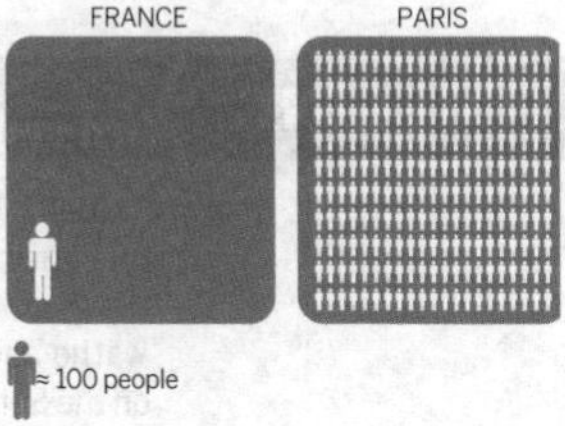

History

Paris, with its cobbled streets, terraced cafes, iconic landmarks and placid Seine waters, really does evoke a certain timelessness. Yet a quick perusal through its tumultuous history reveals a city that has changed and evolved dramatically over the centuries.

In the early Middle Ages, most of today's Paris was either a carpet of fields and vineyards or a boggy, waterlogged marsh.

Early Settlers: the Celts & Romans

The early history of Paris is murky, but the general consensus is that a Celtic tribe known as the Parisii established a fishing village in the area in the 3rd century BC. Years of conflict between the Gauls and Romans ended in 52 BC, when the latter took control of the territory after a decisive victory during Julius Caesar's eight-year Gallic Wars campaign. The Romans promptly established a new town – Lutetia (Lutèce in French) – with the main public buildings (forum, bathhouse, theatre and amphitheatre) all located on the Left Bank, near today's Panthéon. Remnants of both the bathhouse and amphitheatre are still visible.

Though Lutetia was not the capital of its province, it was a prosperous town, with a population of around 8000. However, raids by the Franks and other Germanic tribes during the 3rd century AD left the settlement on the Left Bank scorched and pillaged, and its inhabitants fled to the Île de la Cité, subsequently fortified with stone walls. Christianity was introduced by St-Denis – decapitated on Montmartre in AD 250 for his efforts – and the first church was built on the western part of the island.

The Roman town held out until the late 5th century – mythically saved from Attila the Hun by the piety of Ste-Geneviève, who became the city's patron saint – only to fall when a second wave of Franks overran the area for good.

The Middle Ages: Paris as Capital

One of the key figures in early Parisian history was the Frankish king Clovis I (c 466–511). Clovis was the first ruler to unite what would later become France, to convert to Christianity and to declare Paris

TIMELINE

3rd century BC

Celtic Gauls called Parisii arrive in the Paris area and set up wattle-and-daub huts on the Seine, possibly in the Nanterre area.

52 BC

Roman legions under Titus Labienus crush a Celtic revolt on Mons Lutetius (site of today's Panthéon) and establish the town of Lutetia (Lutèce in French).

AD 250

St-Denis, who brought Christianity to Lutetia, is executed on Montmartre. According to legend, he then carries his head 10km north, to the site of the future royal necropolis of St-Denis.

the capital. Under the Frankish kings the city once again began to expand, and important edifices such as the abbey of St-Germain des Prés and the abbey at St-Denis were erected.

However, the militaristic rulers of the succeeding Carolingian dynasty, beginning with Charles 'the Hammer' Martel (688–741), were almost permanently away fighting wars in the east, and Paris languished, controlled mostly by its counts. When Charles Martel's grandson, Charlemagne (768–814), moved his capital to Aix-la-Chapelle (today's Aachen in Germany), Paris' fate was sealed. Basically a group of separate villages with its centre on the Ile de la Cité, Paris was badly defended throughout the second half of the 9th century and was raided incessantly by Vikings, who eventually established control over northern and northwestern France.

Gallo-Roman Paris (Lutetia) features in several classic Asterix adventures, including *Asterix and the Golden Sickle*.

The Paris counts, whose powers had grown as the Carolingians feuded among themselves, elected one of their own, Hugh Capet, as king at Senlis in 987. He made Paris the royal seat and lived in the renovated palace of the Roman governor on the Île de la Cité (site of the present Palais de Justice). Under the 800 years of Capetian rule that followed, Paris prospered as a centre of politics, commerce, trade, religion and culture.

The city's strategic riverside position ensured its importance throughout the Middle Ages. The first guilds were created in the 11th century, and in the mid-12th century the ship merchants' guild bought the principal river port, by today's Hôtel de Ville (City Hall), from the crown. Frenetic building marked the 12th and 13th centuries. The Basilique de St-Denis was commissioned in 1136 and less than three decades later, work started on Notre Dame. During the reign of Philippe-Auguste (r 1180–1223), the city wall was expanded and fortified with 25 gates and hundreds of protective towers.

In 1292 the medieval city of Paris counted 352 streets, 10 squares and 11 crossroads.

The swampy Marais was drained for agricultural use and settlement, prompting the eventual need for the food markets at Les Halles in 1183 and the Louvre as a riverside fortress in the 13th century. In a bid to resolve ghastly traffic congestion and stinking excrement (by 1200 the city had a population of 200,000), Philippe-Auguste paved four of Paris' main streets with metre-square sandstone blocks. Meanwhile, the Left Bank – particularly in the Latin Quarter – developed as a centre of European learning and erudition. Ill-fated lovers Pierre Abélard and Héloïse penned the finest poetry of the age and treatises on philosophy, Thomas Aquinas taught at the new university, and the Sorbonne opened its scholarly doors.

451

Attila the Hun unexpectedly turns away from Paris to march south; credit is given to the prayers of Geneviève, who later becomes the city's patron saint.

509

Clovis I becomes the first king of the Franks and the first Frankish ruler to convert to Christianity. He declares Paris the seat of his new kingdom.

845–86

Paris is repeatedly raided by Vikings for over four decades, including the siege of 885–86 by Siegfried the Saxon, which lasts 10 months but ends in victory for the French.

987

Five centuries of Merovingian and Carolingian rule ends with the crowning of Hugh Capet; a dynasty that will rule one of Europe's most powerful countries for the next eight centuries.

STAR-CROSSED LOVERS

He was a brilliant 39-year-old philosopher and logician with a reputation for controversial ideas. She was the beautiful niece of a canon at Notre Dame. And like Bogart and Bergman in *Casablanca* and Romeo and Juliet in Verona, they had to fall in love – in medieval Paris of all damned times and places.

In 1118 the wandering scholar Pierre Abélard (1079–1142) found his way to Paris, having clashed with yet another theologian in the provinces. There he was employed by Canon Fulbert of Notre Dame to tutor his niece Héloïse (1101–64). One thing led to another and a son, Astrolabe, was born. Abélard married his sweetheart in secret and when Fulbert found out, he was outraged. He had Abélard castrated and sent Héloïse off to a convent where she eventually became abbess. Abélard took monastic vows at the abbey in St-Denis and continued his studies and controversial writings.

Yet, all the while, the star-crossed lovers corresponded: he sending tender advice on how to run the convent and she writing passionate, poetic letters to her lost lover. The two were reunited only in death; in 1817 their remains were disinterred and brought to Père Lachaise cemetery in the 20e, where they lie together beneath a neo-Gothic tombstone in division 7.

Black Times: War & Death

The Hundred Years' War (1337–1453); the Black Death (1348–49), which killed over a third of Paris' population; and the development of free, independent cities elsewhere in Europe, brought political tension and open insurrection to Paris. In 1420 the dukes of Burgundy, allied with the English, occupied the capital and two years later John Plantagenet, duke of Bedford, was installed as regent of France for the English king, Henry VI, then an infant. Henry was crowned king of France at Notre Dame less than 10 years later, but Paris was almost continuously under siege from the French.

During Louis XIII's reign (1610–43) two uninhabited islets in the Seine – Île Notre Dame and Île aux Vaches – were joined to form the Île de St-Louis.

Around that time a 17-year-old peasant girl known to history as Jeanne d'Arc (Joan of Arc) persuaded the French pretender to the throne that she'd received a divine mission from God to expel the English from France and bring about his coronation as Charles VII. She rallied French troops and defeated the English north of Orléans, and Charles was crowned at Reims. But Joan of Arc failed to take Paris. In 1430 she was captured, convicted of witchcraft and heresy by a tribunal of French ecclesiastics and burned at the stake. Charles VII returned to Paris in 1436, ending over 16 years of occupation, but the English were not entirely driven from French territory for another 17 years.

1066

The so-called Norman Conquest of England ignites almost 300 years of conflict between the Normans in western and northern France and the Capetians in Paris.

1163

Two centuries of nonstop building reaches its zenith with the start of Notre Dame Cathedral under Maurice de Sully, the bishop of Paris, continuing for over a century and a half.

1358

The Hundred Years' War (1337–1453) between France and England and the devastation and poverty caused by the plague lead to the ill-fated peasants' revolt led by Étienne Marcel.

1572

Some 3000 Huguenots who are in Paris to celebrate the wedding of the Protestant Henri of Navarre (the future Henri IV) are slaughtered on 23–24 August.

The Rise of the Royal Court

Under Louis XI (r 1461–83) the city's first printing press was installed at the Sorbonne and churches were built around the city in the Flamboyant Gothic style. But it was during the reign of François I in the early 16th century that Renaissance ideas of scientific and geographic scholarship and discovery really assumed a new importance, as did the value of secular matters over religious life. Writers such as Rabelais, Marot and Ronsard of La Pléiade were influential, as were artist and architect disciples of Michelangelo and Raphael who worked towards a new architectural style designed to reflect the splendour of the monarchy (which was fast moving towards absolutism) and of Paris as the capital of a powerful centralised state. At François I's chateau, superb artisans, many brought over from Italy, blended Italian and French styles to create what is known as the First School of Fontainebleau.

But all this grandeur and show of strength was not enough to stem the tide of Protestant Reformation sweeping Europe in the 1530s, strengthened in France by the ideas of John Calvin. Following the Edict of January 1562, which afforded the Protestants certain rights, the Wars of Religion, which lasted three dozen years, broke out between the Huguenots (French Protestants who received help from the English), the Catholic League (led by the House of Guise) and the Catholic monarchy. On 7 May 1588, on the 'Day of the Barricades', Henri III, who had granted many concessions to the Huguenots, was forced to flee from the Louvre when the Catholic League rose against him. He was assassinated the following year.

Henri IV, founder of the Bourbon dynasty, issued the controversial Edict of Nantes in 1598, guaranteeing the Huguenots many civil and political rights, notably freedom of conscience. Ultra-Catholic Paris refused to allow the new Protestant king to enter the city, and a siege of the capital continued for almost five years. Only when Henri IV embraced Catholicism at the cathedral in St-Denis – '*Paris vaut bien un messe*' (Paris is well worth a Mass), he is reputed to have said during Communion – did the capital submit to him. Henri's rule ended abruptly in 1610 when he was assassinated by a Catholic fanatic when his coach became stuck in traffic along rue de la Ferronnerie, south of Les Halles.

Arguably France's best-known king of this or any other century, Louis XIV (r 1643–1715), aka 'Le Roi Soleil' (the Sun King), ascended the throne at the tender age of five. He involved the kingdom in a series of costly, almost continuous wars with Holland, Austria and England, which gained France territory but nearly bankrupted the treasury. State taxation, imposed to refill the coffers, caused widespread poverty

The population of Paris at the start of François' reign in 1515 was 170,000 – still almost 20% less than it had been some three centuries before, when the Black Death had decimated the city population.

Historical Reads

Seven Ages of Paris (Alistair Horne, 2002)

Parisians: An Adventure History of Paris (Graham Robb, 2010)

The Greater Journey: Americans in Paris (David McCullough, 2011)

Suite Française (Irène Némirovsky, 2006)

The Paris Wife (Paula McLain, 2011)

1589

Henry IV, the first Bourbon king, ascends the throne after renouncing Protestantism.

1643

'Sun King' Louis XIV ascends the throne aged five but only assumes absolute power in 1661.

14 July 1789

The French Revolution begins when a mob arms itself with weapons taken from the Hôtel des Invalides and storms the prison at Bastille, freeing a total of just seven prisoners.

1793

Louis XVI is tried and convicted as citizen 'Louis Capet' (all kings since Hugh Capet were declared to have ruled illegally) and executed; Marie-Antoinette's turn comes nine months later.

and vagrancy, especially in cities. In Versailles, Louis XIV built an extravagant palace and made his courtiers compete with each other for royal favour, thereby quashing the ambitious, feuding aristocracy and creating the first centralised French state. In 1685 he revoked the Edict of Nantes.

Paintings by Jules Hardouin-Mansart in the Royal Chapel at Versailles evoke the idea that the French king was chosen by God and is thus his lieutenant on earth – a divinity the 'Sun King' believed in devoutly.

From Revolution to Republic

During the so-called Age of Enlightenment, the royal court moved back to Paris from Versailles and the city effectively became the centre of Europe. Yet as the 18th century progressed, new economic and social circumstances rendered the *ancien régime* dangerously out of step with the needs of the country.

By the late 1780s, the indecisive Louis XVI and his dominating Vienna-born queen, Marie-Antoinette, had alienated virtually every segment of society. When they tried to neutralise the power of more reform-minded delegates at a meeting of the États-Généraux (States-General) in Versailles from May to June 1789, the masses – spurred by the oratory and inflammatory tracts circulating at places like the Café de Foy at Palais Royal – took to the streets of Paris. On 14 July a mob raided the armoury at the Hôtel des Invalides for rifles, seized 32,000 muskets, and stormed the prison at Bastille. Enter the French Revolution.

At first, the Revolution was in the hands of moderate republicans, the Girondins. France was declared a constitutional monarchy and reforms were introduced, including the adoption of the Déclaration des Droits de l'Homme et du Citoyen (Declaration of the Rights of Man and of the Citizen). But as the masses armed themselves against the external threat to the new government – posed by Austria, Prussia and the exiled French nobles – patriotism and nationalism mixed with extreme fervour and then popularised and radicalised the Revolution. It was not long before the Girondins lost out to the extremist Jacobins, who abolished the monarchy and declared the First Republic. The Assemblée Nationale was replaced by an elected Revolutionary Convention.

Louis XVI was convicted of 'conspiring against the liberty of the nation' in January 1793 and guillotined at place de la Révolution, today's place de la Concorde. Two months later the Jacobins set up the notorious Committee of Public Safety to deal with national defence and try 'traitors'. The subsequent Reign of Terror (September 1793 to July 1794) saw religious freedoms revoked, churches closed and desecrated, cathedrals turned into 'Temples of Reason' and thousands incarcerated in dungeons in La Conciergerie before being beheaded.

After the Reign of Terror faded, a five-man delegation of moderate republicans set itself up to rule the republic as the Directory.

History Museums

Musée Carnavale (Le Marais & Ménilmontant)

Musée National du Moyen Âge (Latin Quarter)

Mémorial de la Shoah (Le Marais & Ménilmontant)

1799

Napoléon Bonaparte overthrows the Directory and seizes control of the government in a coup d'état, opening the doors to 16 years of despotic rule, victory and then defeat.

1815

British and Prussian forces under the Duke of Wellington defeat Napoléon at Waterloo; he is sent into exile for the second time, this time to a remote island in the South Atlantic.

1830

During the July Revolution, revolutionaries seize Hôtel de Ville and overthrow Charles X (r 1824–30). Place de la Bastille's Colonne de Juillet honours those killed.

1848

After more than three decades of monarchy, King Louis-Philippe is ousted and the short-lived Second Republic is established with Napoléon's incompetent nephew at the helm.

Napoléon & Empire

The post-Revolutionary government was far from stable and when Napoléon returned to Paris in 1799, he found a chaotic republic in which few citizens had any faith. In November, when it appeared that the Jacobins were again on the ascendancy in the legislature, Napoléon tricked the delegates into leaving Paris for St-Cloud to the southwest ('for their own protection'), overthrew the discredited Directory and assumed power.

At first, Napoléon took the post of First Consul. In a referendum three years later he was named 'Consul for Life' and his birthday became a national holiday. By December 1804, when he crowned himself 'Emperor of the French' in the presence of Pope Pius VII at Notre Dame, the scope and nature of Napoléon's ambitions were obvious to all. But to consolidate and legitimise his authority, Napoléon needed more victories on the battlefield. So began a seemingly endless series of wars and victories by which France would come to control most of Europe.

In 1812 Napoléon invaded Russia and captured Moscow, only for his army to be quickly wiped out by the brutal Russian winter. Two years later, Allied armies entered Paris, exiled Napoléon to Elba and restored the House of Bourbon to the French throne at the Congress of Vienna (1814–15).

But in early 1815 Napoléon escaped the Mediterranean island, landed in southern France and gathered a large army as he marched towards Paris. On 1 June he reclaimed the throne at celebrations held at the Champs de Mars. But his reign came to an end just three weeks later when his forces were defeated at Waterloo in Belgium. Napoléon was exiled again, this time to St Helena in the South Atlantic, where he died in 1821. In 1840 his remains were moved to Paris' Église du Dôme.

The Second Republic was established and elections in 1848 brought in Napoléon's inept nephew, the German-reared (and -accented) Louis Napoléon Bonaparte, as president. In 1851 he staged a coup d'état and proclaimed himself Emperor Napoléon III of the Second Empire, which lasted until 1870.

France enjoyed significant economic growth at this time, and Paris was transformed by town planner Baron Haussmann (1809–91) into the modern city it is today. Huge swaths of the city were completely rebuilt (demolishing much of medieval Paris in the process), its chaotic narrow streets replaced with the handsome, arrow-straight and wide thoroughfares for which the city is now celebrated.

In 1774 a 100ft section of the rue d'Enfer (today's ave Denfert-Rochereau) disappeared into a sinkhole, revealing an inconceivably precarious network of mining tunnels upon which southern Paris had been built.

From 1784 to 1836, the duke of Chartres turned the now dignified Palais Royal into one of Europe's foremost pleasure gardens – 'the capital of Paris' – home to theatres, casinos, shops, cafes and an estimated 2000 prostitutes.

1852–70

Paris enjoys significant economic growth during the Second Empire of Napoléon III and much of the city is redesigned or rebuilt by Baron Haussmann as the Paris we know today.

1871

Harsh terms inflicted on France by victor Prussia in the Franco-Prussian War leads to open revolt and anarchy during the Paris Commune.

1880s

The Third Republic ushers in the bloody-then-beautiful belle époque, a madly creative era that conceives bohemian Paris, with its decadent nightclubs and artistic cafes.

1889

The Eiffel Tower is completed in time for the opening of the Exposition Universelle (World Exhibition) but is vilified in the press and on the street as the 'metal asparagus' – or worse.

The Belle Époque

Though it would usher in the glittering belle époque (beautiful age), there was nothing particularly attractive about the start of the Third Republic. Born as a provisional government of national defence in September 1870, it was quickly besieged by the Prussians, who laid siege to Paris and demanded National Assembly elections be held. Unfortunately, the first move made by the resultant monarchist-controlled assembly was to ratify the Treaty of Frankfurt, the harsh terms of which – a huge war indemnity and surrender of the provinces of Alsace and Lorraine – helped instigate a civil war between radical Parisians (known as Communards) and the national government. The Communards took control of the city, establishing the Paris Commune, but the French Army eventually regained the capital several months later. It was a chaotic period, with mass executions on both sides, exiles and rampant destruction (both the Palais des Tuileries and the Hôtel de Ville were burned down). The Wall of the Federalists in Cimetière du Père Lachaise is a deathly reminder of the bloodshed.

Haussmann revolutionised Paris' water supply and sewage systems, and created some of the city's loveliest parks. The city's first department stores were built, as were Paris' delightful shop-strewn *passages couverts* (covered passages).

The belle époque launched art nouveau architecture, a whole field of artistic 'isms' from impressionism onwards, and advances in science and engineering, including the construction of the first metro line (1900). World Exhibitions were held in the capital in 1889 (showcasing the Eiffel Tower) and 1901 (in the purpose-built Petit Palais). The Paris of nightclubs and artistic cafes made its first appearance around this time, and Montmartre became a magnet for artists, writers, pimps and prostitutes.

But all was not well in the republic. France was consumed with a desire for revenge after its defeat by Germany, and was looking for scapegoats. The so-called Dreyfus Affair began in 1894 when a Jewish army captain named Alfred Dreyfus was accused of betraying military secrets to Germany; he was then court-martialled and sentenced to life imprisonment on Devil's Island. Liberal politicians and writers succeeded in having the case reopened despite bitter opposition from the army command, right-wing politicians and many Catholic groups – and Dreyfus was vindicated in 1900. This resulted in more rigorous civilian control of the military and, in 1905, the legal separation of the church and the state. When he died in 1935 Dreyfus was laid to rest in the Cimetière de Montparnasse.

Essential Historical Encounters

- *Arènes de Lutèce (Latin Quarter)*
- *Musée National du Moyen Âge (Latin Quarter)*
- *Hôtel des Invalides (St-Germain & Les Invalides)*
- *Les Catacombes (Montparnasse & Southern Paris)*

WWII & Occupation

Two days after the German invasion of Poland on 1 September 1939, Britain and France declared war on Germany. For the first nine months Parisians joked about *le drôle de guerre* – what Britons called 'the pho-

1914

Germany and Austria-Hungary declare war on Russia and France. German troops reach the River Marne 15km east of Paris and the government moves to Bordeaux.

1920s

Paris sparkles as centre of the avant-garde with its new-found liberalism, cutting-edge nightlife and painters pushing into new fields of art like cubism and surrealism.

1940

After over 10 months of *le drôle de guerre* (phoney war), Germany launches the battle for France, and the four-year occupation of Paris under direct German rule begins.

25 August 1944

Spearheaded by Free French units, Allied forces liberate Paris and the city escapes destruction, despite Hitler's orders that it be torched; the war in Europe will end nine months later.

ney war' – in which nothing happened. But the battle for France began in earnest in May 1940 and by 14 June France had capitulated. Paris was occupied, and almost half the population fled the city by car, bicycle or on foot. The British expeditionary force sent to help the French barely managed to avoid capture by retreating to Dunkirk, described so vividly in Ian McEwan's *Atonement* (2001), and crossing the English Channel in small boats. The Maginot Line, a supposedly impregnable wall of fortifications along the Franco-German border, had proved useless – the German armoured divisions simply outflanked it by going through Belgium.

The Germans divided France into two: a zone under direct German rule (along the western coast and the north, including Paris); and a puppet state based in the spa town of Vichy and led by General Philippe Pétain, the ageing WWI hero of the Battle of Verdun. Pétain's collaborationist government and French police forces in German-occupied areas (including Paris) helped the Nazis round up 160,000 French Jews and others for deportation to concentration and extermination camps in Germany and Poland.

After the fall of Paris, General Charles de Gaulle, France's undersecretary of war, fled to London. He set up a French government-in-exile and established the Forces Françaises Libres (Free French Forces), a military force dedicated to fighting the Germans alongside the Allies.

The liberation of France started with the Allied landings in Normandy on D-Day (Jour-J in French): 6 June 1944. On 15 August that same year, Allied forces also landed in southern France. After a brief insurrection by the Resistance and general strikes by the metro and police, Paris was liberated on 25 August by an Allied force spearheaded by Free French units – these units were sent in ahead of the Americans so that the French would have the honour of liberating the capital the following day. Hitler, who visited Paris in June 1940 and loved it, demanded that the city be burned towards the end of the war. It was an order that, thankfully, was not obeyed.

Most historians agree that the overall military effectiveness of the Resistance was limited. But it served as an enormous boost to French morale and has impacted French literature and cinema right up till today.

Postwar Instability

De Gaulle returned to Paris and established a provisional government. But in January 1946 he resigned as president, wrongly believing the move would provoke a popular outcry for his return. A few months later, a new constitution was approved by referendum. De Gaulle formed his own party (Rassemblement du Peuple Français) and spent the next 13 years in opposition.

The Fourth Republic saw a series of unstable coalition cabinets following one after another with bewildering speed (on average, one every

The Extraordinary Adventures of Adèle Blanc-Sec features the swashbuckling adventures of Adèle in early-20th-century Paris. Originally a graphic novel series created by Tardi, it was released as a film in 2010.

1949

Simone de Beauvoir publishes her groundbreaking and very influential study *Le Deuxième Sexe* (The Second Sex) just four years after French women win the right to vote.

1958

De Gaulle returns to power after more than a dozen years in opposition, to form the Fifth Republic.

1962

War in Algeria is brought to an end after claiming the lives of more than 12,000 people; three-quarters of a million Algerian-born French citizens arrive in France.

1968

Paris is rocked by student-led riots that bring the nation and the city to the brink of civil war; as a result de Gaulle is forced to resign the following year.

six months), and economic recovery, helped immeasurably by massive American aid. France's disastrous defeat in Vietnam in 1954 ended its colonial supremacy in Southeast Asia. France also tried to suppress an uprising by Arab nationalists in Algeria, where more than a million French settlers lived.

The Fourth Republic came to an end in 1958, when extreme right-wingers, furious at what they saw as defeatism as opposed to tough action in dealing with the uprising in Algeria, began conspiring in an effort to overthrow the government. De Gaulle was brought back to power to prevent a military coup and possible civil war. He drafted a new constitution that handed considerable powers to the president, at the expense of the National Assembly.

On 15 October 1959, then senator and future president François Mitterrand was involved in a staged assassination attempt on his own life, now known as the infamous Observatory Affair.

Charles de Gaulle & the Fifth Republic

The Fifth Republic was rocked in 1961 by an attempted coup staged in Algiers by a group of right-wing military officers. When it failed, the Organisation de l'Armée Secrète (OAS) – a group of French *colons* (colonists) and sympathisers opposed to Algerian independence – turned to terrorism, trying several times to assassinate de Gaulle and nearly succeeding in August 1962 in the town of Clamart just southwest of Paris.

In 1962, after more than 12,000 had died as a result of this 'civil war', de Gaulle negotiated an end to the war in Algeria. Some 750,000 *pied-noir* (black feet), as Algerian-born French people are known in France, came to France and the capital. Meanwhile, almost all of the other French colonies and protectorates in Africa had demanded and achieved independence. Shrewdly, the French government began a program of economic and military aid to its former colonies to bolster France's waning importance internationally and to create a bloc of French-speaking nations – *la francophonie* – in the developing world.

Paris retained its position as a creative and intellectual centre, particularly in philosophy and film-making, and the 1960s saw large parts of the Marais beautifully restored.

In 1923 French women obtained the right to – wait for it – open their own mail. The right to vote didn't come until 1945, and a woman still needed her husband's permission to open a bank account or get a passport until 1964.

A Pivotal Year

The year 1968 was a watershed. In March a large demonstration in Paris against the war in Vietnam gave impetus to the student movement, and protests by students of the University of Paris peppered the capital for most of spring. In May police broke up yet another demonstration, prompting angry students to occupy the Sorbonne and erect barricades in the Latin Quarter. Workers joined in very quickly, with six million people across France participating in a general strike that virtually paralysed the country. It was a period of creativity and new ideas, with

1977

Jacques Chirac, the first Paris mayor to be elected with real power, assumes office.

1978

The Centre Pompidou, the first of a string of *grands projets*, huge public edifices through which French leaders seek to immortalise themselves, opens to great controversy.

1989

President Mitterrand's *grand projet*, Opéra de Paris Bastille, opens to mark the bicentennial of the French Revolution; IM Pei's Grande Pyramide is unveiled at the Louvre.

2001

Socialist Bertrand Delanoë becomes the first openly gay mayor of Paris (and of any European capital); he is wounded in a knife attack by a homophobic assailant the following year.

slogans like '*L'Imagination au Pouvoir*' (Put Imagination in Power) and '*Sous les Pavés, la Plage*' (Under the Cobblestones, the Beach) – a reference to Parisians' favoured material for building barricades and what they could expect to find beneath them – popping up everywhere.

But such an alliance between workers and students couldn't last long. While the former wanted to reap greater benefits from the consumer market, the latter supposedly wanted to destroy it. De Gaulle took advantage of this division and appealed to people's fear of anarchy. And just as Paris and the rest of France seemed on the verge of revolution, a mighty 100,000-strong crowd of Gaullists came out on the streets of Paris to show their support for the government, thus quashing any idea of revolution. Stability was restored.

The book and film *The Day of the Jackal* portrays a fictional account of the attempts by the OAS (a renegade paramilitary group who fought against Algerian independence) to take de Gaulle's life.

Modern Society

Once stability was restored the government immediately decentralised the higher education system and implemented a series of reforms (including lowering the voting age to 18, and enacting an abortion law) throughout the 1970s to create the modern society France is today.

President Charles de Gaulle resigned in 1969 and was succeeded by the Gaullist leader Georges Pompidou and later Valéry Giscard d'Estaing. Socialist François Mitterrand became president in 1981 and immediately nationalised privately owned banks, large industrial groups and other parts of the economy. A more moderate economic policy in the mid-1980s ensured a second term in office for the then 69-year-old Mitterrand.

Jacques Chirac, mayor of Paris since 1977, took over the presidential baton in 1995 and received high marks in his first few months for his direct words and actions in EU matters and the war in Bosnia. But his decision to resume nuclear testing on the French Polynesian island of Mururoa and a nearby atoll was met with outrage in France and abroad, and when, in 1997, Chirac gambled with an early parliamentary election for June, the move backfired. Chirac remained president but his party, the Rassemblement Pour la République (RPR; Rally for the Republic), lost support, and a coalition of socialists, communists and Greens came to power – under whom France's infamous 35-hour working week was introduced.

Paris is run from the Hôtel de Ville (City Hall) by the *maire* (mayor) with help from 21 *adjoints* (deputy mayors), elected by 163 members of the Conseil de Paris (Council of Paris) and serving terms of six years.

Chirac's second term, starting in 2002, was marred by some of the worst violence seen in Paris since WWII. In autumn 2005, following the death of two teenage boys of North African origin hiding in an electrical substation while on the run from the police, riots broke out in Paris' *cités,* the enormous housing estates encircling the capital where a dispossessed population lives. The violence quickly spread to other

2002

The French franc is thrown onto the scrap heap of history as the country adopts the euro as its official currency, along with 14 other EU member-states.

2004

France bans the wearing of crucifixes, the Islamic headscarf and other overtly religious symbols in state schools.

2005

The French electorate overwhelmingly rejects the EU Constitution; the suburbs surrounding Paris are wracked by rioting youths.

2010

Countrywide strikes and protests briefly paralyse the country after the government announces plans to raise the retirement age from 60 to 62 years.

cities in France and the government called a state of emergency. Only 9000 burnt cars and buildings later was peace in Paris was restored.

The Presidential Pendulum

Presidential elections in 2007 ushered old-school Jacques Chirac out and the dynamic, ambitious and media-savvy Nicolas Sarkozy in. The former interior minister and chairperson of centre-right party Union pour un Mouvement Populaire (UMP) wooed voters with promises of reducing unemployment, job creation, lower income tax, a crackdown on crime and help for France's substantial immigrant population – something that had particular pulling power coming from the son of a Hungarian immigrant father and Greek Jewish-French mother. And the French, fed up with an economically stagnant, socially discontented France, wanted change. A new breed of French president was born.

Contrary to the rigorous economic reform platform on which he'd been elected and against the backdrop of the global recession, Sarkozy struggled to keep the French economy buoyant. Attempts to introduce reforms – eg the scaleback of the extremely generous French pension system – provoked widespread horror and a series of national strikes and protests. Sarkozy's popularity plummeted, paving the way for socialist François Hollande's victory in the 2012 presidential elections.

With France still struggling to restart the economy, Hollande pledged to end austerity measures and reduce unemployment. Many economic policies have thus far proved ineffectual though, and rising anger at Hollande's failure to deliver on campaign promises saw his popularity plunge even faster and further than Sarkozy's – his 20% approval rating is the lowest of any French president in recent history – and resulted in a near total wipeout for French socialists in the 2014 municipal elections. The 2014 election of socialist Anne Hidalgo, Paris' first female mayor, meant the capital was one of the few cities to remain on the political left.

Bertrand Delanoë, a socialist backed by the Green Party, became the first openly gay mayor of Paris (and any European capital) in 2001. He was re-elected for a second term in 2008.

The French receive free education and health care, state-subsidised child care, travel concessions for families, ample leisure time and a 35-hour working week.

2011

Former president Jacques Chirac is found guilty of diverting public funds while serving as mayor of Paris; he gets a suspended prison sentence.

2012

France loses its top AAA credit rating. Economic policy becomes a campaign issue in the run-up to the 2012 presidential elections in late April.

2012

Socialist candidate François Hollande beats Nicolas Sarkozy to become France's new president but his popularity is short-lived.

2014

Spanish-born Anne Hidalgo becomes the first female mayor of Paris after defeating Sarkozy protégé Nathalie Kosciusko-Morizet.

Fashion

'Fashion is a way of life', Yves St Laurent once declared, and most Parisians would agree. To their reckoning, fashion is French and competition from Milan, Tokyo or New York just doesn't cut the mustard. But what few Parisians know is that Parisian *haute couture* (literally 'high sewing') as it exists today was created by an Englishman.

Revolution & Drama

Nicknamed 'the Napoléon of costumers', 20-year-old Englishman Charles Frederick Worth (1825–95) arrived in Paris and revolutionised fashion by banishing the crinoline (stiffened petticoat), lifting hemlines to ankle length and presenting his creations on live models. The House of Worth stayed in the family for four generations until the 1950s.

In the 1990s highly creative, rebel-yell British designers such as Alexander McQueen (1969–2010) and John Galliano (b 1960) dominated Paris' fashion scene. One of the industry's biggest influencers, Gibraltar-born and London-raised Galliano moved to Paris in 1991 and became chief designer at Givenchy in 1995. A year later he moved to Dior, the legendary French fashion house responsible for re-establishing Paris as world fashion capital after WWII. Galliano's first women's collection for Dior was spectacular – models waltzed down a catwalk framed by 500 gold chairs and 4000 roses arranged to re-create the postwar glamour of Christian Dior's 1946 showroom on av Montaigne, 8e, in Paris' legendary Triangle d'Or (Golden Triangle).

The downfall of fashion's talented enfant terrible was dramatic. In 2011 Galliano was caught on camera casting public insults to punters at his local neighbourhood cafe-bar La Perle in Le Marais. He was dismissed by the House of Dior and later found guilty in court of anti-Semitic abuse.

Paris coined the expression *lèche-vitrine* (literally 'window-licker') for window-shopping. 'Tasting' without buying is an art like any other so don't be shy. The fancy couture houses on av Montaigne may seem daunting but, in most, no appointment is necessary and you can simply walk in.

Contemporary Fashion

Outlandish designs by young rising stars such as Serkan Cura (swiftly making a name for himself with work-of-art dresses crafted from feathers and Swarovski crystals) or world-famous couturiers like 'wild child' Jean Paul Gaultier (known for putting men in punky skirts and Madonna in her signature conical bra) might strut down the Paris catwalk during fashion week. But you encounter few Cura- or Gaultier-clad women rubbing shoulders in the metro: Parisian style is generally too conservative for that.

THE SHOW OF SHOWS

The Paris fashion *haute couture* shows fall in late January for the spring/summer collections and early July for autumn/winter ones. But most established couturiers present a more affordable prêt-à-porter (ready-to-wear) line, and many have abandoned *haute couture* altogether. Prêt-à-porter shows are in late January and September. Shows are exclusive affairs, not open to the hoi polloi.

For alternative catwalk action, reserve a spot at the Friday-afternoon fashion show (excluding January, February and August) at department store Galeries Lafayette, 9e.

On the jewellery front, designs by Marion Vidal in the 9e are bold, funky and heavily architecture-influenced.

London-inspired street-wear jumps off the shelves in trendy shops around rue Étienne Marcel in the Louvre & Les Halles neighbourhood, and Le Marais. The Haut Marais, 3e, is known for its young designer boutiques. Names to excite, watch and wear include Moon Young Hee, Valentine Gauthier, Yukiko and Sakina M'sa. Anne Elisabeth, a well-travelled Parisian designer with boutiques in the 1er, 3e and 6e, is a long-standing favourite. Parisian handbag designers include Nat & Nin, Clarisse (Pauline Pin), Kasia Dietz and Jamin Puech.

BCBG & Intello

In upper-crust circles, the *bon chic bon genre* (BCBG) girl shops at department store Le Bon Marché or Chanel, and rarely ventures outside her preferred districts: the 7e, 8e and 16e. Fast-growing brands like Kooples, Maje, Sandro, Comptoir des Cotonniers, and Zadig & Voltaire are huge among BCBG. The chic Left Bank *intello* (intellectual) shops for trendy but highly wearable fashion at upmarket high-street boutiques like Agnès b (created in Paris in 1975 by Versailles designer Agnès Troublé – the 'b' gives a nod to her husband) and Atelier de Production et de Création (APC).

Bobo & Hipster

Bastille, Le Marais and the 10e around Canal St-Martin are stomping grounds of the *bobo* (bourgeois bohemian) – modern bohemians with wealthy bourgeois parents whose style roots itself in nostalgia for that last voyage to India, Tibet or Senegal and that avowed commitment to free trade and beads. The wildest *bobos* wear Kate Mack and dress their kids in romantic rockesque designs by Liza Korn, at home in 10e.

Younger professional *bobos* frequent iconic concept store Colette or smaller concept stores with carefully curated collections like L'Éclaireur and the Broken Arm in Le Marais. Isabel Marant – with boutiques in Le Marais, Bastille and St-Germain des Prés – enjoys cult worship among Parisian *bobos* thanks to her chic but easy style that teams wearable-year-round floral dresses or denim miniskirts with loose knits and lush scarves. Another favourite is Vanessa Bruno, a Parisian brand again known for its wearable, if slightly edgy, fashion: exposed midriffs, zebra stripes and a sportswear spirit enlivened her Spring 2014 collection.

Hipper than hip, Paris' Brooklyn-styled hipster is similar to a *bobo* but younger (typically aged 18 to 25 years) and usually without the money. Parisian hipsters only drink juice that is freshly squeezed and flout big-name or known fashion labels for a 'purist', often vintage, look.

Ready to Wear

Céline, known for its stylish and clever minimalism since 1945, is a luxury label so popular it's practically mainstream in its ready-to-wear, 'fashion for everyone' approach. Chloé is the other big ready-to-wear house, created in 1952 and the first *haute couture* label to introduce (in 1956) a designer ready-to-wear collection. Paris' prêt-à-porter industry was born.

Nostalgia & Recycling

Hipster 'purism' gives an approving nod to secondhand and recycling, while the desire in less ubertrendy circles to have an original Hermès scarf or Chanel black dress never tires.

Vintage

Parisian women play safe with classic designs and monotones, jazzed up by a scarf (those by Hermès, founded by a saddle-maker in 1837, are the most famous) or other simple accessory, hence the fervent nostalgia for the practical designs and modern simplicity of inter-war designer Coco Chanel (1883–1971), celebrated creator of the 1920s' 'little black dress'. Equal enthusiasm for pieces by Givenchy, Féraud and other designers from the 1950s heyday of Paris fashion contribute to the overwhelming demand today for vintage clothing.

Twice a year Parisian auction house Hôtel Drouot hosts *haute-couture* auctions. Collector Didier Ludot has sold the city's finest couture creations of yesteryear in his exclusive twinset of boutiques at Palais Royal since 1975: his legendary boutique, La Petite Robe Noir, showcases little black dresses by designers from the 1920s to the 1990s.

Postvintage

Postvintage fashion is about recycling. Art and fashion studio Andrea Crews, born between new-millennium sex shops in Pigalle and now at home in Le Marais, was among the first to reinvent grandpa's discarded shirts and daughter's has-beens into new hip garments.

Trends of Tomorrow

Each year the city of Paris honours its rising fashion stars with the Grand Prix Création de la Ville de Paris, a prize awarded to the 'Best New Designer' (working in the trade for under three years) and 'Best Confirmed Designer' (at least three years in the fashion biz). The list of prize laureates is tantamount to a who's who of tomorrow's fashion scene.

Talent to watch includes 2013 winner Serkan Cura, who crafts the most exquisite, overtly feminine dresses in his Paris studio using all sorts of feathers, occasionally intermingled with handmade silk flowers or beetle wings; Les Garçons (duo Louis Gerin and Gregory Lamaud), which reinvents classics to dress men in lacy lingerie and luxuriously comfortable homewear; and the label IRM Design (duo Marion Lalanne and Pierre-Alexis Heret), which creates bold, often hand-painted fabrics and cuts for 'strong, charismatic and independent women'. The collection in which IRM Design collaborated with Marseille-born Paris-based knife-painter Françoise Nielly naturally turned heads.

Fashion Museums & Exhibitions

Fondation Pierre Bergé-Yves Saint Laurent (Eiffel Tower & Western Paris), 16e

Musée de la Mode de la Ville de Paris (Eiffel Tower & Western Paris), 16e

Cité de la Mode et du Design (Docks en Seine, Montparnasse & Southern Paris), 13e

Architecture

It took disease, clogged streets, an antiquated sewage system and Baron Georges-Eugène Haussmann to drag architectural Paris out of the Middle Ages and into the modern world – yet since the city's radical transformation by Haussmann in the 19th century, which saw entire parts of the city razed and thousands of people displaced, Paris has never looked back. Its contemporary skyline shimmers with the whole gamut of architectural styles, from Roman arenas and Gothic cathedrals to postmodernist cubes and futuristic skyscrapers.

Above: Ornate foyer of the Palais Garnier opera house (p97)

Gallo-Roman

Traces of Roman Paris can be seen in the residential foundations in the Crypte Archéologique in front of Notre Dame; in the Arènes de Lutèce; and in the frigidarium (cooling room) and other remains of Roman baths dating from around AD 200 at the Musée National du Moyen Age.

The latter museum also contains the Pillier des Nautes (Boatsmen's Pillar), one of the most valuable legacies of the Gallo-Roman period. It is a 2.5m-high monument dedicated to Jupiter and was erected by the boatmen's guild during the reign of Tiberius (AD 14-37) on the Île de la Cité. The boat has become the symbol of Paris, and the city's Latin motto is '*Fluctuat Nec Mergitur*' (Tossed by Waves but Does Not Sink).

Merovingian & Carolingian

Although quite a few churches were built in Paris during the Merovingian and Carolingian periods (6th to 10th centuries), very little of them remain.

When the Merovingian ruler Clovis I made Paris his seat in the early 6th century, he established an abbey on the south bank of the Seine. All that remains is the Tour Clovis, a heavily restored Romanesque tower within the grounds of the prestigious Lycée Henri IV just east of the Panthéon.

Archaeological excavations in the crypt of the 12th-century Basilique de St-Denis have uncovered extensive tombs from the Merovingian and Carolingian periods; the oldest dates from around AD 570.

Designer Rooftops

- *Grand Palais (Champs-Élysées & Grands Boulevards)*
- *Cathédrale de Notre Dame (The Islands)*
- *Galeries Lafayette (Champs-Élysées & Grands Boulevards)*
- *Fondation Louis Vuitton pour La Création (Eiffel Tower & Western Paris)*

Romanesque

A religious revival in the 11th century led to the construction of many *roman* (Romanesque) churches, typically with round arches, heavy walls, few (and small) windows, and a lack of ornamentation that bordered on the austere.

No remaining building in Paris is entirely Romanesque but several have important representative elements. Église St-Germain des Prés, built in the 11th century on the site of the Merovingian ruler Childeric's 6th-century abbey, has been altered many times over the centuries, but the Romanesque bell tower above the west entrance has changed little since AD 1000. The choir, apse and truncated bell tower of Église St-Nicolas des Champs, now part of the Musée des Arts et Métiers, are Romanesque. Église St-Germain l'Auxerrois was built in a mixture of Gothic and Renaissance styles between the 13th and 16th centuries.

Must-See Buildings

- *Eiffel Tower*
- *Louvre pyramid*
- *Basilique de Sacré-Cœur, Montmartre*
- *Centre Pompidou*
- *Cité de l'Architecture et du Patrimoine*

Gothic

The world's first Gothic building was Basilique de St-Denis, which combined various late-Romanesque elements to create a new kind of structural support in which each arch counteracted and complemented the next. The basilica served as a model for many 12th-century French cathedrals, including Notre Dame de Paris and Chartres cathedral.

In the 14th century the Rayonnant – or Radiant – Gothic style, named after the radiating tracery of the rose windows, developed. Interiors became even lighter thanks to broader windows and more translucent stained glass. One of the most influential Rayonnant buildings was Ste-Chapelle, the stained glass of which forms a curtain of glazing on the 1st floor. The two transept facades of Cathédrale de Notre Dame de Paris and the vaulted Salle des Gens d'Armes (Cavalrymen's Hall) in the Conciergerie, the largest surviving medieval hall in Europe, are other fine examples of Rayonnant Gothic style.

By the 15th century, decorative extravagance led to Flamboyant Gothic, so named because the wavy stone carving made the towers appear to be blazing or flaming *(flamboyant)*. Beautifully lacy examples of Flamboyant architecture include the Clocher Neuf (New Bell Tower) at Chartres' cathedral, Église St-Séverin, and Tour St-Jacques, a 52m tower which is all that remains of an early-16th-century church. Inside

The Panthéon (p215)

Église St-Eustache there's some outstanding Flamboyant Gothic arch work holding up the ceiling of the chancel. Several *hôtels particuliers* (private mansions) were also built in this style, including Hôtel de Cluny, now the Musée National du Moyen Âge.

The iconic apartment buildings that line the boulevards of central Paris, with their cream-coloured stone and curvy wrought-iron balconies, are the work of Baron Haussmann (1809–91), prefect of the Seine *département* between 1853 and 1870.

Renaissance

The Renaissance set out to realise a 'rebirth' of classical Greek and Roman culture and first affected France at the end of the 15th century, when Charles VIII began a series of invasions of Italy, returning with some new ideas.

The Early Renaissance style, in which a variety of classical components and decorative motifs (columns, tunnel vaults, round arches, domes etc) were blended with the rich decoration of Flamboyant Gothic, is best exemplified in Paris by Église St-Eustache on the Right Bank and Église St-Étienne du Mont on the Left Bank.

Mannerism was introduced by Italian architects and artists brought to France around 1530 by François I. In 1546 Pierre Lescot designed the richly decorated southwestern corner of the Cour Carrée at the Musée du Louvre.

The Right Bank district of Le Marais remains the best area for Renaissance reminders in Paris proper, with some fine *hôtels particuliers*, such as Hôtel Carnavalet, housing part of the Musée Carnavalet.

Baroque

During the baroque period (tail end of the 16th to late-18th centuries), painting, sculpture and classical architecture were integrated to create structures and interiors of great subtlety, refinement and elegance. With the advent of the baroque, architecture became more pictorial, with painted church ceilings illustrating the Passion of Christ to the faithful, and palaces invoking the power and order of the state.

Salomon de Brosse, who designed the Palais du Luxembourg in the Jardin du Luxembourg in 1615, set the stage for two of France's most prominent early baroque architects: François Mansart, designer of Église Notre Dame du Val-de-Grâce, and his young rival Louis Le Vau, architect of Château de Vaux-le-Vicomte, which served as a model for Louis XIV's palace at Versailles.

Other fine French-baroque examples: Église St-Louis en l'Île, Chapelle de la Sorbonne, Palais Royal, and Hôtel de Sully with its inner courtyard decorated with allegorical figures.

Neoclassicism

Neoclassical architecture emerged about 1740 and had its roots in the renewed interest in classical forms – a search for order, reason and serenity through the adoption of forms and conventions of Graeco-Roman antiquity: columns, geometric forms and traditional ornamentation.

Among the earliest examples of this style are the Italianate facade of Église St-Sulpice; and the Petit Trianon at Versailles, designed by Jacques-Ange Gabriel for Louis XV in 1761. The domed building in Paris housing the Institut de France is a masterpiece of early French neoclassical architecture, but France's greatest neoclassical architect of the 18th century was Jacques-Germain Soufflot, creator of the Panthéon in the Latin Quarter.

Neoclassicism came into its own under Napoléon, who used it extensively for monumental architecture intended to embody the grandeur of imperial France and its capital: the Arc de Triomphe, the Arc de Triomphe du Carrousel, Église de Ste-Marie Madeleine, the Bourse de Commerce, and the Assemblée Nationale in the Palais Bourbon. Fittingly, the climax to this great 19th-century movement was Palais Garnier, the city's opera house designed by Charles Garnier.

HÔTEL DROUAT

A zany structure if ever there was one is auction house Hôtel Drouat. After a late-1970s surrealist facelift by architects Jean-Jacques Fernier and André Biro, the 19th-century Haussmann building was instantly hailed as a modern architectural gem.

Art Nouveau

Art nouveau, which emerged in Europe and the USA in the second half of the 19th century under various names (Jugendstil, Sezessionstil, Stile Liberty), caught on quickly in Paris, and its influence lasted until about 1910. It was characterised by sinuous curves and flowing, asymmetrical forms reminiscent of creeping vines, water lilies, the patterns on insect wings and the flowering boughs of trees. Influenced by the arrival of exotic objets d'art from Japan, art nouveau's French name came from a Paris gallery that featured works in the 'new art' style.

A lush and photogenic architectural style, art nouveau is expressed to perfection in Paris by Hector Guimard's graceful metro entrances and Le Marais synagogue, parts of the interiors in the Musée d'Orsay and the city's main department stores, Le Bon Marché and Galeries Lafayette.

Modern

France's best-known 20th-century architect, Charles-Édouard Jeanneret (aka Le Corbusier) was born in Switzerland but settled in Paris in 1917 at the age of 30. A radical modernist, he tried to adapt buildings to their functions in industrialised society without ignoring the human element. Most of Le Corbusier's work was done outside Paris, though he did design several private residences and the Pavillon Suisse, a dormitory for Swiss students at the Cité Internationale Universitaire in the 14e.

But until 1968, French architects were still being trained almost exclusively at the conformist École de Beaux-Arts, reflected in most of the early impersonal and forgettable 'lipstick tubes' and 'upended shoebox' structures erected in the skyscraper district of La Défense, the Unesco building (1958) in the 7e, and the 210m-tall Tour Montparnasse (1973).

Interesting and frightening were Le Corbusier's plans for Paris that never left the drawing board. Plan Voisin (Neighbour Project; 1925) envisaged wide boulevards linking the Gare Montparnasse with the Seine and lined with skyscrapers. The project would have required bulldozing much of the Latin Quarter.

Contemporary

For centuries France's leaders sought to immortalise themselves by erecting *grands projets* (huge public edifices) in Paris. Georges Pompidou commissioned the once reviled, now much-loved Centre Pompidou. His successor, Valéry Giscard d'Estaing, was instrumental in transforming the derelict Gare d'Orsay train station into the glorious Musée d'Orsay (1986). François Mitterrand surpassed all of the postwar presidents with monumental projects costing taxpayers €4.6 billion: Jean Nouvel's Institut du Monde Arabe (1987), built during this time, mixes modern Arab and Western elements and is arguably one of the city's most beautiful late-20th century buildings. Jacques Chirac orchestrated the magnificent Musée du Quai Branly, a glass, wood and sod structure with 3-hectare experimental garden, also by Jean Nouvel.

Ground-Breaking Designs

Recent years have seen the construction of several modern Parisian landmarks: IM Pei's glass-pyramid entrance at the hitherto sacrosanct and untouchable Musée du Louvre, an architectural cause célèbre that paved the way for Mario Bellini and Rudy Ricciotti's magnificent 'flying carpet' roof atop the museum's Cour Visconti in 2012; the city's second opera house, tile-clad Opéra de Paris Bastille, designed by Uruguayan architect Carlos Ott in 1989; and the monumental Grande Arche de la Défense by Danish architect Johan-Otto von Sprekelsen in the same year; the delightful Conservatoire National Supérieur de Musique et de Danse (1990) and Cité de la Musique (1994), designed by Christian de Portzamparc in the whimsical Parc de la Villette; the four glass towers of the €2 billion Bibliothèque Nationale de France (Dominique Perrault, 1995); and neighbouring M2K Bibliothèque pleasure palace (Wilmotte & Namur, 2003) in a glass shoebox that glimmers at night.

A signature architectural feature of Paris is the vertical garden, or *mur végétal* (vegetation wall). Seeming to defy gravity, these gardens clad walls in chic boutique interiors, outside museums, within spas and elsewhere. The Seine-facing garden at the Musée du Quai Branly, by Patrick Blanc, is Paris' most famous.

The *grand projet* of the new millennium was Jean Nouvel's long-awaited Philharmonie de Paris, a state-of-the-art creation that took three years to build and cost €381 million. On a more human scale is the redeveloped warehouse district known as Masséna Nord, where narrow streets and open blocks link conversions such as the Grands Moulins (an old mill that is now the hub of the new Paris Diderot University), the former SNCF cold-storage warehouse of Les Frigos (now a colourful artists community), and an old factory complete with smokestack (a new architecture school).

If it ever gets off the ground, the sustainable 297m-tall Tour Phare (Lighthouse Tower; www.tour-phare.com) at La Défense will torque like a human torso and, through awnings that are raised and lowered when the sun hits them, use light as a building material. Plans are for it to be completed in 2017.

Recent Renaissance

An utterly fabulous development is the recent renaissance of some of Paris' loveliest art deco buildings: in 2014 the luxury MGallery arm of the Accor hotel group opened a five-star hotel and spa in the legendary Molitor swimming pool complex in western Paris, where the bikini made its first appearance in the 1930s. In Le Marais, thermal-baths-turned-1980s-nightclub Les Bain Douches – another legendary address – opened as luxury hotel Les Bains after years of being abandoned. Preserving as many of the original art deco features as possible was a characteristic of both projects.

Drawing on the city's long-standing tradition of glass in its architecture (there is no more beautiful example than the art nouveau Grand Palais, one of the Paris skyline's most recognisable landmarks thanks to the gargantuan glass dome that tops it) Canadian architect Frank Gehry used 12 enormous glass 'sails' to design the extraordinary Fondation Louis Vuitton pour la Création, which opened in the Bois de Boulogne in late 2014. Glass is likewise a big feature of the 1970s eyesore-turned-contemporary-stunner Forum des Halles shopping centre in the 1er – a curvaceous, curvilinear and glass-topped construction by architects Patrick Berger and Jacques Anziutti, scheduled to be completed in 2016.

Literature

Whether attending a reading at legendary bookshop Shakespeare & Company in the Latin Quarter, browsing bookshelves in a hip wine bar in Le Marais or poring over the latest *bande dessinée (comic strip)* in bookshop Fnac, Parisians have a deep appreciation for the written word, and literature remains essential to their sense of identity. Couple this with the mass of modern literature inspired by the 'City of Lights' and Paris will never leave you short of a good read.

Histoire d'O (Story of O; 1954), Dominique Aury's erotic, sadomasochistic novel written under a pseudonym, has sold more copies outside France than any other contemporary French novel. Most believed it to be the work of a man; it was only 40 years after publication that the author revealed her identity.

Medieval

Paris does not figure largely in early medieval French literature, although the misadventures of Pierre Abélard and Héloïse took place in the capital, as did their mutual correspondence, which ended only with their deaths.

François Villon, the finest poet of the Middle Ages, received the equivalent of a Master of Arts degree from the Sorbonne before he turned 20. Involved in a series of brawls, robberies and illicit escapades, 'Master Villon' (as he became known) was sentenced to be hanged in 1462, supposedly for stabbing a lawyer. However, the sentence was commuted to banishment from Paris for 10 years, and he disappeared forever. Villon left behind a body of poems charged with a highly personal lyricism, among them *Ballade des Pendus* (Ballad of the Hanged Men), in which he writes his own epitaph, and *Ballade des Dames du Temps Jadis,* translated by the English poet and painter Dante Gabriel Rossetti as the 'Ballad of Dead Ladies'.

Renaissance

The great landmarks of French Renaissance literature are the works of François Rabelais, Pierre de Ronsard (and other poets of the Renaissance group of poets known as La Pléiade) and Michel de Montaigne. The exuberant narratives of erstwhile monk Rabelais blend coarse humour with erudition in a vast *oeuvre* that seems to include every kind of person, occupation and jargon to be found in the France of the early 16th century. Rabelais' publisher, Étienne Dolet, was convicted of heresy and blasphemy in 1546, hanged and burned on place Maubert, 5e.

Classical

During the 17th century, François de Malherbe, court poet under Henri IV, brought a new rigour to rhythm in literature. One of his better-known works is his sycophantic *Ode* (1600) to Marie de Médici. Transported by the perfection of Malherbe's verses, Jean de la Fontaine went on to write his charming *Fables* (1668) in the manner of Aesop – though he fell afoul of the Académie Française (French Academy) in the process. A mood of classical tragedy permeates *La Princesse de Clèves* (1678), by Marie de la Fayette, widely regarded as the precursor of the modern character novel.

Eighteenth Century

The literature of the 18th century is dominated by philosophers, among them Voltaire (François-Marie Arouet) and Jean-Jacques Rousseau. Voltaire's political writings, arguing that society is fundamentally opposed to nature, had a profound and lasting influence on the century, and he is buried in the Panthéon. Rousseau's sensitivity to landscape and its moods anticipated romanticism, and the insistence on his own singularity in *Les Confessions* (1782) made it the first modern autobiography. He, too, lies in the Panthéon.

Literary Sights

Maison de Victor Hugo (Le Marais, Ménilmontant & Belleville)

Maison de Balzac (Eiffel Tower & Western Paris)

Musée de la Vie Romantique (Montmartre & Northern Paris)

Musée Carnavalet (Le Marais, Ménilmontant & Belleville)

Art Ludique-Le Musée (Montparnasse & Southern Paris)

French Romanticism

The 19th century produced poet and novelist Victor Hugo, who lived on place des Vosges before fleeing to the Channel Islands during the Second Empire. *Les Misérables* (1862) describes life among the poor of Paris in the early 19th century. *Notre Dame de Paris* (The Hunchback of Notre Dame; 1831), a medieval romance and tragedy revolving around the life of the celebrated cathedral, made Hugo the key figure of French romanticism.

Other influential 19th-century novelists include Stendhal (Marie-Henri Beyle), Honoré de Balzac, Amandine Aurore Lucile Dupin (aka George Sand) and, of course, Alexandre Dumas, who wrote the swashbuckling adventures *Le Compte de Monte Cristo* (The Count of Monte Cristo; 1844) and *Les Trois Mousquetaires* (The Three Musketeers; 1844).

In 1857 two landmarks of French literature were published: *Madame Bovary*, by Gustave Flaubert, and *Les Fleurs du Mal*, by Charles Baudelaire. Both writers were tried for the supposed immorality of their works. Flaubert won his case, and his novel was distributed without censorship. Baudelaire, who moonlighted as a translator in Paris, was obliged to cut half a dozen poems from his work and fined 300 francs.

The aim of Émile Zola, who came to Paris with his close friend, the artist Paul Cézanne, in 1858, was to transform novel-writing from an art to a science by the application of experimentation. His theory may now seem naive, but his work influenced most significant French writers of the late 19th century and is reflected in much 20th-century fiction as well. His novel *Nana* (1880) tells the decadent tale of a young woman who resorts to prostitution to survive the Paris of the Second Empire.

FOREIGN LITERATURE: INTERWAR HEYDAY

Foreigners have found inspiration in Paris since Charles Dickens used the city alongside London as the backdrop to *A Tale of Two Cities* in 1859. The heyday of Paris as a literary setting, however, were the interwar years.

Ernest Hemingway's *The Sun Also Rises* (1926) and the posthumous *A Moveable Feast* (1964) portray bohemian life in Paris between the wars. So many vignettes in the latter – dissing Ford Maddox Ford in a cafe, 'sizing up' F Scott Fitzgerald in a toilet in the Latin Quarter, and overhearing Gertrude Stein and her lover, Alice B Toklas, bitchin' at one another from the sitting room of their salon near the Jardin du Luxembourg – are classic and *très parisien*.

Gertrude Stein let her hair down by assuming her lover's identity in *The Autobiography of Alice B Toklas*, a fascinating account of the author's many years in Paris, her salon on rue de Fleurus, 6e, and her friendships with Matisse, Picasso, Braque, Hemingway and others.

Down and Out in Paris and London (1933) is George Orwell's account of the time he spent working as a *plongeur* (dishwasher) in Paris and living with tramps in the city in the 1930s. Henry Miller's *Tropic of Cancer* (1934) and *Quiet Days in Clichy* (1956) are steamy novels set partly in the French capital. Then there's Anaïs Nin's voluminous diaries and fiction; her published correspondence with Miller is particularly evocative of 1930s Paris.

Symbolism & Surrealism

Paul Verlaine and Stéphane Mallarmé created the symbolist movement, which strove to express states of mind rather than simply detail daily reality. Arthur Rimbaud, in addition to crowding an extraordinary amount of exotic travel into his 37 years and having a tempestuous sexual relationship with Verlaine, produced two enduring pieces of work: *Une Saison en Enfer* (A Season in Hell; 1873) *and Illuminations* (1874). Verlaine died at 39 rue Descartes, 5e, in 1896.

Marcel Proust dominated the early 20th century with his seven-volume novel *À la Recherche du Temps Perdu* (Remembrance of Things Past; 1913–27), which explores the true meaning of past experience recovered from the unconscious by 'involuntary memory'. In 1907 Proust moved from the family home near av des Champs-Élysées to an apartment on bd Haussmann famous for its cork-lined bedroom (now in the Musée Carnavalet). André Gide found his voice in the celebration of gay sensuality and, later, left-wing politics. *Les Faux-Monnayeurs* (The Counterfeiters; 1925) exposes the hypocrisy and self-deception to which people resort in order to fit in with others or deceive themselves.

Literary Cafes

Café de Flore & Les Deux Magots (St-Germain & Les Invalides)

La Belle Hortense, L'Autre Café & Caffè Marcovaldo (Le Marais, Ménilmontant & Belleville)

André Breton wrote French surrealism's three manifestos, although the first use of the word 'surrealist' is attributed to the poet Guillaume Apollinaire, a fellow traveller of surrealism killed in action in WWI. Colette (Sidonie-Gabrielle Colette) enjoyed tweaking the nose of conventionally moral readers. Her best-known work is *Gigi* (1945) but far more interesting is *Paris de Ma Fenêtre* (Paris from My Window; 1944), dealing with the German occupation of Paris. Her view was from 9 rue de Beaujolais in the 1er, overlooking Jardin du Palais Royal.

Existentialism

After WWII, existentialism developed as a significant literary movement around Jean-Paul Sartre, Simone de Beauvoir and Albert Camus, who worked and conversed in the cafes of bd St-Germain in St-German des Prés. All three stressed the importance of the writer's political engagement. De Beauvoir, author of *Le Deuxième Sexe* (The Second Sex; 1949), had a profound influence on feminist thinking. Camus' novel *L'Étranger* (The Stranger; 1942) reveals that the absurd is the condition of modern man, who feels himself an outsider in his world.

No literary genre has a bigger cult following in France than the *bande dessinée* (comic strip) – Paris even has a museum, Art Ludique-Le Musée, dedicated to the art. The genre was originally written for children, but comic strips for adults burst onto the scene in 1959 with René Goscinny and Albert Uderzo's now-iconic *Astérix* series.

Modern Literature

In the late 1950s certain novelists began to look for new ways of organising narrative. The so-called *nouveau roman* (new novel) refers to the works of Nathalie Sarraute, Alain Robbe-Grillet, Boris Vian, Julien Gracq, Michel Butor and others. But these writers never formed a close-knit group, and their experiments took them in divergent directions.

In 1980 Marguerite Yourcenar, best known for her memorable historical novels including *Mémoires d'Hadrien* (Hadrian's Memoirs; 1951), became the first woman to be elected to the Académie Française. Marguerite Duras came to the notice of a larger public in 1984 when she won the Prix Goncourt for *L'Amant* (The Lover).

Philippe Sollers, an editor at *Tel Quel,* a highbrow, left-wing, Paris-based review, was very influential in the 1960s and early 1970s. His 1960s novels were highly experimental, but with *Femmes* (Women; 1983) he returned to a conventional narrative style. Another *Tel Quel* editor, Julia Kristeva, became known for her theoretical writings on literature and psychoanalysis but subsequently turned her hand to fiction: *Les Samuraï* (The Samurai; 1990), a fictionalised account of the heady days of *Tel Quel,* is an interesting document on Paris intelligentsia life.

PRIZE-WINNING READS

Ensure your city-break reading is up to the minute by plumping for the latest winner of the Prix Goncourt, France's most prestigious literary prize. Awarded annually since 1903, it has reflected in recent years the preoccupation in contemporary French literature with issues of race, multiculturalism and immigration. In 2009 Franco-Senegalese writer Marie NDiaye became the first black woman to win the award, with *Trois Femmes Puissantes* (Three Powerful Women; 2012); she burst onto the literary scene aged 21 with *Comédie Classique* (1988), a 200-page novel comprising just one single sentence. In 2013 the prize went to Parisian novelist and screenwriter Pierre Lemaitre for his historical novel *Au Revoir là-haut* (Goodbye Upstairs), set in a traumatised postwar France.

France's other big literary award is the Grand Prix du Roman de l'Académie Française, around since 1918. *Les Onze* by French novelist Pierre Michon (2009 winner), published in English as *The Eleven* (2013), portrays a humble Parisian painter who decorates the homes of Louis XIV's mistresses and goes on to create a Mona Lisa–type masterpiece. Michon's earlier novels, *Small Lives* (2008) and *Masters & Servants* (1997), come equally recommended.

Roland Barthes and Michel Foucault are other notable 1960s and '70s authors and philosophers. In the 1990s French writing focused in a nihilistic way on what France had lost as a nation (identity, international prestige etc), and never more so than in the work of controversial writer Michel Houellebecq, who rose to national prominence in 1998 with his *Les Particules Élémentaires* (Atomised).

Contemporary

Contemporary French writers include Jean Echenoz, Erik Orsenna, Christine Angot (dubbed '*la reine de l'autofiction*', 'the queen of autobiography'), and Paris-based comedian/dramatist Nelly Alard, who had her second novel *Un moment d'un couple* (A Moment of a Couple) published in 2013. Author Yasmina Khadra is actually a man – a former colonel in the Algerian army who adopted his wife's name as a nom de plume.

No contemporary French writer better delves into the mood and politics of the capital's notable ethnic population than Faïza Guène (b 1985), a French literary sensation who writes in an 'urban slang' style. Born and bred on a housing estate outside Paris, her debut novel, *Kiffe Kiffe Demain* (2004), sold in 27 countries and is published in English as *Just Like Tomorrow* (2006). Like the parents of most of her friends, Guène's father moved from a village in western Algeria to northern France in 1952, aged 17, to work in the mines. Only in the 1980s could he return to Algeria, where he met his wife. He returned to France with her – to Les Courtillières housing estate in Seine-St-Denis, where 6000-odd immigrants live like sardines in five-storey blocks stretching for 1.5km. Such is the setting for *Kiffe Kiffe Demain* and for Guène's second (semiautobiographical) novel, *Du Rêve pour les Oeufs* (2006), published in English as *Dreams from the Endz* (2008). Her third novel, *Les Gens du Balto* (2008), published in English as *Bar Balto* (2011), is a series of colloquial, first-person monologues by various characters who live on a street in a Parisian suburb. Her latest work, *Un Homme ça ne pleure pas* (2014), shifts to Nice, in southern France.

France's top-selling writer is Parisian Marc Levy (b 1961). The film rights of his first novel were snapped up to become Stephen Spielberg's *Just Like Heaven* (2005), and his novels have been translated into 42 languages and sold more than 30 million copies worldwide. His latest, *Une autre idée de bonheur* (Another Idea of Happiness; 2014) is set in the US.

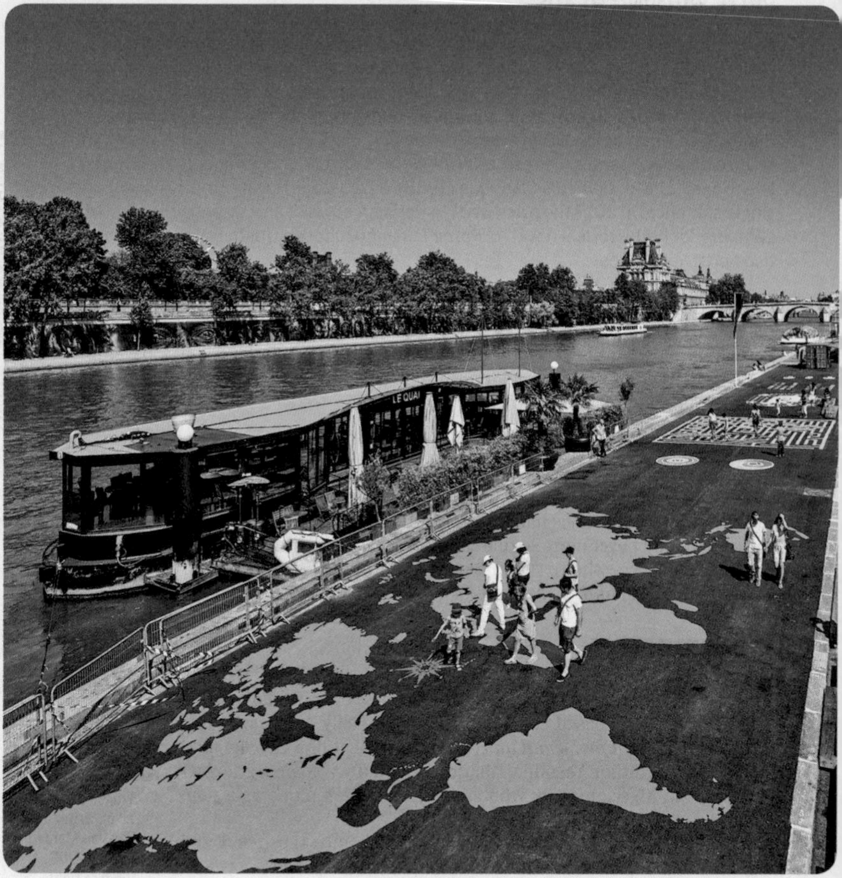

Art

While art in Paris today means anything and everything – bold installations in the metro, monumental wall frescos, mechanical sculpture, suburban tags and other gregarious street art – the city's rich art heritage has its roots firmly embedded in the traditional genres of painting and sculpture.

Above: Art installation outside the Musée d'Orsay

Baroque to Neoclassicism

According to philosopher Voltaire, French painting proper began with baroque painter Nicolas Poussin (1594–1665), the greatest representative of 17th-century classicism, who frequently set scenes from ancient Rome, classical mythology and the Bible in ordered landscapes bathed in golden light.

In the field of sculpture, extravagant and monumental tombs had been commissioned by the nobility from the 14th century, and in Renaissance Paris Pierre Bontemps (c 1507–68) decorated the beautiful tomb of François I at Basilique de St-Denis, and Jean Goujon (c 1510–67) created the Fontaine des Innocents near the Forum des Halles. No sculpture better evokes baroque than the magnificent *Horses of Marly* of Guillaume Coustou (1677–1746), at the entrance to av des Champs-Élysées.

Modern still life pops up with Jean-Baptiste Chardin (1699–1779), who brought the humbler domesticity of the Dutch masters to French art. In 1785 neoclassical artist Jacques Louis David (1748–1825) wooed the public with his vast portraits with clear republican messages. A virtual dictator in matters of art, he advocated a precise, severe classicism.

Jean-Auguste-Dominique Ingres (1780–1867), David's most gifted pupil in Paris, continued the neoclassical tradition. His historical pictures (eg *Oedipus and the Sphinx*, the 1808 version of which is in the Louvre) are now regarded as inferior to his portraits.

Painting Meccas

- *Musée du Louvre (Louvre & Les Halles)*
- *Musée d'Orsay (St-Germain & Les Invalides)*
- *Musée Picasso (Le Marais, Ménilmontant & Belleville)*

Romanticism

One of the Louvre's most gripping paintings, *The Raft of the Medusa* by Théodore Géricault (1791–1824), hovers on the threshold of romanticism; if Géricault had not died early (aged 33) he probably would have become a leader of the movement, along with his friend Eugène Delacroix (1798–1863; find him in the Cimetière du Père Lachaise), best known for his masterpiece commemorating the July Revolution of 1830, *Liberty Leading the People*.

While romantics revamped the subject picture, the Barbizon School effected a parallel transformation of landscape painting. The school derived its name from a village near the Forêt de Fontainebleau where Jean-Baptiste Camille Corot (1796–1875) and Jean-François Millet (1814–75) painted in the open air. The son of a Norman peasant farmer, Millet took many of his subjects from peasant life, and his *L'Angélus* (The Angelus; 1857) is probably the best-known French painting after the *Mona Lisa*. View it in the Musée d'Orsay.

In sculpture, the work of Paris-born Auguste Rodin (1840–1917) overcame the conflict between neoclassicism and romanticism. One of Rodin's most gifted pupils was his lover Camille Claudel (1864–1943), whose work can be seen with Rodin's in the Musée Rodin.

Sculpture Studios

- *Musée Rodin (St-Germain & Les Invalides)*
- *Musée Atelier Zadkine (St-Germain & Les Invalides)*
- *Atelier Brancusi (Louvre & Les Halles)*
- *Musée Bourdelle (Montparnasse & Southern Paris)*

Realism

The realists were all about social comment: Millet anticipated the realist program of Gustave Courbet (1819–77), a prominent member of the Paris Commune whose paintings depicted the drudgery and dignity of working-class lives. In 1850 he broke new ground with *A Burial at Ornans* (in the Musée d'Orsay), painted on a canvas of monumental size reserved until then exclusively for historical paintings.

Édouard Manet (1832–83) used realism to depict Parisian middle classes, yet he included in his pictures numerous references to the Old Masters. His *Déjeuner sur l'Herbe* and *Olympia* were both scandalous, largely because they broke with the traditional treatment of their subject matter. He was a pivotal figure in the transition from realism to impressionism.

One of the best sculptors of this period was François Rude (1784–1855), creator of the relief on the Arc de Triomphe and several pieces in the Musée d'Orsay. By the mid-19th century, memorial statues in public places had replaced sculpted tombs, making such statues all the rage.

Sculptor Jean-Baptiste Carpeaux (1827–75) began as a romantic, but his work in Paris – such as *The Dance* on the Palais Garnier and his fountain in the Jardin du Luxembourg – recalls the gaiety and flamboyance of the baroque era.

Trendy Galleries

- *Maison Rouge (Bastille & Eastern Paris)*
- *Palais de Tokyo (Eiffel Tower & Western Paris)*
- *Fondation Cartier pour l'Art Contemporain (Montparnasse & Southern Paris)*
- *Fondation Louis Vuitton pour la Création (Eiffel Tower & Western Paris)*

Impression, Soleil Levant by Claude Monet

César Baldaccini (1921–98), known simply as César, used iron and scrap metal to create imaginary insects and animals, later graduating to pliable plastics. Among his best-known works are the *Centaur* statue in the 6e and the statuette handed to actors at the Césars (French cinema's equivalent of the Oscars).

Impressionism

Paris' Musée d'Orsay is the crown jewel of impressionism. Initially a term of derision, 'impressionism' was taken from the title of an 1874 experimental painting, *Impression: Soleil Levant* (Impression: Sunrise) by Claude Monet (1840–1926). Monet was the leading figure of the school, and a visit to the Musée d'Orsay unveils a host of other members, among them Alfred Sisley (1839–99), Camille Pissarro (1830–1903), Pierre-Auguste Renoir (1841–1919) and Berthe Morisot (1841–95). The impressionists' main aim was to capture the effects of fleeting light, painting almost universally in the open air – and light came to dominate the content of their painting.

Edgar Degas (1834–1917), buried in Cimetière de Montmartre, was a fellow traveller of the impressionists, but he preferred painting cafe life *(Absinthe)* and in ballet studios *(The Dance Class)* than the great outdoors – several beautiful examples hang in the Musée d'Orsay.

Henri de Toulouse-Lautrec (1864–1901) was a great admirer of Degas but chose subjects one or two notches below: people in the bistros, brothels and music halls of Montmartre (eg *Au Moulin Rouge*). He is best known for his posters and lithographs, in which the distortion of the figures is both satirical and decorative.

Paul Cézanne (1839–1906) is celebrated for his still lifes and landscapes depicting southern France, though he spent many years in Paris after breaking with the impressionists. The name of Paul Gauguin (1848–1903) immediately conjures up studies of Tahitian and Breton women. Both Cézanne and Gauguin were postimpressionists, a catch-all term for the diverse styles that flowed from impressionism.

Bathers at Asnières by Georges Seurat

Pointillism & Symbolism

Pointillism was a technique developed by Georges Seurat (1859–91), who applied paint in small dots or uniform brush strokes of unmixed colour to produce fine 'mosaics' of warm and cool tones. His tableaux *Une Baignade, Asnières* (Bathers at Asnières) is a perfect example.

Henri Rousseau (1844–1910) was a contemporary of the postimpressionists, but his 'naive' art was unaffected by them. His dreamlike pictures of the Paris suburbs and of jungle and desert scenes (eg *The Snake Charmer*) – again in Musée d'Orsay – have influenced art right up to this century. The eerie treatment of mythological subjects by Gustave Moreau (1826–98) can be seen in the artist's studio, now within the Musée Gustave-Moreau in the 9e.

Twentieth-Century Art

Twentieth-century French painting is characterised by a bewildering diversity of styles, including fauvism, named after the slur of a critic who compared the exhibitors at the 1905 Salon d'Automne (Autumn Salon) in Paris with *fauves* (wild animals) because of their wild brushstrokes and radical use of intensely bright colours. Among these 'beastly' painters was Henri Matisse (1869–1954).

Cubism was launched in 1907 with *Les Demoiselles d'Avignon* by Spanish prodigy Pablo Picasso (1881–1973). Cubism, as developed by Picasso, Georges Braque (1882–1963) and Juan Gris (1887–1927), deconstructed the subject into a system of intersecting planes and presented various aspects simultaneously.

In the 1920s and '30s the École de Paris (School of Paris) was formed by a group of expressionists, mostly foreign born.

Both Brazue and Picasso experimented with sculpture and, in the spirit of Dada, Marcel Duchamp exhibited 'found objects', one of which was a urinal, which he mounted, signed and dubbed *Fountain* in 1917.

Keep abreast of current exhibitions, events and happenings with Paris' contemporary art and design magazine *Slash* (www.slash-paris.com), also on Twitter and Facebook.

No piece of French art better captures the rebellious, iconoclastic spirit of Dadism – a Swiss-born literary and artistic movement of revolt – than *Mona Lisa,* by Marcel Duchamp (1887–1968), complete with moustache and goatee. In 1922 German Dadaist Max Ernst (1891–1976) moved to Paris and worked on surrealism, a Dada offshoot that flourished between the wars. Drawing on the theories of Sigmund Freud, it attempted to reunite the conscious and unconscious realms, to permeate everyday life with fantasies and dreams. The most influential of this style in Paris was Spanish-born artist Salvador Dalí (1904–89), who arrived in the French capital in 1929 and painted some of his most seminal works while residing here. To see his work, visit the Dalí Espace Montmartre.

One of the most influential pre-WWII sculptors to emerge in Paris was Romanian-born Constantin Brancusi (1876–1957); view his work at the Atelier Brancusi. Two other Paris-busy sculptors each have a museum devoted to their work: Ossip Zadkine (1890–1967) and Antoine Bourdelle (1861–1929).

METRO ART

No genre is more Parisian than the metro art adorning the 300-plus stations of the city's world-famous Métropolitain. Art themes often relate to the *quartier* (neighbourhood) or name of the station. Montparnasse Bienvenüe, for example, evokes the creation of the metro – it was an engineer named Fulgence Bienvenüe (1852–1936) who oversaw the building of the first 91km from 1886; while Carrefour Pleyel, named in honour of the 18th-century composer and piano-maker Ignace Joseph Pleyel (1757–1831), focuses on classical music.

The following is just a sample of the most interesting stations from an artistic perspective.

➡ **Abbesses** (line 12 metro entrance) The noodlelike pale-green metalwork and glass canopy of the station entrance is one of the finest examples of the work of Hector Guimard (1867–1942), the celebrated French art nouveau architect whose signature style once graced most metro stations. For a complete list of the metro stations that retain *édicules* (shrinelike entranceways) designed by Guimard, see www.parisinconnu.com.

➡ **Assemblée Nationale** (line 12 platform) Gigantic posters of silhouettes in red, white and blue by artist Jean-Charles Blais (b 1956) represent the MPs currently sitting in parliament.

➡ **Bastille** (line 5 platform) A 180-sq-metre ceramic fresco features scenes taken from newspaper engravings published during the Revolution, with illustrations of the destruction of the infamous prison.

➡ **Chaussée d'Antin-Lafayette** (line 7 platform) Large allegorical painting on the vaulted ceiling recalls the Marquis de Lafayette (1757–1834) and his role as general in the American Revolution.

➡ **Cluny–La Sorbonne** (line 10 platform) A large ceramic mosaic replicates the signatures of intellectuals, artists and scientists from the Latin Quarter through history, including Molière (1622–73), Rabelais (c 1483–1553) and Robespierre (1758–96).

➡ **Concorde** (line 12 platform) What look like children's building blocks in white-and-blue ceramic on the walls of the station are 45,000 tiles that spell out the text of the *Déclaration des Droits de l'Homme et du Citoyen* (Declaration of the Rights of Man and of the Citizen), the document setting forth the principles of the French Revolution.

➡ **Palais Royal–Musée du Louvre** (line 1 metro entrance) The zany entrance on place du Palais by Jean-Michel Othoniel (b 1964) is composed of two crown-shaped cupolas (one representing the day, the other night) consisting of 800 red, blue, amber and violet glass balls threaded on an aluminium structure. Sublime.

Above: Métropolitain entrance

Coloured curtain inspired by contemporary art

A bill in 1936 provided for 'the creation of monumental decorations in public buildings' by allotting 1% of building costs to art. The concept mushroomed half a century later (with Daniel Buren) and now there's artwork everywhere: in the Jardin des Tuileries, La Défense, Parc de la Villette, the metro...

WWII ended Paris' role as the world's artistic capital. Many artists left during the occupation, and though some returned after the war, the city never regained its old magnetism.

Contemporary Art

Artists in the 1990s turned to the minutiae of daily urban life to express social and political angst, using new mediums to let rip. Conceptual artist Daniel Buren (b. 1938) reduced his painting to a signature series of vertical 8.7cm-wide stripes that he applies to every surface imaginable – white-marble columns in the courtyard of Paris' Palais Royal included. Partner-in-crime Michel Parmentier (1938–2000) insisted on monochrome painting – blue in 1966, grey in 1967 and red in 1968.

Paris-born conceptual artist Sophie Calle (b. 1953) brazenly exposes her private life in public with eye-catching installations such as 107 women reading and commenting on an email she received from her French lover, dumping her. The resultant work of art – compelling and addictive – was published in the artist's book *Take Care of Yourself.*

Street art is the current buzz word. In 2013 the world's largest collective street-art exhibition, La Tour Paris 13 (www.tourparis13.fr), opened in a derelict apartment block in the 13e *arrondissement* (city district). Its 36 apartments on 13 floors were covered from head to toe with works by 100 international artists. The blockbuster exhibition ran for just one month – lines to get in were hours long – after which the tower was shut and, in April 2014, demolished. Itself an artwork, the three-day demolition was filmed and streamed live on the internet (where the street artworks remain). Galerie Itinerrance (http://itinerrance.fr), an art gallery in the 13e specialising in graffiti art, organised the mind-blowingly successful project.

Film

Be it exploring behind the scenes at an art deco cinema, cosying up on a sofa in a 19th-century Japanese pagoda-turned-cinema to catch art house, or following in the footsteps of iconic screen heroine Amélie Poulain through the streets of Montmartre, Paris is possibly one of the world's most cinematic cities: the French capital has produced a bevy of blockbuster film-makers and stars and is the filming location of countless box-office hits by both home-grown and foreign directors.

Movie Makers & Stars

French cinema has not looked back since 2012 when *The Artist* (2011), a silent B&W romantic comedy set in 1920s Hollywood, won seven BAFTAs and five Oscars to become the most awarded film in French cinema history. Best Director went to Parisian Michel Hazanavicius (b 1967) and Best Original Score went to French composer-pianist Ludovic Bource (b 1970). Best Actor was awarded to charismatic Jean Dujardin (b 1972), a born-and-bred Parisian suburbs lad who started with one-man shows in city bars and cabarets, and made his name with roles as varied as surfer Brice waiting for his wave in *Brice de Nice* (2005), James Bond in *OSS 117: Le Caire, Nid d'Espions* (OSS 117: Cairo Nest of Spies; 2006), the sexiest cowboy around in *Lucky Luke* (2009) and a WWII French soldier in George Clooney's recent *The Monuments Men* (2014).

Another French blockbuster packed with Parisian talent is Anne Fontaine's *Coco Avant Chanel* (Coco Before Chanel; 2009). The movie tells the compelling life story of orphan-turned fashion designer Coco Chanel, played by Audrey Tautou (b 1976), the waifish French actress who conquered stardom with her role as Parisian do-gooder Amélie in Jean-Pierre Jeunet's *Le Fabuleux Destin d'Amélie Poulain* (2001), an earlier Paris classic set in Montmartre.

One of the most successful French-language films ever is *Intouchables* (Untouchable; 2011). Directed by Parisian Éric Toledano and Olivier Nakache, the comic drama is about a billionaire quadriplegic and his live-in Senegalese carer in Paris. Assuming the role of carer is Omar Sy (b 1978), a charismatic actor with a sensational smile, raised in the Parisian suburbs by Senegalese Mauritian parents. The film, which scooped Best Foreign Film at both the Golden Globes and the

1920s

French film flourishes. Sound ushers in René Clair's (1898–1981) world of fantasy and satirical surrealism. Watch Abel Gance's antiwar blockbuster *J'Accuse!* (I Accuse!; 1919), filmed on actual WWI battlefields.

1930s

WWI inspires a new realism: portraits of ordinary lives dominate film. Watch *La Grande Illusion* (The Great Illusion; 1937), based on the trench-warfare experience of director Jean Renoir.

1940s

Surrealists eschew realism. Watch Jean Cocteau's *La Belle et la Bête* (Beauty and the Beast; 1946) and *Orphée* (Orpheus; 1950). WWII saps the film industry of both talent and money.

1950s

Nouvelle Vague (New Wave): small budgets, no stars and real-life subject matter produce uniquely personal films. Watch Jean-Luc Goddard's carefree, B&W celebration of Paris *À Bout de Souffle* (Breathless; 1959).

1980s

Big-name stars, slick production values and nostalgia: generous state subsidies see film-makers switch to costume dramas and comedies in the face of growing competition from the USA.

2000s

Renaissance: *philanthrope* Amélie is the subject of Jean-Pierre Jeunet's *Le Fabuleux Destin d'Amélie Poulain* (2001), the first of a string of French-made films to succeed globally.

BAFTA Awards in 2013, turned Omar Sy into the rags-to-riches darling of French film and an international celebrity.

French-produced *Taken 2* (2012) was directed by Olivier Megaton (b 1965), another product of the Parisian suburbs, who was a graffiti artist before turning his creative hand to film-making – with success.

France's leading lady is Marion Cotillard (b 1975), a Paris girl and the first French woman since 1959 to win an Oscar for her role as Édith Piaf in Olivier Dahan's *La Môme* (La Vie en Rose; 2007). Hugely versatile, the Parisian actress went on to play an amputee in art film *De Rouille et d'Os* (Rust and Bone; 2012) by Parisian director Jacques Audiard (b 1952). In her most recent film, *Deux Jours, Une Nuit* (Two Days, One Night; 2014), screened at the 2014 Cannes International Film Festival, the Paris superstar plays an employee in a solar-panel factory who learns she will lose her job if her coworkers don't each sacrifice €1000 bonuses offered to them.

The world's first paying-public film screening was held in Paris' Grand Café on blvd des Capucines, 9e, in December 1895 by the Lumière brothers, inventors of 'moving pictures'.

Female film-makers are few: enter Pascale Ferrari (b 1960), a very talented director from Paris whose latest film, *Bird People* (2014), takes place in and around a hotel at Paris' Charles de Gaulle airport.

On Location

Paris is the perfect cinematic setting and a natural movie star: look no further than timeless French classics *Hôtel du Nord* (1938), set along the Canal St-Martin, and *Les Enfants du Paradis* (1946), set in 1840s Paris, both directed by Parisian film-maker Marcel Carné (1906–96).

New Wave film director Jean-Luc Godard followed his B&W celebration of Paris in *À Bout de Souffle* (Breathless; 1959) with *Bande à Parte* (Band of Outsiders; 1964), an entertaining gangster film with marvellous scenes in the Louvre.

Cinematic Trips

La Pagode (St-Germain & Les Invalides)

Cinémathèque Française (Bastille & Eastern Paris)

Le Grand Rex (Louvre & Les Halles)

Art Ludique-Le Musée (Montparnasse & Southern Paris)

For decades 'Most Watched French Film' kudos went to *La Grand Vadrouille* (The Great Ramble; 1966), a French comedy in which five British airmen are shot down over German-occupied France in 1942. One is catapulted into Paris' Bois de Vincennes zoo, another into the orchestra pit of Paris' opera house, and so the comic tale unfurls.

No Parisian actress was hotter in the 1990s than Juliette Binoche (b 1964), catapulted to fame after diving into the shimmering, bright-turquoise water of Paris' art deco swimming pool the Piscine de Pontoise in the 5e, in *Bleu* (Blue; 1993), the first in Krzysztof Kieślowski's *Trois Couleurs* (Three Colours) triology. A decade on, Binoche wooed cinema-goers in equal measure with her role as a grieving mother in *Paris je t'aime* (2006), a staggering work comprising 18 short films – each set in a different Parisian *arrondissement* (neighbourhood).

Honoured with the Palme d'Or at Cannes in 2008, Laurent Cantet's *Entre Les Murs* (The Class; 2008) portrays a year in the school life of pupils and teachers in a Parisian surburb. Based on the autobiographical novel of teacher François Begaudeau, the documentary-drama is a brilliant reflection of contemporary multiethnic society.

The city has always been uberchic for foreign film directors, whatever their genre: Bernardo Bertolucci's *Last Tango in Paris* (1972) starred Marlon Brando as a grief-stricken American. Woody Allen's *Everybody Says I Love You* (1996) unfolded on the Left Bank's quai de la Tournelle, while dream scenes in his subsequent *Midnight in Paris* (2011) evoked the city in the 1920s. Martin Scorsese's Oscar-winning children's film *Hugo* (2011) paid tribute to cinema and Parisian film pioneer Georges Méliès through the remarkable adventure of an orphan boy in the 1930s who tends the clocks at a Paris train station. The crazed antics of Gargamel et al in American movie *Smurfs 2* (2013) were shot on location in Paris at Cathédrale Notre Dame de Paris.

Music

From organ recitals bathed in Gothic architectural splendour to some of the world's best rap, music is embedded deep in the Parisian soul. To understand the capital's musical heritage is to enrich your experience of a city where talented musicians audition to perform in the metro, and silent movies with little or no script – simply an extraordinary musical soundtrack – scoop Oscars.

Jazz & French Chansons

Jazz hit Paris in the 1920s with the banana-clad form of Josephine Baker, an African American cabaret dancer. In 1934 a chance meeting between Parisian jazz violinist Stéphane Grappelli (1908–97) and three-fingered Roma guitarist Django Reinhardt (1910–53) in a Montparnasse nightclub led to the formation of the Hot Club of France quintet. Claude Luter and his Dixieland band were hip in the 1950s.

The *chanson française*, a tradition dating from troubadours in the Middle Ages, was eclipsed by the music halls of the early 20th century but was revived in the 1930s by Édith Piaf (1915–63) and Charles Trenet (1913–2001). In the 1950s Left Bank cabarets nurtured singers like Léo Ferré (1916–63), Georges Brassens (1921–81), Claude Nougaro (1929–2004), Jacques Brel (1929–78), Barbara (1930–97) and the very sexy, very Parisian Serge Gainsbourg (1928–91). The genre was revived in the new millennium as *la nouvelle chanson française* by performers like Vincent Delerm (b 1976), Bénabar (b 1969; www.benabar.com), Jeanne Cherhal (b 1978; www.jeannecherhal.net) and Camille (b 1978).

Top Five Albums

- *Histoire de Melody Nelson*, Serge Gainsbourg
- *Moon Safari*, AIR
- *Dante*, Abd al Malik
- *Bankrupt*, Phoenix
- *Paris by Night*, Bob Sinclair

Rock & Pop

French pop has come a long way since the *yéyé* (imitative rock) days of the 1960s as sung by Johnny Hallyday. The distinctive M is the son of singer Louis Chédid; Arthur H is the progeny of pop-rock musician Jacques Higelin; and Thomas Dutronc (www.thomasdutronc.fr) is the offspring of 1960s idols Jacques and Françoise Hardy. Serge Gainsbourg's daughter with Jane Birkin, songwriter-singer and actress Charlotte (b 1971) made her musical debut in 1984 with the single 'Lemon Incest' and – several albums later – released a cover version of the song 'Hey Joe' as soundtrack to the film *Nymphomaniac* (2013), in which she also starred.

Noir Désir was *the* sound of French rock until its lead vocalist, Bertrand Cantat (b 1964), was imprisoned in 2003 for the murder of his girlfriend. Following his early release from prison in 2007, Noir Désir limped along until 2010. The controversial singer, once dubbed the 'Jim Morrison of French rock', later formed the band Détroit with instrumentalist Pascal Humbert. Cantat's powerfully husky voice instantly won fans over, Détroit's first album, *Horizons* (2013), selling 160,000 copies in just six months and tickets for the band's 2014 tour selling like hot cakes.

Indie rock band Phoenix from Versailles – born in the late 1990s in a garage in the Paris suburbs – headlines festivals in the US and UK. Lead singer Thomas Mars (b 1976), his schoolmate Chris Mazzalai (guitar), his brother Laurent Brancowitz (guitar and keyboards) and Deck d'Arcy (keyboards and brass) have five hugely successful albums under their belt and a much-coveted Grammy award.

Always worth a listen is Louise Attaque (http://louiseattaque.com) and Nosfell (www.nosfell.com), one of France's most creative and intense musicians, who sings in his own invented language called 'le klokobetz'. His third album, *Massif Armour* (2014), opens and closes in 'le klokobetz' but otherwise woos listeners with powerful French love lyrics.

David Guetta, Laurent Garnier (www.laurent-garnier.com), Martin Solveig and Bon Sinclair (www.bobsinclar.com) – originally nicknamed 'Chris the French Kiss' – are top Parisian electronica producers and DJs who travel the international circuit.

Electronica

Paris does dance music very well, computer-enhanced Chicago blues and Detroit techno often being mixed with 1960s lounge music and vintage tracks from the likes of Gainsbourg and Brassens to create a distinctly urban and highly portable sound.

Internationally successful bands like Daft Punk and Justice head up the scene. Daft Punk (www.daftalive.com), originally from Versailles, adapts first-wave acid house and techno to its younger roots in pop and indie rock. Its debut album, *Homework* (1997), fused disco, house funk and techno, while the latest, *Random Access Memories* (2013), boldly ditched computer-generated sound for a strong disco beat played by session musicians. Opening track 'Give Life Back to Music' came out as a single in 2014.

World

Paris' world beat is strong: think Algerian *rai* (artists include Cheb Khaled, Natacha Atlas, Jamel, Cheb Mami), Senegalese *mbalax* (Youssou N'Dour), West Indian zouk (Kassav', Zouk Machine) and Cuban salsa. In the late 1980s, bands Mano Negra and Les Négresses Vertes combined many of these elements with brilliant results, as did Manu Chao (b 1961; formerly frontman for Mano Negra; www.manuchao.net), the Paris-born son of Spanish parents.

Magic System from Côte d'Ivoire popularised *zouglou* (a kind of West African rap and dance music) with its album *Premier Gaou*, and Congolese Koffi Olomide (b 1956) still packs the halls. Also try to catch blind singing couple Amadou and Mariam – Rokia Traoré (www.rokiatraore.net) – from Mali, and Franco-Algerian DJ-turned-singer Rachid Taha (www.rachidtaha.fr), whose music mixes Arab and Western musical styles with lyrics in English, Berber and French.

No artist has cemented France's reputation in world music more than Paris-born Franco-Congolese rapper, slam poet and three-time Victoire de la Musique–award winner Abd al Malik (www.abdalmalik.fr). His albums *Gibraltar* (2006), *Dante* (2008) and *Château Rouge* (2010) are classics.

Musical Pilgrimages

- *Serge Gainsbourg's grave, Cimetière du Montparnasse*
- *Jim Morrison's grave, Cimetière du Père Lachaise*
- *La Cigale, Montmartre*
- *Les Bains, Le Marais*
- *Aux Folies and Musée de Édith Piaf, Belleville*

Rap

France is known for its rap, an original 1990s sound spearheaded by Senegal-born, Paris-reared rapper MC Solaar and Suprême NTM (NTM being an acronym for a French expression far too offensive to print). Most big-name rappers are French 20-somethings of Arabic or African origin whose prime preoccupation is the frustrations and fury of fed-up immigrants in the French suburbs. Take hot-shot rapper Disiz La Peste (b 1978), born in Amiens to a Senegalese father and Belgian mother: his third album *Histoires Extra-Ordinaires d'un Jeune de Banlieue* (The Extraordinary Stories of a Youth in the Suburbs; 2005) portrayed just what its title suggested, as did his 'last' album *Disiz the End* (2009), after which he morphed into Peter Punk and created a very different rock-punk-electro sound. In 2011 he returned as rap artist Disiz La Peste, successfully releasing the album *Lucide* in 2012 and its sequel *Trans-Lucide* – opening track entitled 'Fuck les problèmes' – in 2014.

Survival Guide

Transport

ARRIVING IN PARIS

Few roads *don't* lead to Paris, one of the most visited destinations on earth. Practically every major airline flies through one of its three airports, and most European train and bus routes cross it.

Paris is the central point in the French rail network, Société Nationale des Chemins de Fer Français (SNCF), with six train stations that handle passenger traffic to different parts of France and Europe. Each is well connected to the Paris public transportation system, the Régie Autonome des Transports Parisiens (RATP). To buy onward tickets from Paris, visit a station or go to **Voyages SNCF** (www.voyages-sncf.com).

Most trains – and all Trains à Grande Vitesse (TGV) – require advance reservations. As with most tickets, the earlier you book, the better your chances of securing a discounted fare. Mainline stations in Paris have left-luggage offices and/or *consignes* (lockers).

On public transport, children under four years travel free and those aged four to nine years (inclusive) pay half price; exceptions are noted.

Flights, tours and rail tickets can be booked online at www.lonelyplanet.com.

Charles de Gaulle Airport

Most international airlines fly to **Aéroport de Charles de Gaulle** (CDG; www.aeroports-deparis.fr), 28km northeast of central Paris. In French the airport is commonly called 'Roissy' after the suburb in which it is located. A €1.7 billion project to create a high-speed train link between Charles de Gaulle and Gare de l'Est in central Paris is on the table, but no track will be laid until 2017. When complete in 2023, the CDG Express will cut the current 40-odd minute journey to 20 minutes.

Metro & RER Networks

CDG is served by the RER B line (€9.50, approximately 50 minutes, every 10 to 15 minutes), which connects with the Gare du Nord, Châtelet–Les Halles and St-Michel–Notre Dame stations in the city centre. Trains run from 5am to 11pm; there are fewer trains on weekends.

Taxi

A taxi to the city centre takes 40 minutes. During the day, you'll pay around €50; the fare increases 15% between 5pm and 10am and on Sundays. Only take taxis at a clearly marked rank. Never follow anyone who approaches you at the airport and claims to be a driver.

CLIMATE CHANGE & TRAVEL

Every form of transport that relies on carbon-based fuel generates CO_2, the main cause of human-induced climate change. Modern travel is dependent on aeroplanes, which might use less fuel per kilometre per person than most cars but travel much greater distances. The altitude at which aircraft emit gases (including CO_2) and particles also contributes to their climate change impact. Many websites offer 'carbon calculators' that allow people to estimate the carbon emissions generated by their journey and, for those who wish to do so, to offset the impact of the greenhouse gases emitted with contributions to portfolios of climate-friendly initiatives throughout the world. Lonely Planet offsets the carbon footprint of all staff and author travel.

Bus

There are six main bus lines:

➡ **Les Cars Air France line 2** (€17, 1¼ hours, every 20 minutes, 6am to 11pm) Links the airport with the Arc de Triomphe. Children aged two to 11 pay half price.

➡ **Les Cars Air France line 4** (€17.50, every 30 minutes, 6am to 10pm from CDG, 6am to 9.30pm from Paris) Links the airport with Gare de Lyon (50 minutes) in eastern Paris and Gare Montparnasse (55 minutes) in southern Paris. Children aged two to 11 pay half price.

➡ **Roissybus** (€10.50, 45 to 60 minutes, every 15 minutes, 5.30am to 11pm) Links the airport with the Opéra.

➡ **RATP bus 350** (€5.70, 50 minutes, every 30 minutes, 5.30am to 11pm) Links the airport with Gare de l'Est in northern Paris.

➡ **RATP bus 351** (€5.70, 60 minutes, every 30 minutes, 5.30am to 11pm) Links the airport with place de la Nation in eastern Paris.

➡ **Noctilien bus 140 & 143** (€7.60 or four metro tickets, hourly, 12.30am to 5.30pm) Part of the RATP night service, Noctilien has two buses that go to CDG: bus 140 from Gare de l'Est, and 143 from Gare de l'Est and Gare du Nord.

Gare du Nord

Eurostar (www.eurostar.com) The London–Paris line runs from St-Pancras International to Gare du Nord. Voyages take 2¼ hours.

Thalys (www.thalys.com) Thalys trains pull into Paris' Gare du Nord from Brussels, Amsterdam and Cologne.

SPEED- OR CENT-SAVER?

Increasingly popular as a means of getting to/from all three Paris airports is the excellent taxi-sharing scheme **WeCab** (www.wecab.com), whereby you book a taxi in advance and split the ride with other passengers going to the same place as you.

For those seeking speed, not a cent-saver, the hot choice is a *taxi moto* (motorbike taxi), whereby you leap on the back of a bike, driver and helmet provided, and zip past the traffic into town at lightning speed. Companies include **Paris Motos** (☎06 75 67 56 75; www.parismotos.fr) and **Taxi Moto Paris** (☎06 64 65 61 86; http://taxi-motos-paris.com).

Orly Airport

Aéroport d'Orly (ORY; ☎01 70 36 39 50; www.aeroports-deparis.fr) is 19km south of central Paris but, despite being closer than CDG, it is not as frequently used by international airlines, and public transportation options aren't quite as straightforward.

Taxi

A taxi to the city centre takes roughly 30 minutes. During the day, you'll pay between €40 and €55; the fare increases 15% between 5pm and 10am and on Sundays.

Metro & RER Networks

There is no direct train to/from Orly; you'll need to change halfway. Note that while it is possible to take a shuttle to the RER C line, this service is quite long and not recommended.

➡ **RER B** (€10.90, 35 minutes, every four to 12 minutes) This line connects Orly with the St-Michel–Notre Dame, Châtelet–Les Halles and Gare du Nord stations in the city centre. In order to get from Orly to the RER station (Antony), you must first take the Orlyval automatic train. The service runs from 6am to 11pm (fewer on weekends). You only need one ticket to take the two trains.

Bus & Tram

There are several bus lines and a state-of-the-art tram line that serve Orly:

➡ **Air France bus 1** (€12.50, one hour, every 20 minutes, 5am to 10.20pm from Orly, 6am to 11.20pm from Invalides) This bus runs to/from the Gare Montparnasse (35 minutes) in southern Paris, Invalides in the 7e, and the Arc de Triomphe. Children aged two to 11 pay half price.

➡ **Orlybus** (€7.50, 30 minutes, every 15 minutes, 6am to 11.20pm from Orly, 5.35am to 11.05pm from Paris) This bus runs to/from the metro station Denfert Rochereau in southern Paris, making several stops en route.

➡ **Tramway T7** (€1.70, every six minutes, 40 minutes, 5.30am to 12.30am Monday to Saturday, 6.30am to 12.30am Sunday) In service since the end of 2013, this tramway links Orly with Villejuif-Louis Aragon metro station in southern Paris; buy tickets from the machine at the tram stop as no tickets are sold onboard. Pick up traffic updates on Twitter @T7_RATP.

Beauvais Airport

Aéroport de Beauvais (BVA; ☎08 92 68 20 66; www.aeroportbeauvais.com) is 75km north of Paris and is served by a few low-cost airlines.

Before you snap up that bargain, consider if the post-arrival journey is worth it.

➡ **Shuttle** (€17, 1¼ hours) The Beauvais shuttle bus links the airport with metro station Porte de Maillot. See the airport website for details and tickets.

Gare d'Austerlitz

Gare d'Austerlitz is the terminus for a handful of trains from the south, including services from Orléans and Limoges. High-speed trains to/from Barcelona also use Austerlitz. Current renovations will continue until 2020.

Gare de l'Est

Gare de l'Est is the terminus for trains from Strasbourg, Berlin and Vienna. Located in northern Paris.

Gare de Lyon

Gare de Lyon is the terminus for trains from Provence, the Alps, the Riviera and Italy. Also serves Geneva. Located in eastern Paris.

Gare Montparnasse

Gare Montparnasse is the terminus for trains from the southwest and west, including services from Brittany, the Loire, Bordeaux, Toulouse and Spain and Portugal. Some of these services will eventually move to Gare d'Austerlitz (by 2020 once refurbishment is complete). Located in southern Paris.

Gare St-Lazare

Gare St-Lazare is the terminus for trains from Normandy. Located in Clichy, western Paris.

Gare Routiére Internationale de Paris-Galliéni

Eurolines (www.eurolines.fr) connects all major European capitals to Paris' international bus terminal, **Gare Routiére Internationale de Paris-Galliéni** (☎08 92 89 90 91; 28 av du Général de Gaulle; Ⓜ Galliéni). The terminal is in the eastern suburb of Bagnolet; it's about a 15-minute metro ride to the more central République station.

GETTING AROUND PARIS

Getting around Paris is comparatively easy for a big city. Most visitors combine the efficient metro with walking. Buses offer a good view of the city, but can be hard to figure out and slowed by traffic. More tempting is the city's communal bike-share scheme, Vélib'.

Underground Rail

Paris' underground network is run by RATP and consists of two separate but linked systems: the metro and the Réseau Express Régional (RER) suburban train line. The metro has 14 numbered lines; the RER has five main lines (but you'll probably only need to use A, B and C). When buying tickets consider how many zones your journey will cover: there are five concentric transportation zones rippling out from Paris (5 being the furthest), so if you travel from Charles de Gaulle airport to Paris, for instance, you will have to buy a zone 1–5 ticket.

For information on the metro, RER and bus systems, visit www.ratp.fr. Metro maps of various sizes and degrees of detail are available for free at metro ticket windows; several can also be downloaded for free from the RATP website.

Metro

➡ Metro lines are identified by both their number (eg ligne 1; line 1) and their colour, listed on official metro signs and maps.

➡ Signs in metro and RER stations indicate the way to the correct platform for your line. The *direction* signs on each platform indicate the terminus. On lines that split into several branches (such as lines 7 and 13), the terminus of each train is indicated on the cars and on signs on each platform giving the number of minutes until the next and subsequent train.

➡ Signs marked *correspondance* (transfer) show how to reach connecting trains. At stations with many intersecting lines, like Châtelet and Montparnasse Bienvenüe, walking from one platform to the next can take a very long time.

➡ Different station exits are indicated by white-on-blue *sortie* (exit) signs. You can get your bearings by checking the *plan du quartier* (neighbourhood maps) posted at exits.

➡ Each line has its own schedule but trains usually start at around 5.30am, with the last train beginning its run between 12.35am and 1.15am (2.15am on Friday and Saturday).

RER

➡ The RER is faster than the metro but the stops are much further apart. Some attractions, particularly those on the Left Bank (eg the Musée d'Orsay, Eiffel Tower and Panthéon), can be reached far more conveniently by the RER than by the metro.

➡ If you're going out to the suburbs (eg Versailles, Disneyland), ask for help on the platform – finding the right train can be confusing. Also make sure your ticket is for the correct zone.

NAVIGO PASS

If you're staying in Paris longer than a few days, the cheapest and easiest way to use public transport is to get a combined travel pass that allows unlimited travel on the metro, RER and buses for a week, a month or even a year. You can get passes for travel in two to five zones but, unless you'll be using the suburban commuter lines extensively, the basic ticket valid for zones 1 and 2 should be sufficient.

Navigo (www.navigo.fr), like London's Oyster or Hong Kong's Octopus cards, is a system that provides you with a refillable weekly, monthly or yearly unlimited pass that you can recharge at machines in most metro stations. To pass through the station barrier swipe the card across the electronic panel as you go through the turnstiles. Standard Navigo passes, available to anyone with an address in Île de France, are free but take up to three weeks to be issued; ask at the ticket counter for a form or order online via the Navigo website. Otherwise pay €5 for a Navigo Découverte (Navigo Discovery) card, which is issued on the spot but (unlike the standard Navigo pass) not replaceable if lost or stolen. Both passes require a passport photo and can be recharged for periods of one week or more.

A weekly pass costs €20.40 for zones 1 and 2 and is valid Monday to Sunday. It can be purchased from the previous Friday until Thursday; from the next day weekly tickets are available for the following week only. Even if you're in Paris for three or four days, it may work out cheaper than buying *carnets* and will certainly cost less than buying a daily Mobilis or Paris Visite pass. The monthly pass (€67.10 for zones 1 and 2) begins on the first day of each calendar month; you can buy one from the 20th of the preceding month. Both are sold in metro and RER stations from 6.30am to 10pm and at some bus terminals.

Navigo cards can be recharged online.

Tickets & Fares

- The same RATP tickets are valid on the metro, the RER (for travel within the city limits), buses, trams and the Montmartre funicular.
- A ticket – white in colour and called *Le Ticket t+* – costs €1.70 (half price for children aged four to nine years) if bought individually and €13.70 for adults for a *carnet* (book) of 10.
- Tickets are sold at all metro stations. Ticket windows accept most credit cards; however, automated machines *do not* accept North American credit cards.
- One ticket lets you travel between any two metro stations (no return journeys) for a period of 1½ hours, no matter how many transfers are required. You can also use it on the RER for travel within zone 1, which encompasses all of central Paris.
- A single ticket can be used to transfer between buses, but not to transfer from the metro to bus or vice-versa. Transfers are not allowed on Noctilien buses.
- Always keep your ticket until you exit from your station; if you are stopped by a ticket inspector, you will have to pay a fine if you don't have a valid ticket.

TOURIST PASSES

The Mobilis and Paris Visite passes are valid on the metro, RER, SNCF's suburban lines, buses, night buses, trams and Montmartre funicular railway. No photo is needed, but write your card number on the ticket. Passes are sold at larger metro and RER stations, SNCF offices in Paris, and the airports.

The Mobilis card allows unlimited travel for one day and costs €6.80 (two zones) to €16.10 (five zones). Buy it at any metro, RER or SNCF station in the Paris region. Depending on how many times you plan to hop on/off the metro in a day, a *carnet* might work out cheaper.

Paris Visite allows unlimited travel as well as discounted entry to certain museums and other discounts and bonuses. The 'Paris+Suburbs+Airports' pass includes transport to/from the airports and costs €22.85/34.70/48.65/59.50 for one/two/three/five days. The cheaper 'Paris Centre' pass, valid for zones 1 to 3, costs €10.85/17.65/24.10/34.70 for one/two/three/five days. Children aged four to 11 years pay half price.

Bicycle

Vélib'

The **Vélib'** (http://en.velib.paris.fr; day/week subscription €1.70/8, bike hire up to 30min/60min/90min/2hr free/€1/2/4) bike share scheme puts 20,000-odd bikes at the disposal of Parisians and visitors to get around the city. There are some 1800 stations throughout the city, each with anywhere from 20 to 70 bike stands. The bikes are accessible around the clock.

➡ To get a bike, you first need to purchase a one-/seven-day subscription (€1.70/8). There are two ways to do this: either at the terminals found at docking stations or online.

➡ The terminals require a credit card with an embedded smartchip – this means the majority of North Americans cannot subscribe here. But fret not because you can purchase a subscription online. Just be sure to do this before you leave your hotel.

➡ After you authorise a refundable deposit (€150) to pay for the bike should it go missing, you'll receive an ID number and PIN code and you're ready to go.

➡ Bikes are rented in 30-minute intervals: the first half-hour is free, the second is €2, the third and each additional half-hour are €4. If you return a bike before a half-hour is up and then take a new one, you will not be charged.

➡ If the station you want to return your bike to is full, log in to the terminal to get 15 minutes for free to find another station.

➡ Bikes are geared to cyclists aged 14 and over, and are fitted with gears, an antitheft lock with key, reflective strips and front/rear lights. Bring your own helmet (they are not required by law).

➡ In June 2014 the city of Paris launched P'tits Vélib', a bike-sharing scheme for children aged two to 10 years, with bike stations in five sites, including Bois de Bologne, Bois de Vincennes and Les Berges de Seine.

Rentals

Most rental places will require a deposit. Take ID and bank card/credit card.

Au Point Vélo Hollandais (☎01 43 45 85 36; www.pointvelo.com; 83 bd St-Michel, 5e; per day €15; ⏰10.30am-7.30pm Mon-Sat; Ⓜ Cluny-La Sorbonne or RER Luxembourg)

Freescoot (☎01 44 07 06 72; www.freescoot.com; 63 quai de la Tournelle, 5e; bike/tandem from €15/30; ⏰9am-1pm & 2-7pm Mon-Sat year-round, plus Sun mid-Apr–mid-Sep; Ⓜ Maubert-Mutualité)

Gepetto et Vélos (☎01 43 54 19 95; www.gepetto-velos.com; 59 rue du Cardinal Lemoine, 5e; per day €16; ⏰9am-2pm & 3-7pm Tue-Sat year-round, plus Sun mid-Apr–mid-Sep; Ⓜ Cardinal Lemoine)

Paris à Vélo, C'est Sympa (☎01 48 87 60 01; www.parisvelosympa.com; 22 rue Alphonse Baudin, 11e; per day €20; ⏰9.30am-1pm & 2-6pm Mon-Fri, 9am-7pm Sat & Sun Apr-Oct, shorter hours winter; Ⓜ St-Sébastien Froissart)

TREASURE HUNTS

'Treasure hunts' organised by **THATLou** (☎06 86 13 32 12; www.thatlou.com; per person excluding admission fees Louvre/d'Orsay €25/35) inject fun into the potentially tricky affair of navigating some of the city's most vast and overwhelming sights, including the Louvre, Musée d'Orsay and the Latin Quarter. Hunts are in English or French, can be for two people or more, and typically last two hours. Participants form teams (to play alone or against another team) and have to photograph themselves in front of 20 to 30 works of arts ('treasure'). Most hunts are themed – at the Louvre there are 12 themes to choose from, including Love, Kings & Leaders, Beauty & Beasts and so forth – and Daisy de Plume, the talented bilingual hunt creator, also puts together customised hunts.

Bus

Buses can be a fun way to get around – and there are no stairs to climb, meaning they are more widely accessible – but they're slower and less intuitive to figure out than the metro.

Local Buses

Paris' bus system, operated by RATP, runs from 5.30am to 8.30pm Monday to Saturday; after that, certain evening-service lines continue until between midnight and 12.30am. Services are drastically reduced on Sunday and public holidays, when buses run from 7am to 8.30pm.

Night Buses

The RATP runs 47 night bus lines known as **Noctilien** (www.noctilien.fr), which depart hourly from 12.30am to 5.30am. The services pass through the main *gares* (train stations) and cross the major axes of the city before leading out to the suburbs. Look for navy-blue N or Noctilien signs at bus stops. There are two circular lines within Paris (the N01 and N02) that link four main train stations – St-Lazare, Gare de l'Est, Gare de Lyon and Gare Montparnasse – as well as popular nightlife areas (Bastille, Champs-Élysées, Pigalle, St-Germain).

Noctilien services are included on your Mobilis or Paris Visite pass for the zones in which you are travelling. Otherwise you pay a certain number of standard €1.70 metro/bus tickets, depending on the length of your journey.

Tickets & Fares

Normal bus rides embracing one or two bus zones cost

one metro ticket; longer rides require two or even three tickets. Transfers to other buses – but not the metro – are allowed on the same ticket as long as the change takes place 1½ hours between the first and last validation. This does not apply to Noctilien services.

Whatever kind of single-journey ticket you have, you must validate it in the ticket machine near the driver. If you don't have a ticket, the driver can sell you one for €2. If you have a Mobilis or Paris Visite pass, flash it at the driver when you board.

Boat

Batobus (www.batobus.com; Port de Solférino, 7e; 1-/2-day pass €16/18; ⏲10am-9.30pm Apr-Aug, to 7pm rest of year) runs glassed-in trimarans that dock every 20 to 25 minutes at eight small piers along the Seine: Eiffel Tower, Musée d'Orsay, St-Germain des Prés, Notre Dame, Jardin des Plantes, Hôtel de Ville, Musée du Louvre and Champs-Élysées.

Buy tickets online, at ferry stops or tourist offices. You can also buy a two-/three-day ticket that also covers L'Open Tour buses for €45/49.

Taxi

➡ The *prise en charge* (flagfall) is €2.50. Within the city limits, it costs €1 per kilometre for travel between 10am and 5pm Monday to Saturday (*Tarif A;* white light on taxi roof and meter).

➡ At night (5pm to 10am), on Sunday from 7am to midnight, and in the inner suburbs the rate is €1.24 per km (*Tarif B;* orange light).

➡ Travel in the outer suburbs is at *Tarif C*, €1.50 per kilometre (blue light).

➡ There's a €3 surcharge for taking a fourth passenger, but drivers sometimes refuse for insurance reasons. The first piece of baggage is free; additional pieces over 5kg cost €1 extra.

➡ Flagging down a taxi in Paris can be difficult; it's best to find an official taxi stand.

➡ To order a taxi, call or reserve online with **Taxis G7** (☎36 07; www.taxisg7.fr), **Taxis Bleus** (☎01 49 36 10 10; www.taxis-bleus.com) or **Alpha Taxis** (☎01 45 85 85 85; www.alphataxis.com).

➡ Increasingly big in Paris is **Uber** (www.uber.com/cities/paris) taxi, whereby you order a taxi and pay via your smartphone.

Car & Motorcycle

Driving in Paris is defined by the triple hassle of navigation, heavy traffic and parking. It doesn't make sense to use a car to get around, but if you're heading out of the city on an excursion, then your own set of wheels can certainly be useful. If you plan on hiring a car, it's best to do it online and in advance.

Autolib'

Paris' electric-car-share program, **Autolib'** (www.autolib.eu), is similar to bike-share scheme Vélib': pay €9 per half hour to rent a GPS-equipped car in 30-minute intervals, or subscribe for a week/month (€10/25) to benefit from cheaper rates (€7/6.50 per half-hour). Cars can be picked up/dropped off at 1000 available stations around the city and are designed only for short hops; the car battery is good for 250km. Carry your driver's licence and photo ID.

Scooters

Freescoot (☎01 44 07 06 72; www.freescoot.com; 63 quai de la Tournelle, 5e; ⏲9am-1pm & 2-5pm, closed Sun Oct-May) Rents 50/125cc scooters in various intervals (per 24 hours €55/65). Prices include third-party insurance as well as helmets, locks, raingear and gloves. To rent a 50/125cc scooter you must be at least 21/23 years old, respectively, and leave a refundable credit card deposit of €1300/1600. No licence required for smaller scooters.

Left Bank Scooters (☎06 82 70 13 82; www.leftbankscooters.com) Run by a young Australian-British couple, this outfit rents pastel-coloured Vespa XLV 50/125cc scooters for 24 hours at €70/80, including insurance, helmet and wet-weather gear. To rent a 50/125cc scooter, you must be at least 18/20 years old and have a car or motorcycle licence. Credit-card deposit is €1000. This place runs tours as well.

Parking

Parking meters in Paris do not accept coins but require either a chip-enabled credit card or a Paris Carte, available at any *tabac* (tobacconist) for €10 to €30. The machine will issue you a ticket for the allotted time, which should be placed on the dashboard behind the windscreen. Municipal public car parks, of which there are more than 200 in Paris, charge between €2 and €3.50 an hour or €20 to €25 per 24 hours. Most are open 24 hours.

TOURS

Bicycle

Bike About Tours (☎06 18 80 84 92; www.bikeabouttours.com; 4 rue de Lobau, 4e; Ⓜ Hôtel de Ville) This expat-run tour group offers daytime city tours (€30, 3½ hours), trips to Versailles (€80), e-bike tours to Champagne (€135) and private family tours.

HANDS-ON TOURS

Make-up workshops, backstage cabaret tours, fashion designer showroom visits, French table decoration or art embroidery classes, market tours, baking with a Parisian baker: the repertoire of cultural and gourmet tours and behind-the-scenes experiences offered by **Meeting the French** (www.meetingthefrench.fr) is truly outstanding.

Fat Tire Bike Tours (☎01 56 58 10 54; www.fattirebiketours.com) Day and night bike tours of the city, both in central Pais and further afield to Versailles and Monet's garden in Giverny.

Paris à Vélo, C'est Sympa! (☎01 48 87 60 01; www.parisvelosympa.com) Four guided bike tours (adult/child €35/20, three hours), including an evening cycle and a sunrise tour.

Boat

A boat cruise down the Seine is the most relaxing way to watch the city glide by – and is a wonderful way for Paris first-timers to get a quick introduction to the city's main monuments.

Bateaux Parisiens (www.bateauxparisiens.com; Port de la Bourdonnais, 7e; adult/child €14/6; MBir Hakeim or RER Pont de l'Alma) This vast operation runs 1½-hour river circuits with recorded commentary in 13 languages (every 30 minutes 10am to 10.30pm April to September, hourly 10am to 10pm October to March), and a host of themed lunch/dinner cruises. It has two locations: one by the Eiffel Tower, the other south of Notre Dame.

Bateaux-Mouches (☎01 42 25 96 10; www.bateaux-mouches.com; Port de la Conférence, 8e; adult/child €13.50/5.50; ⏱Apr-Dec; MAlma Marceau) The largest river cruise company in Paris and a favourite with tour groups. Cruises (70 minutes) run regularly from 10.15am to 11pm April to September and 13 times a day between 11am and 9pm the rest of the year. Commentary is in French and English. It's located on the Right Bank, just east of the Pont de l'Alma.

Vedettes de Paris (☎01 44 18 19 50; www.vedettesdeparis.fr; Port de Suffren, 7e; adult/child €14/6; MBir Hakeim or Pont de l'Alma) It might be a small company but its one-hour sightseeing cruises on smaller boats are second to none. It runs themed cruises too, including imaginative 'Paris mystery' tours for kids and boats along the river to Cathédrale de Notre Dame (adult single/return ticket €8/14).

Vedettes du Pont Neuf (☎01 46 33 98 38; www.vedettesdupontneuf.fr; Square du Vert Galant, 1er; adult/child €14/7, internet ticket €10/5; MPont Neuf) This company runs one-hour cruises year-round from its centrally located dock at the western tip of Île de la Cité; tickets are cheaper if you buy in advance online. Check its website for details of the wonderful 'Concerts en Seine' the boat company organises – classical music afloat after dusk (tickets €30 to €40).

Bus

Big Bus Paris (http://fra.bigbustours.com; 1-day pass adult/child €29/16) Paris' Les Cars Rouges merged with London's Big Bus Company to create Big Bus Paris. City bus tours are hop-on-off style, with 10 stops around the city. App for iPhone or Android available.

L'Open Tour (www.parisopentour.com; one-day pass adult/child €31/16) Hop-on, hop-off bus tours aboard open-deck buses with four different circuits and 50 stops to jump on/off at – tops for a whirlwind city tour.

Walking

Ça Se Visite (www.ca-se-visite.fr; adult/child on foot €12/10, scooter €15/13) Meet local artists and craftspeople on resident-led 'urban discovery tours' of the northeast (Belleville, Ménilmontant, Canal Saint-Martin, Canal de l'Ourcq, Oberkampf, La Villette) – on foot or *trottinette* (scooter).

Eye Prefer Paris (www.eyeprefe rparistours.com; 3 people €210) New Yorker-turned-Parisian Richard Nahem leads offbeat tours of the city.

Localers (www.localers.com; cost varies) Classic walking tours and behind-the-scenes urban discoveries with local Paris experts: *pétanque*, photo shoots, market tours, cooking classes, foie gras-tasting et al.

Parisien d'un jour – Paris Greeters (www.parisgreeters.fr; by donation) See Paris through local eyes with these two- to three-hour city tours. Volunteers – knowledgeable Parisians passionate about their city in the main – lead groups (maximum six people) to their favourite spots. Minimum two weeks' notice needed.

Paris Walks (☎01 48 09 21 40; www.paris-walks.com; adult/child €12/8) Long established and highly rated by our readers, Paris Walks offers two-hour thematic walking tours (art, fashion, chocolate, the French Revolution etc).

Directory A–Z

Customs Regulations

Residents of non-EU countries must adhere to the following limits:

- **Alcohol** 4L of wine and 1L of spirits
- **Perfume** 50g of perfume and 250cc of eau de toilette
- **Tobacco** 200 cigarettes, 50 cigars or 250g of loose tobacco

For visitors from EU countries, limits only apply for excessive amounts; see www.douane.gouv.fr.

Discount Cards

Almost all museums and monuments in Paris have discounted tickets *(tarif réduit)* for students and seniors (generally over 60 years), provided you have a valid ID. Children often get in for free; the cut-off age for 'child' is anywhere between six and 18 years.

EU citizens under 26 years get in for free at national monuments and museums.

Paris Museum Pass (http://en.parismuseumpass.com; 2/4/6 days €42/56/69) Gets you into 60-odd venues in and around Paris; a huge advantage is that pass holders usually enter larger sights at a different entrance meaning you bypass (or substantially reduce) ridiculously long ticket queues.

Paris City Passport (www.parisinfo.com; 2/3/5 days €71/103/130) Sold at the **Paris Convention & Visitors Bureau** (Office du Tourisme et des Congrès de Paris; www.parisinfo.com; 27 rue des Pyramides, 1er; ⌚9am-7pm May-Oct, 10am-7pm Nov-Apr; ⓂPyramides) and on its website, this handy city pass covers unlimited public transport, admission to some 60 museums in the Paris region (aka a Paris Museum Pass), and a 1hr boat cruise along the Seine. Three- and five-day passes include a hop-on-off open-top bus sightseeing service around central Paris' key sights with **Big Bus Paris** (http://fra.bigbustours.com; 1-day pass adult/child €29/16).

Emergency

- Ambulance (SAMU): ☎15
- Fire: ☎18
- Police: ☎17
- EU-wide emergency: ☎112

Internet Access

Wi-fi (pronounced '*wee*-fee' in France) is available in most Paris hotels, usually at no extra cost, and in some museums.

Free wi-fi is available in 260 public places, including parks, libraries and municipal buildings, between 7am and 11pm daily. In parks look for a purple 'Zone Wi-Fi' sign near the entrance. To connect, select the 'PARIS_WI-FI_' network and connect; sessions are limited to two hours. For complete details and a map of hot spots see www.paris.fr/wifi.

Expect to pay between €4 and €5 per hour for online access in internet cafes; **Milk** (www.milklub.com; 31 bd Sebastopol, 1er; 1/2/3 hr €3.90/6.90/8.90; ⌚24hr; ⓂLes Halles) has several branches in central Paris.

Electricity

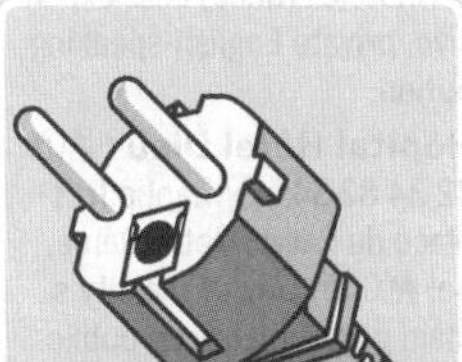

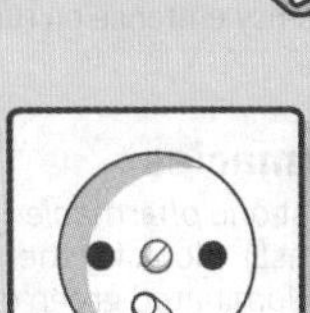

230V/50Hz

Legal Matters

If the police stop you for any reason, be polite and remain calm. They have wide powers of search and seizure and can, without any particular reason, decide to examine your passport, visa, *carte de séjour* (residence permit) and so on. (You are expected to have photo ID on you at *all* times.) Do *not* challenge them.

French police are strict about security. Do not leave baggage unattended; they are quite serious when they say that suspicious objects will be summarily blown up.

Medical Services

Hospitals

Paris has some 50 hospitals including the following:

American Hospital of Paris (☎01 46 41 25 25; www.american-hospital.org; 63 bd Victor Hugo, Neuilly-sur-Seine; Ⓜ Pont de Levallois) Private hospital; emergency 24-hour medical and dental care.

Hertford British Hospital (☎01 47 59 59 59; www.ihfb.org; 3 rue Barbès, Levallois; Ⓜ Anatole France) Less expensive, private English-speaking option.

Hôpital Hôtel Dieu (☎01 42 34 82 34; www.aphp.fr; 1 place du Parvis Notre Dame, 4e; Ⓜ Cité) One of the city's main government-run public hospitals; after 8pm use the emergency entrance on rue de la Cité.

Pharmacies

At least one *pharmacie* (chemist) – look for the large illuminated green cross outside – in each neighbourhood is open with extended hours; find a complete night-owl listing on the Paris Convention & Visitors Bureau website (www.parisinfo.com).

PRACTICALITIES

➜ **Classifieds** Pick up the free FUSAC (France USA Contacts; wwww.fusac.fr) in Anglophone haunts in Paris for classified ads about housing, babysitting, French lessons, part-time jobs and so forth.

➜ **Newspapers and magazines** Parisians read their news in centre-left *Le Monde* (www.lemonde.fr), right-leaning *Le Figaro* (www.lefigaro.fr) and left-leaning *Libération* (www.liberation.fr). *Metro* (http://readmetro.metrofrance.com) is the freebie to pick up outside metro stations, and *Le Parisien* (www.leparisien.fr) is the city-news read.

➜ **Smoking** Smoking is illegal in indoor public spaces, including restaurants and bars (hence the crowds of smokers in doorways and pavement terraces outside).

➜ **TV and DVDs** TV is Secam; DVDs use the PAL system.

➜ **Weights and measures** Paris uses the metric system.

Pharmacie Bader (☎01 43 26 92 66; www.pharmacie-bader.com; 10-12 bd St-Michel, 6e; ⏲9am-9pm; Ⓜ St-Michel)

Pharmacie de la Mairie (☎01 42 78 53 58; http://pharmacie-mairie-paris.com; 9 rue des Archives, 4e; ⏲9am-8pm; Ⓜ Hôtel de Ville)

Pharmacie Les Champs (☎01 45 62 02 41; Galerie des Champs-Élysées, 84 av des Champs-Élysées, 8e; ⏲24hr; Ⓜ George V)

Money

France uses the euro (€), which is divided into 100 centimes. Denominations are €5, €10, €20, €50, €100, €200 and €500 notes, and €0.01, €0.02, €0.05, €0.10, €0.20, €0.50, €1 and €2 coins.

French vendors can be ornery when it comes to breaking a €50 note – don't even bother with bills larger than this.

Check the latest exchange rates on websites such as www.xe.com.

ATMs

ATMs (*distributeur automatique de billets* in French) are widespread. Unless you have particularly high transaction fees, ATMs are usually the best and easiest way to deal with currency exchange. French banks don't generally charge fees to use their ATMs but check with your own bank before you travel to know if/how much they charge for international cash withdrawals.

Changing Money

Cash is not a good way to carry money; it can be stolen and in France you often won't get the best exchange rates.

In Paris, *bureaux de change* are usually more efficient, open longer hours and give better rates than banks – many banks don't even offer exchange services.

Bureaux de change charge anything from 6% to 13% plus €3 or €4 on cash transactions, and 6% to just under 10% (plus €3) to change travellers cheques.

Credit Cards

Visa/Carte Bleue is the most widely accepted credit card in Paris, followed by MasterCard (Eurocard). Amex cards can be useful at more upmarket establishments. In general, all three cards can be used to pay for train travel and restaurant meals and for cash advances. Note that France uses a smartcard with an embedded microchip and PIN. North Americans will thus not be able to use their credit cards at automated machines (such as at a metro station or museum) – they'll have to buy from the ticket window.

Tipping

French law requires that restaurant, cafe and hotel bills include a service charge (usually between 12% and 15%). Taxi drivers expect small tips of between 5% and 10% of the fare, though the usual procedure is to round up to the nearest €1 regardless of the fare.

Travellers Cheques

The most flexible travellers cheques are issued by Amex (in US dollars or euros) and Visa, as they can be changed at many post offices.

Opening Hours

The following list shows *approximate* standard opening hours for businesses. Hours can vary by season; our listings depict peak-season operating hours. Many businesses close for the entire month of August for summer holidays.

- **Banks** 9am-1pm & 2-5pm Mon-Fri, some Sat morning
- **Bars and cafes** 7am-2am
- **Museums** 10am-6pm, closed Mon or Tue
- **Post offices** 8am-7pm Mon-Fri & till noon Sat
- **Restaurants** noon-2pm & 7.30-10.30pm
- **Shops (clothing)** 10am-7pm Mon-Sat, occasionally close in the early afternoon for lunch
- **Shops (food)** 8am-1pm & 4-7.30pm, closed Sun afternoon & sometimes Mon

Post

Most post offices *(bureaux de poste)* are open Monday to Saturday. *Tabacs* (tobacconists) usually sell postage stamps.

The main **post office** (www.laposte.fr; 52 rue du Louvre, 1er; ⏲24hr; Ⓜ Sentier or Les Halles), five blocks north of the eastern end of the Musée du Louvre, is open round the clock, but only for basic services such as sending letters. Other services, including currency exchange, are available only during regular opening hours. Be prepared for long queues.

Each *arrondissement* has its own five-digit postcode, formed by prefixing the number of the *arrondissement* with '750' or '7500' (eg 75001 for the 1er *arrondissement*, 75019 for the 19e). The only exception is the 16e, which has two postcodes: 75016 and 75116. All mail to addresses in France *must* include the postcode.

Public Holidays

There is close to one public holiday a month in France and, in some years, up to four in May alone. Be aware, though, that unlike in the USA or UK, where public holidays usually fall on (or are shifted to) a Monday, in France a *jour férié* (public holiday) is celebrated strictly on the day on which it falls. Thus if May Day falls on a Saturday or Sunday, no provision is made for an extra day off.

The following holidays are observed in Paris:

- **New Year's Day** (Jour de l'An) 1 January
- **Easter Sunday & Monday** (Pâques & Lundi de Pâques) Late March/April
- **May Day** (Fête du Travail) 1 May
- **Victory in Europe Day** (Victoire 1945) 8 May
- **Ascension Thursday** (L'Ascension) May (celebrated on the 40th day after Easter)
- **Whit Monday** (Lundi de Pentecôte) Mid-May to mid-June (seventh Monday after Easter)
- **Bastille Day/National Day** (Fête Nationale) 14 July
- **Assumption Day** (L'Assomption) 15 August
- **All Saints' Day** (La Toussaint) 1 November
- **Armistice Day/Remembrance Day** (Le Onze Novembre) 11 November
- **Christmas** (Noël) 25 December

Safe Travel

In general, Paris is a safe city and random street assaults are rare. The city is generally well lit and there's no reason not to use the metro until it stops running, at some time between 12.30am and just past 1am. As you'll notice, women *do* travel alone on the metro late at night in most areas, though not all who do so report feeling 100% comfortable.

Metro stations that are best avoided late at night include Châtelet–Les Halles and its seemingly endless corridors, Château Rouge in Montmartre, Gare du Nord, Strasbourg St-Denis, Réaumur Sébastopol and Montparnasse Bienvenüe. *Bornes d'alarme* (alarm boxes) are located in the centre of each metro/RER platform and in some station corridors.

Nonviolent crime such as pickpocketing and thefts from handbags and packs is a problem wherever there are crowds, especially packs of tourists. Places to be particularly careful include Montmartre (especially around Sacré Cœur); Pigalle; the areas around Forum des Halles and the Centre Pompidou; the Latin Quarter (especially the rectangle bounded by rue St-Jacques, bd St-Germain, bd St-Michel and quai St-Michel); below the Eiffel Tower; and anywhere on the metro during rush hour (particularly on line 4 and the western part of line 1).

Take the usual precautions: don't carry more money than you need, and keep your credit cards, passport and other documents in a concealed pouch, a hotel safe or a safe-deposit box.

Vigipirate is a security plan devised by the Paris city council to combat terrorism. Both citizens and visitors are asked to report any abandoned luggage or package at all times. When the full Vigipirate scheme is put into action, public litter bins are sealed, left-luggage services in train stations and at airports are unavailable, checks at the entrances to public buildings and tourist sites are increased, and cloakrooms and lockers in museums and at monuments are closed.

Taxes & Refunds

France's value-added tax (VAT) is known as TVA *(taxe sur la valeur ajoutée)* and is 20% on most goods with a few exceptions: for food products and books it's 5.5%, and for medicines it is 2.1%. Prices that include TVA are often marked TTC (*toutes taxes comprises;* literally 'all taxes included').

If you're not an EU resident, you can get a TVA refund provided that: you're aged over 15; you'll be spending less than six months in France; you purchase goods worth at least €175 at a single shop on the same day (not more than 10 of the same item); the goods fit into your luggage; you are taking the goods out of France within three months of purchase; and the shop offers *vente en détaxe* (duty-free sales).

Present a passport at the time of purchase and ask for a *bordereau de vente à l'exportation* (export sales invoice) to be signed by the retailer and yourself. Most shops will refund less than the full amount (about 14%) to which you are entitled, in order to cover the time and expense involved in the refund procedure.

As you leave France or another EU country, have all three pages of the *bordereau* validated by the country's customs officials at the airport or at the border. Customs officials will take one sheet and hand you two. You must post one copy (the pink one) back to the shop and retain the other (green) sheet for your records in case there is any dispute. Once the shop where you made your purchase receives its stamped copy, it will send you a *virement* (fund transfer) in the form you have requested. Be prepared for a wait of up to three months.

If you're flying out of Orly or Charles de Gaulle, certain shops can arrange for you to receive your refund as you're leaving the country, though you must complete the steps outlined above. You must make such arrangements at the time of purchase.

For more information contact the **customs information centre** (☎08 11 20 44 44; www.douane.minefi.gouv.fr; ⏰8.30am-6pm Mon-Fri).

Telephone

There are no area codes in France – you always dial the 10-digit number.

Telephone numbers in Paris always start with 01, unless the number is provided by an internet service provider (ISP), in which case it begins with 09.

Mobile phone numbers throughout France commence with either 06 or 07.

France's country code is 33.

To call abroad from Paris, dial France's international access code (00), the country code, the area code (usually without the initial '0', if there is one) and the local number. International Direct Dial (IDD) calls to almost anywhere in the world can be placed from public telephones. The international reduced rate applies from 7pm to 8am weekdays and all day at the weekend.

Note that while numbers beginning with 08 00, 08 04, 08 05 and 08 09 are toll-free in France, other numbers beginning with 08 are not (costs per minute range from €0.09 to €0.75).

Customer service numbers are generally more expensive than local rates.

Most four-digit numbers starting with 10, 30 or 31 are free of charge.

If you can read basic French, directory enquiries are best done via the *Yellow Pages* (www.pagesjaunes.fr; click on Pages Blanches for the *White Pages*), which will provide more information, including maps, for free. From a mobile phone, use the site http://mobile.pagesjaunes.fr.

Mobile Phones

You can use your mobile/cell phone *(portable)* in France provided it is GSM (the standard in Europe, which is becoming increasingly common elsewhere) and tri-band or quad-band. If you meet the requirements, you can check with your service provider about using it in France, but beware of roaming costs, especially for data.

Rather than staying on your home network, it is usually more convenient to buy a local SIM card from a French provider such as **Orange** (www.orange.fr), **SFR** (www.sfr.fr), **Bouygues** (www.bouyguestelecom.fr) and **Free Mobile** (http://mobile.free.fr) which will give you a local phone number. In order for this to work, you'll need to ensure your phone is 'unlocked', which means you can use another service provider.

Count on paying between €1.90 and €5 for the initial SIM card (with a few minutes of calls included), then €5 for a prepaid Mobicarte recharge card covering anything from €5 to €100 worth of calls plus unlimited texts within France. Deals obviously vary between service providers, so check online what each is currently offering before leaving home. *Tabacs* (tobacconists), mobile phone outlets such as **La Boutique Orange** (16 place de la Madeleine, 8e; ⏲10am-7pm Mon-Sat; Ⓜ Madeleine), supermarkets etc sell Mobicartes.

Phonecards

Although mobile phones and Skype may have killed off the need for public phones, they do still exist. In France they are all phonecard-operated, but in an emergency you can use your credit card to call.

A *télécarte* (phonecard; €7.50/15 for 50/120 calling units) can be purchased at post offices, *tabacs*, supermarkets, SNCF ticket windows, metro stations and anywhere you see a blue sticker reading '*télécarte en vente ici*' (phonecard for sale here).

You can buy prepaid phonecards such as **Allomundo** (www.allomundo.com) that are up to 60% cheaper for calling abroad than the standard *télécarte*. They're usually available in denominations of up to €15 from *tabacs*, newsagents, phone shops and other sales points, especially in ethnic areas such as rue du Faubourg St-Denis (10e), Chinatown (13e) and Belleville (19e and 20e). In general they're valid for two months, but the ones offering the most minutes for the least euros can expire in just a week.

All public phones can receive both domestic and international calls. If you want someone to call you back, just give them France's country code (33) and the 10-digit number, usually written after the words '*Ici le...*' or '*No d'appel*' on the tariff sheet or on a little sign inside the phone box. Remind them to drop the '0' from the initial '01' of the number. When there's an incoming call, the words '*décrochez – appel arrive*' (pick up receiver – incoming call) will appear in the LCD window.

CHARGING DEVICES

There is talk of public transport company RATP jazzing up bus stops of the future with phone-charging stations, but until then charging phones and other devices on the move remains challenging. Carrying your own charger and cable ups the odds dramatically of getting more juice – don't be shy to ask in cafes and restaurants if you can plug in and charge. Ditto for taxi drivers, an increasing number of whom carry a selection of smartphone-compatible cables and chargers. It's easy to recharge at **Bibliothèque Nationale de France** (☎01 53 79 59 59; www.bnf.fr; 11 quai François Mauriac, 13e; temporary exhibitions adult/child from €9/free; ⏲exhibitions 10am-7pm Tue-Sat, 1-7pm Sun, closed early-late Sep; Ⓜ Bibliothèque). Or do it yourself at Gare de Nord, Gare de Montparnasse or Gare de St-Lazare at a pedal-powered charging station.

Time

France uses the 24-hour clock in most cases, with the hours usually separated from the minutes by a lower-case 'h'. Thus, 15h30 is 3.30pm, 00h30 is 12.30am and so on.

France is on Central European Time (like Berlin and Rome), which is one hour ahead of GMT. When it's noon in Paris it's 11am in London, 3am in San Francisco, 6am in New York and and 9pm in Sydney.

Daylight-saving time runs from the last Sunday in March to the last Sunday in October.

Toilets

Public toilets in Paris are signposted *toilettes* or *WC*. The self-cleaning cylindrical toilets you see on Parisian pavements are open 24 hours, are reasonably clean and are free of charge, though, of course, they never seem to be around when you need them. Look for the words *libre* ('available'; green-coloured) or *occupé* ('occupied'; red-coloured).

Cafe owners do not appreciate you using their facilities if you are not a paying customer; however, if you have young children they may make an exception (ask first!). When desperate, try a fast-food chain, major department store or even a big hotel.

There are free public toilets in front of Notre Dame cathedral, near the Arc de Triomphe, east down the steps at Sacré Cœur and at the northwestern entrance to the Jardins des Tuileries.

Tourist Information

The main branch of the **Paris Convention & Visitors Bureau** (Office du Tourisme et des Congrès de Paris; www.parisinfo.com; 27 rue des Pyramides, 1er; ⊙9am-7pm May-Oct, 10am-7pm Nov-Apr; Ⓜ Pyramides) is about 500m northwest of the Louvre.

The bureau maintains a handful of centres elsewhere in Paris, most of which are listed here (websites are the same as for the main office). In addition, find information desks at Charles de Gaulle Airport. For tourist information around Paris, see **Paris Region** (www.visitparisregion.com).

Gare de l'Est Welcome Desk (place du 11 Novembre 1918, 10e; ⊙8am-7pm Mon-Sat; Ⓜ Gare de l'Est) Inside Gare de l'Est train station, facing platforms 1 and 2.

Gare de Lyon Welcome Desk (20 bd Diderot, 12e; ⊙8am-6pm Mon-Sat; Ⓜ Gare de Lyon) Inside Gare de Lyon train station, facing platforms L and M.

Gare du Nord Welcome Desk (18 rue de Dunkerque, 10e; ⊙8am-6pm; Ⓜ Gare du Nord) Inside Gare du Nord station, under the glass roof of the Île de France departure and arrival area (eastern end of station).

Montmartre Welcome Desk (opp 72 bd Rochechouart, 18e; ⊙10am-6pm; Ⓜ Anvers) At the foot of Montmartre.

Syndicate d'Initiative de Montmartre (☎01 42 62 21 21; www.montmartre-guide.com; 21 place du Tertre, 18e; ⊙10am-6pm; Ⓜ Abbesses) Locally run tourist office and shop on Montmartre's most picturesque square. It sells maps of Montmartre and organises tours daily at 2.30pm.

Travellers with Disabilities

Paris is an ancient city and therefore not particularly well equipped for *visiteurs handicapés* (disabled visitors): kerb ramps are few and far between, older public facilities and budget hotels usually lack lifts, and the metro, dating back more than a century, is mostly inaccessible for those in a wheelchair *(fauteuil roulant)*.

But efforts are being made. The tourist office continues its excellent 'Tourisme & Handicap' initiative, in which museums, cultural attractions, hotels and restaurants that provide access or special assistance or facilities for those with physical, mental, visual and/or hearing disabilities display a special logo at their entrances. For a list of the ever-increasing number of places that qualify, visit the website of the Paris Convention & Visitors Bureau (www.parisinfo.com) and click on 'Practical Paris'.

Resources

For information about which cultural venues in Paris are accessible to people with disabilities, surf **Accès Culture** (www.accesculture.org).

Access in Paris, a useful if dated 245-page guide to the French capital for the disabled, can be downloaded in PDF form at **Access Project** (www.accessinparis.org).

Mobile en Ville (☎09 52 29 60 51; www.mobile-en-ville.asso.fr; 8 rue des Mariniers, 14e, Paris) works hard to make independent travel within the city easier for people in wheelchairs. Among other things it organises wheelchair *randonnées* (walks) in and around Paris; those in wheelchairs are pushed by 'walkers' on rollerskates.

Transport

The SNCF has made many of its train carriages more accessible to people with disabilities. A traveller in a wheelchair can travel in both the TGV (*train à grande vitesse;* high-speed train) and in the 1st-class carriage with a 2nd-class ticket on mainline trains provided they make a reservation by phone or at a train station at least a few hours before departure. Details are available in the SNCF booklet *Le Mémento du Voyageur Handicapé* (Handicapped Traveller Summary) available at all train stations. For advice on planning your journey from station to station, contact the SNCF service **Accès Plus** (☎08 90 64 06 50; www.accessibilite.sncf.com).

Metro line 14 was built to be wheelchair-accessible, although in reality it remains extremely challenging to navigate in a chair – unlike Paris buses which are 100% accessible.

For information on accessibility on all forms of public transport in the Paris region, get a copy of the *Guide Practique à l'Usage des Personnes à Mobilité Réduite* (Practical Usage Guide for People with Reduced Mobility) from the **Syndicate des Transports d'Île de France** (☎08 10 64 64 64; www.stif-idf.fr). Its info service for travellers with disabilities, **Info Mobi** (www.infomobi.com), is especially useful.

Taxi company **Horizon** (☎01 47 39 00 91), part of **Taxis G7** (☎36 07; www.taxisg7.fr), has cars especially adapted to carry wheelchairs and drivers trained in helping passengers with disabilities.

Visas

There are no entry requirements for nationals of EU countries. Citizens of Australia, the USA, Canada and New Zealand do not need visas to visit France for up to 90 days. Except for people from a handful of other European countries (including Switzerland), everyone, including citizens of South Africa, needs a so-called Schengen Visa, named after the Schengen Agreement that has abolished passport controls among 26 EU countries and has also been ratified by the non-EU governments of Iceland, Norway and Switzerland. A visa for any of these countries should be valid throughout the Schengen area, but it pays to double-check with the embassy or consulate of each country you intend to visit. Note that the UK and Ireland are not Schengen countries.

Visa fees depend on the current exchange rate, but transit and the various types of short-stay (up to 90 days) visas all cost €60, while a visa allowing stays of more than 90 days costs €99. You will need: your passport (valid for a period of three months beyond the date of your departure from France); a return ticket; proof of sufficient funds to support yourself; supporting documents explaining your stay in France for an extended period; recent passport-size photos; a completed visa form; and the visa fee. Check www.france.diplomatie.fr for the latest visa regulations and the closest French embassy to your current residence.

Titre de Séjour

If you are issued a long-stay visa valid for six months or longer, you may need to apply for a *titre de séjour* (residence permit; also called a *carte de séjour*) after arrival in France. Regulations have been relaxed in recent years; if you are only staying in France for up to 12 months you probably won't need it, but you will need to register with the French Office of Immigration and Integration. Check the website of the **Préfecture de Police** (www.prefecturedepolice.interieur.gouv.fr) first for instructions for all possible situations.

Those holding a passport from one of 31 European countries and seeking to take up residence in France no longer need to acquire a *titre de séjour;* their passport or national ID card is sufficient. Check the website given above to see which countries are included.

Foreigners with non-European passports should check the website of the Préfecture de Police or call ☎01 58 80 80 58.

Visa Extensions

Tourist visas *cannot* be extended except in emergencies (such as medical problems). If you have an urgent problem, contact the Service Étranger (Foreigner Service) at the Préfecture de Police for guidance. If you entered France on the 90-day visa-waiver program (ie you are Australian, Kiwi or American) and you have stayed for 90 days, you must leave the Schengen area for an additional 90 days before you can re-enter.

Work & Student Visas

If you would like to work, study or stay in France for longer than three months, apply to the French embassy or consulate nearest to you for the appropriate *long séjour* (long-stay) visa. Au pairs are granted student visas: they must be arranged *before* you leave home (unless you're an EU resident); the same goes for the year-long working holiday visa *(permis vacances travail)*.

Unless you hold an EU passport or are married to a French national, it's extremely difficult to get a visa that will allow you to work in France. For any sort of long-stay visa, begin the paperwork in your home country several months before you plan to leave. Applications usually cannot be made in a third country nor can tourist visas be turned into student visas after you arrive in France. People with student visas can apply for permission to work part-time; enquire at your place of study.

Women Travellers

Women attract more unwanted attention than men, but female travellers need not walk around Paris in fear: people are rarely assaulted on the street. However, the French seem to have given relatively little thought to sexual harassment *(harcèlement sexuel)*, and many men still think that to stare suavely at a passing woman is to pay her a compliment.

France's national rape crisis hotline, **Viols Femmes Informations** (☎08 00 05 95 95; ⏲10am-7pm Mon-Fri), can be reached toll-free from any telephone, without using a phonecard. It's run by a group called **Collectif Féministe contre le Viol** (CFCV | Feminist Collective Against Rape; ☎08 00 05 95 95; www.cfcv.asso.fr).

In an emergency, call the police (☎17). Medical, psychological and legal services are available to people referred by the police at the **Urgences Médico-Judiciaires** (☎01 42 34 82 85; 1 place du Parvis Notre Dame, 4e; ⏲24hr; Ⓜ St-Michel) inside the Hôtel Dieu.

La Maison des Femmes de Paris (☎01 43 43 41 13; http://maisondesfemmes.free.fr; 163 rue de Charenton, 12e; ⏲11am-7pm Mon-Fri; Ⓜ Reuilly Diderot) is a meeting place for women of all ages and nationalities, with events, workshops and exhibitions scheduled throughout the week.

Language

The sounds used in spoken French can almost all be found in English. If you read our pronunciation guides as if they were English, you'll be understood just fine. There are a couple of sounds to take note of: nasal vowels (represented in our guides by o or u followed by an almost inaudible nasal consonant sound m, n or ng), the 'funny' *u* (ew in our guides) and the deep-in-the-throat *r*. Syllables in French words are, for the most part, equally stressed. As English speakers tend to stress the first syllable, try adding a light stress on the final syllable of French words to compensate.

BASICS

Hello.	*Bonjour.*	bon·zhoor
Goodbye.	*Au revoir.*	o·rer·vwa
Excuse me.	*Excusez-moi.*	ek·skew·zay·mwa
Sorry.	*Pardon.*	par·don
Yes./No.	*Oui./Non.*	wee/non
Please.	*S'il vous plaît.*	seel voo play
Thank you.	*Merci.*	mair·see
You're welcome.	*De rien.*	der ree·en

How are you?
Comment allez-vous? ko·mon ta·lay·voo

Fine, and you?
Bien, merci. Et vous? byun mair·see ay voo

What's your name?
Comment vous appelez-vous? ko·mon voo·za·play voo

My name is ...
Je m'appelle ... zher ma·pel ...

Do you speak English?
Parlez-vous anglais? par·lay·voo ong·glay

I don't understand.
Je ne comprends pas. zher ner kom·pron pa

ACCOMMODATION

Do you have any rooms available?
Est-ce que vous avez des chambres libres? es·ker voo za·vay day shom·brer lee·brer

How much is it per night/person?
Quel est le prix par nuit/personne? kel ay ler pree par nwee/per·son

Is breakfast included?
Est-ce que le petit déjeuner est inclus? es·ker ler per·tee day·zher·nay ayt en·klew

dorm	*dortoir*	dor·twar
guesthouse	*pension*	pon·syon
hotel	*hôtel*	o·tel
youth hostel	*auberge de jeunesse*	o·berzh der zher·nes

a ... room	*une chambre ...*	ewn shom·brer ...
single	*à un lit*	a un lee
double	*avec un grand lit*	a·vek un gron lee

with (a) ...	*avec ...*	a·vek ...
air-con	*climatiseur*	klee·ma·tee·zer
bathroom	*une salle de bains*	ewn sal der bun
window	*fenêtre*	fer·nay·trer

DIRECTIONS

Where's ...?	*Où est ...?*	oo ay ...
What's the address?	*Quelle est l'adresse?*	kel ay la·dres

WANT MORE?

For in-depth language information and handy phrases, check out Lonely Planet's *French Phrasebook*. You'll find it at **shop.lonelyplanet.com**, or you can buy Lonely Planet's iPhone phrasebooks at the Apple App Store.

Signs

Entrée	Entrance
Femmes	Women
Fermé	Closed
Hommes	Men
Interdit	Prohibited
Ouvert	Open
Renseignements	Information
Sortie	Exit
Toilettes/WC	Toilets

Can you write down the address, please?
Est-ce que vous pourriez écrire l'adresse, s'il vous plaît? — es·ker voo poo·ryay ay·kreer la·dres seel voo play

Can you show me (on the map)?
Pouvez-vous m'indiquer (sur la carte)? — poo·vay·voo mun·dee·kay (sewr la kart)

at the corner	*au coin*	o kwun
at the traffic lights	*aux feux*	o fer
behind	*derrière*	dair·ryair
in front of	*devant*	der·von
far (from ...)	*loin (de ...)*	lwun (der ...)
left	*gauche*	gosh
near (to ...)	*près (de ...)*	pray (der ...)
next to ...	*à côté de ...*	a ko·tay der ...
opposite ...	*en face de ...*	on fas der ...
right	*droite*	drwat
straight ahead	*tout droit*	too drwa

EATING & DRINKING

What would you recommend?
Qu'est-ce que vous conseillez? — kes·ker voo kon·say·yay

What's in that dish?
Quels sont les ingrédients? — kel son lay zun·gray·dyon

I'm a vegetarian.
Je suis végétarien/végétarienne. — zher swee vay·zhay·ta·ryun/vay·zhay·ta·ryen (m/f)

I don't eat ...
Je ne mange pas ... — zher ner monzh pa ...

Cheers!
Santé! — son·tay

That was delicious.
C'était délicieux! — say·tay day·lee·syer

Please bring the bill.
Apportez-moi l'addition, s'il vous plaît. — a·por·tay·mwa la·dee·syon seel voo play

I'd like to reserve a table for ...
Je voudrais réserver une table pour ... — zher voo·dray ray·zair·vay ewn ta·bler poor ...

(eight) o'clock	*(vingt) heures*	(vungt) er
(two) people	*(deux) personnes*	(der) pair·son

Key Words

appetiser	*entrée*	on·tray
bottle	*bouteille*	boo·tay
breakfast	*petit déjeuner*	per·tee day·zher·nay
cold	*froid*	frwa
delicatessen	*traiteur*	tray·ter
dinner	*dîner*	dee·nay
fork	*fourchette*	foor·shet
glass	*verre*	vair
grocery store	*épicerie*	ay·pees·ree
hot	*chaud*	sho
knife	*couteau*	koo·to
lunch	*déjeuner*	day·zher·nay
market	*marché*	mar·shay
menu	*carte*	kart
plate	*assiette*	a·syet
spoon	*cuillère*	kwee·yair
wine list	*carte des vins*	kart day vun
with/without	*avec/sans*	a·vek/son

Meat & Fish

beef	*bœuf*	berf
chicken	*poulet*	poo·lay
crab	*crabe*	krab
lamb	*agneau*	a·nyo
oyster	*huître*	wee·trer
pork	*porc*	por
snail	*escargot*	es·kar·go
squid	*calmar*	kal·mar
turkey	*dinde*	dund
veal	*veau*	vo

Fruit & Vegetables

apple	*pomme*	pom
apricot	*abricot*	ab·ree·ko
asparagus	*asperge*	a·spairzh
beans	*haricots*	a·ree·ko
beetroot	*betterave*	be·trav

cabbage	*chou*	shoo
celery	*céleri*	sel·ree
cherry	*cerise*	ser·reez
corn	*maïs*	ma·ees
cucumber	*concombre*	kong·kom·brer
gherkin (pickle)	*cornichon*	kor·nee·shon
grape	*raisin*	ray·zun
leek	*poireau*	pwa·ro
lemon	*citron*	see·tron
lettuce	*laitue*	lay·tew
mushroom	*champignon*	shom·pee·nyon
peach	*pêche*	pesh
peas	*petit pois*	per·tee pwa
(red/green) pepper	*poivron (rouge/vert)*	pwa·vron (roozh/vair)
pineapple	*ananas*	a·na·nas
plum	*prune*	prewn
potato	*pomme de terre*	pom der tair
prune	*pruneau*	prew·no
pumpkin	*citrouille*	see·troo·yer
shallot	*échalote*	eh·sha·lot
spinach	*épinards*	eh·pee·nar
strawberry	*fraise*	frez
tomato	*tomate*	to·mat
turnip	*navet*	na·vay
vegetable	*légume*	lay·gewm

Other

bread	*pain*	pun
butter	*beurre*	ber
cheese	*fromage*	fro·mazh
egg	*œuf*	erf
honey	*miel*	myel
jam	*confiture*	kon·fee·tewr
oil	*huile*	weel
pepper	*poivre*	pwa·vrer
rice	*riz*	ree
salt	*sel*	sel
sugar	*sucre*	sew·krer
vinegar	*vinaigre*	vee·nay·grer

Drinks

beer	*bière*	bee·yair
coffee	*café*	ka·fay
(orange) juice	*jus (d'orange)*	zhew (do·ronzh)
milk	*lait*	lay
red wine	*vin rouge*	vun roozh
tea	*thé*	tay
(mineral) water	*eau (minérale)*	o (mee·nay·ral)
white wine	*vin blanc*	vun blong

EMERGENCIES

Help!
Au secours! — o skoor

Leave me alone!
Fichez-moi la paix! — fee·shay·mwa la pay

I'm lost.
Je suis perdu/perdue. — zhe swee·pair·dew (m/f)

Call a doctor.
Appelez un médecin. — a·play un mayd·sun

Call the police.
Appelez la police. — a·play la po·lees

I'm ill.
Je suis malade. — zher swee ma·lad

It hurts here.
J'ai une douleur ici. — zhay ewn doo·ler ee·see

I'm allergic (to ...).
Je suis allergique (à ...). — zher swee za·lair·zheek (a ...)

SHOPPING & SERVICES

I'd like to buy ...
Je voudrais acheter ... — zher voo·dray ash·tay ...

Can I look at it?
Est-ce que je peux le voir? — es·ker zher per ler vwar

I'm just looking.
Je regarde. — zher rer·gard

I don't like it.
Cela ne me plaît pas. — ser·la ner mer play pa

How much is it?
C'est combien? — say kom·byun

It's too expensive.
C'est trop cher. — say tro shair

There's a mistake in the bill.
Il y a une erreur dans la note. — eel ya ewn ay·rer don la not

bank	*banque*	bonk
internet cafe	*cybercafé*	see·bair·ka·fay
tourist office	*office de tourisme*	o·fees der too·rees·mer

Question Words

What?	*Quoi?*	kwa
When?	*Quand?*	kon
Where?	*Où?*	oo
Who?	*Qui?*	kee
Why?	*Pourquoi?*	poor·kwa

Numbers

1	*un*	un
2	*deux*	der
3	*trois*	trwa
4	*quatre*	ka·trer
5	*cinq*	sungk
6	*six*	sees
7	*sept*	set
8	*huit*	weet
9	*neuf*	nerf
10	*dix*	dees
20	*vingt*	vung
30	*trente*	tront
40	*quarante*	ka·ront
50	*cinquante*	sung·kont
60	*soixante*	swa·sont
70	*soixante-dix*	swa·son·dees
80	*quatre-vingts*	ka·trer·vung
90	*quatre-vingt-dix*	ka·trer·vung·dees
100	*cent*	son
1000	*mille*	meel

TIME & DATES

What time is it?
Quelle heure est-il? kel er ay til

It's (eight) o'clock.
Il est (huit) heures. il ay (weet) er

Half past (10).
(Dix) heures et demie. (deez) er ay day·mee

morning	*matin*	ma·tun
afternoon	*après-midi*	a·pray·mee·dee
evening	*soir*	swar
yesterday	*hier*	yair
today	*aujourd'hui*	o·zhoor·dwee
tomorrow	*demain*	der·mun

Monday	*lundi*	lun·dee
Tuesday	*mardi*	mar·dee
Wednesday	*mercredi*	mair·krer·dee
Thursday	*jeudi*	zher·dee
Friday	*vendredi*	von·drer·dee
Saturday	*samedi*	sam·dee
Sunday	*dimanche*	dee·monsh

TRANSPORT

I want to go to ...
Je voudrais aller à ... zher voo·dray a·lay a ...

Does it stop at ...?
Est-ce qu'il s'arrête à ...? es·kil sa·ret a ...

At what time does it leave/arrive?
À quelle heure est-ce qu'il part/arrive? a kel er es kil par/a·reev

I want to get off here.
Je veux descendre ici. zher ver day·son·drer ee·see

a ... ticket	*un billet ...*	un bee·yay ...
1st-class	*de première classe*	der prem·yair klas
2nd-class	*de deuxième classe*	der der·zyem klas
one-way	*simple*	sum·pler
return	*aller et retour*	a·lay ay rer·toor

aisle seat	*côté couloir*	ko·tay kool·war
boat	*bateau*	ba·to
bus	*bus*	bews
cancelled	*annulé*	a·new·lay
delayed	*en retard*	on rer·tar
first	*premier*	prer·myay
last	*dernier*	dair·nyay
plane	*avion*	a·vyon
platform	*quai*	kay
ticket office	*guichet*	gee·shay
timetable	*horaire*	o·rair
train	*train*	trun
window seat	*côté fenêtre*	ko·tay fe·ne·trer

I'd like to hire a ...	*Je voudrais louer ...*	zher voo·dray loo·way ...
car	*une voiture*	ewn vwa·tewr
bicycle	*un vélo*	un vay·lo
motorcycle	*une moto*	ewn mo·to

child seat	*siège-enfant*	syezh·on·fon
helmet	*casque*	kask
mechanic	*mécanicien*	may·ka·nee·syun
petrol/gas	*essence*	ay·sons
service station	*station-service*	sta·syon·ser·vees

Can I park here?
Est-ce que je peux stationner ici? es·ker zher per sta·syo·nay ee·see

I have a flat tyre.
Mon pneu est à plat. mom pner ay ta pla

I've run out of petrol.
Je suis en panne d'essence. zher swee zon pan day·sons

GLOSSARY

(m) indicates masculine gender, (f) feminine gender, (pl) plural and (adj) adjective

adjoint (m) – deputy mayor

ancien régime (m) – 'old order'; France under the monarchy before the Revolution

apéritif (m) – a drink taken before dinner

arrondissement (m) – one of 20 administrative divisions in Paris; abbreviated on street signs as 1er (1st arrondissement), 2e or 2ème (2nd) etc

auberge (de jeunesse) (f) – (youth) hostel

avenue (f) – avenue (abbreviated av)

banlieues (f pl) – suburbs

belle époque (f) – 'beautiful age'; era of elegance and gaiety characterising fashionable Parisian life roughly from 1870 to 1914

billet (m) – ticket

billeterie (f) – ticket office or window

biologique or **bio** (adj) – organic

boucherie (f) – butcher

boulangerie (f) – bakery

boules (f pl) – a game played with heavy metal balls on a sandy pitch; also called *pétanque*

brasserie (f) – 'brewery'; a restaurant that usually serves food all day long

brioche (f) – small roll or cake, sometimes made with nuts, currants or candied fruit

bureau de change (m) – currency exchange bureau

café du quartier (m) – neighbourhood café

carnet (m) – a book of (usually) 10 bus, tram, metro or other tickets sold at a reduced rate

carrefour (m) – crossroads, intersection

carte (f) – card; menu; map

carte de séjour (f) – residence permit

cave (f) – (wine) cellar

chambre (f) – room

chanson française (f) – 'French song'; traditional musical genre where lyrics are paramount

chansonnier (m) – cabaret singer

charcuterie (f) – a variety of meat products that are cured, smoked or processed, including sausages, hams, pâtés and rillettes; shop selling these products

cimetière (m) – cemetery

consigne (f) – left-luggage office

correspondance (f) – linking tunnel or walkway, eg in the metro; rail or bus connection

cour (f) – courtyard

couvert (m) – covered shopping arcade (also called *galerie*)

dégustation (f) – tasting, sampling

demi (m) – half; 330mL glass of beer

département (m) – administrative division of France

dessert (m) – dessert

eau (f) – water

église (f) – church

entrée (f) – entrance; first course or starter

épicerie (f) – small grocery store

espace (f) – space; outlet

exposition universelle (f) – world exhibition

fête (f) – festival; holiday

ficelle (f) – string; a thinner, crustier 200g version of the baguette not unlike a very thick breadstick

fin de siècle (adj) – 'end of the century'; characteristic of the last years of the 19th century and generally used to indicate decadence

forêt (f) – forest

formule (f) – similar to a *menu* but allows choice of whichever two of three courses you want (eg starter and main course or main course and dessert)

fromagerie (f) – cheese shop

galerie (f) – gallery; covered shopping arcade (also called passage)

galette (f) – a pancake or flat pastry, with a variety of (usually savoury) fillings

gare (f) – railway station

gare routière (f) – bus station

gendarmerie (f) – police station; police force

grand projet (m) – huge, public edifice erected by a government or politician generally in a bid to immortalise themselves

Grands Boulevards (m pl) – 'Great Boulevards'; the eight contiguous broad thoroughfares that stretch from place de la Madeleine eastwards to the place de la République

halles (f pl) – covered food market

hameau (m) – hamlet

hammam (m) – steam room, Turkish bath

haute couture (f) – literally 'high sewing'; the creations of leading designers

haute cuisine (f) – 'high cuisine'; classic French cooking style typified by elaborately prepared multicourse meals

hôtel de ville (m) – city or town hall

hôtel particulier (m) – private mansion

jardin (m) – garden

kir (m) – white wine sweetened with a blackcurrant (or other) liqueur

lycée (m) – secondary school

mairie (f) – city or town hall
marché (m) – market
marché aux puces (m) – flea market
menu (m) – fixed-price meal with two or more courses; see *formule*
musée (m) – museum
musette (f) – accordion music
nocturne (f) – late night opening at a museum, department store etc
orangerie (f) – conservatory for growing citrus fruit
pain (m) – bread
palais de justice (m) – law courts
parc (m) – park
parvis (m) – square in front of a church or public building passage
pastis (m) – an aniseed-flavoured aperitif mixed with water
pâté (m) – potted meat; a thickish paste, often of pork, cooked in a ceramic dish and served cold (similar to terrine)
pâtisserie (f) – cakes and pastries; shop selling these products
pelouse (f) – lawn
pétanque (f) – see boules
pied-noir (m) – 'black foot'; French colonial born in Algeria
place (f) – square or plaza
plan (m) – city map
plan du quartier (m) – map of nearby streets (hung on the wall near metro exits)
plat du jour (m) – daily special in a restaurant
poissonnerie (f) – fishmonger, fish shop
pont (m) – bridge
port (m) – harbour, port
port de plaisance (m) – boat harbour or marina
porte (f) – door; gate in a city wall
poste (f) – post office
préfecture (f) – prefecture; capital city of a département
produits biologique – organic food
quai (m) – quay
quartier (m) – quarter, district, neighbourhood
raï – a type of Algerian popular music
RATP – Régie Autonome des Transports Parisiens; Paris' public transport system
RER – Réseau Express Régional; Paris' suburban train network
résidence (f) – residence; hotel usually intended for longterm stays
rillettes (f pl) – shredded potted meat or fish
rive (f) – bank of a river
rond point (m) – roundabout
rue (f) – street or road
salle (f) – hall; room
salon de thé (m) – tearoom
SNCF – Société Nationale de Chemins de Fer; France's national railway organisation
soldes (m pl) – sale, the sales
sono mondiale (f) – world music
sortie (f) – exit
spectacle (m) – performance, play or theatrical show
square (m) – public garden
syndicat d'initiative (m) – tourist office
tabac (m) – tobacconist (which also sells bus tickets, phonecards etc)
tarif réduit (m) – reduced price (for students, seniors, children etc)
tartine (f) – a slice of bread with any topping or garnish
taxe de séjour (f) – municipal tourist tax
télécarte (f) – phonecard
TGV – train à grande vitesse; high-speed train
tour (f) – tower
tous les jours – every day (eg on timetables)
traiteur (m) – caterer, delicatessen
Vélib' (m) – communal bicycle rental scheme in Paris
vélo (m) – bicycle
version française (m) – literally 'French version': a film dubbed in French
version originale – literally 'original version': a nondubbed film in its original language with French subtitles

Behind the Scenes

SEND US YOUR FEEDBACK

We love to hear from travellers – your comments keep us on our toes and help make our books better. Our well-travelled team reads every word on what you loved or loathed about this book. Although we cannot reply individually to your submissions, we always guarantee that your feedback goes straight to the appropriate authors, in time for the next edition. Each person who sends us information is thanked in the next edition – the most useful submissions are rewarded with a selection of digital PDF chapters.

Visit **lonelyplanet.com/contact** to submit your updates and suggestions or to ask for help. Our award-winning website also features inspirational travel stories, news and discussions.

Note: We may edit, reproduce and incorporate your comments in Lonely Planet products such as guidebooks, websites and digital products, so let us know if you don't want your comments reproduced or your name acknowledged. For a copy of our privacy policy visit lonelyplanet.com/privacy.

OUR READERS

Many thanks to the travellers who used the last edition and wrote to us with helpful hints, useful advice and interesting anecdotes: Sain Alizada, Loren Buchanan, Jill Drake, Michael Rodin, Ellie Sanders, Seraphim Schuchter, Colin Shepherd, Veronika Siebenkotten-Branca, Laurence van Bilderbeek

AUTHOR THANKS

Catherine Le Nevez

Un grand merci to my fellow award-winning Paris authors Chris and Nicola. *Merci mille fois* to Julian, and all of the innumerable Parisians who offered insights and inspiration. *Merci* too to Pierre-Emmanuel, and to everyone at Versailles. Thanks too to Kate Morgan, James Smart, Jo Cooke and all at LP. As ever, *merci encore* to my parents, brother, *belle-sœur* and *neveu* for sustaining my lifelong love of Paris.

Christopher Pitts

Special thanks to my two great co-authors for their advice and input and to all the crew at LP who have put much hard work into making this book what it is. *Bises* as well to the Pavillards and my dearest partners in crime: Perrine, Elliot and Céleste.

Nicola Williams

Un grand merci to the many in Paris who aided and abetted in tracking down the best: font of all Parisian knowledge-extraordinaire Élodie Berta and colleague Herve Guillon (Office de Tourisme et des Congrès), Père Lachaise guru Thierry Le Roi, Louvre treasure-hunt queen Daisy de Plume (THATLou), Mary Winston Nicklin, Jane Bertch at La Cuisine Paris, Parisian photographer Sophie Farrugia, Lindsey Tramuta and Kasia Dietz. Kudos to my very own, extra-special 'Paris with kids' research team Niko, Mischa and Kaya Luefkens.

ACKNOWLEDGMENTS

Illustrations pp112-13, pp204-5 and pp276-7 by Javier Zarracina.

Cover photograph: Basilique du Sacré-Cœur at twilight, Brian Jannsen/Alamy.

THIS BOOK

This 10th edition of Lonely Planet's *Paris* guidebook was written and researched by Catherine Le Nevez, Christopher Pitts and Nicola Williams, who also all wrote and researched the previous edition. This guidebook was commissioned in Lonely Planet's London office, and produced by the following:

Destination Editors Kate Morgan, James Smart

Product Editor Martine Power

Senior Cartographer Valentina Kremenchutskaya

Book Designer Mazzy Prinsep

Assisting Editors Sarah Bailey, Michelle Bennett, Katie Connolly, Justin Flynn, Elizabeth Jones, Kate Kiely, Charlotte Orr, Kirsten Rawlings

Assisting Cartographers Hunor Csutoros, Mark Griffiths, Corey Hutchison

Cover Researcher Naomi Parker

Thanks to Sasha Baskett, Elin Berglund, Dan Corbett, Helvi Cranfield, Brendan Dempsey, Ryan Evans, Larissa Frost, Anna Harris, Jouve India, Kat Marsh, Claire Murphy, Wayne Murphy, Claire Naylor, Karyn Noble, Samantha Russell-Tulip, Dianne Schallmeiner, Ellie Simpson, Lyahna Spencer, Angela Tinson, Samantha Tyson, Lauren Wellicome, Juan Winata

See also separate subindexes for:
- **EATING P372**
- **DRINKING & NIGHTLIFE P374**
- **ENTERTAINMENT P375**
- **SHOPPING P376**
- **SPORTS & ACTIVITIES P377**
- **SLEEPING P377**

Index

Sights 000
Map Pages **000**
Photo Pages **000**

Sights 000
Map Pages **000**
Photo Pages **000**

EATING

ENTERTAINMENT

SPORTS & ACTIVITIES

SLEEPING

Sights 000
Map Pages **000**
Photo Pages **000**

Paris Maps

Sights
- Beach
- Bird Sanctuary
- Buddhist
- Castle/Palace
- Christian
- Confucian
- Hindu
- Islamic
- Jain
- Jewish
- Monument
- Museum/Gallery/Historic Building
- Ruin
- Sento Hot Baths/Onsen
- Shinto
- Sikh
- Taoist
- Winery/Vineyard
- Zoo/Wildlife Sanctuary
- Other Sight

Activities, Courses & Tours
- Bodysurfing
- Diving
- Canoeing/Kayaking
- Course/Tour
- Skiing
- Snorkelling
- Surfing
- Swimming/Pool
- Walking
- Windsurfing
- Other Activity

Sleeping
- Sleeping
- Camping

Eating
- Eating

Drinking & Nightlife
- Drinking & Nightlife
- Cafe

Entertainment
- Entertainment

Shopping
- Shopping

Information
- Bank
- Embassy/Consulate
- Hospital/Medical
- Internet
- Police
- Post Office
- Telephone
- Toilet
- Tourist Information
- Other Information

Geographic
- Beach
- Hut/Shelter
- Lighthouse
- Lookout
- Mountain/Volcano
- Oasis
- Park
- Pass
- Picnic Area
- Waterfall

Population
- Capital (National)
- Capital (State/Province)
- City/Large Town
- Town/Village

Transport
- Airport
- Border crossing
- Bus
- Cable car/Funicular
- Cycling
- Ferry
- Metro station
- Monorail
- Parking
- Petrol station
- S-Bahn/Subway station
- Taxi
- T-bane/Tunnelbana station
- Train station/Railway
- Tram
- Tube station
- U-Bahn/Underground station
- Other Transport

Note: Not all symbols displayed above appear on the maps in this book

Routes
- Tollway
- Freeway
- Primary
- Secondary
- Tertiary
- Lane
- Unsealed road
- Road under construction
- Plaza/Mall
- Steps
- Tunnel
- Pedestrian overpass
- Walking Tour
- Walking Tour detour
- Path/Walking Trail

Boundaries
- International
- State/Province
- Disputed
- Regional/Suburb
- Marine Park
- Cliff
- Wall

Hydrography
- River, Creek
- Intermittent River
- Canal
- Water
- Dry/Salt/Intermittent Lake
- Reef

Areas
- Airport/Runway
- Beach/Desert
- Cemetery (Christian)
- Cemetery (Other)
- Glacier
- Mudflat
- Park/Forest
- Sight (Building)
- Sportsground
- Swamp/Mangrove

MAP INDEX

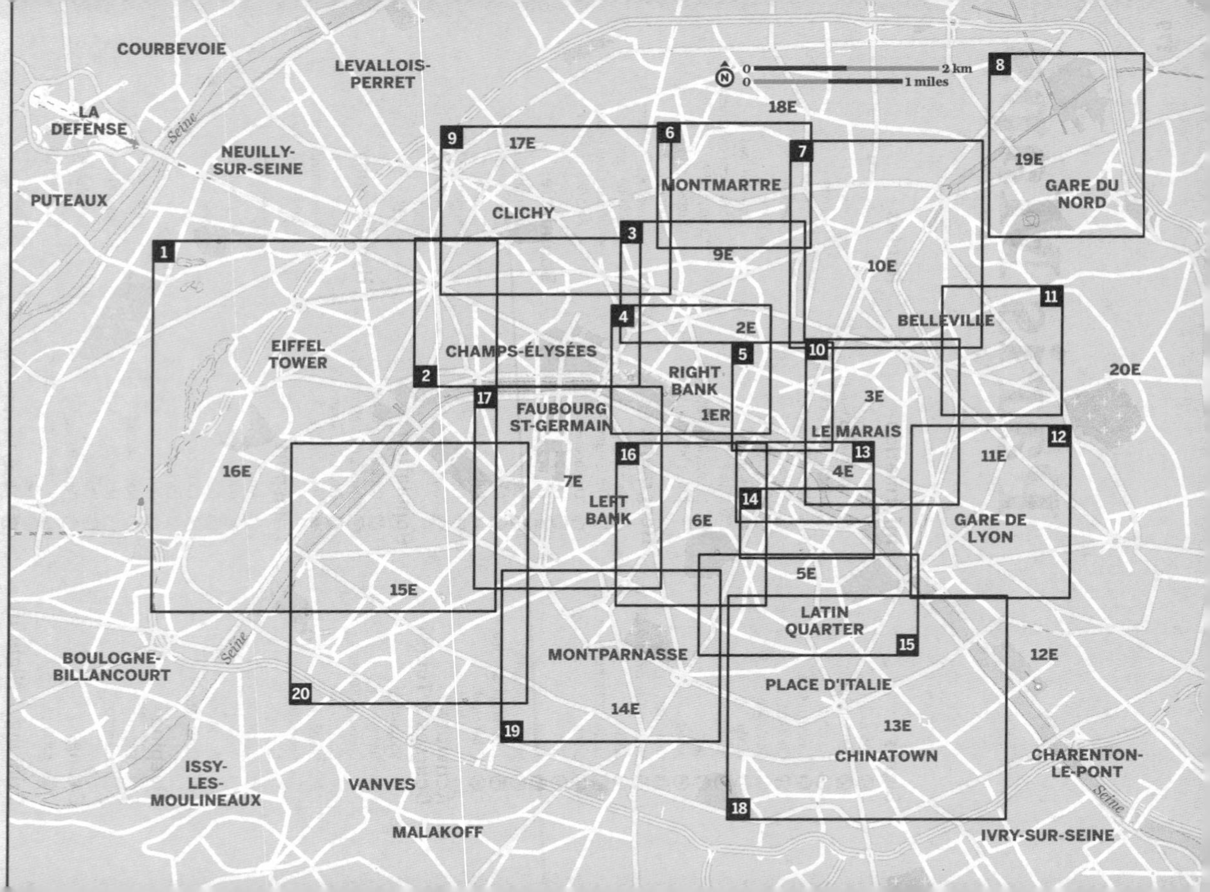

COURBEVOIE
LEVALLOIS-PERRET
LA DEFENSE
PUTEAUX
NEUILLY-SUR-SEINE
Seine
0 2 km
0 1 miles
18E
17E
19E
GARE DU NORD
MONTMARTRE
CLICHY
9E
10E
EIFFEL TOWER
CHAMPS-ÉLYSÉES
BELLEVILLE
2E
RIGHT BANK
1ER
3E
20E
FAUBOURG ST-GERMAIN
LE MARAIS
11E
16E
7E
4E
LEFT BANK
6E
GARE DE LYON
15E
5E
LATIN QUARTER
BOULOGNE-BILLANCOURT
MONTPARNASSE
12E
PLACE D'ITALIE
14E
13E
CHINATOWN
CHARENTON-LE-PONT
ISSY-LES-MOULINEAUX
VANVES
MALAKOFF
IVRY-SUR-SEINE
1
2
3
4
5
6
7
8
9
10
11
12
13
14
15
16
17
18
19
20

EIFFEL TOWER & WESTERN PARIS *Map on p382*

Top Sights (p82)
1 Cité de l'Architecture et du Patrimoine ... E4
2 Eiffel Tower ... F5
3 Musée du Quai Branly ... G4
4 Musée Guimet des Arts Asiatiques ... F3
5 Musée Marmottan Monet ... B5

Sights (p85)
6 Aquarium de Paris Cinéaqua ... F4
7 Flame of Liberty Memorial ... G4
8 Fondation Louis Vuitton ... B1
9 Fondation Pierre Bergé-Yves Saint Laurent ... G3
10 Galerie-Musée Baccarat ... F3
11 Galeries du Panthéon Bouddhique ... F3
12 Jardin d'Acclimatation ... B1
13 Maison de Balzac ... D5
14 Musée Dapper ... E2
15 Musée d'Art Moderne de la Ville de Paris ... G4
16 Musée de la Marine ... E4
17 Musée de la Mode de la Ville de Paris ... F3
18 Musée de l'Homme ... E4
19 Musée du Vin ... E5
20 Palais de Chaillot ... E4
21 Palais de Tokyo ... F4
22 Parc du Champ de Mars ... G5

Eating (p87)
58 Tour Eiffel ... (see 2)
23 Hugo Desnoyer ... B6
24 La Mascotte ... G3
Le Jules Verne ... (see 2)
25 Le Petit Rétro ... E3
26 Les Deux Abeilles ... G4
Les Ombres ... (see 3)
27 Malitourne ... G3
28 Marché Président Wilson ... F3
29 Mes Bocaux ... G3
Monsieur Bleu ... (see 21)
Tokyo Eat ... (see 21)
30 Traiteur Jegado ... G3

Drinking & Nightlife (p90)
31 Bô Zinc Café ... C6
32 Café Branly ... G4
33 St James Paris ... D2
34 Upper Crèmerie ... G2

Entertainment (p91)
35 Les Marionnettes du Champ de Mars ... G5
Yoyo ... (see 21)

Shopping (p92)
36 Patrick Roger ... F2

Sports & Activities (p92)
37 Bateaux Parisiens ... F5
38 Fat Tire Bike Tours ... F5
39 Hippodrome d'Auteuil ... A6
40 Le Chalet des Îles ... B3
41 Vedettes de Paris ... F5

Sleeping (p292)
42 Hôtel du Bois ... F2
43 Hôtel Félicien ... C7
44 Hôtel Molitor ... A7
45 Hôtel Sezz ... E5

EIFFEL TOWER & WESTERN PARIS

Key on p381

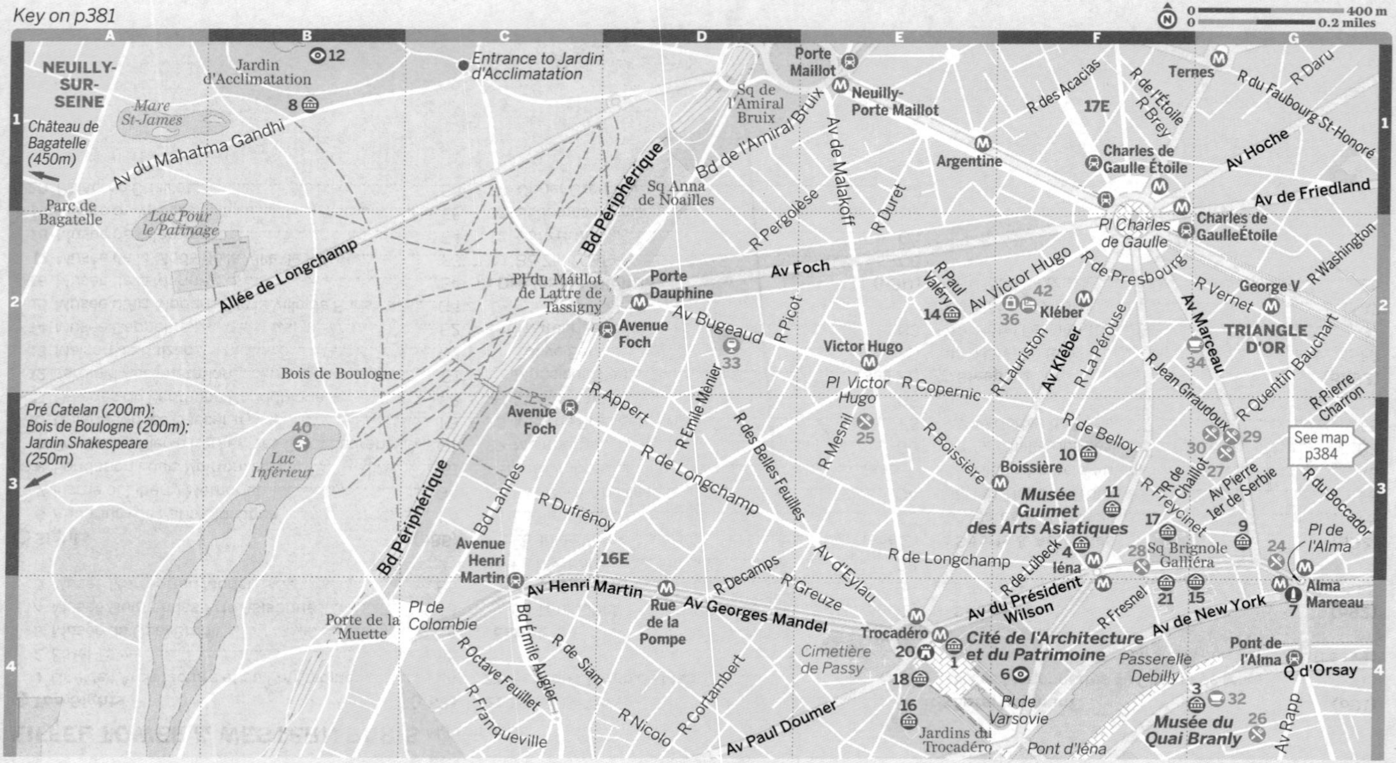

EIFFEL TOWER & WESTERN PARIS

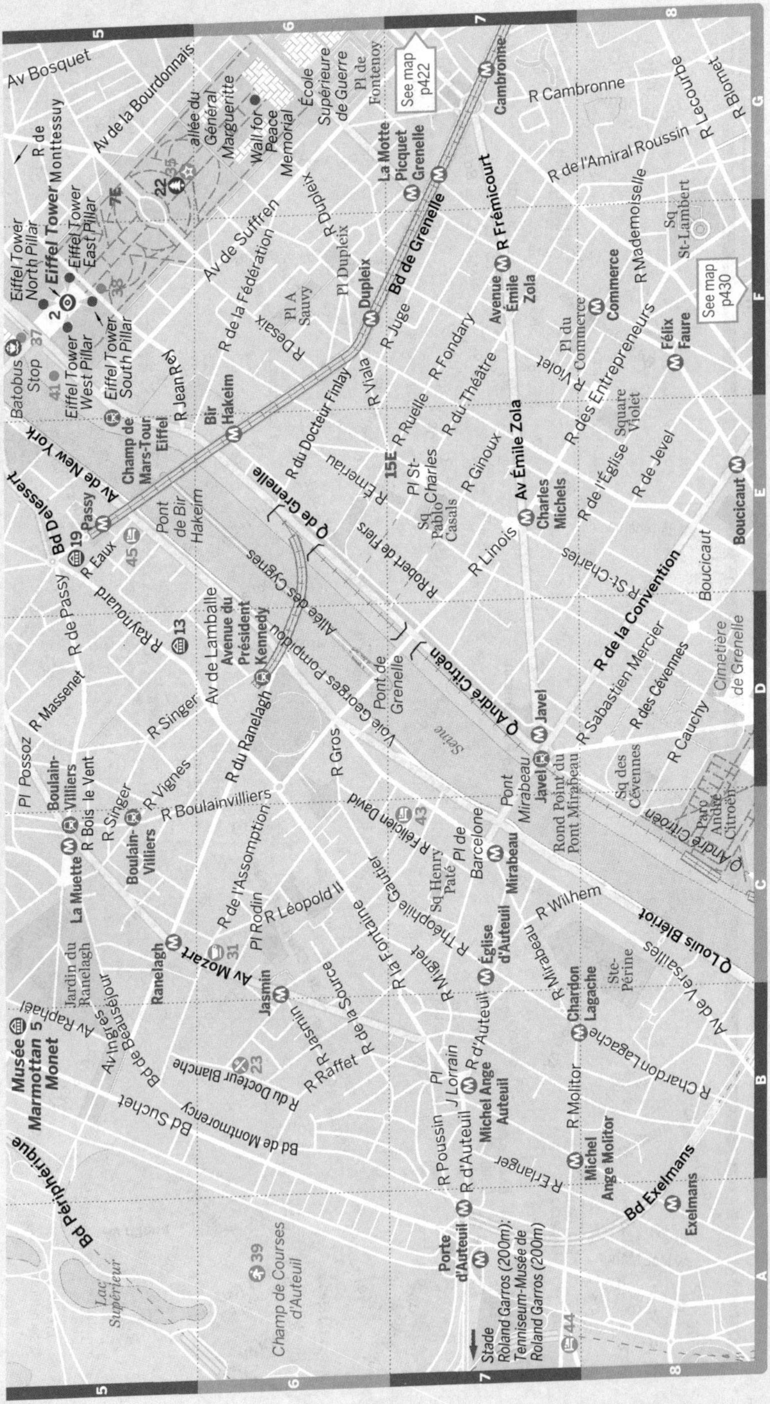

CHAMPS-ÉLYSÉES

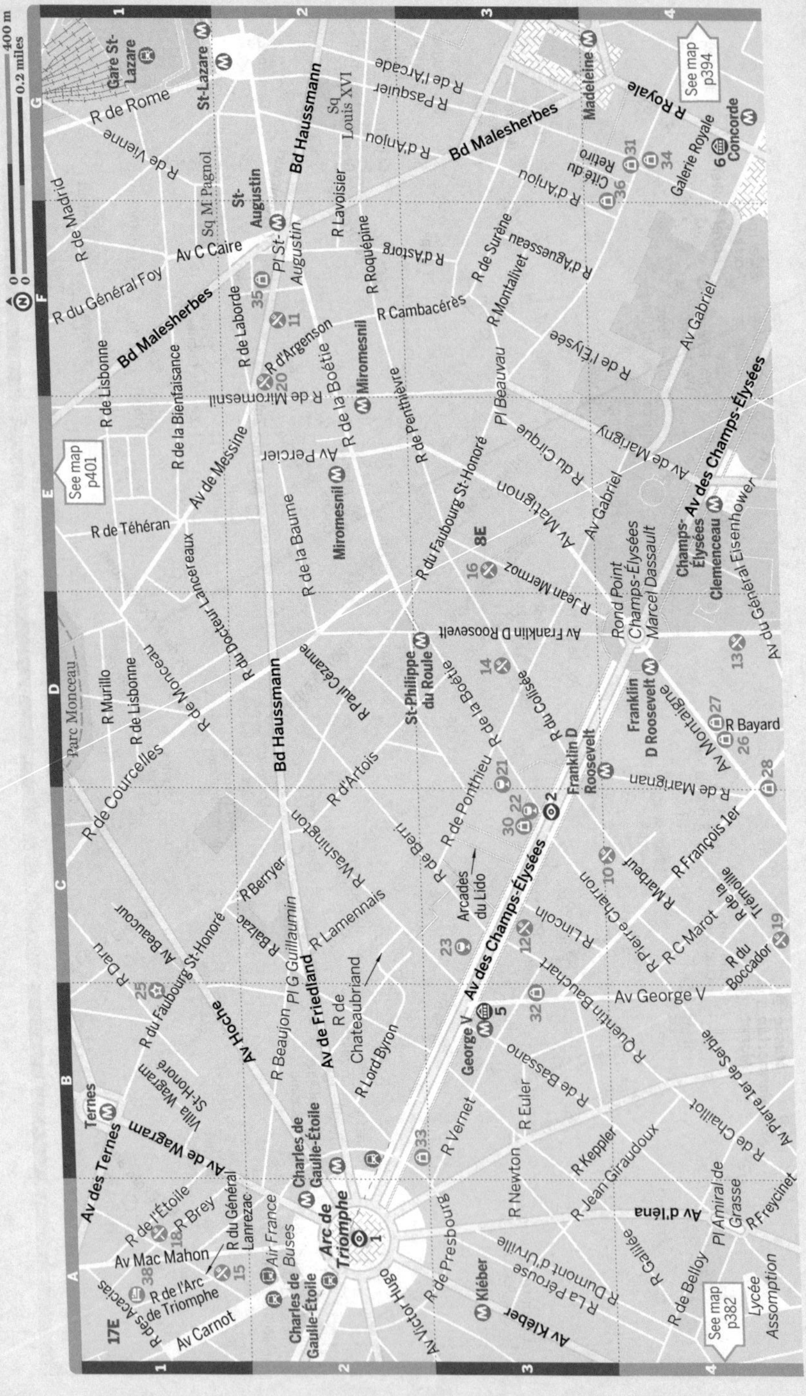

Top Sights (p95)
1 Arc de Triomphe ... A2

Sights (p97)
2 Avenue des Champs-Élysées ... C3
3 Grand Palais ... E5
4 Jardin de la Nouvelle France ... D5
5 Louis Vuitton Espace Culturel ... B3
6 Musée Maxim's ... G4
7 Palais de la Découverte ... E5
8 Petit Palais ... E5
9 Place de la Concorde ... G5

Eating (p100)
10 Aubrac Corner ... C4
11 Bistrot du Sommelier ... F2
12 Ladurée ... C3
13 Lasserre ... D4
14 Le Boudoir ... D3
15 Le Hide ... A1
16 Makoto Aoki ... E3
17 Mini Palais ... E5
18 Pad Thai ... A1
19 Philippe & Jean-Pierre ... C4
20 Raoul Maeder ... F2

Drinking & Nightlife (p104)
21 Charlie Birdy ... D3
22 Le Madam ... C3
23 Queen ... C3
24 ShowCase ... E5

Entertainment (p104)
25 Salle Pleyel ... B1

Shopping (p105)
26 Chanel ... D4
27 Chloé ... D4
28 Christian Dior ... D4
29 Givenchy ... B5
30 Guerlain ... C3
31 Hermès ... G4
32 Jean-Paul Gaultier ... B3
33 Lancel ... B2
34 Lanvin ... G4
35 Les Caves Augé ... F2
Louis Vuitton ... (see 5)
Publicis Drugstore ... (see 33)
36 Yves Saint Laurent ... G4

Sports & Activities (p352)
37 Bateaux-Mouches ... C5

Sleeping (p292)
38 Hidden Hotel ... A1

GRANDS BOULEVARDS

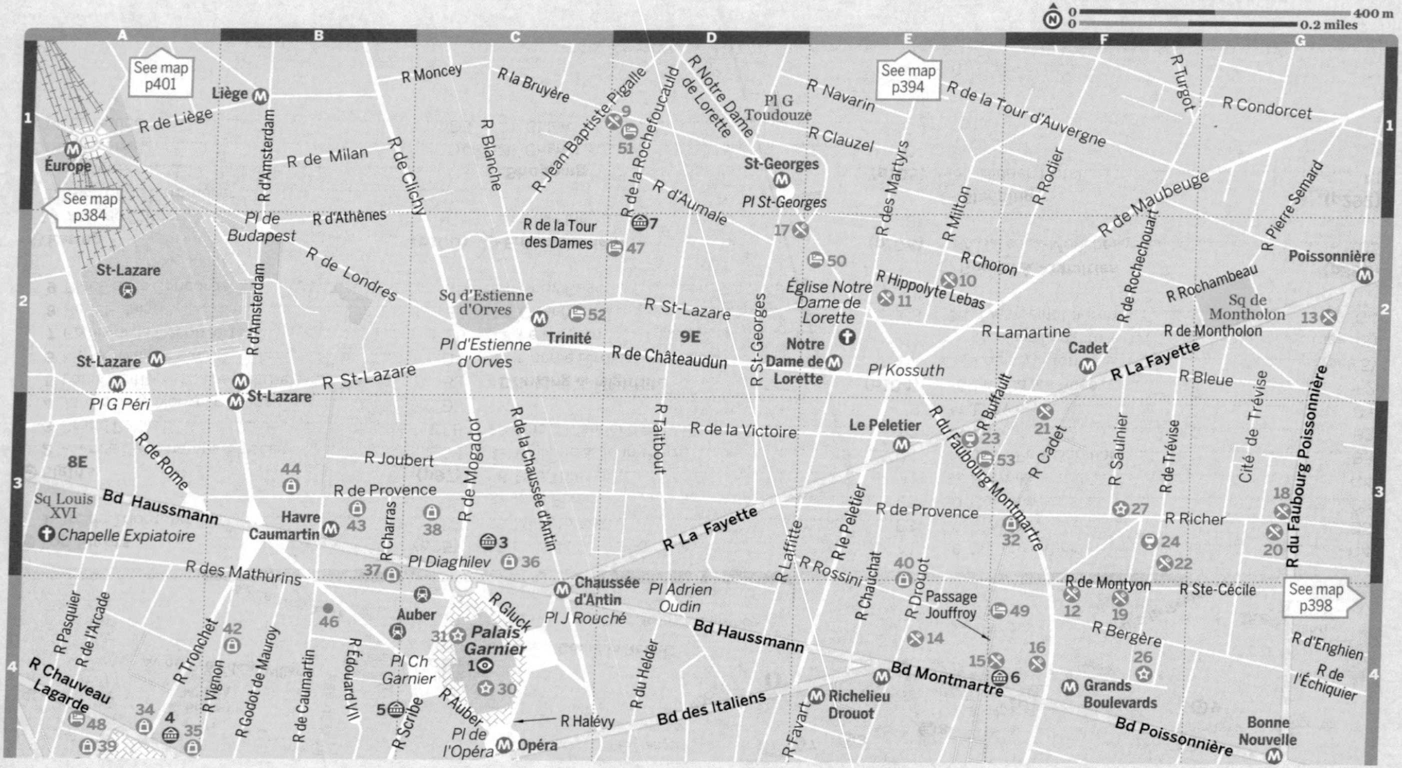

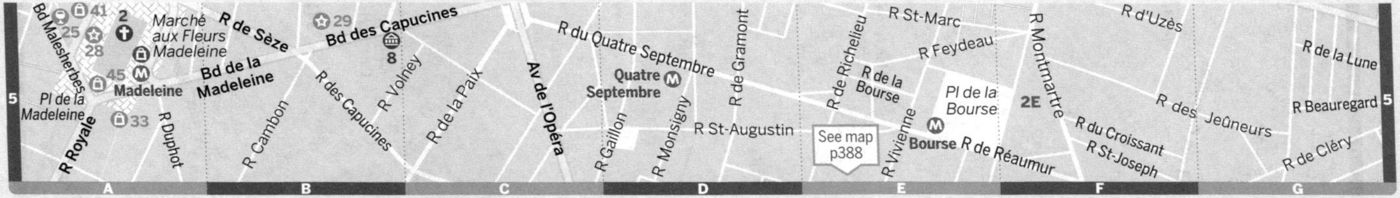

Top Sights (p97)
1 Palais Garnier....C4

Sights (p97)
2 Église de la Madeleine....A5
3 Galerie des Galeries....C3
4 La Pinacothèque....A4
5 Musée du Parfum....B4
6 Musée Grévin....F4
7 Musée National Gustave Moreau....D2
8 Théâtre-Musée des Capucines....B5

Eating (p100)
9 Bistrot La Bruyère....D1
10 Caillebotte....E2
11 Chez Plume....E2
12 Floquifil....F4
13 Le Grenier à Pain....G2
14 Le J'Go....E4
15 Le Valentin....F4
16 Le Zinc des Cavistes....F4
17 Les Coulisses Vintage....D2
Les Pâtes Vivantes....(see 53)
18 L'Office....G3
19 Nouveau Paris-Dakar....F4
20 Richer....G3
21 Stanz....F3
22 SuperNature....F3

Drinking & Nightlife (p104)
23 Au Général La Fayette....E3
24 Autour d'un Verre....F3
25 Le Forum....A5

Entertainment (p104)
26 Au Limonaire....F4
27 Folies-Bergère....F3
28 Kiosque Théâtre Madeleine....A5
29 L'Olympia....B5
30 Palais Garnier....C4
31 Palais Garnier Box Office....C4

Shopping (p105)
32 À la Mère de Famille....F3
33 Boutique Maille....A5
34 ERES....A4
35 Fauchon....A4
36 Galeries Lafayette....C3
37 Galeries Lafayette - Home Design....B3
38 Galeries Lafayette - Men's Store....C3
39 Hédiard....A4
40 Hôtel Drouot....E3
41 La Maison de la Truffe....A5
42 La Maison du Miel....B4
43 Le Printemps....B3
44 Le Printemps de l'Homme....B3
45 Place de la Madeleine....A5

Sports & Activities (p352)
46 L'Open Tour....B4

Sleeping (p292)
47 BVJ Opéra....D2
48 Hôtel Amarante Beau Manoir....A4
49 Hôtel Chopin....F4
50 Hôtel France Albion....E2
51 Hôtel Joyce....D1
52 Hôtel Langlois....C2
53 Hôtel Monte Carlo....E3

Key on p390

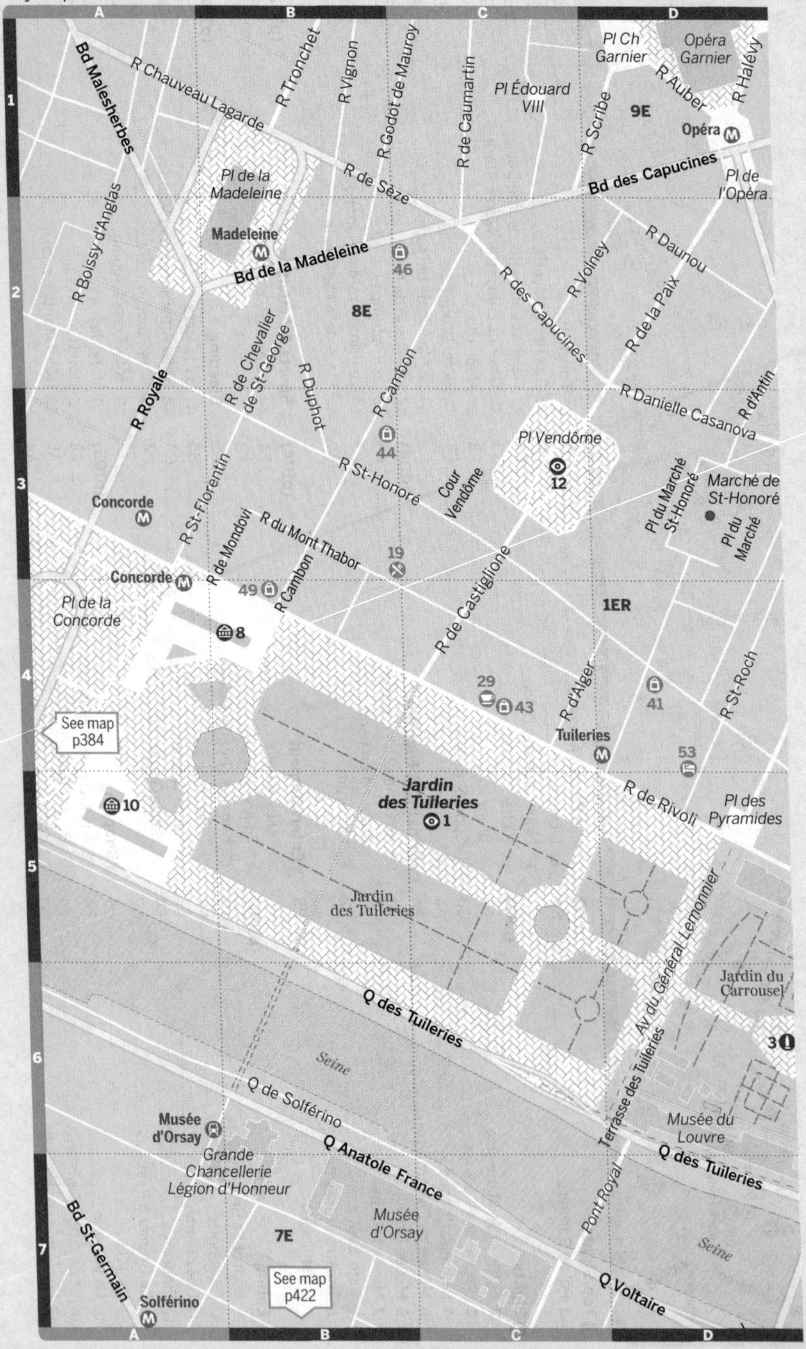

A
B
C
D
1
2
3
4
5
6
7
Bd Malesherbes
R Chauveau Lagarde
R Tronchet
R Vignon
R Godot de Mauroy
R de Caumartin
Pl Ch Garnier
Opéra Garnier
R Halévy
R Auber
Pl Édouard VIII
R Scribe
9E
Opéra
Pl de la Madeleine
R de Sèze
Bd des Capucines
Pl de l'Opéra
R Boissy d'Anglas
Madeleine
Bd de la Madeleine
46
R Daunou
R Volney
R des Capucines
R de la Paix
8E
R Royale
R de Chevalier de St-George
R Duphot
R Cambon
R Danielle Casanova
R d'Antin
Pl Vendôme
44
12
R St-Honoré
Cour Vendôme
Pl du Marché St-Honoré
Marché de St-Honoré
Pl du Marché
Concorde
R St-Florentin
R de Mondovi
R du Mont Thabor
19
Concorde
49
R Cambon
R de Castiglione
1ER
Pl de la Concorde
8
29
43
R d'Alger
41
R St-Roch
See map p384
Tuileries
53
Jardin des Tuileries
1
R de Rivoli
Pl des Pyramides
10
Jardin des Tuileries
Av du Général Lemonnier
Jardin du Carrousel
Q des Tuileries
3
Seine
Terrasse des Tuileries
Q de Solférino
Musée d'Orsay
Musée du Louvre
Grande Chancellerie Légion d'Honneur
Q Anatole France
Q des Tuileries
Pont Royal
Musée d'Orsay
Bd St-Germain
7E
Seine
See map p422
Q Voltaire
Solférino

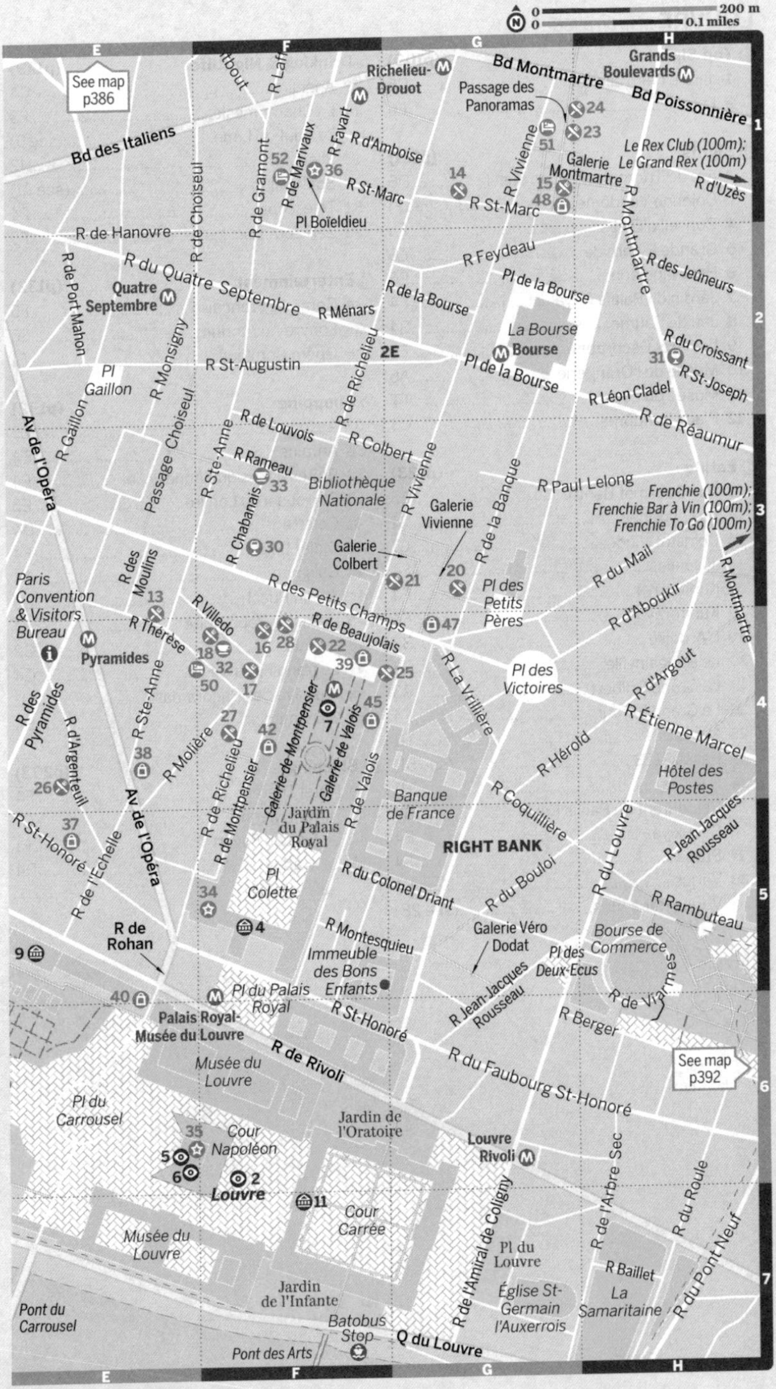
0
200 m
0
0.1 miles
E
F
G
H
1
2
3
4
5
6
7
See map p386
See map p392
Bd des Italiens
Bd Montmartre
Bd Poissonnière
Richelieu-Drouot
Grands Boulevards
Passage des Panoramas
24
23
51
Galerie Montmartre
Le Rex Club (100m); Le Grand Rex (100m)
R d'Uzès
R Favart
R d'Amboise
R de Marivaux
52
36
R de Gramont
R St-Marc
14
15
48
Pl Boïeldieu
R Vivienne
R Montmartre
R de Hanovre
R de Choiseul
R Feydeau
R des Jeûneurs
R du Quatre Septembre
Quatre Septembre
R de Port Mahon
R Ménars
R de la Bourse
Pl de la Bourse
La Bourse
Bourse
R du Croissant
31
R St-Joseph
2E
R St-Augustin
Pl Gaillon
R Monsigny
R de Richelieu
R Léon Cladel
R de Réaumur
R Gaillon
Av de l'Opéra
Passage Choiseul
R de Louvois
R Colbert
R Rameau
R Ste-Anne
33
Bibliothèque Nationale
R Paul Lelong
Frenchie (100m); Frenchie Bar à Vin (100m); Frenchie To Go (100m)
Galerie Vivienne
R de la Banque
R Chabanais
30
Galerie Colbert
21
20
R du Mail
R des Moulins
Paris Convention & Visitors Bureau
13
R des Petits Champs
Pl des Petits Pères
R d'Aboukir
R Villedo
R Thérèse
47
R de Beaujolais
Pyramides
18
16
28
22
R La Vrillière
32
39
25
Pl des Victoires
50
17
R d'Argout
R des Pyramides
Galerie de Montpensier
7
45
R Étienne Marcel
27
42
Galerie de Valois
R Hérold
R d'Argenteuil
38
R Molière
R de Valois
Hôtel des Postes
26
Banque de France
R Coquillière
R de Richelieu
R de Montpensier
Jardin du Palais Royal
R du Louvre
R Jean Jacques Rousseau
37
RIGHT BANK
R St-Honoré
R de l'Echelle
Pl Colette
R du Colonel Driant
R du Bouloi
34
R Rambuteau
4
R Montesquieu
Galerie Véro Dodat
Bourse de Commerce
R de Rohan
9
Immeuble des Bons Enfants
Pl des Deux-Ecus
R de Viarmes
R Jean-Jacques Rousseau
40
Pl du Palais Royal
R St-Honoré
R Berger
Palais Royal-Musée du Louvre
R de Rivoli
R du Faubourg St-Honoré
Musée du Louvre
Pl du Carrousel
35
Cour Napoléon
Jardin de l'Oratoire
Louvre Rivoli
R de l'Arbre Sec
5
6
2
Louvre
11
Cour Carrée
R de l'Amiral de Coligny
R du Roule
Musée du Louvre
Pl du Louvre
R Baillet
R du Pont Neuf
Jardin de l'Infante
Église St-Germain l'Auxerrois
La Samaritaine
Pont du Carrousel
Batobus Stop
Q du Louvre
Pont des Arts

LOUVRE *Map on p388*

LES HALLES *Map on p392*

Map on p392

Top Sights (p109)
1 Centre Pompidou ... G6
2 Église St-Eustache ... C4

Sights (p121)
3 59 Rivoli ... D7
4 Atelier Brancusi ... G6
5 Bourse de Commerce ... B4
6 Église St-Germain l'Auxerrois ... B7
7 Forum des Halles ... D5
8 Musée en Herbe ... B3
9 Musée National d'Art Moderne ... G6
10 Tour Jean sans Peur ... E3
11 Tour St-Jacques ... E8

Eating (p123)
12 Au Rocher de Cancale ... D3
13 Aux Tonneaux des Halles ... D4
14 Beef Club ... C4
15 Blend ... C2
16 Caldo Freddo ... D4
17 Claus ... A5
18 Cojean ... A7
19 Crêpe Dentelle ... D2
20 Dame Tartine ... F7
21 Djakarta Bali ... C5
22 Fée Nature ... C2
Fish Club ... (see 14)
23 Frenchie ... E1
24 Frenchie Bar à Vins ... E1
25 Frenchie To Go ... E1
26 La Bague de Kenza ... A5
27 La Mauvaise Réputation ... C2
28 La Tour de Montlhéry – Chez Denise ... C5
29 Le Bio d'Adam et Eve ... C6
30 Lina's Beautiful Sandwich ... B3
31 Pirouette ... E5
32 Racines 2 ... B6
33 Saveurs Végét'Halles ... D6
34 Spring ... B6
35 Stohrer ... D3
36 Yam'Tcha ... B5

Drinking & Nightlife (p129)
37 Café La Fusée ... G5
38 Depur ... F2
39 Experimental Cocktail Club ... E2
40 Jefrey's ... E2
41 Kong ... B7
42 Le Cœur Fou ... C2
43 Le Fumoir ... A6
44 Le Garde Robe ... B6
45 Le Tambour ... C3
46 Lockwood ... D1
47 Ô Chateau ... C3

Entertainment (p132)
48 Forum des Images ... D5
49 Le Baiser Salé ... E7
50 Sunset & Sunside ... E7
51 Théâtre de la Ville ... E8
52 Théâtre du Châtelet ... D8

Shopping (p132)
53 À La Mère de Famille ... D2
54 AllSaints Spitalfields ... B3
55 Charles Chocolatier ... D4
56 Comptoir de la Gastronomie ... C3
57 E Dehillerin ... B4
58 Galerie Véro Dodat ... A4
59 Kabuki Femme ... E4
60 Kiliwatch ... D3
61 La Fermette ... D2
62 Librairie Gourmande ... C1
63 MORA ... C3
64 Nysa ... D2
65 Room Service ... C2

Sleeping (p293)
66 Edgar ... F1
67 Hôtel Crayon ... A4
68 Hôtel de la Place du Louvre ... A7
69 Hôtel O ... B3
70 Hôtel St-Merry ... F7
71 Hôtel Tiquetonne ... F3
72 Le Relais du Louvre ... B7
73 Les Bains ... G4

LES HALLES

Key on p391

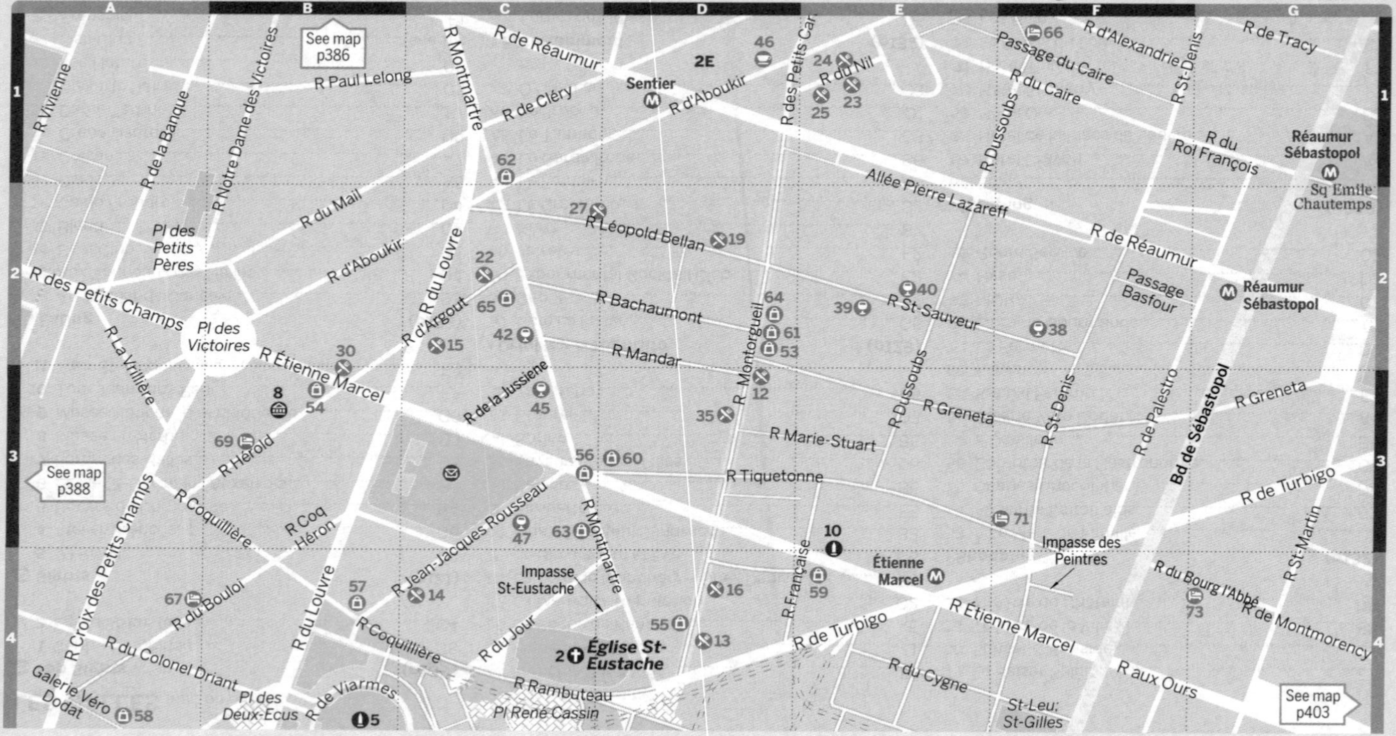
0 200 m
0 0.1 miles
N
A
B
C
D
E
F
G
1
2
3
4
2E
Sentier
Réaumur Sébastopol
Sq Emile Chautemps
Étienne Marcel
Église St-Eustache
Pl des Victoires
Pl des Petits Pères
Pl des Deux-Ecus
Pl René Cassin
St-Leu-St-Gilles
Galerie Véro Dodat
Passage Basfour
Passage du Caire
Impasse des Peintres
Impasse St-Eustache
Allée Pierre Lazareff
Bd de Sébastopol
R de Tracy
R d'Alexandrie
R St-Denis
R du Roi François
R de Réaumur
R du Caire
R Dussoubs
R du Nil
R des Petits Carreaux
R d'Aboukir
R de Cléry
R Montmartre
R Paul Lelong
R Notre Dame des Victoires
R de la Banque
R Vivienne
R des Petits Champs
R La Vrillière
R Croix des Petits Champs
R du Mail
R Étienne Marcel
R Hérold
R Coq Héron
R Coquillière
R du Bouloi
R du Colonel Driant
R du Louvre
R d'Argout
R de la Jussienne
R Jean-Jacques Rousseau
R du Jour
R Rambuteau
R de Viarmes
R Léopold Bellan
R Bachaumont
R Mandar
R Montorgueil
R St-Sauveur
R Greneta
R Marie-Stuart
R Tiquetonne
R Française
R de Turbigo
R du Cygne
R aux Ours
R de Palestro
R St-Martin
R du Bourg l'Abbé
R de Montmorency
See map p386
See map p388
See map p403
2
5
8
10
12
13
14
15
16
19
22
23
24
25
27
30
35
38
39
40
42
45
46
47
53
54
55
56
57
58
59
60
61
62
63
64
65
66
67
69
71
73

LES HALLES

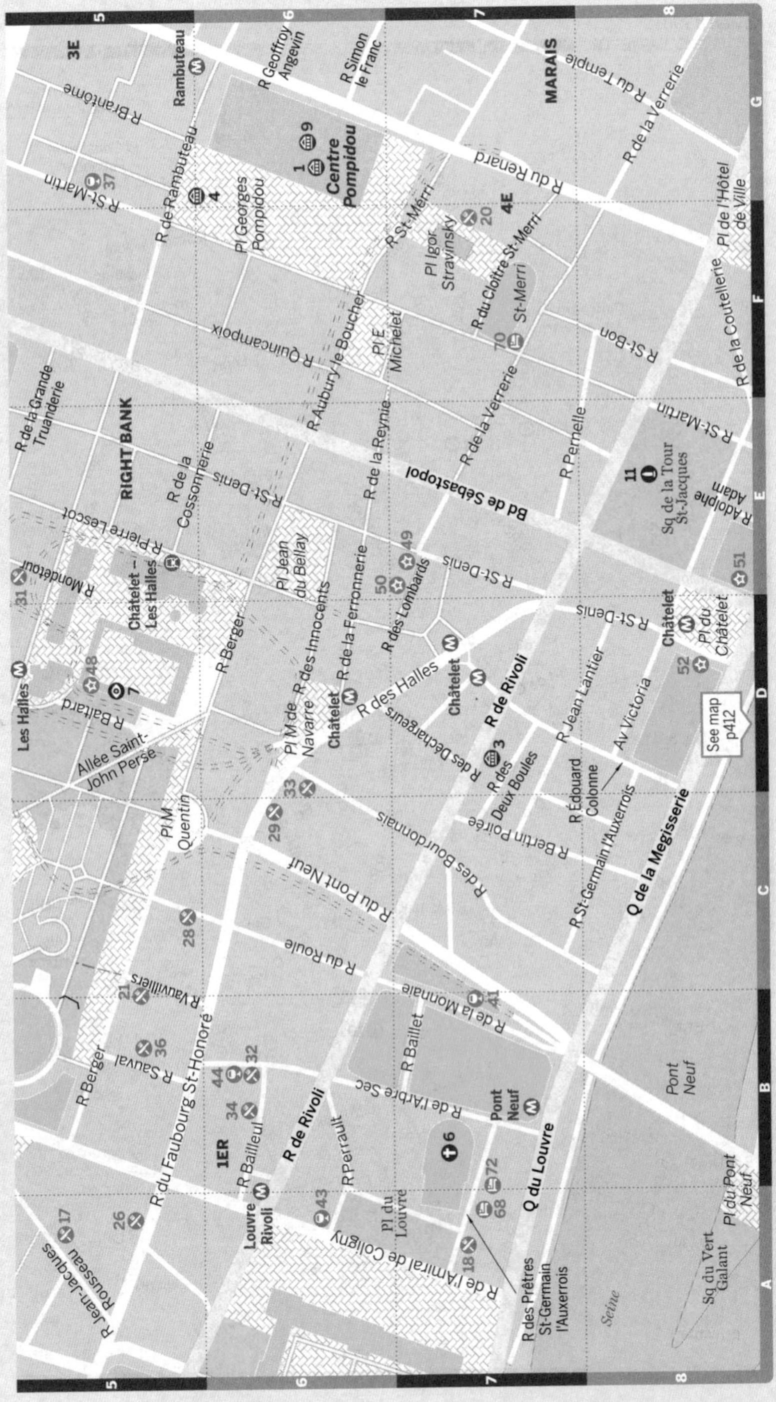

3E
1ER
4E
RIGHT BANK
MARAIS
Rambuteau
R Brantôme
R St-Martin
R de Rambuteau
R Geoffroy Angevin
R Simon le Franc
Centre Pompidou
Pl Georges Pompidou
R du Renard
R du Temple
R de la Verrerie
Pl de l'Hôtel de Ville
R de la Coutellerie
R St-Merri
Pl Igor Stravinsky
R du Cloître St-Merri
St-Merri
R St-Bon
R Quincampoix
R Aubury le Boucher
Pl E Michelet
R de la Grande Truanderie
R de la Cossonnerie
R St-Denis
Bd de Sébastopol
R de la Reynie
R Pernelle
R St-Martin
Sq de la Tour St-Jacques
R Adolphe Adam
R Pierre Lescot
R Mondétour
Châtelet – Les Halles
Pl Jean du Bellay
R de la Ferronnerie
R des Lombards
R St-Denis
Châtelet
Pl du Châtelet
Les Halles
R Baltard
R Berger
R des Innocents
Allée Saint-John Perse
Pl M de Navarre
R des Halles
R de Rivoli
R Jean Lantier
Av Victoria
See map p412
R des Déchargeurs
R des Deux Boules
R Édouard Colonne
R St-Germain l'Auxerrois
Q de la Mégisserie
Pl M Quentin
R Bertin Poirée
R des Bourdonnais
R du Pont Neuf
R du Roule
R Vauvilliers
R de la Monnaie
R Baillet
R Sauval
R de l'Arbre Sec
Pont Neuf
R du Faubourg St-Honoré
R Bailleul
R Perrault
Pl du Louvre
Q du Louvre
Louvre Rivoli
R de l'Amiral de Coligny
R Jean-Jacques Rousseau
R des Prêtres St-Germain l'Auxerrois
Seine
Sq du Vert Galant
Pl du Pont Neuf
1 9 4 20 70 11 49 50 51 31 48 7 52 3 33 29 28 21 41 36 32 44 34 6 72 68 43 26 17 18 37
A B C D E F G
5 6 7 8

Key on p396

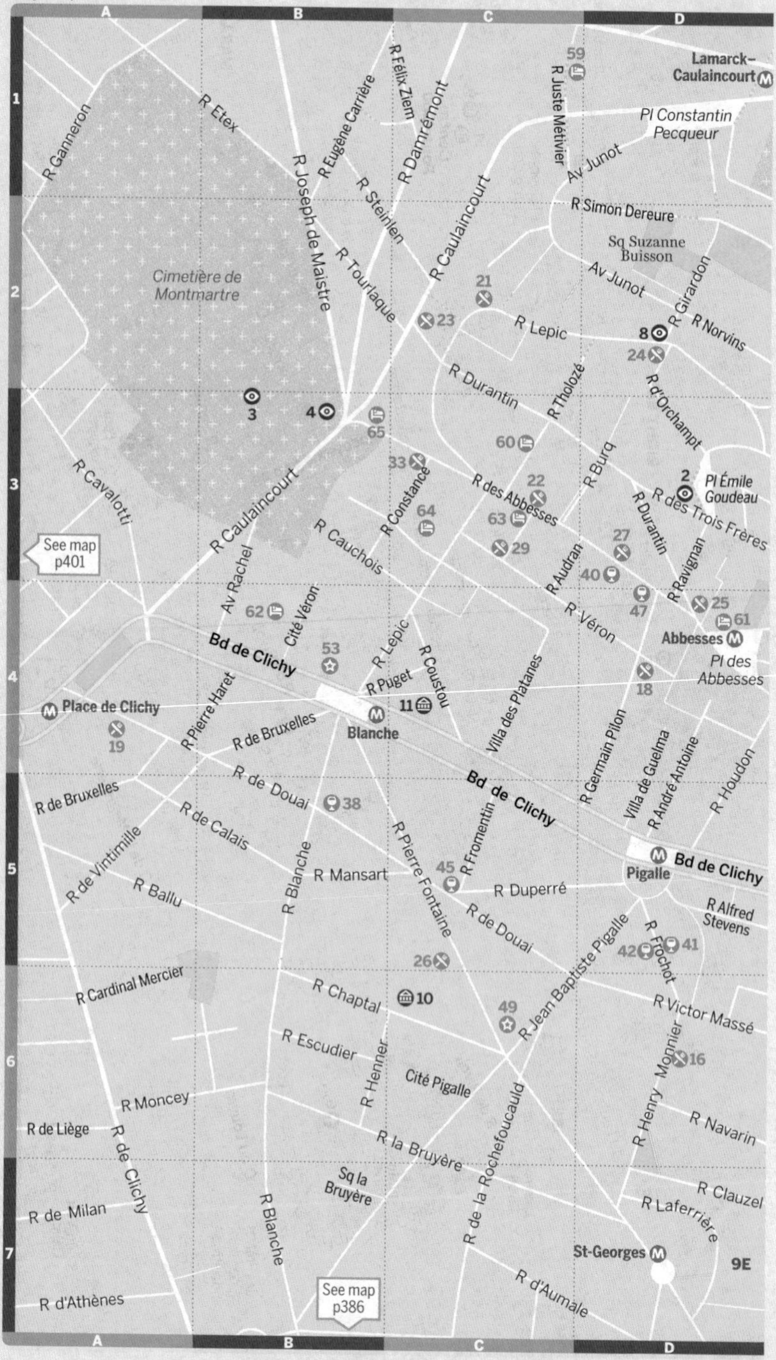

See map p401

See map p386

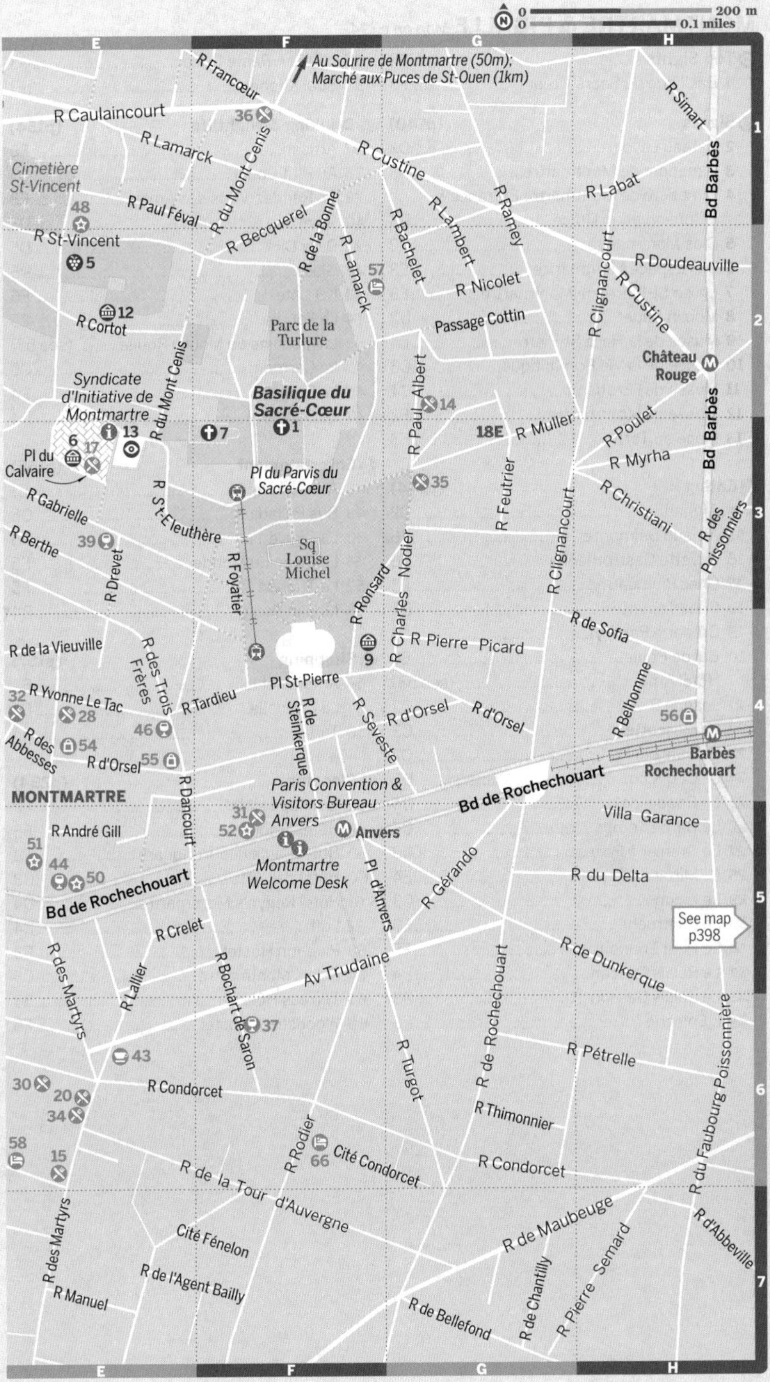
0 200 m
0 0.1 miles
E
F
G
H
1
2
3
4
5
6
7
Au Sourire de Montmartre (50m); Marché aux Puces de St-Ouen (1km)
R Francœur
R Caulaincourt
36
R Lamarck
R du Mont Cenis
R Custine
R Simart
Bd Barbès
Cimetière St-Vincent
48
R Paul Féval
R Becquerel
R de la Bonne
R Lamarck
R Bachelet
R Lambert
R Ramey
R Labat
R St-Vincent
5
57
R Nicolet
R Clignancourt
R Doudeauville
R Custine
12
R Cortot
Parc de la Turlure
Passage Cottin
Château Rouge
Syndicate d'Initiative de Montmartre
R du Mont Cenis
Basilique du Sacré-Cœur
R Paul Albert
14
Bd Barbès
6
13
7
1
18E
R Muller
R Poulet
Pl du Calvaire
17
R Myrha
Pl du Parvis du Sacré-Cœur
35
R Christiani
R Gabrielle
R St-Eleuthère
R Feutrier
R Clignancourt
R des Poissonniers
R Berthe
39
Sq Louise Michel
R Drevet
R Foyatier
R Ronsard
R Charles Nodier
R de Sofia
R de la Vieuville
R des Trois Frères
9
R Pierre Picard
Pl St-Pierre
R Belhomme
32
R Yvonne Le Tac
28
R Tardieu
R de Steinkerque
R Seveste
R d'Orsel
R d'Orsel
56
R des Abbesses
54
46
R d'Orsel
55
Barbès Rochechouart
MONTMARTRE
R Dancourt
Paris Convention & Visitors Bureau Anvers
Bd de Rochechouart
Villa Garance
31
52
Anvers
R André Gill
51
44
50
Montmartre Welcome Desk
Pl d'Anvers
R Gérando
R du Delta
Bd de Rochechouart
R Crelet
See map p398
R de Dunkerque
R des Martyrs
R Lallier
R Bochart de Saron
Av Trudaine
37
R de Rochechouart
R Turgot
R Pétrelle
43
R du Faubourg Poissonnière
30
20
R Condorcet
34
R Thimonnier
58
15
R Rodier
66
Cité Condorcet
R Condorcet
R de la Tour d'Auvergne
R de Maubeuge
R d'Abbeville
Cité Fénelon
R Pierre Semard
R des Martyrs
R de l'Agent Bailly
R Manuel
R de Bellefond
R de Chantilly

MONTMARTRE & PIGALLE *Map on p394*

GARE DU NORD & CANAL ST-MARTIN *Map on p398*

Sights **(p140)**
1 Canal St-Martin ... D6
2 Espace Beaurepaire ... E7
3 Institut des Cultures d'Islam ... B1
4 Institut des Cultures d'Islam (Goutte d'Or) ... C1
5 Musée de l'Évantail ... B8
6 Porte St-Denis ... B8
7 Porte St-Martin ... C8

Eating **(p144)**
8 Abri ... A5
9 Albion ... A5
10 Bistro Bellet ... B6
11 Bob's Juice Bar ... D7
Chez Michel ... (see 20)
12 Du Pain et des Idées ... D7
13 El Nopal ... E5
14 Helmut Newcake ... F7
15 Jambo ... G6
16 Krishna Bhavan ... D3
17 La Cantine de Quentin ... E6
18 La Marine ... E7
19 La Môme ... C2
20 La Pointe du Groin ... B4
21 La Rotonde ... F2
22 Le Cambodge ... E7
23 Le Chansonnier ... E4
24 Le Réveil du Xe ... C7
25 Le Verre Volé ... D7
26 Les Vinaigriers ... D6
27 Marché St-Quentin ... B5
28 Petit Cambodge ... F7
29 Philou ... E7
30 Pink Flamingo ... E6
31 Sésame ... E8
32 Sol Semilla ... D6
33 Sunken Chip ... D6
34 Terminus Nord ... B4
35 Vivant ... A6

Drinking & Nightlife **(p154)**
36 Café Chéri(e) ... G6
37 Chez Jeanette ... B7
38 Chez Prune ... E7
39 Cork & Cavan ... E7
40 DeLaVille Café ... A7
41 Holybelly ... D7
42 Hôtel du Nord ... E6
43 L'Atmosphère ... D6
44 Le Coq ... D8
45 Tuck Shop ... D7
46 Vivant Cave ... A6

Entertainment **(p155)**
47 Alhambra ... D7
48 New Morning ... B6
49 Point Éphémère ... F3

Shopping **(p157)**
50 Antoine et Lili ... D6
51 Artazart ... E7
52 Bazar Éthic ... E7
53 Frivoli ... E7
54 Idéco ... E7
55 La Crèmerie ... D7
56 Liza Korn ... E7
57 Maje ... D7
58 Médecine Douce ... E7

Sports & Activities **(p158)**
Azhar Hammam ... (see 4)

Sleeping **(p294)**
59 A Room in Paris ... B5
60 Auberge de Jeunesse Yves Robert ... D1
61 Hôtel du Nord – Le Pari Vélo ... D8
62 Le Citizen Hotel ... E6
63 République Hôtel ... D8
64 Robinet d'Or ... E5
65 St Christopher's Gare du Nord ... C4

GARE DU NORD & CANAL ST-MARTIN

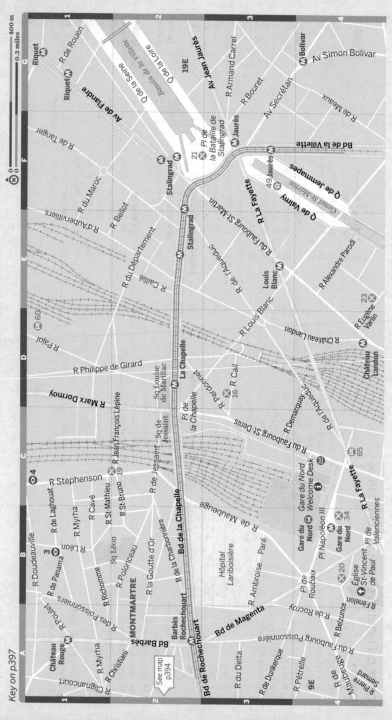

Key on p397

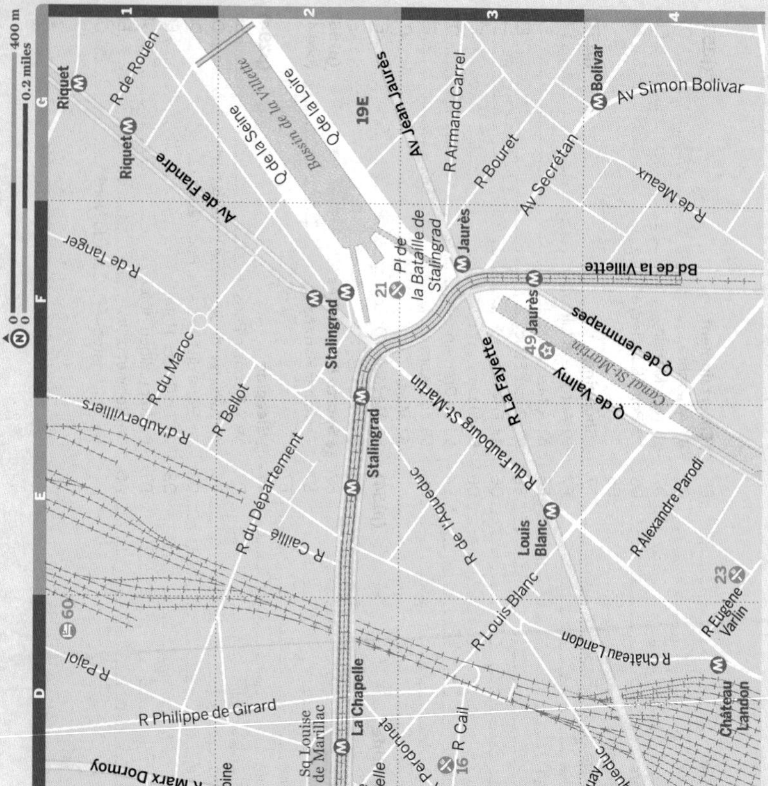

GARE DU NORD & CANAL ST-MARTIN

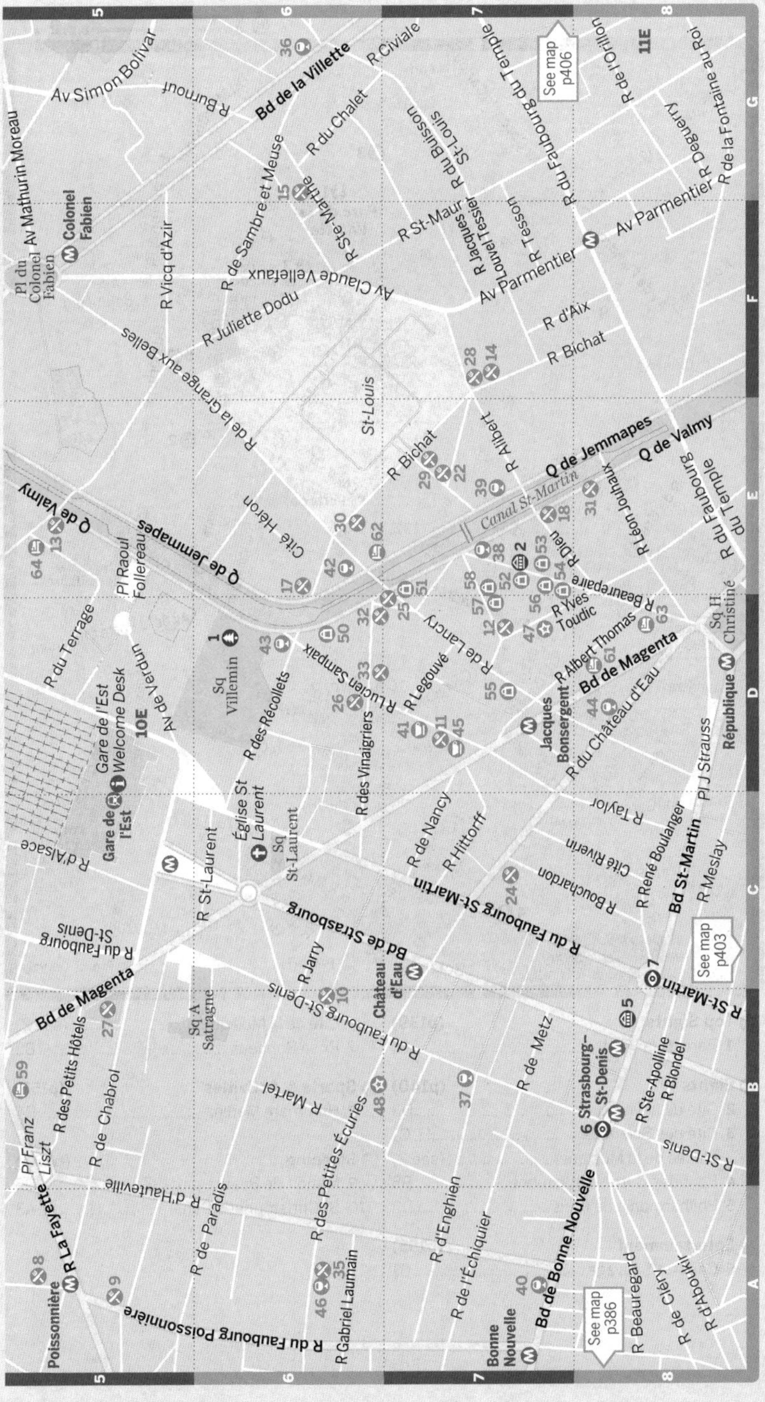

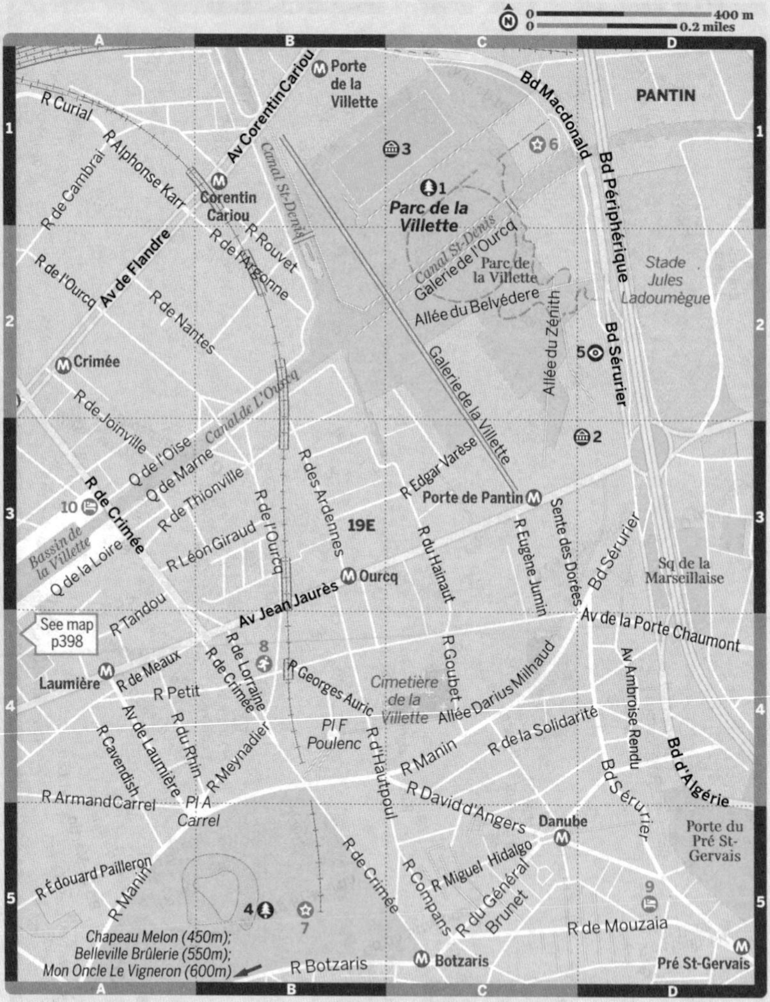

Top Sights (p139)

1 Parc de la Villette C1

Sights (p140)

2 Cité de la Musique D3

3 Cité des Sciences C1

Musée de la Musique .... (see 2)

4 Parc des Buttes-Chaumont B5

5 Philharmonie de Paris D2

Entertainment (p155)

6 Cabaret Sauvage C1

Cité de la Musique .... (see 2)

7 Rosa Bonheur B5

Sports & Activities (p157)

8 Hammam Medina B4

Sleeping (p294)

9 Manoir de Beauregard D5

10 St Christopher's Canal A3

CLICHY & GARE ST-LAZARE

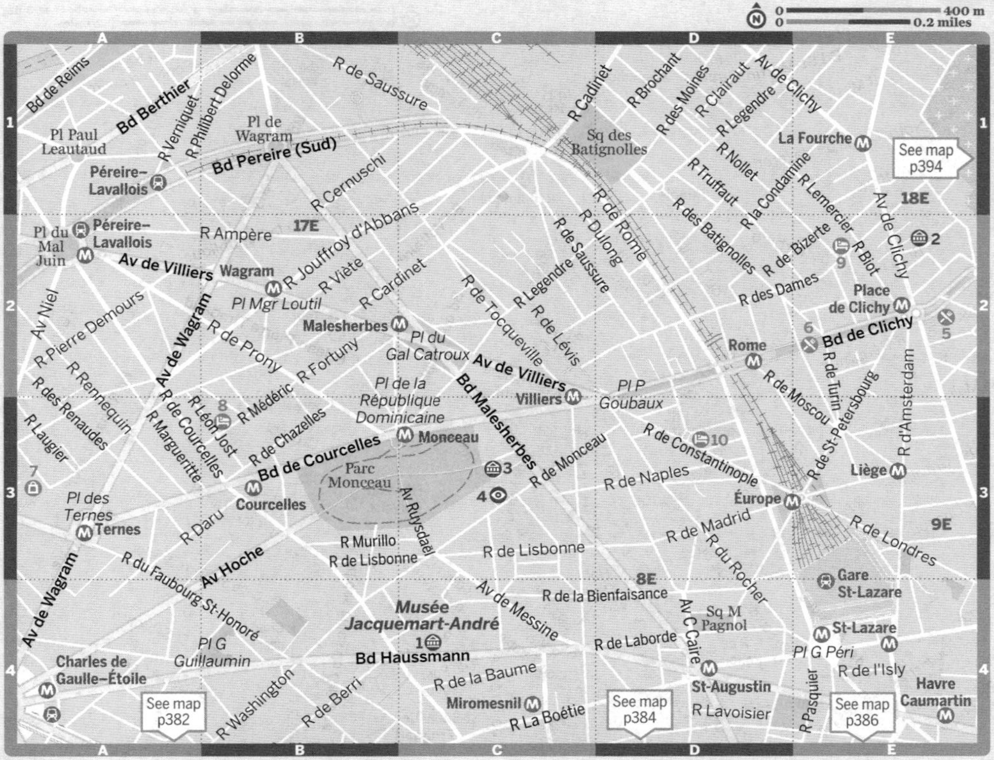

Top Sights (p143)

1 Musée Jacquemart-André C4

Sights (p140)

2 Le Bal E2
3 Musée Cernuschi C3
4 Musée Nissim de Camondo C3

Eating (p144)

Bistro des Dames .... (see 9)
5 Charlot, Roi des Coquillages E2
Le Bal Café .... (see 2)
6 Marché Batignolles-Clichy E2

Shopping (p157)

7 Fromagerie Alléosse A3

Sleeping (p294)

8 BVJ Monceau B3
9 Hôtel Eldorado E2
10 New Orient Hôtel D3

LE MARAIS

Key on p404

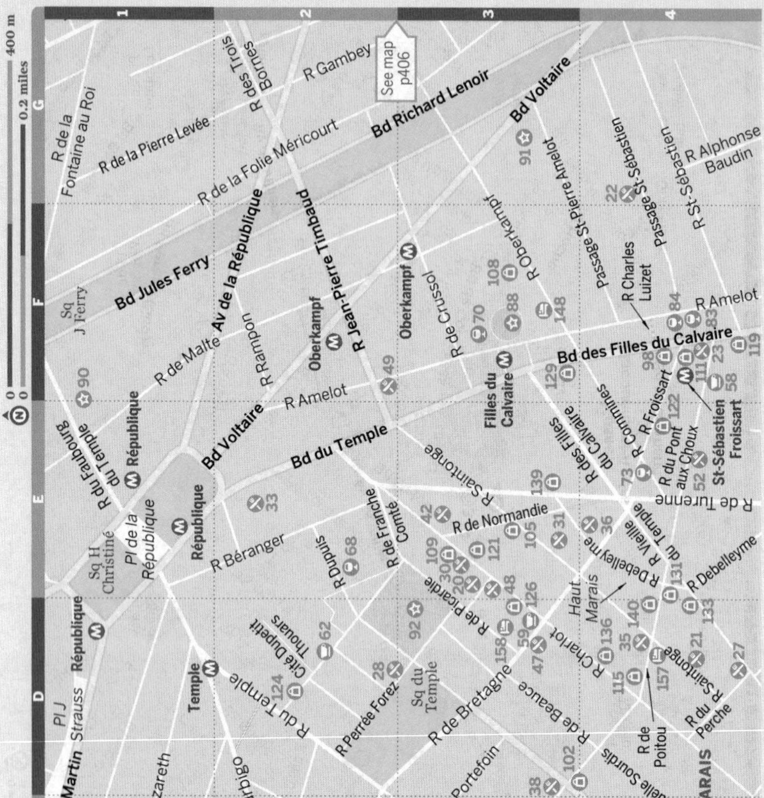

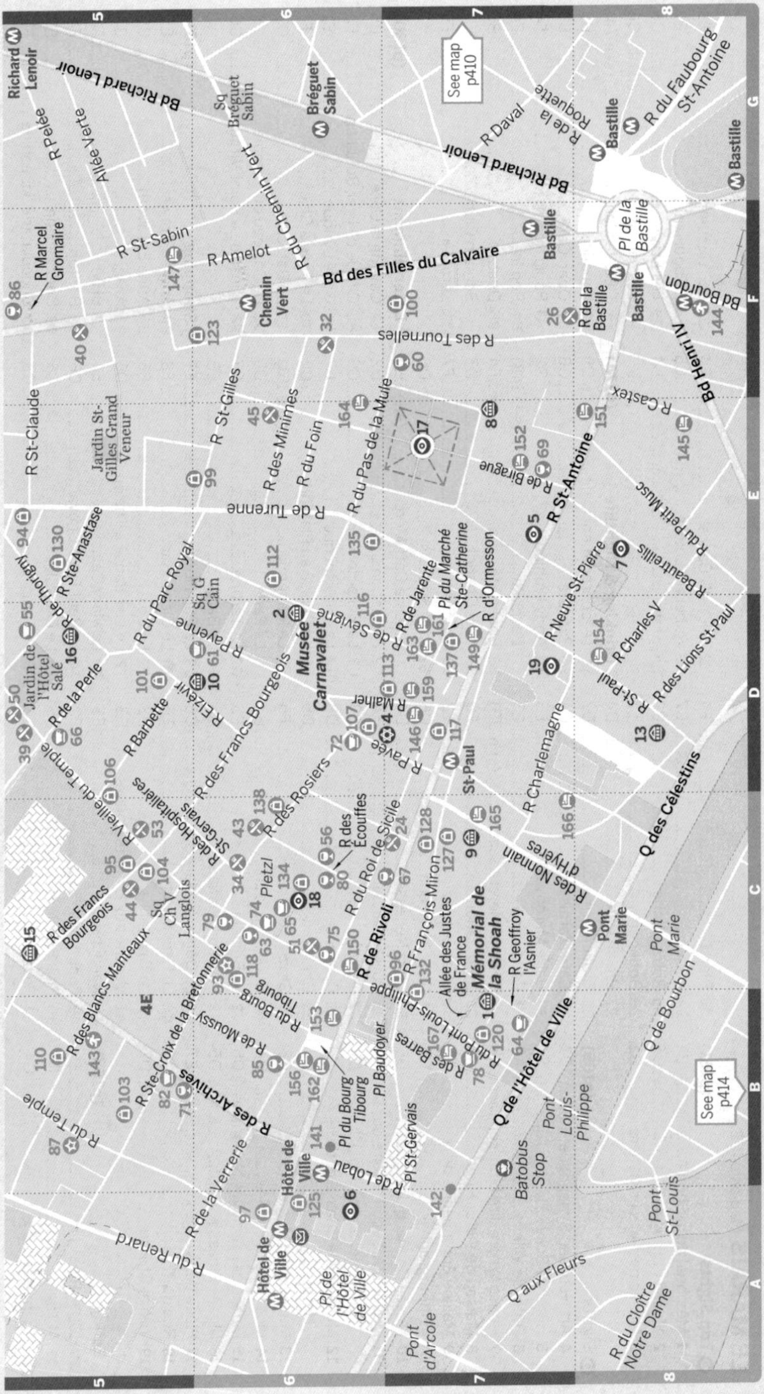
Bd Richard Lenoir
Richard Lenoir
R Pelée
Allée Verte
R St-Sabin
R Marcel Gromaire
R Amelot
Sq Bréguet Sabin
Bréguet Sabin
R du Chemin Vert
Bd des Filles du Calvaire
Chemin Vert
See map p410
R Daval
R de la Roquette
R du Faubourg St-Antoine
Bastille
Pl de la Bastille
R de la Bastille
Bd Bourdon
Bd Henri IV
R des Tournelles
R Castex
R St-Claude
Jardin St-Gilles Grand Veneur
R St-Gilles
R des Minimes
R du Foin
R du Pas de la Mule
R de Birague
R St-Antoine
R du Petit Musc
R de Turenne
R Ste-Anastase
R de Thorigny
R du Parc Royal
Sq G Cain
R Payenne
Musée Carnavalet
R de Sévigné
R de Jarente
Pl du Marché Ste-Catherine
R d'Ormesson
R Neuve St-Pierre
R Beautreillis
R Charles V
R des Lions St-Paul
R St-Paul
Jardin de l'Hôtel Salé
R de la Perle
R Barbette
R Elzévir
R des Francs Bourgeois
R Malher
R Pavée
St-Paul
R Charlemagne
Q des Célestins
R Vieille du Temple
R des Hospitalières St-Gervais
R des Rosiers
R des Écouffes
R du Roi de Sicile
R François Miron
R de Rivoli
R des Nonnains d'Hyères
Pont Marie
R des Francs Bourgeois
Sq Ch V Langlois
Pletzl
R des Blancs Manteaux
R Ste-Croix de la Bretonnerie
R du Bourg Tibourg
R de Moussy
R des Archives
Pl du Bourg Tibourg
Pl Baudoyer
Allée des Justes de France
Mémorial de la Shoah
R Geoffroy l'Asnier
R du Pont Louis-Philippe
R des Barres
Q de l'Hôtel de Ville
Q de Bourbon
See map p414
Pont Louis-Philippe
R du Temple
R de la Verrerie
Hôtel de Ville
R de Lobau
Pl St-Gervais
Batobus Stop
R du Renard
Pl de l'Hôtel de Ville
Pont St-Louis
Q aux Fleurs
Pont d'Arcole
R du Cloître Notre Dame

LE MARAIS *Map on p402*

Top Sights (p161)
1 Mémorial de la Shoah ... B7
2 Musée Carnavalet ... D6
3 Musée des Arts et Métiers ... B2

Sights (p165)
4 Art Nouveau Synagogue ... D7
5 Hôtel de Sully ... E7
6 Hôtel de Ville ... A6
7 House Where Jim Morrison Died ... E8
8 Maison de Victor Hugo ... E7
9 Maison Européenne de la Photographie ... C7
10 Musée Cognacq-Jay ... D6
11 Musée d'Art et d'Histoire du Judaïsme ... B4
12 Musée de la Chasse et de la Nature ... C4
13 Musée de la Magie ... D8
14 Musée de la Poupée ... B4
15 Musée des Archives Nationales ... C5
16 Musée Picasso ... D5
17 Place des Vosges ... E7
18 Rue du Trésor ... C6
19 Village St-Paul ... D7

Eating (p168)
20 100% Bio ... E3
21 Al Taglio ... D4
22 Au Passage ... G4
23 Blend ... F4
24 Boboli ... C7
25 Bob's Kitchen ... B2
26 Bofinger ... F7
27 Breizh Café ... D4
28 Broken Arm ... D2
29 Café Marais ... C4
30 Caffè Marcovaldo ... E3
31 Candelaria ... E3
Cantine Merci ... (see 119)
32 Chez Janou ... F6
33 Chez Jenny ... E2
34 Chez Marianne ... C6
35 Chez Nénesse ... D4
36 Cuisine de Bar ... E4
37 Derrière ... B3
38 Dessance ... D3
39 Glou ... D5
40 Grazie ... F5
41 Huré ... B4
42 La Briciola ... E3
43 L'As du Fallafel ... C6
44 Le Dôme du Marais ... C5
45 Le Petit Marché ... E6
46 Le Taxi Jaune ... B3
47 Marché aux Enfants Rouges ... D3
48 Nanashi ... E3
49 Paperboy ... F2
50 Pink Flamingo ... D5
51 Pozzetto ... C6
52 Rachel's Cakes ... E4
53 Robert et Louise ... C5
54 Stanz ... B4

Drinking & Nightlife (p174)
55 (A)pparemment Café ... D5
56 3w Kafé ... C6
57 Andy Wahloo ... B2
Bespoke ... (see 148)
58 Boot Café ... F4
59 Café Charlot ... D3
60 Café Martini ... F7
61 Café Suédois ... D6
Cinéma Café Merci ... (see 119)
62 Fondation Café ... D2
63 La Belle Hortense ... C6
64 La Caféothèque ... B7
65 La Chaise au Plafond ... C6
La Mangerie ... (see 161)
66 La Perle ... D5
67 La Tartine ... C7
68 Le Barav ... E2
69 Le Cap Horn ... E7
70 Le Clown Bar ... F3
71 Le Cox ... B5
72 Le Loir dans La Théière ... D6
73 Le Mary Céleste ... E4
74 Le Petit Fer à Cheval ... C6
75 Le Pick-Clops ... C6
76 Le Tango ... C3
77 Le Trinquette ... B3
78 L'Ebouillanté ... B7
79 Les Étages ... C6
80 Les Jacasses ... C6
L'Étoile Manquante ... (see 74)
81 Loustic ... B3
82 Open Café ... B5
83 Panic Room ... F4
84 Pop In ... F4
85 Quetzal ... B6
Scream Club ... (see 90)
86 Zéro Zéro ... F5

Entertainment (p180)
87 Café de la Gare ... B5
88 Cirque d'Hiver Bouglione ... F3
89 Gaîté Lyrique ... B1
90 La Favela Chic ... F1
91 Le Bataclan ... G3
92 Le Carreau du Temple ... D3
93 Théâtre Le Point Virgule ... C6

Shopping (p181)
94 Andrea Crews ... E5
95 Anne Elisabeth ... C5
96 Azag ... C7
97 BHV ... A6
98 Bonton ... F4
99 Chez Hélène ... E6
100 Chocolaterie Joséphine Vannier ... F7

101 CSAO ... D5
102 État Libre d'Orange ... D3
103 Fleux ... B5
104 Fragonard ... C5
105 Isabel Marant ... E3
106 Jamin Puech ... D5
107 K Jacques ... D6
108 Kate Mack ... F3
109 La Boutique Extraordinaire ... E3
110 Le Boudoir 26 ... B5
111 Le Labo ... F4
L'Éclair de Génie ... (see 107)
112 L'Éclaireur ... E6
113 L'Éclaireur (Menswear) ... D7
114 L'Épicerie ... B3
115 L'Habilleur ... D4
116 Losco ... D6
117 Maison Georges Larnicol ... D7
118 Mariage Frères ... C6
119 Merci ... F4
120 Mi Amor ... B7
121 Moon Young Hee ... E3
122 Nathalie Sevikïan ... E4
123 Odetta Vintage ... F6
124 Ofr. Librairie ... D2
125 Paris Rendez-Vous ... A6
126 Pauline Pin ... D3
127 Petit Pan ... C7
128 Petit Pan Bébé ... C7
129 Rougier & Plé ... F3
130 Samuel Coraux ... E5
131 Shine ... E4
132 Sic Amor ... B7
133 Surface to Air ... D4
134 Trésor ... C6
135 Tumbleweed ... E6
136 Valentine Gauthier ... D4
137 Vert d'Absinthe ... D7
138 Vintage Désir ... C6
139 Violette et Léonie ... E3
140 Virginie Monroe ... D4

Sports & Activities (p186)

141 Bike About Tours ... B6
142 La Cuisine Paris ... A7
143 Les Bains du Marais ... B5
144 Nomadeshop ... F8
Rollers & Coquillages ... (see 144)

Sleeping (p297)

145 Castex Hôtel ... E8
146 Grand Hôtel Malher ... D7
147 Hôtel Bastille de Launay ... F5
148 Hôtel Beaumarchais ... F3
149 Hôtel Caron ... D7
150 Hôtel Caron de Beaumarchais ... C6
151 Hôtel de la Herse d'Or ... E8
152 Hôtel de la Place des Vosges ... E7
153 Hôtel de Nice ... B6
154 Hôtel du 7e Art ... D8
155 Hôtel du Haut Marais ... C3
156 Hôtel du Loiret ... B6
157 Hôtel du Petit Moulin ... D4
158 Hôtel du Vieux Saule ... D3
159 Hôtel Emile ... D7
160 Hôtel Georgette ... B3
161 Hôtel Jeanne d'Arc ... D7
162 Hôtel Rivoli ... B6
163 Hôtel Saint Paul de Marais ... D7
164 Le Pavillon de la Reine ... E6
165 MIJE Fourcy ... C7
166 MIJE Le Fauconnier ... C7
167 MIJE Maubuisson ... B7

MÉNILMONTANT & BELLEVILLE

Key on p408

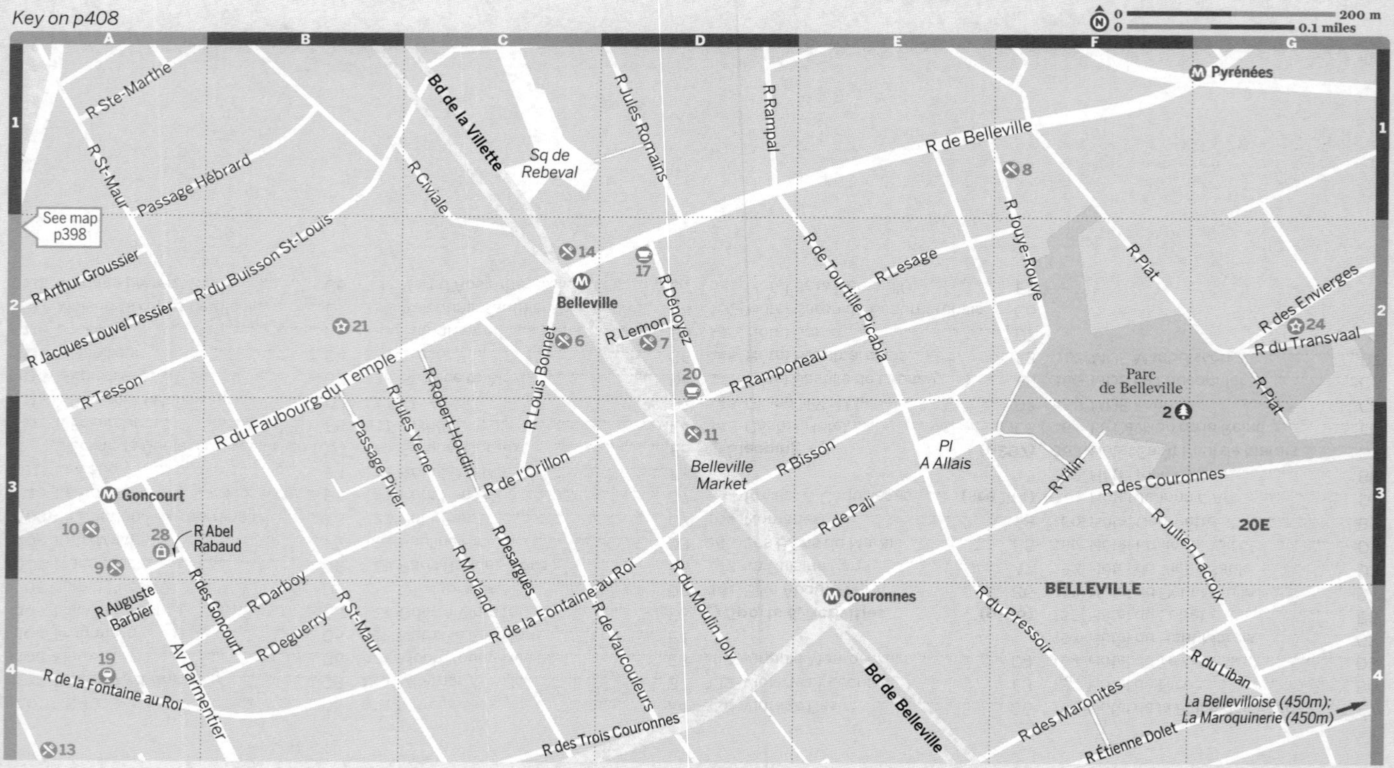

MÉNILMONTANT & BELLEVILLE

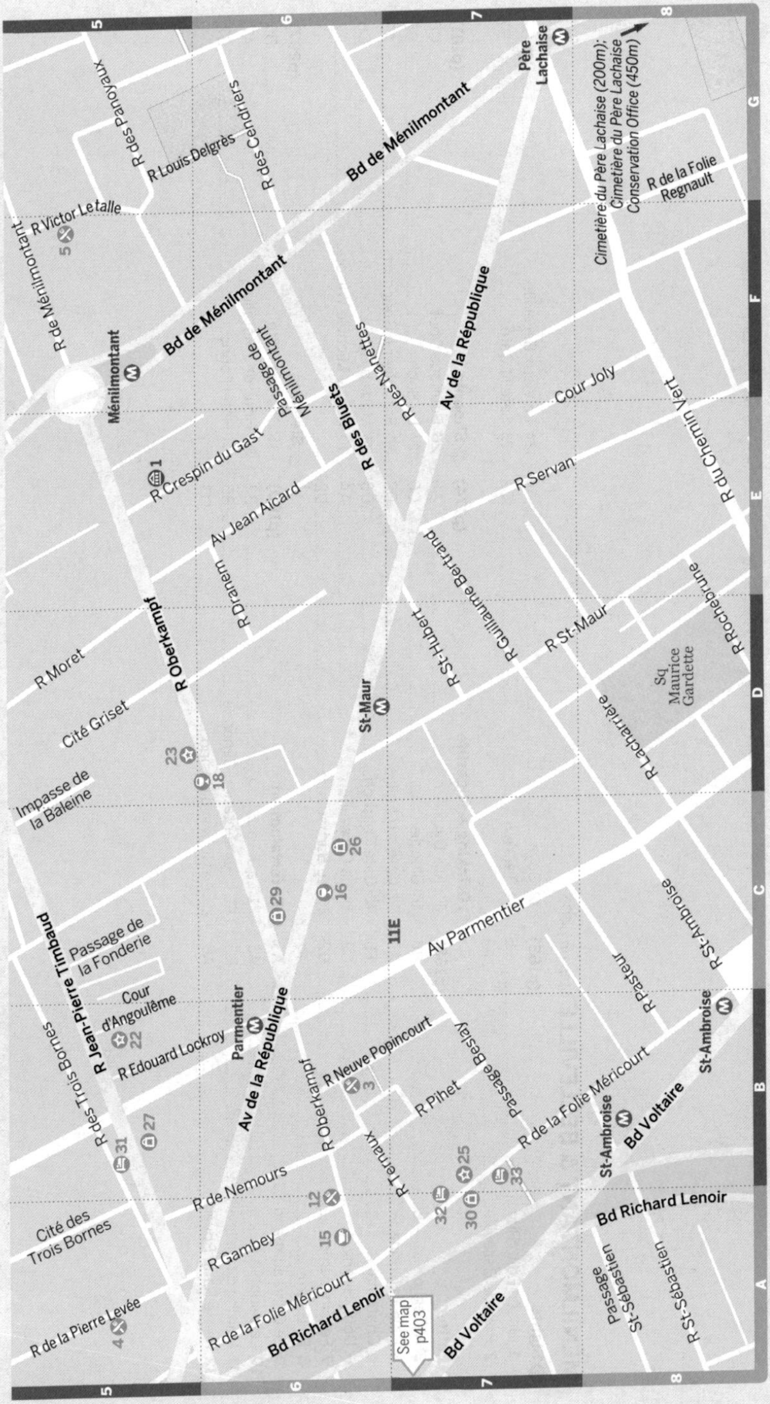

MÉNILMONTANT & BELLEVILLE *Map on p406*

Sights **(p165)**
1 Musée Édith Piaf E5
2 Parc de Belleville F3

Eating **(p168)**
3 Al Taglio B6
4 Blue Valentine A5
5 Chatomat F5
6 Dong Huong C2
7 Felicity Lemon D2
8 Le Baratin F1
9 Le Chateaubriand A3
10 Le Dauphin A3
11 Marché de Belleville D3
12 Pierre Sang Boyer A6
13 Soya A4
14 Tai Yien C2

Drinking & Nightlife **(p174)**
15 Aux Deux Amis A6
16 Bloodies C6
17 Café aux Folies D2
18 Café Charbon D6
19 La Caravane A4
20 Le Barbouquin D2

Entertainment **(p180)**
21 La Java B2
22 L'Alimentation Générale B5
23 Le Nouveau Casino D5
24 Le Vieux Belleville G2
25 Satellit Café B7

Shopping **(p181)**
26 Boutique Obut C6
27 By Sophie B5
28 Fromagerie Goncourt A3
29 Made by Moi C6
30 Puzzle Michèle Wilson A7

Sleeping **(p297)**
31 Cosmos Hôtel B5
32 Hôtel des Métallos A7
33 Hôtel Fabric B7

BASTILLE & EASTERN PARIS *Map on p410*

Sights (p189)
1 Maison Rouge ... A6
2 Opéra Bastille ... B4
3 Place de la Bastille ... B4
4 Promenade Plantée ... C6

Eating (p191)
5 40/60 ... E4
6 À La Banane Ivoirienne ... E5
7 À la Biche au Bois ... B6
8 À La Renaissance ... D2
9 Agua Limón ... D5
10 Au Vieux Chêne ... F5
11 Bar à Soupes ... D4
12 Bistrot Mélac ... G3
13 Bistrot Paul Bert ... F4
14 Bones ... E2
15 Chalet Savoyard ... D4
16 Chez Paul ... C4
17 Chez Ramulaud ... G5
18 CheZaline ... D2
19 Clamato ... E3
20 Cocotte et Canou ... F3
21 Crêperie Bretonne ... E4
22 Gentle Gourmet Café ... A6
23 Le 6 Paul Bert ... F4
24 Le Cotte Rôti ... D6
25 Le Siffleur de Ballons ... E5
26 Le Souk ... D3
27 Le Square Trousseau ... D5
28 Le Train Bleu ... C7
29 Le Viaduc Café ... C6
30 L'Ébauchoir ... E5
31 L'Écailler du Bistrot ... F4
32 L'Encrier ... C6
33 Les Amis de Messina ... F5
34 Les Domaines Qui Montent ... E2
35 Marché Bastille ... B3
36 Marché d'Aligre ... D6
37 Miss Lunch at Première Pression Provence ... D5
38 Moisan ... D5
39 Paris Hanoï ... E4
40 Pink Flamingo ... D5
41 Septime ... E4
42 Swann et Vincent ... C5
43 Table ... C5
44 Unico ... F4
45 Yard ... G1

Drinking & Nightlife (p196)
46 Barrio Latino ... C4
47 Café Titon ... G4
48 La Fée Verte ... D2
49 La Liberté ... F5
50 Le Baron Rouge ... D5
51 Le Bistrot du Peintre ... D4
52 Le China ... C5
53 Le Pure Café ... F4
54 Les Funambules ... F5
55 Mojito Lab ... C3
56 Pause Café ... D4
57 Sanz by Bizz'art ... C4
58 Septime La Cave ... E3
59 Tape Bar ... B3
60 Troll Café ... D5
61 Twenty One Sound Bar ... E4

Entertainment (p198)
62 Badaboum ... D3
63 La Chapelle des Lombards ... C3
64 Le Balajo ... B3
65 Le Motel ... D4
66 Opéra Bastille ... B4
67 Opéra Bastille Box Office ... B4

Shopping (p198)
68 El Galpon ... F4
69 Fermob ... C5
70 La Cocotte ... F5
71 La Manufacture de Chocolat ... B3
72 Marché aux Puces d'Aligre ... D6
73 My Crazy Pop ... D5
Viaduc des Arts ... (see 4)

Sleeping (p300)
74 Hi Matic ... E3
75 Hôtel Daval ... B3
76 Hôtel Paris Bastille ... B5
77 Standard Design Hôtel ... C3

BASTILLE & EASTERN PARIS

Key on p409

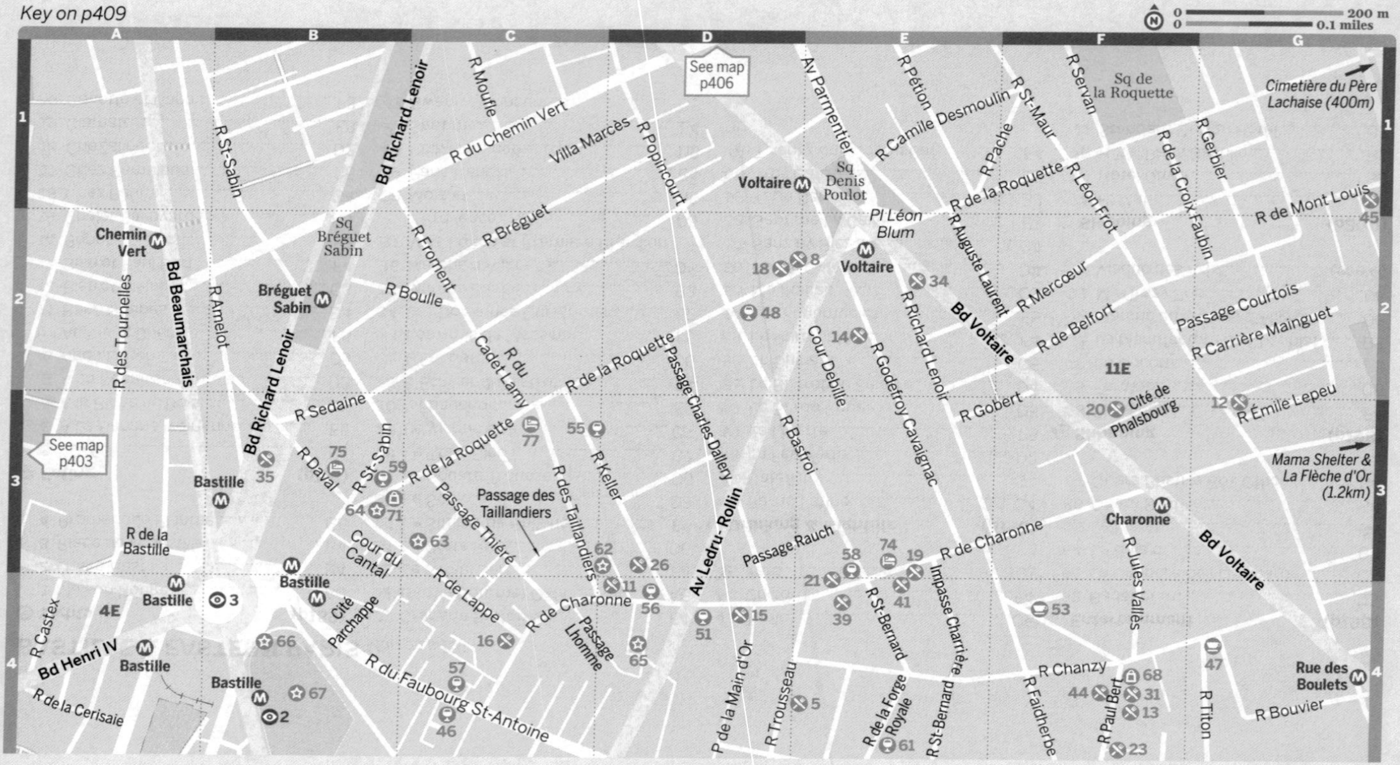

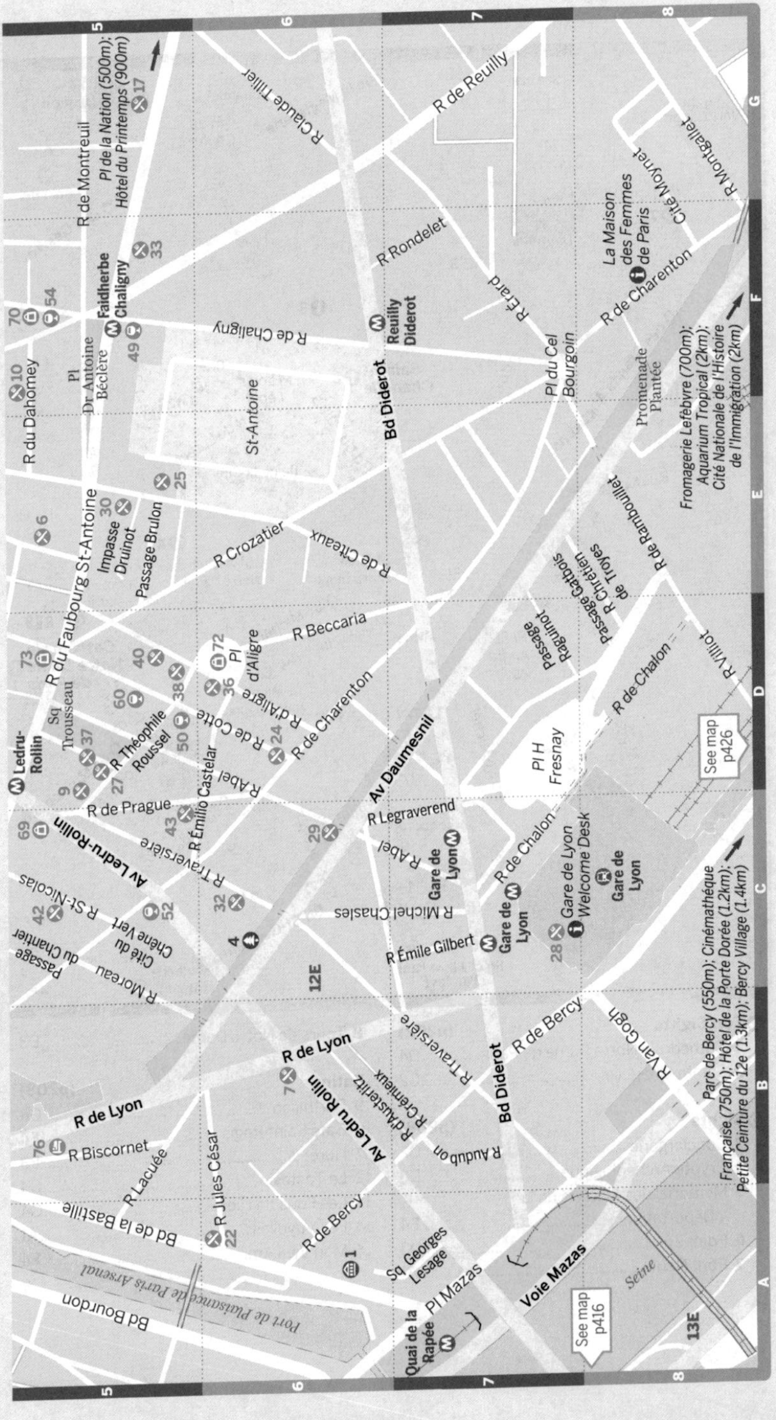
R de Montreuil
Pl de la Nation (500m); Hôtel du Printemps (900m)
17
R Claude Tillier
R de Reuilly
R Montgallet
Cité Moynet
La Maison des Femmes de Paris
R de Charenton
R Rondelet
33
R du Dahomey
10
70
54
Faidherbe Chaligny
49
R de Chaligny
Pl Dr Antoine Béclère
St-Antoine
Reuilly Diderot
Bd Diderot
R Erard
Pl du Cel Bourgoin
Promenade Plantée
Fromagerie Lefèbvre (700m); Aquarium Tropical (2km); Cité Nationale de l'Histoire de l'Immigration (2km)
6
30
25
R du Faubourg St-Antoine
Impasse Druinot
Passage Brulon
R Crozatier
R de Cîteaux
R de Rambouillet
Passage Gatbois
R Chrétien de Troyes
Passage Raguinot
R Beccaria
73
72
Pl d'Aligre
40
38
36
60
Sq Trousseau
R d'Aligre
R de Cotte
R de Charenton
R Villiot
R de Chalon
Ledru-Rollin
37
50
24
R Théophile Roussel
9
27
R Abel
Av Daumesnil
Pl H Fresnay
See map p426
R de Prague
43
R Émilio Castelar
69
Av Ledru-Rollin
R Traversière
29
R Legraverend
R Abel
Gare de Lyon
R de Chalon
Gare de Lyon Welcome Desk
Gare de Lyon
R St-Nicolas
42
52
32
R Michel Chasles
Gare de Lyon
28
Cité du Chêne Vert
Passage du Chantier
4
R Émile Gilbert
R Moreau
12E
R Traversière
R de Bercy
R Van Gogh
Parc de Bercy (550m); Cinémathèque Française (750m); Hôtel de la Porte Dorée (1.2km); Petite Ceinture du 12e (1.3km); Bercy Village (1.4km)
R de Lyon
7
Av Ledru Rollin
R Crémieux
R d'Austerlitz
Bd Diderot
R Biscornet
76
R Audubon
R Lacuée
R Jules César
22
Bd de la Bastille
R de Bercy
1
Sq Georges Lesage
Port de Plaisance de Paris Arsenal
Bd Bourdon
Pl Mazas
Voie Mazas
Seine
Quai de la Rapée
See map p416
13E
A
B
C
D
E
F
G
5
6
7
8

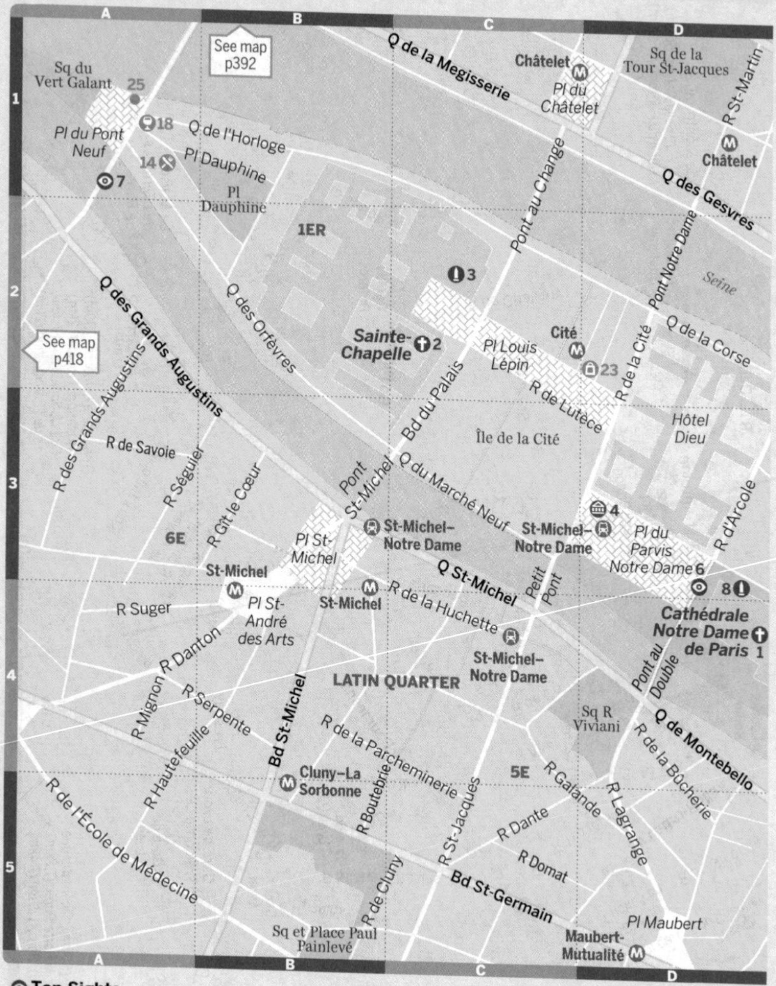

Top Sights (p202)

1 Cathédrale Notre Dame de Paris............D4
2 Sainte-Chapelle............C2

Sights (p208)

3 Conciergerie............C2
4 Crypte Archéologique............D3
5 Mémorial des Martyrs de la Déportation............E4
6 Point Zéro............D3
7 Pont Neuf............A1
8 Tours de Notre Dame............D3

Eating (p208)

9 Berthillon............G4
10 Café Saint Régis............F4
11 Huré............E3
12 Le Tastevin............G4
13 Les Fous de l'Île............G4
14 Les Voyelles............A1
15 Mon Vieil Ami............F4

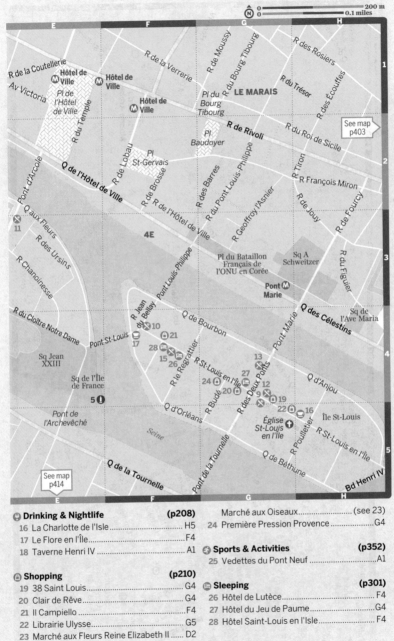

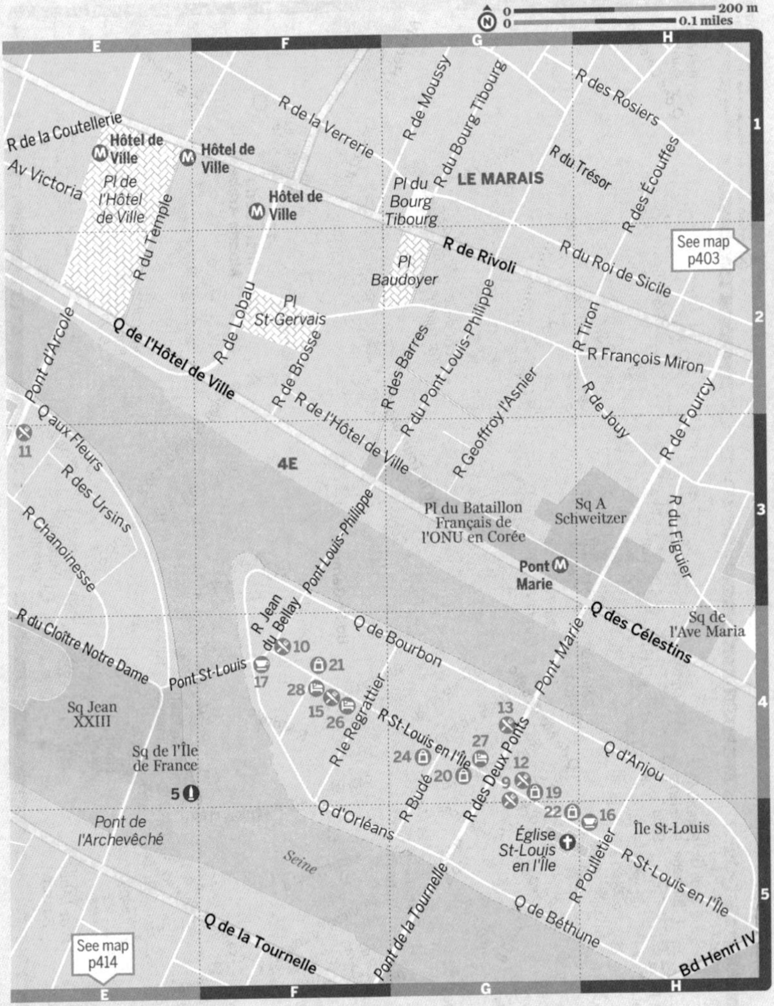

Drinking & Nightlife (p208)

16 La Charlotte de l'Isle H5
17 Le Flore en l'Île F4
18 Taverne Henri IV A1

Shopping (p210)

19 38 Saint Louis G4
20 Clair de Rêve G4
21 Il Campiello F4
22 Librairie Ulysse G5
23 Marché aux Fleurs Reine Elizabeth II D2
Marché aux Oiseaux .... (see 23)
24 Première Pression Provence G4

Sports & Activities (p352)

25 Vedettes du Pont Neuf A1

Sleeping (p301)

26 Hôtel de Lutèce F4
27 Hôtel du Jeu de Paume G4
28 Hôtel Saint-Louis en l'Isle F4

LATIN QUARTER NORTH

Key on p415

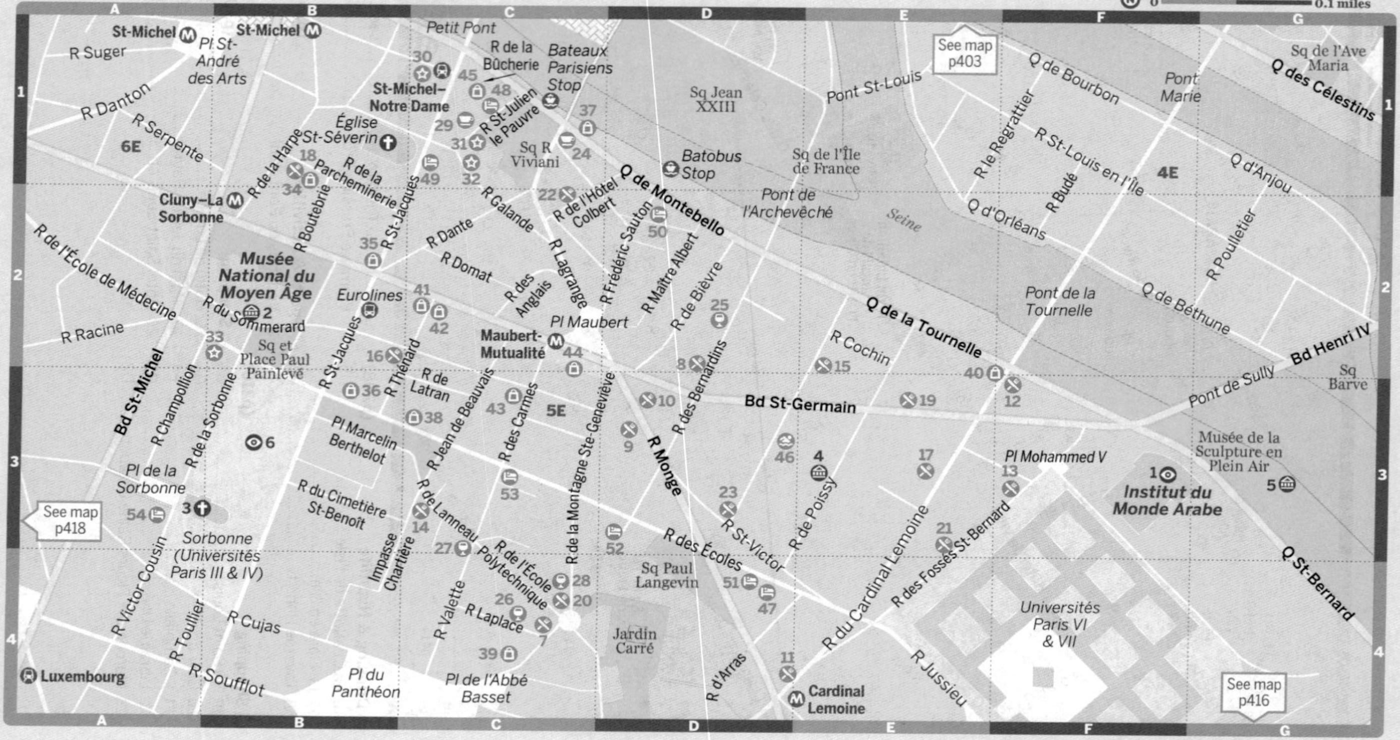

LATIN QUARTER NORTH *Map on p414*

Top Sights (p213)
1 Institut du Monde Arabe ... F3
2 Musée National du Moyen Âge ... B2

Sights (p214)
3 Chapelle de la Sorbonne ... A3
4 Collège des Bernardins ... E3
5 Musée de la Sculpture en Plein Air ... G3
6 Sorbonne ... B3

Eating (p216)
7 58 Qualité Street ... C4
8 Anahuacalli ... D2
9 Boulangerie Eric Kayser ... D3
10 Ciel ... D3
11 Kootchi ... D4
12 La Tour d'Argent ... F3
13 L'AOC ... F3
14 Le Coupe-Chou ... C3
15 Le Petit Pontoise ... E2
16 Le Pré Verre ... B2
17 Le Puits de Légumes ... E3
18 Lengué ... B1
19 Les Pâtes Vivantes ... E3
20 Les Pipos ... C4
21 Moissonnier ... E3
22 Sola ... C2
23 Terroir Parisien ... D3

Drinking & Nightlife (p221)
24 Café Panis ... C1
25 Curio Parlor Cocktail Club ... D2
26 Le Piano Vache ... C4
27 Le Pub St-Hilaire ... C3
28 Le Violon Dingue ... C4
29 Tea Caddy ... C1

Entertainment (p224)
30 Caveau de la Huchette ... C1
31 Église St-Julien le Pauvre ... C1
32 Le Caveau des Oubliettes ... C1
33 Le Champo ... B2

Shopping (p225)
34 Abbey Bookshop ... B1
35 Album ... B2
36 Au Vieux Campeur ... B3
37 Bouquinistes ... C1
38 Crocodisc ... C3
39 Crocojazz ... C4
Fromagerie Laurent Dubois ... (see 44)
40 La Tour d'Argent Boutique ... E2
41 Librairie de Voyage ... C2
42 Librairie Eyrolles ... C2
43 Magie ... C3
44 Marché Maubert ... C2
45 Shakespeare & Company ... C1

Sports & Activities (p227)
46 Piscine Pontoise ... D3

Sleeping (p301)
47 Familia Hôtel ... D4
48 Hôtel Esmeralda ... C1
49 Hôtel Henri IV Rive Gauche ... C1
50 Hôtel les Degrés de Notre Dame ... D2
51 Hôtel Minerve ... D4
52 Hôtel Résidence Henri IV ... D3
53 Hôtel St-Jacques ... C3
54 Select Hôtel ... A3

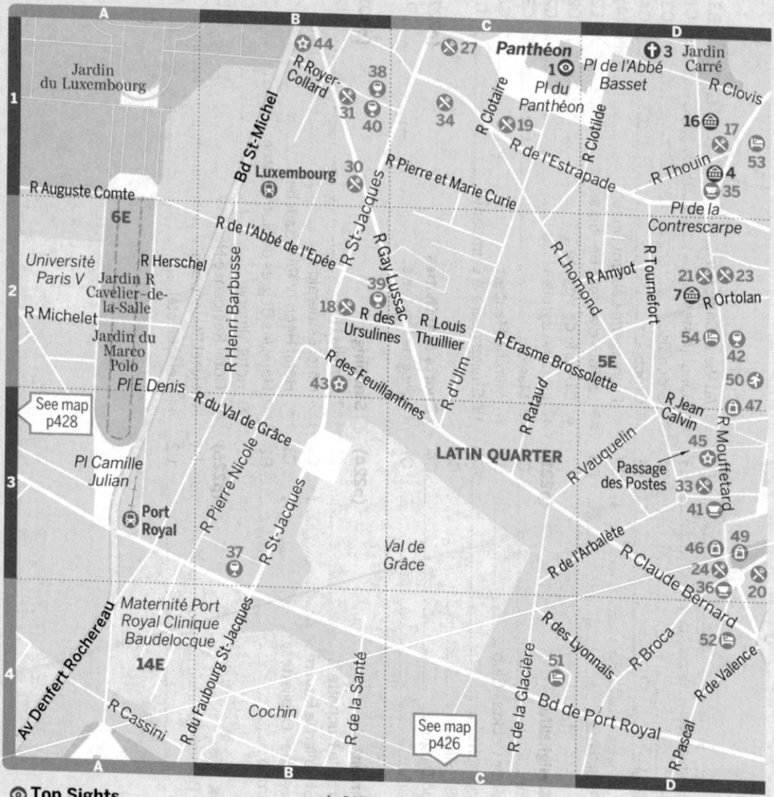

Top Sights (p215)

1 Panthéon...C1

Sights (p214)

2 Arènes de Lutèce...E1
3 Église St Étienne du Mont...D1
4 Ernest Hemingway's apartment...D1
5 Galerie d'Anatomie Comparée et de Paléontologie...G2
6 Galerie de Minéralogie et de Géologie...F3
Galerie des Enfants...(see 8)
7 George Orwell's boarding house...D2
8 Grande Galerie de l'Évolution...F2
9 James Joyce's flat...E1
10 Jardin des Plantes...G1
11 Jardin des Plantes Entrance...H2
12 Les Grandes Serres...F2
13 Ménagerie du Jardin des Plantes...G1
14 Mosquée de Paris...E2
15 Muséum National d'Histoire Naturelle...F2
16 Paul Verlaine's Garret...D1

Eating (p216)

17 Bonjour Vietnam...D1
18 Boulangerie Bruno Solques...B2
19 Café de la Nouvelle Mairie...C1
20 Cave Mavrommatis...D3
21 Chez Nicos...D2
22 Dans Les Landes...E4
23 Gelati d'Alberto...D2
24 La Salle à Manger...D3
25 L'Agrume...F4
26 Le Buisson Ardent...E1
27 Le Comptoir du Panthéon...C1
28 Le Jardin des Pâtes...E2
29 Le Pot O'Lait...E3
30 Les Papilles...B1
31 Machu Picchu...B1

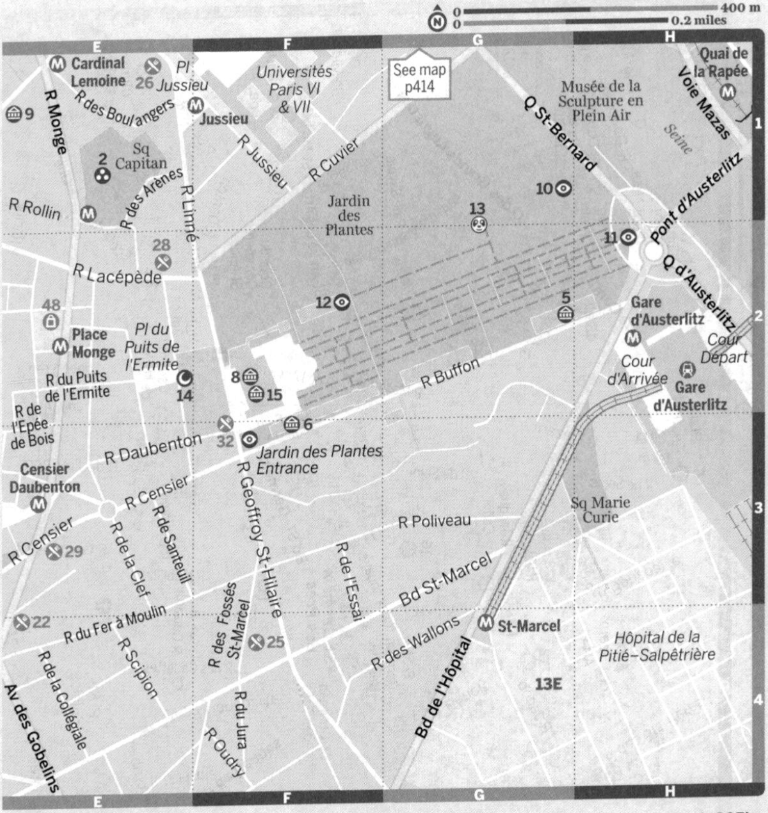

32 Mosquée de Paris F3
33 Petits Plats de Marc D3
34 Tashi Delek C1

Drinking & Nightlife **(p221)**

35 Café Delmas D1
36 Cave La Bourgogne D3
37 L'Académie de la Bière B3
38 Le Crocodile B1
39 Le Mauzac B2
40 Le Pantalon B1
41 Le Verre à Pied D3
42 Le Vieux Chêne D2

Entertainment **(p224)**

43 Café Universel B2
44 Le Petit Journal St-Michel B1
45 L'Epée de Bois D3

Shopping **(p225)**

46 Androuet D3
47 Chocolats Mococha D2
Delizius .... (see 46)
48 Marché Monge E2
49 Marché Mouffetard D3

Sports & Activities **(p227)**

50 Bowling Mouffetard D2
Hammam de la Mosquée de Paris .... (see 32)

Sleeping **(p301)**

51 Five Hotel C4
52 Hôtel de l'Espérance D4
53 Hôtel des Grandes Écoles D1
54 Young & Happy D2

ST-GERMAIN

Key on p420

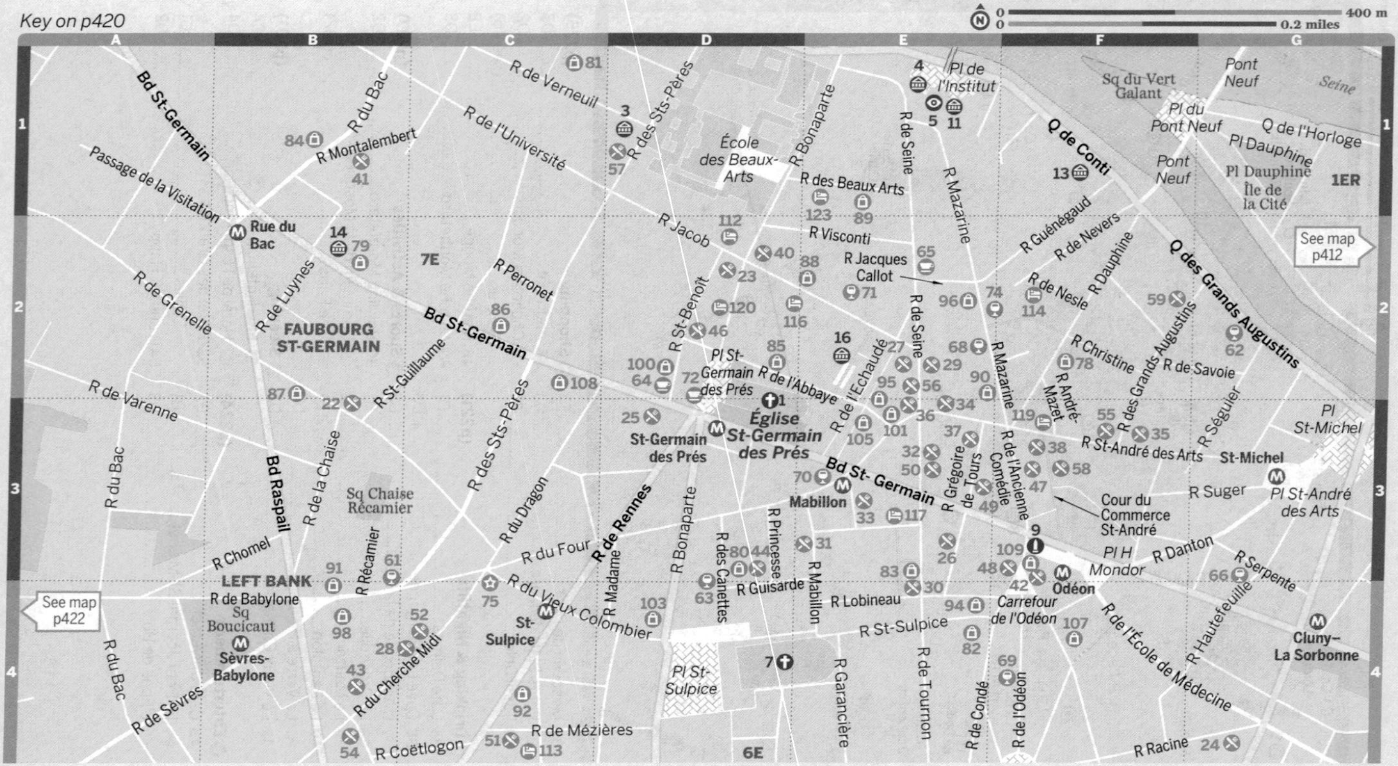

ST-GERMAIN

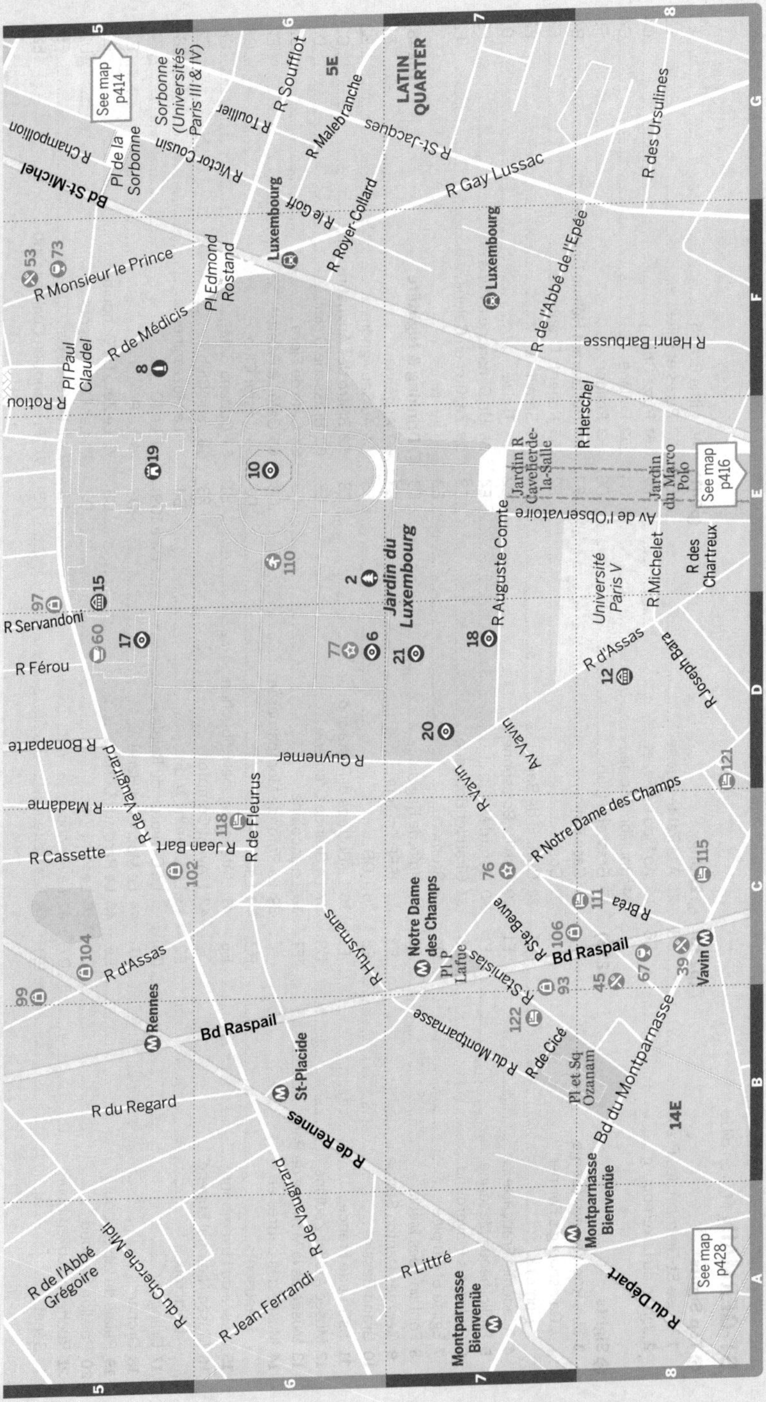
See map p414
See map p416
See map p428
Bd St-Michel
R Champollion
Pl de la Sorbonne
Sorbonne
Sorbonne (Universités Paris III & IV)
R Victor Cousin
R Toullier
R Soufflot
5E
R Malebranche
LATIN QUARTER
R St-Jacques
R Gay Lussac
R des Ursulines
R le Goff
Luxembourg
R Royer-Collard
Pl Edmond Rostand
R Monsieur le Prince
R de Médicis
Pl Paul Claudel
R Rotrou
R de l'Abbé de l'Epée
R Henri Barbusse
R Herschel
Jardin R Cavelier-de-la-Salle
Jardin du Marco Polo
Av de l'Observatoire
Jardin du Luxembourg
R Auguste Comte
Université Paris V
R Michelet
R des Chartreux
R Servandoni
R Férou
R d'Assas
R Joseph Bara
R Bonaparte
R Guynemer
Av Vavin
R Vavin
R Madame
R de Vaugirard
R Jean Bart
R de Fleurus
R Cassette
R Notre Dame des Champs
R Huysmans
Notre Dame des Champs
Pl P Lafue
R Ste-Beuve
R Bréa
Bd Raspail
R Stanislas
Vavin
Rennes
R du Montparnasse
R de Cicé
Pl et Sq Ozanam
Bd du Montparnasse
14E
St-Placide
R du Regard
R de Rennes
R de Vaugirard
Montparnasse Bienvenüe
R de l'Abbé Grégoire
R du Cherche Midi
R Jean Ferrandi
R Littré
R du Départ
53
73
8
19
10
110
2
97
15
60
17
77
6
21
18
12
20
121
118
102
76
115
111
106
104
99
122
93
45
67
39
A
B
C
D
E
F
G
5
6
7
8

ST-GERMAIN *Map on p418*

Top Sights (p230)

1 Église St-Germain des Prés ... D3
2 Jardin du Luxembourg ... E6

Sights (p238)

3 5bis Rue Verneuil (Serge Gainsbourg's Former Home) ... D1
4 Académie Française ... E1
5 Bibliothèque Mazarine ... E1
6 Children's Playground ... D6
7 Église St-Sulpice ... D4
8 Fontaine des Médici ... F5
9 Georges Danton Statue ... F3
10 Grand Bassin ... E6
11 Institut de France ... E1
12 Musée Atelier Zadkine ... D8
13 Musée de la Monnaie de Paris ... F1
14 Musée des Lettres et Manuscrits ... B2
15 Musée du Luxembourg ... E5
16 Musée National Eugène Delacroix ... E2
17 Orangery ... D5
18 Orchards ... D7
19 Palais du Luxembourg ... E5
20 Pavillon Davioud ... D7
21 Rucher du Luxembourg ... D7
Sénat ... (see 19)

Eating (p241)

22 À la Petite Chaise ... B3
23 Au Pied de Fouet ... D2
24 Bouillon Racine ... G4
25 Brasserie Lipp ... D3
26 Casa Bini ... E3
27 Cosi ... E2
28 Cuisine de Bar ... C4
29 Fish La Boissonnerie ... E2
30 Gérard Mulot ... E4
31 Giraudet Boutique ... E3
32 Grom ... E3
33 Huîterie Regis ... E3
34 JSFP Traiteur ... E3
35 KGB ... F3
36 La Bottega di Pastavino ... E3
37 La Grande Crèmerie ... E3
38 La Jacobine ... F3
39 La Rotonde Montparnasse ... C8
40 Ladurée ... D2
41 L'Atelier de Joël Robuchon ... B1
42 L'Avant Comptoir ... F3
43 Le Cherche Midi ... B4
Le Comptoir du Relais ... (see 109)
44 Le Mâchon d'Henri ... D3
45 Le Parc aux Cerfs ... C8
46 Le Petit Zinc ... D2
47 Le Procope ... F3
48 Les Éditeurs ... F3
49 Little Breizh ... E3
50 Pères et Filles ... E3
51 Pizza Chic ... C4
52 Poilâne ... C4
53 Polidor ... F5
54 Restaurant Hélène Darroze ... B4
55 Roger la Grenouille ... F3
56 Semilla ... E2
57 Treize ... D1
58 Un Dimanche à Paris ... F3
59 Ze Kitchen Galerie ... F2

Drinking & Nightlife (p248)

60 Angelina ... D5
61 Au Sauvignon ... B3
62 Bistro des Augustins ... G2
63 Brasserie O'Neil ... D3
64 Café de Flore ... D2
65 Café La Palette ... E2
66 Castor Club ... G3
67 Cubana Café ... C8
68 Jane Club ... E2
La Mezzanine ... (see 68)
69 Le 10 ... F4
70 Le Pré ... E3
71 Le Zéro De Conduite ... E2
72 Les Deux Magots ... D2
73 L'Urgence Bar ... F5
74 Prescription Cocktail Club ... E2

Entertainment (p251)

75 Comédie Française Théâtre du Vieux Colombier ... C4
76 Le Lucernaire ... C7
77 Théâtre du Luxembourg ... D6

Shopping (p252)

78 A La Recherche De Jane ... F2
79 Alexandra Sojfer ... B2
80 Au Plat d'Étain ... D3
81 Carré Rive Gauche ... C1
82 Cave St-Sulpice ... E4
83 Cire Trudon ... E3
84 Deyrolle ... B1
85 Flamant Home Interiors ... D2
86 Fragonard Boutique ... C2
87 Frédéric Malle ... B2
88 Gab & Jo ... E2
89 Galerie Loft ... E1
90 Hapart ... E2
91 Hermès ... B4
92 JB Guanti ... C4
93 La Clef des Marques ... C7
94 La Crèmerie ... E4
95 La Dernière Goutte ... E3
96 La Galerie Moderne ... E2
97 La Maison de Poupée ... E5
98 La Maison du Chocolat ... B4
99 Le Bain Rose ... C5
100 Le Chocolat Alain Ducasse ... D2
101 Le Dépôt-Vente de Buci ... E3
102 Pâtisserie Sadaharu Aoki ... C5
103 Pierre Hermé ... D4
104 Plastiques ... C5
105 Ragtime ... E3
106 Rouge et Noir ... C7
107 San Francisco Book Company ... F4
108 Sonia Rykiel ... C2
109 Theatr'Hall ... F3

Sports & Activities

110 Shetland Ponies for Hire ... E6

Sleeping (p303)

111 Hôtel Danemark ... C8
112 Hôtel d'Angleterre ... D2
113 Hôtel de l'Abbaye Saint Germain ... C4
114 Hôtel de Nesle ... F2
115 Hôtel des Académies et des Arts ... C8
116 Hôtel des Marronniers ... D2
117 Hôtel Le Clément ... E3
118 Hôtel Perreyve ... C6
119 Hôtel St-André des Arts ... F3
120 Hôtel St-Germain des Prés ... D2
121 L'Apostrophe ... D8
122 Le Six ... B7
123 L'Hôtel ... E1

LES INVALIDES

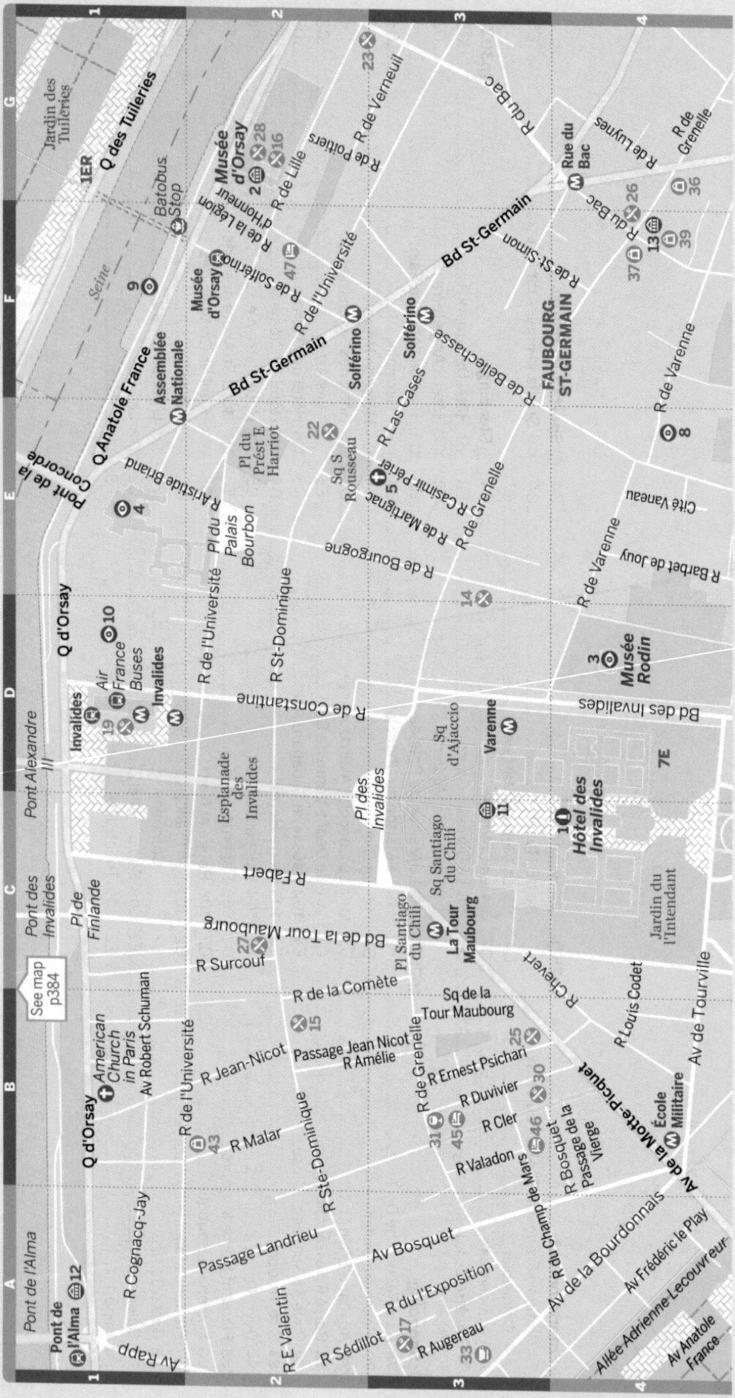

Key on p424

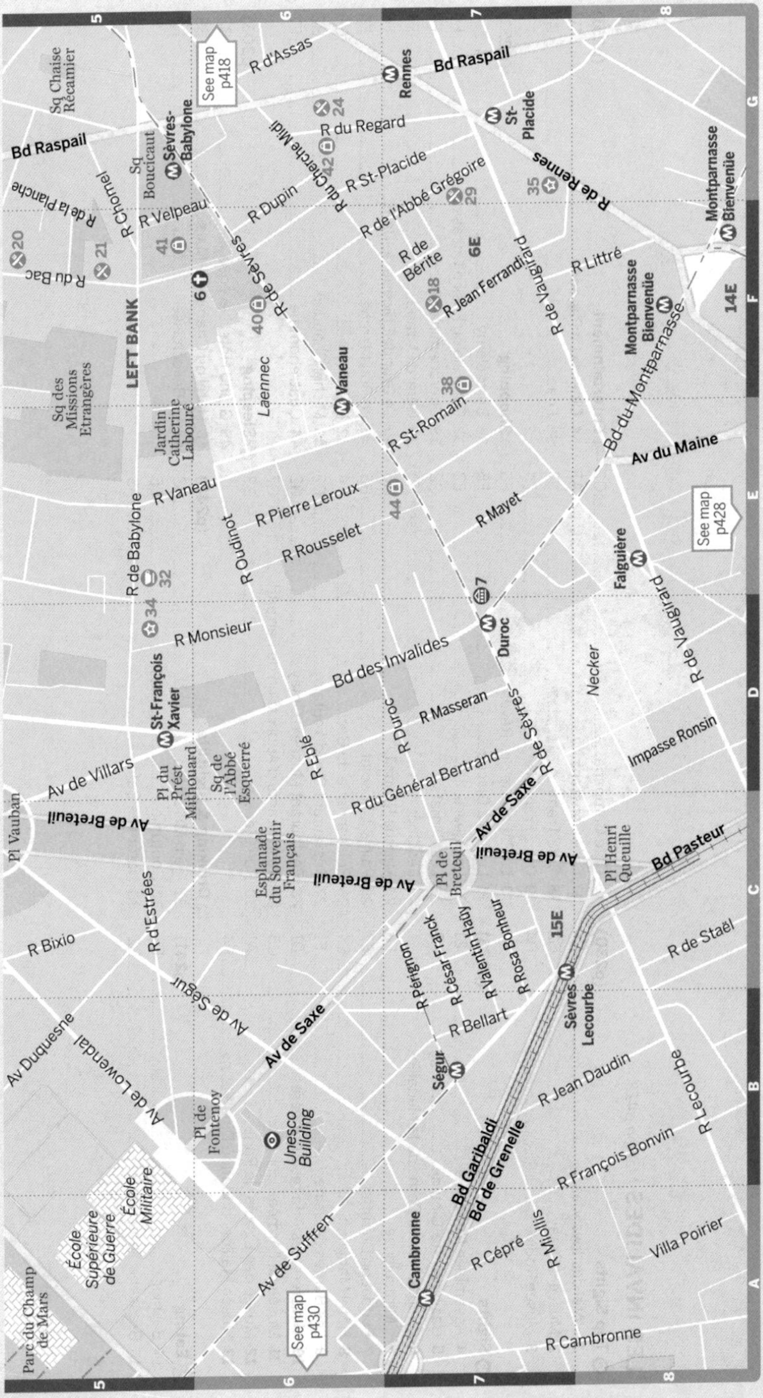

Bd Raspail
R d'Assas
See map p418
Rennes
Sq Chaise Récamier
Sèvres-Babylone
Sq Boucicaut
R du Regard
24
42
R du Cherche Midi
St-Placide
R St-Placide
R Chomel
R de la Planche
R Velpeau
R Dupin
R de l'Abbé Grégoire
29
R de Rennes
35
Montparnasse Bienvenüe
20
21
R du Bac
41
6
R de Sèvres
R de Bérite
6E
R Jean Ferrandi
R de Vaugirard
R Littré
18
40
LEFT BANK
Sq des Missions Etrangères
Laennec
Vaneau
38
R St-Romain
Bd du Montparnasse
14E
Jardin Catherine Labouré
R Vaneau
R Oudinot
R Pierre Leroux
44
Av du Maine
R Rousselet
R Mayet
See map p428
R de Babylone
32
34
7
Falguière
R Monsieur
Duroc
Bd des Invalides
Necker
St-François Xavier
R Duroc
R Masseran
R de Sèvres
Impasse Ronsin
Av de Villars
Pl du Prést Mithouard
Sq de l'Abbé Esquerré
R Eblé
R du Général Bertrand
Pl Vauban
Av de Breteuil
Esplanade du Souvenir Français
Av de Saxe
Pl de Breteuil
Pl Henri Queuille
Bd Pasteur
R d'Estrées
R Bixio
R Pérignon
R César Franck
R Valentin Haüy
R Rosa Bonheur
15E
R de Staël
Av de Ségur
Sèvres Lecourbe
Av Duquesne
Av de Lowendal
R Bellart
Ségur
R Jean Daudin
Pl de Fontenoy
Unesco Building
Bd Garibaldi
Bd de Grenelle
R Lecourbe
École Militaire
École Supérieure de Guerre
R François Bonvin
Av de Suffren
Cambronne
R Cépré
R Miollis
Villa Poirier
Parc du Champ de Mars
See map p430
R Cambronne

LES INVALIDES *Map on p422*

Top Sights (p230)
1 Hôtel des Invalides ... C4
2 Musée d'Orsay ... G2
3 Musée Rodin ... D4

Sights (p238)
4 Assemblée Nationale ... E1
5 Basilique Ste-Clotilde ... E3
6 Chapelle Notre Dame de la Medaille Miraculeuse ... F6
7 Fondation Dubuffet ... E7
8 Hôtel Matignon ... E4
9 Les Berges de Seine ... F1
10 Ministère des Affaires Étrangères ... D1
11 Musée de l'Armée ... C3
12 Musée des Égouts de Paris ... A1
13 Musée Maillol-Fondation Dina Vierny ... F4

Eating (p241)
14 Besnier ... E3
15 Brasserie Thoumieux ... B2
16 Café Campana ... G2
17 Café Constant ... A3
18 Café Trama ... F7
19 Chez Françoise ... D1
20 La Pâtisserie des Rêves ... F5
21 Le Bac à Glaces ... F5
22 Le Square ... E2
23 Les Climats ... G2
Les Cocottes ... (see 17)
24 Marché Raspail ... G6
25 Pain & Chocolat ... B3
26 Poissonnerie du Bac ... F4
27 Restaurant David Toutain ... C2
28 Restaurant Musée d'Orsay ... G2
29 Restaurants d'Application de Ferrandi ... G7
30 Rue Cler ... B3

Drinking & Nightlife (p248)
31 Alain Milliat ... B3
32 Coutume ... E5
33 Natur'elle Café ... A3

Entertainment (p251)
34 Cinéma La Pagode ... D5
35 Fnac ... G7

Shopping (p252)
36 Barthélémy ... G4
37 Centrale du Fusil d'Occasion ... F4
38 Chercheminippes ... F7
39 Gérard Durand ... F4
40 La Grande Épicerie de Paris ... F6
41 Le Bon Marché ... F5
42 L'Embellie ... G6
43 Michel Chaudun ... B2
44 Quatrehomme ... E7

Sleeping (p303)
45 Grand Hôtel Lévèque ... B3
46 Hôtel du Champ-de-Mars ... B3
47 Le Bellechasse ... F2

PLACE D'ITALIE & CHINATOWN *Map on p426*

Sights **(p261)**
- Art Ludique-Le Musée .... (see 2)
- 1 Bibliothèque Nationale de France H3
- 2 Docks en Seine G1
- 3 Galerie Itinerrance H4
- 4 Manufacture des Gobelins C3
- 5 Parc Montsouris A7

Eating **(p265)**
- 6 Au Petit Marguery C2
- 7 Chez Gladines C5
- 8 Chez Nathalie C5
- 9 Entoto A3
- 10 Hao Hao E7
- 11 La Chine Masséna E7
- 12 La Tropicale D4
- 13 L'Auberge du 15 .... A2
- 14 L'Auberge du Roi Gradlon B3
- 15 Laurent Duchêne B5
- 16 Le Temps des Cérises C5
- 17 L'Ourcine B3
- 18 Pho 14 .... D5
- 19 Restaurant Variations E2

Drinking & Nightlife **(p268)**
- 20 Bateau El Alamein H3
- 21 Frog & British Library H4
- 22 La Dame de Canton H3
- 23 La Folie en Tête B5
- 24 La Fût Gueuze D2
- 25 Le Batofar H3
- 26 Le Djoon G2
- 27 Le Merle Moqueur C5
- 28 Sputnik C5
- Tandem .... (see 28)

Entertainment **(p270)**
- 29 MK2 Bibliothèque G4
- 30 Péniche l'Improviste F1
- 31 Petit Bain H3

Shopping **(p270)**
- 32 La Petite Chaloupe C2
- 33 Tang Frères F6

Sports & Activities **(p272)**
- 34 Piscine de la Butte Aux Cailles C5
- 35 Piscine Joséphine Baker H2

Sleeping **(p305)**
- 36 Hôtel La Demeure D2
- 37 Hôtel La Manufacture D3
- 38 Hôtel Saint Charles B5
- 39 Oops C3

PLACE D'ITALIE & CHINATOWN

Key on p425

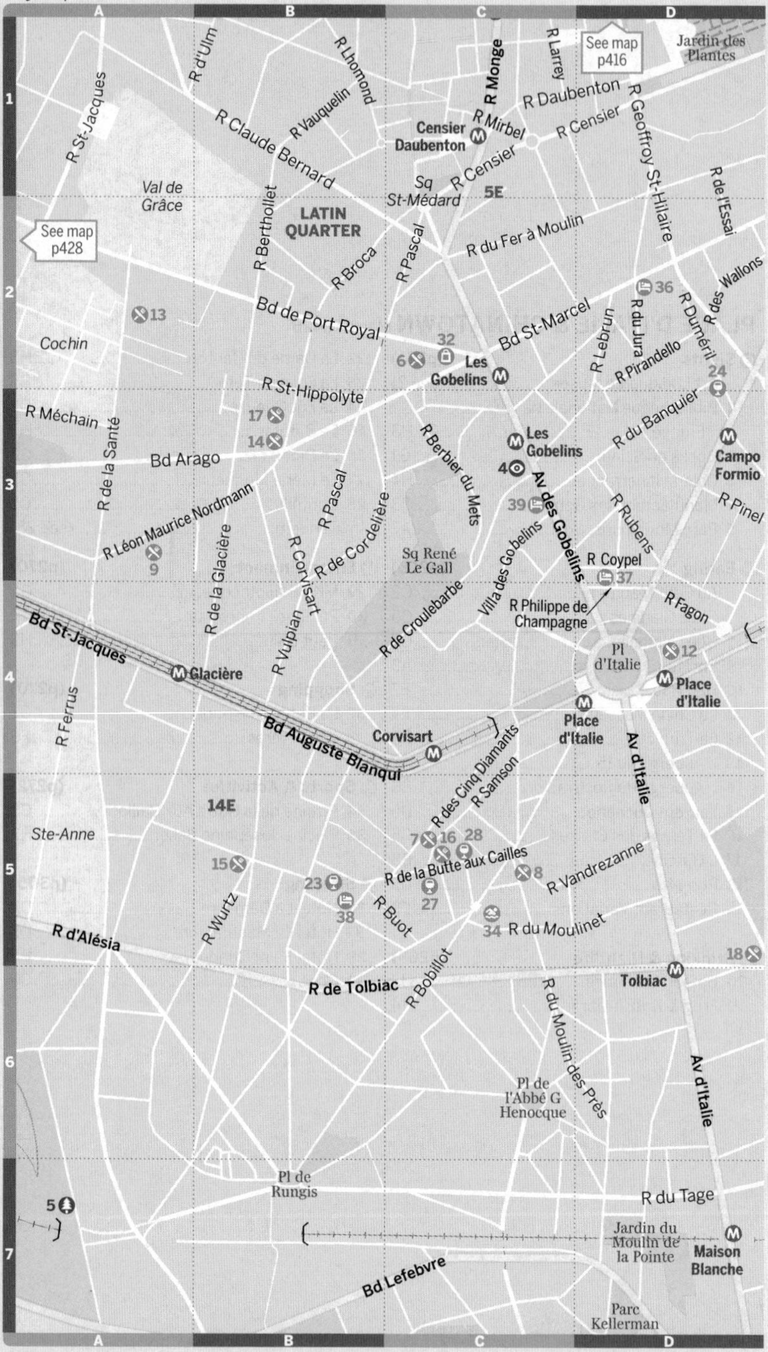

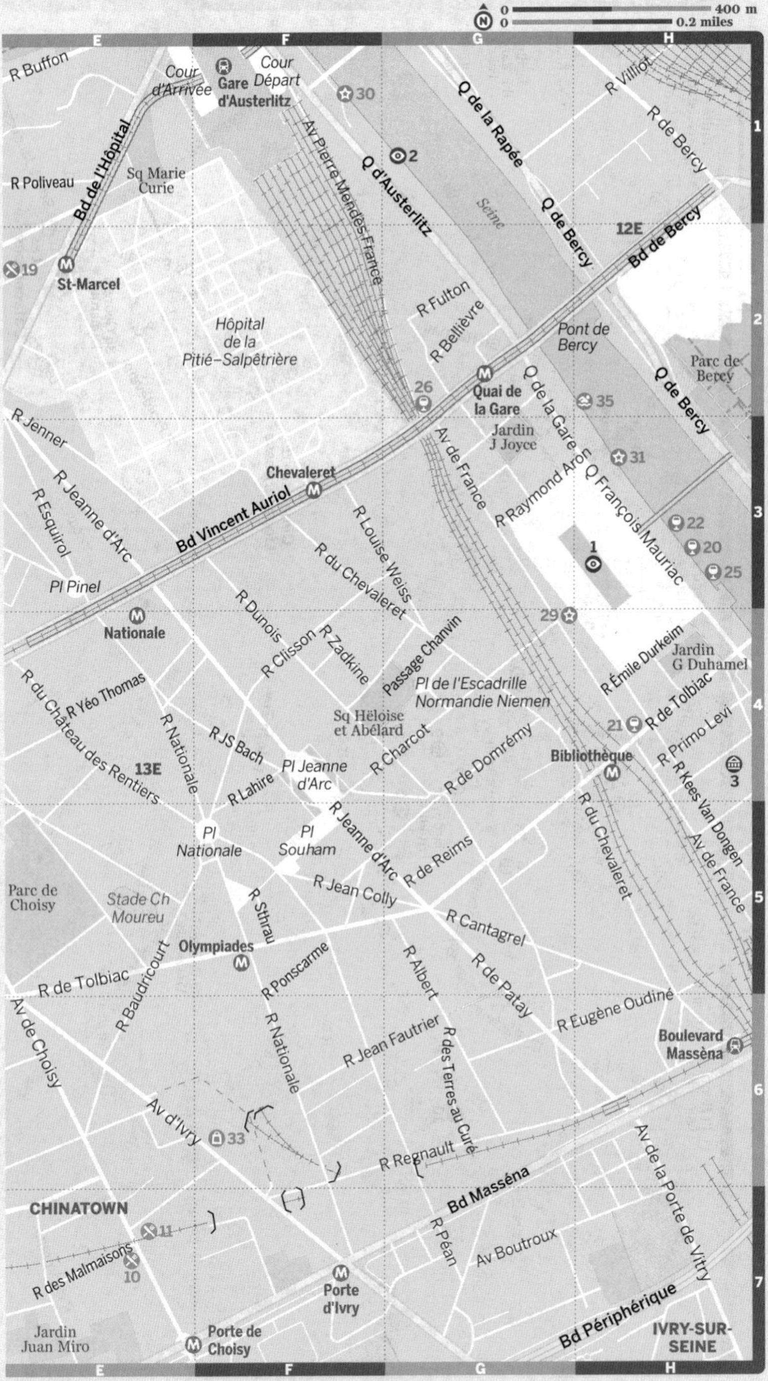

0 400 m
0 0.2 miles
N
E
F
G
H
1
2
3
4
5
6
7
R Buffon
Cour d'Arrivée
Gare d'Austerlitz
Cour Départ
30
R Villiot
Q de la Rapée
R de Bercy
Bd de l'Hôpital
Av Pierre Mendès France
Q d'Austerlitz
2
R Poliveau
Sq Marie Curie
Seine
Q de Bercy
12E
Bd de Bercy
19
St-Marcel
R Fulton
R Bellièvre
Hôpital de la Pitié–Salpêtrière
Pont de Bercy
Parc de Bercy
Quai de la Gare
26
Q de la Gare
35
Q de Bercy
R Jenner
Av de France
Jardin J Joyce
31
Chevaleret
R Raymond Aron
Q François Mauriac
R Jeanne d'Arc
R Esquirol
Bd Vincent Auriol
R Louise Weiss
22
20
R du Chevaleret
1
25
Pl Pinel
R Dunois
29
Nationale
R Clisson
R Zadkine
Passage Chanvin
R Émile Durkeim
Jardin G Duhamel
R du Château des Rentiers
R Yéo Thomas
Pl de l'Escadrille Normandie Niemen
R de Tolbiac
21
R Nationale
R JS Bach
Sq Hèloise et Abélard
R Charcot
R Primo Levi
13E
Pl Jeanne d'Arc
R de Domrémy
Bibliothèque
3
R Lahire
R Kees Van Dongen
R Jeanne d'Arc
R du Chevaleret
Pl Nationale
Pl Souham
Av de France
R de Reims
Parc de Choisy
Stade Ch Moureu
R Jean Colly
R Sthrau
R Cantagrel
Olympiades
R Albert
R Baudricourt
R Ponscarme
R de Patay
R de Tolbiac
R Eugène Oudiné
Av de Choisy
R Nationale
R Jean Fautrier
R des Terres au Curé
Boulevard Massèna
Av d'Ivry
33
Av de la Porte de Vitry
R Regnault
Bd Masséna
CHINATOWN
11
R Péan
Av Boutroux
R des Malmaisons
10
Porte d'Ivry
Bd Périphérique
Jardin Juan Miro
Porte de Choisy
IVRY-SUR-SEINE

MONTPARNASSE

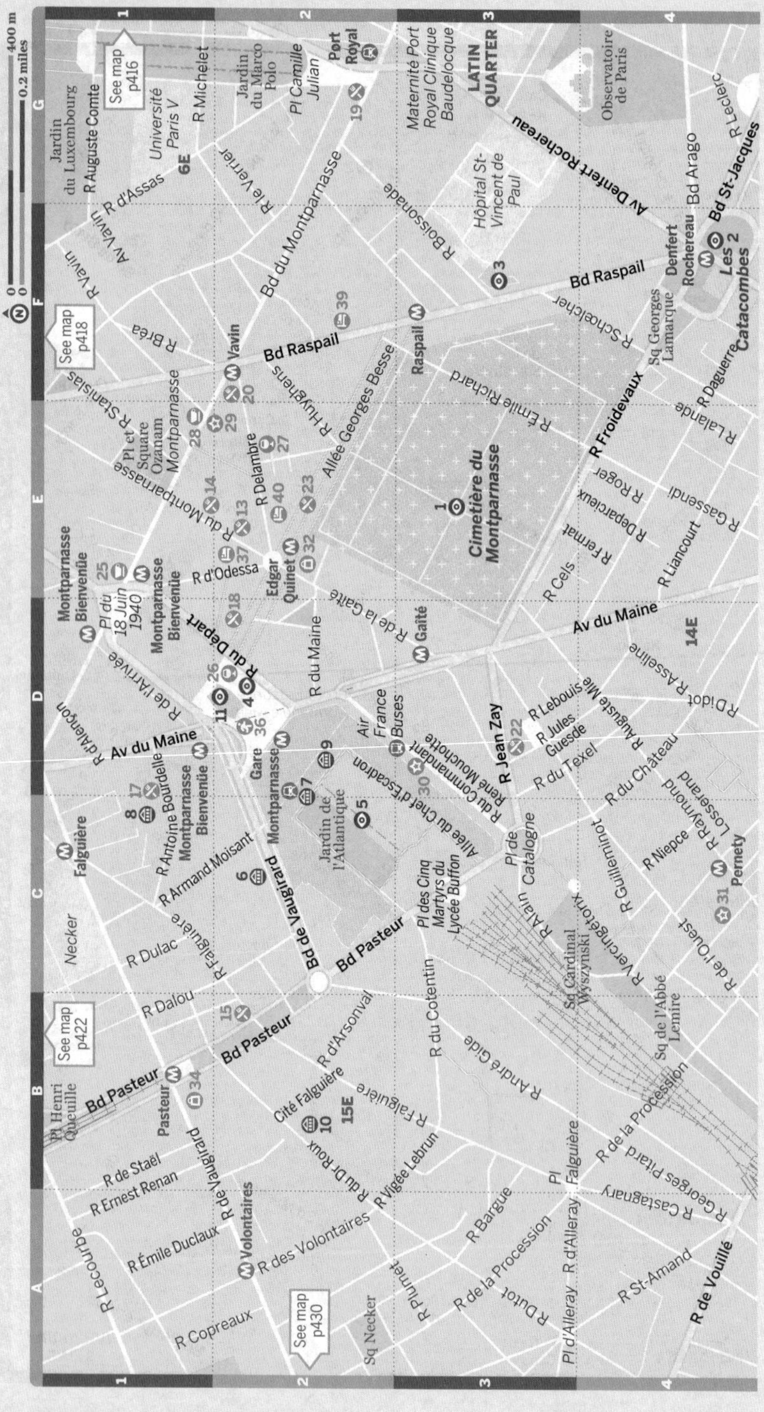

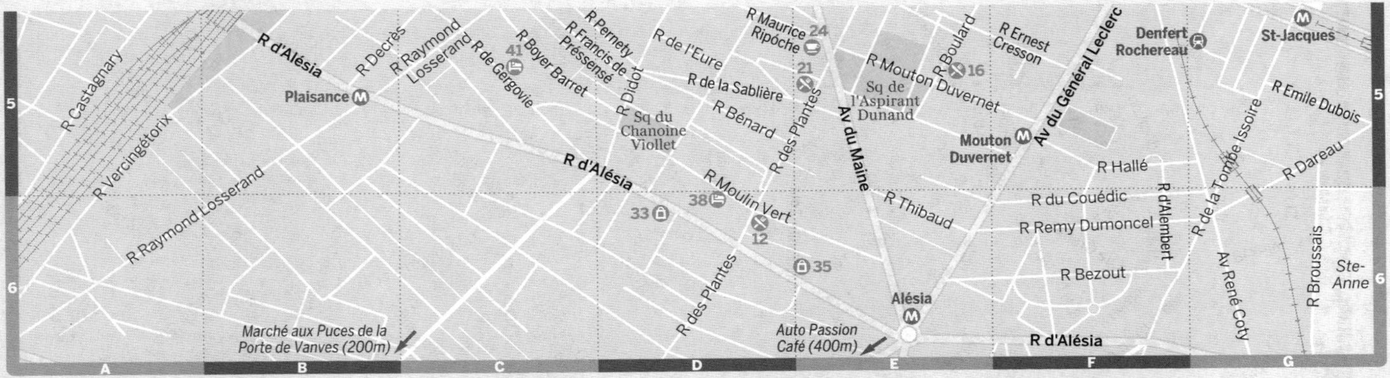

Top Sights (p258)

1 Cimetière du Montparnasse E3
2 Les Catacombes F4

Sights (p259)

3 Fondation Cartier pour l'Art Contemporain F3
4 Gare Montparnasse D2
5 Jardin de l'Atlantique C2
6 L'Adresse C2
7 Mémorial du Maréchal Leclerc de Hauteclocque et de la Libération de Paris D2
8 Musée Bourdelle C1
9 Musée Jean Moulin D2
10 Musée Pasteur B2
11 Tour Montparnasse D2

Eating (p262)

12 Au Moulin Vert D6
13 Crêperie Josselin E2
14 Crêperie Plougastel E1
15 Des Gâteaux et du Pain B2
16 Jeu de Quilles E5
17 La Cabane à Huîtres D1
18 La Cerisaie D2
19 La Closerie des Lilas G2
La Coupole ....(see 29)
Le Ciel de Paris ....(see 11)
20 Le Dôme F2
21 Le Sévéro E5
22 Marché Brancusi D3
23 Marché Edgar Quinet E2

Drinking & Nightlife (p268)

24 Félicie E5
25 La Ruche E1
26 Le Redlight D2
27 Le Rosebud E2
28 Le Select E1

Entertainment (p270)

29 Dancing La Coupole E2
30 Le Petit Journal Montparnasse D3
31 L'Entrepôt C4

Shopping (p270)

32 Adam Montparnasse E2
33 Naf Naf Stock D6
34 Pierre Hermé B1
35 Sonia Rykiel E6

Sports & Activities (p272)

36 Pari Roller D2

Sleeping (p305)

37 Celtic Hôtel E2
38 Hôtel de la Loire D6
39 Hôtel de la Paix F2
40 Hôtel Delambre E2
41 La Maison C5

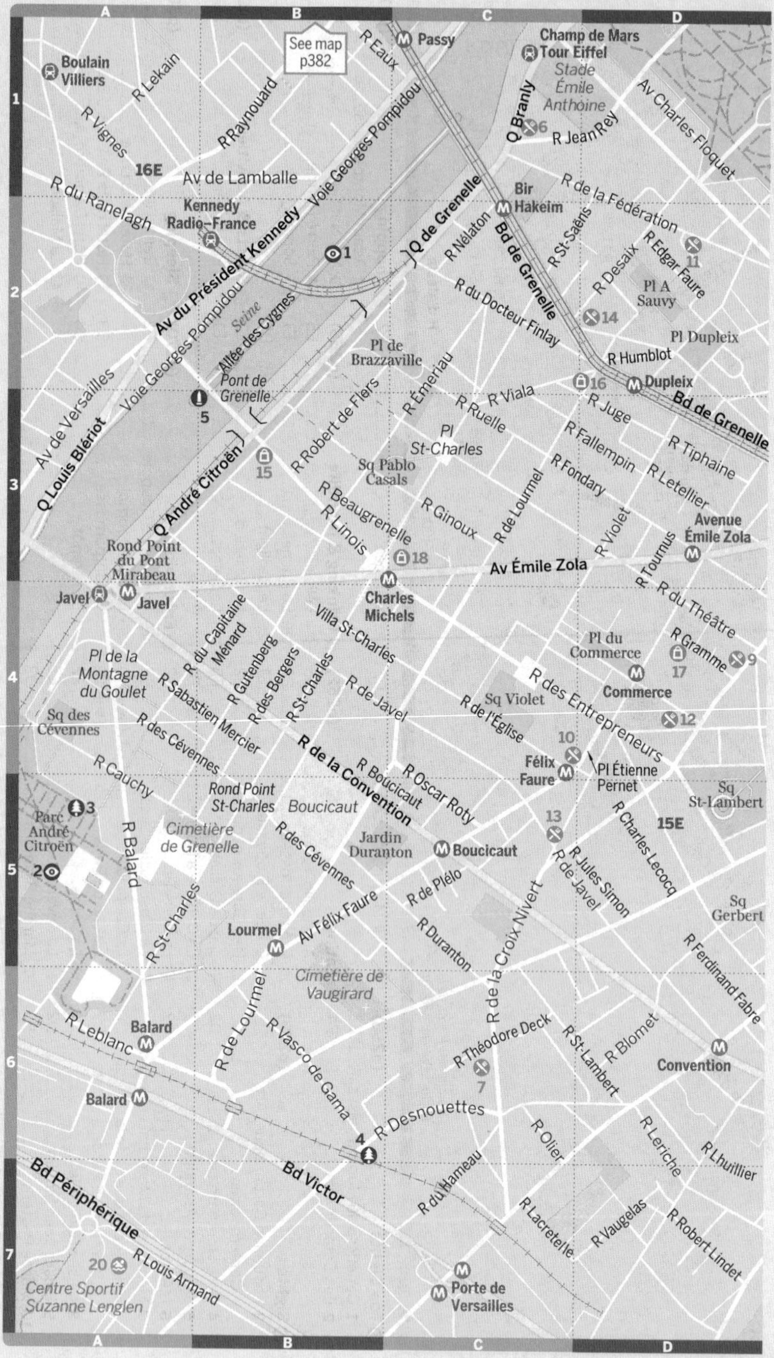
A
B
C
D
1
2
3
4
5
6
7
See map p382
Boulain Villiers
R Lekain
R Raynouard
R Vignes
16E
Av de Lamballe
R du Ranelagh
Kennedy Radio–France
Av du Président Kennedy
Voie Georges Pompidou
Seine
Allée des Cygnes
Pont de Grenelle
Av de Versailles
Q Louis Blériot
Q André Citroën
Q de Grenelle
R Eaux
Passy
Champ de Mars Tour Eiffel
Stade Émile Anthoine
Q Branly
R Jean Rey
Av Charles Floquet
Bir Hakeim
Bd de Grenelle
R Nélaton
R St-Saëns
R de la Fédération
R Edgar Faure
R Desaix
Pl A Sauvy
Pl Dupleix
R du Docteur Finlay
R Humblot
Dupleix
Pl de Brazzaville
R Émeriau
R Robert de Flers
R Viala
R Ruelle
R Juge
R Fallempin
R Tiphaine
R Letellier
R Fondary
Pl St-Charles
Sq Pablo Casals
R Beaugrenelle
R Linois
R Ginoux
R de Lourmel
R Violet
R Tournus
Avenue Émile Zola
Av Émile Zola
Charles Michels
Rond Point du Pont Mirabeau
Javel
R du Capitaine Ménard
Villa St-Charles
R du Théâtre
R Gramme
Pl du Commerce
Commerce
Pl de la Montagne du Goulet
R Sabastien Mercier
R Gutenberg
R des Bergers
R St-Charles
R de Javel
R de l'Église
Sq Violet
R des Entrepreneurs
Sq des Cévennes
R des Cévennes
R de la Convention
R Boucicaut
R Oscar Roty
Félix Faure
Pl Étienne Pernet
R Cauchy
Rond Point St-Charles
Boucicaut
Sq St-Lambert
15E
Parc André Citroën
R Balard
Cimetière de Grenelle
Jardin Duranton
R Charles Lecocq
R Jules Simon
R de Javel
Sq Gerbert
R de Plélo
Av Félix Faure
R Duranton
R de la Croix Nivert
Lourmel
Cimetière de Vaugirard
R Ferdinand Fabre
R Leblanc
Balard
R Vasco de Gama
R Théodore Deck
R St-Lambert
R Blomet
Convention
R Desnouettes
R Olier
R Leriche
R Lhuillier
Bd Victor
R du Hameau
Bd Périphérique
R Lacretelle
R Vaugelas
R Robert Lindet
R Louis Armand
Centre Sportif Suzanne Lenglen
Porte de Versailles

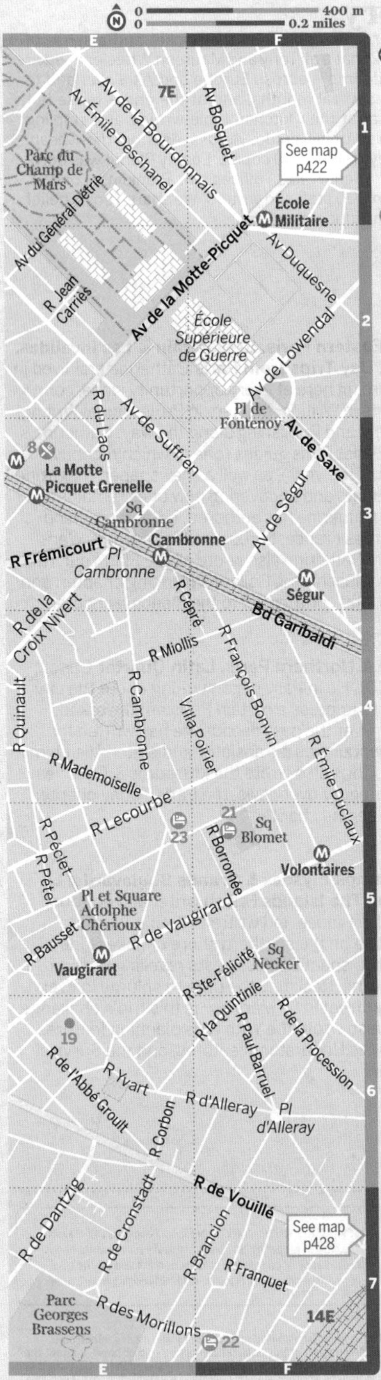

Sights **(p259)**

1 Île aux Cygnes ... B2
2 Le Ballon Air de Paris ... A5
3 Parc André-Citroën ... A5
4 Petite Ceinture du 15e ... B6
5 Statue of Liberty Replica ... B3

Eating **(p262)**

6 Choux d'Enfer ... C1
7 Jadis ... C6
8 La Gauloise ... E3
9 La Véraison ... D4
10 Le Banyan ... C4
11 Le Casse Noix ... D2
12 Le Cristal De Sel ... D4
13 Les Trois Garçons ... C5
14 Poilâne ... D2

Shopping **(p270)**

15 Beaugrenelle ... B3
16 Fromagerie Laurent Dubois ... D2
17 Le Petit Bazar ... D4
18 Mistigriff ... C3

Sports & Activities **(p272)**

19 École Le Cordon Bleu ... E6
20 Forest Hill Aquaboulevard ... A7

Sleeping **(p305)**

21 Aloha Hostel ... F5
22 Arty Paris ... F7
23 Hôtel Carladez Cambronne ... E5

Our Story

A beat-up old car, a few dollars in the pocket and a sense of adventure. In 1972 that's all Tony and Maureen Wheeler needed for the trip of a lifetime – across Europe and Asia overland to Australia. It took several months, and at the end – broke but inspired – they sat at their kitchen table writing and stapling together their first travel guide, *Across Asia on the Cheap*. Within a week they'd sold 1500 copies. Lonely Planet was born.

Today, Lonely Planet has offices in Franklin, London, Melbourne, Oakland, Beijing and Delhi, with more than 600 staff and writers. We share Tony's belief that 'a great guidebook should do three things: inform, educate and amuse'.

Our Writers

Catherine Le Nevez

Coordinating Author, Bastille & Eastern Paris, St-Germain & Les Invalides, Montparnasse & Southern Paris, Day Trips from Paris Catherine first lived in Paris aged four and she's been returning here at every opportunity since, completing her Doctorate of Creative Arts in Writing, Masters in Professional Writing, and post-grad qualifications in Editing and Publishing along the way. Catherine's writing includes numerous Lonely Planet Paris guides (one of which recently won the British Travel Press Awards travel guidebook of the year), as well as newspaper, magazine and online articles. Revisiting her favourite Parisian haunts and uncovering new ones remains a highlight of this and every assignment. Outside Paris, Catherine has authored, co-authored and contributed to scores of Lonely Planet guidebooks across France, Europe and far beyond. Wanderlust aside, Paris remains her favourite city on earth. Catherine also wrote all the Plan Your Trip chapters (with the exception of the With Kids chapter, Museums & Galleries planning chapter, and the Eating and Parks & Activities category overviews), and contributed to the Sleeping chapter.

Christopher Pitts

Louvre & Les Halles, Montmartre & Northern Paris, Latin Quarter Christopher Pitts first moved to Paris in 2001. He initially began writing about the city as a means to buy baguettes – and to impress a certain Parisian (it worked, they're now married with two kids). Over the past decade, he has written for various publications, in addition to working as a translator and editor. Visit him online at www.christopherpitts.net. Chris also wrote the Museums & Galleries planning chapter, the Eating and Parks & Activities category overviews, the Paris Today chapter and the History chapter. He also contributed to the Sleeping chapter.

Nicola Williams

Eiffel Tower & Western Paris; Champs-Élysées & Grands Boulevards; Le Marais, Ménilmontant & Belleville; The Islands British writer and editorial consultant Nicola Williams has lived in France and written about it for more than a decade. From her hillside house on the southern shore of Lake Geneva, it's an easy hop to Paris where she has spent endless years revelling in its extraordinary art, architecture and cuisine. Resisting the urge to splurge in every boutique she passed while walking the length of every street in Le Marais was this trip's challenge. Nicola can be found on Twitter at @Tripalong. Nicola also wrote the With Kids planning feature, the Fashion, Architecture, Literature, Art, Film and Music Understand features, and the Survival Guide. Nicola also contributed to the Sleeping chapter.

Published by Lonely Planet Publications Pty Ltd
ABN 36 005 607 983
10th edition – Jan 2015
ISBN 978 1 74321 555 5

10 9 8 7 6 5 4 3 2 1
Printed in China